The Sociology of Health, Healing, and Illness

With thorough coverage of inequality in health care access and practice, this leading textbook has been widely acclaimed by teachers as the most accessible of any available. It introduces and integrates recent research in medical sociology, and emphasizes the importance of race, class, and gender throughout.

This new edition leads students through the complexities of the evolving Affordable Care Act. It significantly expands coverage of medical technology, end-of-life issues, and alternative and complementary health care—topics that students typically debate in the classroom. Many new text boxes and enhancements in pedagogy grace this new edition, which is essential in the fast-changing area of health care.

New to this edition:

- More text boxes relating the social aspects of medicine to students' lives.
- Expanded coverage leading students through the complex impacts of the ACA and health care reform.
- Expanded coverage of medical technology, end-of-life issues, and alternative and complementary health care.
- 'Health and the Internet' sections are updated and renovated toward student assignments.
- New end-of-chapter lists of terms, with key terms as flash cards on the companion website.
- An updated test bank.

Gregory L. Weiss earned his Ph.D. from Purdue University and is now Professor Emeritus of Sociology at Roanoke College. During his career, he has been an honored teacher (winning numerous college, state-wide, regional (SSS), and national (ASA's Section on Teaching and Learning)) awards, a dedicated researcher and writer (author of *Grass Roots Medicine* and co-author of *Experiencing Social Research* and the ASA publication on *Creating an Effective Sociology Assessment Program* as well as dozens of scholarly articles), and active in the community in a variety of health- and animal-related organizations.

Lynne E. Lonnquist also earned her Ph.D. from Purdue University. She has taught at a variety of institutions, including Mary Baldwin College (where she also served as Professor of Sociology and Director of the Adult Degree Program) and at Roanoke College. Recently, she has served as a mental health educator and counselor as well as Director of the Center for Growth and Well Being in Roanoke, Virginia. She has been active in numerous local, state, regional, and national sociological and mental health organizations.

NINTH EDITION

THE SOCIOLOGY OF HEALTH, HEALING, AND ILLNESS

Gregory L. Weiss and Lynne E. Lonnquist

Routledge
Taylor & Francis Group

NEW YORK AND LONDON

Ninth edition published 2017
by Routledge
711 Third Avenue, New York, NY 10017

and by Routledge
2 Park Square, Milton Park, Abingdon, Oxon, OX14 4RN

Routledge is an imprint of the Taylor & Francis Group, an informa business

First edition published 1994 by Prentice Hall
Eighth edition published 2015 by Pearson

Library of Congress Cataloging in Publication Data
Names: Weiss, Gregory L., author. | Lonnquist, Lynne E., author.
Title: The sociology of health, healing, and illness / Gregory L. Weiss,
Lynne E. Lonnquist.
Description: Ninth edition. | New York, NY : Routledge, 2017. | Includes
bibliographical references and index.
Identifiers: LCCN 2016032180| ISBN 9781138647725 (hbk) | ISBN
9781138647732
(pbk) | ISBN 9781315626901 (ebk)
Subjects: LCSH: Social medicine—United States. | Medical ethics--United
States. | Medical care--United States.
Classification: LCC RA418.3.U6 W45 2017 | DDC 362.10973—dc23

ISBN: 978-1-138-64772-5 (hbk)
ISBN: 978-1-138-64773-2 (pbk)
ISBN: 978-1-315-62690-1 (ebk)

Typeset in Times New Roman
by RefineCatch Limited, Bungay, Suffolk

To Janet and to Dan

Contents

CHAPTER FOUR
SOCIETY, DISEASE, AND ILLNESS   76

CHAPTER FIVE
SOCIAL STRESS   113

CHAPTER SIX
HEALTH BEHAVIOR   141

CHAPTER SEVEN
EXPERIENCING ILLNESS AND DISABILITY   171

CHAPTER EIGHT
PHYSICIANS AND THE PROFESSION OF MEDICINE   203

CHAPTER NINE
MEDICAL EDUCATION AND THE SOCIALIZATION OF PHYSICIANS   233

CHAPTER THIRTEEN
PROFESSIONAL AND ETHICAL OBLIGATIONS OF PHYSICIANS IN THE PHYSICIAN–PATIENT RELATIONSHIP   348

CHAPTER FOURTEEN
THE HEALTH CARE SYSTEM OF THE UNITED STATES   371

CHAPTER FIFTEEN
HEALTH CARE DELIVERY   418

CHAPTER SIXTEEN
THE SOCIAL IMPLICATIONS OF ADVANCED HEALTH CARE TECHNOLOGY   448

CHAPTER SEVENTEEN
COMPARATIVE HEALTH CARE SYSTEMS   481

Preface

The ninth edition of this textbook has been updated to reflect the very important changes that have occurred in the United States health care system in the last three years, and in matters related to the sociology of health, healing, and illness. It reflects medical sociology's commitment to analyzing patterns of disease and illness, health- and illness-related behaviors, the health care professions, and the health care system.

In preparing this ninth edition we have sought to retain and strengthen the emphases and features of the earlier editions, to thoroughly update patterns, trends, and statistics, and to present new material that reflects important changes in health care in society and important advancements in medical sociology.

KEY EMPHASES WITHIN THE TEXT

This edition of the text maintains the same five emphases as the earlier editions. First, we provide broad coverage of the traditional subject matter of medical sociology, and include both new perspectives and new research findings on this material. The core areas of medical sociology (the influence of the social environment on health and illness, health and illness behavior, health care practitioners and their relationships to patients, and the health care system) all receive significant attention within the text. Naturally, statistics throughout the text have been updated to provide timely analysis of patterns and trends. Recent research findings and thought have been incorporated in every chapter. Attention devoted to relatively new areas in the field has not reduced coverage of traditional areas such as social stress, illness behavior, and the physician–patient relationship.

Second, we have continued to emphasize emerging areas of analysis in medical sociology and recent work within the field. Recent health care reform efforts in both the public and private domains continue to have dramatic effects on almost every aspect of health care. We describe these effects throughout the text.

We also continue to incorporate key medical ethics issues throughout the text. These issues represent some of the most important health-related debates occurring in the United States today, and many medical sociologists have acknowledged the importance of understanding these policy debates and setting them within a sociological context. We have attempted to provide balanced and comprehensive coverage of several of these issues (especially in Chapters 13 and 16 and in the discussion questions and cases at the ends of chapters).

We work hard to keep this book as up to date as possible and to reflect the most recent developments related to health, healing, and illness. For example, this ninth edition provides extended analysis of a wide range of topics, including the following:

- Several new "In the Field" boxes, including emphasis on climate change, the Flint water crisis, mental health concerns among college students, the opioid crisis, heart attacks in women, the emergence of e-cigarettes, the military health care system, concierge medicine, and the broken end-of-life care system
- The early experience with the implementation of the Patient Protection and Affordable Care Act, including its successes and failures and continuing efforts to dismantle it; a special section focuses more specifically on ongoing key issues related to the ACA (Medicaid

expansion, contraceptive requirements, and people still left out of the system)

- Introduction of key new concepts, such as biomedicalization, physician burnout, integrative medicine, specialty drugs, the sociology of bio-knowledge, and mHealth
- Increased coverage of infectious diseases, including Ebola and Zika
- Increased coverage of disease and illness in developing countries
- Additional coverage of the causes of life expectancy and mortality
- A reworking of information on HIV/AIDS to reflect progress in treatment
- Coverage of the recent changes in the MCAT exam and the Doctor of Nursing degree
- Coverage of the expansion of exclusive provider organizations
- The continuing controversy about the HPV vaccine
- Additional coverage in developments related to palliative care
- Additional coverage of the relationship between medical providers and medical industries
- Increased analysis of the movement toward patient-centered care and the importance of health literacy and patient activation
- Additional information on health care technology
- A brief look at health applications as part of the changing technology in medicine
- Increased attention to the globalization of health care
- Significant recent developments in the health care systems of Canada, China, and the United Kingdom, and increased attention to European models for health insurance

Third, the extensive coverage of gender, race, and class issues as they relate to health, healing, and illness has been maintained. Throughout the textbook, we examine issues in the light of race, class, and gender. We want students to constantly

be exposed to the important influence of these factors on matters related to health and illness. The chapters on social epidemiology, social stress, health and illness behaviors, the profession of medicine and medical education, and the physician–patient relationship all give special emphasis to these matters.

Fourth, we continue to emphasize key social policy questions. Timely questions and issues addressed include regular, routine HIV checks (Chapter 4), the provision of clean needles to people using injectable drugs (Chapter 6), mandating HPV vaccinations (Chapter 6), public financing of medical education (Chapter 9), the reconfiguration of traditional responsibilities of hospital nurses (Chapter 10), the use of strikes by medical providers (Chapter 10), religious exemption laws (Chapter 11), the legal status of medical marijuana (Chapter 11), the Affordable Care Act (Chapter 14), the effects of consolidation and merger among American hospitals and the pressures placed on the viability of public hospitals (Chapter 15), and the use and possible abuse of advanced health care technologies (Chapter 16).

Fifth, we have attempted to prepare a text that is informative. We want readers to become aware of many of the understandings of health, healing, and illness that we have because of medical sociology, and to become intrigued by the provocative issues and debates that exist in medical sociology and in the health care field. We also want readers to find this book readable and interesting.

Both of us have enjoyed structuring our classrooms to enable as much reflection, critical thinking, and student participation as possible. We have found that there is simply not time for some of the classroom activities that we most enjoy (e.g., reading and then discussing a provocative paperback, watching a good documentary and critically analyzing it together, or using student panels to introduce issues) if we feel obligated to lecture on all the material in each chapter.

On the other hand, we do want students to become familiar with the important contributions of the field. When we use this book, we do spend some time lecturing on parts of it, adding to certain discussions and presenting some of the material in an alternative manner. However, our students are able to grasp much of the book on their own, enabling us to supplement and create additional types of learning experiences.

What are the key pedagogical features of this text?

- Clear organization within chapters and a clear writing style
- Interesting boxed inserts ("In the Field") that provide illustrations of key points made in the chapters
- Interesting boxed inserts ("In Comparative Focus") that examine a selected health topic or issue in another country or countries
- Meaningful tables and charts with the most recent data available at the time of writing this edition of the book
- Illustrative photographs, many of which were taken specifically for use in this book
- Chapter summaries
- End-of-chapter "Health on the Internet" references and questions
- End-of-chapter "Discussion Cases"
- End-of-chapter "Glossary" sections
- References conveniently provided at the end of each chapter
- A Glossary is available as an e-Resource at www.routledge.com/9781138647732

Three additional facets of the book are important to us and help to describe its place within the field. First, we consider one of the strengths of the book to be the large number of research studies cited to illustrate key points. We do this to demonstrate to students the empirical basis of sociology, the origin of sociological knowledge, and the fascinating types of research conducted in medical sociology. We hope it inspires students to consider interesting research projects.

We have worked hard to identify theoretically meaningful and methodologically sound studies that contribute important knowledge to our understanding of health, healing, and illness. While making heavy use of research conducted by medical sociologists, we also include appropriate material from the other social sciences, from the government, and from the medical professional literature. We believe that this is helpful in forming the most comprehensive understanding of the topics covered in the book.

A second facet of our book that is important to us is that we provide balanced coverage on key issues. This does not mean that our book lacks critical perspective or analysis. In fact, readers will find no shortage of critical questions being asked. However, our objective is to expose students to arguments on both sides of the issues, and to challenge them to consider the soundness of reasoning and quality of evidence that are offered.

Finally, we hope that this text reflects a genuine understanding of some very important and complex issues. Both of us have had many opportunities to experience various dimensions of the health care system. Between the two of us, we have been able to apply and extend our medical sociological training through work in a free health clinic, in a family planning clinic, in family counseling, in hospital bioethics groups, on the human rights committee of a state psychiatric hospital, on the Navajo reservation, and in voluntary health agencies. Although we have not substituted our personal experiences for more general understandings developed through sound theory and research, we believe that our experiences have helped us to develop a better understanding of certain issues and assisted us in being able to illustrate important concepts and patterns.

Ultimately, our hopes for student-readers remain the same as with the earlier editions—that they gain an appreciation of how the sociological perspective and social theory contribute to an understanding of health, healing, and illness, and of the manner in which social research is used to study these processes. In addition, we hope that readers perceive some of the many wonderfully exciting issues that are studied by medical sociologists.

ACKNOWLEDGMENTS

We are deeply grateful to the many people who have made helpful suggestions and comments to us about the first eight editions of this book. Our appreciation is extended to the following individuals: James R. Marshall, SUNY–Buffalo, School of Medicine; Lu Ann Aday, University of Texas, School of Public Health; Paul B. Brezina, County College of Morris; Janet Hankin, Wayne State University; Naoko Oyabu-Mathis, Mount Union College; Judith Levy, University of Illinois at Chicago; Mike Farrall, Creighton University; John Collette, University of Utah; Raymond P. Dorney, Merimack College; C. Allen Haney, University of Houston; Arthur Griel, Alfred College; Larry D. Hall, Spring Hill College; Patricia Rieker, Simmons College; Deborah Potter, Brandeis University; John Schumacher, University of Maryland, Baltimore County; Lisa Jean Moore, College of Staten Island; Ilona Hansen, Winona State University; William H. Haas III, University of North Carolina at Asheville; Robert D. Ruth, Davidson College; Eldon L. Wegner, University of Hawaii at Manoa; Diane S. Shinberg, University of Memphis; Juyeon Son, University of Wisconsin Oshkosh; Matthew Carlson, Portland State University; Linda Grant, University of Georgia; Ande Kidanemariam, Northeastern State University; Mark Bird, College of Southern Nevada; Daphne Pedersen, University of North Dakota; Abby Johnston, Baptist College of Health Sciences; and Angelique Harris, Marquette University.

We would also like to thank Janet Jonas for her terrific photographs, and the librarians at Fintel Library (especially Jeffrey Martin) at Roanoke College and the Health Sciences Library at the University of Virginia.

Gregory L. Weiss
Lynne E. Lonnquist

CHAPTER I

A Brief Introduction to the Sociology of Health, Healing, and Illness

Learning Objectives

- Identify and explain the major historical factors that led to the development of medical sociology as a subfield of sociology.

- Identify and give specific examples of the four major categories of focus within medical sociology.

- Explain how the sociological perspective, sociological theory, and social research methods can be applied to the study of health, healing, and illness.

- Discuss the orientation of medical sociologists to their research in this early part of the twenty-first century.

Through much of the first half of the twentieth century, matters pertaining to health, healing, and illness were viewed as being primarily within the domain of physicians, other health care practitioners, and scholars in the chemical and biological sciences. Neither medicine nor sociology paid much attention to each other. This has changed dramatically in the ensuing years as the paths of sociology and medicine have increasingly converged. This chapter presents a brief introduction to the sociology of health, healing, and illness—a subfield of sociology commonly referred to as medical sociology.

DEFINITION OF MEDICAL SOCIOLOGY

Ruderman (1981:927) defines **medical sociology** as "the study of health care as it is institutionalized in a society, and of health, or illness, and its relationship to social factors." The Committee on Certification in Medical Sociology (1986:1) of the American Sociological Association (ASA) provided the following elaboration:

Medical sociology is the subfield which applies the perspectives, conceptualizations, theories, and methodologies of sociology to phenomena having to do with human health and disease. As a specialization, medical sociology encompasses a body of knowledge which places health and disease in a social, cultural, and behavioral context. Included within its subject matter are descriptions and explanations or theories relating to the distribution of diseases among various population groups; the behaviors or actions taken by individuals to maintain, enhance, or restore health or cope with illness, disease, or disability; people's attitudes and beliefs about health, disease, disability and medical care providers and organizations; medical occupations or professions and the organization, financing, and delivery of medical care services; medicine as a social institution and its relationship

1

to other social institutions; cultural values and societal responses with respect to health, illness, and disability; and the role of social factors in the etiology of disease, especially functional and emotion-related.

Clearly, the focus of medical sociology is broader than just "medicine." In fact, the title of this book was intentionally selected to connote that medical sociology includes a focus on health (in the positive sense of social, psychological, and emotional wellness), healing (the personal and institutional responses to perceived disease and illness), and illness (as an interference with health).

Sociologists study health, healing, and illness because they are a central part of the human experience, because they help us to understand how society works, and because they reflect patterns of social relationships. Sociologists emphasize that explanations for health and illness and for healing practices must go beyond biological and individualistic factors by examining the important influence of social context.

HISTORICAL DEVELOPMENT OF MEDICAL SOCIOLOGY

Setting the Foundation: The Importance of Social Factors on Health and Illness

It is difficult to identify any specific event as the "starting point" of the field of medical sociology. Certainly, some of the basic insights of the field were present among society's earliest philosophers and physicians. Many physicians in ancient times (see Chapter 2) perceived an essential interrelationship among social and economic conditions, lifestyle, and health and illness. This understanding has been an integral part of medical thinking in some (though not all) civilizations since then. Often cited as a key historical figure who paved the way for medical sociology is Rudolf Virchow, the great

mid-nineteenth-century physician (and the founder of modern pathology). Virchow identified social and economic conditions as being primary causes of an epidemic of typhus fever in 1847, and lobbied for improved living conditions for the poor as a primary preventive technique. Arguing against biomedical reductionism—attempting to reduce every disease and illness to a biological cause—Virchow contended that medicine is largely a social science that needs to consider the influence of social structure on the creation of both health and illness.

The Turn of the Century: Development of Social Medicine

The last decades of the nineteenth century and the first decades of the twentieth century were a period of heightened awareness in both the United States and Europe of the need for social programs to respond to health crises. These were years of social upheaval caused in part by the effects of the Industrial Revolution and rapid urban growth (and, in the United States, a tremendous influx of largely poor and unskilled immigrants). In 1915, Alfred Grotjahn published a classic work, *Soziale Pathologie*, documenting the role of social factors in disease and illness and urging the development of a social science framework for working with communities and providers in reducing health problems. The term **social medicine** was coined to refer to efforts to improve public health.

However, an important crosscurrent was occurring simultaneously. The discovery of the germ theory of disease enabled physicians to more successfully treat the acute infectious diseases that plagued society. This reinforced a belief that medicine could rely solely on biological science. The discipline of sociology was still in its infancy and was not able to provide sufficient documentation of the need for a complementary focus on social conditions.

The Early to Mid-Twentieth Century: More Studies on Health and Medicine

Several important precursors to the development of medical sociology occurred in the first half of the twentieth century. Social surveys became an important research technique, and many focused on health and living conditions. Sociologists often worked with charity organizations and settlement houses, which also became subjects for study. By the 1930s and 1940s, many sociological studies of the medical field, including Talcott Parsons' 1939 work on the medical professions, appeared. Political scientist Oliver Garceau (1941) contributed to the political sociology of medicine by analyzing the political life of the American Medical Association. George Rosen (1944) studied increasing specialization in medicine. Oswald Hall (1946) studied the informal organization of medical practice in an American city (Rosen, 1976).

The 1950s and 1960s: The Formal Subdiscipline Emerges

The emergence of medical sociology as a field of study occurred in the 1950s and 1960s. The most important developments then pertain to changes in health, healing, and illness, external recognition of the field, and its institutionalization within sociology.

Changes in Health, Healing, and Illness. Based on analysis by Rodney Coe (1970) and others, the development of medical sociology was facilitated by four changes that had occurred or were occurring in medicine in the 1950s and 1960s. These are as follows:

1. *Changing patterns of morbidity and mortality.* During this time, the primary causes of sickness and death shifted from acute infectious diseases (e.g., influenza and tuberculosis) to chronic, degenerative diseases (e.g., heart disease and cancer). Because the factors that lead to degenerative diseases are more obviously interwoven with social patterns and lifestyle, the necessity for sociological contributions became more apparent.

2. *The impact of preventive medicine and public health.* In the 1800s and early 1900s, the field of public health focused primarily on bacteriology (linking particular germs to diseases) and immunology (preventing disease occurrence). As the twentieth century progressed, however, it became apparent that protection of public health also required consideration of social factors such as poverty, malnutrition, and congested living areas—all of obvious interest to sociologists.

3. *The impact of modern psychiatry.* The development of the field of psychiatry led to increased interest in the psychophysiological basis for many diseases and illnesses, in the importance of effective interaction between patients and practitioners, and in the use of patients' social environment as part of therapy.

4. *The impact of administrative medicine.* Throughout the twentieth century, the organizational complexity of the medical field—in the settings in which care is delivered, in the ownership of medical facilities, and in the bureaucracies that were created to regulate and finance medical care—expanded enormously. The abilities of sociologists to analyze organizations and structures, identify those who are harmed as well as those who gain by various arrangements, and examine the consequences of alternative techniques were increasingly useful skills in organizationally complex environments.

External Recognition and Legitimation. Two key events during the 1950s and 1960s contributed to the increased interest in and legitimation of medical sociology. First, medical schools began to hire sociologists for their faculties. Although medical sociology was not always well integrated into the curriculum, the move symbolized an increasing recognition of sociology's potential contribution to understanding disease and illness. Second, government agencies and private foundations initiated significant financial funding for medical sociology. The National Institutes of Health and the National Institute of Mental Health sponsored sociological research in medicine and subsidized training programs for graduate students in sociology. (Both authors of this book received fellowships from the U.S. Public Health Service for their graduate education.) The Russell Sage Foundation provided significant funding of programs to increase the use of social science research within medicine.

Institutionalization of Medical Sociology. Finally, two additional events are especially noteworthy in the institutionalization of medical sociology. In 1959, medical sociology was accepted as a formal section of the ASA—an important step in bringing recognition to a field and enabling recruitment of new members. Second, in 1965, the ASA assumed control of an existing journal in medical sociology and renamed it the *Journal of Health and Social Behavior*. Now the official ASA journal for medical sociology, it is a key mechanism for medical sociologists to share their research findings.

Since then the field has flourished. The ASA section on medical sociology currently has approximately 1,000 members (there are about 13,000 ASA members), and is the third largest special interest section within the association. Medical sociologists publish in a wide variety of journals in sociology, public health, and medicine, and are increasingly employed in health planning, community health education, education of health professionals, government at all levels, and health care administration in addition to colleges and universities. See the "In the Field" box on Major Topics in Medical Sociology for one way of organizing the major topics within medical sociology.

 IN THE FIELD

MAJOR TOPICS IN MEDICAL SOCIOLOGY

The four major categories of interest in medical sociology with specific topics of analysis and sample research questions (that will be answered in the appropriate chapters) are as follows:

Category #1: The Relationship Between the Social Environment and Health and Illness

Social Epidemiology—the study of patterns and trends in the causes and distribution of disease and illness within a population. Research question: Why is the infant mortality rate higher for African Americans?

Social Stress—the study of the imbalance or unease created when demands on a person exceed resources to deal with them. Research question: Why do women report higher levels of stress?

Category #2: Health and Illness Behavior

Health Behavior—the study of behaviors intended to promote positive health. Research question: Why does society focus on changing individual behaviors rather than the social circumstances that influence individual behaviors?

Experiencing Illness and Disability—the study of the ways that people perceive, interpret, and act in response to illness and disability. Research question: What factors cause people to interpret medical symptoms in very different ways?

Category #3: Health Care Practitioners and Their Relationship with Patients

Physicians and the Profession of Medicine—the study of medicine as a profession and the role of medicine within society. Research question: How does the high number of medical malpractice suits influence physicians and the practice of medicine?

Medical Education and the Socialization of Physicians—the study of the education and socialization of physicians in medical schools. Research question: What are the key value orientations that students learn in medical school?

Nurses, Advanced Practice Practitioners, and Allied Health Workers—the study of issues pertaining to non-physician health care providers. Research question: Why are physicians more supportive of physician assistants than they are of nurse practitioners?

Alternative and Complementary Healing Practices—the study of healers and healing practices outside conventional medicine. Research question: Why do many people simultaneously use both medical doctors and alternative healers?

The Physician–Patient Relationship—the study of patterns in the way that physicians and patients relate to each other and factors that influence these patterns. Research question: To what extent do male and female physicians interact differently with patients?

Category #4: The Health Care System

The Health Care System—the study of the organization, regulation, financing, and important problems in the health care system and recent health care reform legislation and activity. Research question: What effect will health care reform have on the health care system?

Health Care Delivery—the study of the organizations and agencies (including hospitals) that provide health care services. Research question: What are the consequences for society of for-profit versus not-for-profit hospitals?

The Social Effects of Health Care Technology—the study of the social consequences and public policy choices of new health care technologies. Research question: What are the supporting and opposing arguments for legalizing physician-assisted death?

Comparative Health Care Systems—the study of health care systems in other countries. Research question: Why are most health care systems around the world currently undergoing significant change?

Foundational and Emerging Areas of Interest

All fields of inquiry are built on certain foundational topics, yet remain open to new and emerging areas of interest. The "In the Field" box on Major Topics in Medical Sociology identifies the foundational topics within this field. Within these major topics in medical sociology, four particular and interrelated areas are of rapidly expanding interest.

Issues Related to Health Care Reform. Concerns about the high costs of health care and the lack of access that millions of Americans have had to quality health care have led to recent reform efforts in the United States. A massive shift from traditional health insurance plans to managed care networks, such as health maintenance organizations, occurred throughout the 1990s and early 2000s, and major health care reform legislation (the Patient Protection and Affordable Care Act—commonly known as the Affordable Care Act or Obamacare) was passed in 2010. Hankin and Wright (2010:S10), in an editorial entitled "Reflections on Fifty Years of Medical Sociology" in the *Journal of Health and Social Behavior*, state:

> The work for medical sociologists is just beginning as we enter a new era of health care reform. Not only can we offer insights about how to implement reform, but we can also examine the intended and unintended consequences of transforming the health care system and the extent to which these structural changes actually improve population health.

These changes have had tremendous effects on the health care system, and are examined throughout this book.

Issues Related to Technological Advancements in Medicine.   Rapid advancements in medical technologies have dramatically changed the practice of medicine and how we conceptualize the human body. Medical sociologists increasingly are examining these technologies and their effects on the delivery of health care, the financing and regulation of health care, the provision of information to patients, the sharing of information among patients, and the reform of the health care system.

> Across the half-century lifespan of the (ASA) Medical Sociology Section, during which sweeping changes have impacted American society as a whole, technologies have changed dramatically, too, from large "machines at the bedside" to tiny pills and devices that enter into and transform human bodies, and information technologies that have altered if not restructured health care provision. (Casper and Morrison, 2010:S121)

Many of these technologies—from life-saving technologies to the significant development of

use of social media by health care providers and patients—are examined in this text.

Issues Related to Medical Ethics.   These technological advancements in medicine have raised important and provocative ethical questions. Sociological analysis and insights are extremely important in genuinely understanding these matters (DeVries et al., 2007). In recent years, medical sociologists have become more active in studying (1) values, attitudes, and behaviors of people relative to ethical issues in medicine (e.g., attitudes about genetic research and human cloning) and how they are influenced by various social factors, (2) social policy questions (e.g., on new reproductive technologies or the termination of treatment for the terminally ill), and (3) social movements (e.g., the pro-life and pro-choice movements) that have developed around interest in ethical issues in medicine. DeVries and Subedi (1998:xiii) describe sociology's role as "lifting bioethics out of its clinical setting, examining the way it defines and solves ethical problems, the modes of reasoning it employs, and its influence on medical practice."

Issues Related to Globalization.   The increasing globalization of the world is readily apparent with respect to health and medicine. Recent disease epidemics—such as Ebola and SARS—demonstrate that the spread of disease from country to country now occurs on a worldwide basis. As the provision of health care becomes more and more expensive, countries around the world find it increasingly difficult to sustain an adequate health care system. Collaboration among countries with respect to health care provision continues to grow. In several chapters in this book, the increasing attention given by medical sociology to global health care issues is described.

SOCIOLOGY'S CONTRIBUTION TO UNDERSTANDING HEALTH, HEALING, AND ILLNESS

Sociology is "the scientific study of social life, social change, and the social causes and consequences of human behavior" (American Sociological Association, 2013:1). It is the discipline with primary responsibility for studying social interactions among people, groups and organizations, and social institutions, and examining how these interactions influence and are influenced by the larger culture and social structure of society.

Three particular aspects of sociology contribute in important ways to understanding health, healing, and illness: (1) the sociological perspective, (2) the construction of social theories to explain why things happen as they do, and (3) the scientific foundation of the discipline.

The Sociological Perspective

Sociology is one of many perspectives that are used to acquire knowledge about the world. History, biology, chemistry, anthropology, psychology, economics, political science, philosophy and religion, clinical medicine, and other disciplines all contribute to our understanding of the medical field. Sociology's primary focus is to understand social interaction, groups and organizations, and how social context and the social environment influence attitudes, behaviors, and social organization.

The **sociological perspective** requires an ability to think about things in a manner other than that to which many individuals are accustomed. Often we think very individualistically about human behavior. If a particular teenager begins smoking cigarettes, or a particular man is very reluctant to see a physician when ill, or a particular medical resident feels abused by superiors, we may attempt to understand the behavior by focusing on the particular individual or the

C. Wright Mills (1916–1962) coined the term "sociological imagination" to refer to the ability to see how individuals' *personal* troubles are influenced by large-scale, social *(public)* issues. © Archive Photos/Getty Images.

particular situation. However, sociology attempts to understand these behaviors by placing them in social context—that is, by looking for social patterns and examining the influence of social forces or circumstances that have an impact on individual behavior.

C. Wright Mills, an enormously influential sociologist, referred to this ability to see how larger social patterns (public issues) influence individual behavior (personal troubles) as **sociological imagination** (Mills, 1959). Consider the following:

1. Almost all adult smokers began smoking as teenagers; few adults begin smoking.
2. Men are more reluctant than women to see a physician.

3. Pharmaceutical drugs are more expensive in the United States than in any other country.

How do we understand these very important social patterns that have a significant influence on health and illness in the United States? Sociologists attempt to understand these patterns by placing them in social context. It is not just one adult smoker who started as a teen—that is the common pattern. So we try to find the social forces and the social arrangements that make it common for teens but not for adults to initiate smoking.

It is not just one man who is more reluctant than one woman to see a physician. If it was, there might be an individual explanation. But in fact men in general show more reluctance than women in general, so we are talking about some social force that influences men and women differently. What is it that creates this greater physician-aversion for men?

Finally, it is not just one drug that is more expensive in the United States than in other countries. If it was, there might be something in particular about that drug. But in fact almost all drugs are more expensive—many are much, much more expensive—so there must be some larger explanation. This is what Mills meant when he said that sociologists try to identify and explain the "public issues" (the larger social forces) that lead to "personal troubles."

The Construction of Social Theories

Sociology is an effort to identify and describe social patterns and then to find cause-and-effect relationships that explain the patterns. In *Invitation to Sociology* (1963), Peter Berger describes sociology as searching for the general in the particular—attempting to determine how particular facts or individual behaviors may generate as well as reflect social patterns. Whether the focus is delinquency, family interaction, or medicine, sociologists attempt to identify patterns in attitudes and behaviors.

All science, natural and social, assumes that there is some underlying order in the universe. Events, whether they involve molecules or human beings, are not haphazard. They follow a pattern that is sufficiently regular for us to be able to make generalizations—statements that apply not just to a specific case but to most cases of the same type . . . Generalizations are crucial to science because they place isolated, seemingly meaningless events in patterns we can understand. It then becomes possible to analyze relationships of cause and effect and thus to explain why something happens and to predict that it will happen again under the same conditions in the future. (Robertson, 1987:6)

Major Theoretical Orientations in Sociology That Guide the Effort to Find Explanations. Three major theoretical orientations have dominated the field of sociology. These orientations are fundamental images of society that guide sociological thinking and the process of searching for explanations.

Functionalism (or structural functionalism) views society as a system (a structure) with interdependent parts (e.g., the family, the economy, and medicine) that work together to produce relative stability. Each of these parts is assumed to have positive consequences (or functions) and may have negative consequences (or dysfunctions) for the society as a whole. When each part operates properly, a stable and relatively harmonious society exists.

Given this image of society, functionalists are adept at identifying the effective integration of societal parts. For example, functionalists might identify the manner in which the value that America places on science and discovery has led to significant advancements in medical knowledge and to the development of new forms of medical technology.

Conflict theory views society as a system largely dominated by social inequality and social conflict. Societies are viewed as being in a constant state of change, characterized by disagreements over goals and values, competition among groups with unequal amounts of power, and hostility. Conflict theorists perceive whatever societal order exists to be dictated by the most powerful groups, rather than being based on the value consensus envisioned by functionalists.

Given this image of society, conflict theorists are skillful at utilizing a critical perspective and at identifying social inequities. In this regard, medical sociologists have an opportunity to comment critically on perceived problems and inequities in the health care system and to offer a critical perspective on the functioning of the system. For example, conflict theorists point out that a primary reason why many low-income women conceive premature, low-birth-weight babies is their inability to access adequate prenatal care.

While functionalism and conflict theory view society from a macro perspective (examining society as a whole), **interactionism** (or symbolic interactionism) focuses on small-scale, day-to-day interactions among people. Society is viewed as the ultimate outcome of an infinite number of episodes of interaction each day in which individuals interpret social messages and base their responses on these interpretations.

In medicine, interactionists have shown how physicians sometimes utilize particular communication strategies (e.g., using brief, close-ended questions and interrupting patient comments) to reinforce dominance and bolster role distance.

The Scientific Foundation of the Discipline

Charon and Vigilant (2008) have stated that sociology rests on both an objective and critical foundation. Sociology is a social science, and through much of its formative years, researchers typically followed the same basic model of science and scientific research as did their colleagues in the natural and physical sciences. These techniques rely on empirical procedures

used to obtain quantifiable data designed to test specific hypotheses. Scientists are expected to maintain objectivity in the conduct of their research—that is, to attempt to prevent biases from influencing the conduct of the work or the conclusions drawn.

The Scientific Process. A model of the **scientific process** is provided in Figure 1–1. According to this model, once a particular sociological question has been identified, the researcher scours the literature (typically books and journals) to learn what research has already been done and determine what is already known about the subject. This work guides the researcher in formulating a *theory,* or general explanation, about why things happen as they do regarding the particular issue being studied.

Based on this theory, the researcher deduces one or more specific *hypotheses* (specific statements predicting what will be found in the research). These hypotheses must be capable of being found to be accurate or inaccurate. Research is then designed to test the accuracy of the hypotheses, a sample of people is selected

Figure 1–1 The Scientific Process

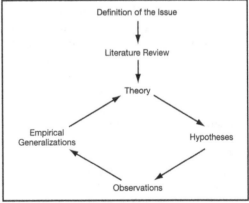

Source: Adapted from Walter L. Wallace (ed.). *Sociological Theory: An Introduction,* Copyright (1969) by Aldine Publishers. Reprinted by permission of Aldine Transaction, a division of Transaction Publishers.

from the population for study, and data are collected.

Once the data have been collected and analyzed, the researcher seeks to draw empirical generalizations from the research. Conclusions are drawn about the accuracy of the hypotheses and the appropriateness of the theory that guided the research. The research may lend additional credence to the theory, or suggest that the theory needs to be modified, or be so inconsistent with the theory that a major revision is needed. If the results of the research are published or presented, the study will join others on the subject and be available for the next researcher doing a literature review in the area.

Data-Collection Techniques.   Some of the most important data-collection techniques used by medical sociologists are briefly described here. Other techniques, such as specific epidemiological techniques, are described where appropriate in the text.

1. *Survey research.* **Survey research** is the most commonly used data-gathering technique in sociology. It involves the systematic collection of information about attitudes and behaviors through personal or telephone interviews or self-administered questionnaires (increasingly done online). Survey research is particularly helpful in studying attitudes or values—subjects that cannot easily be studied in other ways—and obtaining self-reported data on health and response to illness. Proper sampling techniques must be followed so that the sample is representative of the population of interest.

2. *Experimental research.* **Experimental research**—that is, seeking to identify cause-and-effect relationships between specified variables in carefully controlled conditions—is typically conducted in a laboratory, but can be done in natural settings. In the ideal case, two groups—the experimental group and the control group—are formed. The groups should be as similar as possible, except that only the experimental group receives the independent variable (the potential "cause"). Whatever change occurs in the dependent variable (the potential "effect") from the beginning to the end of the experiment can then be attributed to the independent variable. Experimental research can be used in health settings for purposes such as testing the effectiveness of health education materials, innovations in teaching medical students, and new payment mechanisms.

3. *Observational research.* **Observational research**—that is, the systematic observation of people in their natural environment—has also been a valuable data-collection technique for medical sociologists. While it is more difficult to be systematic when using this technique (although an extensive array of techniques to support systematic study is available), it does enable observation of actual behaviors rather than reports of behavior or behaviors performed in artificial settings. Important observational studies have been conducted in such diverse settings as hospitals, mortality review conferences, and patient self-help groups.

4. *Use of existing statistics.* Many demographers (those who study population size, composition, and distribution) and other medical sociologists study health problems and society's reaction to them by drawing upon recorded vital and social statistics. Researchers may examine birth and death records, medical charts and insurance forms, and any compiled statistics on mortality, morbidity, medical resources, or any other aspect of health care systems.

Getting at Socially Constructed Reality. Although the scientific method continues to dominate in sociology, most sociologists acknowledge that reality is often more subjective than objective. These perspectives direct sociology to help us to understand the "socially constructed" nature of belief systems about health, illness, and healing practices. Cultures vary in their perception of what constitutes good health, in factors that shape health (e.g., Chinese belief in the presence of a vital spirit in the body), and in views of appropriate healing procedures (e.g., the importance of social support in Navajo healing). These perspectives are examined further in this text in chapters on social stress, illness behavior, and alternative healing practices.

THE ROLE OF THE MEDICAL SOCIOLOGIST IN THE TWENTY-FIRST CENTURY

What will be the future role of the medical sociologist? Perhaps three aspects will be most important.

First, the most important objective of the medical sociologist will continue to be to demonstrate and emphasize the important influence of cultural, social-structural, and institutional forces on health, healing, and illness. Medical sociologists must be ever more vigilant in using their "theoretical and methodological skills to address interesting and important questions" in order to ensure that the sociological perspective continues to influence public discussion (Pescosolido and Kronenfeld, 1995:19).

Second, medical sociologists need to maintain their spirit of free and critical inquiry (Bloom, 1990). Responding to an article which suggested that some physicians were concerned about sociologists' more liberal ideology, Mechanic (1990:89) wrote:

It seems clear that these commentators . . . prefer a sociology that is adjunct to medical activity and accepting of its basic premises. Such a sociology would simply be a servant to medicine, not fulfilling its larger responsibility to understand medicine as a social, political, and legal endeavor; to challenge its curative and technological

imperatives; to examine equity of care in relation to class, race, gender, age, character of illness, and geographic area; and to study the appropriate goals and objectives for health care in the context of an aging society with an illness trajectory dominated by chronic disease.

Finally, medical sociologists should continue to seek interdisciplinary collaboration. In the early years of the field, medical sociologists debated whether their primary focus should be on the **sociology of medicine** (i.e., advancing sociological theory and method through research in the medical field) or on the **sociology in medicine** (i.e., making practical contributions to the practice of medicine) (Straus, 1957). While many medical sociologists have clearly identified more with one or the other of these approaches, the distinction has blurred over time, and today most researchers understand that good sociological research can simultaneously contribute to the development of medical sociology *and* to improved health care (Bird, Conrad, and Fremont, 2000). Many refer to this as being **sociology with medicine**. Straus (1999) has suggested that it is even possible to take a critical perspective while working in a medical setting, as long as it is perceived to be constructive, objective, and not blatantly antagonistic.

Mechanic (1995:1492) has noted that "the major health problems facing national systems are complex and multifaceted and not easily amenable to analysis from the perspective of any single discipline." Coe (1997:6) has encouraged working with other social scientists (as well as others involved in health research) as a way of creating "opportunities to strengthen a sociological perspective" and deepening "our understanding of the complexities of human behavior in the context of health and illness." Zussman (2000) has written persuasively about how genuine understanding of ethical issues in medicine can be derived by utilizing both normative reflection (the primary approach of medical ethics) and empirical description (the primary contribution of sociology). Brown (2013) has called for interdisciplinary work among medical sociologists and environmental sociologists, and linking of their work with environmental health science. Several medical sociologists (Fremont and Bird, 1999; Pescosolido, 2006, 2011; Seabrook and Avison, 2010) have recently urged greater efforts to integrate social and biological explanations of matters related to health, healing, and illness.

SUMMARY

Medical sociology emerged as a scholarly field of inquiry in the 1950s and 1960s. Four factors were primarily responsible for this emergence: (1) a shift from acute infectious diseases to chronic degenerative diseases as major sources of morbidity and mortality, (2) increased focus on behavioral factors related to health and illness, (3) increased recognition of the importance of the patient–physician relationship, and (4) the increasingly complex structure of the health care system. Simultaneously, outside agencies (e.g., medical schools and government agencies) were taking an increasing interest in the field, and medical sociology was becoming institutionalized as a special interest section in the ASA.

Sociology's contributions to the study of health, healing, and illness emanate from the sociological perspective (the understanding that human behavior is largely shaped by the groups to which people belong and by the social interaction that takes place within those groups), sociology-based theoretical approaches (functionalism, conflict theory, and interactionism), and the scientific foundation and critical perspective of the discipline.

The most important tasks of medical sociology are to demonstrate and emphasize the important influence of cultural, social-structural, and institutional forces on health, healing, and illness, and to maintain a spirit of free and critical inquiry while recognizing the interdisciplinary basis of health and illness.

HEALTH ON THE INTERNET

This chapter discusses recent calls for health researchers in various disciplines to work more closely together. Learn more about three of the social science disciplines that investigate health, healing, and illness by checking out their websites.

Medical sociology: www.asanet.org/
    medicalsociology/

Medical anthropology: www.medanthro.net
Health psychology: www.health-psych.org

What is the main focus of each of these three fields? What similarities and differences do you note?

DISCUSSION QUESTIONS

1. In order to understand better the approach and work of medical sociologists, select a recent article from the *Journal of Health and Social Behavior* or *Social Science and*

Medicine or any journal assigned by your professor. Identify its main subject, theoretical approach, data-collection technique, and main findings. How does the approach of a medical sociologist differ from that of a medical journalist or that of a layperson attempting to understand some subject related to health, healing, and illness? Identify a specific question related to medical sociology or an issue that you might be interested in studying.

2. The health and medical sector is an extraordinarily broad and important component of society. One way of identifying the importance of health, healing, and illness in society is to note the extent to which the social institution of medicine is closely interwoven with all or almost all other social institutions. Identify how the social institution of medicine interrelates with each of these other social institutions:

science	government	economy
education	family	law
religion	the arts	recreation

GLOSSARY

conflict theory	social medicine
experimental research	sociological imagination
functionalism	sociological perspective
interactionism	sociology in medicine
medical sociology	sociology of medicine
observational research	sociology with medicine
scientific process	survey research

REFERENCES

American Sociological Association. 2013 *What is Sociology?* www.asanet.org/employment/careers21st_whatissociology.cfm.

American Sociological Association, Committee on Certification in Sociology. 1986 *Guidelines for the Certification Process in Medical Sociology.* Washington, DC: American Sociological Association.

Berger, Peter L. 1963 *Invitation to Sociology: A Humanistic Perspective.* New York: Doubleday.

Bird, Chloe E., Peter Conrad, and Allen M. Fremont. 2000 "Medical Sociology at the Millennium." Pp. 1–10 in *Handbook of Medical Sociology*, 5th ed., Chloe E. Bird, Peter Conrad, and Allen M. Fremont (eds.). Upper Saddle River, NJ: Prentice Hall.

Bloom, Samuel W. 1990 "Episodes in the Institutionalization of Medical Sociology: A Personal View." *Journal of Health and Social Behavior*, 31:1–10.

Brown, Phil. 2013 "Integrating Medical and Environmental Sociology with Environmental Health." *Journal of Health and Social Behavior*, 54:145–164.

Casper, Monica J., and Daniel R. Morrison. 2010 "Medical Sociology and Technology: Critical Engagements." *Journal of Health and Social Behavior*, 51:S120–S132.

Charon, Joel, and Lee G. Vigilant. 2008 *The Meaning of Sociology*, 8th ed. Upper Saddle River, NJ: Prentice Hall.

Coe, Rodney M. 1970 *Sociology of Medicine.* New York: McGraw-Hill.

———. 1997 "The Magic of Science and the Science of Magic: An Essay on the Process of Healing." *Journal of Health and Social Behavior*, 38:1–8.

DeVries, Raymond, and Janardan Subedi. 1998 *Bioethics and Society: Constructing the Ethical Enterprise.* Upper Saddle River, NJ: Prentice Hall.

DeVries, Raymond, Leigh Turner, Kristina Orfali, and Charles L. Bosk. 2007 *The View from Here: Bioethics and the Social Sciences.* London: Blackwell.

Fremont, Allen M., and Chloe E. Bird. 1999 "Integrating Sociological and Biological Models: An Editorial." *Journal of Health and Social Behavior*, 40:126–129.

Garceau, Oliver. 1941 *The Political Life of the American Medical Association.* Cambridge, MA: Harvard University Press.

Grotjahn, Alfred. 1915 *Soziale Pathologie.* Berlin: August Hirschwald Verlag.

Hall, Oswald. 1946 "The Informal Organization of the Medical Profession." *Canadian Journal of Economic and Political Science*, 12:30–44.

Hankin, Janet R., and Erik R. Wright. 2010 "Reflections on Fifty Years of Medical Sociology." *Journal of Health and Social Behavior*, 51:S10.

Mechanic, David. 1990 "The Role of Sociology in Health Affairs." *Health Affairs*, 9:85–97.

———. 1995 "Emerging Trends in the Application of the Social Sciences to Health and Medicine." *Social Science and Medicine*, 40:1491–1496.

Mills, C. Wright. 1959 *The Sociological Imagination.* New York: Oxford University Press.

Parsons, Talcott. 1939 "The Professions and Social Structure." *Social Forces*, 17:457–467.

Pescosolido, Bernice A. 2006 "Of Pride and Prejudice: The Role of Sociology and Social Networks in Integrating the Health Sciences." *Journal of Health and Social Behavior*, 47:189–208.

———. 2011 "Taking the 'Promise' Seriously: Medical Sociology's Role in Health, Illness, and Healing in a Time of Social Change." Pp. 3–20 in *Handbook of the Sociology of Health, Illness, and Healing: A Blueprint for the 21st Century*, Bernice A. Pescosolido, Jack K. Martin, Jane D. McLeod, and Anne Rogers (eds.). New York: Springer.

Pescosolido, Bernice A. and Jennie J. Kronenfeld. 1995 "Health, Illness, and Healing in an Uncertain Era: Challenges from and for Medical Sociology." *Journal of Health and Social Behavior*, Extra Issue:5–33.

Robertson, Ian. 1987 *Sociology*, 3rd ed. New York: Worth Publishers.

Rosen, George. 1944 *The Specialization of Medicine.* New York: Froben Press.

———. 1976 "Social Science and Health in the United States in the Twentieth Century." *Clio Medica*, 11:245–268.

Ruderman, Florence A. 1981 "What Is Medical Sociology?" *Journal of the American Medical Association*, 245:927–929.

Seabrook, James A., and William R. Avison. 2010 "Genotype–Environment Interaction and Sociology: Contributions and Complexities." *Social Science and Medicine*, 70:1277–1284.

Straus, Robert. 1957 "The Nature and Status of Medical Sociology." *American Sociological Review*, 22:200–204.

———. 1999 "Medical Sociology: A Personal Fifty-Year Perspective." *Journal of Health and Social Behavior*, 40:103–110.

Wallace, Walter L. (ed.). 1969 *Sociological Theory: An Introduction.* Chicago, IL: Aldine Publishing Company.

Zussman, Robert. 2000 "The Contributions of Sociology to Medical Ethics." *Hastings Center Report*, 30:7–11.

CHAPTER 2

The Development of Scientific Medicine

Learning Objectives

- Explain how medical belief systems fluctuated from the earliest civilizations to the Hippocratic Era to the Medieval Era to the Renaissance and to the development of scientific medicine with today's focus on technology in medicine.

- Identify and discuss three significant contributions of Hippocrates (the "Father of Medicine") to the understanding of health, healing, and illness.

- Describe the practice of medicine in early America.

- Identify and discuss the effects of the Civil War on medical understanding and on the practice of medicine.

- Compare and contrast the views of Paul Starr and Vicente Navarro on the "cultural authority of medicine."

Today's healing practices and health care systems have developed through centuries of efforts to understand disease and illness and to find effective means to protect and restore health. Understanding this historical development is important both as an end in itself and as a means to a better understanding of current patterns.

Compiled histories of medicine are not in short supply, but few of these histories attempt to place the development of medicine within a societal context. A "sociological approach to the history of medicine" includes at least the following: (1) a "sociology of medical knowledge"—that is, the ways in which societies "socially construct" medical knowledge; (2) the development and evolution of the primary activities in which physicians engage, including patient education, prevention, examination and diagnosis, prognosis, curative techniques, and palliative care (relief from suffering); (3) the evolution

of the organization of medical practice, including medical specialization and the relationship to hospitals and corporations; (4) the development of hospitals and their changing role within society; and (5) the development and evolution of public health measures, including nutrition, sanitation, and public education (McKeown, 1970; White, 2009).

This chapter gives some attention to all of these themes, but focuses primarily on the first theme by describing the historical development of scientific medicine and tracing the ascendancy of scientific medical authority in America. It demonstrates that the discovery and acceptance of medical knowledge can be understood only in social context and are, at the very least, partially dependent on both cultural values (including orientation toward medicine) and the configuration of powerful interests within the society. In particular, notice the following:

1. The "constantly shifting character" (Cassady, 1991) of medicine as understanding of disease causation shifts between a supernatural and scientific basis, as the role and popularity of alternative healing philosophies ebb and flow, and as the emphasis within medicine centers more on preventive care or curative care.
2. The constant struggle of physicians and medical researchers to discover causes of disease and effective cures for them, and the typically long time lag before major discoveries are accepted and have any impact on patient care.
3. The important impact on medicine of other major institutions in society, including the government, religion, the family, and science.
4. The constantly evolving view within societies of the nature and inevitability of disease and of the patient's responsibility for self-care.

A BRIEF HISTORY OF MEDICINE

One of the most significant events in the development of scientific medicine occurred when it was discovered that many diseases can be traced to specific causes such as bacteria, viruses, parasites, and genetic impairments. Chief credit for this discovery is typically assigned to Louis Pasteur's formulation of the germ theory of disease in the 1860s and 1870s. Prior to this time, both lay and professional understanding of the causes of disease and illness had evolved through a multitude of approaches and explanations. The first part of this chapter traces this development of scientific medical knowledge.

EARLY HUMANS

Although the first forms of writing did not appear until between 4000 and 3000 BC, paleontologists have used human remnants such as teeth, bones, and mummies, as well as works of art, to study early disease and its treatment. They have learned that disease and injury are as old as humankind (and the presence of bacteria and viruses far older). There is evidence of tumors, fractures, parasitic diseases, arthritis, osteomyelitis, and dental caries that pre-date written communication. How did early humans interpret these medical calamities?

> Primitive man, noting the rising and setting of the sun and moon, the progress of the seasons, the birth, growth, and inevitable death of plants, animals, and humans, did not take long to arrive at the supposition that these phenomena did not occur by chance ... it seemed logical to suppose that they were ordered by some all-powerful god, or gods, and equally logical was the belief that fortune and misfortune were signs of the gods' pleasure or displeasure. (Camp, 1977:11)

Supernatural Belief Systems

These "magico-religious" or **supernatural explanations of disease** evolved into complex belief systems. Diseases were caused either by direct intervention of a god or spirit or through a sorcerer (a mortal in control of supernatural forces) or through the intrusion of some foreign object into the body. This "object" might have been a spirit or demon, or even something more tangible, such as a stone or pebble (Magner, 2005).

Early humans used several divination procedures (e.g., crystal gazing or trances) to read the intentions of the supernatural. Once the diagnosis was made, appropriate cures were employed. Religious rituals such as prayer, magic spells, and exorcism were used when the origin of the disease was traced to supernatural forces, and more physical means including a "sucking-out" procedure, artificially induced vomiting, and "bloodletting" (draining blood from the body to extract the foreign presence or redistribute the blood, a practice that survived for centuries) were used in cases of object intrusion (Magner, 2005).

The most amazing procedure used was skull **trephination**—utilizing sharpened stones to

Trephination is considered by many to be the first surgical technique. It involved carving a circular section from the skull in order to reduce pressure or to release evil spirits causing sickness. It likely started as long as 7,000 years ago and continued for perhaps 2,500 years. © Paul Bevitt/Alamy Stock Photo.

drill or carve a hole in the skull. The exact purpose of trephination is unknown, but many believe it was done to release evil spirits. The holes drilled were of various sizes and configurations depending upon the diagnosis. Fossil studies demonstrate that many of the patients survived the surgery, and some of them received additional trephinations years after the original one (Kennedy, 2004).

The First Physicians

Specialists (often religious figures) emerged to serve as intermediaries with the gods. Known as the **shaman** (or the "witch doctor" or "medicine man"), this was typically a highly revered, much-feared individual who often provided effective

medical care. Many were adept at observing animals and noting the plants and herbs they used for relief, and many practiced trial-and-error medicine—experimenting with a variety of substances or procedures until the most effective ones were identified. The kinds of diseases that were most common in early societies—rheumatic diseases, digestive disorders, skin diseases, and gynecological disorders—were problems more amenable to cures available at the time than would be epidemic diseases, such as typhoid, measles, and smallpox, which many believe were not yet present.

Of course, these techniques were only part of the medical arsenal of the shaman. Prayer and incantation, ritualistic dancing, and sacrifices were also used to capture the attention of the gods. These techniques also increased the patient's confidence in the cures being attempted—an important psychotherapeutic benefit (Magner, 2005).

THE EGYPTIAN CIVILIZATION

Of the various ancient civilizations whose medical practices have been studied in some depth, Egypt has received the most attention. This is due to its reputation as an especially healthy civilization, and to an abundance of written material and other forms of evidence (medical writings preserved on the papyrus reed and well-preserved mummies) that exist from the 3,000-year Egyptian civilization. Of interest is the fact that many Egyptian physicians gave credit to earlier African civilizations (see the accompanying box, "The Contributions of Imhotep and Ancient Africans to Medicine").

The most important development in Egyptian medicine is the evolution of physicians into specialists, as most of them focused on a particular disease or a particular part of the body. Physicians were also religious leaders, and each was devoted to a different god. As a result, they

---

IN THE FIELD

THE CONTRIBUTIONS OF IMHOTEP AND ANCIENT AFRICANS TO MEDICINE

A considerable body of knowledge attests to the fact that Africans in antiquity made significant contributions to medicine and may have been the originators of medical practice. Although current medical history texts give little attention to the contributions to medicine of people of color, Greek philosophers, historians, and physicians—who are given much credit—wrote of what they learned from the writings and oral traditions of Africans.

Some now refer to Imhotep—an African engineer, architect, scribe, priest, builder of tombs, and possibly a physician, who lived in the 2600s B.C.—as the "Historical Father of Medicine." He is known to have been an advisor to the king, to have built impressive tombs and possibly the first hospital, and to have produced journals (now lost) on surgery, anatomy, pathology, diagnosis, and experimental scientific observation. His legend grew following his death, and he became a deified figure in Egypt (Makah and Jalil, 2009; Pickett, 1992).

---

tended to focus on whatever diseases were associated with their deity. Not surprisingly, given the hot and dusty desert conditions, most physicians specialized in eye care.

Egyptian medicine also produced two noteworthy documents: the **Code of Hammurabi** (a Babylonian king who lived from 1728 to 1686 BC), which is possibly the first codified set of guidelines regarding responsibilities of physicians, and the *Ebers Papyrus*—a type of medical textbook summarizing extant knowledge about several disease categories that offered tips on diagnosis, prognosis, and therapeutic measures, including over 800 specific prescriptions (Magner, 2005).

GREEK AND ROMAN SOCIETIES

One of the most remarkable civilizations of all was that of Greece during the last 2,000 years BC The substantial contribution of the Greeks to medicine is consistent with their contributions to philosophy, art, theater, sculpture, government, and other areas.

In the beginning part of this era, religion and medicine were still inextricably linked. Apollo, the sun god, was also god of health and medicine and believed to be the inventor of the healing art. According to Greek legend, Aesculapius was the son of Apollo and such a brilliant healer that by the eighth century he was considered the Greek god of health. Temples called "asklepieia" were created where priest-physicians practiced the healing ceremony of incubation or "temple sleep."

Patients who came to the temple would purify themselves (bathe), fast, read about the cures of former patients, and make offerings to Aesculapius. They would be given drugs to induce sleep. During the night, harmless "sacred" snakes would crawl around the patients and lick their wounds, after which attendants would apply salves. Lore has it that cures were invariably produced (Magner, 2005).

Hippocrates—the "Father of Medicine"

Simultaneously, a more empirically based medicine was developing, and many physicians enjoyed favorable reputations. The most renowned of these physicians is certainly **Hippocrates** of Cos (460–377 BC)—the "Father of Medicine." Hippocrates was born in Cos, was well educated, became a successful and much beloved physician, and was an esteemed teacher. He is best known for three major contributions:

1. *The principle of natural, rather than supernatural, explanations for disease.* Hippocrates taught that disease is a natural process and that symptoms are reactions of the body to disease. He further emphasized that the chief function of the physician is to aid the natural forces of the body. With this principle, sick people ceased to be considered as sinners, and sinners began to be thought of as sick people. Hippocrates emphasized that the body possessed its own means of recovery, and that a healthy man was one in a balanced mental and physical state because of complete harmony of all the humors (Green, 1968:31).

   Hippocrates subscribed to the **humoral theory of disease**—a dominant approach for centuries. The humoral theory postulates that there are four natural elements in the world (air, earth, fire, and water) and four natural properties (hot, cold, dry, and wet). In the body the elements are blood (hot), phlegm (cold), yellow bile (dry), and black bile (wet). A person is healthy when these four humors are in balance and when the individual is in balance with the environment. Therefore, one seeks moderation in life so as not to upset the balance. Sickness is created by imbalance. These imbalances are detected by physical symptoms. A warm forehead (fever) indicates excessive heat; a runny nose is a sign of excessive phlegm. Appropriate cures seek to restore balance. For example, cold food was a remedy for heat-related diseases, and a very dry environment was created for the patient with excessive phlegm.

Hippocrates of Cos, the "Father of Medicine," advocated natural rather than supernatural explanations for disease. © INTERFOTO/Alamy.

2. *His writings.* One of the most important sets of medical writings ever collated is the *Corpus Hippocraticum*—more than 70 books, monographs, and essays covering a variety of aspects of medicine. Hippocrates wrote of the importance of observing disease progression, and described his own copious note taking of medical histories, symptoms, and reactions to therapy when treating his patients. He encouraged physicians to treat the whole patient, not just a particular organ or a particular symptom (Porter, 2006).

3. *His teaching of human compassion and ethical standards as illustrated in the Hippocratic Oath.* The first section of the **Hippocratic Oath** (see the accompanying box, "The Hippocratic Oath") expresses reciprocal

commitments made by physicians and their apprentices, and establishes teaching as a primary obligation of the physician. The second portion of the oath is a brief summary of ethical guidelines. Some of the pledges—for example, against performing abortion, cutting for stone, and facilitating a suicide—raise questions, since all were common practice at the time and were activities in which Hippocratic physicians are known to have engaged (Nuland, 1995). Nevertheless, the oath commanded significant attention then as it does now (even though most physicians no longer pledge to it).

Despite the popularity of Hippocrates, Greece could be described as an "open medical marketplace" that was comprised of several types of religious, magical, and empirical medical practitioners. Because there was no medical licensing, anyone could be a healer, and patients used the services of practitioners representing a multitude of medical philosophies.

Roman Medicine

Medicine did not flourish in Rome. Roman households ministered to the sick in their own families, often using treatments similar to those used in early societies. Beginning in the third century BC (Rome was founded in 753 BC), Greek physicians began filtering into Rome. At first, these physicians were persecuted, partly out of a

---

IN THE FIELD

THE HIPPOCRATIC OATH

I swear by Apollo the physician, and Aesculapius, Hygeia, and Panacea and all the gods and goddesses, that, according to my ability and judgment, I will keep this oath and this covenant:

To reckon him who taught me this Art equally dear to me as my parents, to share my substance with him, and relieve his necessities if required; to look upon his offspring on the same footing as my own brothers, and to teach them this Art, if they shall wish to learn it, without fee or stipulation; and that by precept, lecture, and every other mode of instruction, I will impart a knowledge of the Art to my own sons, and those of my teachers, and to disciples who have signed the covenant and have taken an oath according to the law of medicine, but no one else.

I will follow that system of regimen which, according to my ability and judgment, I consider for the benefit of my patients, and abstain from whatever is deleterious and mischievous.

I will give no deadly medicine to anyone if asked, nor suggest any such counsel; and in like manner I will not give to a woman an abortive remedy. With purity and with holiness I will pass my life and practice my Art.

I will not cut persons labouring under the stone, but will leave this to be done by such men as are practitioners of this work.

Into whatever houses I enter, I will go into them for the benefit of the sick, and will abstain from every voluntary act of mischief and corruption; and, further, from the seduction of females or males, of freemen and slaves.

Whatever, in connection with my professional practice, or not in connection with it, I see or hear, in the life of men, which ought not to be spoken of abroad, I will not divulge, as reckoning that all such should be kept secret.

While I continue to keep this Oath unviolated, may it be granted to me to enjoy life and practice the Art, respected by all men, in all times. But should I trespass and violate this Oath, may the reverse be my lot.

jealousy that Rome was not producing its own physicians. Cato the Censor (234–149 BC), the man given credit for being the first important writer in Latin, prohibited all in his family from using these physicians (he relied instead on raw cabbage taken internally and rubbed on the body as a medicinal cure). Pliny the Elder himself is said to have remarked that "The honour of a Roman does not permit him to make medicine his profession, and the Romans who begin to study it are mercenary deserters to the Greeks" (Camp, 1977).

Perhaps for this reason, physicians openly competed for status and reputation. Aggressive self-promotion and public humiliation of rivals were not uncommon. Physicians sought out medical cases that had been difficult to solve and attempted public, "spectacular" diagnoses or cures that would be widely publicized and, when successful, would lead to improvement in social standing (Mattern, 1999).

Asclepiades

The arrival of Asclepiades (a Greek physician born in Asia Minor in 124 BC) initiated a general increased regard for physicians. Skeptical of the idea of the "self-healing" potential of the body, Asclepiades believed that health and illness were determined by the condition of the pores. If the pores were either too open or too closed, illness would result. He prescribed massage, diet (wine was a common recommendation), and baths as techniques to alter the structure of the pores (Magner, 2005). Asclepiades became a popular figure, founded a school that survived his death in 60 BC, and influenced Julius Caesar to decree in 46 BC that Greek slave-doctors were free and had full rights of citizenship.

Roman Contributions to Medicine

Rome's major medical contributions were to the field of public health. Recognizing that unsanitary conditions contributed to the spread of disease, the government constructed a system of aqueducts to obtain pure water, built an elaborate system of public baths, passed ordinances requiring street cleanliness, and established a system of hospitals to tend to the sick.

Galen

The other most pivotal figure of this era is Galen, a physician whose ideas dominated much of medicine for the next 12 centuries. Born in Asia Minor in AD 131, he studied Hippocratic medicine (and its rival theories) and eventually migrated to Rome at the age of 34. There he became famous as a physician, author, and medical researcher.

Galen made extensive contributions to the understanding of anatomy. Since he was prevented by Roman law from using human cadavers for study, Galen relied on the dissection of monkeys and pigs and on the study of the skeletons of criminals. Based on these studies, he refuted several common medical notions (e.g., that the heart was the origin of the nerves, and that blood vessels originated in the brain) and added to the existing knowledge about bones, muscle groups, the brain, and various nerves. Yet he could not be dissuaded from his belief in "pneuma"—that certain vital spirits (but not blood) circulated throughout the body (Magner, 2005).

Galen, a rather dogmatic individual who was absolutely convinced that his ideas were accurate, vehemently discouraged others from further investigating his work. Although we now know many of his theories to be false, they were extremely influential during his time and for several subsequent centuries. On the other hand, his title as the "Father of Experimental Physiology" seems well deserved, as he was probably the foremost medical experimentalist until the 1600s.

THE MEDIEVAL ERA

The end of the Western Roman Empire is generally pegged at AD 476, when the conquest of Europe by the barbarians was completed. In the East, the Byzantine Empire (based in Constantinople) survived and became a center of civilization. The time period between (roughly) AD 500 and AD 1500 is referred to as the Medieval Era.

Monastic Medicine

Medical practice in the first half of this era is referred to as **monastic medicine**, since medicine was based in the monastery. Medical practice was officially controlled by the early Christian Church in Byzantium (which later became Constantinople and then Istanbul), which was extremely hostile to physicians. This hostility was based on two precepts: (1) disease and illness are beneficial in that they test one's faith and commitment to God and the church, and (2) all illnesses occur as punishment by God, possession by the devil, or the result of witchcraft.

These religious causes required religious cures—typically prayer, penitence, or intercession of saints. Particular diseases and body parts were believed to have a patron saint who could inflict pain and enact cure. For example, if one had a toothache, prayer was made to Saint Apollonia. According to the church, private physicians represented a form of blasphemy in their efforts to cure disease apart from religious intervention. In reality, many people from all stations in life considered secular healing to be an appropriate complement to religious healing, and often used the services of herbalists, midwives, wise women, and lay specialists. These practitioners are largely responsible for preserving much of the medical knowledge that had been passed on to them and ensuring its transmission to later generations (Bennett, 2000).

Arabic Medicine

The commonwealth of Islam was founded in 622 by Mohammed. During the next 100 years, his followers conquered almost half of the world known at that time. By 1000, the Arab Empire extended from Spain to India. The Arabs were intensely interested in medicine. They built famous teaching hospitals, bestowed high prestige on private physicians, and basically served as the link between Greek medicine and Renaissance medicine (Magner, 2005).

Scholastic Medicine

The second half of the Medieval Era is referred to as the time of **scholastic medicine**. In 1130, a proclamation from the Council of Clermont forbade monks from practicing medicine because

---

IN THE FIELD

A MEDIEVAL JOKE

If you want to be cured of	Apply it
I don't know what	I don't know where
Take this herb of	And you will be cured
I don't know what name	I don't know when

it was too disruptive to the peace and order of monastic sequestration. Rather than shifting medicine to the private sector, medical practice became the province of the secular clergy, and universities began to play a prominent role in the education of physicians. Although it is impossible to fix the precise date at which universities in the modern sense first developed, twelfth- and thirteenth-century schools became centers where a variety of disciplines were taught (probably the most important legacy of the Middle Ages) (Magner, 2005).

Two other occurrences during this era are significant. (1) There were numerous devastating epidemics (leprosy reached a peak in the thirteenth century, epidemics of scurvy were common, and the Bubonic Plague—**Black Death**—caught hold in Europe in the 1340s and killed an estimated 43 million people in 20 years) that made clear the total helplessness of physicians to restrain disease (Porter, 2006). (2) The earliest hospitals developed in the monastic period (although they were mostly places of refuge for the poor, the clergy did provide caring concern for those who came to them).

MEDICINE IN THE RENAISSANCE

The fifteenth and sixteenth centuries—the Renaissance—represent a rebirth in the arts and philosophy, scientific endeavor, technological advancement, and medicine. The scholarly blinders of the Middle Ages were discarded in favor of *humanism*, which stressed the dignity of the individual, the importance of this life (and not solely the afterlife), and spiritual freedom.

Andreas Vesalius

A key early event of the Renaissance was the refutation (at long last) of many of Galen's ideas. Andreas Vesalius (1514–1564), a product of a Brussels medical family, contradicted

Galen's description of anatomy. Using corpses purchased from grave robbers, he discovered that Galen's descriptions accurately portrayed monkeys but, in many respects, not humans. For centuries, people had believed that Galen's conclusions were based on human dissection, yet they were not! Vesalius contended that if Galen was wrong about anatomy, he might be wrong about his other medical conclusions (e.g., pneuma). Yet allegiance to Galen's ideas was so strong that Vesalius was dismissed from his university position for this heresy, and his career as an anatomist was finished (although he later became a court physician). It was not until 1628 that Englishman William Harvey demonstrated conclusively that blood circulates throughout the body in an action stimulated by the heart (Kennedy, 2004).

Paracelsus

The humoral theory of disease also came under attack. Philippus Aureolus Theophrastus Bombastus von Hohenheim (1493–1541)—Paracelsus, for short—held that God revealed medical truth to humans through revelation. A devotee of astrology and alchemy (the chemistry of the day), he criticized the humoral theory, spent much of his life searching for specific pharmacological remedies, and produced some modest successes. Although often disliked for his attacks on Galen, and a thoroughly contradictory fellow, Paracelsus is nevertheless an important figure in medical history.

Medical Specialization

During the Renaissance, the medical specialization that had begun to develop in the ninth or tenth century became more pronounced. *Physicians* were those who had graduated from a school of medicine. They provided diagnosis and consultation and were expected to bear themselves as gentlemen so as to match the demeanor of their wealthy patients. *Surgeons* were lower in status because they practiced skills learned in apprenticeship. Their primary responsibilities were to treat external complaints (e.g., wounds and abscesses), repair broken bones, and perform minor surgeries. In some areas, *barber surgeons* were available to perform major surgery (often on the war-wounded), and many also practiced bloodletting. Approximately equal in prestige to surgeons, *apothecaries* dispensed herbs and spices prescribed by physicians and, especially in the countryside, often took on the physician's duties. Nevertheless, self-medication and lay healing were very common in the Renaissance, and families placed priority on staying well.

MEDICINE FROM 1600 TO 1900

The Seventeenth Century

The development of modern science is the key event of the seventeenth century.

> This scientific revolution replaced previous concepts with new ideas of matter and its properties, new applications of mathematics to physics, and new methods of experimentation. By 1700, a "new world" view had taken form. Modern science rested on interchange and mutual verification of scientific ideas and information by investigators in many countries and these needs were satisfied by the development of scientific societies and publications. (Green, 1968:83)

In part, this scientific revolution was stimulated by several scientist-philosophers of the century, most notably Francis Bacon (1561–1626) and René Descartes (1596–1650). Bacon argued for "natural" explanations for events that could be understood through systematic observation and experimentation. Descartes invented analytical geometry and, through his work on momentum, vision, reflex actions, and a mind–body duality, laid the basis for a science of physiology.

William Harvey. The most important physiological advancement in the century was the confirmation by Englishman William Harvey (1578–1657) of the circulation of blood. Though the idea had been suggested by others earlier in history, Harvey was the first to offer experimental and quantitative proof.

Throughout his life, Harvey was a clinician-researcher. He maintained a clinical practice of medicine (in his later years being physician to kings and other members of the aristocracy) while he devoted himself to medical investigation in anatomy and physiology. Primarily through analysis of dissected and vivisected animals, observation of the weakening heartbeat of animals as they were about to die, and various forms of experimentation on human heartbeat, Harvey proved that the contraction of the heart drove blood into the major arteries toward the body's peripheries (and that cardiac valves prevented blood from re-entering the heart through the arteries). When the heart is resting between beats, it is filled with blood that has been carried to it by the veins. Although Harvey's finding removed a key obstacle to medical progress, the discovery was met with skepticism by some and open hostility by others. It had little influence on the treatment of patients during Harvey's time (even in his own practice), as physicians waited for further substantiation of his main ideas (Nuland, 1995).

Clinical Medicine. How did all this scientific theorizing affect patient treatment? The answer is very little. Even those theories now known to be accurate were met with skepticism, and the process of incorporating new knowledge or techniques into medical practice was quite slow. Medical superstitions were common, routine treatments often dangerous, and quackery quite prevalent. On the other hand, some seventeenth-century physicians focused their attention on the physician–patient relationship and on the body's self-healing capacity, and in this way maintained the Hippocratic tradition.

The Eighteenth Century

The eighteenth century—the "Age of Enlightenment"—is marked by efforts to collate the advancements of the preceding century and further refine knowledge in all fields, including medicine. People perceived that they were living at a special time of rapid growth, more open intellectual inquiry, advancement in the arts, literature, philosophy, and science, and freer political expression.

Development of a Modern Concept of Pathology. Although medical progress had been achieved in many areas, understanding of disease causation in the early eighteenth century was little different than it had been 2,500 years earlier. Many still advocated the humoral theory or some variation of it; others traced disease to climactic conditions, or focused on structural explanations such as the condition of the pores.

The understanding that diseases are attached to particular organs is traceable to Giovanni Battista Morgagni (1682–1771), an Italian physician and professor of anatomy at the University of Padua. Based on his systematic and thorough note taking of patients' symptoms, Morgagni developed the "anatomical concept of disease"—that diseases could be traced to particular pathology or disturbance in individual organs. Hence, he directed medicine to seek the originating localized disturbance in a particular organ. It may seem strange to us today that for so long physicians did not connect patients' symptoms with the corresponding pathological condition. And even those who challenged the prevailing notions of the day, like Andreas Vesalius and William Harvey, relied primarily on the old ways in the actual treatment of their own patients.

The Emergence of Public Health and Preventive Medicine. The eighteenth century also witnessed a return to interest in public health. Attention was focused on the unsanitary conditions that prevailed in industry, the armed forces, prisons, and hospitals. The lack of public sanitation in cities and contaminated water supplies were seen as significant threats to health. Individuals were encouraged to attend more to personal hygiene.

The foremost accomplishment of this movement was the discovery of an effective preventive measure against smallpox, a leading cause of death among children. Edward Jenner (1749–1823), a British country doctor, had heard that milkmaids infected by cowpox developed an immunity to smallpox. Through experimentation (on humans), Jenner demonstrated that persons inoculated with cowpox (i.e., vaccinated) would not develop the disease. Although initially regarded with suspicion, it was a signal event in the history of preventive medicine (Magner, 2005).

Alternative Paths of Medicine. While discussing the advancement of ideas later confirmed by science, competing theories and treatments of the day are often overlooked. The discoveries of Morgagni and Jenner, for example, do not mean that medicine was not simultaneously taking alternative routes. For example, William Cullen of Edinburgh (1712–1790) founded a medical system based on "nervous forces"—that all diseases were a result of over-stimulation or an inability to respond to stimulation. Appropriate cures were found in stimulants and depressants. Edinburgh-trained James Graham established a "Temple of Health and Hymen" in London. The temple was filled with beautiful young virgins attired in skimpy costumes who would sing to the sick—an approach that seemed logical to Graham, who believed that illness could only be cured in the presence of beautiful sights and sounds (Camp, 1977).

The Nineteenth Century

Many eighteenth- and nineteenth-century inventions stimulated a rapid growth in the iron and textile industries and led to the Industrial Revolution. Industrialization began in England and then spread to the rest of Europe and the United States. The development of large industries with many jobs pulled large numbers of workers into concentrated areas. The world was not prepared to deal with the consequences of this urbanization process. The cities that grew up around the industries were severely overcrowded, typically unsanitary, and often lacked safe procedures for food and water storage. These conditions produced a very unhealthy living environment.

Hospital Medicine. The first half of the nineteenth century is known mostly for the importance that physicians and medical researchers attached to clinical observation. Whereas medicine in the Middle Ages had been centered in monasteries and libraries, and in the Renaissance (as in antiquity) had been centered on the individual sickbed, in the nineteenth century, for the first time, it was centered on the hospital.

Hospitals had existed for centuries, but increased rapidly in number in the 1800s in response to the massive number of people migrating into the newly developing cities. Communicable diseases became commonplace; many of the urban migrants contracted typhoid fever and tuberculosis. Admission to a hospital was the only resort. These patients provided an unprecedented opportunity for clinicians and researchers to observe the sick and search for common patterns in their symptomology, disease progression, and response to medication. By the 1830s, especially in Paris, physician-researchers were increasingly taking advantage of the opportunity to separate patients by condition and specialize in particular conditions in order to expand medical knowledge (Weisz, 2003). Simultaneous advances in science and technology (e.g., the invention of the stethoscope by Laennec) were extremely important events of this era, but the immediate course of medicine was more strongly influenced by clinical observation in hospitals.

Laboratory Medicine. The laboratory became the focus in the second half of the century. The work of Morgagni and others had fixed attention on pathology in particular organs, but no one knew what caused something in the organ to go awry. Many theories existed, and each sought "the" answer to unlock this key mystery. The absence of a correct answer to this question was repeatedly made obvious by the absence of effective cures.

> They bled their patients, and they puked them and purged them and blistered them as their professional forefathers had always done; they confused the metabolisms of the sick with dazzling combinations of botanicals whose real actions were only partially known, and often not known at all. They stimulated in cases whose cause was thought to be too little excitation, and they tried to induce a touch of torpor when the opposite was the case. In short, except when the need for amputation or lancing was obvious, the healers didn't really know what they were doing. (Nuland, 1995:306)

Discovery of the Cell. The answer to the mystery is, of course, the cell, and credit for its discovery and interpretation goes to the German pathologist Rudolf Virchow (1821–1902). Virchow pinpointed the cell as the basic physiological matter, and understood that disease begins with some alteration in the normally functioning, healthy cell. Effective treatment depends on restoring the cell to normality (or at least terminating its abnormal development).

Ironically, while Virchow's discovery of the human cell appropriately led to study of the physiological changes involved in disease progression, Virchow was a leading proponent of the importance of environmental influences on health and illness. He understood that one's social class position, occupation, and involvement in social networks had as much to do with creating sickness as cellular changes. He referred to medicine as a "social science" and as the "science of man," and sought to influence societal conditions that have a negative impact on human health (Kennedy, 2004). The final 30 years of his life were largely devoted to explorations in the fields of anthropology and archaeology, the development of public health measures in his home town of Berlin, and advocating for democratic reform and political and cultural freedom in Germany. He was a much beloved figure in Germany at the time of his death.

The Germ Theory of Disease. One more question remained. What causes a cell to begin to change? What substance or condition initiates the disease process? At various points in history, medical researchers had speculated on the existence of microorganisms, but the speculation never inspired any substantial following. From the 1830s through the 1860s, various researchers observed bacteria under the microscope (minute organisms were first observed under a microscope by its inventor, Leeuwenhoek, in 1675), but their significance was not understood at the time.

The key figure in the development of the **germ theory of disease** is Louis Pasteur (1822–1895), a French chemist, now called the "Father of Modern Medicine." In 1857, Pasteur countered prevailing understandings by demonstrating that fermentation (he lived in the wine region) was not solely a chemical event but also the result of various microorganisms. By 1862, he had disproved the notion that bacteria were spontaneously generated.

However, it was not until 1877, after 20 years of research on microorganisms, that Pasteur turned to human diseases. He identified the specific bacteria involved in anthrax and chicken cholera and, with several of his pupils, identified other disease-causing bacteria, and developed effective vaccinations against them. By 1881, the germ theory of disease was generally accepted.

Louis Pasteur, called the "Father of Modern Medicine," is credited with discovering the role of microorganisms as a cause of many human diseases. © Georgios Kollidas /Fotolia.

With the impetus provided by Pasteur, one bacteriological discovery after another occurred. Between 1878 and 1887, the causative agents for gonorrhea, typhoid fever, leprosy, malaria, tuberculosis, cholera, diphtheria, tetanus, pneumonia, and epidemic meningitis were discovered (Magner, 2005).

The success of these efforts inspired an exciting period in medical history. Researchers would focus on a particular disease, identify the organism that caused it, determine how it invaded the body, and identify a vaccine that would prevent it. The mass media—newspapers, magazines, health education pamphlets, radio, motion pictures, and even comic books—joined in and promoted medical advancements (Hansen, 2009).

At first, however, it was understood only that vaccines worked. It required another ten years to understand why—that the body produces antibodies in response to the presence of a disease, and that these antibodies remain in the body to fight the disease on future exposures (Magner, 2005).

Progress in Surgery.   Considerable progress in surgery also occurred during this time due to three essential advancements: (1) an understanding of the "localized" nature of disease (when surgeons believed that diseases were caused by generalized forces, like humors, it made little sense to remove a particular area or organ); (2) an ability to control the patient's pain in the surgical process (which occurred in incremental stages based on trial and error throughout the nineteenth century); and (3) an ability to prevent wound infection. Throughout history, surgeons recognized that almost all surgeries (even "successful" surgery) resulted in a frequently fatal infection in the wound site. ("The operation was a success, but the patient died.") Surgery performed in hospitals was especially likely to result in infection.

The importance of "asepsis" (surgical cleanliness) was discovered by Sir Joseph Lister (1827–1912), an English surgeon. Lister's concern was prompted by the very large percentage (almost half) of his amputation patients who died as a result of infection. At first convinced that infection was caused by the air that came into contact with the wound, Lister altered his thinking when he read descriptions of Pasteur's work. By the mid-1860s, he realized that sepsis (an inflammatory response throughout the body to infection) was caused by bacteria in the air rather than by the air itself. Lister learned that applying carbolic acid to the wound, his hands, the surgical instruments, and the dressings used to close the wound prevented sepsis from occurring (Magner, 2005).

THE ASCENDANCY OF MEDICAL AUTHORITY IN AMERICA

Early America

The earliest explorers to America found that Native Americans relied mostly on supernatural explanations for disease and illness. Diagnosis of disease and illness and treatment were often assigned to separate individuals. Treatment of the sick was typically assigned to a "medicine man" who could intercede with the gods and, it was hoped, drive off evil spirits. Among the most common ailments were those related to the active and difficult lifestyle—fractures, dislocations, and wounds.

The Early Colonists.   The earliest colonists endured an excruciatingly difficult voyage across the ocean (typically requiring three or more months) only to be met with tremendous hardship upon arrival. Although warned about the danger of disease by their sponsor, the London Company, the Jamestown settlers in 1607 were more concerned about being attacked by Indians. They selected a site for their new home that had a military advantage (being able to see up and down the river) but was limited by an inadequate food supply and brackish water. Six months after their arrival, 60 of the 100 who landed had died from dietary disorders or other diseases.

The Plymouth Colony in Massachusetts had a similar experience. Due to an outbreak of scurvy and other diseases, only 50 of the 102 arrivals survived the first three months. Epidemics and other infectious diseases (e.g., malaria, dysentery, typhoid fever, influenza, smallpox, scarlet fever, yellow fever, and consumption—tuberculosis) were the primary killers during the colonial years (Green, 1968).

The colonists also brought with them from Europe several contagious diseases (e.g., measles, smallpox, and mumps) that had been unknown in the Americas. Lacking immunity to these diseases, Native American populations

were very susceptible to them and were decimated in continuing outbreaks. Some historians
estimate that up to 90 percent of Native
Americans died in this process (Cassady, 1991).

Although health problems were rampant in
the colonies, conditions for slaves were especially bad. Subjected to massive overwork, poor
food, housing, and sanitation, and inadequate
medical care, the health of slaves was very poor
in both an absolute and relative sense.

Early Medical Practitioners.   Medical
care was provided by colonists (often clergy)
who had some formal education (not necessarily
in medicine). The only known medical work
published in America in the 1600s was by the
Reverend Thomas Thatcher of the Old South
Church in Boston. The Reverend Cotton Mather
(1663–1728) (precocious, vain, and fanatical
about witches) is often called the first significant
figure in American medicine. Though a full-time
clergyman, Mather read widely about medicine,
wrote numerous treatises and books on anatomy
and therapeutic medicine, and is known for an
understanding of inoculation far beyond that of
his contemporaries.

There were a few trained physicians and
surgeons who had migrated to the colonies from
Europe, and it was common for young men to
attach themselves to these physicians as apprentices (typically for four to seven years). However,
in colonial America, people from all walks of life
took up medicine and referred to themselves as
physicians. Many added the physician's duties to
another job, such as food merchant, wig maker, or
cloth manufacturer (Starr, 1982). Much medical
care was delivered by the apothecary. Although
apothecaries primarily made their living by
providing drugs and medical preparations, they
also gave medical advice, dressed wounds, and
even performed amputations (Magner, 2005).

Obviously, in such conditions, there was little
in the way of professionalized medicine. The first
comprehensive hospital in the United States (the
Pennsylvania Hospital in Philadelphia) was not
built until 1751 (and the second not until 20 years
later in New York); the first efforts to license
medicine came in 1760 (in New York); the first
formalized medical school (at the College of
Philadelphia) was established in 1765; and the
first state medical society (in New Jersey) organized in 1766.

Domestic Medicine.   Given these conditions,
it is not surprising that families assumed primary
responsibility for protecting the health of family
members and providing therapeutic agents when
they were sick. Women stored medicinal herbs
just as they did preserves, made up syrups, salves,
and lotions, bandaged injuries, and were expected
to tend to sick family members. They called on
other family and friends in the community for
advice, and sometimes sought the assistance of an
older woman in the community known for her
healing knowledge (Cassady, 1991; Starr, 1982).

Domestic medicine was supported by an
ideology that individuals and families were
capable of providing for the ill. Texts on domestic
medicine (typically written by physicians) were
available, as was advice through newspapers and
almanacs as well as word of mouth. Medical
jargon was criticized as being unnecessary and
discouraging people from family treatment.

The Revolution to the Mid-1800s

Although there were only about 3,500 physicians
in the country at the start of the Revolutionary
War (and only 400 of these had a university
medical degree), medicine was making progress.
Many of the physicians were as competent as the
times allowed, and they took their responsibility
to apprentices seriously. Many of America's
founders, such as Benjamin Franklin, John
Adams, and Thomas Jefferson, were captivated
by the spirit of science, although that developed
in medicine in America only much later (Abrams,
2013).

Americans who could afford formal medical education often traveled to the University of Edinburgh, then considered the world's finest medical school, or other European centers. By the turn of the century, the country had established four medical schools (Pennsylvania, Columbia, Harvard, and Dartmouth), each of which sought to offer excellence in medical training (but with a minimum of faculty members; Dartmouth had a one-man medical faculty for over a decade).

The most famous American physician of this era was Benjamin Rush (1745–1813), who, after serving an apprenticeship in the colonies, earned a medical degree from the University of Edinburgh. Rush, a signer of the Declaration of Independence and a strong advocate for temperance and the abolition of slavery, wrote extensively on his medical observations and made substantial contributions to the understanding of yellow fever and psychological problems. He argued against the common stigmatization of the mentally ill, and urged that those with mental health problems be treated with kindness and humaneness (Magner, 2005).

Nevertheless, he preached and practiced many of the medical errors of the day. He believed that all symptoms and sickness were traceable to just one disease—a "morbid excitement" induced by "capillary tension," and he recommended and used bloodletting and purging as common cures (Magner, 2005).

America's experience in the Revolutionary War highlighted the lack of accurate knowledge about disease causation and treatment. The annual death rate in the Continental army was approximately 20 percent; 90 percent of war deaths were the direct result of disease (Green,

---

IN THE FIELD

THE DEATH OF A PRESIDENT

In December 1799, the president went out riding and got caught in a cold freezing rain, hail, and snow. When he returned to the house, he went to dinner without changing his wet clothes. He quickly came down with a cold, hoarseness, and a severe sore throat.

He was feeling worse the next morning, and three physicians were called in. A mixture of molasses, vinegar, and butter was provided, but it brought on near-fatal choking. A short time later, a bloodletter was added to the team. At various points during the day, blood was removed from the patient: 12 to 14 ounces at 7:30 A.M., an additional 18 ounces at 9:30 A.M., and another 18 ounces at 11:00 A.M. Despite continued pleadings by his wife for caution, another 32 ounces of blood were let at 3:00 P.M. At 4:00 P.M., calomel (mercurous chloride) and tartar emetic (antimony potassium tartrate) were administered.

After a brief spell of improvement, his condition began to weaken. Various poultices and compresses were applied. Around 10:00 P.M., he whispered burial instructions to a friend. A few minutes later, the recently retired first president of the United States, George Washington, died.

Did the attempted cure kill the former president? It is clear that the bloodletting did not help and probably hastened Washington's death. It is now generally agreed that Washington had acute bacterial epiglottis. The youngest of the three physicians had argued unsuccessfully to do a very new technique at the time, a tracheotomy, to assist Washington's breathing. That might have worked and prolonged his life (Morens, 1999; Wallenborn, 1997).

1968). See the accompanying box, "The Death of a President," on the use of bloodletting as a factor in George Washington's death.

Frontier Medicine. In the early nineteenth century, many of America's most important contributions to medicine occurred in the expanding Midwestern region of the country. This is explained by the extremely difficult life lived by those on the frontier and their suscepti-bility to disease. Life was difficult, and food was often in short supply (Steele, 2005).

Although families typically practiced home-made remedies (based on both trial and error and superstition), there were some remarkable medical achievements. Ephraim McDowell (1771–1830), an Edinburgh-trained physician practicing in Danville, Kentucky, was the first to successfully practice ovariotomies (in 1809, he removed a 22½-pound ovarian tumor from a woman who had originally thought herself preg-nant). The experience of William Beaumont (1785–1853) with a young accidental gunshot victim led to experiments on digestion (Green, 1968). Daniel Drake (1785–1870) wrote about the influence on health of physical and social environmental factors (e.g., climate, diet, ethnicity, lifestyle, and occupation), encouraged collaboration among physicians, and was a strong proponent of physician licensure.

The Status of Medicine. Despite these advancements, medicine remained a very down-graded occupation. Physicians had little genuine understanding of disease causation, and few effective treatments. Sometimes their cures were helpful (e.g., using willow bark, a source of aspirin, or rose hips, the ripened fruit of the rose bush and a good source of vitamin C, for fevers). Other remedies may not have been helpful, but neither were they harmful (e.g., using fried daisies for a compress, or putting feverish patients in a tent with burning tobacco). However, some cures were very harmful (e.g.,

bleeding, purging, amputation for any broken limb, and trephination).

Alternative Philosophies. For a variety of reasons, physicians were poorly paid (and often not paid at all). These reasons include: (1) the fact that family medicine was preferred by many, (2) the difficulty in seeing a substantial number of patients in a day (people lived far apart and efficient transportation was lacking), (3) the inability of many patients to pay for care (much care was provided on credit but never reimbursed), and (4) the fact that many people offered themselves as physicians (without licensure requirements, there was virtually unlimited entry into the field). Given these conditions, many could not justify the cost of formal education. Through the first half of the 1800s, then, physicians enjoyed little prestige (Starr, 1982).

Many alternative healing philosophies (medical sects) competed throughout this time period. "Thomsonianism" was created by Samuel Thompson (1769–1843), a New Hampshirite, who had had unhappy experiences with "regular" physicians. His motto was "Every man his own physician." He believed that disease resulted from insufficient heat, and could be countered by measures that would restore natural heat (e.g., steam baths that would promote intense sweating, and "hot" botanicals such as red pepper). Over three decades, Thompson's influence grew, and he attracted many followers (Steele, 2005).

A second important medical sect, homeop-athy, was founded by a German physician, Samuel Hahnemann (1755–1843), who viewed diseases as being primarily of the spirit. Homeopaths believed that diseases could be cured by drugs that produced the same symp-toms when given to a healthy person (the homeo-pathic law of "similars"—that like cures like). The rationale was that after a patient had taken a homeopathic medicine, their natural disease would be displaced by a weaker, but similar, artificial disease that the body could more easily overcome (Starr, 1982). For example, homeopaths view coughing as the body's effort to deal with foreign substances in the lung. Whereas medical doctors would typically try to suppress the cough, homeopaths would regard this as stifling the body's natural curative processes.

Conventional physicians (who were referred to as allopaths and as practicing allopathic medicine) were vocally critical of homeopaths and others who practiced forms of medicine contrary to the allopaths. They sought to discredit them, often refused to interact with them, and attempted to drive them from the field of medicine. You can read more about the relationship between conventional and alternative medicine in Chapter 11.

1850 Onward

At least three events of major significance during the second half of the nineteenth century and the first half of the twentieth century combined to "professionalize" medicine.

The Civil War.   As has frequently occurred, war dramatizes both the technological strengths and weaknesses of a society. Despite the ferocity of battle between the Union and Confederate forces, disease and illness represented the most lethal forces of the Civil War. An estimated 618,000 persons were killed during the Civil War—one-third from battle fatalities and two-thirds from disease and illness. Diarrhea and dysentery were the major killers, while numerous deaths were caused by smallpox, typhoid, yellow fever, pneumonia, scarlet fever, and infection from surgical procedures.

The wounded often lay on the battlefield for days until a conflict subsided and they could be moved. Wounds commonly became infected. Surgery was very primitive. Although anesthesia was often used, it typically took the form of alcohol or opium. In some instances, the patient was hit in the jaw to knock him out, or else the patient would simply bite down on a piece of wood or even a bullet (hence the expression "bite the bullet") as a distraction.

To remove a bullet, the surgeon would put his unwashed hand in the open wound, squish around until the bullet was found, and pull it out. Scalpels used for amputation (there were approximately 60,000 amputations during the Civil War—75 percent of all operations) were not washed, the blade was often dull, and whatever sharpening occurred was done on the surgeon's boot sole. Surgeons bragged about the speed with which they could amputate a limb (the best were called 1½-minute men). Almost everyone got infections, and many died from them. For comparison purposes, in Vietnam, 1 in every 75 wounded soldiers died, whereas in World War Two, 1 in 33 wounded died, and in the Civil War, 1 in 7 wounded died.

The lack of effective medical care was obviously frustrating and in fact inspired several ways of improving care both on the battlefield and in society in general. Military physicians were encouraged to systematically observe their patients and to undertake whatever kind of experimentation might produce helpful knowledge (Devine, 2014). Professional nursing was begun during the Civil War as a means of assisting in the treatment of wounded soldiers. The ambulance corps was initiated to move the wounded from the battlefield to field hospitals. These experiences helped medical personnel to learn about sanitation and other public health measures.

Medical Advancements.   As discussed earlier, the discovery by Pasteur that microorganisms cause disease is considered by many to be the single most important medical discovery ever made. Coupled with Lister's recognition of the importance of sepsis, and the discovery by Wilhelm Roentgen (1845–1923) of X-rays and their diagnostic utility in the 1890s, much improved disease diagnosis was possible. These advancements meant that knowledge existed that required specialized training.

The germ theory of disease stimulated a massive and effective assault on infectious disease through prevention (immunization) and treatment. The decades from the 1920s through to the 1940s represent years of peak pharmacological success—a time when one "magical bullet" after another was discovered. Insulin was discovered in 1921, and vitamin C was isolated in 1928 (enabling better understanding of vitamin deficiency diseases), the same year that a vaccine for yellow fever was produced. The potential for sulfa drugs (in preventing the growth or multiplication of bacteria) was realized in the 1930s, and the ability of penicillin to kill bacteria was fully understood by the 1940s. For a time, great optimism was engendered that all diseases and illnesses could be eradicated.

An unfortunate consequence of this focus on germ-caused disease was the turning away of attention from the "whole person." Some of the most valuable lessons to be learned from the Hippocratic tradition, such as the influence of lifestyle, the importance of inner harmony and moderation in life, the mind–body connection, and the importance of person-oriented medicine, were lost in the rush to identify microorganismic culprits and methods of conquering them. It would be decades before the importance of these themes would be remembered.

The Organization of Professional Medicine. During the first half of the nineteenth century, several localities and states formed professional medical societies. While there was considerable variation in their objectives and activities, each focused primarily on promoting the professionalization of medicine. On May 5, 1847, 250 physicians representing many of these medical societies and some medical schools met in Philadelphia to establish a national medical society, the **American Medical Association (AMA)**.

The motivation to establish the AMA was partly ideological and partly economic. Competition from homeopaths and other alternative healers was limiting financial success for physicians and reducing pride in the field. Physicians openly sought more esteem and condemned those who used alternative approaches (Magner, 2005; Steele, 2005). In part, the motivation for creating the AMA was similar to Hippocrates' motivation for writing his famous oath—to establish visible standards for the practice of medicine so as to gain greater confidence from the general public.

The AMA identified its chief goals as (1) the promotion of the science and art of medicine, (2) the betterment of public health, (3) the standardization of requirements for medical degrees, (4) the development of an internal system of licensing and regulation, and (5) the development of a code of medical ethics.

However, it would be years before the AMA would develop into an important force in medicine. Several states and some medical schools opposed uniform standards in education and licensing requirements. There was general public sentiment against legitimizing a particular medical orientation, as it was not clear that the brand of medicine offered by the AMA was superior to the many alternative healing philosophies in existence.

Forces Stimulating Professionalization

Three pivotal events strengthened the position of the AMA in medicine. First, the discovery of the germ theory of disease offered medical schools a sound approach to disease causation and treatment, and provided the public with a clear rationale for preferring formally trained physicians.

Second, the AMA was eventually successful in achieving one of its key goals—**medical licensure** requirements. The AMA and the country's top medical schools argued that licensure would restrict the practice of medicine to those who had been formally trained and were able to demonstrate competency. Opposition stemmed both from those who wanted to maximize the choices people had available for medical practitioners and from the administrations of many of the lower-quality medical schools who feared that their graduates would not be able to pass a licensure exam. By the early 1900s, the battle had largely been won, as most states required a license to practice medicine.

These two events were necessary, but not sufficient in the AMA's drive for professional authority. By 1900, there were approximately 110,000 physicians in the United States, but only 8,000 of them belonged to the AMA. Reorganization of the AMA in 1901 (tightening the relationship among local, state, and national associations and increasing the power of the AMA's governing board) provided a boost to the association, but one more thing was needed—control of medical education.

In the late 1800s and early 1900s, there was considerable variation in the quality of America's medical schools. More than 400 medical schools had been created in the United States in the 1800s (more than twice as many as exist today.) Some, like Harvard and Johns Hopkins, offered sound training in the basic sciences and substantial clinical experience under close supervision, and had excellent resources. The majority, however, were not linked to a university and did not have access to the faculty, library resources, and facilities provided in the better schools. In many cases, admission standards were non-existent, and there was no training provided in the basic sciences, and little or no clinical supervision. As late as the 1870s, one physician was quoted as saying that "It is very well understood among college boys that after a man has failed in scholarship, failed in writing, failed in speaking, failed in every purpose for which he entered college; after he has dropped down from class to

class; after he has been kicked out of college; there is one unfailing city of refuge—the profession of medicine" (Numbers, 1985:186).

The Flexner Report.   The AMA contracted with the Carnegie Foundation to study the quality of medical education. They hired Abraham Flexner to conduct a comprehensive study of all the medical schools in the United States and Canada. Upon hearing of this study, many schools closed immediately rather than risk being condemned. Flexner's team visited the 155 remaining schools. His final report, the **Flexner Report**, issued in 1910, praised the efforts of many schools (Harvard, Western Reserve, McGill, Toronto, and especially Johns Hopkins) but lambasted those that offered inferior programs. He recommended that the number of schools be reduced to 31 and that medical education be subjected to formal regulation.

The Great Trade of 1910

The only national standards available for accrediting medical schools were those that had been prepared by the Council on Medical Education (CME) of the AMA. In 1910, the states and the federal government made a deal with the AMA. In return for providing the best and most efficient health care system, the states and the federal government gave the CME monopoly over the production and licensing of physicians, including the power to establish standards for medical schools. In this **Great Trade of 1910**, the AMA was given a near-exclusive right to regulate the medical profession. With the power of knowledge supplied by the germ theory of disease and the organizational legitimacy provided by the states and the federal government, the powerful position of the AMA was secured. In turn, the AMA institutionalized scientific medicine as the foundation of America's health care system.

PERSPECTIVES ON THE ASCENDANCY OF MEDICAL AUTHORITY

Attempts to interpret and explain the ascendancy of scientific medicine and professionalized medicine (i.e., medical authority) in the United States have followed various lines. Two contrasting approaches—those of Paul Starr and Vicente Navarro—are summarized here.

Paul Starr

Paul Starr's *The Social Transformation of American Medicine* (1982) is a fascinating and well-documented description and analysis of the evolution of the medical profession in America. Starr (who won the Pulitzer Prize for this work) describes the rise of medical authority in America, as medicine was transformed from a relatively weak and poorly regarded occupation into a powerful and prestigious "sovereign" profession, and how the efforts of medicine to maintain professional autonomy by limiting government control have left it open to being taken over by corporatization. The second of these points will be examined in later chapters. The first point addresses the bases for the ascendancy of medical authority in America, and is discussed here.

Starr acknowledges the synergistic relationship between the advance of science and the professionalization of medicine, but contends that something more than the former is needed to explain medicine's acquisition of economic power and political influence in America, and its ability to shape the health care system. Paul Wolpe summarizes this point.

A profession's power rests on its consensually granted authority over a specific, cultural tradition. Knowledge and maintenance of that tradition is the profession's social capital, and it must guard that capital from challenges while projecting an aura of confidence, competence, trust, and self-criticism. Professions institutionalize control over social capital by establishing licensing proce-

dures, internally-run educational institutions, and self-regulation. But institutional legitimacy, while somewhat self-sustaining, also depends on ongoing public acceptance of a profession's claim of exclusive expertise over a realm of specialized knowledge. Lacking broad coercive powers, professions have developed strategies to protect their socially granted right to interpret their particular cultural tradition. (Wolpe, 1985:409)

Starr suggests that professions develop authority in order to maintain their position. This includes social authority (Max Weber's notion of controlling actions through commands; authority is typically built into laws or rules or bureaucratic protocol) and cultural authority (which Starr defines as "the probability that particular definitions of reality and judgments of meaning and value will prevail as valid and true") (Starr, 1982:13). **Cultural authority of medicine** is manifested in the "awe and respect from the general public and legislators" that allow medicine to set its own conditions of practice (e.g., site of care and payment mechanism) (Anderson, 1983:1243). While social authority can be legislated, professions must "persuade" publics that they are deserving of cultural authority.

The triumph of the regular profession depended on belief rather than force, on its growing cultural authority rather than sheer power, on the success of its claims to competence and understanding rather than the strong arm of the police. To see the rise of the profession as coercive is to underestimate how deeply its authority penetrated the beliefs of ordinary people and how firmly it had seized the imagination even of its rivals. (Starr, 1982:229)

What structural changes in medicine resulted from this "social transformation"? Starr (1982) delineates five key changes. (1) The growth of hospitals created a desire for hospital privileges and referrals, which caused physicians to become more colleague dependent and less patient dependent. (2) Gaining control of medical education and the licensure process enabled the profession to restrict entry into the field and shape the evolution of the profession. (3) Having medicine viewed as a special type of field legitimated the expenditure of enormous sums of public money for hospital construction, medical education, medical research, and public health. (4) Physicians gained nearly complete control over conditions of medical practice (e.g., the setting of fees), and established significant political influence. (5) Medicine established very clear professional boundaries that were to be respected by others.

By the 1920s, the ascendancy of medical authority was clear. According to Starr, this occurred largely because the public believed in professionalized medicine (giving it "cultural authority") and allowing it to secure its position of dominance. Although the sovereignty of medicine would not peak for several decades (probably around 1970), its prominent position and ability to control the health care system were firmly established.

Vicente Navarro

An alternative view of the ascendancy of medical authority in America is presented by sociologists and medical historians who follow a social conflict approach. Vicente Navarro, a Marxist scholar who has written extensively about medicine, disagrees with three assumptions he finds in Starr's approach.

> Starr's interpretation of America sees the past and present structure of power in the United States as reflecting the wishes of the majority of Americans. To see the structure of power in America as the outcome of what Americans want, however, is to beg the question of which Americans. If by Americans it is meant the majority of Americans, then two assumptions are being made. One is that

the majority of Americans share a set of beliefs, values, and wants that provide an ideological cohesiveness to the totality of the unit called America. The other assumption is that the majority of Americans have had and continue to have the power to determine what happens both in the private sector of America (through market forces) and in the public sector (through representative public institutions). To these two assumptions Starr adds a third: the dominant ideologies and positions become dominant through their powers of persuasion rather than through coercion and repression of alternative ideologies and positions. (Navarro, 1984:515)

Navarro emphasizes that Americans have been and continue to be "divided into classes, races, genders, and other power groupings, each with its own interests, set of beliefs, and wants that are in continuous conflict and struggle" (Navarro, 1984:515). These groups have different levels of power, and interact within a dominant–dominated framework. In society in general and within medicine, powerful groups are decisive due to the resources they have acquired. They get their way not because they successfully persuade, but because they have sufficient power to coerce and repress the less powerful.

According to Navarro, the ascendancy of medical authority occurred (and the corporatization of medicine is now occurring) not because people willed it and not because they were persuaded that it was in their interests, but because it served the interests of powerful societal groups (the government, those sufficiently wealthy to afford medical education and private health care, and the corporate sector). These groups determine what options are provided for society, and ignore values and preferences (e.g., for universal coverage for health care) that they judge not to be in their interest.

SUMMARY

The study of the history of medicine is important both to understand earlier peoples and events and to decipher ways in which modern ideas and practices have evolved. Understanding of disease shifted from supernatural explanations in early humans, to a slightly more empirical basis in Egyptian society, to natural causes in the Greco-Roman era. Hippocrates, the "Father of Medicine," encouraged careful observation of sickness in patients, a close relationship between physician and patient, and ethical guidelines for physician behavior.

The centrality of religion's role in medicine re-emerged during the Medieval Era, but ultimately became overshadowed by the scientific perspective during the Renaissance. Particularly important was Pasteur's discovery of the germ theory of disease. Diseases were common in colonial America, trained physicians were few, accurate medical knowledge was limited, and most families cared for their own sick members. Physicians had little training, low prestige, and earned little money. The gradual implementation of the germ theory of disease led to other medical discoveries, much improved medical care, and widespread public health and disease prevention programs.

The AMA was established in 1847, although it did not become a powerful voice for medicine for several decades. The two key events in the institutionalization of the AMA were (1) the establishment of licensure requirements in states, thus controlling entry into the field, and (2) the federal government's granting of authority to the AMA to control standards in medical education.

Paul Starr emphasizes that medical authority ascended in the United States largely because the medical profession persuaded people that such power was in their best interest. Vicente Navarro contends that the profession of medicine and the health care system have evolved in ways determined by powerful groups.

HEALTH ON THE INTERNET

There are several informative sites about Hippocrates, his writings, and recent updates of his work. Read the Introductory Note, the Oath of Hippocrates, and the Law of Hippocrates at

www.bartleby.com/38/1/.

Consider the following questions:

1. The final paragraph of the Introductory Note contains an aphorism about the art of the physician. What is the meaning of this statement? What does it say about the physician–patient relationship? Have you observed any occasions when a physician seemed to be practicing this art?

2. Point 2 in the Law of Hippocrates identifies several personal traits that Hippocrates believes should be found in persons seeking to become a physician. What do these traits say about Hippocrates' view of physicians? Are any of the traits surprising to you?

3. In what ways is the Law of Hippocrates consistent with the Oath of Hippocrates, and in what ways does it differ?

4. There are now many contemporaneously written oaths to which physicians and other health care providers pledge. Search online, identify one alternative oath, and compare and contrast it with the Hippocratic Oath.

DISCUSSION QUESTION

In his seminal work, *The Structure of Scientific Revolutions* (published in 1962), Thomas Kuhn describes the history of science as a series of eras each guided by a dominant paradigm (i.e., a theoretical perspective or general understanding of things). This is "normal science," and it is sustained through education and research apprenticeships whereby young scientists are socialized into the prevailing paradigm.

Occasionally, new theoretical insights or empirical findings appear that question the dominant paradigm. If these "anomalies" are infrequent or isolated occurrences, consensus around the dominant paradigm will be undisturbed. However, if these contradictory perspectives persist and are accepted, a "scientific revolution" may occur wherein the old paradigm is replaced by a new one. Kuhn sees scientific progress as occurring through revolutions rather than evolutions.

Based on your reading of this chapter and other familiarity you have with the history of medicine, would you say Kuhn's view is or is not applicable to the advancement of medical knowledge? Has the progression of medical knowledge and the understanding of the causes of disease occurred incrementally in an evolutionary process? Or have there been one or more revolutions in understanding disease and illness wherein new paradigms have become accepted?

GLOSSARY

American Medical Association (AMA)
Black Death
Code of Hammurabi
cultural authority of medicine
domestic medicine
Flexner Report
germ theory of disease
Great Trade of 1910
Hippocrates

Hippocratic Oath
humoral theory of disease
medical licensure
monastic medicine
scholastic medicine
shaman
supernatural explanations of disease
trephination

REFERENCES

Abrams, Jeanne E. 2013 *Revolutionary Medicine: The Founding Fathers and Mothers in Sickness and in Health.* New York: New York University Press.

Anderson, Odin. 1983 "Book Review of the Social Transformation of American Medicine." *Medical Care,* 21:1243–1245.

Bennett, David. 2000 "Medical Practice and Manuscripts in Byzantium." *Social History of Medicine,* 13:279–291.

Camp, John. 1974, 1977 *The Healer's Art: The Doctor through History.* New York: Taplinger Publishing Company.

Cassady, James H. 1991 *Medicine in America: A Short History.* Baltimore, MD: The Johns Hopkins University Press.

Devine, Shauna. 2014 *Learning from the Wounded: Civil War and the Rise of American Medical Science.* Chapel Hill, NC: The University of North Carolina Press.

Green, John R. 1968 *Medical History for Students.* Springfield, IL: Charles C. Thomas.

Hansen, Bert. 2009 *Picturing Medical Progress from Pasteur to Polio: A History of Mass Media Images and Popular Attitudes in America.* New Brunswick, NJ: Rutgers University Press.

Kennedy, Michael. 2004 *A Short History of Disease, Science, and Medicine.* Cranston, RI: The Writer's Collective.

Kuhn, Thomas S. 1962 *The Structure of Scientific Revolutions.* Chicago, IL: University of Chicago Press.

McKeown, Thomas. 1970 "A Sociological Approach to the History of Medicine." *Medical History*, 4:342–351.

Magner, Lois N. 2005 *A History of Medicine*, 2nd ed. Boca Raton, FL: Taylor & Francis.

Makah, Jonathan, and Marques Jalil. 2009 *The Healing of the Gods: Imhotep, Health and Healing in Ancient Kemet (Egypt)*. Seattle, WA: CreateSpace Independent Publishing Platform.

Mattern, Susan P. 1999 "Physicians and the Roman Imperial Aristocracy: The Patronage of Therapeutics." *Bulletin of the History of Medicine*, 73:1–18.

Morens, David M. 1999 "Death of a President." *New England Journal of Medicine*, 341:1845–1849.

Navarro, Vicente. 1984 "Medical History as Justification Rather than Explanation: A Critique of Starr's *The Social Transformation of American Medicine*." *International Journal of Health Services*, 14:511–527.

Nuland, Sherwin B. 1995 *Doctors: The Biography of Medicine*. New York: Knopf.

Numbers, Ronald L. 1985 "The Rise and Fall of the American Medical Profession." Pp. 185–196 in *Sickness and Health in America: Readings in the History of Medicine and Public Health* (2nd ed.), Judith W. Leavitt and Ronald L. Numbers (eds.). Madison, WI: University of Wisconsin Press.

Pickett, Anthony C. 1992 "The Oath of Imhotep: In Recognition of African Contributions to Western Medicine." *Journal of the National Medical Association*, 84:636–637.

Porter, Roy. 2006 *The Cambridge History of Medicine*. Cambridge, MA: Cambridge University Press.

Starr, Paul. 1982 *The Social Transformation of American Medicine*. New York: Basic Books, Inc., Publishers.

Steele, Volney. 2005 *Bleed, Blister, and Purge*. Missoula, MT: Mountain Press Publishing Company.

Wallenborn, White M. 1997 "George Washington's Terminal Illness: A Modern Medical Analysis of the Last Illness and Death of George Washington." *The Papers of George Washington*. www.gwpapers.virginia.edu/articles/wallenborn.html.

Weisz, George. 2003 "Medical Specialization in the Nineteenth Century." *Bulletin of the History of Medicine*, 77:536–575.

White, Kevin. 2009 *An Introduction to the Sociology of Health and Illness*. London: Sage Publications.

Wolpe, Paul R. 1985 "The Maintenance of Professional Authority: Acupuncture and the American Physician." *Social Problems*, 32:409–424.

CHAPTER 3

Social Epidemiology

Learning Objectives

- Define the term "social epidemiology," and identify the major research techniques used by epidemiologists.
- Identify and describe the five major stages of the epidemiological transition. Discuss the changing presence of acute infectious diseases and chronic degenerative diseases during these stages.
- Explain the poor performance of the United States relative to other countries regarding life expectancy and infant mortality.
- Explain the manner in which social class, race, and gender influence life expectancy, infant mortality, and morbidity in the United States.
- Describe how the meaning of "disability" has changed in the United States in the last 20 years. Identify social factors that influence the likelihood of disability.

The field of social epidemiology focuses on understanding the causes and distribution of diseases and impairments within a population. Early in the history of the field, epidemiologists concentrated primarily on identifying the microorganisms responsible for epidemics of acute infectious diseases. Utilizing the germ theory of disease (see Chapter 2), epidemiologists achieved much success in identifying the responsible agents. As populations became less susceptible to infectious diseases and less likely to die from them, chronic degenerative diseases such as coronary heart disease and cancer became more prominent.

Gradually, the focus of **epidemiology** broadened to address the importance of social characteristics (including gender, race, and social class), lifestyle, and the social and physical environment (including such things as employment status, stress, exposure to toxic substances, and participation in social networks) in relation to disease and illness. This expanded focus on the influence of social and cultural factors on the risk of death and disease is often referred to as **social epidemiology**, and now represents a major thrust of many (although not all) epidemiologists, whatever their disciplinary background (Friis, 2010).

THE WORK OF THE EPIDEMIOLOGIST

The work of the epidemiologist has been compared to that of a detective or investigator. Epidemiologists scrutinize data on death and disease within societies, often searching for patterns or linkages within population subgroups (e.g., among men or women, or among people living in cities or rural areas) or other meaningful changes over time. If a pattern or trend is discerned, the task of the epidemiologist is to explain it—that is, to identify a cause-and-effect relationship. This may require an understanding of how the disease is contracted, how it has been or could be spread, and why it is more common among some groups of people than others.

Increasingly, epidemiologists subscribe to a "web of causation" approach based on their belief that most disease patterns need to be explained by a complex of factors involving the disease agent, the human host, and the social and physical environment. McKinlay (1996) has suggested the addition of a fourth target—social systems. Thinking of influences such as government reimbursement policies, priorities of hospitals and other organizations, and the behavior of health providers, he argues that individual health behaviors cannot sensibly be separated from system influences.

Although epidemiologists are constantly at work studying disease and illness patterns, the public often hears of their work when an emergency situation occurs. Just in the last few years in the United States, there have, for example, been salmonella "scares" traced to contaminated irrigation waters on a serrano pepper farm in Mexico, to a peanut corporation, and to imported peppers, as well as a hepatitis scare traced to an unsanitary dentist's office in Oklahoma. The swine flu virus, the Zika virus, and the Ebola

virus have recently created international scares. When people begin to get sick, experts are called in to study those who are afflicted, determine what they have in common, test for contaminated products, and get harmful products removed from store shelves.

The Zika virus is a mosquito-borne virus that was first identified in the Zika Forest of Uganda in monkeys in 1947 and in humans in 1952. The first outbreaks in human populations occurred in 2007 in Yap (South Pacific) and in 2013 in French Polynesia. Additional large outbreaks occurred in 2015 in Brazil and Columbia, and in other areas in Africa. By 2016, the virus had appeared in more than 60 countries. It is most likely to take hold in hot, steamy climates with abundant mosquitos. Once an infected mosquito gets into a country (e.g., on an international traveler), it can reproduce and spread the virus. The virus can also be spread through sexual transmission. It has been linked to microcephaly (small head and underdeveloped brain) in infants, and to Guillain–Barré syndrome in adults. At the time of writing of this edition, epidemiologists around the world were searching for a means of killing the infected mosquitos or

A photo taken in June 2016 showing a Brazilian mother holding her baby, who was born with microcephaly caused by the Zika virus. © Xinhua/ Alamy Stock Photo.

preventing them from spreading the virus. Human populations have been encouraged to take increased precautions to prevent mosquito bites. Some countries have discouraged women from getting pregnant until more is known about the disease. Another emergency situation, the swine flu pandemic of 2009–2010, is described in the accompanying box.

IN COMPARATIVE FOCUS

THE SWINE FLU PANDEMIC

On April 24, 2009, the World Health Organization (WHO) announced that the United States and Mexico had reported a collective 27 confirmed cases of swine influenza A/H1N1. The WHO acknowledged that these illnesses were of major concern because they were human cases associated with an animal influenza virus. It further commended the United States and Mexico for their proactive reporting, and stated that it would be collaborating to further characterize the outbreak.

Two days later, the United States went from having 9 confirmed cases in two states to having 20 confirmed cases in five states. In a second situational update, the WHO acknowledged that these influenza cases were caused by a new subtype of influenza, H1N1, which was previously unidentified in swine or humans. By April 28, four days after the initial report, the United States had 64 confirmed cases of H1N1, Mexico had 26 confirmed cases with seven related deaths, and the flu strain had appeared in five other countries. Although the WHO did not advise the restriction of regular travel or the closure of borders, it was considered sensible for ill individuals to delay international travel, and for people who had developed symptoms after international travel to seek medical attention.

The new influenza virus spread at a rapid rate. The WHO noted that during previous pandemics, the influenza virus had taken more than 6 months to spread as widely as the H1N1 virus took to spread in less than 6 weeks. To further complicate matters, H1N1 has symptoms that are quite similar to those of the seasonal flu strain. Such symptoms include fever, cough, headache, muscle and joint pain, sore throat and a runny nose, and sometimes vomiting and diarrhea. Whereas most people who contracted H1N1 experienced mild symptoms and recovered fully, swine flu produced unusual patterns of death and illness. Most of the deaths occurred in young, otherwise healthy adults. Additional populations who were at high risk for contracting H1N1 included pregnant women, infants and children under the age of 2 years, and people with chronic health problems or compromised immune systems. It has been suggested that this influenza had such an effect on young people because they had no natural immunity, whereas members of the population aged 65 years or older were affected less than would be expected.

On June 11, 2009, the WHO raised the level of pandemic alert from Phase 5 to Phase 6 (the highest level), indicating that a global pandemic was under way. They predicted that up to two billion people would be infected. At that time, 74 countries had reported laboratory-confirmed infections. The response in the United States was on a large scale. Massive prevention-oriented publicity campaigns were enacted, state and local governments communicated periodically to area residents, many colleges and universities developed plans, some schools and mass meetings were cancelled, and more than 80 million doses of the H1N1 vaccine were administered.

A year later, the pandemic had declined to a simmering level. In August 2010, the WHO announced that the pandemic was over. Eventually, 18,000 deaths in 213 countries were clinically confirmed, but experts agreed that almost 300,000 people in total had died, and some estimated that the number was closer to 600,000. Most of the deaths occurred in South-East Asia and Africa. In the United States, about 60 million people contracted H1N1, 265,000 were hospitalized, and 12,000 died.

As the pandemic threat subsided, the WHO and Centers for Disease Control and Prevention (CDC) attempted to analyze their response to the crisis. Critics charged that the threat was overblown, and that the number of deaths was only about one-third of the annual toll from seasonal flu. Concerns were expressed that an insufficient number of vaccines had been made readily available in the important initial stages of the pandemic. Ultimately, it became clear that some states in the United States had a well-developed emergency preparedness plan, whereas others did not.

In conducting their work, epidemiologists utilize a variety of data-gathering techniques, including (1) examination of medical records and databases from physicians, hospitals, schools, employers, insurance companies, public health departments, and birth and death records, (2) systematic health examinations, (3) health-focused surveys, and (4) experimentation under tightly controlled conditions.

The leading health surveillance organization in the world is the **World Health Organization (WHO)**, which was created in 1948 under the auspices of the United Nations. It is headquartered in Geneva, Switzerland, with offices located around the world. The WHO monitors the world health situation and world health trends, provides technical support to countries with their health care systems and enters into programmatic partnerships, establishes norms and protocols, and helps to set the world health research agenda.

In 1950, the United States created a nationwide system of disease surveillance, now called the **Centers for Disease Control and Prevention (CDC)**. CDC is located in Atlanta. It provides ongoing evaluations of disease conditions and systematic responses to these conditions. Through this national surveillance system, data are now analyzed to define outbreaks of disease, characterize the extent of the outbreak, determine likely effects of the

The World Health Organization, centered in Geneva, Switzerland, is the leading epidemiological agency in the world. It provides leadership in global health matters regarding health policies, medical research, and assessment of health trends, and also provides technical support to countries around the world. © yui/Shutterstock.

disease on the population. and identify and make efforts to control or stop it. The CDC reports these data weekly to health departments, government agencies, academic facilities, and the public through the *Morbidity and Mortality Weekly Report (MMWR)*.

THE EPIDEMIOLOGICAL TRANSITION

Prior to large-scale migrations of people and urbanization, the threat of infectious (communicable) disease and epidemics was minimal.

However, once people began to move from one region of the world to another, and once crowded and unsanitary cities emerged within nations, **acute infectious diseases** [e.g., pneumonia and tuberculosis (TB)] began to spread more quickly and lingered longer. As societies further develop and modernize, morbidity and mortality change systematically to **chronic degenerative diseases** (e.g., heart disease and cancer). To capture this **epidemiological transition**, Omran (1971) divided the mortality experience of humankind into three stages—the Age of Pestilence and Famine, the Age of Receding Pandemics, and the Age of Degenerative and Human-Made Diseases.

The Age of Pestilence and Famine existed throughout the world for thousands of years, and still exists in many of the world's developing countries. Factors including lack of proper nutrition, poor sanitation, and unclean drinking water lead to continuing epidemics of infectious and parasitic diseases, such as influenza, pneumonia, diarrhea, smallpox, and TB.

Infants, children, and women of reproductive age are at particularly high risk during this era, and are even now often the victims of nutrition-related diseases. Infant mortality rates (IMRs) remain very high today in many developing countries, where more than 1 in every 10 babies dies during the first year of life. Moreover, adult health in developing countries is a serious and continuing problem. Data reveal that in industrialized market-based economies, the risk of death between the ages of 15 and 60 years is 12 percent for males and 5 percent for females. The corresponding figures for sub-Saharan Africa, a developing area, are 38 percent for males and 32 percent for females. Historically, life expectancy during the Age of Pestilence and Famine was between 20 and 40 years, although life expectancy in most of the world's developing countries today exceeds that. In several African countries, however, life expectancy remains less than 60 years.

In the late 1800s and early 1900s, industrialization and urbanization led to an increase in societal wealth. Significant improvements occurred in sanitation (e.g., cleaner water supplies and more effective sewage systems) and standard of living (especially in the availability of nutritious food). Advances in medical knowledge and public health swept across countries. These changes led to the Age of Receding Pandemics—a transition stage—in which the risk of death from infectious and parasitic diseases declined, and the risk of death from degenerative diseases increased. People began to survive into older age, and, as they did so, became more likely to experience and die from heart disease, cancer, and other chronic degenerative diseases. Historically, during this stage, life expectancy was about 50 years.

The Age of Degenerative and Human-Made Diseases arrived in the mid-1900s with the stabilization of death from acute infectious diseases at a relatively low level, and with mortality from degenerative diseases significantly increasing and becoming the most common cause of death. During this third stage, mortality rates dropped considerably from earlier times, and life expectancy reached approximately 70 years or more.

At one time, it was generally believed that the decline in mortality experienced during the third period put life expectancy at about its biological limit. However, in the mid-1960s, an unexpected and rapid decline in deaths from major degenerative diseases began to occur. This decline first affected middle-aged people, but eventually the lives of older people were also extended.

Thus, modern societies have entered a fourth period of epidemiological transition—the Age of Delayed Degenerative Diseases. During this era, the risk of dying from chronic degenerative diseases continues, but is pushed back to older ages. Both reduction in behavioral risk factors (e.g., a decline in cigarette smoking and improvements in blood pressure control) and advances in medical technology have been responsible for this shift (Olshansky and Ault, 1986).

Recently, Gaziano (2010) has proposed that a fifth epidemiological stage—the Age of Obesity and Inactivity—is now under way, and indeed has been for the last few decades. He suggests that the progress made in postponing disease and mortality to later stages of life is beginning to be undermined by an epidemic of obesity. Data show that more than two-thirds of American adults are overweight, and one-third meet the definition of being obese. Almost 75 percent of American adult males are overweight (Flegal et al., 2010). If not addressed, this excess weight will lead to an increased risk of coronary heart disease, stroke, hypertension, diabetes, cancer, joint disease, sleep apnea, asthma, and other chronic conditions.

The Age of Delayed Degenerative Diseases and the Age of Obesity and Inactivity raise new questions about the health of the population. Will the prolonging of life continue? If so, will that result in additional years of health or additional years of disability? Will healthier lifestyles and the postponement of chronic disease retard the aging process? Will death from other diseases increase? Will there be continued outbreaks of epidemic disease (e.g., AIDS and the recent increases in rates of TB)? The box "Disease Epidemics of the Present" illustrates this possibility.

IN THE FIELD

DISEASE EPIDEMICS OF THE PRESENT

In May 1995, a 36-year-old man was admitted to the hospital in Kikwit, Zaire, with a fever and diarrhea. Soon, however, blood began seeping out of every orifice of his body, and his internal organs became liquefied. He died on the fourth day, the same day that a nun and a nurse who had cared for him became ill. Others on the hospital staff became sick. Epidemiological experts in lethal viruses (who were referred to by one author as "disease cowboys") stationed at the World Health Organization collected their equipment and materials and immediately flew to Kikwit. They gathered samples and dispatched them to the Centers for Disease Control and Prevention. Their verdict, as feared, was Ebola virus.

Ebola first surfaced in 1976 in Zaire and the Sudan. The disease is carried by fruit bats living in West Africa, and can be transmitted to humans through a bite, the consumption of a diseased bat, or by another animal that has been bitten by a bat. The virus is spread through direct contact with bodily fluids of someone who is infected. The fatality rate is between 50 percent and 90 percent. There is no vaccine and no treatment. Ebola was contained in this episode within a couple of weeks, but only after it had killed 228 of 289 victims.

Was this Ebola outbreak a rare and unduplicated experience? No. In the last couple of decades, more than 20 fearsome viruses have surfaced around the world, including HIV (which had caused more than 35 million deaths in the world) and Lassa (which affects between 300,000 and 500,000 people annually in West Africa). Many observers believe that these outbreaks are due to the unceasing devastation of the ecosystem—including destruction of the ozone layer and the rainforest, and the continual accumulation of chemicals in the environment—which has opened these viruses to the human host.

In March 2014, an even larger outbreak of the Ebola virus emerged in the country of Guinea in West Africa, and quickly spread to its neighbors in Liberia, and Sierra Leone. These are extremely poor countries where conflict and civil war have

(Continued)

(Continued)

destroyed the education system and the health care system. There are only one or two doctors available for every 100,000 people (Chan, 2014). In July, an Ebola case was confirmed to have been spread through air travel, thus meaning that all countries were vulnerable.

The United States became directly involved, and its lack of preparedness became evident in September when a man who had recently flown into the country from Liberia presented himself at a hospital in Dallas with symptoms consistent with Ebola. Rather than being quarantined as health experts had recommended, he was examined, given some antibiotics, and sent home. (He was rushed back to the hospital 3 days later with intensified symptoms, and he ultimately died.) Two of the nurses who treated him contracted Ebola, but they recovered. (One of them sued her hospital for failing to properly train and equip nurses to treat Ebola.) A small number of medical providers who treated Ebola patients in West Africa and contracted the virus returned to the United States, and one of these physicians also died. Many physicians, nurses, and health experts decried that the United States was not more prepared to handle an epidemic. It was clear that much time had been lost by countries and organizations around the world in responding to the initial outbreak in West Africa. By mid-January 2016, all three West African nations were declared to be Ebola-free.

Once an organized response began, the effort was impressive. The World Health Organization, the Centers for Disease Control and Prevention, the United Nations Security Council, the World Bank and private groups such as Doctors Without Borders contributed urgently needed medical providers and supplies. President Obama sent in 3,000 military personnel to help to coordinate disaster relief, build more hospitals, and train health care workers. The virus was contained by late 2015, but only after there were more than 27,000 cases and more than 11,000 deaths.

What did the United States learn from this experience? Almost everyone agrees that the level of preparedness to handle disease epidemics needs to be increased. Better intelligence gathering, more sharing of information among and within countries, and improved electronic monitoring have all been called for (Carney and Weber, 2015). In June 2015, the Department of Health and Human Services designated 55 hospitals and 9 regional facilities as being specially trained to handle Ebola patients. This includes provider training, use of medical equipment and supplies, and some structural changes. However, the likelihood is that the next epidemic may be a different disease, perhaps one more contagious than Ebola, and perhaps one that hits at a much higher level. There is still considerable concern that more anticipation and preparation are needed.

One thing is certain—unless the Age of Obesity and Inactivity dramatically reverses recent improvements in life expectancy, all segments of the elderly population are expected to increase in absolute numbers. The CDC (2003) has projected that the United States population aged 65 years or over will increase to 71.0 million in 2030 (having been only 16.7 million in 1960 and 35.0 million in 2000).

Recent Alarming Trends in Infectious Diseases

In the last several years, societies around the world have had to deal with two alarming epidemiological trends—the emergence of new diseases, and the declining ability to successfully treat some diseases already present.

First, with regard to new diseases, Zika virus, Middle East respiratory syndrome (MERS), bird flu, swine flu, and numerous others have captured worldwide attention in the last few years. Since 1980, the world has been confronted with about three new pathogens a year. What is causing this surge in new diseases? At least five important explanations exist.

1. *Continued growth in the world population.* More people require more available land, and increased numbers of people are forced to live in crowded, urban environments.
2. *Increased travel.* An increase in the number of travelers throughout the world increases the chances of a pathogen being contracted in one area and unwittingly transported to another.
3. *Climate change.* Vector-borne diseases are those that are spread by insects, such as mosquitos, and other invertebrates, such as ticks and spiders. The life cycles of vectors depend on climactic factors, but generally they thrive in warmer climates where they increasingly breed and feed off animals and, in some cases, humans.
4. *Deforestation and natural habitat loss.* Cleared land collects rainwater better than rainforests, thus providing more suitable breeding grounds for mosquitos. Lyme disease is on the rise because of our encroachment upon and fragmentation of woodland habitat in the United States. The Nipah virus is a newly discovered pathogen that is causing considerable public health concern because of its ability to infect a broad range of animals, and its high lethality among humans. It was first detected in Malaysia. Habitat loss caused a mass exodus of Nipah virus-carrying fruit bats as they searched for food. This led the bats to cultivated fruit farms that were planted next to pig farms. Unfortunately, the pigs were highly susceptible to the Nipah virus, and then in turn these pigs passed the virus on to humans (Akhtar, 2016:2).

5. *The global trade in wildlife and production of animals for food.* About two-thirds of the emerging pathogens come from other animals. As demand for food, skins, and entertainment increases, so does the risk of infectious disease. The United States is one of the largest importers and exporters of animals (Akhtar, 2016).

Second, epidemiologists have discovered a pattern that could be tremendously disruptive to the epidemiological transition. Several infectious diseases, including TB, syphilis, gonorrhea, and bacterial pneumonia, are becoming increasingly resistant to the antibiotics that have been successful in defeating them. Malaria (spread by a parasite) was all but eradicated in the world in 1965. Today, however, it infects more than 200 million people annually and kills more than 600,000. Diphtheria (an upper respiratory illness caused by a bacterium) is very rare in the United States, but affects up to 200,000 people in Russia each year. Approximately 2 billion people worldwide are infected with TB (a bacterial disease, usually of the lungs), 9 million people annually develop active TB, and about 1.5 million people die from it. Once almost conquered in the United States, this disease has now re-emerged with more than 9,000 cases per year.

Several patterns related to infectious disease are evident in these two problems. First, they represent a global problem. About one-third of all deaths in the world today are attributable to infectious disease—the single biggest killer. Second, these diseases are becoming an increasing threat in the United States. Combined, they now represent the third leading cause of death in the United States, and the mortality rate from infectious disease has jumped in the last 20 years. Third, many of the previously successful antibiotic treatments for these diseases are no longer effective. Some infectious diseases have become resistant to traditional drugs, and more will become so. For example, the WHO estimated that 440,000 people in the world had multidrug-resistant TB (i.e., neither of the two most effective drugs against TB could defeat the virus) in 2008, and that a third of these individuals died (World Health Organization, 2010). Methicillin-resistant *Staphylococcus aureus* (commonly known as MRSA) has long been a problem in hospitals, and the number of patients contracting it spiked in the 1990s (when more than 125,000 people in the United States were hospitalized each year with this infection). Recent studies show that the incidence of MRSA in hospitals has now significantly decreased. And, finally, the response to infectious disease must be at the worldwide level. Yet both the CDC and the WHO are on record as expressing the view that the state of preparedness for outbreaks of disease epidemics is inadequate.

This chapter offers an introduction to several key concepts and measurement techniques in epidemiology—life expectancy, mortality, infant mortality, maternal mortality, morbidity, and disability—and examines current rates and trends within the United States and around the world.

LIFE EXPECTANCY AND MORTALITY

Life Expectancy

Using both current mortality data and projections, **life expectancy** rates reflect the average number of years that a person born in a given year can expect to live. The average life expectancy throughout the world is about 70 years, but this statistic camouflages significant variation. Life expectancy is about 78 years in modern countries (with several countries now having a life expectancy of more than 80 years), but only about 67 years in developing countries (with some still in the forties and fifties). Life expectancy has increased significantly in most countries in the last 20 years, especially in several

large developing countries, such as China and India.

Despite the fact that it spends significantly more money on health care than any other country, the United States fares poorly in relation to others. Among countries with a population of at least 5 million, the United States rates only 22nd highest in life expectancy, and among all countries, it is 43rd.

About two-thirds of the gap between the United States and other countries is explained by Americans' higher likelihood of dying before the age of 50 years. The most important reason for this discrepancy is that Americans are much more likely to die from causes other than disease. These causes include drug poisoning (largely from alcohol, prescription opioid abuse, and heroin), gun-related violence (both suicide and homicide—the rate of firearm homicides is 20 times higher in the United States than in other countries), and motor-vehicle crashes (Ho, 2013; Storrs, 2016). Table 3–1 identifies estimated life expectancy in the year 2015 for some of the world's countries that have a population of more than 5 million.

Trends.   Since 1900, life expectancy in the United States has increased by more than 30 years, from 47 to 79.7 years (in 2015). This does not mean that a significant increase has occurred in the life span (the maximum biological age). In the early part of the century, death for both males and females often occurred in the first year of life, and often during childbirth in females. These deaths significantly reduced average life expectancy. Males and females who survived these stages could expect to live on average almost as long as males and females do today.

Longer life expectancy together with a lower fertility rate (i.e., the rate of reproduction of women in their most fertile years—age 15 to 44 years) has resulted in a larger proportion of the United States population being over 65 years of age. Just 4 percent of the population was 65

TABLE 3–1   Life Expectancy in the Year 2015 (Estimates) in Countries With a Population of More Than 5 Million

Country	Life Expectancy in 2015
Japan	84.7
Singapore	84.7
Hong Kong	82.9
Switzerland	82.5
Israel	82.3
Australia	82.2
Italy	82.1
Sweden	82.0
Canada	81.8
France	81.8
Norway	81.7
Spain	81.6
Austria	81.4
Netherlands	81.2
Belgium	80.9
Finland	80.8
Germany	80.6
United Kingdom	80.5
Greece	80.4
Taiwan	80.0
South Korea	80.0
United States	79.7 (22nd) (43rd among all 224 countries)
Lowest 10	
Chad	49.8
Afghanistan	50.9
Central African Republic	51.8
Somalia	52.0
Zambia	52.2
Mozambique	52.9
Nigeria	53.0
Uganda	54.9
Burkina Faso	55.1
Niger	55.1

Source: Central Intelligence Agency. 2016b "Life Expectancy at Birth," *The World Factbook*, www.cia.gov/library/publications//the-world-factbook

years or older in 1900. Today it is 13 percent, and people aged 65 years or older are the fastest increasing segment of the population.

This "aging" of the American population has many implications. The greater number of elderly persons will require significant increases

in the supply of primary and specialty health care, short-term hospitalization, and extended care. Their numbers will also provide a formidable voting bloc and lobbying force to ensure that their needs will not be overlooked. Because extended care can be very expensive, increasing numbers of the elderly may need to reside with their adult children, thus requiring a family member to take on a full-time caregiving role, or necessitating the use of home health care services. Many elderly persons and their families will be faced with having to determine the relative value of quality versus quantity of life and the extent to which high-technology medicine will be employed (Sade, 2012).

Mortality

Mortality refers to the number of deaths in a population. Whereas death itself is easy to document, determining the actual cause can be problematic because death may result from a combination of many factors. In the United States, an attempt is made to classify each death according to the *International Statistical Classification of Diseases, Injuries, and Causes of Death*, which consists of a detailed list of categories of diseases and injuries. Although this system is valuable, it is not totally reliable due to the problems in diagnosing the actual underlying cause of death—something that is especially difficult for some chronic diseases.

Measurement.   Mortality rates are reported in ratios such as the **crude death rate (CDR)**. The crude death rate refers to the number of deaths per year per 1,000 people in a population. In 2015, the crude death rate worldwide was 7.8, and the rate in the United States was 8.2. Lesotho had the highest death rate in the world (14.9), and Qatar had the lowest (1.5).

Trends.   The crude death rate in the United States has declined by almost 50 percent since 1900, and continues to drop slowly. The largest decrease has been for females, both black and white, while the least reduction has been for black males.

In addition, the major causes of death have changed substantially (see Table 3-2). Today, death is most likely to result from a chronic degenerative disease. Almost 75 percent of deaths in the United States are due to heart disease, cancer, stroke, diabetes, lung disease, or cirrhosis, whereas in 1900 the major killers were infectious diseases such as influenza and pneumonia, gastrointestinal diseases, and TB. However, deaths from almost all chronic, degenerative diseases are occurring at later ages. To an increasing extent, people are now dying of multiple system diseases—being afflicted with more than one fatal disease.

Sociodemographic Variations in Life Expectancy

Socioeconomic Status (SES).   People with high socioeconomic status have a distinct

advantage over the less affluent with regard to life expectancy. The effect of income and level of education on life expectancy is clear, and has been shown to hold for both men and women and in a variety of racial and ethnic groups. People with low incomes live approximately 7 years less than the more affluent, and, in all groups, those with less than a high-school degree have the shortest life expectancy, whereas those with a college degree or higher level of education have the highest life expectancy (Montez et al., 2011). Among white males, college and graduate degree holders have on average about 12 additional years of life expectancy compared with those with less than a high-school degree (Olshansky et al., 2012). Moreover, this disparity in life expectancy by education has been increasing in recent years (Spittel, Riley, and Kaplan, 2015).

What is the explanation for this relationship and for the fact that it is becoming stronger? There are many reasons why the more highly educated may live longer. **Fundamental cause theory (FCT)** has often been used to focus on the importance of personal resources such as knowledge, money, power, prestige, and social connections to explain the life expectancy advantage of the more educated (Masters, Link, and Phelan, 2015). For example, higher levels of education are associated with greater opportunities for employment, economic security, a sense of personal control, social ties, less overall stress, healthier and safer living and working environments, and a more nutritious diet. Due to the fact that the more highly educated tend to have more financial resources, they have greater access to health services, and they use more preventive and curative services.

But why is this factor becoming more and more important? Hayward et al. have proposed that societal technological change has elevated the importance of educational attainment—particularly advanced education—for enabling access to health care knowledge and other health care resources, and that this may be reflected in

TABLE 3–2   The Ten Leading Causes of Death in the United States, 1900 and 2015

1900	2015
1. Influenza and pneumonia	Heart disease (611,000)
2. Tuberculosis	Cancer (585,000)
3. Gastroenteritis	Lung disease (149,000)
4. Heart disease	Accidents (131,000)
5. Cerebral hemorrhage	Stroke (129,000)
6. Kidney disease	Alzheimer's disease (85,000)
7. Accidents	Diabetes (76,000)
8. Cancer	Influenza and pneumonia (57,000)
9. Certain diseases of infancy	Kidney disease (47,000)
10. Diphtheria	Suicide (41,000)

Source: Centers for Disease Control and Prevention, National Center for Health Statistics. 2015 *Leading Causes of Death for 2013*. www.cdc.gov/nchs.

TABLE 3–3   Life Expectancy by Race and Gender, 2013

Average Years of Life Remaining	Expectation of Life in Years				
	Total	White		Black	
		Male	Female	Male	Female
At birth	78.8	76.7	81.4	72.3	78.4

Source: Centers for Disease Control and Prevention, National Center for Health Statistics. 2014b "Life Expectancy by Race, Sex, and Age, 2013." www.cdc.gov/nchs.

longer life expectancy (Hayward, Hummer, and Sassoon, 2015).

Race and Ethnicity.   In the United States, white people have a much longer life expectancy than most racial and ethnic minority groups. Life expectancy for African Americans lagged behind that for the total population throughout the twentieth century, but since 1990 the gap has decreased. However, in 2013, whites still lived an average of 4 years longer than blacks (see Table 3–3). The leading causes of death for blacks are the same as for whites (heart disease, cancer, lung diseases, and stroke), although blacks die from these diseases at an earlier age.

See the box "What Explains the Continuing Racial Differences in Mortality?" for a further examination of this issue.

Hispanics are now the largest racial/ethnic minority group in the United States, comprising about 17.5 percent of the population. Although Hispanics (a broad term covering several groups with important differences) are more likely than non-Hispanic whites to be below the poverty level and less likely to have health insurance— conditions almost universally related to poorer health and higher death rates—they have a lower death rate. On average, Hispanics have a life expectancy of about 81 years—2 or 3 years more than the national average. This is sometimes referred to as the "Hispanic Epidemiological Paradox."

Some have suggested that this is a matter of selective migration—that healthier Hispanics have been more likely to migrate to the United States. However, this explanation has been largely disproved. On the other hand, it has been

---

IN THE FIELD

WHAT EXPLAINS THE CONTINUING RACIAL DIFFERENCES IN MORTALITY?

Continuing racial differences in life expectancy and mortality represent an obvious and critical social disparity in the United States. In 2013, whites in the United States averaged more than 4 years longer life expectancy than blacks. This represented some reduction in the disparity in the last 15 years, but is still a large difference.

Healthy People 2020, a document published by the United States Department of Health and Human Services, identified the goals of achieving health equity, eliminating disparities, and improving the health of all groups as key during the 2010s (United States Department of Health and Human Services, 2010).

(Continued)

(*Continued*)

What causes this racial mortality disparity? Extensive research has pointed to a variety of both macro-level factors (social class differences, racial residential segregation, and historical and continuing racial discrimination) that structure and limit personal resources (education, occupation, income, and health insurance), and micro-level social and individual lifestyle factors (stress exposure, diet, exercise, and lack of medical care) (Sudano and Baker, 2006).

The link between some of these factors and mortality may be more apparent than it is for others, but research has documented all these factors as influences. For example, what impact does racial residential segregation have on mortality? As Williams and Jackson (2005) explain, due to residential segregation, blacks often live in poorer neighborhoods than do whites of similar income. Neighborhood affects educational and employment opportunities, which in turn influence income and access to health insurance. High unemployment rates and low wages are associated with higher rates of out-of-wedlock births and single-parent households, which are in turn related to lower levels of supervision and elevated rates of violent behavior. Poorer neighborhoods are more often exposed to environmental toxins. Perception of neighborhood safety relates to the ability to get adequate physical exercise. Both the tobacco and alcohol industries often target their products at poorer neighborhoods. Thus the neighborhood in which one lives is associated with a wide variety of factors that ultimately influence mortality rate.

One study determined that approximately 38 percent of the racial mortality differential is due to income differences (blacks are three times more likely than whites to be below the poverty level), about 31 percent is due to blacks having more high-risk factors (such as cigarette smoking and generally higher incidences of hypertension, high cholesterol levels, and diabetes), and

the remaining 31 percent is due to less access to health services, and differences in social and physical environment (Otten et al., 1990). In a study that also included Hispanics, Sudano and Baker (2006) identified education, income, and net worth as being more influential than lifestyle and health insurance.

In 2003, the Institute of Medicine published *Unequal Treatment: Confronting Racial and Ethnic Disparities in Health Care* (Smedley, Stith, and Nelson, 2003)—a book based on thorough investigation of research on black–white health differentials. While acknowledging the important influences described above, the book focused attention on what health care providers and health care systems could do to reduce or eliminate the disparity. Part of their analysis examines racial differences in health care services even after socioeconomic differences are controlled. They highlight several studies which show that differences between blacks and whites in treatment for heart disease are not explained by severity of disease or by other clinical factors, and that these treatment differences lead to higher mortality for black patients. Other studies have documented racial differences in the use of diagnostic tests, in the provision of cancer treatment, and in drug therapy for AIDS patients.

A key part of *Unequal Treatment* relates to recommendations on what can be done at both the macro and micro levels in order to address these disparities. For example, it is recommended that all health care providers be made aware that these inequities exist despite what may be the best intentions of individual health care providers. To enhance ability and skill in working with patients from diverse backgrounds, all future providers should undergo some cross-cultural education that focuses on (1) *attitudes* (cultural sensitivity and awareness), (2) *knowledge* (of cultural groups), and (3) *skills* (in working with patients of a different cultural background).

discovered that Hispanics are significantly less likely than whites to smoke cigarettes, and that this has led to lower death rates from heart disease and cancer, and to an overall lower death rate (Fenelon, 2013). Efforts are now under way to determine whether the lower death rate may also be due to dietary factors and/or the strong family life and support networks found in many Hispanic families.

Asian and Pacific Islanders, another strikingly diverse population, represent about 6.5 percent of the population. Included among this group are some well-established Asian American populations (Japanese, Chinese, and Filipinos) and many recent immigrants and refugees from South-East Asia. The Asian-American population is one of the healthiest groups in the country, and with the longest life expectancy. Overall life expectancy is about 87 years—well above the national average. Female (89 years) and male (84 years) life expectancies both exceed their counterparts in other groups. Leading causes of death mirror those of other population groups, but rates are lower. As with the Hispanic groups, the lower rate of cigarette smoking contributes significantly to this advantage.

Gender. Females have a longer life expectancy than males. At birth, female infants can expect to live about 81 years, compared with just 76 years for male infants. Within racial groups, white female infants are expected to live almost 5 years longer than their white male counterparts, and black females about 6 years longer than black male infants. Mortality rates for all four leading causes of death in the United States—heart disease, cancer, lung disease, and stroke—are higher for men than for women.

Females have a biological advantage over males from the beginning of life, as demonstrated by lower mortality rates at both the prenatal and neonatal (i.e., first 28 days) stages of life. However, the sizeable gap in expected years of life between men and women can be traced to an interrelationship among several biological and sociocultural influences. A discussion of these factors is provided in the box "Why Do Women Live Longer than Men?"

INFANT MORTALITY

Measurement

Approximately 130 million babies are born alive in the world each year (more than 350,000 births occur each day in the world). About 3 million of them die in the first year of life (1 million babies die on the day they are born), and an additional 2.6 million are stillborn. More than 90 percent of these deaths occur in the developing world. **Infant mortality rate** is defined as the number of deaths of persons less than 1 year of age for every 1,000 babies born.

Epidemiologists divide infant mortality rate into two components—the **neonatal mortality rate** (deaths among infants in the first 28 days of life) and the **post-neonatal mortality rate** (deaths between 29 days and 1 year of life). Although infant mortality rates are sometimes used as an indicator of the quality of health care within a country, the post-neonatal mortality rate is actually a better indicator for two reasons. First, deaths in the first 28 days of life are often a direct consequence of genetic problems or difficulties in the birthing process. Second, using the neonatal rate to assess quality or delivery of care creates an illogical situation. The better health care technology gets at sustaining an early life, but one that it cannot sustain over the long term, the higher the neonatal mortality rate and the lower the evaluation of the health care system (i.e., babies who die during birth are not counted in infant mortality rates, but babies who are sustained and given a chance at life but die in the first 28 days are counted). The post-neonatal mortality rate is a better reflection of babies who die due to socioenvironmental conditions.

IN THE FIELD

WHY DO WOMEN LIVE LONGER THAN MEN?

In the United States, women live approximately 5 years longer than men. Is this an inescapable gender-based feature? No. In the early part of the twentieth century, there was little difference in life expectancy between men and women, and by 1920, women lived only about 2 years longer than men. Although women live longer than men in all industrialized countries, in some agriculturally based societies, men live longer than women. These patterns reflect the importance of social and cultural influences, not genetic determination. Systematic analyses of gender differentials in mortality point to two primary reasons: (1) differences in health-related behaviors and circumstances, and (2) differences in the manner in which health services are used.

In the United States, women are more likely to experience acute illnesses such as upper respiratory tract infections and gastroenteritis and have higher rates of certain chronic debilitating (but not usually life-threatening) conditions such as anemia, thyroid conditions, colitis, and arthritis. Men are more likely to have life-threatening chronic conditions such as cancer, stroke, and liver disease (Bird and Rieker, 2008).

This pattern can be traced to behavioral differences. Over most of the age span, males are more likely than females to die of cancer. This can be traced to a greater likelihood of cigarette smoking, men's greater propensity to

drink alcohol excessively, and men being more likely to be exposed to cancer-causing agents in the workplace. Gender differences in reproductive anatomy and the effects of sex hormones also play a role and help to explain the greater likelihood of women dying from certain types of cancer, such as breast cancer.

Men are more likely to die in automobile accidents (studies show that men drive more miles but also drive faster, less cautiously, and violate more traffic regulations), to die in on-the-job accidents, to commit suicide, or to be victims of homicide. Whether or not male sex hormones create a predisposition to more aggressive behavior, socialization experiences relative to alcohol consumption, use of guns, physical risk taking, and assumption of risky jobs set the pattern (Stillion and McDowell, 2001–2002).

In addition, women are more likely than men to seek medical care. Women perceive more symptoms, take them more seriously, and are more willing to see a physician about them. They are more likely to have a regular source of medical care, use more preventive care, see physicians more often, be prescribed medications, and be hospitalized (Bird and Rieker, 2008). Often, men would benefit from earlier and increased medical attention as a means of earlier diagnosis of and intervention in diseases that become life-threatening.

Both the infant mortality rate and post-neonatal mortality rates are considered strong measures of a country's health care, because they reflect social and economic conditions including public health practices, the overall health of women, the quality of health care services, and the access people have to health care services.

Trends

The infant mortality rate (IMR) in the United States has steadily declined since the early 1900s, although there has been little reduction in the last 3 years. Between 1950 and 2015, the mortality rate for infants dropped from 29.2/1,000 live births to a rate of 5.9 (about 23,000 babies per year). The long-term

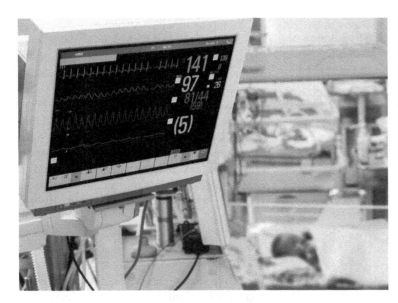

Hospital neonatal intensive care units provide specialized intensive care for sick and premature newborns. Despite their prevalence in the United States, the U.S. infant mortality rate lags behind that of most modern countries. © beerkoff/Fotolia.

improvement is a result of factors such as improved socioeconomic status, better housing and nutrition, clean water, and pasteurized milk. Medical discoveries such as antibiotics and immunizations, better prenatal care and delivery, and technological breakthroughs in infant care (such as neonatal intensive care and new surgical techniques) have also been important.

Despite this decrease in the infant mortality rate, the United States ranks far below most nations that have comparable (or even fewer) resources (see Table 3–4). Japan, Singapore, Norway, and Finland are world leaders—all with an infant mortality rate at or below 2.5. In recent years, most of these countries have experienced a more rapid reduction in the rate of infant deaths than the United States.

Countries with the highest infant mortality rates are mostly located in sub-Saharan Africa. In the countries with the highest rates of all—Afghanistan and Mali—the rate is more than 100, which means that more than 1 in 10 babies die in the first year of life. The United States rate ranks only 30th best among countries with a population of more than 5 million, and only 58th best among all countries in the world. Of the world's 26 highest-income countries, the United States ranks lowest in terms of infant mortality rate.

Some researchers have asked if there are differences among countries in the method by which infant mortality is calculated, and, if so, whether this differential reporting contributes to the relatively higher IMR in the United States. The answer to the first part of this question is yes—some countries use a variation of the IMR formula, and this variation contributes to a modest reduction in the rate of infant deaths. Most countries—including the United States—consider all babies born when calculating IMR. Some other countries—for example, Ireland and Poland—consider only babies with a birth weight of at least 500 g. Thus the smallest and most vulnerable babies—those most likely to die—are excluded. This has the consequence of lowering their IMR. France and the Netherlands include only babies with a birth weight of at least 500 g, or of at least 22 weeks' gestation.

However, in response to the second part of the question, researchers have calculated the magnitude of the difference in the IMR caused

TABLE 3–4 Infant Mortality Rates in 2015 in Countries with a Population of More Than 5 Million

Country	Number of Deaths Under 1 year/1,000 Live Births
Japan	2.1
Singapore	2.5
Norway	2.5
Finland	2.5
Sweden	2.6
Czech Republic	2.6
Hong Kong	2.7
France	3.3
Italy	3.3
Spain	3.3
Belgium	3.4
Germany	3.4
Austria	3.5
Israel	3.6
Belarus	3.6
Netherlands	3.6
Switzerland	3.7
South Korea	3.9
Denmark	4.1
Australia	4.4
United Kingdom	4.4
Taiwan	4.4
Poland	4.5
Cuba	4.6
Canada	4.7
Greece	4.7
Hungary	5.0
Slovakia	5.3
United States	5.9 (30th) (58th among all 224 countries)

Highest 10

Afghanistan	115.1
Mali	102.2
Somalia	98.4
Central African Republic	90.6
Chad	88.7
Niger	84.6
Angola	78.3
Burkina Faso	75.3
Nigeria	72.7
Sierra Leone	71.7

Source: Central Intelligence Agency. 2016a "Infant Mortality." *The World Factbook*. www.cia.gov/library/publications.

by the formula variations, and have discovered that they have a very small overall effect. Given that most countries use the same formula as the United States, and given the small number of babies excluded from being counted in the other countries relative to the number of births counted, there is validity in comparing countries internationally. Although there might be some modest movement upward or downward in the ranking for any given country, there should be considerable consistency. In all calculations, the United States has a high relative IMR (Heisler, 2012).

Causes

By far the single most hazardous condition for infants is low birth weight. About 8 percent of all live births are considered to be low birth weight (less than 2,500 g—about 5½ pounds), and an additional 1.5 percent are very low birth weight (less than 1,500 g). Low birth weight is the primary determinant of approximately 75 percent of all deaths in the first month, and 60 percent of all infant deaths. Low-birth-weight babies are also at risk of congenital anomalies such as malformations of the brain and spine, heart defects, and long-term disabilities such as cerebral palsy, autism, mental retardation, and vision and hearing impairments.

What factors increase the likelihood of a baby being low birth weight? At a micro level, low birth weight has been linked to the age of the mother (younger females have a more difficult time sustaining a healthy pregnancy), maternal smoking and use of alcohol or other drugs, and inadequate prenatal care. About two-thirds of low-birth-weight babies are born prematurely. (Prematurity is defined as being before the 37th week of a typical 40-week pregnancy.)

Estimates are that half of the infant deaths due to low birth weight would be preventable with early and adequate prenatal care (most women at risk for delivering a low-birth-weight baby can be identified at an initial visit, and monitored for factors such as inadequate nutrition, substance use, hypertension, urinary tract infections, and other potential risks to the fetus). Important issues such as weight gain, exercise, breast-feeding, and immunizations can be discussed.

In the United States, 4 to 5 percent of mothers who give birth have received late or no prenatal care. Mothers who do not receive prenatal care are three times more likely to give birth to a low-weight baby, and their babies are five times more likely to die in the first year of life. Many European countries attribute their lower infant mortality rate to the provision of early and adequate prenatal care to all women.

At a macro level, several social structural (social, economic, and political) factors directly impinge on the infant mortality rate. One recent study of state infant mortality levels compared the influence of social structural factors (such as percentage of persons in poverty, percentage of blacks and Hispanics in the population, amount of residential segregation, and political voting patterns) and health services variables (such as number of physicians relative to the population, and proportion of state expenditures on health care). The researchers found that the social structural factors were more strongly related to the rate of infant mortality (Bird and Bauman, 1995). Despite the appeal of focusing only on individual-level explanatory factors, it is very important to consider the influence of social structural factors as determinants of infant mortality.

Variations by Socioeconomic Status and Race

The overall infant mortality rate masks a significant discrepancy that exists among families of differing socioeconomic status and among families of differing racial and ethnic background. For example, lower-income women and black women are more likely to give birth in their teenage years and experience more health problems during pregnancy, but they are less likely to receive early and adequate prenatal care. In the United States in 2014, 4.3 percent of white women received late or no prenatal care, but the corresponding percentages were 5.7 percent for Asian women, 7.5 percent for Hispanic women, 9.7 percent for black women, and 10.8 percent for American Indian/Alaskan Native women (www.cdc.gov/nchs/vitalstats.htm). These factors lead to a higher likelihood of giving birth prematurely and of having a low-birth-weight baby, and a higher infant mortality rate. The IMR is 1 to 1½ times higher in families below the poverty level than in those above it, and twice as high among black families compared with white families.

Several excellent studies have emphasized the importance of social structural factors as explanations for the differences in black and white infant mortality rates. LaVeist (1993) has documented the effects of poverty (the fact that blacks are more likely to be below the poverty level), racial segregation (segregated black, urban communities being more likely to be toxic environments lacking in city services and medical services and having an inflated cost of living), and political empowerment (the black infant mortality rate is lower in cities with greater black political power, perhaps due to reduced feelings of hopelessness and greater availability of and inclination to use appropriate health services). Table 3–5 shows the relationship between infant mortality and race/ethnic background of the mother.

MATERNAL MORTALITY

Every day in the world, more than 800 women die from pregnancy- or childbirth-related complications. This adds up to more than 300,000 maternal deaths each year. More than 95 percent of these deaths occur in the developing world. Although this number is very large,

TABLE 3–5   Infant Deaths per 1,000 Live Births by Race of Mother, United States, 2012

Race/Ethnic Origin	Percent
Asian/Pacific Islander	4.1
Central/South American	4.1
Cuban	5.0
Mexican	5.0
White	5.1
Overall	**6.0**
Puerto Rican	6.9
American Indian/Alaskan Native	8.4
Black	10.9

Source: Centers for Disease Control and Prevention, National Center for Health Statistics. 2014a "Infant Deaths Per 1,000 Live Births by Race of Mother, United States, 2012." www.cdc.gov/nchs.

it actually represents a reduction of more than 40 percent since 1990. Several sub-Saharan African nations have decreased their rate by more than half during this time.

The **maternal mortality rate (MMR)** is defined as the number of women who die in the process of giving birth for every 100,000 live births. The rate is about 12 per 100,000 live births in developed countries, but about 240 per 100,000 live births in developing countries. The risk of a woman in a developing country dying from a pregnancy- or birth-related cause during her lifetime is about 33 times higher than for a woman in a developed country.

Why do women die during the birth process? The most common reason is that they die from complications during and immediately following childbirth. Most of these complications develop during pregnancy, but others exist before pregnancy and are worsened by it. Around 75 percent of these complications result from one or more of five conditions—severe bleeding (mostly occurring after birth), infections (mostly also occurring post birth), eclampsia or elevated blood pressure during pregnancy, complications of delivery, and unsafe abortions. Other complications result from having certain diseases (e.g., malaria or AIDS) during pregnancy.

Most of these complications develop during pregnancy, and most are preventable or treatable. The provision of adequate family planning and prenatal care services as well as post-partum care, and clean, safe surgical procedures attended by a skilled health worker—such as a physician, nurse, or midwife—would dramatically reduce the MMR even further (World Health Organization, 2015). It is also essential that pregnant women in whom complications develop have access to emergency obstetrical care. This entails upgrading rural health centers and referral hospitals and ensuring that they have the necessary drugs, supplies, and equipment, such as magnesium sulfate for eclampsia, antibiotics for infection, and basic surgical equipment for Cesarean sections (Rosenfield, Min, and Freedman, 2007).

The accompanying box, "Mortality Patterns in Developing Countries," discusses some further explanations for the higher mortality rates in those countries.

In contrast to the decreasing maternal mortality rate in most countries, the rate in the United States has been increasing—from about 7/100,000 in the late 1980s to almost 18/100,000 at the time of writing this edition. In 2015, only eight countries in the world (including war-torn Afghanistan and South Sudan) were experiencing an increase in MMR.

Why is this occurring? A small portion of the increase is due to more accurate record-keeping. However, more important factors are more obesity-related complications (e.g., hypertension and diabetes), more women giving birth at later ages, a dramatic increase in the number of Cesarean section births, and continued absence of appropriate prenatal care for some women (World Health Organization, 2015). In 2013, about one-third of births in the United States were Cesarean sections, whereas the World

IN COMPARATIVE FOCUS

MORTALITY PATTERNS IN DEVELOPING COUNTRIES

Worldwide, life expectancy increased more in the twentieth century and the first part of the twenty-first century than in all previous human history, and the biggest increases have been in the most recent years. Average life expectancy in the world increased from just 48 years in 1955 to 66 years at the turn of the century, to 70 years in 2013, and is expected to increase to about 73 years by 2025.

These data, of course, camouflage continuing disparities between the world's wealthiest and poorest nations. In 1996, 76 percent of the deaths reported in Africa were of people younger than 50 years; the corresponding figure in Europe was just 15 percent. By 2025, the percentage in Africa is predicted to decrease to 57 percent, while the figure for Europe should decrease to 7 percent—both marked improvements, but a continuing very large disparity (Hager, 1998).

Maternal mortality rates remain at a very high level in many developing countries. The United Nations Children's Fund estimates that more than 300,000 women die during pregnancy and childbirth each year. More than 95 percent of these deaths occur in the Third World. It is estimated that 30 percent of births worldwide occur without any trained person in attendance, and maternal mortality is especially high in these situations.

While still at a high level, infant mortality rates have been slowly decreasing throughout the developing world. In many developing countries, the focus is more on "child mortality" (i.e., death in the first 5 years of life) than solely on infant mortality. This is because children aged 2 to 5 years are at continued high risk in these countries—a situation unlike that in industrialized countries. Worldwide, an estimated 7 million children die each year (more than 19,000 per day) before their fifth birthday. Although this is an extremely high number, it is a very large decrease since 1990, when about 12 million children under the age of 5 years died each year. The major

causes of these deaths are lack of access to clean water, inadequate nutrition, expensive vaccines, and lack of skilled birthing attendants.

The experience of Pakistan, the world's sixth largest country, with a population of more than 170 million people, illustrates the influence of economic and social development on infant mortality rates. Despite having a high infant mortality rate, little progress has been made in reducing the number of infant deaths. Pakistan has the highest rate of first-day deaths in the world, and more than 200,000 babies die annually in the first year of life. Concerned about this pattern, Sohail Agha studied national, community, and household data and two national surveys, and identified two primary factors that accounted for the lack of progress.

First, Pakistan has considerable socioeconomic inequality that has resulted in the concentration of political power in a powerful rural elite. Throughout the 1980s and early 1990s, economic planning was built around the "trickle-down theory"—that efforts should be made to promote economic flourishing of the upper classes with the expectation that their success would filter down to the lower classes. The failure of this policy resulted in substantial disparities in income, education, nutrition, and access to quality housing, sanitary conditions, and clean water—all factors implicated in infant mortality rates.

Second, Agha identified gender inequity as contributing to the high infant mortality rate. Relative to Pakistani men, women tend to be poor, illiterate, less educated, and have low social and legal status. This may contribute to a lack of priority being given to women's and children's health. In addition, more highly educated women generally prefer to have fewer children, stopping procreation at an earlier age, and having more space between births—all factors that have a positive effect on the health and sustainability of newborns (Agha, 2000).

Health Organization recommends that this figure should be only about 10 to 15 percent.

Significant variations in maternal mortality rate exist among population subgroups in the United States. Black women are four times more likely than white women to die, and unmarried women have an MMR nearly three times higher than that of married women. The risk of death decreases as level of education increases, with women under 20 years of age who have not graduated from high school at highest risk.

Lack of prenatal care continues to be a major risk factor for maternal mortality in the United States. Because one out of four pregnant women in the United States experiences a major complication, such as high blood pressure or a hemorrhage, prenatal care can be of as much benefit to a pregnant woman as to her fetus.

MORBIDITY

Morbidity refers to the amount of disease, impairment, and accident in a population. For several reasons, this concept is more difficult to measure than mortality. The definition of illness varies considerably from one individual to another and from one group to another. Some people have a disease and do not realize it; others think they have a disease although there is no clinical confirmation of this. Even if one is sick, home care may be used instead of professional care, so the illness is never officially reported. In cases where a physician is consulted, the results of the examination may or may not be reported, since the law does not require the reporting of all diseases. While certain communicable diseases, such as TB, polio, measles, mumps, and chicken pox, are reportable, others, such as cancer and heart disease, are not. If written records (e.g., hospital records) are used, only the professionally treated cases will be counted, resulting in an underestimation of the number of cases.

Much of the morbidity data we rely on is gathered through health surveys such as the National Health Interview Survey. Although sampling techniques are now very successful in representing a population, accurate data still depend upon respondents' memories, and reporting still reflects individual perceptions of illness.

Measurement

Two epidemiological techniques—incidence and prevalence—are used extensively to determine the social and ecological distribution of disease and illness.

Incidence and Prevalence.   The **incidence** of disease, impairment, or accident refers to the number of new cases added to the population within a given time period. For example, one could report on the incidence of AIDS in the United States during the last year—this would be interpreted as the number of people newly diagnosed with AIDS in the last 12 months. **Prevalence** refers to the total number of cases of a condition present at a given time. For example, the prevalence of AIDS in the United States today would be the total number of living people who have been diagnosed with AIDS. Together, incidence and prevalence help to identify disease patterns.

Patterns and Sociodemographic Variations in Morbidity

One aggregate approach for summarizing the extent to which morbidity exists involves collecting information on **restricted-activity days,** which are defined as days on which a person cuts down on their activities for more than half of the day because of illness or injury. In the United States, in 2001, the average person experienced 11.3 restricted-activity days. As summarized in Table 3–6, illness and injury were higher for the poor than for the wealthy, for

TABLE 3–6 Number of Restricted-Activity Days by Selected Characteristics, 2001

Characteristic	Average Number of Restricted-Activity Days
Total population	11.3
Male	10.4
Female	12.1
White	10.7
Black	15.8
Hispanic	11.4
Poor	15.2
High income	9.8
Perceived fair/poor health	23.3
Perceived excellent health	6.8

Source: Agency for Health Care Research and Quality, Medical Expenditure Panel Survey. 2010 *Restricted Activity Days in the United States*. Washington, DC: USDHHS.

blacks than for whites or Hispanics, for females than for males, and for those who perceive themselves to be in poor or only fair health.

The next section briefly examines the relationship between morbidity and age, socioeconomic status, race, and gender. This information is supplemented by the box, "The Important Link between Health and Involvement in Positive Social Relationships."

Age. The health of children in the United States has changed dramatically in the past four decades. One by one, the major infectious diseases that used to imperil children have been eliminated or significantly reduced by widespread immunization. Smallpox has been eliminated, and polio will be soon. Diphtheria, scarlet fever, cholera, tetanus, pneumonia, measles, mumps, and whooping cough are increasingly uncommon in this country; however, many of these diseases continue to plague children in developing countries. Although more than 75 percent of children in the United States get all their immunizations by their third birthday, some children, especially in inner-city and rural

areas, do not. In addition, some individuals and organizations have recently made the charge that the basic immunizations can cause allergic reactions and increase the likelihood of conditions such as crib death. Though some parents are now feeling ambivalent about immunizations, most epidemiologists emphasize that the country needs to remain vigilant in ensuring that children are immunized against these diseases.

As the prevalence of these infectious diseases has decreased, epidemiologists have focused increased attention on four other conditions that contribute to morbidity among children and adolescents:

1. ***Poor diet and lack of exercise.*** Poor nutrition, lack of exercise, and the resulting obesity among adolescents have become major problems. Estimates are that more than 30 percent of adolescents are overweight or obese, and this figure has been increasing. The percentage of children aged 6–11 years who are obese jumped from 7 percent in 1980 to 18 percent in 2012. The percentage of adolescents and teenagers aged 12–19 years who are obese increased from 5 percent to 21 percent during the same period.

This pattern has been created by twin conditions—an increasing percentage of adolescents eating less nutritious, high-fat, high-sugar diets (as per most fast food) and a decreasing percentage getting the recommended amount of exercise. While these same patterns characterize adults, patterns set in adolescence are especially difficult to break.

Poor diet and lack of exercise are related to elevated risks for many diseases, including heart disease, cancer, diabetes, depression, and stroke.

2. ***Use of tobacco, alcohol, and other drugs.*** Cigarette smoking among young people has decreased in the last few years, but is still at a high level. About 25 percent of high-school

students and about 8 percent of middle-school students smoke cigarettes. Added to this are many more who use smokeless tobacco, hookahs, or electronic cigarettes. Males are slightly more likely than females to smoke cigarettes, and whites are about twice as likely to do so as blacks, with the percentage for Hispanics in the middle.

Alcohol use has also decreased slightly in the last few years, but is still at a high level. About 35 percent of high-school students drink alcohol (21 percent binge drink, more than 10 percent drive after drinking, and 22 percent had ridden with someone who had been drinking).

Illicit drugs other than marijuana include LSD and other hallucinogens, cocaine, heroin and other narcotics, amphetamines, barbiturates, and tranquillizers not taken under a doctor's care. After peaking in the 1960s, the use of illicit drugs other than marijuana declined during the 1970s, 1980s, and 1990s, stabilized but increased slightly in the early 2000s, and in most cases is now increasing again at a rapid pace. Almost 30 percent of high-school students report having used illicit drugs in the last year. About 10 percent of Americans have been diagnosed with a drug use disorder.

In recent years, a major heroin epidemic has occurred, and there are more than 500,000 current users. Most of them are young white men with low incomes who first became hooked on prescription opiates—such as Percocet and Vicodin—and then switched to heroin because it is less expensive.

Cigarette smoking is related to an increased likelihood of developing many chronic diseases, including cancer, heart disease, depression, and lung disease. Underage drinking is associated with a variety of health problems, including impaired brain development, memory problems, alcohol poisoning, alcohol dependence, and car crashes. More than 4,000 underage young people die each year from crashes that occurred after excessive drinking. The health problems associated with illicit drug use depend upon the specific drug, but are many, and can be very serious. More than 40,000 people die from drug overdoses each year—more than half of these deaths are from prescription pills, and about 10,000 are due to heroin.

3. *Sexual activity and pregnancy.* In the last several years, teenage sexual activity has declined somewhat and contraceptive use has increased. About 50 percent of teens are sexually active (approximately 20 percent by the age of 15 years, 60 percent by 18 years, and 70 percent by 19 years), about one in seven has had at least four sexual partners, and about 30 percent do not routinely use a condom (regular condom use has increased among teenagers, although sexually active 9th graders are more likely to regularly use a contraceptive than sexually active 12th graders). This means that a substantial percentage of teenagers are susceptible to sexually transmitted infections and early pregnancy (about 600,000 teenage girls get pregnant each year).

The rate of childbearing by teenagers has been on a long-term decline. The rates of teenage pregnancies, teenage births, and teenage abortion in the United States are now at historic lows. However, the teenage birth rate in the United States is still substantially higher than it is in other developed countries. Sexually active individuals who do not use condom protection are at increased risk of HIV, other sexually transmitted diseases, and unintended pregnancy. Teenage mothers are less likely to finish school and to be employed, and are more likely to have low-birth-weight babies.

4. *Violence.* Physical abuse is an increasingly recognized problem, as are emotional and sexual abuse. Substantial increases in reported physical and sexual abuse cases have occurred since 1980, although the increase is partially

due to improved reporting. In 2014, an estimated 702,000 children in the United States (about 14 percent of all children) were confirmed by Child Protective Services to have been the victims of some form of maltreatment. Maltreatment includes neglect, physical abuse, emotional abuse, custodial interference, and sexual abuse. Almost 1,600 children died that year as a result of the maltreatment.

Children who experience maltreatment are more likely to suffer from a wide variety of negative health outcomes, including impaired brain development, impaired cognitive learning, and depression, and to be at higher risk for heart disease, lung disease, liver disease, high blood pressure, and cancer.

At the other end of the age spectrum, the level of health among the elderly has improved in recent years as a result of better diet, more exercise, and more advanced and accessible health care. Despite the fact that health problems increase in the later years, older people now tend to rate their own health status as good, and fewer report disabling physical conditions. This assessment is consistent with physician evaluations, and seems realistic in relation to the reduced requirements of the elderly for active levels of functioning, since most are no longer parenting or working.

This assessment is also despite the fact that, as people in their later years get older, they are more likely to experience multiple health ailments, such as heart disease, cancer, high blood pressure, diabetes, declining cognitive ability, hearing impairment, and arthritis. It is not uncommon for those over 65 to be seeing multiple physicians (e.g., primary care physician, cardiologist, pulmonologist, oncologist, and others) and to be taking ten or more prescriptions on a regular basis.

Many believe that the human life span is relatively finite and fixed, at about 85 years on average, and that improvements in health will compress the onset of morbidity and disability into the later years of life. This will result in an improved quality of life and a reduced need for medical care. Others argue that life expectancy is rising more rapidly than the rate at which onset of morbidity is being postponed. They predict that gains in life expectancy will be accompanied by additional years of chronic illness and disability.

Socioeconomic Status.   Nearly one in every seven Americans lives in a family with an income below the federal poverty level, and more than 20 percent of children under 18 years of age are in such families. House, Kessler, and Herzog (1990) have investigated the relationship between socioeconomic status and level of health (measured by number of chronic conditions, functional status, and limitation of daily activities) at various ages. They discovered a vast amount of preventable morbidity and functional limitations in the lower socioeconomic stratum of American society, and that the discrepancy between the poor and non-poor was especially great for those between the ages of 35 and 75 years.

The disadvantages in terms of health status in middle and early old age are explained by the vulnerability of this group to a number of psychosocial and environmental risk factors. These include greater exposure to physical, chemical, biological, and psychosocial hazards, increased stress due to employment insecurity and inadequate financial resources, and higher participation rates in various harmful behaviors, such as smoking and alcohol consumption, as well as poorer eating habits and lack of exercise. Variation in these risk factors among socioeconomic groups appears to be relatively small in early adulthood, greater during middle and early old age, and then relatively small again in older age (House, Kessler, and Herzog, 1990).

Figure 3–1 is a representation of one model of how poverty influences morbidity and mortality.

Figure 3–1 The Cycle of Poverty and Pathology

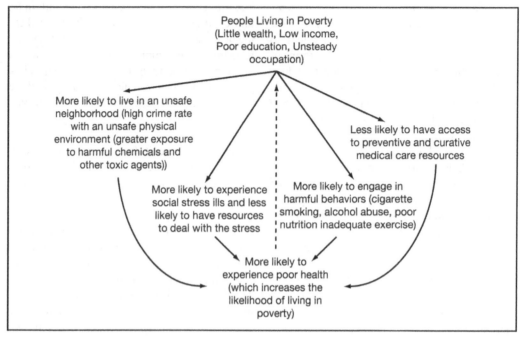

Source: Adapted from Diana B. Dutton, "Social Class, Health, and Illness," pp. 31–62 in *Applications of Social Science to Clinical Medicine and Health Policy*, Linda H. Aiken and David Mechanic, eds. Copyright 1986 by Rutgers, the State University. Reprinted by permission of Rutgers University Press.

Persons in the lower social class are more likely to live and work in areas with hazardous chemico-physical conditions, and are less likely to be involved in supportive social networks. These conditions lead to higher levels of psychological stress. The poor are more likely to engage in certain health-damaging behaviors (e.g., cigarette smoking and getting too little exercise, although heavy drinking occurs more in higher SES groups) in part due to the high level of stress (Shaw et al., 2014). The harmful lifestyle behaviors, the high levels of stress, and the lack of support networks all contribute to increased morbidity and a greater likelihood of mortality. Since the poor often cannot afford preventive or therapeutic care, health problems frequently do not receive immediate attention, and serious conditions worsen.

Race and Ethnicity. One of the most discouraging health-related trends in the United States in the last decade has been the worsening state of health of African Americans. Rates of morbidity are higher for blacks than for whites for most diseases, including heart disease, cancer, diabetes, pneumonia and influenza, liver disease and cirrhosis, accidental injuries, and AIDS. Blacks experience more health problems than whites early in life, and their health deteriorates more rapidly. Some, but not all, of this health disadvantage is due to the lower economic standing of blacks. However, at all ages and at all levels of socioeconomic standing, blacks have more health problems than whites (Ferraro and Farmer, 1996).

Research has found that race creates an added burden on the health of blacks. Williams (2012) contends that this added burden derives from three primary factors:

1. Indicators of SES are not equivalent across race. Blacks and Hispanics have lower levels of earning, less wealth, and less purchasing power at every educational level.
2. Health is affected by economic adversity over the life course—not just at the current time. Thus, there is a cumulative health hardship.
3. Discrimination—both institutional (e.g., residential segregation that leads to more health-harmful neighborhoods in which minorities live) and individual (which has been found to be a significant source of health-harming psychological distress).

The health of Asians and Pacific Islanders is as varied as the people are diverse. The level of health of those born within the United States and established in the culture is very similar to that of the population as a whole, but on most major indicators, Asians and Pacific Islanders are the healthiest of all racial/ethnic groups in the country. In general, Chinese, Japanese, and Korean Americans are more likely than Vietnamese or Filipino Americans to have positive health outcomes.

However, Asian Americans are at especially high risk for certain diseases. Asian Americans are the only segment of the United States population for whom cancer is the leading cause of death. Rates of lung cancer (due mostly to higher rates of cigarette smoking), liver cancer, and stomach cancer are a particular problem. Rates of hepatitis B and tuberculosis are also higher than in the general population.

Most Hispanic groups—especially Mexican and Cuban Americans—compare favorably with whites on rates of morbidity, and fare better than blacks. On the other hand, Puerto Ricans fare less well than whites on indicators of morbidity. Rates of diabetes, tuberculosis, and HIV/AIDS are all of special concern. As with other groups, Hispanics below the poverty level are at special risk.

The Mexican Americans who are most at risk of morbidity are the approximately 1 million farmworkers who do exhausting work, have high rates of accidents, and have limited access to health care providers. Groups on both sides of the United States–Mexico border contend with serious air and water pollution, poor sanitation, considerable overcrowding, and illegally dumped hazardous wastes.

Gender.   Although men have a higher prevalence of fatal conditions and thus higher mortality rates, women have higher morbidity rates for most acute illnesses (including infectious and respiratory diseases) and most chronic conditions. Five reasons have been offered to account for gender differences in morbidity:

1. *Biological risks.* Males are at some health disadvantage because of women's intrinsic protection from certain gene and hormonal differences. Reproductive conditions (pregnancy, childbirth, and disorders of puerperium) account for a substantial amount—but not all—of the morbidity differential even at ages 17 to 44 years.
2. *Acquired risks due to differences in work and leisure activities, lifestyle and health habits, and psychological distress.* Acquired risks are different for men and women. Some health-harming lifestyle behaviors, such as smoking cigarettes, excessive alcohol consumption, and occupational hazards, are more common among men. Others, such as less active leisure activities, being overweight, stress and unhappiness, and role pressures are associated more with women. Most analysts perceive this to be the most important explanation for gender differences in mortality, and an important part of the explanation for gender differences in morbidity.
3. *Psychosocial aspects of symptoms and care.* People perceive symptoms, assess their

severity, and decide what to do to relieve or cure health problems differently. Gender differences in responding to illness may stem from childhood or adult socialization that it is more acceptable for women to reflect upon and discuss symptoms and concerns. The presence of physiological conditions such as menstruation, pregnancy, breast-feeding, and menopause may encourage women to pay more attention to their bodies and be more observant of physiological changes. Much research has confirmed that women place higher value on health and have more of a preventive orientation toward health. This may be the other most important explanatory factor in morbidity differentials.

4. *Health-reporting behavior.* Women are more willing to acknowledge symptoms and illness and to seek care. In one study, women were discovered to be significantly more likely than men to report headache-related disability and seek health care services for their headaches, even after controlling for severity of the head-ache (Celetano, Linet, and Stewart, 1990). Depending on the source of the data, part of these differences may relate to continuing differences in the socioeconomic position of men and women. Women are less likely than men to be employed, so they can more easily arrange a medical visit. If a family member is ill, it is more likely that the woman will call in sick, since women on average earn less than men, and in many families it is the wife's "duty" to take care of sick children or to be at home on school holidays.

5. *Prior experience with health care and care-takers.* Men use fewer health care services. As a result of their greater participation in self-care and greater attentiveness to health status, women may derive more benefit from seeing a health care provider and receive more positive reinforcement for their atten-tiveness (Verbrugge, 1990).

DISABILITY

What it means to be "disabled" or to have a **disability** has undergone significant revision in the last 25 years. Historically, the mindset in Western societies has been that disability is a personal tragedy and an individual failing. Typically, the focus has been on deficits, abnor-malities, and functional limitations. Often, definitions of disability focused solely on having at least one designated disabling physical condition. For example, a person with one arm or leg would be considered to have a disability. Societal attitudes ranged from sympathy to indifference to exclusion (Barnes and Mercer, 2010).

Many sociologists believe that this approach focuses too much on the individual outside of any social context. They prefer a **social model of disability** which posits that restrictions in activities or functions experienced by individ-uals are the result of a society that has not made appropriate accommodations. According to David Mechanic:

> In the older conception, while disability deserved public sympathy and assistance, it was viewed in essence as a personal problem that required considerable withdrawal from usual activities. The contemporary view has had a transformative influence in its implication that persons with almost any impairment can meet most of the demands of everyday living if they adopt appro-priate attitudes and if physical, social, and attitu-dinal barriers are removed. (1995:1210)

From this perspective, disability occurs only when there is an absence of "fit" between the capabilities of persons and the physical environ-ment in which they live. This gap can partially be addressed at the individual level (e.g., by modi-fying the impairment, increasing patient motiva-tion, and teaching coping strategies), but must also be addressed through social policy and envi-ronmental remediation (e.g., by providing assis-tive devices, removing unnecessary physical

---

IN THE FIELD

THE IMPORTANT LINK BETWEEN HEALTH AND INVOLVEMENT IN POSITIVE SOCIAL RELATIONSHIPS

The important influence of social relationships on human attitudes and behaviors is well documented by sociologists and other social scientists. In the last 30 years, medical sociologists have attempted to understand better the impact of social relationships on health and illness. A key finding is that engagement in positive social relationships has a significant impact on health. Adults who are more socially connected have healthier lives and longer life expectancy than their more socially isolated peers. They are less likely to suffer from a host of diseases and illnesses (including heart disease, high blood pressure, and cancer), and do better when these diseases occur (Umberson and Montez, 2010).

How does participation in positive social relationships benefit health? Umberson and Montez (2010) identify three pathways. First, social relationships increase the likelihood of engaging in healthy behaviors and being able to withdraw from unhealthy behaviors. Interaction with others may create a sense of responsibility toward them (e.g., a parent may become more health conscious as a role model for children or to be better able to care for them). This is a behavioral explanation.

Beyond this first benefit but related to it is **social capital theory**, which posits that there may be valuable resources found within our social networks. These resources might provide helpful health information, assist in enabling

health-promoting behaviors, increase access to beneficial resources, and add to an individual's self-esteem and positive self-concept (Song and Lin, 2009).

Second, the psychosocial explanation asserts that social relationships can provide a variety of psychosocial benefits. They may be an important source of emotional support, enhance mental health, assist in handling stress, and provide for greater happiness and purpose in life. As an example, a recent study of Latino sexual minorities found that those who were actively involved in local lesbian, gay, bisexual, and transgender (LGBT) organizations were better able to deal with social stigmatization, felt higher levels of social support, and were less likely to engage in potentially health-harming sexual risk behaviors (Ramirez-Valles et al., 2010).

Third, research has found that supportive relationships with others have beneficial effects on the immune system, the endocrine system, and the cardiovascular system, and reduce the negative bodily effects of social stress. This is a physiological explanation.

Of course, not all social relationships are positive, and participation in a negative relationship can exact health detriments in addition to failing to provide health benefits. In both cases, participation in social relationships influences health throughout the life course and has a cumulative impact on health.

---

barriers, and ensuring fair treatment). In the last few years an abundance of research has clearly demonstrated the importance of the "built environment" in reducing barriers to full participation in society (Barnes and Mercer, 2010; Clarke et al., 2011).

The World Health Organization (2013:1) defines disabilities as:

an umbrella term, covering impairments, activity limitations, and participation restrictions. An *impairment* is a problem in body function or structure; an *activity limitation* is a difficulty encountered by an individual in executing a task or action; while a *participation restriction* is a problem experienced by an individual in involvement in life situations. Disability is a complex phenomenon, reflecting an interaction between features of a person's body and features of the society in which he or she lives.

An example of this evolution in thinking would be to consider the situation of a disabled person failing to find employment. Traditionally, society may have focused on this as an individual shortcoming. However, given that the employment rate is much lower for disabled persons than for the rest of the population, it may be viewed more as a structural problem—that work environments are configured in such a way as to be inappropriate for people with disabilities—or even as reflecting discriminatory attitudes toward disabled people (Barnes and Mercer, 2010).

See the accompanying box, "The Importance of the Americans with Disabilities Act."

Measurement of disability varies from one study to another—that is, the identification of

---

IN THE FIELD

THE IMPORTANCE OF THE AMERICANS WITH DISABILITIES ACT

Throughout much of its history, the United States made few efforts to attempt to create a society in which people with disabilities could participate as freely and fully as possible. The virtually impenetrable barriers that occurred throughout workplaces and public settings prevented full participation of individuals with functional limitations.

The signature change in this approach occurred in 1990 with the passage of the Americans with Disabilities Act (ADA). The ADA was a civil rights law that came on the heels of racial and gender legislation and was "a social promise of equality and inclusion into all facets of life, while offering an inspiring model that much of the world would come to embrace" (Gostin, 2015:2231).

In 2015, 25 years after the passage of the ADA, many individuals and groups reflected on the consequences of the legislation and on Supreme Court interpretations and rulings relative to it. Many pointed out important changes in access to public services, such as crosswalks with curb cuts for wheelchair access, more buildings that can be entered with floors that can be changed without climbing steps, pedestrian signals that assist people with vision difficulties, and more accessible vehicles.

Despite these changes, the substantial disparities that remain in employment, housing, transportation, and other areas often lead to less access and ultimately to poorer health for those with disabilities. For example, access problems remain for using some types of diagnostic imaging equipment and even equipment as basic as a weight scale, for participating in certain types of wellness programs, for communicating for deaf people, and in having medical providers feel comfortable and competent in working with people with disabilities. The Supreme Court has heard several cases that require interpretation of the ADA, and especially early on, they defined disability so narrowly that they prevented many of the advancements which Congress intended. Therefore, in 2008, Congress passed with broad support new legislation (the ADA Amendments Act of 2008) that had the effect of overturning many decisions and adding protections for a more broadly defined group of disabled persons. The Patient Protection and Affordable Care Act—referred to as the ACA or Obamacare (see Chapter 14)—was passed in 2010 and contains provisions specifically to address health inequities for people with disabilities. These include such things as more systematic data gathering, new standards for medical equipment to increase accessibility, and helping health care professionals to become more competent in "disability culture" (Peacock, Iezzoni, and Harkin, 2015).

who is and who is not disabled or what is and what is not a disability is not always the same. Nevertheless, in 2011, the World Health Organization and the World Bank published a report which estimated that 1 billion people around the world live with some form of disability, and that 80 percent of these individuals live in developing countries. According to the report, those with disabilities are more than twice as likely to find health care providers unprepared to meet their needs, nearly three times more likely to be denied care, and four times more likely to be treated badly (World Health Organization and World Bank, 2011).

According to a CDC survey conducted in 2013 using the **Behavioral Risk Factor Surveillance System** (BRFSS), slightly more than 20 percent of the United States population reported one or more disabilities. Typically about two-thirds of reported disabilities are considered to be severe.

Table 3–7 identifies the percentage of selected population subgroups with a disability, Table 3–8 reports the percentage of the population with specific disabling conditions, and Table 3–9 shows the median family income and percentage employed for people without an identified disability and for people with specific functional limitations.

Blacks and Hispanics are slightly more likely than whites to have a disability. Females report more disabilities than males, lose more days from school and work, and have more days confined to bed than males. The likelihood of having a disability is highest among those with the least education, and it decreases as the level of education increases. Many surveys have found that people in the lowest-income groups are around three or four times more likely to have a disability as people in higher-income groups. Their lack of financial means often results in not gaining access to needed services. This in turn often hinders the successful

TABLE 3–7   Percentage of the United States Population with One or More Disabilities, 2013

Characteristic	Percentage
With any physical difficulty	22.2
Male	19.8
Female	24.4
Age 18–44 years	15.7
Age 45–64 years	26.2
Age ≥ 65 years	35.5
White	20.6
Black	29.0
Hispanic	25.9
Less than high-school degree	39.8
High-school degree	26.0
Some college	22.9
College degree or more	11.8

Source: Elizabeth A. Courtney-Long et al. 2015 "Prevalence of Disability and Disability Type Among Adults – United States, 2013." *Morbidity and Mortality Weekly Report* (Atlanta, Georgia: Centers for Disease Control and Protection), 64:777–783.

TABLE 3–8   Prevalence of Any Disability and Disability Type Among Individuals Aged 18 or Older, United States, 2013

Disability Status in United States Population	Percentage
With any disability (some people with more than one disability)	22.2
Vision difficulty	4.6
Cognition difficulty	10.6
Mobility difficulty	13.0
Self-care difficulty	3.6
Independent living difficulty	6.5

Source: Elizabeth A. Courtney-Long et al. 2015 "Prevalence of Disability and Disability Type Among Adults – United States, 2013." *Morbidity and Mortality Weekly Report* (Atlanta, Georgia: Centers for Disease Control and Protection), 64:777–783.

management of a chronic medical condition, and makes it more difficult to live successfully in the community (Allen and More, 1997).

TABLE 3–9   Social Correlates of Disability, Age 21 to 64 Years, 2010

	Percentage	Median Household Income	Percentage Employed
Disability Type			
No disability	83.4	$55,134	79.1
Seeing	2.3	$31,112	41.7
Hearing	1.9	$37,562	55.5
Walking	6.6	$28,475	28.7
Speaking	1.0	$29,415	34.0
Lifting	5.0	$28,307	27.3
Pushing/pulling	6.8	$29,772	31.7

Source: United States Bureau of the Census, *Survey of Income and Program Participation* (Washington, DC: United States Bureau of the Census, 2010).

Disability is very much related to age—persons aged 65 years or older are around two to three times more likely than younger people to have a disability. However, disability among seniors has been declining for the last two decades. Better nutrition, higher levels of education, improved economic status, and medical advances have all contributed to this important change.

Health status and disability status are often related, as many health problems arise from or are related to the main cause of disability. These secondary conditions are often linked to living conditions. For example, pressure sores and musculoskeletal disorders are common among those who are confined to a wheelchair or bed. Not only can these complicating medical conditions arise from immobility or inactivity, but they may also be a result of the progression of the original disabling condition, such as visual impairment among diabetics. Studies continue to show that people with physical limitations are more likely to experience depression and negative feelings and less likely to experience positive emotions (Caputo and Simon, 2013).

Of course, it is possible for a person to be disabled and yet be in good health (e.g., someone who is blind). In 2010, among people aged 65 years or older, about 42 percent of the severely disabled and 72 percent of the non-severely disabled were in good, very good, or excellent health. About 92 percent of those without a disability reported the same positive health status.

SUMMARY

Prior to large-scale migration and urbanization, acute infectious diseases and epidemics presented relatively little threat to humans. The development of easier modes of travel and the emergence of cities brought with them outbreaks of infectious disease. With the discovery of the germ theory of disease and other advances in medicine, as well as greater understanding of the importance of social factors in the transmission of diseases, the threat of infectious diseases was reduced and replaced by a higher incidence and greater likelihood of death from chronic degenerative diseases.

The average number of years of life to be expected from birth—that is, life expectancy—has increased dramatically in the United States during the last 100 years, but still lags behind that in many other countries. Significant improvements have also been made in the infant mortality rate and the maternal mortality rate, although the United States still has higher rates than those in most other modern countries.

Sociodemographic characteristics are significant predictors of life expectancy, infant and maternal mortality, morbidity, and disability within the population. In general, the poor and African Americans are most vulnerable to illness, disability, and death. Men have a significantly higher mortality rate than women, although women experience more morbidity.

HEALTH ON THE INTERNET

A good way to stay abreast of mortality and morbidity data is to check the CDC's *Morbidity and Mortality Weekly Report* on the Internet (www.cdc.gov/mmwr/). After you enter the website, click on "Y" in the top A–Z Index, and then click on "Youth Violence."

How are *interpersonal violence* and *youth violence* defined (see left-hand menu)? What are the four types of *risk factors* and the three types of *protective factors* associated with youth violence? What are some *consequences* of youth violence? What are some *prevention strategies* for youth violence? What is the significance of violence being included in the website of a center for "disease control?"

DISCUSSION CASES

1. This chapter demonstrates how much valuable information epidemiologists provide for understanding and controlling diseases. However, data gathering can conflict with the rights of individuals. For example, identification of individuals with sexually transmitted infections, collection of names of their sexual partners, and contacting these partners can certainly infringe on the autonomy and privacy of the individuals even as they assist in promoting public health. It is therefore extremely important that the responsibilities of epidemiologists be carried out while adhering to ethical principles of respect, justice, and equity.

   Discuss these issues as they relate to the following case. Thomas Hoskins is a 21-year-old full-time college student who is also employed 30 hours per week. The pressures of school, work, and a marriage on the rocks have been adding up for him. Three weeks ago, he went out with a few friends, had too much to drink, and ended up sleeping with a woman he met at the bar. Tests confirm that he now has gonorrhea. While giving him an injection, his physician tells him that all sexually transmitted diseases must be reported to the state health department.

   Thomas is panic stricken. He fears that his wife will somehow find out (she has friends who work for the health department), and that if she does, their marriage will be over. He pleads with the physician to make an exception to his duty to report. This is his first extramarital sexual contact, and he assures the physician it will be his last.

   Should the physician make an exception in this case and not comply with the state mandatory reporting law? Or should physicians always report regardless of the circumstances?

2. Life expectancy in the United States has increased to about 80 years and is continuing to increase. Many respected demographers anticipate that life expectancy will top out at

around 88 years for females and 82 years for males. However, Donald Loria, a professor at the New Jersey Medical School, believes that the average could reach 100 years in the next few decades just with continued gradual increases, and 110 or 120 years with revolutionary advances in health and medicine (Curtis, 2004). Some others do not see this as being likely or possible.

But what if this happened? What if average life expectancy reached 100 or 110 years by mid-century? Identify the changes that would occur in social institutions if 30 or 40 percent of the population was aged 65 years or older (up from today's 13.5 percent). If we knew that this change was going to occur within the next five decades, what social planning could be done to try to accommodate it?

GLOSSARY

acute infectious diseases
Behavioral Risk Factor Surveillance System (BRFSS)
Centers for Disease Control and Prevention (CDC)
chronic degenerative diseases
crude death rate (CDR)
disability
epidemiological transition
epidemiology
fundamental cause theory
incidence
infant mortality rate (IMR)

life expectancy
maternal mortality rate (MMR)
morbidity
mortality
neonatal mortality rate
post-neonatal mortality rate
prevalence
restricted-activity days
social capital theory
social epidemiology
social model of disability
World Health Organization (WHO)

REFERENCES

Agency for Health Care Research and Quality, Medical Expenditure Panel Survey. 2010 *Restricted Activity Days in the United States*. Washington, DC: USDHHS.

Agha, Sohail. 2000 "The Determinants of Infant Mortality in Pakistan." *Social Science and Medicine*, 51:199–208.

Akhtar, Aysha. 2016 "Why Are We Seeing an Explosion of New Viruses Like Zika?" *HuffPost World Economic Forum*. www.huffingtonpost.com/aysha-akhtar/.

Allen Susan M., and Vincent More. 1997 "The Prevalence and Consequences of Unmet Need." *Medical Care*, 35:1132–1148.

Barnes, Colin, and Geof Mercer. 2010 *Exploring Disability: A Sociological Introduction*, 2nd ed. Malden, MA: Polity Press.

Bird, Chloe E., and Patricia P. Rieker. 2008 *Gender and Health: The Effects of Constrained Choices and Social Policies*. New York: Cambridge University Press.

Bird, Sheryl T., and Karl E. Bauman. 1995 "The Relationship Between Structural and Health Services Variables and State-Level Infant Mortality in the United States." *American Journal of Public Health*, 85:26–29.

Caputo, Jennifer, and Robin W. Simon. 2013 "Physical Limitation and Emotional Well-Being: Gender and Marital Status Variations." *Journal of Health and Social Behavior*, 54: 241–257.

Carney, Timothy J., and David J. Weber. 2015 "Public Health Intelligence: Learning from the

Ebola Crisis." *American Journal of Public Health*, 105:1740–1744.

Celetano, David D., Martha S. Linet, and Walter F. Stewart. 1990 "Gender Differences in the Experience of Headache." *Social Science and Medicine*, 30:1289–1295.

Centers for Disease Control and Prevention. National Center for Health Statistics. 2003 "Public Health and Aging: Trends in Aging—United States and Worldwide." www.cdc.gov/mmwr/preview/mmwrhtml/mm5206a2.htm

———. 2014a "Infant Deaths Per 1,000 Live Births by Race of Mother, United States, 2012." www.cdc.gov/nchs.

———. 2014b "Life Expectancy by Race, Sex, and Age, 2013." www.cdc.gov/nchs.

———. 2015 "Leading Causes of Death for 2013." www.cdc.gov/nchs.

Central Intelligence Agency. 2016a "Infant Mortality." *The World Factbook*, www.cia.gov/library/publications/the-world-factbook.

———. 2016b "Life Expectancy at Birth." *The World Factbook*, www.cia.gov/library/publications/the-world-factbook.

Chan, Margaret. 2014 "Ebola Virus Disease in West Africa—No Early End to the Outbreak." *New England Journal of Medicine*, 371: 1183–1185.

Clarke, Phillipa J., Jennifer A. Ailshire, Els R. Nieuwenhuijsen, and Marike W. de Kleijn-de Frankrijker. 2011 "Participation Among Adults With Disability: The Role of the Urban Environment." *Social Science and Medicine*, 72:1674–1684.

Courtney-Long, Elizabeth A., Dianna D. Carroll, Qing C. Zhang, Alissa C. Stevens, Shannon Griffin-Blake, Brian S. Armour, and Vincent A. Campbell. 2015 "Prevalence of Disability and Disability Type Among Adults—United States, 2013." *Morbidity and Mortality Weekly Report*, 64 (July 31):777–783.

Curtis, Wayne. 2004 "The Methuselah Report." *AARP Bulletin*, 43:5–7.

Dutton, Diana B. 1986 "Social Class, Health, and Illness." Pp. 31–62 in *Applications of Social Science to Clinical Medicine and Health Policy*, Linda H. Aiken and David Mechanic (eds.). New Brunswick, NJ: Rutgers University Press.

Fenelon, Andrew. 2013 "Revisiting the Hispanic Mortality Advantage in the United States: The Role of Smoking." *Social Science and Medicine*, 82:1–9.

Ferraro, Kenneth F., and Melissa Farmer. 1996 "Double Jeopardy to Health Hypothesis for African-Americans: Analysis and Critique." *Journal of Health and Social Behavior*, 37:27–43.

Flegal, Katherine M., Margaret D. Carroll, Cynthia L. Ogden, and Lester R. Curtin. 2010 "Prevalence and Trends in Obesity Among U.S. Adults, 1999–2008." *Journal of the American Medical Association*, 303:235–241.

Friis, Robert H. 2010 *Epidemiology 101*. Sudbury, MA: Jones and Bartlett Learning.

Gaziano, J. Michael. 2010 "Fifth Phase of the Epidemiologic Transition: The Age of Obesity and Inactivity." *Journal of the American Medical Association*, 303:275–276.

Gostin, Leonard, O. 2015 "The Americans with Disabilities Act at 25: The Highest Expression of American Values." *Journal of the American Medical Association*, 313:2231–2235.

Hager, Mary. 1998 "The World Health Organization Has Seen the Future, and It's Full of Good Health." *Newsweek*, June 1, p. 10.

Hayward, Mark D., Robert A. Hummer, and Isaac Sassoon. 2015 "Trends and Group Differences in the Association Between Educational Attainment and U.S. Adult Mortality: Implications for Understanding Education's Causal Influence." *Social Science and Medicine*, 127:8–18.

Heisler, Elayne J. 2012 *The U.S. Infant Mortality Rate: International Comparisons, Underlying Factors, and Federal Programs*. Washington, DC: Congressional Research Service. www.fas.org/sgp/crs/misc/R41378.pdf.

Ho, Jessica Y. 2013 "Mortality Under Age 50 Accounts for Much of the Fact That US Life Expectancy Lags That of Other High-Income Countries." *Health Affairs*, 32:459–467.

House, James S., Ronald Kessler, and A. Regula Herzog. 1990 "Age, Socioeconomic Status, and Health." *The Milbank Quarterly*, 68:383–411.

LaVeist, Thomas A. 1993 "Segregation, Poverty, and Empowerment: Health Consequences for African Americans." *The Milbank Quarterly*, 71:41–64.

McKinlay, John B. 1996 "Some Contributions from the Social System to Gender Inequalities in Heart Disease." *Journal of Health and Social Behavior*, 37:1–26.

Masters, Ryan K., Bruce G. Link, and Jo C. Phelan. 2015 "Trends in Educational Gradients of 'Preventable Mortality': A Test of Fundamental

Cause Theory." *Social Science and Medicine*, 127:19–28.

Mechanic, David. 1995 "Sociological Dimensions of Illness Behavior." *Social Science and Medicine*, 41:1207–1216.

Montez, Jennifer K., Robert A. Hummer, Mark D. Hayward, Hweyoung Woo, and Richard G. Rogers. 2011 "Trends in the Educational Gradient of U.S. Adult Mortality from 1986 through 2006 by Race, Gender, and Age Group." *Research on Aging*, 33:145–171.

Olshansky, S. Jay, and A. Brian Ault. 1986 "The Fourth State of the Epidemiologic Transition: The Age of Delayed Degenerative Diseases." *The Milbank Quarterly*, 64:355–391.

Olshansky, S. Jay, Toni Antonucci, Lisa Berkman, Robert H. Binstock, Axel Boersch-Supan, John T. Cacioppo, Bruce A. Carnes, Laura L. Carstensen, Linda P. Fried, Dana P. Goldman, James Jackson, Martin Kohli, John Rother, Yuhui Zheng, and John Rowe. 2012 "Differences in Life Expectancy Due to Race and Educational Differences Are Widening, and Many May Not Catch Up." *Health Affairs*, 8:1803–1813.

Omran, A.R. 1971 "The Epidemiologic Transition: A Theory of the Epidemiology of Population Change." *Milbank Memorial Fund Quarterly*, 49:309–338.

Otten, Mac W., Steven M. Teutsch, David F. Williamson, and James F. Marks. 1990 "The Effect of Known Risk Factors on the Excess Mortality of Black Adults in the United States." *Journal of the American Medical Association*, 263:845–850.

Peacock, Georgina, Lisa I. Iezzoni, and Thomas R. Harkin. 2015 "Health Care for Americans with Disabilities—25 Years after the ADA." *New England Journal of Medicine*, 373:892–893.

Ramirez-Valles, Jesus, Lisa M. Kuhns, Richard T. Campbell, and Rafael M. Diaz. 2010 "Social Integration and Health: Community Involvement, Stigmatized Identities, and Sexual Risk in Latino Sexual Minorities." *Journal of Health and Social Behavior*, 51:30–47.

Rosenfield, Allan, Caroline J. Min, and Lynn P. Freedman. 2007 "Making Motherhood Safe in Developing Countries." *New England Journal of Medicine*, 356:1395–1397.

Sade, Robert M. 2012 "The Graying of America: Challenges and Controversies." *Journal of Law, Medicine and Ethics*, 40:6–9.

Shaw, Benjamin A., Kelly McGeever, Elizabeth Vasquez, Neda Agahi, and Stefan Fors. 2014 "Socioeconomic Inequalities in Health After Age 50: Are Health Risk Behaviors to Blame?" *Social Science and Medicine*, 101:52–60.

Smedley, Brian D., Adrienne Y. Stith, and Alan R. Nelson (eds.). 2003 *Unequal Treatment: Confronting Racial and Ethnic Disparities in Health Care*. Washington, DC: Institute of Medicine.

Song, Lijun, and Nan Lin. 2009 "Social Capital and Health Inequality: Evidence from Taiwan." *Journal of Health and Social Behavior*, 50: 149–163.

Spittel, Michael L., William T. Riley, and Robert M. Kaplan. 2015 "Educational Attainment and Life Expectancy: A Perspective from the NIH Office of Behavioral and Social Sciences Research." *Social Sciences and Medicine*, 127:203–205.

Stillion, Judith M., and Eugene E. McDowell. 2001–2002 "The Early Demise of the 'Stronger' Sex: Gender-Related Causes of Sex Differences in Longevity." *Omega*, 44:301–318.

Storrs, Carina. 2016 "Why Americans Don't live as Long as Europeans." www.cnn.com/2016/health/american-life-expectancy-shorter-than-europeans/index,html.

Sudano, Joseph J., and David W. Baker. 2006 "Explaining US Racial/Ethnic Disparities in Health Declines and Mortality in Late Middle Ages: The Roles of Socioeconomic Status, Health Behaviors, and Health Insurance." *Social Science and Medicine*, 62:909–922.

Umberson, Debra, and Jennifer K. Montez. 2010 "Social Relationships and Health: A Flashpoint for Health Policy." *Journal of Health and Social Behavior*, 51:S54–S66.

United States Bureau of the Census. 2010 *Survey of Income and Program Participation*. Washington, DC: USGPO.

United States Department of Health and Human Services. 2010 *Healthy People 2020*. Washington, DC: DHHS.

Verbrugge, Lois M. 1990 "Pathways of Health and Death." Pp. 41–79 in *Women, Health and Medicine—A Historical Handbook*, Rima D. Apple (ed.). New York: Garland Publishing, Inc.

Williams, David R. 2012 "Miles To Go Before We Sleep: Racial Inequities in Health." *Journal of Health and Social Behavior*, 53:279–295.

Williams, David R., and Pamela B. Jackson. 2005 "Social Sources of Racial Disparities in Health." *Health Affairs*, 24:325–334.

World Health Organization. 2010 "Multidrug and Extensively Drug Resistant Tuberculosis: 2010 Global Report on Surveillance and Response." www.who.int/tb/features_archive/m_xdrtb_facts/en/.

———. 2013 "Disabilities." www.who.int/topics/disabilities/en/.

———. 2015 "Maternal Mortality." www.who.int/mediacentre/factsheets/fs348/en/.

World Health Organization and World Bank. 2011 *World Report on Disability*. Geneva, Switzerland: World Health Organization.

CHAPTER 4

Society, Disease, and Illness

Learning Objectives

- Distinguish between "fundamental causes," "proximate risk factors," and "genetic factors" as causes of disease.

- Identify and discuss three important patterns of disease in the world's developing countries.

- Explain the traditional under-representation of women and racial and ethnic minorities

in medical research. Discuss the harm created by this under-representation.

- Identify and discuss the most important fundamental causes of disease that are discussed in this chapter.

- Identify and explain the most important proximate risk factors related to heart disease and to cancer—the two leading causes of death in the United States.

The types of diseases that are most common within a society and their distribution among the population are determined by a wide range of factors that include the presence of disease agents, characteristics of the social, economic, physical, and biological environment, and demographic characteristics and lifestyles of the people. In every society these factors lead to some groups being more vulnerable to disease than others, and being more likely to contract specific diseases.

THE SOCIAL ETIOLOGY OF DISEASE

Explaining both the occurrence of particular **acute infectious diseases** and **chronic degenerative diseases** within a society and their distribution within the population begins with identification of the cause or causes of each disease (i.e., their **etiology**). After the **germ theory of disease** was discovered in the late 1800s, the identification of the bacterium or

virus responsible for most acute infectious diseases was relatively straightforward. However, tracing the origin of most chronic degenerative diseases has been more complicated, due to at least four reasons:

1. Most chronic degenerative diseases, such as cancer and coronary heart disease, have multiple causes. Rather than being traceable to the presence of a particular bacterium or virus, factors related to diet, exercise, personality type, smoking and drinking behavior, stress, social support, and others interrelate in countless configurations. It is very difficult to measure the amount, duration, and effects of each factor on an individual.

2. With many chronic degenerative diseases, there is a long latency period between the influence and the consequence. Cancer often appears 20 to 30 or more years after exposure to the carcinogenic substance, making it difficult to determine cause-and-effect relationships. Moreover, not everyone who is

exposed to a harmful lifestyle or a carcino-genic substance will contract degenerative disease (e.g., some lifetime smokers never get lung cancer).

3. It is very difficult to determine how much of a behavior or how much of a substance is necessary to trigger a disease. Some researchers point out that almost any substance taken in sufficiently large quanti-ties can be health damaging. Many regula-tions on substances in society are based on the idea that there is a threshold of exposure below which there is no danger to health. Other researchers disagree, saying that there are only lower levels of danger.

4. The validity of generalizations from animal testing to humans is an unresolved question. For example, the amount of a substance required to cause cancer in an animal may not realistically indicate the amount to which humans can safely be exposed. There are many toxicologists on both sides of this issue. Some years ago, when limits on human consumption of saccharin were contemplated based on laboratory tests on rats, one wag suggested that diet soft drinks should be labeled "Warning: Extensive use of this product has been shown by scientists to be dangerous to your rat's health."

To fully understand disease causation and distribution, it is important to understand both **social determinants of health** (fundamental causes and proximate risk factors) and genetic factors.

Social Determinants of Health

In their 1994 book, *Why Are Some People Healthy and Others Not? The Determinants of Health of Populations*, economist Robert Evans, epidemiologist Morris Barer, and political scien-tist Theodore Marmor sought to explain why diseases are not randomly distributed within societies. They synthesized research done in several disciplines and included studies conducted in the United States and in other countries. While not discounting the influence of heredity on disease causation, they concluded that the primary determinants of the health of people and of the distribution of diseases within society are embedded in the social structure of society.

Hertzman, Frank, and Evans (1994) identify six possible causal pathways through which one's position in the social structure can deter-mine health status or the likelihood of disease:

1. *Physical environment.* Some individuals are more likely than others to be exposed to the potentially harmful effects of physical, chem-ical, and biological agents. The presence of harmful substances in the workplace (e.g., hydrocarbons in coal), in the home (e.g., lead paint chipping from the walls), or in the neighborhood (e.g., proximity to a landfill) serves as a pathway to ill health. See the accompanying box, "Climate Change and Health."

2. *Social environment (and psychological response).* Some persons live in a more stressful social environment than others (e.g., at the workplace or school, within the family, or with social responsibilities), and some have less access to supportive social relation-ships. This can lead to greater likelihood of ill health.

3. *Differential susceptibility.* The opportunities that individuals have for occupational success have been shown to be partially influenced by physical traits such as appearance and height. A tall person with an attractive appear-ance may gain some occupational advantages over a shorter person with a more disheveled appearance. These advantages may ulti-mately translate into circumstances (e.g., higher and more secure income) that lead to health benefits.

IN THE FIELD

CLIMATE CHANGE AND HEALTH

The interrelated issues of *climate change* and *global warming* have become entangled in political discourse in the United States, and the scientific understanding of climate change and the medical consequences of it are sometimes lost in political posturing. The international scientific community overwhelmingly accepts the idea that climate change is occurring and that it is largely a consequence of particular human behaviors. Global surface temperatures today are about 0.6 degrees Celsius higher than the average for the last century. The year 2014 was the hottest year in recorded history at that time. The following year, 2015, was even hotter than 2014. Atmospheric carbon dioxide was at its highest level in at least 800,000 years. Ocean temperatures have warmed, amounts of snow and ice have diminished, and the sea level has risen. Extreme temperature events (sometimes hot and sometimes cold, sometimes wet and sometimes dry) are causing considerable disruption to ecosystems, agriculture, the availability of clean air and water, and a host of human health conditions.

Surveys have found that 97 percent of climate scientists have concluded that it is very likely that climate change is due to human activities, especially the increasing release of greenhouse gases into the atmosphere. The primary source of this problem is the reliance on fossil fuels (e.g., coal, oil, and gas) as they are used to provide electricity, heat, transportation, and industrial energy. The greenhouse gases build up in the earth's atmosphere, thus causing heat from the earth to become trapped. This leads to a rise in temperature and increased likelihood of situations like floods and droughts.

This has an impact on human health in important but indirect ways. There are no diseases that directly result from climate change. However, climate change is a "risk amplifier"—it makes other diseases more likely. Heart attacks and heart failure increase substantially in very warm weather. Many infectious diseases flourish in very warm weather. Warm weather attracts mosquitos which can carry with them diseases such as malaria and West Nile virus. Lung cancer, asthma, and other respiratory diseases could increase due to the presence of more toxins in the air. Expected declines in crop productivity and availability of clean water could lead to more nutritional diseases and increased diarrheal problems. Environmental conditions could lead to increases in neurological diseases such as Parkinson's disease and Alzheimer's disease (Krueger, Biedrzycki, and Hoverter, 2015).

Due to the obvious health-related considerations, health care leaders from around the world are now becoming increasingly involved in efforts to reduce greenhouse gases. Conferences have been held around the world for physicians, nurses, public health specialists, and other health care professionals. The World Health Organization, the Centers for Disease Control and Prevention, the World Medical Association, and several national medical associations are taking leadership on the health issues, are serving as role models in changing their sources of energy, are educating the public that climate change is a serious health-related issue and not just fodder for political bickering, and are demonstrating the importance of global connectedness in addressing vital issues.

4. *Individual lifestyle.* Some people live a healthier lifestyle than others, and lifestyle decisions are often shaped by social forces. For example, it is little wonder that individuals who grow up in a family of cigarette smokers are themselves more likely to smoke. People who perceive their neighborhood to be safe are more likely to get adequate physical exercise through walking or jogging than those who do not feel safe in their neighborhood.

5. *Differential access to/response to health care services.* Differences in health status may result from systematic differences in access to health care services, in differential propensity to use services, and in differential benefit of services received. All of these factors relate strongly to financial resources.

6. *Reverse causality.* In this pathway, a person's health status influences their position in the social structure, rather than the other way round as is commonly assumed. For example, the relationship between income and sickness might exist because the sick become poor rather than because the poor become sick. However, with the exception of chronic mental illness, the authors find little empirical support for this pathway.

These social determinants of health can be divided into two specific types of factors—**fundamental causes** and **proximate risk factors.** *Proximate risk factors* of disease and illness refer to health-related individual behaviors, and include diet, exercise, use of tobacco and alcohol, control of stress, and other aspects of lifestyle. Epidemiologists have amassed volumes of research that link these factors to the onset of specific diseases and illnesses, and this will be examined in depth later in this chapter and in Chapters 5 and 6. *Fundamental causes* of disease and illness refer to underlying social conditions such as socioeconomic status, social inequality, community and neighborhood

characteristics, exposure to stressful life events, and access to a supportive social network. These fundamental causes help to shape health and disease by influencing participation in proximate risk factors (e.g., influencing the likelihood of smoking cigarettes) and by providing access to important resources (e.g., money and social connectedness) that can bolster health and enable receipt of preventive or curative medical care (Link and Phelan, 1995, 2000).

> Key resources such as knowledge, money, power, prestige, and beneficial social connections can be used no matter what the risk and protective factors are in a given circumstance.... If the problem is cholera, for example, a person with greater resources is better able to avoid areas where the disease is rampant, and highly resourced communities are better able to prohibit entry of infected persons. If the problem is heart disease, a person with greater resources is better able to maintain a heart-healthy lifestyle and get the best medical treatment available. (Phelan, Link, and Tehranifar, 2010:S29)

An example of an underlying social condition that has a significant impact on the occurrence of disease and illness and is a component of SES is education. In Chapter 3, the advantage that the highly educated have in terms of life expectancy was discussed. Not surprisingly, this advantage also exists with respect to disease and illness. The fact that more highly educated people are healthier has been well documented, and has been shown to occur through four pathways. First, well-educated persons are more likely to be employed, work full-time at a fulfilling job, and have a high income with little economic hardship—all of which have a positive impact on health. Second, the well-educated have a greater sense of control over their lives and health, and have higher levels of social support—both of which are associated with good health. Third, well-educated persons are less likely to smoke and more likely to get adequate exercise and to drink in moderation—all of which have a positive impact on health

IN THE FIELD

TOXIC AIR AND AMERICA'S SCHOOLS

Air samples taken outside Meredith Hitchens Elementary School in Addyston, Ohio, a suburb of Cincinnati, showed high levels of chemicals coming from the plastics company across the street. The Ohio Environmental Protection Agency (EPA) concluded that the risk of getting cancer there was 50 times higher than what the state considers acceptable. School district officials closed the school. The air outside 435 other schools across the country appears to be even worse.

The newspaper *USA Today*, working with researchers from Johns Hopkins University and the University of Massachusetts, Amherst, spent eight months using the most up-to-date computer modeling process for tracking industrial pollutants outside schools across the nation. Their research led to a ranking of 127,800 public, private, and parochial schools based on the level of nearby toxic chemicals and health hazards. The findings are important because children are especially susceptible to airborne pollutants, as they breathe in more air

relative to their weight than adults do (Heath, Morrison, and Reed, 2008; Morrison and Heath, 2008).

How could such a condition exist? Many states have no laws regulating where schools can be built. In building new schools, school districts often look for inexpensive land (10 percent of the 435 worst schools had been built in the last decade). Inexpensive land can often be found near heavy (and often polluting) industry. Throughout most of the first decade of the 2000s, the EPA was less aggressive in pursuing polluting industries and had never done research of this type around the nation's schools. Few people want a school built in proximity to their home. Residents of low-income communities typically have less influence on local decision making than do residents of more well-to-do communities. One result of this is that low-income schools are more likely to be located near polluting industries, and the children of those schools are more likely to have to deal with unclean air.

IN THE FIELD

THE WATER CRISIS IN FLINT, MICHIGAN

Flint, Michigan is a community of 100,000 largely poor and black people. It was once a thriving automobile city in which General Motors had situated its first factory. However, in the late 1960s, General Motors began disinvesting in the community, factory jobs were lost, and urban decay began to settle in. Many prosperous residents moved to the suburbs or out of the Flint area altogether.

By the early 2000s, city finances were a shambles, and debt was being accumulated.

Contrary to the wishes of the people, the governor appointed an emergency town administrator to deal with the economic problems. Drastic measures were taken—many town officials were fired, salaries and benefits were reduced, and fees went up. Officially, the financial emergency ended in 2005.

Some progress occurred over the next ten years (some abandoned buildings were destroyed, and a new factory was created), but General Motors continued its move out of town. In its heyday, General Motors employed 80,000 people in Flint. By 2006, only 8,000 employees remained. By 2011, another financial emergency was declared (the city was bankrupt), and another administrator was appointed by the governor. In 2014, in order to save money, the decision was made to switch the town water supply from Detroit's system using Lake Huron water to the Flint River.

Shortly after the water supply transition, the General Motors plant complained that the water was creating rust on newly machined parts, and the plant was given permission to change to a different water supplier. For months, city residents also complained that their water was contaminated. It was discolored, smelly, and foul tasting, and skin rashes appeared after people had bathed in it. It was found to contain dangerous bacteria. When the city added chlorine to the water to attempt to kill the bacteria, it became corrosive.

When they did not get an adequate response at the local or state level, or from the Environmental Protection Agency representative in the area, local residents hired scientists to investigate their water. They found that the corrosive water was causing a dangerously high level of lead to leach from the aged pipes. By that time, Flint residents had been consuming the water for a year. High levels of lead can lead to a variety of physical health and other problems, including anemia, decreased IQ, and slower growth. Some of the damage might not be manifested for years, and the developmental problems are not reversible. One of Michigan's

Labor and community activists in Lansing, Michigan, picket Governor Rick Snyder's annual State of the State speech, calling for him to resign because of the state's handling of the water crisis in Flint. © Jim West/Alamy Stock Photo.

senators stated that a key problem was that officials simply did not listen to what the people were saying.

(Margolis, 2013; Ross and Wu, 1995). Finally, more highly educated people are more likely to have health insurance and are better able to obtain medical care.

For two specific examples of the importance of fundamental causes in the United States, see the boxes "Toxic Air and America's Schools" and "The Water Crisis in Flint, Michigan."

Genetic Factors in Health

Knowledge about the role of genetic transmission in disease and illness has increased substantially in the last several years with the successful mapping of the approximately 25,000 genes within each human. The **Human Genome Project** began in 1990 with the goal of assigning each gene to its proper location on a chromosome. The work that was conducted in the United States (about 60 percent), England (30 percent), and elsewhere was largely completed in 2000. This knowledge is being used to better understand the role of genes with respect to a variety of diseases.

Given the importance of fundamental causes and proximate risk factors in affecting disease and illness, what role is played by genetic transmission? Essentially, genes affect disease and illness in two primary ways:

1. *As the specific cause of approximately 4,000 "genetic diseases," including Down syndrome, cystic fibrosis, Tay–Sachs disease, Huntington's disease, and sickle-cell anemia.* Some diseases are monogenic—that is, they can be traced to a single gene. For example, chromosome 21 is the site of genes for Down syndrome, Lou Gehrig's disease, and epilepsy. More diseases are polygenic—that is, they result from several genes acting together. These are more complicated causal relationships about which much more needs to be known.

   While genetic diseases represent a small component of all diseases, they are especially apparent early in life. About 25 percent of all admissions of people under 18 years of age to United States hospitals are for a genetic disease or condition, and genetic conditions are the second leading cause of death for children between the ages of 1 and 4 years.

2. *As a factor that increases the likelihood of occurrence of many other diseases, including heart disease, some types of cancer, Alzheimer's disease, and diabetes.* In these cases, an individual's genetic makeup renders it either more or less likely that environmental factors will trigger a particular disease. An even greater number of diseases follow this multifactorial path in which interplay between the genes and the environment causes a disease to occur.

Some laypeople have become so excited by the new knowledge about genes and their implications for disease and illness that they have envisioned a future in which all disease can be understood through genetic roots. However, this perspective ignores all our existing knowledge about social pathways to disease and illness. Both genetic and sociological lines of research need to continue, along with efforts to integrate the two perspectives, or at least to utilize both of them in seeking to understand why disease and illness occur as they do (Fletcher and Conley, 2013). As an illustration, Bearman (2008) cites the fact that the genetic tendency to obesity can only be observed in societies that produce a surplus of food. This example points to the need for the work of both biologists and sociologists to unravel the contributions of genes and social factors to particular diseases and conditions.

This is exactly what Pescosolido et al. (2008) did in a study that attempted to understand alcohol dependence. Using data from the Collaborative Study on the Genetics of Alcoholism, they tested propositions about alcohol dependence based on three sociological theories and on the influence of the GABRA-2 gene (which has been linked to alcoholism). They found strong evidence that the GABRA-2 gene increases the likelihood of alcohol dependence, but that this influence was largely true only for men, that childhood deprivation enhances the gene's expression in alcohol dependence, and that living within a strong socially supportive network almost completely eliminates the effects of the gene. Thus, in this case, consideration of both genetic and social influences provides the most complete understanding. As more is learned about the genetic origin of or influence on particular diseases and on the interplay between genes and social factors, advances in preventive medicine and patient outcomes are likely (Tuckson, Newcomer, and De Sa, 2013).

Medical research is a foundation for advances in understanding disease causation and the evaluation of new therapeutic agents. The National Institutes of Health (NIH) is the leading medical research organization in the United States. © Tyler Olson/ Fotolia.

THE INTERRELATIONSHIP OF PROXIMATE RISK FACTORS AND FUNDAMENTAL CAUSES: THE CASE OF DEVELOPING COUNTRIES

In chapter 3, we used the *epidemiological transition* to explain the general shift from acute infectious diseases to chronic degenerative diseases within societies as they modernize. Because the pace of this transition has accelerated in recent years, developing countries in the world today are confronted with a **double disease burden**. While they are still at a point in development in which they have to deal with acute infectious diseases (such as malaria and tuberculosis), they are already facing increased rates of the chronic degenerative diseases (such as heart disease and cancer) that predominate in industrialized countries.

For example, while the level of world hunger is still at a staggering level (almost 800 million undernourished people in the world), several large countries—including China and Brazil— have significantly reduced their number of malnourished in the last few decades. In several poor countries, although the number of deaths among newborns and children is still shockingly high, fewer children are dying before age 5. These advances are occurring largely in shifts from agrarian-based societies to industrialized societies. With this industrialization process, however, people are adopting more affluent Western lifestyles, including high-fat diets (and popularity of fast foods), greater use of tobacco and alcohol, and less physical activity. These changes will lead to an increased incidence of chronic, degenerative diseases. Almost 7 percent of the world's children under age 5 are overweight or obese. About 80 percent of the world's cigarette smokers live in low- and middle-income countries. China and India, the world's two largest countries, have huge populations today with diabetes and high blood pressure, a sign that increased rates of heart disease are likely in the near future. (In the 1990s, 4 percent of Chinese people had diabetes; by 2015, the figure was 12 percent.) See the accompanying box, "Disease and Illness Patterns in Worldwide Perspective."

To assist in handling this critical situation in developing countries, a broad program for research and empowerment called the **health transition (HT)** has been developed (Caldwell,

---

IN COMPARATIVE FOCUS

DISEASE AND ILLNESS PATTERNS IN WORLDWIDE PERSPECTIVE

The main causes of death and sickness around the world have changed significantly in the last 10 to 20 years, with chronic degenerative diseases becoming more and more important. The *Global Burden of Disease Study*, published in 2012 in *The Lancet*, is a collaboration of 486 scientists in 302 institutions in 50 countries and an effort to understand death, sickness, and disability in countries around the world.

The study found that people are living longer nearly everywhere around the world and fewer children are dying, but that people are more often dealing with chronic degenerative diseases (diseases that occur later in life). Sixty percent of deaths worldwide are due to chronic degenerative diseases (Venkat, Ali, and Koplan, 2010). Key findings are that heart disease and stroke are the leading causes of death around the world, that diabetes, lung cancer, and motor vehicle accidents are becoming increasingly common causes of death, and that certain conditions such as malnutrition and childhood infectious diseases are decreasing as causes of death. However, the health of people aged 10 to 24 years has not kept pace with that of older persons, and injuries (especially from traffic accidents), suicide, homicide, AIDS, and complications of childbirth account for most deaths in this age category. Mental health problems in people of all ages continue to be of great concern (Holtz, 2013).

In 2014 the World Health Organization identified the following ten facts as being key to understanding world disease patterns.

1. Life expectancy at birth had increased globally by 6 years since 1990.
2. Around 6.6 million children under the age of 5 years die each year (most could be saved with simple interventions).
3. Preterm birth is the leading killer of newborn babies worldwide.
4. Cardiovascular diseases are the leading causes of death in the world (most could be prevented or delayed by healthy diet, regular physical exercise, and by not using tobacco).
5. Most HIV/AIDS deaths occur in Africa (and many people do not know they are infected).
6. Every day, about 800 women die due to complications of pregnancy and childbirth.
7. Mental disorders such as depression are among the 20 leading causes of disability.
8. Tobacco kills nearly 6 million people each year.
9. Almost one in ten adults has diabetes.
10. Nearly 3,500 people die in road crashes every day (increasing vehicle ownership in developing countries will probably increase this number).

1993). The program is grounded in three themes (Gallagher, Stewart, and Stratton, 2000):

1. *The importance of equitable distribution of income and wealth.* Health progress occurs more rapidly in countries without huge disparities in wealth. Some countries that are relatively poor but which do not have sharp divisions in wealth (e.g., China and Cuba) have made more headway in reducing death rates than some relatively wealthier countries with greater inequality (e.g., Iran).
2. *The importance of public and community health.* It is commonly accepted that the decline in the death rate in industrialized countries resulted more from public health measures than from advances in clinical medicine. Therefore, developing countries are being urged to invest in social policies that emphasize improvements in food and water supply, sanitation, access to primary health care, community development, and greater opportunities for women in education, employment, and public life. Countries are being discouraged from investing available funds in high-technology medicine that has much more limited impact.
3. *The importance of lifestyle and behavioral factors.* While proximate risk factors such as diet, tobacco smoking, and sexual behavior are important in industrialized countries because of their link to chronic diseases, they are especially important in developing countries because of their link to infectious diseases. Thus, emphasis is encouraged on such behaviors as drinking only safe water (which might necessitate considerable travel and inconvenience), limiting family size to a number that can be economically supported, and using a condom for non-monogamous sex.

In the remainder of this chapter, five significant but very different diseases and conditions in American society are examined. Coronary heart disease and cancer are the two leading causes of death in the United States. HIV/AIDS is a relatively recently identified disease that quickly became a worldwide epidemic. It appears to be in transition from a fatal disease to a controllable chronic condition. Alzheimer's disease was first identified in the early 1900s as a disease of mental deterioration in mid- and late-adult life. It is currently the only one of the ten leading causes of death in the United States for which there is no treatment or cure. Mental illness and severe mental disorders have long been studied, and a considerable body of research has developed around their etiology. Nevertheless, they are still sometimes considered to be less "legitimate" than physical diseases and illnesses, and they often receive less government funding.

CORONARY HEART DISEASE (CHD)

The Cardiovascular System

The body's cardiovascular system transports necessary nutrients, oxygen, and water to all the body's tissues, carries substances such as disease-fighting antibodies to wherever they are needed in the body, and removes carbon dioxide and other waste products. The pumping of the heart stimulates the flow of blood, which is the transportation system. For the heart to function properly (it beats about 100,000 times a day, pumping about 1,800 gallons of blood), it must receive an adequate supply of blood from the three main coronary arteries and their smaller branches. Heart disease occurs when this system is disrupted.

Coronary heart disease (CHD, sometimes called ischemic heart disease) occurs when the inner surface (or inner layers) of any artery become thickened, resulting in a narrowing and

IN THE FIELD

THE HISTORICAL UNDER-REPRESENTATION OF WOMEN AND RACIAL AND ETHNIC MINORITIES IN BIOMEDICAL RESEARCH

The physiology and social position of women and men and blacks and whites differ in ways that relate to disease and illness. Gender and racial/ethnic groups show different propensities to different diseases. Therapeutic and pharmacological agents affect people differently. For these reasons, biomedical research must be conducted on samples that reflect population differences (within or among studies) if they are to benefit all people. Amazingly, this is often not the case. Dresser summarized the issue in 1992.

> The failure to include women in research populations is ubiquitous. An NIH-sponsored study showing that heart attacks were reduced when subjects took one aspirin every other day was conducted on men, and the relationship between low-cholesterol diets and cardiovascular disease has been almost exclusively studied in men. Yet coronary heart disease is the leading cause of death in women. Similarly, the first twenty years of a major federal study on health and aging included only men. Yet two-thirds of the elderly population are women. The recent announcement that aspirin can help to prevent migraine headaches is based on data from males only, even though women suffer from migraines up to three times as often as men.
>
> The list goes on: studies on AIDS treatment frequently omit women, the fastest growing infected population. An investigation of the possible relationship between caffeine and heart disease involved 45,589 male research subjects ... Moreover, the customary research subject not only is male, but is a white male. African Americans, Latinos, and other racial and ethnic groups have typically been excluded. (Dresser, 1992:24)

What was the outcome of this bias? As an example, of the ten prescription drugs that were withdrawn from the market between 1997 and 2000, eight caused a more adverse reaction in women than in men. Two of the drugs caused a rare but dangerous form of heart arrhythmia in

some women who took them. These unanticipated reactions occurred because the drugs had not been adequately tested on women.

Criticism of this research discrimination led to a major research initiative—the Women's Health Initiative—which was started in 1991 to study heart disease and stroke, cancer, and osteoporosis in women of all races and all socioeconomic strata. The successful effort to bring this issue to public attention and to enlist Congress in creating this program was directed by a number of important groups, including many sociologists (Auerbach and Figert, 1995). Spending on women's health research reached an all-time high.

Two years later, the National Institutes of Health Revitalization Act of 1993, which required that all federally funded studies include women as well as men, and racial and ethnic minorities as well as whites, was passed. Additional policies were implemented in 2001.

However, change has come slowly. In 2015, for example, the Food and Drug Administration approved a prescription drug for women with low libido. One limitation was that one could not consume alcohol while taking the drug, or one would risk serious side effects. This conclusion came from a study that included 25 individuals—23 men and 2 women. Despite the fact that men and women metabolize alcohol differently, the study essentially ignored female subjects (Shumaker, 2015). Some research has found that heart failure clinical trials still overrepresent younger, white males in their study populations, suggesting that more attention needs to be paid to this area (Heiat, Gross, and Krumholz, 2002).

How have researchers justified these discriminatory practices? Some have cited research tradition (Duster, 2006). Some have cited the benefits of studies with homogenous samples—the more alike the samples, the more that variation can be attributed to the intervention under study. Some have argued that women would complicate studies by their hormonal changes during the menstrual cycle, that research could be jeopardized by women who become pregnant during the research, and that women are more difficult to obtain as volunteers.

However, none of these reasons is adequate. Critics point out that comparable studies could be conducted on groups other than white males, or statistical controls could be used within heterogeneous samples. Hormonal changes during the menstrual cycle are part of reality; rather than being viewed as somehow distorting the results, efforts need to be made to understand the influence of personality type on heart disease and the influence of aspirin on migraine headaches, and so on, in women, given their particular physiology. It has been argued that, logically, it would make just as much sense to say that the absence of a menstrual cycle ought to disqualify males for fear of skewed results (Dresser, 1992; Merton, 1993).

The need for more medical research and more sociologically informed medical research on traditionally under-represented groups is complicated by the fact that there has been little increase in the budget for the National Institutes of Health (NIH)—the primary medical research organization in the United States—in recent years. Without a stronger commitment by the federal government, progress in understanding and treating diseases and in understanding differences among racial, ethnic, and gender groups will also stagnate (Loscalzo, 2006).

---

hardening of the artery, which decreases the amount of blood that can flow through it. This is usually caused by a build-up of cholesterol plaques and other fatty substances or a blood clot. If the blood flow is severely restricted, the person may feel a tightening sensation or squeezing feeling in the chest that may radiate into the left arm and elsewhere. CHD is the most common form of cardiovascular disease.

If a coronary artery becomes completely blocked, the heart may not receive enough blood to fulfill its normal workload. This may lead to a heart attack—that is, sudden and irreversible damage to the heart muscle. Other forms of heart disease can occur involving the heart valves, the veins, or the heart muscle itself. Heart disease is the most common cause of death in the United States.

Prevalence, Incidence, and Mortality

In 2014, about 27 million living adults in the United States had been diagnosed with heart disease (more than 10 percent of the adult population). More than 600,000 people die each year from heart disease, which makes this the leading cause of death in the United States. It is the most common cause of death for both men and women. Every year about 735,000 Americans have a heart attack, and 15 percent die from it.

Heart disease has often been considered a man's disease in the United States, and much more research has been conducted on heart disease in males than in females. However, this is a misperception. Men and women are about equally likely to have heart disease, but because there are more women than men in the population, more women than men have heart disease, and more women than men die from it each year. Heart disease is the leading cause of death for both men and women (about 1 in 4 deaths for both males and females is due to heart disease), but women are more likely to die from a heart attack than men are. Under the age of 50 years, heart attacks in women are twice as likely to be fatal as those in men. See the accompanying box, "Differing Treatment for Women's Heart Attacks."

IN THE FIELD

DIFFERING TREATMENT FOR WOMEN'S HEART ATTACKS

Why do women heart attack victims fare worse than men? Data show that heart attacks strike more women than men in the United States, that death rates from heart disease are higher for women than for men, and that women who have a heart attack have longer stays in hospital and more complications while they are there.

Recent research has discovered several explanations for these findings. People—including physicians—may still think of heart disease as being more of a "man's disease." Research has shown that women who have certain conditions, such as high cholesterol and high blood pressure, are less likely than men to be told that these are risk factors for heart disease, and are less likely to have beneficial medications such as statins prescribed.

Heart attacks are often manifested differently in women and men. While both women and men may feel tightness or pain in the chest, women are more likely to display symptoms such as nausea, vomiting, shortness of breath,

and pain in the back or jaw. If not familiar with these different symptoms, neither the woman nor her physician may immediately suspect a heart attack.

Finally, when women under the age of 55 years arrive at a hospital in the midst of a heart attack, research has discovered that they are less likely to receive angioplasty or a stent to immediately open clogged arteries, and are more likely to die in the hospital during that visit than are men in the same situation. If the artery blockages do not look so severe as those commonly observed in males (even though they may actually be doing more harm to the arteries), medical providers may not be as quick to diagnose heart disease.

All of these conditions could be remedied by comprehensive research on women's heart disease. However, only about 20 percent of subjects in clinical trials for heart disease are women, and even when they are included, researchers often do not focus on gender differences in their analysis.

Heart disease is the leading cause of death among whites, blacks, Hispanics, and American Indians/Alaskan Natives, although death rates are considerably higher for blacks. Heart disease is second only to cancer for Asian Americans and Pacific Islanders. Disproportionately high rates of CHD deaths are found in black men (a heart disease death rate twice that in white women) and among people living in the southeastern part of the country.

Etiology

The five major proximate risk factors for CHD are (1) cigarette smoking, (2) poor diet (especially if reflected by high levels of

cholesterol and high blood sugar), (3) physical inactivity, (4) obesity (mostly resulting from poor diet and lack of exercise), and (5) high blood pressure (this is both a disease and a risk factor for other diseases).

Cigarette Smoking. The World Health Organization has called tobacco the single biggest cause of premature adult death throughout the world—it kills about 6 million people annually, and is predicted to kill 8 million annually by 2030. Given current projections, half of all those in the world who smoke cigarettes—about 650 million people—will eventually die from tobacco smoking. Studies in the United States have determined that cigarette smoking is the biggest risk

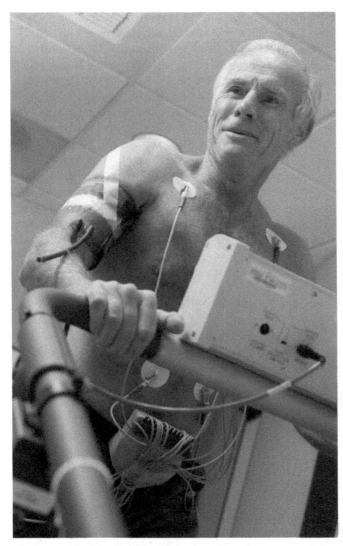

Advances in treatment of heart disease have led to the creation of many cardiac rehabilitation centers around the country. These facilities include heart and healthy living education, constantly monitored physical exercise, and emotional support for living healthily and happily with coronary heart disease. © Dennis MacDonald/Photoedit – SPT311DM 032 001.

factor for sudden cardiac death, that smokers have a two to four times higher risk than non-smokers of having a heart attack, and that smokers are approximately 30 percent more likely than non-smokers to experience fatal coronary heart disease.

Moreover, there is extensive danger in breathing in **environmental tobacco smoke (ETS)**—that is, other people's tobacco smoke.

Never-smokers living with smokers had a 1 to 3 percent greater chance of developing heart disease than never-smokers living with non-smokers. Nationally, this equates to approximately 45,000 deaths from CHD annually as a result of breathing ETS.

Poor Diet.   Eating well with a diet high in fruits and vegetables, whole grains and high-fiber foods, and fish, and low in saturated and trans fats, cholesterol, and salt is a heart health protector. Those who eat poor diets often end up with high levels of blood sugar and cholesterol. *Cholesterol* is a type of fat (lipid) that can build up in the bloodstream. It is transported in the bloodstream via lipoproteins. Most blood cholesterol is carried into the circulatory system by low-density lipoproteins (LDLs), where it may be deposited and accumulate on the arterial walls, causing restriction of blood flow. Cholesterol is also carried on high-density lipoproteins (HDLs), which actually help to remove the plaque from the arteries. The greater the ratio of LDL to HDL, the more likely it is that cholesterol plaque build-up will occur. As this ratio increases, the risk of heart disease increases. People with high cholesterol levels have about twice the risk of heart disease as people with lower levels.

Physical Inactivity.   Not engaging in sufficient physical activity can lead to heart disease both directly and indirectly (by increasing the likelihood of developing other medical conditions, such as high blood pressure, high cholesterol, and high blood sugar, that also increase the risk of heart disease).

Obesity.   According to national surveys of body mass index (BMI), which measures the composition of the body, only 30 percent of American adults are of a healthy weight. Approximately one-third are overweight, and another one-third are obese (i.e., significantly overweight). Obesity increases the likelihood that cholesterol, blood sugar, and blood pressure will all be too high. Being overweight increases the likelihood of heart disease, and being obese significantly increases the likelihood of heart disease—especially if the extra weight is concentrated around the waist. Obesity is a major factor in more than 100,000 deaths from heart disease in the United States annually.

High Blood Pressure.   Approximately one-third of American adults have high blood pressure (defined as a pressure of 140/90 mmHg or higher, or taking antihypertensive drugs), which is the major cause of strokes and deaths from strokes, and one of the major causes of heart attacks and deaths from heart attacks. Several factors are associated with high blood pressure. Generally, the older people get, the more likely they are to develop high blood pressure. People whose parents have high blood pressure are more likely to develop it, and blacks are more likely than whites to suffer from the disease. When a person has high blood pressure together with obesity, smoking, high blood cholesterol levels, or diabetes, the risk of stroke or heart attack increases substantially.

Other   Factors.   Other   factors   that contribute to the risk of heart disease include family history (having a family history of heart disease, especially in one's parents or siblings and at an early age, elevates the personal risk for the disease), diabetes (which increases the risk of developing CHD partly due to the effects that the disease has on cholesterol and blood sugar levels), and poor dental health, such as chronic gum disease. High levels of social stress can underlie all of these proximate risk factors and contribute directly to CHD.

Trends

The death rate from heart disease has declined steadily and dramatically over the past few decades (by 50 percent in the last 35 years and by about 25 percent just in the last 10 years). The percentage of deaths due to heart disease has declined, and heart failure typically now occurs much later in life (usually after the age of 70 years). Much of this sharp decline is due to changing lifestyle. The reduction in the number of cigarette smokers is most important, but changes in diet (and more effective drugs) have brought

Getting adequate exercise is one of the most important activities in which people can engage to prevent heart disease and other chronic degenerative diseases. However, too few Americans actually get the recommended amount of weekly exercise. © AntonioDiaz/ Fotolia.

cholesterol levels down, and blood pressure levels are lower than a decade ago. Improved medical therapies, including initial treatment for those with chest pain or having a heart attack, bypass surgery, and long-term rehabilitation, also play a role.

Worldwide.   Globally, cardiovascular diseases (primarily coronary heart disease and stroke) are responsible for about 31 percent of all deaths, and represent the most common cause of death throughout the world. Heart disease alone is responsible for more than seven million deaths each year—more than 13 percent of all deaths.

CANCER

Cancer is a group of diseases characterized by the uncontrolled growth (often forming masses of tissue called tumors) and spread of abnormal cells. Normally the body's cells reproduce themselves in an orderly manner, with worn-out or injured tissues being replaced or repaired. Should abnormal (cancer) cells develop, the body's immune system will usually defeat and eliminate them. Tumors that are "benign" are non-cancerous and do not spread, whereas "malignant" tumors

are cancerous. When the cancer cells remain at their original site, the disease is said to be localized; when they spread and invade other organs or tissue, the disease is said to have metastasized.

Cancer can cause considerable pain. This occurs as various tubes within the body (e.g., esophageal, intestinal, and urinary bladder) become obstructed or as the expanding tumor destroys additional healthy tissue. Infections often occur. A cancerous tumor unsuccessfully removed or destroyed eventually causes death.

Prevalence, Incidence, and Mortality

Current estimates are that 14.5 million Americans alive now have been diagnosed with cancer (some are now cancer-free), and an additional 1.7 million people are diagnosed with cancer each year. About one in two males and slightly more than one in three females will be diagnosed with cancer at some point in their lifetime. These figures do not include the estimated 2 million cases of skin cancer (which are discussed later in this chapter) diagnosed annually. About 77 percent of all cancers are diagnosed in persons age 55 years or older (American Cancer Society, 2016).

Cancer is the second leading cause of death in the United States, claiming almost 600,000 lives each year. Among adults aged 40 to 79 years, cancer is the leading cause of death. Almost one death in four is caused by cancer. Due mostly to cigarette smoking, the national death rate from cancer rose for most of the twentieth century, and peaked in 1991. The rate has fallen since then, due mainly to a decrease in the number of cigarette smokers.

Table 4–1 lists the most common sites of newly diagnosed cancer, by incidence and by mortality, for males and females. For males, the prostate, the lungs, and the colon and rectum are the most common new cancer sites, but lung cancer is by far the most lethal cancer, accounting for 27 percent of all male cancer deaths. For females, the breast, the lungs, and the colon and rectum are the most common new cancer sites, and lung cancer is the most common fatal site, accounting for 26 percent of all female cancer deaths.

Cancer usually develops in older people; 86 percent of all cancer diagnoses are in people aged 50 years or older. People of lower socioeconomic status have a much higher likelihood of developing cancer and dying from it than those with higher SES. This is especially true with regard to education. White, Hispanic, and black males with less than a high-school education are almost three times more likely to die

TABLE 4–1   Leading Sites of New Cancer Cases and Deaths, 2016 Estimates

Estimated New Cases		Estimated Deaths	
Female	Male	Female	Male
Breast 246,660 (29%)	Prostate 180,890 (21%)	Lung and bronchus 72,160 (26%)	Lung and bronchus 85,920 (27%)
Lung and bronchus 106,470 (13%)	Lung and bronchus 117,920 (13%)	Breast 40,450 (14%)	Prostate 26,120 (8%)
Colon and rectum 63,670 (8%)	Colon and rectum 70,820 (8%)	Colon and rectum 23,170 (8%)	Colon and rectum 26,020 (8%)
Uterine corpus 60,050 (7%)	Urinary bladder 58,950 (7%)	Pancreas 20,330 (7%)	Pancreas 21,450 (7%)
Thyroid 49,350 (6%)	Skin melanoma 46,870 (6%)	Ovary 14,240 (5%)	Liver 18,280 (6%)
Non-Hodgkin lymphoma 32,410 (4%)	Non-Hodgkin lymphoma 40,430 (5%)	Uterine 10,470 (4%)	Leukemia 14,130 (4%)
Skin melanoma 29,510 (3%)	Kidney 39,650 (5%)	Leukemia 10,270 (4%)	Esophagus 12,720 (4%)
Leukemia 26,050 (3%)	Oral and pharynx 34,780 (4%)	Liver 8,890 (3%)	Urinary bladder 11,820 (4%)
Pancreas 25,400 (3%)	Leukemia 34,090 (4%)	Non-Hodgkin lymphoma 8,630 (3%)	Non-Hodgkin lymphoma 11,520 (4%)
Kidney 23,050 (3%)	Liver 28,410 (3%)	Brain and nervous system 6,610 (2%)	Brain and nervous system 9,440 (3%)
All sites 843,820 (100%)	All sites 841,390 (100%)	All sites 281,400 (100%)	All sites 314,290 (100%)

*Excludes basal and squamous cell skin cancers and *in situ* carcinoma, except urinary bladder.

Source: Data from the American Cancer Society, *Cancer Facts and Figures—2016,* Atlanta, GA: American Cancer Society, Inc.

from cancer than their counterparts with a college education or higher. The disparity is highest for lung cancer, reflecting the higher rate of smoking among those with less education, but it also reflects less physical activity and poor diet among these groups, and slow treatment once cancer has developed.

Cancer incidence and mortality rates at almost all body sites are higher for blacks than for whites. The 5-year survival rate for cancer is 9 percent higher in whites. Studies of racial disparities in cancer point to socioeconomic explanations. African Americans are more likely to be in poverty, and to have a lower level of education, and are less likely to have health insurance. The lack of health insurance leads to less preventive care, later detection of cancer, and less likelihood of high-quality treatment.

Hispanics, Asian Americans and Pacific Islanders, and American Indians and Alaskan Natives overall have somewhat lower cancer incidence and mortality rates than whites. However, all these groups have a higher rate of cancer due to infection (especially in the stomach, liver, and cervix). Because lifestyle relates so closely to cancer risk, these groups are being studied in order to determine the reasons for their overall lower susceptibility.

Etiology

The World Health Organization estimates that up to 90 percent of all cancers are environmentally induced or related. Environmental cancer-producing substances, or *carcinogens*, are found in the food and drugs we ingest, the water we drink, the air we breathe, the occupations we pursue, and the substances with which we come into contact. Particular carcinogens are related to the development of cancer in particular locations. Five important proximate risk factors are (1) cigarette smoking, (2) poor diet, (3) excessive alcohol consumption, (4) obesity, and (5) overexposure to sunlight.

Cigarette Smoking. The strong relationship between cigarette smoking and heart disease is duplicated for cancer. Smoking is associated with high rates of lung cancer as well as cancer of the mouth, pharynx, larynx, esophagus, pancreas, uterine cervix, kidney, and bladder. The American Cancer Society estimates that cigarette smoking is responsible for almost one-third of all cancer deaths, and for almost 80 percent of all lung cancer deaths. Lung cancer mortality rates are 15 to 20 times higher for current male smokers and more than 13 times higher for current female smokers compared with lifetime never-smokers. Alone, smoking greatly increases risk, but with other carcinogens (e.g., poor diet), the risk is even greater. Half of those who continue to smoke throughout their life will die from a tobacco-related disease.

Environmental tobacco smoke has also been identified as a cause of cancer in non-smokers, with an estimated 7,330 lung cancer deaths per year and more than 45,000 heart disease deaths per year attributable to ETS. Secondary smoke may have especially serious effects on fetuses and young children. A mother who smokes is more likely than a non-smoker to have a spontaneous abortion, and much more likely to produce a low-birth-weight infant (with a greater chance of dying in the first year of life). Infants born to women who smoked during pregnancy are also more likely to die from sudden infant death syndrome. In addition, children of parents who smoke have a higher incidence of impaired lung function, bronchitis, pneumonia, and middle ear infections than children of non-smokers (American Cancer Society, 2016).

Poor Diet. Research has demonstrated a clear link between diet and the incidence of cancer. Experts have concluded that diet may be related to as many as 35 percent of all cancer deaths. In general, the type of diet that protects heart health also protects against cancer.

Studies based on international variations in cancer mortality have been illuminating. For example, higher rates of cancers of the colon, rectum, breast, and prostate are found in Western countries in which diets are relatively high in meat and fat but low in fruits, vegetables, and whole grains. On the other hand, stomach cancer rates are higher in countries in which diets are relatively high in starch, contain small amounts of meats and fats, and frequently use pickled, salted, smoked, or other preserved foods. High-fiber foods have been shown to lower the risk of colon cancer, and diets rich in vitamins A and C reduce the risk for cancers of the larynx, esophagus, stomach, and lung.

Excessive Alcohol Consumption.   Drinking in moderation can have some health benefits, but excessive alcohol consumption is a risk factor for cancer as it is for heart disease. Excessive alcohol consumption is the primary cause of cirrhosis of the liver, a very grave disease that puts people at high risk of developing liver cancer, a type of cancer with a generally poor prognosis. Cancers of the mouth, larynx, throat, and esophagus have all been linked to excessive alcohol consumption, especially in combination with the use of tobacco products. For each of these cancers the risk increases substantially with intake of more than two drinks per day.

Obesity.   People who are obese are at increased risk for several types of cancer, including breast, colon and rectum, esophagus, gall bladder, kidney, pancreas, uterus, and thyroid. In the United States, obesity may be a prime contributor in about 5 percent of cancer cases. However, a nutritious diet and adequate physical activity bolster general health and the body's ability to ward off disease.

Overexposure to Sunlight.   Almost all the five million cases of non-melanoma skin cancer

diagnosed each year in the United States are considered to be sun related. If detected early, these cancers are fairly routine to remove. Much more dangerous is malignant melanoma skin cancer, which is not so much related to the amount of sun exposure over a lifetime but rather to one or a couple of intense episodes of sunburn (often early in life).

In the United States, risk of overexposure to ultraviolet radiation also occurs during skin tanning. The association of tanning and skin cancer in adulthood is well established and is especially apparent among individuals with early childhood and adolescent exposure (use of a tanning bed before the age of 30 years increases the risk of melanoma by 75 percent. The National Institutes of Health have declared tanning beds to be a carcinogen, and the World Health Organization lists tanning beds with the most dangerous types of cancer-causing substances (Ladizinski et al., 2013).

Nevertheless, there are over 50,000 indoor tanning facilities in the United States, and it is a US$5 billion annual industry. An estimated 30 million Americans use tanning beds each year, with college students being heavy users. Recently, some states and localities have tightened their regulations to prevent use of tanning beds by people under the age of 18 years, and the Food and Drug Administration has recommended making this the national law. Some countries have outlawed all use of tanning beds.

Other Factors.   Other factors that are considered primary carcinogens include exposure to harmful substances (e.g., hydrocarbons and benzene) in the workplace, excessive exposure to radiation, and excessive exposure to environmental pollutants (e.g., petroleum products, synthetic organic chemicals, and insecticides). About 5 percent of all cancers are strongly hereditary. In these cases an inherited gene alteration confers a high risk of developing a particular type of cancer.

Trends

The key trend with regard to cancer is the increasing rate of survival for people with a cancer diagnosis. In the early 1900s, few people diagnosed with cancer had any likelihood of long-term survival. By the 1930s, about 20 percent of cancer patients survived at least 5 years. This percentage increased to about 50 percent in the 1970s, to about 60 percent in the 1990s, and is now 69 percent. Table 4–2 shows the 5-year survival rates for selected cancer sites for 1989–1995 and 2005–2011. Moreover, up to 80 percent of children now survive cancer, and recent efforts to protect them against long-term complications have been increasingly successful.

Improved survival rates are due both to early detection of cancer and to significantly improved treatment effectiveness. The probability of early detection and survival varies considerably according to the cancer's anatomical location. However, if cancer is still localized when detected, the survival rate for most types of cancer leaps to over 80 percent (American Cancer Society, 2016).

Worldwide.   Globally, there are about 14 million new cases of cancer diagnosed each year. About one in seven deaths is due to cancer—about 18 million deaths per year. Cancer is the second leading cause of death (after heart disease) throughout high-income countries, and is the third leading cause of death in low- and middle-income countries (after heart disease and infectious/parasitic diseases). However, although better screening and lifestyle changes (especially a decrease in cigarette smoking) have reduced the prevalence of cancer in high-income countries, cancer rates are increasing in low- and middle-income countries. This is due to the fact that, as countries modernize, they often take on more traditional Western-style behaviors such as eating more junk food, smoking, and not taking enough exercise (Torre et al., 2015).

HIV/AIDS

Acquired immunodeficiency syndrome (AIDS) is an infectious disease caused by the *human immunodeficiency virus (HIV)*. If untreated, HIV disables the immune system and enables normally controllable infections to overcome the body and ultimately kill the person. Unlike some other viruses, the human body cannot get rid of HIV.

TABLE 4–2   Five-Year Survival Rates (Percent) for Selected Cancer Sites

Site	1987–1989	2005–2011	Percentage Point Difference
Prostate	83	99	16
Kidney	57	74	17
Cervix uterus	70	69	−1
All sites	55	69	14
Colon and rectum	60	66	6
Oral	54	66	12
Leukemia	43	62	19
Ovary	38	46	8
Lung and bronchus	13	18	5
Pancreas	4	8	4

Source: American Cancer Society, *Cancer Facts and Figures—2016*, Atlanta, GA: American Cancer Society, 2016.

Without treatment, persons who have contracted the HIV virus typically remain in a latent (asymptomatic) stage for up to 8 to 10 years (with early treatment, it is much longer). During this time, the person may show no symptoms but is capable of transmitting the virus to others. In fact, studies indicate that the virus may be 100 to 1,000 times more contagious during the first 2 months after infection. Because tests to identify the presence in the body of antibodies to HIV—the means by which exposure to the virus is determined—are not reliable for up to 2 months following exposure, these months represent a critical time for transmission.

The transition to AIDS itself occurs when significant suppression of the body's immune system begins to lead to other medical conditions or diseases. Common among these are chronic, unexplained weight loss, chronic fevers, night sweats, constant diarrhea, swollen glands, and thrush (a thick, white coating on the tongue). As AIDS progresses, the patient typically experiences debilitating bouts of pneumonia, chronic herpes infections, seizures, and dementia, and ultimately death.

Prevalence, Incidence, and Mortality

Because HIV has such a long latency period, and because most Americans have never been tested for exposure to the HIV virus, it is difficult to calculate precisely the number of individuals who are HIV-positive. Epidemiologists use two estimation methods. The first method involves *back calculation*, taking into consideration the information available on incubation times and the change in trends of AIDS incidence (all states are required to report AIDS cases to the Centers for Disease Control and Prevention [CDC] to estimate the number of persons already exposed to the virus). The second method uses *seroprevalence* data (confirming the presence of antibodies to the virus) from CDC surveys of specific groups

such as blood donors, civilian applicants for military service, childbearing women, ambulatory patients, and federal prisoners.

By using both methods, the CDC estimates that approximately 1.2 million Americans are currently infected with HIV (with more than 150,000 of these individuals being unaware of this). By the end of 2012, 658,000 people in the United States had died from AIDS, and there are now about 13,000 deaths per year. New HIV infections peaked at about 150,000 a year in the mid-1980s, but have decreased to around 50,000 annually since then (Centers for Disease Control and Prevention, 2016).

About 75 percent of those with HIV/AIDS (and 80 percent of new cases) are male. HIV is most commonly transmitted between the ages of 25 and 34 years, although the age of transmission has been dropping even lower). Blacks and Hispanics constitute a disproportionate number of persons with HIV/AIDS, although there is no evidence that race per se is a biological risk factor for vulnerability to the disease. Blacks account for about 39 percent of newly diagnosed HIV infections, whites for about 35 percent, and Hispanics/Latinos for about 22 percent. Over the course of their lifetimes, 1 in 16 black men will be diagnosed with HIV infection, as will 1 in 33 Native Hawaiian/Other Pacific Islander men, 1 in 36 Hispanic/Latino men, 1 in 100 American Indian/Alaskan Native men, 1 in 102 white men, and 1 in 145 Asian men.

The death rate from AIDS is about three times higher for black males than for white males, and more than 20 times higher for black females than for white females. Rates for Hispanic males and females were about 2 times and 3.5 times higher, respectively, than the rates for their white counterparts. High rates of unemployment and despair in inner-city areas, with associated drug use and less accurate knowledge about AIDS, help to account for the higher rates among blacks and Hispanics (Centers for Disease Control and Prevention, 2016).

Etiology

HIV is transmitted through the exchange of bodily fluids—blood, semen, pre-seminal fluid, rectal fluids, vaginal fluids, and breast milk—from a person who has HIV. These fluids must come in contact with a mucous membrane or damaged tissue or be directly injected into the bloodstream (from a needle or syringe) for transmission to occur. Mucous membranes are found inside the rectum, vagina, penis, and mouth. Therefore exchange can occur through coital sex, anal sex (a common means of transmission for gay men because the tissue of the rectal wall is very thin and easily penetrated by the virus), or oral sex (extremely rare but theoretically possible), through the passing of HIV-contaminated blood (e.g., via a blood transfusion, sharing of needles by intravenous drug users, or reuse of contaminated needles for medical injections), and from an infected mother to a child (either prenatally or through breastfeeding) (Centers for Disease Control and Prevention, 2016).

The three most common transmission methods in the United States are male-to-male sexual contact (53 percent), heterosexual contact (32 percent), and injection drug use (17 percent). Research has determined that HIV is more easily transmitted from men to women than vice versa, in part because the vagina is a more receptive contact surface than a man's penis. The risk of transmission of infection from mother to child during pregnancy, birth, or breastfeeding is high in the case of an HIV-positive mother who is not taking medication. However, recommendations to test all pregnant women for HIV and start HIV treatment immediately have led to a reduction in the number of babies who are born with HIV.

Trends

The most remarkable development in recent years with regard to HIV/AIDS is the discovery of both effective prevention and therapy. The most groundbreaking treatment method is pre-exposure prophylaxis (PrEP)—a daily pill that can be taken by persons who are HIV-negative. Research indicates that it lowers the risk of HIV infection by up to 92 percent when taken consistently. The CDC and the United States Preventive Services Task Force recommend that all persons aged 15 to 65 years (as well as younger and older people at increased risk) and all pregnant women be tested for HIV on a regular basis, and that those in high-risk groups be tested annually and take PrEP. The cost of PrEP is about US$13,000 per year per patient.

In addition, after years of research around the world, an effective antiretroviral therapy (ART) has been discovered for HIV. For HIV-positive individuals who receive ART, life expectancy at diagnosis approximates that of uninfected persons. There are still some complications—some countries struggle to find the resources to pay for all of the needed ART, some ART recipients develop health problems from long-term therapy or from multidrug interactions, and affected individuals must commit to treatment that may interfere with life's other responsibilities. Nevertheless, ART is an extraordinary step forward (Fauci, Marston, and Folkers, 2014).

Perhaps the most troublesome recent trend is that while the number of diagnoses of HIV are dropping for certain groups (heterosexuals, intravenous drug users, and black women), the rates for black gay and bisexual men are only starting to level off, and the rates for Latino gay and bisexual men have actually increased. Many of these individuals are not getting continuing ART. In 2014, just under 50 percent of gay and bisexual men who had been diagnosed with HIV were receiving ART treatment, despite the fact that there are programs available to finance ART for people who cannot afford it. Why is this? It may be due to denial, or because the need is not understood by the patient or their physician (studies show that many physicians are unaware of recent PrEP drugs), or due to perceived stigma, or because so much time and effort is consumed by life's day-to-day struggle for adequate housing, food, employment, and other basic needs.

To see an online interactive visual of the distribution of AIDS cases in the United States, go to Emory University's website (www.AIDSVu.org) and click on the national map.

Worldwide. In the late 1970s, HIV spread silently around the world, unrecognized and unnoticed. Although the first case was officially recognized in the United States in 1981, the vast scope of the infection was not realized until the mid-1980s. It is now considered to be a worldwide pandemic or plague. Although an accurate prevalence rate is difficult to determine, it is estimated that in 2014 approximately 37 million people worldwide were infected with HIV, with 2 million more being infected each year. An estimated 1.2 million people died of AIDS that year. Altogether, more than 39 million people have died from AIDS-related diseases (globally, AIDS is the sixth most common cause of death). Figure 4–1 portrays the global AIDS situation.

ALZHEIMER'S DISEASE

Alzheimer's disease (AD) is a chronic degenerative dementing illness of the central nervous system. It is the most common cause of *dementia*—a condition that involves personality change, emotional instability, disorientation, memory loss, loss of verbal abilities, and an inability to care for oneself. Other specific symptoms of AD include intellectual impairment, depression, agitation, and delusions.

In order to diagnose AD, an extensive evaluation is necessary, which includes a complete medical history, interviews with the patient and family members, mental status examination, physical and neurological examination, and formal neuropsychological testing. Multiple

clinical trials are currently under way to slow or stop the progression of AD.

Currently, there are some medications available to help people carry out everyday activities, to slow down the progression of loss of thinking, memory, or speaking skills, and to assist with certain behavioral symptoms. However, they do not stop or reverse the underlying disease process, and typically only help for a few months to a couple of years. Researchers are also exploring several lifestyle factors (e.g., diet, exercise, stress, and sleep problems) that may influence the risk of AD and age-related cognitive decline. Many studies have found links between brain health and heart disease, diabetes, and depression. Taking steps to reduce the risk of those conditions— through physical exercise, not smoking, limiting intake of high-fat and high-sugar foods, cholesterol and blood pressure control, and maintaining social and intellectual engagement as one ages— may also reduce one's risk of AD.

In 2011, Congress enacted the National Plan to Address Alzheimer's Disease. It set a target date of 2025 for developing methods of prevention and effective treatment. Nevertheless, relative to funding for other leading causes of death, Alzheimer's disease research is severely underfunded.

Prevalence, Incidence, and Mortality

It is difficult to determine the prevalence of AD for a number of reasons. Because the onset of the disease is often extremely slow and the symptoms may go unnoticed or misinterpreted, and because there is no cure for the disease, many people with AD may not have sought medical attention. In the United States, more than 5 million people have AD (see Figure 4-2). About 1 in 20 people aged 65 to 74 years, about 1 in 5 people aged 75 to 84 years, and nearly half of those aged 85 years or older) have AD. Because more women live to older ages, they account for nearly two-thirds of

Figure 4–1   Global HIV Trends, 1990–2013

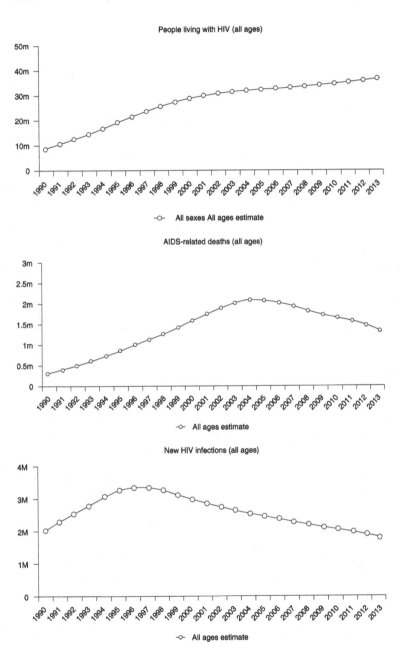

Source: Data from UNAIDS (2016) *Data and Analysis*. Geneva, Switzerland: UNAIDS. www.aidsinfo.unaids.org/.

IN COMPARATIVE FOCUS

AIDS: THE KILLING FIELDS IN AFRICA

The devastating effects of HIV/AIDS take their greatest toll on the world's less developed countries. While HIV rates have stabilized and/or declined in most developed countries and in an increasing number of developing countries (especially in sub-Saharan Africa and the Caribbean), they continue to escalate in some other developing countries (especially in North Africa, the Middle East, Eastern Europe, and Central Asia). Today, 95 percent of people infected with HIV live in a developing country.

Historically, sub-Saharan Africa was the site of the greatest problems. In the early and mid-2000s, for 16 countries in the world—all in sub-Saharan Africa—more than 10 percent of their population aged 15 to 49 years were HIV infected. In South Africa and Zimbabwe the figure was more than 20 percent.

In addition to its human toll, AIDS wreaks havoc on the entire social fabric of nations. Because most of those infected had acquired HIV by their twenties or thirties, there was a significant shortfall of workers and an increase in the number of people unable to financially support themselves in these countries. Life expectancy dropped sharply. Millions of children were orphaned (more than 20 million children worldwide have lost one or both parents to AIDS). In some countries, there were more people in their sixties and seventies than in their thirties and forties, which meant that there was inadequate support for the elders. Some countries experienced a significant drop in their national wealth.

Why did HIV/AIDS spread so rapidly in sub-Saharan Africa? Several circumstances had an effect. Many African men in rural villages form a migrant labor pool that migrates to large cities, mining areas, or large commercial farming areas. Their wives typically remain at home to take care of the children. These long absences from home make common the use of prostitutes (most of whom are infected) or multiple sexual partners, thus increasing the opportunities for the virus to be spread. The desire to have a large family led many men to be reluctant to use a condom when back home, which meant that their wives then became vulnerable to infection. In addition, health education programs were frequently unsuccessful, leaving many rural areas where knowledge of HIV/AIDS was inadequate.

Finally, there was simply not enough money to provide the necessary care. During this time, the United States spent almost US$900 million annually fighting about 55,000 new AIDS cases a year, while all of Africa spent about US$150 million fighting 4 million new cases a year. There was insufficient medicine in most of these countries, and stark inability to pay for AIDS treatment. Despite the increasing effectiveness of drug combinations in reducing suffering and extending life, only about 2 percent of Africans with AIDS were getting treatment as late as 2003 and 2004.

In 2003, new efforts were initiated in the United States and around the world to commit more money to battling HIV/AIDS in the developing world. The United States pledged increased contributions (up to US$3 billion in 2004); the World Health Organization and the United Nations started a new program to bring antiretroviral drugs to those afflicted; the United Nations, the World Bank, the Global Fund to Fight AIDS, Tuberculosis, and Malaria, and former President Clinton created a joint plan to buy and distribute inexpensive, generic AIDS drugs in poor countries; and actor Richard Gere with MTV and VH1 and two of India's largest entertainment networks began creating AIDS Awareness Programs.

Over the last decade, marked progress has been made. Globally, new AIDS cases have decreased by almost 35 percent, and AIDS-related mortality has decreased by 42 percent. Although not all sub-Saharan African countries have lowered the number of new infections or involved more patients in drug programs, many others have made significant progress (Kaiser Family Foundation, 2016; Tucker, 2013).

Figure 4–2   Number of Alzheimer's Cases

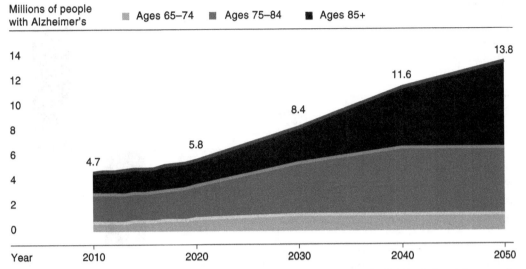

Source: Data from Alzheimer's Association, *Alzheimer's Facts and Figures*, 2015, Chicago, IL: Alzheimer's Association. www.alz. org/alzheimers_disease_facts_and_figures.asp.

Alzheimer's sufferers. More than 80,000 people die from AD each year, and the numbers are increasing.

In addition to age, race influences the likelihood of contracting Alzheimer's. African Americans are almost twice as likely as whites to have AD and other forms of dementia, and Hispanics are about 1.5 times more likely to have one of these conditions. The late-onset form of AD is most common among blacks. In 2013, scientists identified a new gene mutation that is linked to AD and is more common among blacks. This finding has opened up new areas of research.

The progression of AD varies from person to person. On average, a person afflicted with AD survives for up to 10 years or more before dying, although some individuals have survived for up to 25 years. Alzheimer's is now the sixth leading cause of death among adults in the United States, and is growing more rapidly as a cause of death than any other condition (see Figure 4-3).

Etiology

Although significant progress in understanding the etiology of AD has been made in the last few years, scientists do not yet know the exact cause. It is increasingly accepted that there is more than one pathway to developing AD. Currently the two most promising lines of explanation relate to two kinds of brain abnormalities. The first is a plaque comprised of beta amyloid that forms on brain cells. When the immune system activates to address the problem, the brain becomes inflamed. Over time, these plaques build up in the brain. The second abnormality is the presence of molecular tangles inside brain cells, which can ultimately kill the cells.

Researchers have now identified three genes that, when mutated, cause abnormalities in our brain cells. These mutations are inheritable, and virtually everyone who inherits one develops AD by the age of 60 years. However, later-onset AD also has a large genetic component, with individuals who have one affected parent being

Figure 4–3   Percentage Changes in Selected Causes of Death (All Ages) Between 2000 and 2013

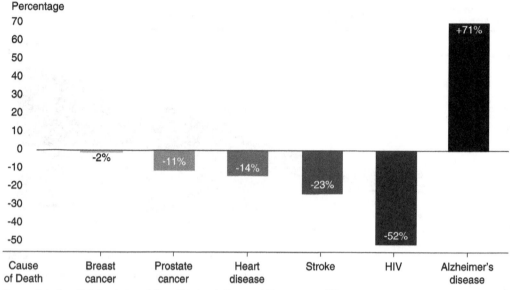

Source: Data from Alzheimer's Association, *Alzheimer's Facts and Figures*, 2015, Chicago, IL: Alzheimer's Association. www.alz. org/alzheimers_disease_facts_and_figures.asp.

three times more likely to develop AD, and those with two affected parents being five times more likely to do so. It appears that the genes are not causative of AD, but simply make one more susceptible to it when exposed to certain environmental triggers. Much current research is focused on understanding these triggers, and researchers are making headway in finding a drug that could melt away the plaque. Currently, the most definitive diagnosis of AD is made after death, by examining the brain tissue for plaques and tangles.

Trends

Projections indicate that, without an effective cure or preventive mechanism, the prevalence of AD will increase substantially in the next 50 years as the numbers of people in the oldest age groups increase. By the year 2050, it is estimated that more than almost 14 million people in the United States will have AD.

This trend will affect health care and the health care system in important ways. There will be a need for more caregivers for advanced cases, and additional lines of support for partners and other family members. In 2012, there were more than 15 million caregivers for people with dementia, and they gave more than 17.5 billion hours of unpaid care. Awareness of these needs in the medical community has increased dramatically in the last three decades, and is largely a result of research and focus by sociologists and the efforts of a small number of dedicated neuroscientists, the National Institute on Aging (NIA), and the Alzheimer's Disease and Related Disorders Association (ADRDA) advocacy group (Alzheimer's Association, 2015).

There will also be important financial consequences. The annual costs of caring for Alzheimer's patients and those with other forms of dementia are expected to increase from US$203 billion in 2013 to US$1.2 trillion in 2050, when people aged 65 years or older will represent 20 percent of the population. Because Medicare and Medicaid pay for approximately 70 percent of AD-related costs, the financial stability of these programs will be challenged (Alzheimer's Association, 2015).

Worldwide. Current estimates are that more than 44 million people worldwide have AD. Extensions of life expectancy in countries around the world suggest a more than tripling of AD cases to 135 million by 2050.

MENTAL ILLNESS

It is difficult to define mental illness, in part due to the sociocultural basis for determining what orientations or behaviors are indicative of a mentally ill person. Some conditions (e.g., homosexuality) that were once considered to be mental illness are no longer categorized as such. Some conditions (e.g., having visions) that are considered to be evidence of mental illness in some cultures are considered perfectly natural in others. Research even indicates that members of different cultures manifest very different symptoms in response to the same clinical psychopathology—for example, schizophrenics in some cultures are loud and aggressive, whereas in other cultures they are quiet and withdrawn.

Moreover, everyone has impairments in functioning or "problems in living" from time to time, and many people consult with mental health professionals such as psychiatrists, clinical psychologists, social workers, and marriage and family counselors about these problems. Most are seeking help with marital or other family relationships, work-related problems, stress, or a lack of self-confidence. Some conditions are more intense, persist for longer, and require more significant treatment.

Although mental illness can be categorized in a variety of ways, the most common mental illnesses include the following (Medline Plus, 2014; WebMD, 2016):

1. *Anxiety disorders*, which are the most common types of mental illness, involve an unusually grave form of fear or dread about certain situations. Although everyone experiences anxiousness sometimes, these disorders refer to a persistently high level of anxiety that may result in a physiological change, such as chest pains. Anxiety disorders include phobias (an abnormally intense level of fear about something that may be harmless), obsessive–compulsive disorders (behaviors that must be performed in order to avoid anxiety or respond to an obsession), and post-traumatic stress disorder (experiencing a traumatic event and then continuing to feel the trauma even after the event has ended).

2. *Mood disorders* (also called affective disorders) affect a person's day-to-day emotional state, and may manifest in lasting feelings of excessive sadness or hopelessness (*depression*), periods of extreme happiness, or fluctuations between the two (*bipolar disorder*).

3. *Psychotic disorders* are severe mental disorders that involve abnormal thinking or perception. These include hallucinations (seeing or hearing things that are not real), delusions (believing things that are not true despite evidence to the contrary), incoherent speech, and *schizophrenia* (which may involve a combination of these symptoms).

4. *Eating disorders* involve a preoccupation with food and an irrational fear of being fat. Examples of these disorders include anorexia nervosa (self-starvation), bulimia (periods of overeating followed by purging), and cycles of binge-eating.

5. *Impulse control and addiction disorders* are manifested in individuals who cannot resist engaging in behaviors that may be harmful to them, and which they wish to avoid. These include kleptomania (stealing), compulsive

gambling, and compulsive use of alcohol and/or other drugs.

6. *Personality disorders* refer to extreme and persistent personality traits that are distressing to the individual and typically cause problems in their interactions with other people. These conditions include paranoia (extreme distrustfulness of other people) and antisocial personality disorder (extreme and distressing personality traits that disrupt normal social functioning).

7. *Obsessive–compulsive disorder* (OCD) occurs when people are plagued by constant thoughts or fears that cause them to perform certain rituals or routines. The disturbing thoughts are called obsessions, and the rituals

are called compulsions. An example is a person with an unreasonable fear of germs who constantly washes their hands.

8. *Post-traumatic stress disorder* (PTSD) refers to conditions that can develop following a traumatic and/or terrifying event, such as a sexual or physical assault, the unexpected death of a loved one, or a natural disaster. People with PTSD often have lasting and frightening thoughts and memories of the event, and tend to be emotionally numb.

See the accompanying box, "College Students and Mental Health Concerns," for a discussion of the kinds of mental disorders that

---

IN THE FIELD

COLLEGE STUDENTS AND MENTAL HEALTH CONCERNS

All the available research data agree that college students now report a higher incidence of mental illness than ever before. About one college student in four has a diagnosable mental disorder. Of those who present at the counseling center, about one in five has a serious (as opposed to mild or moderate) mental health concern. Anxiety has long been the most common issue among students, but today it is being experienced at a more intense and overwhelming level. Within the last 12 months, nearly one student in six has been diagnosed with or treated for anxiety. Reports of depression (experienced by more than one-third of students at some point during college, and the most common reason for dropping out of college) and social anxiety have also increased over time. Many students report being overwhelmed by their responsibilities, and that these feelings are harming their academic performance.

Causes include increasing academic pressure, the demands of multiple responsibilities

(e.g., school, work, organizations, and family), overprotective parents, and compulsive engagement with social media. Some college counseling center directors believe that the generation of students that are coming to college today are not as resilient as earlier generations were, and are less independent. They have a more difficult time when they have to struggle to succeed, especially if they read on social media how well everyone else is supposedly doing.

About half of those who seek care at the mental health center have already had some form of counseling before college, and one in three have previously been treated with psychiatric medications. However, these rates have remained stable over time. Higher rates may also be due in part to a greater willingness to seek treatment due to the reduction in stigma associated with mental disorders, and to increased efforts to encourage students in need to visit the counseling center (Center for Collegiate Mental Health, 2016).

are most commonly experienced by college students.

The most widely used classification system for mental disorders is the ***Diagnostic and Statistical Manual of Mental Disorders, Fifth Edition (DSM-V)*** (2013), prepared by a Task Force of the American Psychiatric Association. It is the system used by mental health professionals, many social workers, the courts, and insurance providers. The *DSM-V* assesses each disorder on the basis of the nature and severity of clinical symptoms, relevant history, related physical illnesses, and recent adaptive functioning, especially with regard to the quality of social relationships.

The *DSM* is a very controversial document. Critics charge that its definitions of disorders and the ability of clinicians to apply those definitions lack validity because they are subjectively based. An example is the fact that homosexuality was listed as a mental disorder through the first two editions of the book. When a large number of members of the American Psychiatric Association (APA) challenged this perspective in the 1970s, the APA voted to delete homosexuality from the list of disorders. Critics charged that nothing "objective" about homosexuality had changed—only its subjective interpretation. Horwitz (2007) contends that *DSM* diagnoses sometimes fail to distinguish between genuine individual pathology and entirely understandable distress caused by discouraging life experiences such as chronic subordination, the inability to achieve valued goals, and the loss of important attachments. Others posit that the *DSM* lacks reliability—that is, it is used inconsistently by different clinicians. Studies have shown that clinicians often disagree about diagnosis and do not uniformly attach defined conditions. Studies which show that the race or gender of a patient influences the diagnosis offer further evidence of a lack of reliability. Many mental health organizations have asked for an independent review of the document. The *DSM* is widely used and

has some utility, but carries with it some serious problems.

Prevalence, Incidence, and Mortality

There are several major data sources that are now used to estimate the prevalence of mental disorders in the population. Population surveys (such as those conducted by CDC's National Health Interview Survey and the Behavioral Risk Factor Surveillance Survey) and surveys of health-care use measure the occurrence of mental illness, associated risk behaviors (e.g., alcohol and drug abuse) and chronic conditions, and use of mental health-related care and clinical services.

In the United States, an estimated 25 percent of adults experience some form of mental illness (other than substance abuse) each year. This is equivalent to about 45 million people. About 20 percent of these cases would be classified as being severe. Most of these disorders are treatable, but estimates are that—because of potential stigma and financial concerns—many do not seek needed treatment. An estimated 50 percent of people will experience at least one mental illness during their lifetime.

It is estimated that one in five children between the ages of 3 and 17 years will have a diagnosable mental disorder in any given year. The most common mental disorder among children is attention deficit hyperactivity disorder (ADHD), which occurs in nearly 7 percent of children. With regard to other disorders, 3.5 percent of children currently have behavioral or conduct problems, 3 percent suffer from anxiety, about 2 percent have depression, and about 1 percent has autism. About two out of 1,000 children aged 6 to 17 years have Tourette syndrome. Boys are more prone to ADHD, behavioral or conduct problems, autism, anxiety, and Tourette syndrome. Girls are more likely to have depression (Centers for Disease Control and Prevention, 2013).

IN THE FIELD

THE EFFECTS OF NEIGHBORHOOD ON MENTAL HEALTH

Considerable research has found that neighborhood context has an important effect on psychological distress and mental health. Disordered neighborhoods, common in disadvantaged areas, may produce several psychological states in residents, including anxiety, anger, depression, and subjective alienation—that is, a sense of separation between oneself and others. Often this heightens one's sense of powerlessness and of mistrust of others. Ross (2011) has theorized that mistrust is likely to develop in neighborhoods where perceived threat is common and where resources to deal with the threat are scarce. A strong sense of personal control might be helpful in reducing the negative effects of this environment, but that orientation is often eroded by the environment. Feeling a sense of powerlessness and mistrust is in itself psychologically distressing.

These negative effects begin in childhood and carry through to later life. Because neighborhoods are often the limit of adolescents' social world, living in a violent and threatening neighborhood has an influence early on about thoughts about self (self-efficacy), which in turn affects emotional health. Studies in disadvantaged neighborhoods have found high levels of anxiety and depression among young people (Dupere, Leventhal, and Vitaro, 2012), and that these adolescent experiences can negatively affect cognitive health in later life. This negative influence has been linked especially to personal socioeconomic status—that is, the decline in mental health was most apparent in those who themselves were poor in addition to living in a disadvantaged neighborhood (Aneshensel et al., 2011).

Medical sociologists typically employ a "social consequences" approach when studying mental illness—that is, they examine how social arrangements and social processes affect mental health and the likelihood of obtaining treatment for mental health problems (Aneshensel, 2005). Among the aspects of social structure commonly studied are socioeconomic status, race, gender, and marital status. See the accompanying box, "The Effects of Neighborhood on Mental Health."

Socioeconomic Status and Race. With the possible exception of anxiety and mood disorders, social science research has found the highest levels of psychological distress among socially disadvantaged groups. Rates of schizophrenia, personality disorders characterized mainly by antisocial behavior and substance abuse, and depression are highest in the lowest socioeconomic groups.

There are three possible explanations for the high prevalence of mental disorders among the poor. The *genetic* explanation asserts that genetic inheritance predisposes members of the lower class to mental disorders. This theory has not received research support. The *social selection/drift* explanation maintains that mentally ill people may drift downward in the social structure, or that mentally healthy individuals tend to be upwardly mobile, thus leaving a "residue" of mentally ill people. Although research indicates that mental health problems do tend to prevent upward social mobility, it has not been found that they lead to downward mobility. A third explanation—*social causation*—posits that people in lower socioeconomic groups live in a social environment that is more stressful, and that they are more vulnerable to the effects of this stress because they lack the personal and financial resources to obtain the help that they need (Aneshensel, 2009). The economic deprivation, dangerous physical environment, less healthy lifestyle, and unstable personal relationships that often accompany poverty all threaten mental health (Eaton, Muntaner, and Sapag, 2010). This approach has received the most empirical support, although none of these three explanations is totally satisfactory.

The relationship between race and mental health disorders depends upon the particular disorder being studied. Although blacks are more likely than whites to be in the lower socioeconomic strata, they do not have higher overall rates of mental illness and disorder (Williams, Costa, and Leavell, 2010). In cases of particular disorders in which rates for blacks are higher than for whites, socioeconomic status accounts for most of the gap (Spence, Adkins, and Dupre, 2011).

Gender.   In contrast to the clear differences between men's and women's physical health, the overall incidence of mental illness in men and women is about the same. However, the overall rates do camouflage differences in the likelihood of developing specific illnesses. For example, rates of mood and anxiety disorders—including depression—are consistently higher in women, and rates of personality disorders, substance abuse, and suicide are consistently higher in men (Bird and Rieker, 2008). These differences are due to both biological and sociocultural factors. Some research has focused on hormonal differences and chromosomal differences between women and men as explanatory factors for differential mental health, but the evidence is insufficient to allow conclusions to be drawn. On the other hand, it is known that differences in behavior are at least partially the result of socialization into prescribed roles for males and females. This pattern is examined in more detail in Chapter 5.

Marital Status.   Research consistently finds that married people experience better mental health than unmarried people, and that married men are even healthier mentally than married women. This is partially due to the social and emotional support received from stable, supportive relationships that can serve to protect one from the psychological consequences of difficult life situations. It may also reflect the fact that the mentally ill are less likely to be married, and thus the differences between levels of mental health are a result of a selection process rather than of marriage itself (Turner and Gartrell, 1978).

One recent study (Frech and Williams, 2007) discovered that both men and women who were depressed prior to their marriage experienced greater psychological benefits from marriage than those who were not previously depressed. They postulate that the added emotional support and companionship of marriage and the reduction in social isolation by linking the person to a wider circle of friends and relatives are responsible for this benefit. This benefit was significant for those who were depressed prior to the marriage, but only modest for those who were not. All men and women experience greater benefits from a marriage when it offers a high level of happiness and a low level of conflict. Thus it should be understood that the benefits of marriage for mental health vary based on certain conditions and circumstances.

Etiology

There are three primary approaches to understanding the etiology of mental illness—the biogenic or physiological approach (also called the medical model), the environmental or social approach, and a combination of the two, the *gene–environment approach*. The traditional biogenic view of mental illness is that it is an observable and measurable condition, stemming from individual psychological or biological pathology, which is amenable to proper treatment.

Many sociologists have challenged this way of thinking and support a social approach. They argue that definitions of mental illness rely more on subjective social judgments than on objective facts. Thoits (1985) believes that the mental illness label is applied when a behavior is inconsistent with (1) *cognitive norms* (i.e., one's thinking is at odds with norms), (2) *performance norms* (i.e., one's behavior is at odds with norms), or (3) *feeling norms* (i.e., one's feelings are at odds with the range, intensity, and duration of feeling expected in a given situation). She believes that violations of feeling norms are the most common basis for labeling someone as mentally ill.

Finally, a third school of thought advocates for a combination of the two approaches. Those who support the gene–environment approach contend that neither biogenic nor social factors can be dismissed, and that a comprehensive explanation requires both.

Trends

Some sociologists who focus on the "sociology of mental health" have challenged the desirability of thinking in terms of clinical diagnoses at all, and suggest that we instead focus on measurements that reflect the true range of human feelings and emotions. Mirowsky and Ross (2002:152) encourage a "human science" that centers on life "as people feel it, sense it, and understand it," and that includes consideration of human suffering even if it does not fall within pre-formulated diagnostic categories. Kessler (2002) also sees greater value in thinking in terms of dimensional assessments (placing each individual on a continuum of psychological distress without identifying a specific point at which a mental illness is established), rather than the traditional procedure of making categorical assessments (each individual either has or does not have a mental illness). These ideas have genuine potential for reshaping our whole approach to understanding human suffering and mental distress.

A positive development is that public discourse about mental health and mental illness is perhaps more open than ever before, and more people than ever are seeking treatment. Nevertheless, mental disorders continue to receive less public attention than physical ailments, despite the very large percentage of people who experience some type of mental disorder each year. In the political arena, coverage of mental health services was a controversial provision in the failed Clinton health care reform package in the early 1990s and the successful Obama reform legislation of 2010. For some, providing for mental health needs lacked the legitimacy of providing coverage for other diseases. Perhaps the biggest battle yet to be won in treating mental disorders is to convince politicians and others of the vast importance of making these services available.

Worldwide. More than 450 million people across the globe suffer from mental illnesses. Schizophrenia, depression, epilepsy, dementia, alcohol dependence, and other mental, neurological, and substance-use disorders make up 13% of the global disease burden, surpassing both cardiovascular disease and cancer. According to the World Health Organization (WHO), mental illnesses account for more disability in developed countries than any other group of illnesses, including cancer and heart disease.

SUMMARY

Social epidemiologists help us to understand the social etiology (causes) and distribution of disease and illness. In addition to the disease agent, they give attention to proximate risk factors, fundamental causes (underlying social conditions), and genetic factors. The *epidemiological transition* explains the historical shift from dominance of acute infectious diseases to dominance of chronic degenerative diseases.

In the United States, heart disease and cancer are the two most common causes of death. Together, they account for over 1.2 million deaths annually. Although the rate of heart disease has decreased substantially in recent decades, it remains the number one killer of Americans. Overall, cancer rates increased until 1991, but have leveled off in the 2000s. Both diseases are influenced by fundamental causes and proximate risk factors. Cigarette smoking, diet, and physical exercise are major risk factors for both diseases. High blood cholesterol, high blood pressure, and social stress are also major risk factors for heart disease, while excessive consumption of alcohol, overexposure to the sun, and overexposure to environmental pollutants are other key risk factors for cancer.

AIDS begins with HIV infection and is transmitted by body fluids through sexual activity, unsterile needles, infected blood supplies, and the placenta. It is a major health problem around the world, and its impact has been particularly severe in Africa. Progress has been made in developing drugs to decrease the likelihood of contracting AIDS, and in long-term survival rates. The disease is currently in transition from a fatal disease to a chronic disease.

Alzheimer's disease is a disease of mental deterioration that begins in mid- to late life and affects millions of people in the United States and especially in other developed countries. There have been advances in our understanding of the disease, but there is still no cure or treatment for it.

Approximately one in four Americans experiences some form of mental disorder each year. Although patterns vary by type of mental illness, people in lower socioeconomic groups experience more mental illness (for many reasons, including neighborhood disorder, higher levels of stress, and less access to medical resources).

HEALTH ON THE INTERNET

Life expectancy varies considerably from state to state. During 2013 to 2014, the longest life expectancies were in residents of Hawaii (81.3 years), Minnesota (81.1 years), Connecticut (80.8 years), California (80.8 years), and Massachusetts (80.5 years). The shortest life expectancies were in residents of Mississippi (75.0 years), West Virginia (75.4 years), Alabama (75.4 years), Louisiana (75.7 years), and Oklahoma (75.9 years). (You can check your state's average at www.worldlifeexpectancy.com/usa/life-expectancy.) What factors might plausibly cause the average life expectancy to vary so much from state to state? Select five or six factors that you think might be most influential.

Then go to the website www.americas healthrankings.org, which is put together by the United Health Foundation. First, under "State Data," click on "Annual Data." Then click on your home state or any other state of particular interest. How many of your factors were examined? Then click on the states with the longest life expectancy and the shortest life expectancy, and compare and contrast their overall health participation. Now, what factors do you identify as being most related to life expectancy?

DISCUSSION CASE

Consider the following issue related to social epidemiology:

The World Health Organization, the United Nations Programme on HIV/AIDS, the Centers for Disease Control and Prevention, and the United States Preventive Services Task Force have all recently called for routine HIV testing without specific consent in all doctors' offices, clinics, and hospitals unless patients explicitly refuse to be tested. The WHO and UN have emphasized the importance of testing even healthy-looking individuals. They point out that this would lead to increased life expectancy for those who are HIV-positive (with proper medication, those diagnosed early with the disease can now basically expect to have a normal length of life, whereas those diagnosed with AIDS in the latter stages die within months), and reduce the likelihood that those who are HIV-positive but unaware of this (an estimated 200,000 more people in the United States) would pass the

disease on to others (drugs have now reduced the likelihood of transmitting the disease by 96 percent). However, a significant backlash has occurred among people who do not wish to see pretest counseling eliminated, and who say that the lingering stigma associated with AIDS makes the risk of disclosure too great, especially when many people still cannot access treatment.

Address the following questions:

1. What are the individual and societal consequences of offering regular routine HIV testing?
2. What values underlie the arguments for and against this proposal?
3. Should our society support/adopt this approach?

GLOSSARY

acute infectious diseases
chronic degenerative diseases
Diagnostic and Statistical Manual of Mental Disorders, Fifth Edition (DSM-V)
double disease burden
environmental tobacco smoke (ETS)
etiology

fundamental causes
germ theory of disease
health transition (HT)
Human Genome Project
proximate risk factors
social determinants of health

REFERENCES

Alzheimer's Association. 2015 *Alzheimer's Facts and Figures.* Chicago, IL: Alzheimer's Association. www.alz.org/alzheimers_disease_facts_and_figures.asp.

American Cancer Society. 2016 *Cancer Facts and Figures—2016.* Atlanta, GA: American Cancer Society.

American Psychiatric Association. 2013 *Diagnostic and Statistical Manual of Mental Disorders, Fifth Edition (DSM-5).* Arlington, VA: American Psychiatric Association Publishing.

Aneshensel, Carol S. 2005 "Research in Mental Health: Social Etiology Versus Social

Consequences." *Journal of Health and Social Behavior,* 48:221–228.

——. 2009 "Toward Explaining Mental Health Disparities." *Journal of Health and Social Behavior,* 50:377–394.

Aneshensel, Carol S., Michelle J. Ko, Joshua Chodosh, and Richard G. Wright. 2011 "The Urban Neighborhood and Cognitive Functioning in Late Middle Age." *Journal of Health and Social Behavior,* 52:163–179.

Auerbach, Judith D., and Anne E. Figert. 1995 "Women's Health Research: Public Policy and Sociology." *Journal of Health and Social Behavior,* 36(Extra Issue):115–131.

Bearman, Peter. 2008 "Exploring Genetics and Social Structure." *American Journal of Sociology*, 114:v–x.

Bird, Chloe E., and Patricia P. Rieker. 2008 *Gender and Health: The Effects of Constrained Choices and Social Policies.* New York: Cambridge University Press.

Caldwell, John C. 1993 "Health Transition: The Cultural, Social, and Behavioural Determinants of Health in the Third World." *Social Science and Medicine*, 36:125–135.

Center for Collegiate Mental Health. 2016 *2015 Annual Report.* University Park, PA: Pennsylvania State University.

Centers for Disease Control and Prevention. 2013 "Mental Health Surveillance among Children – United States, 2005-2011." www.cdc.gov/mmwr/ preview/mmwrhtml.

——. 2016 "HIV/AIDS." www.cdc.gov/hiv/.

Dresser, Rebecca. 1992 "Wanted: Single, White Male for Medical Research." *Hastings Center Report*, 22:24–29.

Dupere, Veronique, Tama Leventhal, and Frank Vitaro. 2012 "Neighborhood Processes, Self-Efficacy, and Adolescent Mental Health." *Journal of Health and Social Behavior*, 53:183–198.

Duster, Troy. 2006 "Lessons from History: Why Race and Ethnicity Have Played a Major Role in Biomedical Research." *The Journal of Law, Medicine, and Ethics*, 34:487–496.

Eaton, William W., Carles Muntaner, and Jaime C. Sapag. 2010 "Socioeconomic Stratification and Mental Disorders." Pp. 226–255 in *A Handbook for the Study of Mental Health: Social Contexts, Theories, and Systems* (2nd ed.), Theresa L. Scheid and Tony N. Brown (eds.). New York: Cambridge University Press.

Evans, Robert G., Morris L. Barer, and Theodore R. Marmor. 1994 *Why Are Some People Healthy and Others Not? The Determinants of Health of Populations.* New York: Aldine de Gruyter.

Fauci, Anthony S., Hilary D. Marston, and Gregory K. Folkers. 2014 "An HIV Cure: Feasibility, Discovery, and Implementation." *Journal of the American Medical Association*, 312:335–336.

Fletcher, Jason M., and Dalton Conley. 2013 "The Challenge of Causal Inference in Gene–Environment Interaction Research: Leveraging Research Designs from the Social Sciences." *American Journal of Public Health*, 103: S42–S45.

Frech, Adrianne, and Kristi Williams. 2007 "Depression and the Psychological Benefits of

Entering Marriage." *Journal of Health and Social Behavior*, 48:149–163.

Gallagher, Eugene B., Thomas J. Stewart, and Terry Stratton. 2000 "The Sociology of Health in Developing Countries." Pp. 389–397 in *Handbook of Medical Sociology* (5th ed.), Chloe Bird, Peter Conrad, and Allen M. Fremont (eds.). Upper Saddle River, NJ: Prentice Hall.

Heath, Brad, Blake Morrison, and Dan Reed. 2008 "When Schools Are Built, Toxic Air Rarely Considered." *USA Today*, December 30, pp. 1–2.

Heiat, Asefeh, Cary P. Gross, and Harlan M. Krumholz. 2002 "Representation of the Elderly, Women, and Minorities in Heart Failure Clinic Studies." *Archives of Internal Medicine*, 162:1682–1688.

Hertzman, C., J. Frank, and R.G. Evans. 1994 "Heterogeneities in Health Status and the Determinants of Population Health." Pp. 67–92 in *Why Are Some People Healthy and Others Not? The Determinants of Health of Populations*, Robert G. Evans, Morris L. Barer, and Theodore R. Marmor (eds.). New York: Aldine de Gruyter.

Holtz, Carol S. 2013 *Global Health Care: Issues and Policies* (2nd ed.). Burlington, MA: Jones and Bartlett.

Horwitz, Allan V. 2007 "Transforming Normality into Pathology: The *DSM* and the Outcomes of Stressful Social Arrangements." *Journal of Health and Social Behavior*, 48:211–222.

Kaiser Family Foundation. 2016 *The Global HIV/ AIDS Epidemic.* kff.org/global-health-policy/fact-sheet/the-global-hivaids-epidemic/.

Kessler, Ronald C. 2002 "The Categorical Versus Dimensional Assessment Controversy in the Sociology of Mental Illness." *Journal of Health and Social Behavior*, 43:171–188.

Krueger, J., Paul Biedrzycki, and Sara P. Hoverter. 2015 "Human Health Impacts of Climate Change: Implications for the Practice and Law of Public Health." *Journal of Law, Medicine, and Ethics*, 43:79–82.

Ladizinski, Barry, Kachiu C. Lee, Renata Ladizinski, and Daniel G. Federman. 2013 "Indoor Tanning Amongst Young Adults: Time to Stop Sleeping on the Banning of Sunbeds." *Journal of General Internal Medicine*, 28:1551–1553.

Link, Bruce G., and Jo C. Phelan. 1995 "Social Conditions as Fundamental Causes of Disease." *Journal of Health and Social Behavior*, Extra Issue:80–94.

——. 2000 "Evaluating the Fundamental Cause Explanation for Social Disparities in Health."

Pp. 33–46 in *Handbook of Medical Sociology* (5th ed.), Chloe E. Bird, Peter Conrad, and Allen M. Fremont (eds.). Upper Saddle River, NJ: Prentice Hall.

Loscalzo, Joseph. 2006 "The NIH Budget and the Future of Biomedical Research." *New England Journal of Medicine*, 354:1665–1667.

Margolis, Rachel. 2013 "Educational Differences in Healthy Behavior Changes and Adherence among Middle-Aged Americans." *Journal of Health and Social Behavior*, 54:353–368.

MedlinePlus. 2014 "Mental Disorders." www.nlm. nih.gov/medlineplus/mentaldisorders.html.

Merton, Vanessa. 1993 "The Exclusion of Pregnant, Pregnable, and Once-Pregnable People (a.k.a. Women) from Biomedical Research." *American Journal of Law and Medicine*, 19:379–445.

Mirowsky, John, and Catherine E. Ross. 2002 "Measurement for a Human Science." *Journal of Health and Social Behavior*, 43:152–170.

Morrison, Blake, and Brad Heath. 2008 "Health Risks Stack Up for School Kids near Industry." *USA Today*, December 8, pp. 1, 6, 7, 10, 11.

Pescosolido, Bernice A., Brea L. Perry, J. Scott Long, Jack K. Martin, John I. Nurnberger, and Victor Hesselbrock. 2008 "Under the Influence of Genetics: How Transdisciplinarity Leads Us to Rethink Social Pathways to Illness." *American Journal of Sociology*, 114:S171–S201.

Phelan, Jo C., Bruce G. Link, and Parisa Tehranifar. 2010 "Social Conditions as Fundamental Causes of Health Inequalities: Theory, Evidence, and Policy Implications." *Journal of Health and Social Behavior*, 51:S28–S40.

Ross, Catherine E. 2011 "Collective Threat, Trust, and the Sense of Personal Control." *Journal of Health and Social Behavior*, 52:287–296.

Ross, Catherine E., and Chia-ling Wu. 1995 "The Links between Education and Health." *American Sociological Review*, 60:719–745.

Shumaker, Erin. 2015 "Sexism in the Doctor's Office Starts Here." www.huffingtonpost.com/entry/women-are-excluded-from-clinical-trials.

Spence, Naomi J., Daniel E. Adkins, and Matthew E. Dupre. 2011 "Racial Differences in Depression Trajectories among Older Women: Socioeconomic, Family, and Health Influences." *Journal of Health and Social Behavior*, 52: 444–459.

Thoits, Peggy A. 1985 "Self-Labeling Processes in Mental Illness: The Role of Emotional Deviance." *American Journal of Sociology*, 91:221–249.

Torre, Lindsey A., Rebecca L. Siegel, Elizabeth M. Ward, and Ahmedin Jemal. 2015 "Global Cancer Incidence and Mortality Rates and Trends—An Update." *Cancer Epidemiology Biomarkers & Prevention*. http://cebp.aacrjournals.org/content/25/1/16.full.

Tucker, Charlotte. 2013 "Blueprint for Fighting HIV Aims for Global AIDS-Free Generation." *The Nation's Health*, February, pp. 1, 18.

Tuckson, Reed V., Lee Newcomer, and Jeanne M. De Sa. 2013 "Accessing Genomic Medicine: Affordability, Diffusion, and Disparities." *Journal of the American Medical Association*, 309:1469–1470.

Turner, R. Jay, and John W. Gartrell. 1978 "Social Factors in Psychiatric Outcome: Toward the Resolution of Interpretive Controversies." *American Sociological Review*, 43:368–382.

UNAIDS. 2016 *Data and Analysis*. www.unaids. org/en/dataanalysis/.

Venkat Narayan, K.M., Mohammed K. Ali, and Jeffrey P. Koplan. 2010 "Global Noncommunicable Diseases—Where Worlds Meet." *New England Journal of Medicine*, 363:1196–1198.

WebMD. 2016 "Types of Mental Illness." www. webmd.com/mental-health/mental-health-types-illness.

Williams, David R., Manuela Costa, and Jacinta P. Leavell. 2010 "Race and Mental Health: Patterns and Challenges." Pp. 268–290 in *A Handbook for the Study of Mental Health: Social Contexts, Theories, and Systems* (2nd ed.), Teresa L. Scheid and Tony N. Brown (eds.) New York: Cambridge University Press.

World Health Organization. 2014 *Ten Facts on the State of Global Health*. www.who.int/features/factfiles/global_burden/en/ index.html.

CHAPTER 5

Social Stress

Learning Objectives

- Explain the process of social stress as presented in the stress model, including reference to social stressors, appraisal, mediators, and stress outcomes.

- Distinguish between life events and chronic strains as they affect social stress. Identify and explain the five key types of chronic strains.

- Apply the concept "social construction of reality" to the appraisal process.

- Identify and discuss the major ways in which individuals cope with stress and use social support to deal with it.

- Explain how social class, race, sexual orientation, and gender can each affect social stress.

There may be few health-related concepts that have captured both the research interest of scientific investigators and the popular imagination as much as "social stress." This reflects both the substantive appeal of the concept for researchers in medicine and the biological and behavioral sciences, and attempts by individuals to understand and take responsibility for their own health.

This chapter presents a brief description of the historical development of the concept, an introduction to the various ways in which stress is conceptualized, and a model of social stress that attempts to capture its causes, mediating effects, and outcomes. Current research into stress as it is related to social class, race, sexual orientation, and gender is also presented.

DEFINITION OF STRESS

The term "stress" is used in almost countless ways. It can refer to events or circumstances (e.g., an examination) that cause us unease, to the general unease we feel during such events, to the specific bodily responses to such events

(e.g., rapid heartbeat), or to the mind's and body's attempts to deal with the unease in order to recapture a sense of wellness.

Most researchers include in the concept of stress some reference to the resulting state in an individual who has experienced various demands. Stoklos (1986:35) defines **stress** as "a state of imbalance within a person, elicited by an actual or perceived disparity between environmental demands and the person's capacity to cope with these demands." Stress occurs in response to "strainful and threatening circumstances in the environment" and has clearer boundaries than states such as anxiety or depression, which are more global, more diffuse, and may exist "even in the absence of specific threats" (Pearlin and Schooler, 1978:4).

HISTORICAL DEVELOPMENT OF THE STRESS CONCEPT

The idea of stress has existed for centuries. As discussed in Chapter 2, such historical luminaries as Hippocrates believed in the humoral theory of illness—that positive health results from a mind and body in harmony—and this is perhaps the earliest characterization of an individual who is not "stressed out." Hippocrates' belief in the self-healing powers of the body is also consistent with an understanding of the body's adaptation to stress.

Historical records indicate that in the four-teenth century the term was equated with hard-ship and affliction, and in nineteenth-century medicine, stress was cited as a cause of ill health, as many diseases were attributed by physicians to conditions of "melancholia," "grief," or "despair." Clearly, by the 1800s, there was widespread recognition of the link between mind and body.

Ironically, Pasteur's demonstration that bacteria cause disease (the germ theory of disease) led many physicians and medical researchers to confine their attention to such germ-caused diseases in the hope of finding specific disease etiology and appropriate "magic bullets." In doing so, many of them abandoned interest in the less concrete areas of attitudes and emotions.

Walter Cannon and Hans Selye

Early in the twentieth century, Walter Cannon, an American physiologist, used the term **homeo-stasis** to describe a state in which the body's physiological processes are in balance and are properly coordinated. He identified many highly specific physiological (adaptive) changes made by the body in response to hunger, thirst, extreme cold, pain, and intense emotions.

Cannon described a "fight or flight" reaction. When circumstances offered the opportunity for success (or there was no choice), humans would fight; in the face of overwhelming odds, they would seek flight. Physiological changes such as sugar entering the bloodstream to provide a rapid source of energy, heavy breathing to provide more oxygen, and acceleration of the heart to provide more fuel and oxygen occur to enhance the individual's reaction.

However, Cannon noted that whereas this resource mobilization was quite functional for early humans, today it is often activated when it is not really useful—on a first date, for example—and may be harmful as it exhausts the individual.

Hans Selye, an endocrinologist at McGill University, is often cited as the classic figure in stress research. Hoping to discover a new sex hormone, Selye experimentally injected labora-tory rats with hormones. Typical reactions were enlarged adrenal glands, shrunken immune systems, and bleeding ulcers. To confirm these effects, he injected non-hormonal substances into a control group of rats and, surprisingly, observed a similar reaction. He realized that the response was a general reaction rather than a substance-specific one. The physiological reac-tion was termed "stress," and the trio of responses (alarm, adaptation, and exhaustion) was called the "general adaptation syndrome."

Based on this work, Selye eventually pinpointed a truth with which people could immediately identify—in our daily lives, we all experience stressful situations. These situations upset our body's equilibrium—our homeo-stasis—and make us more susceptible to mild diseases and illnesses. If stressful situations persist over an extended period of time, the body's resources become depleted and more severe disease or illnesses—or even death—may result.

A MODEL OF SOCIAL STRESS

Several researchers have developed models to describe the processes involved in stress. The model presented in Figure 5–1 is influenced by several of these models, but especially by Morton Lieberman (1982), Pearlin and Aneshensel (1986), and Pearlin and Bierman (2013).

While stress is a broad intellectual concept, this model highlights the importance of using the sociological perspective to understand the following areas:

1. The nature and dynamics of how social forces and circumstances (stressors) create stressful situations.
2. How the perception or appraisal of stressors affects the manner in which they are handled.
3. How the appraisal of stressors affects the enactment of social roles (and strain created in these roles).

Figure 5–1   A Model of the Stress Process

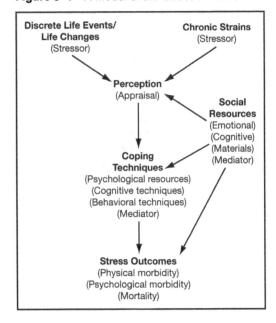

4. How social resources influence the likelihood of stressful circumstances occurring, the appraisal of these circumstances, the extent to which role enactment is problematic, the ability of individuals to cope and the coping mechanisms they use, and the extent to which the stressful circumstances result in negative stress outcomes.

STRESSORS

A primary concern of many sociologists is the identification of stressors—that is, social factors or social forces that contribute to stress. The cataloging of these forces is a difficult task, however, as they range from the broadest of social forces and large-scale social organization (a macro perspective) on the one hand, to the personal social environments in which people function on a day-to-day basis (a micro perspective) on the other.

Stressors and the Sociological Perspective

Attempts to understand human behavior must, of course, consider the importance of broader social forces and social organization. A key insight of sociology is that all human behavior, even that which seems to be very individualistic, is shaped by larger forces in the social environment.

As an example, the French sociologist Émile Durkheim (1858–1917) helped to stimulate interest in identifying ways in which individual behaviors are shaped by larger social forces. In his book *Suicide*, first published in 1897 (and translated in 1951), Durkheim focused on what might seem to be the most individual of human behaviors, and described how it is influenced by social forces. Durkheim asked the following questions: If suicide is an entirely personal, individual behavior, why do rates of suicide vary from one social group to another? Why are suicide rates higher among men than women, among the unmarried than the married, and among Protestants than Catholics? And why do patterns in suicide rates persist over time?

Durkheim found his answer in the extent and nature to which individuals were integrated into a group or society. On this basis, he explained suicide as being most likely to occur (1) when an individual is insufficiently integrated within a group and has few social bonds (e.g., an elderly person whose lifetime partner dies and who feels as if there is little reason to go on living), (2) when an individual identifies so strongly with a social group that they are willing to sacrifice their life for the group (e.g., a kamikaze pilot), or (3) when an individual feels a sense of normlessness during times when society's norms and values are undergoing upheaval or rapid change (e.g., during periods of rapid economic upturn or downturn). Durkheim's analysis is an excellent example of the **sociological imagination** (see Chapter 1). It is an ability to see how personal troubles (e.g., thoughts of suicide) are influenced by wider social forces (e.g., changes in the state of the economy or the extent of social integration). This is the same perspective that we take in order to understand social stress. The box "Are Cell Phones a Social Stressor? The Impact of Cultural Change" provides an example of individual lifestyle (and stress) being affected by a technological change.

IN THE FIELD

ARE CELL PHONES A SOCIAL STRESSOR? THE IMPACT OF CULTURAL CHANGE

Sociologists and psychologists are accustomed to describing life events and chronic strains as being key social stressors. Yet macro-scale global events and changes in culture and social structure, such as war and natural disasters, are also apparent causes of today's high and increasing levels of stress (Wheaton and Montazer, 2009). For example, research has shown a general elevation in perceived level of stress in the United States following the terrorist attacks in New York City on September 11, 2001 (Richman, Cloninger, and Rospenda, 2008).

Could a technological change as simple as the cell phone be part of stress-producing cultural change? Consider the following:

1. *Cell phones are one example (but only one example) of the accelerating rate of new technologies within society.* Ask yourself what technologies exist in society today that did not exist when your parents were your age. Consider the fields of medicine, communication, information technology, transportation, and recreation. Changes within these areas and others represent some of the most transformative changes ever within our society.

2. *Cell phones are a major contributor to peoples' constant accessibility and corresponding decline in privacy.* When the parents of today's 18- to 25-year-olds were in college, the most common form of communication with family and friends back home was a personal letter, and a common source of information was the hard-copy (a term that did not exist) encyclopedia. With the speeding up of communication by e-mail, texting, tweeting, twittering, and social networking, we are now almost constantly "on." We can "connect" to almost anyone immediately, and we are constantly available to others. Information about anything is almost immediately available to us, and information about us is easily accessible by others. All of us have had the experience of having to listen in on loud individuals' cell phone conversations. Menzies (2005) in *No Time: Stress and the Crisis of Modern Life* refers to this as the decline of the "face-to-face world" and the emergence of the "hyperworld." Agus (2011) asserts that technologies such as those on smartphones allow even very short periods of time to be productive or entertaining. By constantly keeping our brains busy with digital input, we are missing out on the

benefits of down time—allowing the brain to process, to create, and even to rest.

3. *Cell phones contribute to the compression of time and space.* Work occupies an increasing part of our lives, while leisure time diminishes. We feel pressure not only to do one thing at a time but also to multitask in order to accomplish things simultaneously. We need constantly changing images to retain our attention. The reading of books has declined. Life is more fragmented. A comment from your bf may cause u 2 lol. Altheide (1995) states that "An increasing array of life is processed rather than lived, recorded rather than remembered and tracked rather than understood." Trying to keep up makes it difficult not to exceed your "optimal level of stimulation" (Blonna, 2007).

Does everyone experience cell phone technology in the same way? Not at all. The Pew Internet and American Life Project (Lenhart et al., 2010) reports that teens are far more likely to consider the cell phone an indispensable part of life. Four out of five have slept with their cell phone; some keep it under their pillow to awaken them for late-night texts. More than half of teens text every day, and teens send or receive on average 1,500 text messages each month. (The average adult texts ten times per day.) More than half of all teens use their cell phone to access the Internet, record video, and play music on a regular basis. The corresponding percentages for adults are far lower but increasing. The cell phone industry itself is not very popular with either adults or teens; it receives more complaints than any other industry. It is not clear whether adults or teens will be more likely to access a new website created by Consumers Union, called escapecellhell.org.

Types of Stressors

In recent years, sociologists have distinguished between two major types of stressors—specific **life events**, and more enduring life problems called **chronic strains**.

Life Events. Life events are important specific events or experiences that interrupt an individual's usual activities and require some adjustment. A distinction is made between anticipated (or scheduled) life events (e.g., marriage, divorce, or the beginning or ending of a school year) and unanticipated (unscheduled) life events (e.g., the death of a loved one, a sudden failure, the sudden loss of a job, or learning of a terminal illness). Recent research has begun to explore the importance of anticipatory events—that is, those that might happen in the future (e.g., failing out of school or being a victim of a crime). The very anticipation of such events might in itself be a stressor.

In order to determine the effects of these specific life events on stress level, researchers have employed three kinds of techniques: (1) studies of the psychiatric effects of specific events, such as reactions to combat and natural and human disasters, (2) comparison of the number and types of life events experienced by psychiatric patients prior to their hospital admission with those for a non-patient control group, and (3) general population surveys examining the relationship between life events, stress, and illness. Researchers have developed a variety of specific scales to measure exposure to stressful life events. One popular scale—the Social Readjustment Rating Scale (Holmes and Rahe, 1967)—contains a list of 43 events that were evaluated by a panel of judges with regard to the level of readjustment that each required. The most stressful life events were identified as being the death of a spouse, a divorce, marital separation, and a jail term. At the other end of the scale were minor violations of the law,

Christmas, vacations, and a change in eating habits.

Does experiencing undesirable life events have a negative impact on health? Yes, although even in cases where the life event is traumatizing, the effect may not be large, and in most cases it does not persist over a long period of time. Researchers do continue to detect a relationship between adverse life events and certain depressive disorders (Dohrenwend, 2000), but the effects are not large and they generally dissipate within 3 months (Avison and Turner, 1988).

Chronic Strains. The second major type of stressor—now often referred to as chronic strains—refers to the relatively enduring problems, conflicts, and threats that people typically face in their daily lives. The most common bases for these types of stressors are family problems with partners, parents, or children; love or sex problems; problems at work or in school; and problems in any site that involves competition. A meaningful way to organize these chronic stressors is to focus on problems that occur within the boundaries of major social roles and role sets. These are likely to be important problems because the relationships that exist in role sets are usually enduring. Because they also tend to be extremely important relationships (e.g., with a partner, child, boss, or teacher), strains that develop are likely to be of great significance to the individual (Pearlin, 1989).

Pearlin (1989:245) uses the concept of "role strain" to refer to "the hardships, challenges, and conflicts or other problems that people come to experience as they engage over time in normal social roles." The five most common types of role strain are listed below.

1. *Role overload* occurs when the combination of all the role demands placed on an individual exceed that individual's ability to meet them. Within the workplace, there is evidence that work overload is most likely to be experienced by those at opposite ends of the spectrum—by salaried, white-collar workers and by the least-skilled, blue-collar workers. For different reasons, both may feel little control over their work demands—an important predictor of job stress. Excessive workload may also be experienced by the homemaker in overseeing house maintenance, food preparation, and child-rearing functions, as well as increasingly playing the caregiver role for parents who are unable to live independently. Primary caregivers and those caring for elders with significant needs must often resort to taking unpaid leave, reducing their working hours, rearranging their work schedule, or even leaving the workforce altogether.

2. *Interpersonal conflicts within role sets* include problems and difficulties that arise within complementary role sets, such as wife–husband, parent–child, and worker–supervisor conflicts, and are the types of strain that often touch people most deeply. Marriage (or engaging in a long-term relationship) is typically the center of our most intimate relationships, the context of many of our most far-reaching decisions (e.g., about children, major purchases, degree of equalitarianism), and the role set in which many spend the most time. Therefore it has the potential for great bliss as well as significant interpersonal conflict. High rates of separation and divorce, emotional and physical abuse within families, and reported levels of marital dissatisfaction all reflect high levels of stress. Pearlin pinpointed one aspect of this conflict:

One of the more common elements of discord—and one of the more stressful—involves a breakdown in reciprocity. By reciprocity and its failure, I mean the sense of inequity people have about their marriages ... people see themselves in marital relationships where ... they invest more than their partner in the relationship, and are more considerate of their partners than they think their partners are of them. (1983:10)

Pearlin (1983) identifies other common sources of strain in marriages: (1) a perception that the spouse does not recognize or accept "quintessential" elements of one's self—that he or she fails to authenticate what is judged to be an especially prized aspect of the self-image; (2) a belief that the spouse is failing to fulfill basic marital expectations such as wage earning or housekeeping; and (3) a feeling that the spouse is failing to provide even minimal levels of affection or that sexual relations are insufficiently satisfying. The lack of physical as well as emotional intimacy clearly relates to marital stress.

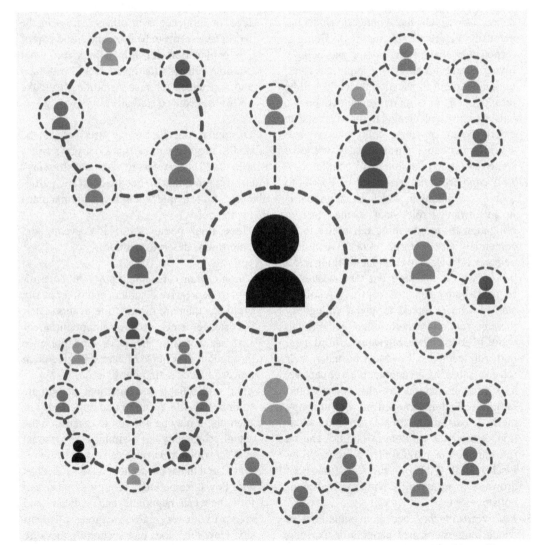

Sociological research increasingly shows that participation in positive social relationships with others is an important contributor to good physical and mental health and can play a significant role in recovering from illness. © djvstock/Fotolia

3. *Inter-role conflict* occurs when the demands of two or more roles held by a person are incompatible, and these demands cannot simultaneously be met. On a small scale, genuine conflict occurs whenever any health care worker is "on call" and gets called in to the hospital just as he or she is about to participate in a family function (say, for example, a one-showing only of a play or dance for which the youngest child has earnestly practiced for months). Being a responsible health care worker and being a loving parent are both very important roles, but on the night in question the child will be disappointed. In a marriage of two people who are equally dedicated to their careers, an elderly parent or young child who requires significant attention during the day will force some resolution of an inter-role conflict.

4. *Role captivity* is the term used by Pearlin to describe situations in which an individual is in an unwanted role—that is, they feel an obligation to do one thing but prefer to do something else (Pearlin, 1983). A retired person who wishes to continue working and a person who is working but who wishes to retire are both held in role captivity. A college student who is forced to attend college by their parents and a college-age person who wants to go to college but cannot afford it are both role captives. Anyone who hates their job and is longing for another is a role captive. The captive situation can also occur within families. Feeling trapped in an unhappy marriage can be an extremely stressful situation. Sometimes children in families can be role captives, as is illustrated by research by Fischer et al. (2000) on the stressfulness of growing up in a family with parental alcoholism.

5. *Role restructuring* occurs in situations in which long-established patterns or expectations undergo considerable restructuring. Pearlin (1989) offers such examples as a rebellious adolescent who desires more independence, an apprentice who grows frustrated with their mentor as the craft is learned, and adult children who must take on increased responsibilities for aging parents. He notes that the transition can be more difficult when it is forced by circumstances (rather than voluntary effort), and when the transition involves some redistribution of status, privilege, or influence over others. Stress in the workplace seems to be increasing, and part of the explanation for this is anxiety about possible job loss (as businesses down-size) and rearranged job responsibilities (to make up for the reduced staff size).

Of course, not all chronic stressors can be related to problems in carrying out one's roles. Pearlin (1989) also refers to "ambient stressors" to identify those that do not attach to any particular role. An example would be living in a place that is too noisy.

Three final points about life events and chronic strains deserve attention:

1. Chronic strains are a more powerful determinant of depressive disorders and other health problems than are discrete life events. Their persistence, emergence in important areas such as marriage and work, and presence throughout the course of each day give them powerful force within our lives.

2. Valid and reliable measurement of chronic strains (like life events) is complicated. For example, it may be difficult to determine the actual "chronicity" of a strain. Interpersonal conflict within a marriage can rarely be represented as a linear phenomenon—it often ebbs and flows, sometimes swinging back and forth between happiness and sadness, and does so with very uneven degrees of intensity. How then does one accurately measure the length of time for which discord has occurred?

Moreover, the specific array of stressors being faced undergoes change during the life course—what is very stressful to an early teen would typically be very different to what is confronting someone in the later years. In addition, stressors may accumulate over time so that determination of the consequences of any single stressor becomes more difficult. What may seem rather straightforward to measure is actually quite complex.

3. Life events and chronic strains may accumulate over time and often overlap. The occurrence of specific life events may alter the existence or meaning of chronic strains. An example is the effect of sudden job loss (a discrete life event) on division of labor within the household (possibly a chronic strain). Moreover, life events may create new strains or magnify existing strains, as might occur if the sudden job loss created ongoing marital discord. This helps to explain the fact that the cumulative amount of stress experienced during childhood can have a long-term negative impact on psychological distress and increases the risk of poor mental health later in life (Bjorkenstam et al., 2015).

APPRAISAL OF STRESSORS

Appraisal and the Sociological Perspective

Within sociology, **interactionism** is a micro-level perspective that focuses on small-scale everyday patterns of social interaction. Interactionists believe that social life is comprised of a myriad number of episodes of daily social interactions in which people communicate verbally and non-verbally and engage in a constant process of interpreting others' messages and responding to these interpretations. According to interactionism, the world is not so much imposed upon the individual, dictating or strongly influencing behavior, as it is

created by the individual through the exchange of these verbal and non-verbal symbols. Berger and Luckmann (1967) assigned the term **social construction of reality** to identify this pattern.

A classic example of the interactionist perspective is found in the work of W.I. Thomas (1863–1947). Thomas recognized that individuals are affected by events only to the extent to which those events are perceived. In other words, neither life events nor chronic strains are in and of themselves stressful. They are simply situations or occurrences in which the likelihood of a stressful response is increased. It is the perception of these events and their interpretation—what an individual believes the implications of the events or strains to be—that is stressful. The **Thomas theorem** is often summarized as "if situations are defined as real, they are real in their consequences." It is the perceived world, whether it is perceived accurately or not, that becomes the basis for response (Thomas and Thomas, 1928).

The Appraisal Process. Whenever any potentially stressful life event or chronic strain occurs, we immediately evaluate or appraise its significance for us. We may attempt to recreate the circumstances that surrounded some similar event in the past and recall how it affected us then, or attempt to systematically remember anything that we have heard or read about the event. We may ask ourselves "Have I ever handled anything like this before? If so, what happened? Can I get through this on my own? Do I need help? Who can help?"

This is done in order to determine the likely consequences of the event for us. If these are negative, we will probably calculate how much damage has already occurred and what threat of additional damage remains. We may assess the availability of resources to help deal with the event. We will calculate the stressfulness of the event not only in absolute terms but also relative to whatever helping resources are available.

The appraisal process does not involve the "real" event, but the individual's *perception* of the real event. To the extent that perceptions differ, individuals will respond differently to the same "real" circumstances. Being laid off from a job may be perceived by some as a tragic event, whereas others may view it as an unsolicited step in searching for a better job.

MEDIATORS OF STRESS: COPING AND SOCIAL SUPPORT

The same stressful circumstances do not lead to the same stress outcomes in all people. Other factors exist that modify the stressor–stress outcome relationship. These additional factors are referred to as **mediators of stress**; they are so identified because research has demonstrated their potential to influence or modify (i.e., mediate) the effects of stressors. This section focuses on coping and social support—the two types of mediators that have received the most attention.

Mediators and the Sociological Perspective

Several sociological concepts and perspectives contribute to an understanding of the mediating role of coping and social support. A classic illustration of the way the social environment influences our self-image (and thus our feelings of confidence in dealing with social stress) is Charles Horton Cooley's (1864–1929) theory of the **looking-glass self**. Cooley illustrated the way that reality is socially constructed by describing the process by which each person develops a self-image. According to this theory, we come to see ourselves as we believe other people see us. Consciously or subconsciously, we attempt to interpret how we are viewed by others (and the judgment being placed on that view), and we gradually develop a self-image consistent with what we perceive (Cooley,

1964). If I believe that people with whom I interact see me as a very humorous person, I will probably see myself that way. However, if others never laugh at my jokes and convey to me that I need a sense-of-humor transplant, I'm not likely to see myself as being very funny.

Coping

Coping refers to the personal responses that people make in order to prevent, avoid, or control emotional distress. It includes efforts to (1) eliminate or modify the stressful situation so that it will not be a continuing problem, (2) control the meaning of the problem, by "cognitively neutralizing" the situation, and (3) control the stress created by the situation (e.g., through stress management techniques).

Specific Coping Techniques. There are three types of specific coping techniques—psychological resources, cognitive techniques, and behavioral techniques.

1. *Psychological resources* are "the personality characteristics that people draw upon to help them withstand threats posed by events and objects in their environment" (Pearlin and Schooler, 1978:5). Three such characteristics have received the most attention:
   a. Individuals with positive feelings about self—*positive self-esteem*—have been shown to cope better with stressful situations. This may be due to greater self-confidence, a feeling that one is held in high regard by others (recall Cooley's looking-glass self), and/or a real or perceived assessment of one's previous ability to handle the stressful situation (Thoits, 2013).
   b. Individuals with a feeling of being in control, controlling their own destiny, and being able to master situations (i.e., *internal control*) have been shown to cope

better with stressors than individuals who see themselves as being less competent and who believe that their life is controlled by luck, fate, or outside others (i.e., *external control*). People who have a high sense of mastery of situations are less likely to report negative stress outcomes (Gadalla, 2009; Ross and Mirowsky, 2013).

  c. Individuals characterized by a trait referred to by Kobasa (1979) as *hardiness* are better able to handle stress. Hardy individuals exhibit a strong commitment to work, family, friends, and other causes and interests, accept change as a challenge rather than as a foe, and have a feeling of personal control over their life (internal control).

2. *Cognitive techniques* involve the assignment of specific interpretations to a stressful event in order to control its meaning (i.e., to neutralize its stressfulness). In the light of some potentially stressful event, one might respond by denying that the event is happening or by telling oneself that the event is not as crucial as it might seem, that it will be over soon, that it might even be a good challenge, or that other people have been in this situation and survived. Many people rely on their spiritual beliefs or participation in religious activities to help them to find meaning in uncontrollable life events.

3. *Behavioral techniques* can also be used to help cope with a stressful event. Individuals might focus on developing and implementing a plan to reduce or eliminate the stressor. Some individuals use biofeedback or yoga or other meditative techniques to help to reduce stressfulness (research supports the health value of these techniques). Many people try to get their mind off the object of despair by engaging in an alternative, distracting activity, such as listening to music, engaging in some physical activity (increasingly,

exercise is being shown by research to be an especially helpful mediator of stress, in both the short and long term), or using alcohol or some other drug. More than one of our students has resorted to the old adage "When the going gets tough, the tough go shopping."

Are all coping techniques equally effective in all situations? The answer is no. Research has shown that different coping techniques are most effective in different situations. Most people use different coping techniques in different situations (e.g., in parental versus marital situations), and different people effectively use different coping techniques in the same situation. The larger and more varied one's coping repertoire, the more likely it is that one can cope with any stressful situation. In general, however, problem-focused strategies that deal directly with the stressor lead to more positive health outcomes than strategies that include mentally distancing oneself from the stressor, wishful thinking, self-blame, and simply emphasizing the positive. Individuals who have effective coping strategies develop confidence in their ability to deal with stressors, and experience fewer uncontrollable events and more controllable events in their lives (Thoits, 2006).

There have been several interesting studies of the specific kinds of coping techniques used in particular circumstances. For example, Schwab (1990) identified five primary coping strategies used by married couples who had experienced the death of a child: (1) seeking a release of tension through talking, crying, exercising, and writing about the death, (2) concentrating on avoiding painful thoughts and feelings by engaging in diversionary activities such as work around the house, (3) cognitively dealing with the situation by reading materials on loss and grief, (4) helping others and/or contributing to a cause, and (5) relying on religiously based beliefs that their child is in a better place and that the family will someday be reunited.

Social Support

Social support refers to resources that people receive from their social relationships and social networks and their membership of groups (Blonna, 2007). This support may be (1) emotional (e.g., caring, concern, sympathy, and encouragement), (2) cognitive (e.g., information and advice useful in dealing with problems), or (3) material (e.g., child care and transportation).

The most important social relationships with respect to health tend to vary over the life course—parents typically are most important for children, peer networks become increasingly important in adolescence, intimate partners are key in adulthood, and adult children often become most important in later life (Umberson, Crosnoe, and Reczek, 2010).

Although the extent to which people are integrated into families, friendship networks, occupational or school groups, and religious and civic groups varies, research confirms that social support has a direct impact on health and is an extremely important mediator of the effects of stress. This effect occurs as early as adolescence, through the teenage and adult years, and into later life. In all cases, the more social ties people have, the better their health (Yang et al., 2016).

The Effect of Social Support on Stress and Stress Outcomes. People who have meaningful social ties and perceive positive social support tend to have better physical and mental health and are better able to adjust to such events as loss of a partner, unemployment, serious illness, and criminal victimization. Conversely, people who feel that they are isolated (i.e., who feel lonely and do not have social support) or who feel socially disconnected (i.e., who have a small social network and infrequently participate in social activities) experience higher levels of physical and mental health problems (Cornwell and Waite, 2009). Two primary models have been developed to explain this relationship.

The **main effects model of social support** asserts that social support contributes directly to well-being and positive health, and that these beneficial effects occur even in the absence of stress. The overall sense of well-being that social support provides, the feeling of being accepted, the knowledge that others care and are available, and the degree of comfort within one's social environment may contribute to inner feelings of contentment and outer expressions of good health.

The **buffering effects model of social support** asserts that the beneficial effects of social support occur only in the presence of stress. By acting as a buffer, social support may decrease the likelihood of negative stress outcomes occurring as a response to high stress levels. The support offered by others, according to this model, provides some sense of security and confidence that stressful circumstances can be handled, and perhaps even that specific assistance in handling the situation will be available. Research has shown that people with larger social networks and with stronger ties to those in their networks are better able to avoid illness and to recover from it (Smith and Christakis, 2008).

Although research findings are not completely consistent, the wealth of evidence shows that both types of effects occur—that social support does contribute directly to positive health, and that it serves an important buffering effect at times of high stress (Thoits, 2011).

There is evidence that coping techniques and social support work together in mediating stress. Yang (2006) focused on the increase in depressive symptoms among older adults as they became more functionally limited. The adults who had positive self-esteem and a sense of control (coping mechanisms) and who had a confidant and were satisfied with their social support (social support mechanisms) best handled the decline in functional abilities.

Recent sociological research has raised cautions about a decline in the level of social support that people today have available to them. McPherson, Smith-Lovin, and Brashears (2006) studied the number of close friends and confidants that people currently had compared with 20 years earlier. In 1985, the average American had three persons in whom to confide, and only 10 percent had no confidant. In 2004, the average number of confidants had decreased to two, and almost 25 percent of individuals had no close friend. Given that social support is one of the key mechanisms for preventing and dealing with stress, the decline in the number of people who have readily available support is a cause for concern.

Finally, the complexity of the relationship between social support and stress must be emphasized. Often it is impossible to disentangle stressors and their mediators. This is something of a "double whammy"—certain circumstances both add to the stressfulness of life and detract from available social support at the same time. For example, much research has confirmed the stressfulness of unemployment and its relationship to depression. However, research has demonstrated that unemployment carries an extra burden. Following job loss, social support from one's partner and fellow workers often diminishes. At the very time when social support is especially needed, it becomes less readily offered. Thus the psychological distress traditionally linked to job loss may actually be due to both job loss and the reduction in social support that often accompanies it.

A recent study (McGee and Thompson, 2015) focused on this very issue among adults aged 18 to 25 years. Almost a quarter of these adults (23 percent) were unemployed at the time of the study, and 12 percent of them were experiencing depression. A key study finding is that the odds of being depressed were three times higher for the unemployed than for the employed. The authors suggested that this relationship could be due to factors such as feelings of uncertainty about transitioning to adulthood, delays in achieving goals, the stigma related to unemployment, and changes in their social network and social relationships.

STRESS OUTCOMES

In one sense, identification of specific "outcomes" or "ills" of stress is remarkably simple—all of us can relate various ailments that we have suffered to stress. In another sense, however, making specific linkages can be quite difficult because stress leads to a wide variety of outcomes through a wide variety of pathways. In any case, it is clear that when one's level of stress cannot successfully be mediated through coping and social support, negative stress outcomes are likely to occur. In other words, stress has a very significant impact on ill health.

In attempting to bring some order to the variety of ills produced by stress, Brown (1984) suggested the following categorization:

1. **Bona fide emotional disturbances** such as anxiety, insomnia, tension headaches, depression, neuroses, phobias, hysterias, and hypochondriasis. These are major factors in aging, sexual impotency, alcoholism, drug abuse, sleep disorders, and learning problems.
2. **Abnormal behaviors** such as compulsive behaviors, aggression, withdrawal, criminal activities, battered child/partner/parent syndrome, and sexual deviation. Some research is now beginning to examine "road rage" and other types of rage as a response to accumulated stress.
3. **Psychosomatic illnesses** such as hypertension, coronary heart disease, ulcers, and colitis.
4. **Worsening of genuine organic illnesses** such as epilepsy, migraine, herpes zoster, coronary thrombosis, and rheumatic arthritis.

Grouped somewhat differently, we might say that unchecked stress increases the likelihood of psychological morbidity (e.g., anxiety and depression), physical morbidity (e.g., coronary heart disease and cancer), and mortality (Pearlin and Aneshensel, 1986).

Pathways between Stress and Disease

Stress responses may be produced voluntarily or involuntarily (see Figure 5–2). A sudden noise or other unanticipated event works through the hypothalamus in the brain (the center of primitive and automatic responses), which stimulates the sympathetic nervous system (and the larger brain system), which arouses the body for action. The cerebral cortex then evaluates the genuine danger presented by the stressor and determines whether the state of arousal is necessary.

The pathway for voluntary responses begins in the cerebral cortex, which assesses and interprets the stressor, and then moves through the

Figure 5–2   The Physiological Pathways of the Stress Response

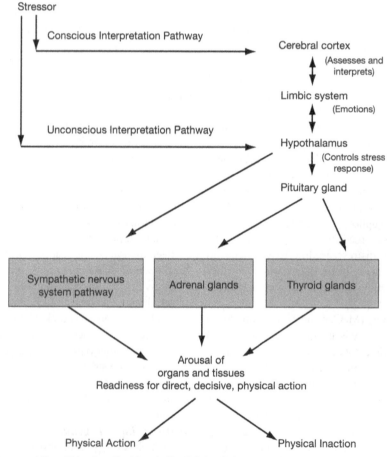

Source: Clint Bruess and Glenn Richardson. *Decisions for Health* (4th ed.). (Dubuque, IA: Brown and Benchmark Publishers, 1995.)

limbic system (the center of emotions) and the hypothalamus to the pituitary gland, which activates the adrenal glands and thyroid gland to secrete hormones to trigger the body's stress response (if that is judged to be appropriate by the cerebral cortex).

The specific responses made by the body include a sharp increase in blood pressure and increased respiration (to increase the availability of oxygen), an increase in blood sugar levels (to provide energy for muscles), increased muscle tension (to enable quick applications of strength), a release of thyroid hormone (to speed up metabolism for energy), a release of cholesterol in the blood (for endurance fuel), and a release of endorphins (the body's natural painkillers). Ultimately, stress may lead to disease through the wearing down of bodily organs, through a weakening of the body's immune system, or through the development of health-impairing behaviors (e.g., increased cigarette smoking or alcohol consumption) in reaction to stress.

THE ROLE OF SOCIOECONOMIC STATUS, RACE, SEXUAL ORIENTATION, AND GENDER IN SOCIAL STRESS

Sociologists have clearly shown the importance of social structure in influencing exposure to stressors, and to access to social and personal resources to deal with the stressors. Especially helpful have been studies that have examined the relationship between social stress and key demographic factors such as socioeconomic status, race, sexual orientation, and gender. Each of these factors influences stress and the likelihood of negative health outcomes influenced by stress.

Socioeconomic Status (SES)

People with lower socioeconomic status have higher rates of psychological distress and mental health problems than the more affluent. There are two main possible explanations for this. The **exposure hypothesis** asserts that people with lower socioeconomic status are exposed to more stressful life experiences than those in the middle or upper classes, that higher rates of distress are a logical result of this exposure (Lantz et al., 2005), and that these stressful experiences (such as economic strain) are of the type that accumulate over the course of one's life (Pearlin et al., 2005).

An example would be the fact that people with more education often have less psychological distress than those with less education. People with a higher level of education tend to have higher-paying and more fulfilling jobs that offer more mental challenge and work autonomy and tend to have more economic resources (Mirowsky and Ross, 2003). A second example relates to the neighborhood in which one lives. Living in a neighborhood in which there are abundant social stressors such as crime, harassment, and various forms of disorder and decay has been shown to increase distress and ultimately to lead to negative health outcomes (Hill, Ross, and Angel, 2005). Individuals living in areas with high levels of industrial activity may stress about the industrial pollution and hazardous wastes to which they are exposed, and feel a sense of powerlessness because they do not have the financial resources to relocate (Downey and Van Willigen, 2005).

The **vulnerability hypothesis** asserts that stressful life experiences have a greater impact on those with lower socioeconomic status, and a greater capacity to lead to negative stress outcomes (Turner and Lloyd, 1999). This greater vulnerability has been traced to three factors— inadequate financial resources, greater use of ineffective coping strategies, and less access to social support networks (McLeod and Kessler, 1990).

First, people with lower socioeconomic status not only experience more of several stressful life events (e.g., job instability and loss, chronic health problems, and poorer quality of housing) but, by definition, also have fewer financial resources available to deal with these problems. For example, purchasing health insurance might be recognized as a partial solution to health care worries, but financial limitations may eliminate this option.

Second, people with lower socioeconomic status are less likely to have psychological traits (e.g., high self-esteem, internal control, and confidence in dealing with stressors) that buffer stress, and they are more likely to use ineffective coping strategies (e.g., avoidance) in responding to stressful situations. These patterns may be linked to socialization experiences. For example, growing up in a family that is unable to secure the health care that it needs may encourage feelings of powerlessness and external control.

Third, aspects of living with low socioeconomic status may reduce the likelihood of establishing or maintaining supportive social resources. While the evidence is mixed on this point, it does appear, for example, that people with lower socioeconomic status are less likely to have a confidant on whom they can rely.

Race

For more than 30 years, research has demonstrated that African Americans have higher rates of psychological distress than whites. A key question is whether this difference can solely or largely be attributed to an economic disparity, or whether perception of racial discrimination exerts a strong independent effect on stress level.

Much research has pointed out that the effects of social class on many outcomes (e.g., educational attainment and financial achievement) vary depending on one's race, and that social class and race may both contribute to higher levels of distress. Kessler and Neighbors (1986) posited that racial differences in distress might be largest in the lower class (especially in the case of competent blacks whose aspirations have been thwarted by discrimination) or in the upper class (especially in the case of financially successful blacks who are feeling status inconsistency). Their analysis of eight studies (a pooled sample of 22,000 respondents) determined that race continues to be an important predictor of distress even when class is controlled, and that blacks experience more distress than whites at all levels of income. Considerable recent research has shown that perceiving racial discrimination is highly stressful, and that the heightened stress does increase the likelihood of negative health outcomes (Grollman, 2012; Meyer, Schwartz, and Frost, 2008; Priest et al., 2013).

Despite the higher level of psychological distress, African Americans do not experience higher levels of negative mental health than whites. This may be due to the pattern in which blacks are more likely than whites to have access to social support. The group solidarity that often exists among members of minority groups may have important stress-buffering effects (Lincoln, Chatters, and Taylor, 2003; Lopez et al., 2012). In addition, having a strong sense of ethnic identity (e.g., strong group pride and cultural commitment to the group) can be a buffer against the stress of racial and ethnic discrimination and help to prevent negative health outcomes (Mossakowski, 2003).

A question also emerges about the experience of individuals who hold more than one disadvantaged status. For example, a gay black man might experience prejudice and discrimination because he is black *and* because he is gay. The **double disadvantage hypothesis** asserts that people who hold more than one disadvantaged status may experience worse health than their counterparts with only one disadvantaged status or with none. The evidence with regard to this hypothesis is mixed, but recently Grollman (2014) used national survey data in the United

States and found a strong relationship between holding multiple disadvantaged statuses and health. Peoples with multiple disadvantaged statuses were more likely than others to experience major depression, poor physical health, and functional limitations. In part, this was due to a greater likelihood of exposure to interpersonal discrimination.

Sexual Orientation

In the last two decades, an increasing number of studies have focused on the physical and mental health status of lesbian, gay, bisexual, and transgender (LGBT) people and on the role of social stress in their health. Although research samples have often been small, research has found that sexual minorities have more physical and mental health problems than heterosexuals. Several scholars have identified the stress associated with being a minority group member in a heteronormative society as underlying these health differences (e.g., Frost, Lehavot, and Meyer, 2015).

Ueno (2010) has identified six specific mechanisms that contribute to this greater stress:

1. Being more likely to experience physical and sexual victimization
2. Being more likely to experience discrimination (including name-calling and job discrimination)
3. Being more likely to experience negative life events (including job loss and friend dissolution)
4. Being more likely to experience chronic strains (including arguments with parents)
5. Being more likely to experience a deficiency in psychosocial resources (including family rejection)
6. Being more likely to experience a deficiency in psychological resources (including lower self-esteem and possible internalization of others' homophobia).

The path by which these mechanisms may affect sexual-minority individuals has been studied by Green (2008). He found that urban gay males faced significant stressors in their everyday lives, including avoidance by others, stigmatization, and rejection. These stressors led directly to lowered self-esteem, a perceived lack of social support, and a decrease in feelings of personal control, and they led to greater feelings of anxiety and depression.

In addition, recent studies of the role of stress in the lives of transgender people have found that they frequently feel stigmatized in health care encounters, they find that medical providers have not received training in dealing with their particular needs and thus interact with them with ambivalence and uncertainty, and that these experiences push the transgendered away from receiving adequate medical care. This also leads to higher rates of negative health experiences (Hughto, Reisner, and Pachankis 2015; Poteat, German, and Kerrigan 2013).

There is even a clear-cut influence of the level of anti-gay prejudice in the community in which one lives, and negative health outcomes for sexual-minority group members. Studies show elevated risks of depression, cardiovascular diseases, suicide, and homicide for gay, lesbian, bisexual, and transgendered people living in communities with high levels of prejudice against them. One study found that these differences translated into a shorter life expectancy (by approximately 12 years) for sexual minority group members living in areas with high levels of prejudice (Hatzenbuehler et al., 2014). This is consistent with research which found that same-sex couples living in states with legally sanctioned marriage reported better health than those living in states with antigay constitutional amendments (Kail, Acosta, and Wright, 2015).

The extra stress and extra difficulties in obtaining appropriate medical care due to being in a sexual minority group clearly affect morbidity and mortality.

Gender

Women have higher rates (perhaps double) of psychological distress and depression than men. As Rosenfield (1989:77) has summarized, these differences are found "across cultures, over time, in different age groups, in rural as well as urban areas, and in treated as well as untreated populations." Consistently, these differences are greater among the married than the unmarried, although distress is greater in women regardless of marital status.

As important as this pattern is in sociological analysis and clinical application, only recently has significant attention been focused on women as subjects in stress research. This lack of attention has been especially obvious in the area of occupational health research, where early research on women was often conducted primarily in order to secure a better understanding of men's stress. The consequence of this inattention is that much remains to be learned about the reasons for the high rates of distress in women.

A wide variety of plausible explanations for the gender disparity in stress have been advanced and tested.

1. Women are exposed to more discrete, stressful life events than are men. This differential exposure hypothesis has not been supported by most research studies. However, some research has highlighted the importance of the fact that women are much more likely than men to take on the caregiver role and to be affected by it, and Keith (1993) found that the higher levels of distress in older women (compared with older men) are due to their greater likelihood of having financial problems.

2. Women include more people in their social network, care more about these people, and are more emotionally involved in the lives of people around them. Consequently, they are more apt to feel stress when others in their network are feeling stress (Kessler and McLeod, 1984). Women are more likely than men to be both providers and recipients of support, although both men and women rely more on women for support during stressful times. Whereas married women use both their spouse and their friends as confidants, married men tend to rely solely on their wives (Edwards, Nazroo, and Brown, 1998).

3. Women are more vulnerable than men to stress due to their socialization to respond more passively, to introject rather than to express anger, and to use less effective coping skills (Kessler and McLeod, 1984). There is some research to support this notion. In a study of coping techniques used by college students, male students used more problem-focused coping (cognitive and behavioral attempts to control the meaning of the situation) whereas female students were more likely to use emotion-focused coping (attempting to regulate emotional responses elicited by the situation). Both male and female students rated the problem-focused techniques as being more effective (Ptacek, Smith, and Zanas, 1992). Countering this research is the fact that women appear to cope with many crises as well as or better than men (e.g., women typically deal better with the death of a partner, with financial difficulties, and with marital separation and divorce).

4. Continuing power differences between women and men in society and within families lead to the gender disparity in distress. Rosenfield (1989, 1992), focusing on married couples, has argued that women's relative lack of decision-making power within the family and the lesser resources and decreased prestige attached to the conventional feminine role of housewife cause and reflect this power differential. How does this affect psychological state?

Low power implies less actual control over the environment and thus lower perceptions of personal control. With diminished assessments of their ability to act on and affect their social world, individuals experience greater psychological distress. Thus ... women have higher rates of anxious and depressive symptoms because their positions of lower power produce lower actual control and thus lower perceived control than those of men. (Rosenfield, 1989:77–78)

5. A final perspective on this issue asserts that the size of the gender disparity in social stress has been exaggerated and misinterpreted. Aneshensel, Rutter, and Lachenbruch (1991) argue that most stress research has focused on a single disorder or stress outcome and then has assumed that those who have this disorder are victims of stress and those without the disorder are not. For example, much of the research which has found that women report higher rates of depression than men has concluded that women experience more stress. However, they argue that most research has focused on outcomes that are more common in women, and has neglected to study anti-social personality and alcohol abuse–dependence disorders that are more common among men. If the full gamut of stress outcomes is considered, women and men may be found to experience comparable levels of stress.

Gender, Work, and Psychological Distress. An important implication of these explanations is that women's different levels and types of participation in the workplace create conditions that lead to the gender disparity in distress. This suggests an avenue for study, namely comparing women who are full-time workers outside the home (both married and unmarried) with those who are employed part-time and those who are not employed outside the home. If it is simply a matter of "social roles," the benefits and liabilities of working should be the same for men and women. If, on the other hand, the effects of employment are conditional

on gender (a sex-role perspective), other factors related to expectations for men and women must be involved (Gore and Mangione, 1983).

Studies addressing these questions have not always produced a coherent picture. Some research has found a reduced disparity in gender distress when the wife is employed, but other research has not. Moreover, some of the research that identifies smaller differences traces them to increased distress in males rather than a decrease in distress in females. Most research has pointed to positive effects for women who work outside the home, but other research has failed to find differences between employed women and housewives. Even when such a difference is discovered, both groups of women have higher distress scores than employed men. The box "Does Marriage Lead to More or Less Stress?" adds to this discussion.

Efforts to sort through these research findings have produced three primary perspectives—role overload, role enhancement, and role context. The "role overload" perspective is based on the proposition that there is only so much time and energy available in the day. When women have to combine homemaking, child-rearing, and full-time employment responsibilities, there is role overload—too much work and too many responsibilities, which is obviously a stressful situation. The same combination of activities may not overload men because they engage in considerably fewer homemaking and child-rearing activities—even when their partner is employed. Because many women feel primary responsibility for household obligations, and many men do not, it can be more psychologically distressing for women to occupy the multiple roles of partner, parent, and worker. A study of dual-career couples in the United States, Sweden, and the Netherlands found that working women in all three countries do more household chores and child care and make more compromises with their job than do their partners (Gjerdingen et al., 2000).

This same pattern exists relative to work positions that extend beyond specified hours. Does the frequency of receiving work-related contact outside of normal working hours (potential inter-role conflict) create guilt for individuals? The answer is yes, but for women only. Such contact does not lead to feelings of guilt or distress for men, but these consequences do occur for women—there is a gendered difference in the way that home and work responsibilities are experienced (Glavin, Schieman, and Reid, 2011).

The "role enhancement perspective" asserts that the more roles any person fulfills, the greater are the opportunities for social contacts, satisfaction, and self-esteem, and consequently better health and psychological well-being. According to this theory, feelings of anxiety or depression ought to be inversely related to the number of role involvements. This may occur directly or indirectly as contacts made through employment often become the most important non-kin source of social support for women who work outside the home.

IN THE FIELD

DOES MARRIAGE LEAD TO MORE OR LESS STRESS?

Married people report less stress than those who are not married (see Figure 5–3).

Compared with married adults of the same age, those who are single, cohabiting, divorced, or widowed all have higher levels of psychological distress, anxiety, and depression. (Very young married adults are the only exception— they report as much depression as their unmarried counterparts.) This relationship is strong and cannot be explained by a selection factor (i.e., that those with higher well-being are more likely to get married) (Mirowsky and Ross, 2003).

Why does this relationship occur? The most important reason is that married people have higher-quality, more supportive relationships. They receive more emotional support—a greater sense of being cared about, loved, esteemed, and valued as a person. Although there is much variation, in general they are happier in their personal relationships. Married people are also more likely to experience economic well-being and less likely to experience economic hardship or crisis (Mirowsky and Ross, 2003).

Is it better to be happily single than unhappily married? The answer is yes. Studies show that it is healthier to live alone than with a partner who does not provide supportive qualities. One 12-year study found that happily married women in their forties and fifties were less likely to develop heart disease and stroke than their single counterparts, but that single women were less likely to develop these conditions than the unhappily married (Troxel et al., 2005). Over the last few decades, the health of single individuals has become more similar to that of married people, while the health of the widowed, divorced, and separated compared with married people has got even worse (Liu and Umberson, 2008).

Do men and women benefit equally from marriage in terms of health? The answer is no. Although both benefit, men benefit more. There are three main reasons for this. (1) Women experience greater child-rearing stress because they often have primary child-rearing responsibility. (2) Women more often experience work–family conflict because they have more child-rearing responsibilities whether or not they are employed outside the home. (3) Wives tend to provide more emotional support for husbands than husbands do for wives.

Figure 5–3   Marital Status and Health

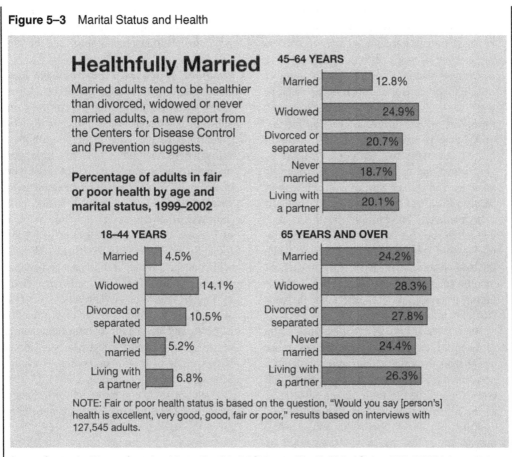

Healthfully Married

Married adults tend to be healthier than divorced, widowed or never married adults, a new report from the Centers for Disease Control and Prevention suggests.

Percentage of adults in fair or poor health by age and marital status, 1999–2002

45–64 YEARS

Married	12.8%
Widowed	24.9%
Divorced or separated	20.7%
Never married	18.7%
Living with a partner	20.1%

18–44 YEARS

Married	4.5%
Widowed	14.1%
Divorced or separated	10.5%
Never married	5.2%
Living with a partner	6.8%

65 YEARS AND OVER

Married	24.2%
Widowed	28.3%
Divorced or separated	27.8%
Never married	24.4%
Living with a partner	26.3%

NOTE: Fair or poor health status is based on the question, "Would you say [person's] health is excellent, very good, good, fair or poor," results based on interviews with 127,545 adults.

Source: Centers for Disease Control and Prevention. "Marital Status and Health: United States, 1999–2002." Advance Data, Number 351 (Atlanta, GA: Centers for Disease Control and Prevention, 2004).

The third perspective—the "role context perspective"—asserts that employment outside the home has neither inherently positive nor inherently negative consequences for stress level, but rather it is dependent on particular factors within the personal, family, and work environments, and on the "meaning" that is attached to work and familial roles (Simon, 1997). What are these additional factors?

1. *The woman's desire to work outside the home.* Waldron and Herold (1986) have demonstrated the importance of attitude toward the effects of employment. Based on a national sample of middle-aged women, they found that for women who desired to work outside the home, employment had beneficial effects and non-employment had detrimental effects. No specific effects were noted for women who had unfavorable or neutral attitudes toward outside employment.

2. *The woman's perception of the balance of benefits and liabilities in outside employment.* The greater the "role integration"—that

is, the balance of role satisfaction and role stress within and between roles—the greater is the sense of well-being. This is related to the number of roles. Thoits (1986) posits a curvilinear relationship between the number of role involvements and well-being—that is, there is role enhancement up to a certain threshold, whereupon role overload begins. Well-being is also affected by the compatibility of the work role with other roles (e.g., child care), the extent to which each can be handled, and the amount of spousal support received for the work career. Spousal support is jeopardized, however, if the husband is distressed by his wife's outside employment—something that often happens when the husband's relative share of the household income decreases or demands that his contribution to household domestic labor increase (Rosenfield, 1992).

Bird (1999) discovered that inequity in the division of household labor creates more stress than does the actual amount of labor performed. Her research confirmed that women continued to do a higher percentage of household chores, and that husbands' contributions were about the amount that they desired, but that wives' contributions went beyond the point of maximum psychological benefit. This may explain why there are health benefits for women who work, but that these benefits diminish when work is combined with care of a young child (Schnittker, 2007).

In addition, perception of the trajectory of one's work career (whether one perceives career movement in an upward or downward direction, and whether one perceives responsibilities and compensation to be appropriate for one's position) affects work satisfaction and ultimately health. Both objective and subjective occupational mobility predict health patterns—upward mobility is associated with better health, and downward mobility is associated with worse health. However, perception of mobility is the better predictor (Wilkinson, Shippee, and Ferraro, 2012).

3. *Qualities of the work environment itself.* Because women, on average, occupy lower-level work positions than men, they are subject to greater stress relative to work conditions, sexual harassment, and job instability. These positions often offer little work autonomy or control, and have less work complexity. Work complexity refers to the amount of variability in the job, and is an indicator of its degree of challenge, its level of interest, the extent to which it is psychologically gratifying, and the likelihood that it will contribute to the individual's self-esteem (Pugliesi, 1995). These job factors are related to higher levels of psychological distress. Workplaces in which gender discrimination is perceived add another important source of stress for women, and it has been linked with negative health outcomes (Pavalko, Mossakowski, and Hamilton, 2003).

Even when women move into positions of increased job authority, there are not necessarily the same benefits as there are for men. Pudrovska and Karraker (2014) studied the relationship between gender, job authority, and depression. They defined job authority as having the ability to hire and fire and to influence pay. As expected, they found that men without authority in their position were more likely to experience depression than men in authority positions. However, the reverse was found for women—those without job authority were less depressed than women with job authority.

What could cause this contrary pattern? The authors contend that the difference is due to gendered cultural expectations for men and women in the workplace. The exercise of job authority may be seen as being consistent with traditional masculine stereotypes that emphasize power, ambition, and dominance. For women, however, exercising job authority may be inconsistent with traditional normative expectations, such as nurturance, empathy, and attachment. This may lead to a workplace that is more accepting of male authority than of female authority—a situation that increases stress and has a negative impact on health for female decision makers.

Over the last few decades, the proportion of women who work has increased, and women have moved in larger numbers into professional, managerial, and highly skilled positions. These positions offer higher salaries, better benefits, and more work control. All of these factors are beneficial to health. At the same time, pressures on workers to work longer hours, be more productive, and work non-standard schedules have also increased. This may have led to some changes in the background of women who choose to stay at home to rear children full time, thus further complicating this relationship (Pavalko, Gong, and Long, 2007).

According to Rosenfield (1989), women's employment does give them greater power and a greater sense of personal control. These are health enhancers. However, something else occurs simultaneously—something that occurs with lesser intensity for men—and that is the likelihood of role overload when work responsibilities are added to being the primary household/child caretaker. This role overload decreases feelings of personal control—with a negative impact on health. The complex maze of possibilities within this configuration of roles will require substantial additional research if it is to be fully understood.

SUMMARY

Stress has been defined as "a state of imbalance within a person, elicited by an actual or perceived disparity between environmental demands and the person's capacity to cope with these demands." The configuration of the stress process can be stated in this way: Various stressful situations (or stressors) occur and are appraised by the individual as to their degree of threat. Individuals are forced to cope with those involving some threat; stressors that are unsuccessfully resolved lead to negative stress outcomes. Throughout the process, social support can help to mediate the stress–stress outcome relationship.

Stressors are of two basic types—specific life events and chronic strains (the latter being more enduring problems in everyday life). Pearlin has classified chronic strains according to problems created in discharging our role obligations: (1) role overload, (2) interpersonal problems within role sets, (3) inter-role conflict, (4) role captivity, and (5) role restructuring and to ambient stressors—those that are enduring but not tied to occupancy of a particular role.

Interpretation and appraisal of stressors are key aspects of the stress process. It is the perceived threat, rather than the actual threat, to which a person responds. If a threat is perceived, the individual may activate certain coping responses (psychological, cognitive, and behavioral techniques) from his or her repertoire and also use social support. Negative stress outcomes occur through the individual's taking on certain health-impairing behaviors, such as cigarette smoking, or through specific psychophysiological changes, including a weakening of the immune system.

Certain groups have higher rates of psychological distress—those with lower socioeconomic status (who are exposed to more stressful life events and have fewer resources with which to combat them), African Americans, sexual minorities, and females (possibly due to women being exposed to more stressful life events, caring more about others' problems, being especially vulnerable to stress due to the effects of socialization, and responding to having less access to power within families and within society). Employment affects stress level differently for women than for men; this may be due to the fact that women often maintain primary responsibility for household tasks and child rearing, even when they are in the labor force.

HEALTH ON THE INTERNET

A significant trend in the United States is the rapidly increasing number of households that are caring for elderly relatives (often taking them into their homes). More than 44 million Americans (more than one in five) provide this caregiving today—a collective 37 billion hours of unpaid caregiving worth US$470 billion. Ten million of these caregivers are "millennials" (aged 18 to 34 years) who are caring for adult family members. The number is expected to increase in the coming years. This trend is a consequence of both the increasing number of people living into their eighties and nineties, often with limitation on their ability to care for themselves, *and* the very high cost of assisted living and nursing home care. Research has found that providing care has a negative impact on both the physical and mental health of the caregiver.

To learn more about the relationship between caregiving and social stress, check out the following:

www.womenshealth.gov/publications/
our-publications/fact-sheet/caregiver-
stress.cfm#b

Answer the following questions: How is "caregiver" defined? Who provides caregiving services? What activities do caregivers often provide?

What is **caregiver stress**? What are the signs and symptoms of caregiver stress? How does caregiver stress affect health? What can caregivers do to prevent or relieve stress?

DISCUSSION CASE

The stress process as it relates to socioeconomic status, race, sexual orientation, and gender was discussed in this chapter. Think about social stress as it relates to racial and ethnic minorities and female students at your college or university. Are racial/ethnic minority and/or female students more likely (or less likely) to face any particular stressful discrete life events than those faced by all students? Are racial/ethnic minority and/or female students more likely (or less likely) to face any of the five sources of chronic strain (role overload, interpersonal conflicts within role sets, inter-role conflict, role captivity, and role restructuring) or ambient stressors than those faced by all students?

Do racial/ethnic minority students cope with stress or use social support differently to other students? Do female students cope with stress or use social support differently to male students?

GLOSSARY

buffering effects model of social support
caregiver stress
chronic strains
coping
double disadvantage hypothesis
exposure hypothesis
homeostasis
interactionism
life events

looking-glass self
main effects model of social support
mediators of stress
social construction of reality
social support
sociological imagination
stress
Thomas theorem
vulnerability hypothesis

REFERENCES

Agus, David B. 2011 *The End of Illness*. New York: Free Press.

Altheide, David. 1995 *An Ecology of Communication: Cultural Formats of Control*. Piscataway, NJ: Aldine Transaction.

Aneshensel, Carol S., Carolyn M. Rutter, and Peter A. Lachenbruch. 1991 "Social Structure, Stress, and Mental Health: Competing Conceptual and Analytic Models." *American Sociological Review*, 56:166–178.

Avison, William R., and R. Jay Turner. 1988 "Stressful Life Events and Depressive Symptoms: Disaggregating the Effects of Acute Stressors and Chronic Strains." *Journal of Health and Social Behavior*, 29:253–264.

Berger, Peter L., and Thomas Luckmann. 1967 *The Social Construction of Reality: A Treatise in the Sociology of Knowledge*. Garden City, NY: Anchor Books.

Bird, Chloe E. 1999 "Gender, Household Labor, and Psychological Distress: The Impact of the Amount and Division of Housework." *Journal of Health and Social Behavior*, 40:32–45.

Bjorkenstam, Emma, Bo Burstrom, Lars Brannstrom, Bo Vinnerljung, Charlotte Bjorkenstam, and Anne R. Pebley. 2015 "Cumulative Exposure to Childhood Stressors and Subsequent Psychological Distress." *Social Science and Medicine*, 142:109–117.

Blonna, Richard. 2007 *Coping With Stress in a Changing World*, 4th ed. Boston, MA: McGraw-Hill.

Brown, Barbara B. 1984 *Between Health and Illness*. New York: Bantam Books.

Bruess, Clint, and Glenn Richardson. 1995 *Decisions for Health*, 4th ed. Dubuque, IA: Brown & Benchmark Publishers.

Centers for Disease Control and Prevention. 2004 "Marital Status and Health: United States, 1999–2002." Advance Data, Number 351. Atlanta, GA: Centers for Disease Control and Prevention.

Cooley, Charles H. 1964 *Human Nature and the Social Order*. New York: Schocken.

Cornwell, Erin Y., and Linda J. Waite. 2009 "Social Disconnectedness, Perceived Isolation, and Health Among Older Adults." *Journal of Health and Social Behavior*, 50:31–48.

Dohrenwend, Bruce P. 2000 "The Role of Adversity and Stress in Psychopathology: Some Evidence and Its Implications for Theory and Research." *Journal of Health and Social Behavior*, 41:1–19.

Downey, Liam, and Marieke Van Willigen. 2005 "Environmental Stressors: The Mental Health Impacts of Living near Industrial Activity." *Journal of Health and Social Behavior*, 46:289–305.

Durkheim, Émile. (trans.) 1951 *Suicide: A Study in Sociology*. New York: The Free Press.

Edwards, Angela C., James Y. Nazroo, and George W. Brown. 1998 "Gender Differences in Marital Support Following a Shared Life Event." *Social Science and Medicine*, 46:1077–1085.

Fischer, Kathy E., Mark Kittleson, Roberta Ogletree, Kathleen Welshimer, Paula Woehlke, and John Benshoff. 2000 "The Relationship of Parental Alcoholism and Family Dysfunction to Stress Among College Students." *Journal of American College Health*, 48:151–156.

Frost, David M., Keren Lehavot, and Ilan H. Meyer. 2015 "Minority Stress and Physical Health Among Sexual Minority Group Members." *Journal of Behavioral Medicine*, 38:1–8.

Gadalla, Tahany M. 2009 "Determinants, Correlates and Mediators of Psychological Distress: A Longitudinal Study." *Social Science and Medicine*, 68:2199–2205.

Gjerdingen, Dwenda, Patricia McGovern, Marrie Bekker, Ulf Lundberg, and Tineke Willemsen. 2000 "Women's Work Roles and Their Impact on Health, Well-Being, and Career: Comparisons between the United States, Sweden, and the Netherlands." *Women and Health*, 31:1–20.

Glavin, Paul, Scott Schieman, and Sarah Reid. 2011 "Boundary-Spanning Work Demands and Their Consequences for Guilt and Psychological Distress." *Journal of Health and Social Behavior*, 52:43–57.

Gore, Susan, and Thomas W. Mangione. 1983 "Social Roles, Sex Roles and Psychological Distress: Additive and Interactive Models of Sex Differences." *Journal of Health and Social Behavior*, 24:300–312.

Green, Adam I. 2008 "Health and Sexual Status in an Urban Gay Enclave: An Application of the Stress Process Model." *Journal of Health and Social Behavior*, 49:436–451.

Grollman, Eric A. 2012 "Multiple Forms of Perceived Discrimination and Health among Adolescents and Young Adults." *Journal of Health and Social Behavior*, 53:199–214.

——. 2014 "Multiple Disadvantaged Statuses and Health: The Role of Multiple Forms of Discrimination." *Journal of Health and Social Behavior*, 55:3–19.

Hatzenbuehler, Mark L., Anna Bellatorre, Yeonjin Lee, Brian K. Finch, Peter Muennig, and Kevin Fiscella. 2014 "Structural Stigma and All-Cause Mortality in Sexual Minority Populations." *Social Science and Medicine*, 103:33–41.

Hill, Terrence D., Catherine E. Ross, and Ronald J. Angel. 2005 "Neighborhood Disorder, Psychophysiological Distress, and Health." *Journal of Health and Social Behavior*, 46: 170–186.

Holmes, Thomas H., and Richard H. Rahe. 1967 "The Social Readjustment Rating Scale." *Journal of Psychosomatic Research*, 11:213–218.

Hughto, Jaclyn M. W., Sari L. Reisner, and John E. Pachankis. 2015 "Transgender Stigma and Health: A Critical Review of Stigma

Determinants, Mechanisms, and Interventions." *Social Science and Medicine*, 147:222–231.

Kail, Ben L., Katie L. Acosta, and Eric R. Wright. 2015 "State-Level Marriage Equality and the Health of Same-Sex Couples." *American Journal of Public Health*, 105:1101–1105.

Keith, Verna M. 1993 "Gender, Financial Strain, and Psychological Distress among Older Adults." *Research on Aging*, 15:123–147.

Kessler, Ronald C., and Jane D. McLeod. 1984 "Sex Differences in Vulnerability to Undesirable Life Events." *American Sociological Review*, 49:620–631.

Kessler, Ronald C., and Harold W. Neighbors. 1986 "A New Perspective on the Relationships Among Race, Social Class, and Psychological Distress." *Journal of Health and Social Behavior*, 27:107–115.

Kobasa, Suzanne C. 1979 "Stressful Life Events, Personality, and Health: An Inquiry into Hardiness." *Journal of Personality and Social Psychology*, 37:1–11.

Lantz, Paula M., James S. House, Richard P. Mero, and David R. Williams. 2005 "Stress, Life Events, and Socioeconomic Disparities in Health: Results from the Americans' Changing Lives Study." *Journal of Health and Social Behavior*, 46:274–288.

Lenhart, Amanda, Rich Ling, Scott Campbell, and Kristen Purcell. 2010 *Teens and Mobile Phones*. Washington, DC: Pew Research Center. www.pewinternet.org/Reports/2010/Teens-and-Mobile-Phones.aspx.

Lieberman, Morton A. 1982 "The Effects of Social Supports on Responses to Stress." Pp. 764–783 in *Handbook of Stress: Theoretical and Clinical Aspects*, Leo Goldberger and Shlomo Breznitz (eds.). New York: The Free Press.

Lincoln, Karen D., Linda M. Chatters, and Robert J. Taylor. 2003 "Psychological Distress Among Black and White Americans: Differential Effects of Social Support, Negative Interaction, and Personal Control." *Journal of Health and Social Behavior*, 44:390–407.

Liu, Hui, and Debra Umberson. 2008 "The Times They Are A Changin': Marital Status and Health Differentials from 1972 to 2002." *Journal of Health and Social Behavior*, 49:239–253.

Lopez, Corina, Michael Antoni, Erin Fekete, and Frank Penedo. 2012 "Ethnic Identity and Perceived Stress in HIV+ Minority Women: The Role of Coping Self-Efficacy and Social

Support." *International Journal of Behavioral Medicine*, 19:23–28.

McGee, Robin E., and Nancy J. Thompson. 2015 "Unemployment and Depression among Emerging Adults in 12 States, Behavioral Risk Factor Surveillance System, 2010." *Preventing Chronic Disease*, 12:E38. doi: 10.5888/pcd12.140451.

McLeod, Jane D., and Ronald C. Kessler. 1990 "Socioeconomic Status Differences in Vulnerability to Undesirable Life Events." *Journal of Health and Social Behavior*, 31:162–172.

McPherson, Miller, Lynn Smith-Lovin, and Matthew E. Brashears. 2006 "Social Isolation in America: Changes in Core Discussion Networks Over Two Decades." *American Sociological Review*, 71:353–375.

Menzies, Heather. 2005 *No Time: Stress and the Crisis of Modern Life*. Vancouver: Douglas & McIntyre.

Meyer, Ilan H., Sharon Schwartz, and David M. Frost. 2008 "Social Patterning of Stress and Coping: Does Disadvantaged Social Statuses Confer More Stress and Fewer Coping Resources?" *Social Science and Medicine*, 67:368–379.

Mirowsky, John, and Catherine E. Ross. 2003 *Social Causes of Psychological Distress*, 2nd ed. Hawthorne, NY: Aldine de Gruyter.

Mossakowski, Krysia N. 2003 "Coping With Perceived Discrimination: Does Ethnic Identity Protect Mental Health?" *Journal of Health and Social Behavior*, 44:318–331.

Pavalko, Eliza K., Krysia N. Mossakowski, and Vanessa J. Hamilton. 2003 "Does Perceived Discrimination Affect Health? Longitudinal Relationships between Work Discrimination and Women's Physical and Emotional Health." *Journal of Health and Social Behavior*, 43:18–33.

Pavalko, Eliza K., Fang Gong, and J. Scott Long. 2007 "Women's Work, Cohort Change, and Health." *Journal of Health and Social Behavior*, 48:352–368.

Pearlin, Leonard I. 1983 "Role Strains and Personal Stress." Pp. 3–32 in *Psychosocial Stress: Trends in Theory and Research*, Howard B. Kaplan (ed.). New York: Academic Press.

——. 1989 "The Sociological Study of Stress." *Journal of Health and Social Behavior*, 30:241–256.

Pearlin, Leonard I., and Carmi Schooler. 1978 "The Structure of Coping." *Journal of Health and Social Behavior*, 19:2–21.

Pearlin, Leonard I., and Carol S. Aneshensel. 1986 "Coping and Social Supports: Their Functions and Applications." Pp. 417–437 in *Application of Social Science to Clinical Medicine and Health Policy*, Linda H. Aiken and David Mechanic (eds.). New Brunswick, NJ: Rutgers University Press.

Pearlin, Leonard I., and Alex Bierman. 2013 "Current Issues and Future Directions in Research into the Stress Process." Pp. 325–340 in *Handbook of the Sociology of Mental Health*, Carol S. Aneshensel, Jo C. Phelan, and Alex Bierman (eds.). New York: Springer.

Pearlin, Leonard I., Scott Schieman, Elena M. Fazio, and Stephen C. Meersman. 2005 "Stress, Health, and the Life Course: Some Conceptual Perspectives." *Journal of Health and Social Behavior*, 46:205–219.

Poteat, Tonia, Danielle German, and Deanna Kerrigan. 2013 "Managing Uncertainty: A Grounded Theory of Stigma in Transgender Health Care Encounters." *Social Science and Medicine*, 84:22–29.

Priest, Naomi, Yin Paradies, Brigid Trenery, Mandy Truong, Saffron Karlsen, and Yvonne Kelly. 2013 "A Systematic Review of Studies Examining the Relationship Between Reported Racism and Health and Wellbeing for Children and Young People." *Social Science and Medicine*, 95:115–127.

Ptacek, J.T., Ronald E. Smith, and John Zanas. 1992 "Gender, Appraisal, and Coping: A Longitudinal Analysis." *Journal of Personality*, 60:747–770.

Pudrovska, Tetyana, and Amelia Karraker. 2014 "Gender, Job Authority, and Depression." *Journal of Health and Social Behavior*, 55:424–441.

Pugliesi, Karen. 1995 "Work and Well-Being: Gender Differences in the Psychological Consequences of Employment." *Journal of Health and Social Behavior*, 36:57–71.

Richman, Judith A., Lea Cloninger, and Kathleen M. Rospenda. 2008 "Macro-level Stressors, Terrorism, and Mental Health Outcomes: Broadening the Stress Paradigm," *American Journal of Public Health*, 98:323–329.

Rosenfield, Sarah. 1989 "The Effects of Women's Employment: Personal Control and Sex Differences in Mental Health." *Journal of Health and Social Behavior*, 30:77–91.

——. 1992 "The Costs of Sharing: Wives' Employment and Husbands' Mental Health." *Journal of Health and Social Behavior*, 33:213–225.

Ross, Catherine E., and John Mirowsky. 2013 "The Sense of Personal Control: Social Structural Causes and Emotional Consequences." Pp. 379–402 in *Handbook of the Sociology of Mental Health,* Carol S. Aneshensel, Jo C. Phelan, and Alex Bierman (eds.). New York: Springer.

Schnittker, Jason. 2007 "Working More and Feeling Better: Women's Health, Employment, and Family Life, 1974–2004." *American Sociological Review,* 72:221–238.

Schwab, Reiko. 1990 "Paternal and Maternal Coping with the Death of a Child." *Death Studies,* 14:407–422.

Simon, Robin W. 1997 "The Meanings Individuals Attach to Role Identities and Their Implications for Mental Health." *Journal of Health and Social Behavior,* 38:256–274.

Smith, Kristen P., and Nicholas A. Christakis. 2008 "Social Networks and Health." *Annual Review of Sociology,* 34:405–429.

Stoklos, D. 1986 "A Congruence Analysis of Human Stress." Pp. 35–64 in *Stress and Anxiety: A Sourcebook of Theory and Research*, Charles D. Spielberger and Irwin G. Sarason (eds.). Washington, DC: Hemisphere.

Thoits, Peggy A. 1986 "Multiple Identities: Examining Gender and Marital Status Differences in Distress." *American Sociological Review,* 51:259–272.

——. 2006 "Personal Agency in the Stress Process." *Journal of Health and Social Behavior,* 47:309–323.

——. 2011 "Mechanisms Linking Social Ties and Support to Physical and Mental Health." *Journal of Health and Social Behavior,* 52:145–161.

——. 2013 "Self, Identity, Stress, and Mental Health." Pp. 357–377 in *Handbook of the Sociology of Mental Health,* Carol S. Aneshensel, Jo C. Phelan, and Alex Bierman (eds.). New York: Springer.

Thomas, William I., and Dorothy S. Thomas. 1928 *The Child in America: Behavior Problems and Programs.* New York: Alfred A. Knopf.

Troxel, Wendy M., Karen A. Matthews, Linda C. Gallo, and Lewis H. Kuller. 2005 "Marital Quality and Occurrence of the Metabolic Syndrome in Women." *Archives of Internal Medicine,* 165:1022–1027.

Turner, R. Jay, and Donald A. Lloyd. 1999 "The Stress Process and the Social Distribution of Depression." *Journal of Health and Social Behavior,* 40:374–404.

Ueno, Koji. 2010 "Mental Health Differences Between Young Adults With and Without Same-Sex Contact: A Simultaneous Examination of Underlying Mechanisms." *Journal of Health and Social Behavior,* 51:391–407.

Umberson, Debra, Robert Crosnoe, and Corinne Reczek. 2010 "Social Relationships and Health Behavior." *Annual Review of Sociology,* 36:139–157.

Waldron, Ingrid, and Joan Herold. 1986 "Employment, Attitudes toward Employment, and Women's Health." *Women and Health,* 11:79–98.

Wheaton, Blair, and Shirin Montazer. 2009 "Stressors, Stress, and Distress." Pp. 171–199 in *A Handbook for the Study of Mental Health: Social Context, Theories, and Systems* (2nd ed.), Teresa L. Scheid, and Tony N. Brown (eds.). New York: Cambridge University Press.

Wilkinson, Lindsay R., Tetyana P. Shippee, and Kenneth R. Ferraro. 2012 "Does Occupational Mobility Influence Health Among Working Women? Comparing Objective and Subjective Measures of Work Trajectories." *Journal of Health and Social Behavior,* 53:432–447.

Yang, Yang, C. 2006 "How Does Functional Disability Affect Depressive Symptoms in Late Life? The Role of Perceived Social Support and Psychological Resources." *Journal of Health and Social Behavior,* 47:355–372.

Yang, Yang C., Courtney Boen, Karen Gerkin, Ting Li, Kristen Schorpp, and Kathleen M. Harris. 2016 "Social Relationships and Physiological Determinants of Longevity across the Human Life Span." *Proceedings of the National Academy of Sciences of the United States of America,* 113:578–583.

CHAPTER 6

Health Behavior

Learning Objectives

- Identify and define the key dimensions of "health."
- Identify and distinguish between the four dimensions of health behavior—prevention, detection, promotion, and protection.
- Explain the difference between a "macro" and a "micro" approach to understand participation in health behaviors. Discuss

these factors as they relate to engaging in adequate physical exercise or smoking cigarettes.

- Distinguish between the *health belief model* and the *theory of reasoned action* in terms of the factors emphasized as being important influences on participation in health behavior.

In the last few decades, medical sociology, like the medical profession and society in general, has been focusing more attention than ever on health and health-related behaviors. This focus has produced some important questions. What does it mean to be "healthy" or "well"? To what extent do people engage in behaviors that will promote health or prevent disease—or at least not engage in health-damaging behaviors? What are the strongest influences on participation in these positive and negative health behaviors? How do society and culture encourage people to live a healthy or non-healthy lifestyle? To what extent should public policy attempt to regulate health-enhancing and health-harming behaviors?

THE CONCEPT OF HEALTH

Most clinicians and laypeople have come to understand that health is a broad-based concept that is comprised of several dimensions. John Ware (1986) reviewed the literature of studies

on health and identified six primary orientations (or dimensions) used by researchers:

1. *Physical functioning.* A focus on physical ability to take care of self, being mobile and participating in physical activities, ability to perform everyday activities, and limiting the number of days confined to bed.
2. *Mental health.* A focus on positive emotional health, psychological well-being, control of emotions and behaviors, and limiting feelings of anxiety and depression.
3. *Social well-being.* A focus on visiting with or speaking on the telephone with friends and family, and on the number of close friends and acquaintances.
4. *Role functioning.* A focus on freedom of limitations in discharging usual role activities, such as work or school.
5. *General health perceptions.* A focus on positive self-assessment of current health status, and on limiting the amount of pain that is being experienced.

6. *Symptoms.* A focus on limiting the number of physical and psychophysiological symptoms.

The Biomedical Focus

The traditional **biomedical definition of health** focuses solely on an individual's physiological state and the presence or absence of symptoms of sickness. **Health** is defined simply as the absence of disease or physiological malfunction. It is not a positive state, but the absence of a negative state—if you're not sick, you're well. According to Wolinsky (1988), the biomedical model makes four primary assumptions that limit its utility for completely understanding health and illness:

1. The presence of disease, its diagnosis, and its treatment are all completely objective phenomena—symptoms and signs provide accurate and unbiased information from which valid diagnosis can unfailingly be made. However, this assumption is faulty. For example, studies have found that individuals' cultural background affects not only their reaction to symptoms but also how these symptoms are reported to physicians, and that the presentation of symptoms can influence diagnosis.
2. Only medical professionals are capable of defining health and illness. In reality, however, both the patient and his or her significant others are involved in the process. While one must not discount the power that society has granted to physicians for defining health and illness, a great deal of diagnosis and treatment takes place outside the physician's office.
3. Health and illness should be defined solely in terms of physiological malfunction. In fact, people are not merely biological beings; they are also psychological and social creatures, and state of health is affected by all three aspects.

4. Health is defined as merely the absence of disease. This focuses attention on the malfunctioning part of the organism but excludes the rest of the positively functioning being. Thus much may be learned about disease, but little is known about health.

The Sociological (Sociocultural) Definition of Health

Sociologists typically consider all six dimensions in defining health, and emphasize the social and cultural aspects of health and illness. This approach focuses on an individual's capacity to perform roles and tasks of everyday living, and acknowledges that there are social differences in defining health.

Capacity to Perform Roles and Tasks. Objecting to the biomedical definition, Talcott Parsons suggested that health be viewed as the ability to comply with social norms. In a **sociological definition of health**, he defined health as "the state of optimum capacity of an individual for the effective performance of the roles and tasks for which he has been socialized" (Parsons, 1972:173). Note the almost completely opposite orientation of this definition to the biomedical approach—no assumption is made that disease can be objectified, the focus is much broader (and more socially relevant) than mere physiological malfunctioning, the individual's own definition of his or her health is given centrality (rather than the physician's definition), and the definition is stated in positive terms. According to this approach, health is not just the lack of something—it is a positive capacity to fulfill one's roles; it is not just a physiological condition—it includes all the dimensions of individuals that affect social participation.

Social Differences in Defining Health. Twaddle (1974) sees health as being defined more by social than by physical criteria. He views health and illness as being on a continuum between the perfect state of health and the perfect state of illness (death). While "normal" health and illness fall somewhere between the two extremes, what may be considered a healthy state for one person may be considered unhealthy by another. Perception of health is relative to one's culture (e.g., being 10 pounds overweight is suggestive of ill health in some cultures but is socially approved in others) and one's position in the social structure (e.g., back pain that may cause a salaried worker to miss a day of work might be ignored by an hourly wage worker), and is influenced by social criteria.

Research has demonstrated that social factors do influence how individuals define personal health status. For example, data from the Health and Lifestyle Survey, a national survey of men and women living in England, Wales, and Scotland, show that personal definitions of health vary by age, gender, and perceived level of health (Blaxter, 2010). Young men conceptualize health in terms of physical strength and fitness, whereas women are more focused on energy, vitality, and the ability to cope. Older men and women consider health in terms of function as well as a state of contentment and happiness. Women of all ages often include social relationships in their definitions, whereas men rarely do so.

The World Health Organization Definition

The World Health Organization takes an inclusive approach by defining health as a state of complete physical, social, and mental well-being, and not merely the absence of disease or infirmity. This definition suggests that health relates to one's ability to cope with everyday activities, and to being a fully functioning human being—physically, socially, and emotionally. In this sense, health is a resource for everyday life. It is a positive concept that emphasizes social and personal resources as well as physical capacities (World Health Organization, 2016).

HEALTH BEHAVIOR

When medical sociologists first began to study **health behavior**, they conceptualized it as an activity undertaken by a person believing him- or herself to be healthy for the purpose of preventing health problems. In recent years, sociologists have recognized that health behavior actually consists of several dimensions and types of activities. Alonzo (1993) has identified four separate dimensions:

1. *Prevention.* The goal of preventive health behavior (prevention) is to minimize the risk of disease, injury, and disability. **Health-protective behaviors (HPBs)** include participating in regular exercise, maintaining a favorable weight and healthy diet, not smoking, and obtaining immunizations against communicable diseases.
2. *Detection.* Detection involves activities to detect disease, injury, or disability before symptoms appear, and includes medical examinations (e.g., taking blood pressure) or screenings for specific diseases.
3. *Promotion.* Health promotion activities consist of efforts to encourage and persuade individuals to engage in HPBs and to avoid or disengage from health-harming behaviors.
4. *Protection.* Health protection activities occur at the societal rather than the individual level, and include efforts to make the environment in which people live as healthy as possible. This involves monitoring the physical and social environments in which people live, physical structures and infrastructures, systems of transportation, available food, air, and water, and places of work, and developing social and economic policies that permit and encourage good health.

DESCRIBING INDIVIDUAL HEALTH BEHAVIORS

Prevention

Health-protective behaviors (HPBs) are individual actions taken to protect, promote, or maintain health. These actions are both prescriptive (e.g., eating a nutritious diet, wearing a seat belt when in a car, and getting adequate exercise) and proscriptive (e.g., avoiding unsafe driving, not smoking, and avoiding excessive alcohol consumption) in nature.

Today, the primary gauge of participation in healthy lifestyles is the **Behavioral Risk Factor Surveillance System (BRFSS)**, a survey conducted by the Centers for Disease Control and Prevention in conjunction with the states and territories. The survey consists of annual household telephone interviews conducted by state health departments. Participation in several key health-related behaviors is presented in Table 6–1.

The summary picture of participation in healthy lifestyles for American adults is very poor. Most Americans eat a poor diet (high in sugar, salt, and trans fats, and low in fruits and vegetables), take too little physical exercise, and almost one in five smokes cigarettes (the single most health-harmful behavior). Poor diet and inadequate exercise combine to lead to obesity (the second most dangerous lifestyle pattern). Excessive alcohol consumption is the behavior that contributes to the third largest number of deaths in the United States. Unlike the percentage of smokers (which is going down) or the percentage of people who are obese (which is going up), the percentage of people who drink excessively has remained at about the same level for at least the last decade.

The Multidimensional Basis of HPBs. Almost all research has discovered individual HPBs to have very small intercorrelations. This means that individual behaviors are often not related—engaging in one particular HPB (e.g., drinking in moderation) does not automatically mean (or even increase the chances of) engaging in another HPB (e.g., taking adequate exercise). For example, men are much more likely than women *both* to take more exercise and to drink immoderately (perhaps both reflecting a traditional male ethic).

Nevertheless, some consistent relationships between HPBs do exist. Some studies have found a positive relationship between smoking and alcohol consumption and between alcohol consumption and poor dietary habits. While level of exercise is highly dependent on age, in general those who eat nutritiously are more likely to exercise than those who have a poor diet. In fact, among those over 60 years of age, smokers and drinkers with a good diet are more than twice as likely to exercise vigorously as non-smokers and non-drinkers with a poor diet.

Correlates of Participation in HPBs. Participation in many of the HPBs is related to such sociodemographic characteristics as age, gender, race, level of education, and income.

TABLE 6–1   The 2000 and 2013 Behavioral Risk Factor Surveillance System for 50 States and DC

Behavioral Risk	Percentage Participating	
	2000	2013
Current smoker	20.0	19.0
Overweight/obese	61.6	64.8
Consume too few fruits and vegetables (2009 data)	76.9	76.6
Take too little physical exercise	78.2	79.5
Binge drinker		16.8

Centers for Disease Control and Prevention (CDC), *Behavioral Risk Factor Surveillance System Survey Data*, Atlanta, GA: U.S. Department of Health and Human Services, Centers for Disease Control and Prevention, 2016.

Studies have consistently found that females are more likely than males to engage in HPBs. Women are more likely to wear seat belts, less likely to smoke cigarettes and be heavy smokers, and less likely to drink alcohol excessively (men are three to four times more likely to be classified as problem drinkers). Women are even much more likely than men to wash their hands after coughing, sneezing, handling money, and especially after using a public restroom (88 percent of women do so, compared with only 67 percent of men). However, a much higher percentage of men than women take adequate exercise. Overall, though, women—especially young women—are much more likely to lead a healthy lifestyle.

Level of education, occupation, and income also affect participation in HPBs. People with high incomes are more likely to have a healthy lifestyle, especially older people. People working in occupations that require higher levels of education lead healthier lifestyles than those working in jobs that require less education. Lower levels of education are strongly associated with smoking and are linked to obesity and lack of exercise. People with lower incomes are more likely to smoke, less likely to exercise, and less likely to wear a seat belt.

Financial means even affect something as personal as birth control. Studies have long shown that a key reason why the teen birth rate is much higher in the United States than in other modern countries is that the U.S. provides less comprehensive sex education starting at an earlier age, and provides less access to contraceptives, especially those that are most effective in preventing pregnancy. A study published in the *New England Journal of Medicine* in 2014 found that when adolescent girls were given free birth control and encouraged to use the most effective methods of pregnancy prevention (long-acting reversible methods such as IUDs and implants, rather than birth control pills and condoms), the rates of pregnancy, abortion, and births all declined dramatically. When they were given information about effectiveness and free access, 72 percent of the adolescent girls selected IUDs or implants, whereas only 5 percent in a comparative group in the population did so (Secura et al., 2014).

In Colorado, a 6-year study (from 2009 to 2015) in which more than 30,000 women were given free, long-acting contraceptives found that there was a significant decrease in teen pregnancy rates, teen abortions, and teen births, and the state saved US$80 million. On the other hand, in Texas and other states that have recently made sharp cuts in family planning services, including free access to contraceptives, the rates of teen pregnancy, teen abortion, and teen birth have increased.

Black women are more likely to be obese and less likely to be physically active than white women, although these differences may be explained by differences in education, income, social networks, and life events. On the other hand, the smoking rates of black and white women are nearly identical, and about the same percentage of blacks and whites use seat belts.

The box on "Binge Drinking on College Campuses" addresses an important behavioral phenomenon among college students.

Detection

Today, a wide range of health-screening procedures are available, including periodic physical examinations, eye and dental examinations, blood pressure and cholesterol readings, prenatal and well-baby care, and screenings to detect cancer. These procedures are designed to identify and monitor health problems. Much research has demonstrated considerable health and cost benefits of participation in these services.

Correlates of Participation in Detection Services. Because these detection services are so effective, the question arises as to why some

IN THE FIELD

BINGE DRINKING ON COLLEGE CAMPUSES

In response to several binge drinking-related deaths among college students in the early 1990s, the Harvard School of Public Health conducted a national survey in 1993 in order to accurately describe the prevalence of binge drinking on campus. They defined binge drinking as the consumption of at least five drinks in a row for males or four drinks in a row for females during the 2 weeks prior to the survey. Based on this definition, they determined that 44 percent of students were binge drinkers.

Prompted by the publicity surrounding the deaths and the widely disseminated findings of the study, many institutions decided to challenge the traditional notion that binge drinking is simply part of the college experience. Drinking awareness and education courses were developed, alcohol counselors were employed, and more stringent college rules were established. However, follow-up surveys conducted throughout the mid- and late 1990s and early 2000s found that the percentage of binge drinkers on campus remained essentially unchanged. What had happened? Why did all the interventions basically not make a dent in the rate of binge drinking?

Close analysis of the data revealed that at least two significant changes did occur during this time period. Reflecting some increasing polarization on campus, both the rate of abstention (which is about 20 percent) and the rate of *frequent* binge drinking—three or more binges in the previous two weeks (which is over 20 percent)—increased during this time. Furthermore, whereas binge drinking among dormitory residents actually declined, it increased among students living off campus, especially among those living in fraternity and sorority houses. Thus the gaps between non-drinkers/light drinkers and intensive drinkers, and between Greeks and non-Greeks, had widened. The study found that while binging occurs among all campus subgroups, the rate is especially high among white male fraternity members (Caudill et al., 2006).

To what extent are students aware of binge drinking on their campus, and to what extent do they view it as a problem? The Harvard survey discovered that around 50 percent of students underestimated the binge drinking rate on their campus (29 percent overestimated it, and only 13 percent were on target). Binge drinkers were especially likely to *overestimate* the campus rate. Researchers found little evidence of a healthy alcohol-related social norm among fraternity members. Many view their level of consumption as being the same as that of their close friends (positive reinforcement), and they do not regard binging as a negative health behavior (Keeling, 2002).

Recently, many institutions have undertaken systematic research projects to test the effectiveness of various types of interventions. Perhaps most popular has been a *social norms approach to binge drinking*. The underlying theory of this approach is based on the evidence that students generally misperceive the frequency with which their peers engage in unhealthy behaviors, and that their own behavior is influenced by this misperception. Students who overestimate the percentage of binge drinkers—that is, who think binging is very common—on their campus are most likely to become binge drinkers themselves (Martens et al., 2006). Thus institutions have sought to create a more accurate impression among students about the actual percentage of binge drinkers on campus.

Studies have also shown that students who anticipate positive outcomes (e.g., socially or sexually) from binging are more likely to binge drink than students who have observed or recall negative outcomes (McBride et al., 2014). In response, many colleges are attempting to educate their students about the link between binging and a variety of negative outcomes, including suicide, violence, alcohol poisoning, and sexual assault.

It is not yet clear how successful these programs will be. On the one hand, the percentage of students who binge drink remains steady at around 40 percent. On the other hand, several limited experiments have found that participation in programs that emphasize the non-drinking or non-binging segment of students or emphasize more explicit discussion of the negative outcomes of binging have the potential to reduce the likelihood of problem and binge drinking (Hagman, Clifford, and Noel, 2007; Turner, Perkins, and Bauerle, 2008).

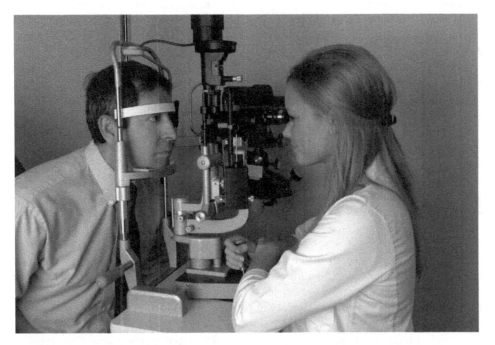

Undergoing routine eye examinations can be an effective "detection" behavior to monitor eye health and to identify any eye diseases or deterioration at an early stage.
© Gino Santa Maria/Fotolia.

people do not use them. One important reason is that the cost of some of these services discourages participation of people with low incomes and inadequate or no health insurance. In the United States, low-income women receive less prenatal care, and children from poor families are less likely than children in more affluent families to have a routine physical examination.

Studies comparing the use of preventive health measures by those who have and those who do not have health insurance illustrate the importance of financial status. Numerous studies have found that individuals who do not incur any expense when using preventive care services are much more likely than those who pay out of pocket to receive preventive health care services.

Cost of services can also be calculated in terms of factors other than available financial resources—for example, not having access to a physician, not being able to get off work (without loss of wages) to visit a physician, and, ultimately, becoming accustomed to going without care. When funds are unavailable or physicians are inaccessible, some families forgo detection services in the hope that they will be able to stay well without them.

Similarly, many poor parents forgo any medical contacts for themselves so that whatever funds are available can be used for their children. Research on families who receive services at free health clinics—where services are typically offered at no charge by volunteer physicians and dentists—has found that many parents bring their children to the clinic for preventive or therapeutic care, but do not ask to be seen themselves. Often, when staff inquire about this, the parent acknowledges having some medical problems that could be addressed by clinic staff. However, the parent has become so accustomed to doing without medical care that no request for personal services is made (Weiss, 2006).

Research has also discovered that level of education and racial/ethnic identity influence receipt of detection services. If other variables are held constant, people with a higher level of education tend to obtain more detection services, and whites tend to obtain more services than blacks or Hispanics. However, the influence of racial/ethnic group membership varies according to the specific type of detection service.

Healthy People 2010 and 2020

Every 10 years, the Department of Health and Human Services publishes a document containing broad national health goals and very specific targeted objectives for the following decade. *Healthy People 2010* was published in January 2000 and was designed to serve as the basis for the development of similar plans in communities and states across the country. Like previous documents published in 1980 and 1990, the document called upon the best scientific knowledge and a broad cross section of individuals from around the country.

The two overarching goals established for the first decade of the millennium were (1) to increase the quality and years of healthy life (i.e., to increase life expectancy and improve quality of life), and (2) to eliminate health disparities among population subgroups. Identified in the document were the ten "leading health indicators" for the nation: (1) physical activity, (2) overweight and obesity, (3) tobacco use, (4) substance abuse, (5) responsible sexual behavior, (6) mental health, (7) injury and violence, (8) environmental quality, (9) immunization, and (10) access to health care (United States Department of Health and Human Services, 2000).

Developing Healthy People 2020 was published in 2010 with the mission of improving health by strengthening health policy and practice, identifying nationwide health improvement priorities, and increasing public health awareness of the social determinants of health, disease, and disability. The planning committee identified four specific objectives for the decade:

- To eliminate preventable disease, disability, injury, and premature death
- To eliminate health disparities and improve health for all groups
- To create social and physical environments that promote good health for all
- To promote healthy development and healthy behaviors at every stage of life.

Jonathan Fielding, who is public health director in Los Angeles County and chaired the advisory committee developing the *2020* document, said:

We can't achieve what we want without looking at education, jobs, public health infrastructure, recognizing that poverty is a poison... it can't just be left to public health. We need to have elected leaders think about the health implications of what they do—tax policy, mass transit, agricultural subsidies—we need people in all sectors to be thinking about health implications. (Fielding, 2009:1)

The accompanying box, "Providing Prenatal Care in Western Europe," illustrates an important public health initiative in Western European countries.

EXPLAINING HEALTH BEHAVIOR

In the late nineteenth century, Max Weber identified both *macro* factors (social-structural conditions) and *micro* factors (personal choices) as being important influences on the formation of lifestyle. He referred to the impact of social-structural conditions and the opportunities afforded in life as "life chances", and the impact of personal choices as "life conduct," and argued that they are interlinked and interdependent (Weber, 1922/1978). This interdependence of life chances and life conduct can be particularly

---

IN COMPARATIVE FOCUS

PROVIDING PRENATAL CARE IN WESTERN EUROPE

The fact that many countries in the world have a lower infant mortality rate than the United States was documented in Chapter 3. A key part of the explanation for this pattern is that a higher percentage of babies born in the United States have low birth weight. Epidemiologists state that the most effective means of reducing the number of low-birth-weight babies is increasing access to prenatal care for all pregnant women.

Why do other countries fare better than the United States? McQuide, Delvaux, and Buekens (2000) examined the situation in 17 Western European nations and determined that all of them provide comprehensive and accessible prenatal care at no charge to all women. In contrast to the United States, no woman is ever turned aside due to inability to pay or lack of available services. All of these countries offer universal coverage for health services, readily available prenatal clinics, and special outreach programs for high-risk pregnant women and postpartum care. In some countries there are additional pregnancy (financial) allowances and the provision of prenatal care at work sites.

How do these countries afford this? The irony is that they actually save money by guaranteeing prenatal care to all women. Studies conducted in the United States have found that the average hospital delivery charge is almost twice as much for women who have not received prenatal care as for those who have (because of the greater likelihood of problem births), and that significantly higher expenses are incurred at least through childhood and adolescence (Henderson, 1994). Those who advocate guaranteeing prenatal care in the United States cite economic as well as moral reasons for their rationale.

If the United States guaranteed accessible prenatal care, would the infant mortality differential between the poor and the non-poor disappear? Much of it would, but probably not all of it. Continuing differences in such areas as nutrition, general health of the mother, and health knowledge may mean that some differential would remain (as it has in other countries), but the social class difference is much smaller in other countries than in the United States.

helpful in relation to health and illness. After all, certain life chances (e.g., socioeconomic status) can influence individual health behaviors (e.g., getting an annual medical checkup), and certain behaviors (e.g., excessive alcohol consumption) can be health damaging and negatively affect one's life chances. In the United States, without question, more attention has been directed to examining participation in health behaviors from the micro perspective. This section of the chapter reviews contributions from both approaches.

The Macro Approach to Health Behavior

Several medical sociologists have criticized the almost exclusive focus that policy makers and the general public have given to personal choices and individual behaviors in considering health behaviors. The late Irving Zola creatively captured this criticism in an oft-quoted metaphor:

> You know, sometimes it feels like this. There I am standing by the shore of a swiftly flowing river and I hear the cry of a drowning man. So I jump into the river, put my arms around him, pull him to shore and apply artificial respiration. Just when he begins to breathe, there is another cry for help. So I jump into the river, reach him, pull him to shore, apply artificial respiration, and then just as he begins to breathe, another cry for help. So back in the river again, reaching, pulling, applying, breathing and then another yell. Again and again, without end, goes the sequence. You know, I am so busy jumping in, pulling them to shore, applying artificial respiration, that I have **no** time to see who the hell is upstream pushing them all in. (Zola in McKinlay, 1974:502–503)

What are the upstream factors? Cohen, Scribner, and Farley (2000) identify four types of health-related macro-level factors that have a direct impact on individual behaviors. These include:

1. *The availability of protective or harmful consumer products* (e.g., tobacco, high-fat foods, sterile needles, and condoms).

2. *Physical structures/physical characteristics of products* (e.g., childproof medical containers, seat belts, and well-lit neighborhood streets).

3. *Social structures and policies* (e.g., enforcement of fines for selling tobacco to those who are underage, and provision of community day-care services).

4. *Media and cultural messages* (e.g., advertisements for alcohol products).

John McKinlay (1974) cogently argues that with regard to preventive health actions, we have spent most of our time downstream being preoccupied with encouraging people to avoid risky behaviors, while we have neglected the consumer products, physical structures, social structures, and media messages upstream that create and promote the options of risky behaviors. He states that a significantly greater impact on health is achieved by legislative acts that raise taxes or restrict advertising on cigarette manufacturers than by a multitude of efforts to persuade individual smokers to quit. Yet most efforts are directed downstream at the individual smokers rather than upstream at the tobacco industry.

In concurring with McKinlay, Nancy Milio (1981) states that the paramount factor in shaping the overall health status of society is the range of available health choices, rather than the personal choices made by individuals at any given time. Moreover, the range of choices is largely shaped by policy decisions in both government and private organizations. To have a real impact on the health of the people, she argues, it is national-level policy that must be affected. An example of this is the increase in the percentage of drivers using a seat belt—the largest increase in participation in a health-related behavior in the United States in the last 30 years. The significant upsurge in seat-belt usage occurred in the mid-1980s, when states began requiring their use. These legislative acts had far more effect on seat-belt usage than all

---

IN THE FIELD

SYRINGE EXCHANGE PROGRAMS

One of the most common methods of transmission of HIV and hepatitis C is the sharing of contaminated needles. The percentage of AIDS cases traced to injectable drug use varies widely from state to state, but ranges from under 10 percent to almost 50 percent, with most states being in the teens. A particularly dramatic example of disease transmission occurred in 2015 in and near a small town (with a population of 4,200) in Indiana. Over a period of a few months, 181 new cases of HIV were diagnosed. Most were caused by the sharing of contaminated needles that were used to inject the powerful painkiller Opana. The number of cases that were occurring gave this small community an HIV incidence rate higher than that in any country of sub-Saharan Africa.

Public health officials and medical associations and societies have for years been urging states to allow over-the-counter sale of syringes in pharmacies and/or allow drug users to exchange used needles for sterile ones in the hope of preventing disease. They have also lobbied the federal government to help to subsidize these programs.

States that offer syringe exchange programs have reported considerable success in reducing the percentage of AIDS and hepatitis C cases caused by use of infected needles. The programs have been called an excellent example of an evidence-based approach to reducing the risk of AIDS. By 2010, all states allowed either over-the-counter sales of syringes or had exchange programs, or both. Needle exchange programs exist in 35 states, although there are only about 230 programs operating in the country.

In the case described above, Indiana passed a state law allowing needle exchanges in communities experiencing a disease outbreak, although the money can be used only for education, substance abuse programs, referrals to medical providers, and support services. Local governments or non-profit organizations must buy the needles. In the ensuing 2 months, needle sharing in the community dropped by 85 percent. The ban on federal funding was also lifted, so that the programs have a reasonable chance of success.

These programs do not have unanimous support. Many Republicans, some Democrats, and many in the drug law enforcement and drug control communities have opposed them for being an implicit endorsement of the use of injectable drugs. They argue that the emphasis should be on treatment for drug abuse rather than reducing its dangers. However, at this point in time, the public health orientation that focuses on prevention of harms is prevailing.

---

the public education "Buckle Up" campaigns combined.

The accompanying box, "Syringe Exchange Programs," describes an interesting policy choice.

The Macro Approach and Cigarette Smoking. The use of tobacco kills more than 400,000 Americans each year and is predicted to lead to the deaths of 1 billion people worldwide in the twenty-first century. For decades, efforts in the United States were focused on encouraging individual smokers to quit. However, these efforts occurred against a backdrop of formal and informal (upstream) social policies that subsidized the tobacco industry, prevented measures that would discourage tobacco use, and allowed marketing campaigns that even the tobacco industry now acknowledges were dishonest. In the mid-1960s, about 40 percent of American adults smoked cigarettes.

In the last few years, important strides have been taken in creating upstream, "macro" social policies to reduce the number of smokers and the social costs and health damages due to smoking. These policies include:

1. ***Ending agricultural subsidies to tobacco farmers.*** Beginning in the 1930s, the government offered a program to stabilize the price of tobacco and encourage small farmers to stick with tobacco as their primary crop. In 2004, legislation was signed to end this program (over a 10-year period). Part of the program termination is a US$10.1 billion payout to tobacco farmers, but at least the program will end.

2. ***Taxing tobacco products at a higher level.*** Until the last few years, the federal government and most state governments continued to tax tobacco products at a low level—especially relative to other countries like the United Kingdom, Canada, Norway, and Denmark, where the cigarette tax was several times higher per pack. Substantial research shows that as the price of cigarettes increases, the number of people, especially teenagers, who are able and willing to purchase them decreases. In the last 10 years, the federal government and many state governments have significantly increased the tax on cigarettes, and the percentage of overall smokers and especially teenage smokers has correspondingly decreased. Between 1997 and 2007, the percentage of teenagers who smoke has been reduced by almost 50 percent.
Recently, the percentage of smokers has stabilized (at just under 20 percent), and part of the reason why the decline has stopped is that some states have chosen not to measurably increase the cigarette tax (in 2015, the state cigarette tax in New York was US$4.35 per pack; in Missouri, it was 17 cents per pack). States that have done the least to use taxes to discourage smoking are Missouri, Virginia, Georgia, North Dakota, North Carolina, West Virginia, and South Carolina, States that have done the most are New York, Rhode Island, Connecticut, Massachusetts, and Washington.

3. ***Developing creative anti-taxing public health campaigns.*** Tobacco companies are fully aware that 90 percent of all smokers begin smoking during their teenage years. Their strategy has often been to target adolescents because they may be very susceptible to marketing techniques, and once they are hooked it may be difficult for them to stop. For years, these marketing campaigns went largely unchallenged. Now, public health departments, schools, and others have begun to create their own marketing campaigns to discourage smoking. Some of these campaigns appear on television, but effective use is also being made of social networking sites (Durkin, Biener, and Wakefield, 2009).

Bans on cigarette smoking in public buildings are one of several "macro-level" public health measures designed to reduce use of tobacco products. Photo courtesy of Janet Jonas.

4. *Creating and enforcing strict smoking bans.* Since the Surgeon General reported "massive and conclusive scientific evidence" in 2006 that breathing in the smoke of other smokers can lead to significant health problems (an estimated 50,000 people die each year from breathing in second-hand smoke), significant action has been taken to eliminate smoking in restaurants, bars, office buildings, apartments and condos, workplaces, and other buildings. Recently, CVS Health, which operates nearly 8,000 CVS stores and pharmacies, voluntarily chose to stop selling cigarettes, cigars, and other tobacco products—a loss of US$2 billion in annual revenue. Other efforts are underway to raise the legal smoking age. Four states have raised the age to 19 years, and Hawaii, California, and about 100 local jurisdictions have raised the age to 21 years. Studies in the United States and abroad have found that this increased minimum age leads to a significant decrease in the number of people who choose to smoke as an adult.

5. *Holding the tobacco industry financially responsible for health damages resulting from their false claims.* In 1998, 46 states reached a joint settlement with the four largest tobacco manufacturers for tobacco-related health care costs annually and in perpetuity. The settlement is estimated to be worth US$246 billion in the first 25 years. The states agreed to spend a significant portion of the settlement funds on tobacco education programs for children, smoking cessation programs, and health care. However, there is some controversy about the legitimacy of the ways in which some states are spending their settlement funds.

6. *Closely regulating the tobacco industry.* In 2009, President Obama signed legislation to give the U.S. Food and Drug Administration (FDA) the authority to regulate tobacco products and their marketing. Long a priority of the public health community, the law includes such components as banning the following: outdoor tobacco advertising near schools and playgrounds, tobacco brand sponsorship of sports teams, free giveaways of non-tobacco items with tobacco purchases, and the sale of cigarettes and smokeless tobacco from vending machines. Penalties were increased for retailers who sell tobacco products to minors. It bans tobacco products from using terms that have been found to be misleading, such as "light" and "low tar," and allows the FDA to monitor other tobacco company claims.

The tobacco industry and members of national, state, and local legislatures who support them and their interests have certainly not surrendered efforts to convince the public, especially teenagers, to smoke cigarettes. Before they were banned, Camel cigarettes sometimes came with promotional giveaways such as berry-flavored lip balm, cell phone jewelry, purses, and wristbands. They have developed new cigarette brands with a variety of exotic flavors that appeal to adolescents. (The FDA immediately banned the sale of candy-, fruit-, and clove-flavored cigarettes, but menthol-flavored cigarettes, which are especially popular among some teens, remain on the market.) When significant tax increases went into effect for roll-your-own tobacco, companies began marketing it as pipe tobacco (even though it would still be used for cigarettes) to avoid the tax. Two of the nation's largest cigarette makers—R.J. Reynolds Tobacco Company and Lorillard Tobacco Company—and several smaller manufacturers and retailers have filed a lawsuit against the marketing restrictions announced by the FDA. One means of bypassing these regulations in the United States is to increase markets overseas—especially in less developed countries—a concern to the global health community (Gostin, 2007). A second means is described in the box "The Emerging E-Cigarette Industry."

IN THE FIELD

THE EMERGING E-CIGARETTE INDUSTRY

In the last few years, the tobacco industry has also created a large e-cigarette (electronic nicotine delivery systems) market. E-cigarettes are typically battery-operated, cigarette-shaped devices that hold a cartridge of a liquid which usually contains nicotine and other chemicals. When in use, the battery powers an atomizer that vaporizes the liquid for the user to inhale. Sweet flavorings can be added, and research has shown these to be especially popular with younger people. By the end of 2015, e-cigarettes were an almost US$3 billion dollar industry. An estimated 15 to 20 percent of adults and teenagers used e-cigarettes in 2015, about 5 percent of these on a daily or almost daily basis.

Proponents say that e-cigarettes are less harmful than tobacco and can be used to curb reliance on tobacco smoking. High satisfaction rates are reported by users, and some studies have found users reporting a decreased desire to smoke cigarettes. Because they do not burn tobacco, they do not produce carbon monoxide (which can lead to heart disease) or tar (which can clog the lungs).

However, e-cigarettes do contain nicotine, which can have a negative effect on the heart and can interfere with fetal development. Large doses can be especially harmful to children. E-cigarettes may also contain a variety of other chemicals that can cause respiratory and

Vapour enthusiasts inhaling from their e-cigarettes as thousands of vapourists attend the 2nd annual Vapour Festival in 2014. © David Bagnall/Alamy Stock Photo.

nervous system problems. There also appear to be dangers from second-hand smoke. Recent research reviews of 38 studies (Kalkhoran and Glantz, 2016) and 20 studies (Sutfin et al., 2015) found that trying e-cigarettes did not deter people from cigarette smoking, and that the odds of quitting smoking were actually 28 percent lower for those using e-cigarettes.

The World Health Organization and various United States groups and agencies have encouraged the establishing of tight regulations for the industry, including a ban on indoor use, restrictions on advertising, and strong penalties for selling to minors. In 2015, the Center for Health and the Environment (CHE) chastised the tobacco industry for attempting to weaken and circumvent various laws. CHE sued 19 e-cigarette companies for failing to warn consumers about the reproductive health threats from nicotine in their products. Later that year, CHE filed legal actions against more than 60 companies for failing to warn consumers about exposure to nicotine and/or one or both of two cancer-causing chemicals, formaldehyde and acetaldehyde, from e-cigarettes, as required by California law (Cox, 2015). In 2016, the Food and Drug Administration was given responsibility for regulating all aspects of e-cigarettes, including ingredients, warning labels, and health risks.

The industry has also been reported to have created "front groups"—seemingly independent groups that support industry claims and promote industry positions. Among others, in 1994, R.J. Reynolds created the "Get Government Off Our Back" group, but kept its own involvement secret. The group appeared to outsiders as a group of generally disaffected citizens who supported the tobacco industry against external criticism, rather than what it actually was—an industry interest group (Apollonio and Bero, 2007). Acting more directly, the industry has attempted to prevent policy-relevant research from being conducted by bringing lawsuits against researchers testing for the damage caused by tobacco and getting their research funding cut off (Landman and Glantz, 2009), and has attempted to use its influence to stop anti-tobacco media campaigns or control their influence (Ibrahim and Glantz, 2007). In 2013, the percentage of adult smokers (19 percent) in the United States had dropped by slightly more than half in the previous five decades. Some studies have reported an even sharper drop to about 17 percent.

The Macro Approach and Obesity.   In the United States, 68 percent of the adult population are at least 10 pounds over their recommended body weight (compared with only 25 percent in 1960). Recent statistics show that 34 percent of adults are *overweight* (i.e., from 10 to 30 pounds over a healthy weight) and 34 percent of adults are *obese* (i.e., more than 30 pounds over a healthy weight). Of those in the latter category, 2 percent (about 4 million people) are *extremely obese* (more than 100 pounds over a healthy weight). About 32 percent of kids are overweight or obese. Obesity is a problem for both women and men, and for whites, blacks, Hispanics, and Asian Americans.

On average, individual weight in the United States increased by 1 to 2 pounds per year for the last decades of the twentieth century and the first decade of the twenty-first century. Between 1986 and 2000, there was a 216 percent increase in the number of obese individuals and a 389 percent increase in the number of extremely obese individuals. The World Health Organization emphasizes that exploding rates of obesity are a worldwide problem (there are almost 2 billion overweight people in the world), but the United States has the largest percentage of obese population. Obesity increases dramatically in the late teens and twenties, but an alarmingly high percentage of children and adolescents are overweight. The percentage of obese 12- to 19-year-olds more than tripled between 1976 and 2000. In addition, research shows that overweight children are likely to become overweight adults. After years of increases, it appears that these percentages are beginning to level off at these extremely high levels.

The consequences of this pattern are clear. Obesity increases the likelihood of premature death, heart disease, diabetes, cancer, high blood pressure, arthritis, depression, Alzheimer's disease, injury, and days lost from work, and leads to significantly greater lifetime medical costs (Haskell, Blair, and Hill, 2009). Estimates are that overweight non-smokers lose 3 years of life, obese non-smokers lose 7 years, and obese smokers lose 13 years.

What has caused this dramatic shift toward weight gain? There is some genetic predisposition to obesity (e.g., genes that influence appetite control and faulty versions of a particular gene that causes food to be stored as fat rather than burned), and there are physiological influences on hunger. For some individuals, these factors are the primary culprit. However, these factors have not changed over time and do not explain the escalating figures for the population. Instead, many social scientists and many in the public health community point to the fact that we have evolved into an **obesogenic culture** filled with influences that push people toward health-harming behaviors such as unhealthy eating and absence of a physically active lifestyle. This characterization is consistent with a macro approach to understanding health behaviors.

The signs of this obesogenic culture are evident. The dietary habits of Americans have changed significantly in the last four decades. Whereas dining in a restaurant was once the exception, it is now the common pattern for many families. Restaurants often prepare foods in ways that provide a very high number of calories and saturated fats. Portion size has become a major marketing technique, and many restaurants provide meals that are double, triple, or more the recommended portion size. Research shows that the more we are served, the more we eat. Fast-food restaurants—perhaps by far the biggest culprit—have become enormously popular during these years. People who eat in fast-food restaurants at least twice a week are about 50 percent more likely to be obese. Many of the "most bang for the buck" foods available in grocery stores are notoriously unhealthy. People are eating more and more, the foods we eat are larger in portion size and contain more calories and fat, and we consume many more calories per day than we require. The average adult American ate an estimated 140 more pounds of food in the year 2000 than in 1990.

For young people, eating nutritiously may be even more of a challenge. The nutritional quality of lunches served at schools has long been criticized, and many schools have long had snack vending machines that offer sugary soft drinks, candy, cookies, regular potato chips, and other unhealthy foods. Studies show that on school days many students get a substantial percentage of their calories from these foods. It is only recently that serious, critical attention has been given to these issues. In 2010, Congress passed the *Healthy, Hunger-Free Kids Act* with strengthened nutrition guidelines and provision for free lunches for children who could not afford to pay.

Fast-food restaurants are often located near schools, and many students eat meals or snacks there. Studies have found that students whose school is within half a mile of a fast-food restaurant consume more soft drinks, eat fewer fruits and vegetables, and are more likely to be overweight (Davis and Carpenter, 2009). Whether the restaurant sells fast food or not, the children's menu at many restaurants is packed with calories, and some dishes offer as many calories as a child needs in an entire day.

Advertisers have targeted children and adolescents with heavy campaigns involving food-related messages. Research has found that almost all of these ads feature junk food. In one study, 34 percent of the ads intended for children were for candy and snacks, 29 percent for sugary cereals, 10 percent for beverages, 10 percent for fast food, 4 percent for dairy products, 4 percent for prepared foods, and the rest for breads, pastries, and dine-in restaurants (Kaiser Family Foundation, 2007). The CDC has reported that an overwhelming percentage of commercials in TV shows aimed at kids under 12 years of age are for products containing too much sugar, too much saturated fat, and too much sodium (Schermbeck and Powell, 2015).

In addition, research has shown that parents are increasingly likely to view their overweight sons and daughters as being of appropriate weight. Because parents who recognize that their children are overweight are more likely to try to help their youngsters slim down, this misperception means that early weight gains are often ignored (Duncan et al., 2015).

The twin cause of the shift toward an overweight and obese population is the decrease in the number of people getting adequate physical exercise. According to most surveys, only about 20 percent of American adults engage in the recommended levels of physical activity—that is, at least 30 minutes of moderate-intensity physical activity for a minimum of 5 days per week, or at least 30 minutes of high-intensity physical activity for a minimum of 3 days per week. About 40 percent of adults get no physical exercise. For young people, levels of physical activity drop markedly between the ages of 9 years (about 3 hours daily of physical activity) and 15 years (about 50 minutes of daily physical activity), and then drop again with the start of college. The feared "freshman 15" (pounds of weight gain) is in actuality a typical gain of 6 to 9 pounds for first-year college students. The most common reasons are a dramatic increase in beer drinking and a further significant decrease in physical activity.

If we conclude that many of the causes of population weight gain are traceable to changes in culture and society, what would be some possible "macro-level" solutions to combat unhealthy eating?

1. A requirement that restaurants post calorie information on menus. Now implemented in New York City for chain restaurants, and being studied in other cities, research has found that such information does influence selection and intake. If a substantial number of diners were to select lower-calorie options, restaurants might offer more of them (Roberto et al., 2010). Some restaurants—including fast-food restaurants—have added nutritional options to their menus.

2. A requirement that schools offer nutritious lunches. Have you ever wondered why school lunches are often based around cheeseburgers, roast beef with gravy, and sausage pizza? It is due to the Farm Bill legislation that requires the U.S. Department of Agriculture to purchase commodity foods such as meat and dairy products—but rarely fruits and vegetables—in order to bolster agricultural businesses by buying their surpluses and ensuring that prices remain at a certain level. These surplus commodity foods are then given to schools for their lunch programs. As a result, many of the foods served are not the healthiest choices (Salsbury, 2007). The Obama administration has made necessary changes to this program. Some soft drink manufacturers are pulling out of schools.

3. Regulation of food advertising directed at children and adolescents, with some limits or required balance with healthy food products.

4. A tax on sugary beverages and sugary foods to discourage their purchase and to generate money to assist healthy eating programs.

This option has been suggested in some cities but has met with strong opposition. (There was a very significant 25 percent decrease in non-diet soda consumption in the United States between 2000 and 2015.)

5. Government legislation that requires the food industry to produce healthier foods. For example, in 2015 the Food and Drug Administration enacted a policy that gives food manufacturers 3 years to remove trans fat from their products. Research has clearly demonstrated that no amount of trans fat is safe for human consumption.

Some macro-level solutions to deal with the lack of physical exercise are as follows:

1. A significant effort to construct "built" environments that encourage rather than discourage physical exercise. Substantial research shows that many more people engage in physical exercise when they have safe, appropriate facilities in which to do so. Communities could start building "complete roads" (that provide space for cars, bikes, and pedestrians to use safely), sidewalks for safe walking or jogging, urban parks for recreational use, greenways (walking paths), community recreation centers, and better-lit neighborhoods (Hunter et al., 2015).

2. Commitment to genuine physical education classes in schools, with an emphasis on activities that students can incorporate throughout their life (i.e., more emphasis on walking, strength training, or aerobics than on dodgeball).

3. Community-wide weight reduction efforts with a strong social support component and incentives.

4. Systematic development of employee wellness programs that emphasize physical exercise.

Reasons for Lack of Attention to Macro Factors. Why is so little attention devoted to macro-level factors? At least three reasons seem important. First, using social policy and the force of laws to regulate individual behavior is viewed by some as contradicting the cultural value of individualism. Alonzo (1993) points out that people are willing to cede to the government's prevention activities that they cannot undertake for themselves—for example, inspecting the safety of each bridge. However, people are more reluctant to empower the government to protect them from their own behaviors. Many believe that allowing the government to go too far upstream oversteps its legitimate role in a free society. The accompanying box, "The Controversy Regarding the Human Papillomavirus (HPV) Vaccination," illustrates this point.

Second, the value of individualism carries over into the political economy. Donahue and

IN THE FIELD

THE CONTROVERSY REGARDING THE HUMAN PAPILLOMAVIRUS (HPV) VACCINATION

It is not uncommon for public health interests and individual choice to come into conflict. On the one hand, when the public health community is convinced that taking some particular action, such as being vaccinated against a disease, is overwhelmingly in the public interest, they may seek to have the service made widely available and even mandated. At the same time, people who are unconvinced of the value of the action or who in principle oppose government mandates on individual behavior object to such plans. These conflicts are especially complex in two circumstances—when the action involves children and adolescents, and when failure to take the action could jeopardize the health of others.

A situation of this type has occurred in the last few years with the development of a vaccine to protect against the human papillomavirus (HPV)—an infection that causes cervical cancer. About one in four teenage girls in the United States gets a sexually transmitted infection (STI), and the most common one is HPV. About 50 percent of women and men acquire some form of HPV during their lifetime. About half of the 14 million new infections annually are in women aged between 15 and 24 years. Many of the 150 types of HPV come and go without presenting any symptoms. However, those that linger can lead to cervical cancer, genital warts, and other cancers of the genitals or anus. Almost 100 percent of cervical cancer cases are related to HPV. About 20,000 women and 8,000 men in the United States develop cancer caused by HPV each year.

In 2006, a vaccine to guard against HPV was developed, and a federal advisory committee on immunizations recommended that all girls aged 11 or 12 years receive the three-dose vaccination. There are now three vaccines on the market. The vaccines can be used for girls and women between the ages of 9 and 26 years, but the ages of 11 and 12 years were selected in order to vaccinate girls before they become sexually active and thus at risk. The vaccine is not effective against all forms of HPV, but it is effective against the strains that cause 70 percent of cervical cancer and 90 percent of genital warts. (A new vaccine protects against 90 percent of cervical cancers.) The drug has only relatively rare and minor side effects. Condoms provide some (but less than 100 percent) protection. Males can also get both the high-risk and low-risk strains of HPV, although the high-risk strains cause more problems for women. The scientific community generally endorsed the vaccine as a safe and effective public health intervention (Balog, 2009). Surveys showed that most parents supported it (Brewer and Fazekas, 2007).

Within the space of a year, legislators in almost half of the states introduced mandatory vaccination bills with parental opt-out provisions. Support was strong among both Democrats and Republicans, as sponsors of the bills represented both parties. Then opponents became more vocal. Opposition for some was based on interference with parental rights. For others, the vaccination mandate seemed to license or even encourage sexual promiscuity for very young girls, and was viewed as unnecessary for those who were not sexually active. (Research has found that girls who receive the vaccine do not become more promiscuous.) Some worried that Merck & Company, the manufacturers of the drug, were lobbying too forcefully and had not done sufficient research on the drug (Rothman and Rothman, 2009). Some argued that the vaccine was dangerous, although research has not found this to be true.

What is the latest on HPV vaccination? Many countries around the world use the vaccine, and it is free for women in the target age group. In the United States, only Virginia, Rhode Island, and DC have mandatory HPV vaccination, although it is available in all states. The vaccine is expensive (US$390 for the three-shot protocol), but there are several programs that pay for most or all of the cost in cases of financial need. However, only about 40 percent of girls aged 11 and 12 years (and about 20 percent of boys) receive the full set of injections.

McGuire (1995) use the term *marketplace strategy* to describe the view that the government's primary obligation is to stay out of the marketplace so that individual consumers can exercise their own judgment about what to purchase and how to live. Of course, the view that the medical marketplace is completely open is inaccurate. Corporations and the government itself have a strong influence on health (e.g., through the location of toxic dumps), and corporations contribute sizable amounts of money to political candidates each year hoping to influence the political process. For example, in recent years the tobacco industry has contributed millions of dollars each year to members of Congress. Whether these contributions have influenced the reluctance of Congress to increase the cigarette tax—a measure that has broad public support—can only be surmised, but the more money a member has received, the less likely he or she has been to support tobacco control legislation (Moore et al., 1994).

Third, the absence of attention to macro-level factors enables society to forgo dealing with the wealth of research that establishes a direct relationship between individuals' social and physical environment and their health status. Studies have shown that even a small increase in years of education for an individual—or in average years of education for a population—has a greater impact on health status than the available quantity of health resources. However, by focusing on the individual, and solely affixing responsibility for health behavior at that level, the important effects of poverty and unemployment, racism, and lack of educational opportunity can be ignored (Becker, 1993).

The Micro Approach to Health Behavior

The importance of macro-level factors does not negate the importance of understanding factors that influence individual decisions about health behaviors. Several micro-level theories have been developed to explain health behavior. This section of the chapter describes two theories that have received significant attention.

The Health Belief Model. The **health belief model (HBM)** provides a paradigm for understanding why some individuals engage in HPBs, while others behave in knowingly unhealthy ways. The model recognizes that, in making health decisions, individuals consider both health-related and non-health-related consequences of behavior.

Development of the HBM (Becker, 1974) was sparked by the concern of many public health researchers in the 1950s and 1960s that few people were altering their behavior (e.g., ceasing to smoke) *despite* public health warnings. Developed by a group of social psychologists, the basic premise of the HBM is that the likelihood of engaging in preventive health behavior is influenced by certain beliefs about a given condition (such as developing cancer) rather than by objective facts.

According to the HBM, individuals will take preventive health action only when the following four conditions exist:

1. The individual feels susceptible or vulnerable to a certain disease or condition.
2. The individual feels that contracting the disease would have serious consequences.
3. The individual believes that taking the preventive action would effectively reduce their susceptibility to the disease (or at least reduce its seriousness if contracted).
4. The individual does not face serious barriers (e.g., inconvenience, expense, pain, or trauma) in engaging in the healthy behavior.

In addition, the individual typically needs some cue or stimulus to act (e.g., media attention, or a friend contracting a disease), and confidence that they can succeed in performing the behavior (this is referred to as self-efficacy).

These perceptions can be influenced by several non-health factors, including demographic (age, gender, socioeconomic status, and race/ethnicity), sociopsychological (personality, peer, and reference group pressure), and structural (knowledge about the disease, prior contact with the disease) factors.

The HBM has been shown to be an effective predictor of preventive health action in studies focusing on such behaviors as breast self-examination, patient compliance with regimens, getting an influenza vaccination, seeking dental care, dietary compliance among obese children, keeping follow-up appointments, use of sunscreen, and cigarette smoking cessation. These studies have shown that taking preventive health action is more likely when perceived vulnerability to a serious disease or illness is high and when a preventive health action is perceived to be effective in avoiding a negative outcome. These studies generally report that the HBM is applicable across population subgroups.

However, limitations of the HBM have also been identified. A key limitation is that the model is structured to focus on preventive health action relative to a particular disease or illness. To use the model, one must assess perceptions of a particular disease and perceptions of the efficacy of taking action to prevent that disease. Although the model has been helpful in examining these disease-specific behaviors, it is less applicable to understanding preventive health actions in general or to predicting the likelihood of engaging in general health- promoting behavior unrelated to fear of a particular disease.

The Health Belief Model and AIDS Risk and Reduction among Young People. The HBM has been used to explain why some young people voluntarily protect themselves against HIV infection, while others remain knowingly vulnerable. Without question, many young people are at risk of AIDS. More than half of all children in the United States engage in some

kind of sexual behavior before the age of 13 years, and more than 75 percent of males and females have engaged in sexual intercourse by the age of 19 years. The high rate of pregnancy among teenagers (more than a million pregnancies per year, with 80 percent being unplanned) and the very high rates of sexually transmitted infections (STIs) (especially gonorrhea, syphilis, and chlamydia) among the young (about half of the 20 million new cases of STIs each year occur among individuals aged 15 to 24 years) testify to the lack of safe sex practices. In addition, about one-third of diagnosed cases of AIDS are people between the ages of 20 and 29 years. Given the long incubation period, most of these people were infected during their teenage years.

According to the HBM, individuals have differing perceptions regarding their susceptibility to infection as well as the seriousness of HIV/AIDS. For example, a gay man may feel particularly vulnerable due to the high incidence of AIDS in this group, and may recognize its seriousness if he has witnessed the illness and death of friends. These perceptions must be complemented by information about the methods of transmission and the precautions that must be taken to avoid transmission.

However, individuals may still fail to take precautions. Some trust that medical technology will find a solution to the problem (which may be a reflection of incorrect information as well as a form of denial of individual risk), others may not have been exposed to a triggering event (e.g., the death of a friend), and some may calculate that perceived barriers (e.g., sacrificing sexual pleasure) outweigh the perceived benefits of preventive action. Individuals must also feel capable of making the recommended behavioral changes, and believe that those changes will actually make a difference. In high-prevalence areas, some may continue to engage in unsafe practices because they believe they are already exposed.

A study of more than 300 introductory psychology students in California postulated that three factors (perceptions of personal vulnerability, sexual behavior history, and homophobia) would predict levels of worry about contracting an STI, and in turn that worry would predict behavioral change to safer sex practices. These predictions were supported by the research, although somewhat different patterns were found for female and male students. For both females and males, worry was a strong predictor of risk reduction behaviors. However, only females were influenced by sexual behavior history (e.g., number of partners, and having had an STD), and only males were influenced by perceived vulnerability and homophobia. Thus gender was identified as a key influence on the processes within the HBM (Cochran and Peplau, 1991).

A more recent study of 245 undergraduate students examined the sexual history and risk beliefs of the students relative to the likelihood of accepting various hypothetical HIV vaccines. Students who were most accepting of the vaccines were those with the greatest behavioral risks and highest perceived susceptibility to HIV accompanied by the lowest personal invulnerability beliefs—all consistent with the HBM model (Ravert and Zimet, 2009).

The Theory of Reasoned Action. Developed by Ajzen and Fishbein (1973), the central premise of the **theory of reasoned action (TRA)** is that intention to perform a behavior precedes actual performance of the behavior. The intention to behave in a particular way is influenced by attitude toward the behavior (how enjoyable or unenjoyable is this behavior?), social norms (is this an expected behavior in society?), messages conveyed by significant others (do others want me to engage in this behavior?), and the importance to the individual of complying with the relevant social norms and wishes of others.

Actual participation in a preventive health action would be preceded by beliefs, attitudes, and norms that encourage the action and an intention to engage in it. Similar to the HBM, background characteristics of the individual and certain personality and other social-psychological traits can be important influences. Unlike the HBM, the TRA is almost entirely rational and does not include a significant emotional component (like perceived susceptibility to disease). In addition, the TRA includes more explicit consideration of social influences by incorporating the wishes of significant others for the individual and the desire of the individual to comply with these wishes. Vanlandingham et al. (1995) determined that the TRA was a better predictor than the HBM of using safe sex practices precisely because it places more emphasis on peer group influence.

The Theory of Reasoned Action and the Cessation of Smoking. Although the TRA has not in general been as successful as the HBM in predicting preventive health actions, it has been more effective in predicting smokers who attempt to stop smoking. One study that was based on a general household survey determined that behavioral intention was a critical precursor to actual attempts to cease smoking, and that it was a more powerful predictor than any of the individual items in the HBM (which was also tested). Although the researchers preferred the HBM for other reasons, they concluded that the intention to engage in a preventive health action is an important influence of the action (Mullen, Hersey, and Iverson, 1987).

Although not specifically testing the TRA, Christakis and Fowler (2008) have examined the extent to which groups of people quit smoking together. They studied a densely interconnected group of more than 12,000 people who were repeatedly assessed over a 32-year period. Within the group, they found discernible clusters of smokers and non-smokers. During the study

Fitness centers have become increasingly popular in communities and on college campuses throughout the country. They enable vigorous exercise throughout the year and can add a social dimension to physical conditioning. © Photographee.eu/Fotolia.

period, whole groups of smokers ceased smoking at the same time. Smoking cessation by a spouse, a sibling, a friend, or a coworker in a small firm all increased the likelihood of an individual stopping smoking. Moreover, smokers were increasingly moved to the periphery of the network. All these patterns are consistent with the importance of social norms and social influences. Additional research has pointed to increased stigma being attached to cigarette smoking—another form of social influence (Stuber, Galea, and Link, 2008).

Other Social-Psychological and Social-Structural Influences. Two additional variables with potential explanatory power for health behavior have been studied. First, the underlying theory of **health locus of control (HLC)** is that healthy behaviors are selected by

individuals based on the expectation that they will actually lead to positively valued health outcomes. That is, those who feel they have control over their own health (internal locus of control) and who place high value on their health are more likely to engage in HPBs than those who feel powerless to control their own health, and who believe health to be determined by luck, chance, or fate (external locus of control) (Jackson, Tucker, and Herman, 2007).

Second, several studies have shown that individuals engaged in ongoing *interpersonal relationships* with family members, friends, and coworkers are more likely to participate in HPBs. Among adults, this often occurs as significant others attempt to influence and persuade the individual to practice a healthy lifestyle. For example, among a group of employees enrolled in a work-site health promotion program, friends, relatives, and coworkers were positive influences in changing health-related behaviors initially and encouraging subjects to maintain these changes over time (Zimmerman and Conner, 1989). This pattern of influence also occurs within marriages, although wives are more likely to try to influence their husband's behavior than the other way around. This may help to explain why there is a significant health benefit for men in getting married, although not for women. Broman (1993) has further established this relationship in his research showing that disengagement from social relationships is often accompanied by an increase in health-harming behaviors.

The influence of other people is particularly strong among adolescents. Research has identified both perceived peer and parental approval of alcohol use to be important determinants of drinking behavior among teenagers. Adolescents who reported high parental approval of alcohol use also reported high levels of alcohol use by their friends. In a study of health care practices during the first 3 years of college, both parents and peers were found to have a significant influence on students' alcohol consumption, diet, exercise, and seat-belt use. The researchers concluded that the direct modeling of behavior was the most important avenue of influence by both parents and peers (Lau, Quadrel, and Hartman, 1990).

SUMMARY

The World Health Organization defines health as a state of complete physical, social, and mental well-being. Sociological approaches to understanding health emphasize the social and cultural aspects of health and illness and an ability to function in various social roles.

In general, the lifestyle of Americans includes many health-harming aspects. About 20 percent of adults continue to smoke cigarettes (the most health-harming behavior), about two-thirds are overweight or obese due to poor diet and lack of physical exercise, and about 5 percent are heavy drinkers. Binge drinking occurs in all population subgroups, but continues to be a particular problem among college students. Because

preventive health care often involves direct or indirect costs, people on a low income have been much less likely to receive it.

Explanations for participation in healthy lifestyles adopt both a macro and micro approach. Macro approaches focus on the important influence of social structure (including poverty, unemployment, and racism) on ill health, and on the potential of social policy to influence participation in HPBs. Micro approaches, like the HBM and the TRA, focus on individual decision making and the process of determining whether or not to participate in specific preventive health actions. Both perspectives are important in understanding health behavior.

HEALTH ON THE INTERNET

In recent years, epidemiologists have carefully examined the consequences of being distracted while driving. Although there could be many sources of distraction, primary attention has been focused on talking on a cell phone or texting

while driving. One study found that talking on a cell phone while driving increased the risk of an accident by four times—making it approximately the same risk as driving while intoxicated (Strayer, Drews, and Crouch, 2006). A second study found that the likelihood of a collision while texting during driving was 23 times greater than when undistracted (Virginia Tech Transportation Institute, 2009). The National Safety Council reports that 28 percent of all automobile crashes are caused by drivers talking on a cell phone or texting while driving (Ship, 2010).

People in all age groups engage in distracted driving, although the percentages are highest in adults aged 18 to 29 years. About 75 percent of people in this age group talk on a cell phone while driving, 68 percent text message, and 48 percent access the Internet on their phone. The Department of Transportation reports that in 2013 more than 3,000 people were killed and nearly 425,000 were injured in accidents caused by distracted drivers. In recent years the number of deaths of teenage drivers has sharply increased. Currently, 46 states and the District of Columbia ban texting while driving, and 14 states plus DC ban the use of hand-held cell phones while driving. Studies show that an overwhelming percentage of teenagers believe that texting while driving will eventually lead to an accident or even being killed, but few have abandoned the practice.

Recent studies have also shown increased dangers for distracted pedestrians. Pedestrians who are using cell phones show the same reduced situation awareness, distracted attention, and unsafe behavior as drivers do (Nasar and Troyer, 2013). Visits to emergency rooms for injuries suffered by distracted pedestrians doubled between 2004 and 2010.

In 2011 the National Transportation Safety Board proposed that all states should prohibit all drivers from using portable electronic devices such as cell phones while driving. The recommendation urged a ban even on hands-free devices with headphones, due to their threat of distraction. The Department of Transportation has also launched a website: www.distraction.gov.

Scan through this website, and then answer the following questions: (1) Given the evidence on danger, why do so many adults of all ages—but especially younger drivers—continue to talk on their cell phone, text, and access the Internet while driving? (2) Would you support the National Transportation Safety Board (NTSB) recommended ban on all use of portable electronic devices while driving? (3) What, if anything, would you propose in addition to or instead of this recommendation to reduce the negative consequences of distracted driving?

DISCUSSION CASES

Case 1

American businesses are becoming more active in monitoring the lifestyle of employees. Business leaders argue that these regulatory activities are justified in order to maintain a high level of on-the-job performance and hold down cost increases for health insurance by having a healthier workforce with fewer costly episodes of disease and illness. Critics of the increased monitoring activities contend that employers have no right to interfere in the private lives of workers. While job performance can and should be evaluated, they argue, attempting to control lifestyle decisions in off-the-job hours is inappropriate and an invasion of privacy.

Businesses are now using several types of monitoring activities, including:

1. *Drug screening of all employees*. The Occupational Safety and Health Administration (OSHA) estimates that 65 percent of all work-related accidents and 40 percent of workplace fatalities are traceable to substance abuse. The Metropolitan

Insurance Company estimates that substance abuse costs employers US$85 billion annually. In response, many companies (about 80 percent of Fortune 500 companies) have instituted urine drug testing for all employees—white collar and blue collar. These tests can show the presence of such substances as amphetamines, barbiturates, cocaine, marijuana, and opiates. Companies have a variety of policies for dealing with those identified as drug users, including first-time warnings, drug education classes, job suspension or termination, and in the case of work situations related to public safety (e.g., firefighters and railroad engineers), prosecution.

2. *Programs of incentives for participation in company wellness programs.* Because most companies provide health insurance benefits to full-time employees, the company benefits financially (through lower insurance premiums) when employees are healthy. In response, more than half of large employers now offer company wellness programs to facilitate employee health. These can involve a wide range of activities, including exercise classes, cholesterol and weight monitoring, on-site blood tests, and health education programs. In order to encourage participation, companies may offer a positive incentive (e.g., a reduction in health insurance cost for the employee) or a negative one (e.g., refusal of the company to pay for any of the employee's health insurance). Both the government and the courts have approved these programs.

3. *Programs of incentives and mandates for specific lifestyles.* Some businesses have established financial reward/penalty systems for workers' lifestyles. Based on "behavioral economics," workers who maintain a certain level of fitness or who do not smoke or who have a cholesterol count below a designated level are given cash bonuses (or the company pays more of the premium for health benefits). Workers who do not meet these lifestyle standards pay a financial penalty (or pay more of the health insurance premium).

Other businesses have developed even more stringent plans. Some employers refuse to hire people (or fire current employees) who smoke cigarettes (a practice that is legal in 21 states), are overweight, have high cholesterol readings, or in at least one case, ride a motorcycle. To date, courts have sent mixed signals on the legality of these provisions.

What are the social implications of programs of drug screening and wellness program and lifestyle incentives and mandates? What would be the consequences if every company established plans like these? Are these programs an invasion of worker privacy? Are there any significant differences between these three types of programs?

Do programs now being initiated by middle and secondary schools to drug test all students raise the same issues as employee drug testing, or are these programs different? Since the Supreme Court decision in 2002 that random testing of student athletes and students participating in extracurricular activities does not violate students' privacy, many schools around the country have instituted these programs. A Kansas school district does not allow students who have not consented to be drug tested to participate in or attend athletic events, field trips, driver's education courses, or school plays. An Indiana school district is drug testing not only athletes but also those who drive to campus or want to attend a school dance, prom, or school party. What additional issues, if any, are raised by these student drug-testing programs?

Case 2

Since 1984, the national minimum legal age for drinking alcohol has been 21 years. In 2009, a group of 135 college and university presidents endorsed the Amethyst Initiative—an advocacy proposal that comments on the failure of current policies to socialize young people to handle alcohol responsibly, and that encourages study and public debate about finding better ideas. Included among the ideas for debate was lowering the legal drinking age to 18 years. Estimates are that each year about 5,000 people under the age of 21 years die as a result of underage drinking (from motor vehicle crashes, homicides, suicides, etc.).

Proponents argue that the current drinking age has not stopped excessive alcohol consumption, but it has pushed it out of the open to places where it cannot be monitored. Rather than reducing driving after drinking, it may actually be leading to an increase as parties move from on-campus to off-campus. Opponents of lowering the drinking age argue that such a move would simply push the dangers of excessive alcohol consumption—to personal health and safety and to that of others—to a younger age, and that it might lead to an increase in driving after drinking among this age group. Meanwhile, social scientists and public health experts have begun to try to document the likely effects of maintaining the current policy or revising it (Wechsler and Nelson, 2010).

What would you identify as being the likely consequences—positive and/or negative—of lowering the drinking age to 18 years? As a social scientist, how could you study this issue? What are the key arguments on both sides of the issue?

Case 3

In this chapter we have discussed the recent controversy regarding whether or not the vaccination for the human papillomavirus should be mandated. What do you consider to be the main arguments in favor of and against such a mandate? How does the fact that public health organizations have recommended the vaccination for individuals under the legal age of consent affect this policy question?

GLOSSARY

Behavioral Risk Factor Surveillance System (BRFSS)
biomedical definition of health
health
health behavior
health belief model (HBM)

health locus of control (HLC)
health protective behaviors (HPBs)
obesogenic culture
sociological definition of health
theory of reasoned action (TRA)

REFERENCES

Ajzen, Icek, and Martin Fishbein. 1973 *Belief, Attitude, Intention, and Behavior*. Reading, MA: Addison-Wesley.

Alonzo, Angelo A. 1993 "Health Behavior: Issues, Contradictions, and Dilemmas." *Social Science and Medicine*, 37:1019–1034.

Apollonio, Dorie E., and Lisa Ann Bero. 2007 "Creating Industry Front Groups: The Tobacco Industry and 'Get Government off Our Back.'" *American Journal of Public Health*, 97: 419–427.

Balog, Joseph E. 2009 "The Moral Justification for a Compulsory Human Papillomavirus Vaccination Program." *American Journal of Public Health*, 99:616–622.

Becker, Marshall H. (ed.). 1974 *The Health Belief Model and Personal Health Behavior*. San Francisco, CA: Society for Public Health Education, Inc.

———. 1993 "A Medical Sociologist Looks at Health Promotion." *Journal of Health and Social Behavior*, 34:1–6.

Blaxter, Mildred. 2010 *Health*, 2nd ed. Cambridge: Polity Press.

Brewer, Noel T., and Karah Fazekas. 2007 "Predictors of HPV Vaccine Acceptability: A Theory-Informed, Systematic Review." *Preventive Medicine*, 45:107–114.

Broman, Clifford L. 1993 "Social Relationships and Health-Related Behavior." *Journal of Behavioral Medicine,* 16:335–350.

Caudill, Barry D., Scott B. Crosse, Bernadette Campbell, Jan Howard, Bill Luckey, and Howard T. Blane. 2006 "High-Risk Drinking Among College Fraternity Members: A National Perspective." *Journal of American College Health*, 55:141–155.

Centers for Disease Control and Prevention. 2016 *Behavioral Risk Factor Surveillance System.* Atlanta, GA: CDC.

Christakis, Nicholas A., and James H. Fowler. 2008 "The Collective Dynamics of Smoking in a Large Social Network." *The New England Journal of Medicine*, 358:2249–2258.

Cochran, Susan D., and Letitia A. Peplau. 1991 "Sexual Risk Reduction Behaviors Among Young Heterosexual Adults." *Social Science and Medicine*, 33:25–36.

Cohen, Deborah A., Richard A. Scribner, and Thomas A. Farley. 2000 "A Structural Model of Health Behavior: A Pragmatic Approach to Explain and Influence Health Behaviors at the Population Level." *Preventive Medicine*, 30:146–154.

Cox, Caroline. 2015 *A Smoking Gun: Cancer-Causing Chemicals in E-Cigarettes*. Oakland, CA: Center for Environmental Health.

Davis, Brennan, and Christopher Carpenter. 2009 "Proximity of Fast-Food Restaurants to Schools and Adolescent Obesity." *American Journal of Public Health*, 99:505–510.

Donahue, John M., and Meredith B. McGuire. 1995 "The Political Economy of Responsibility in Health and Illness." *Social Science and Medicine*, 40:47–53.

Duncan, Dustin T., Andrew R. Hansen, Wei Wang, Fei Yan, and Jian Zhang. 2015 "Change in Misperception of Child's Body Weight among Parents of American Preschool Children." *Childhood Obesity*, 11: 384–393.

Durkin, Sarah J., Lois Biener, and Melanie A. Wakefield. 2009 "Effects of Different Types of Antismoking Ads on Reducing Disparities in Smoking Cessation among Socioeconomic Subgroups." *American Journal of Public Health,* 99:2217–2223.

Fielding, Jonathan. 2009 Quoted in "Healthy People 2020 Tackling Social Determinants of Health," by Kim Krisberg. *The Nation's Health*, December, 2008/January, 2009, pp. 1, 24–25.

Gostin, Lawrence O. 2007 "The 'Tobacco Wars' – Global Litigation Strategies." *Journal of the American Medical Association*, 298:2537–2539.

Hagman, Brett T., Patricia R. Clifford, and Nora E. Noel. 2007 "Social Norms Theory-Based Interventions: Testing the Feasibility of a Purported Mechanism of Action." *Journal of American College Health*, 56:293–298.

Haskell, William L., Steven N. Blair, and James O. Hill. 2009 "Physical Activity: Health Outcomes and Importance for Public Health Policy." *Preventive Medicine*, 49:280–282.

Henderson, James W. 1994 "The Cost Effectiveness of Prenatal Care." *Health Care Financing Review*, 15:21–32.

Hunter, Ruth F., Hayley Christian, Jenny Veitch, Thomas Astell-Burt, J. Aaron Hipp, and Jasper Schipperijn. 2015 "The Impact of Interventions to Promote Physical Activity in Urban Green Space: A Systematic Review and Recommendations for Future Research." *Social Science and Medicine*, 124:246–256.

Ibrahim, Jennifer K., and Stanton A. Glantz. 2007 "The Rise and Fall of Tobacco Control Media Campaigns, 1967–2006." *American Journal of Public Health*, 97:1383–1396.

Jackson, Erin S., Carolyn M. Tucker, and Keith C. Herman. 2007 "Health Value, Perceived Social Support, and Health Self-Efficacy as Factors in a Health-Promoting Lifestyle." *Journal of American College Health*, 2007:69–74.

Kaiser Family Foundation. 2007 "New Study Finds That Food is the Top Product Seen by Children." Kaiser Family Foundation. www.kff.org/other/event/new-study-finds-that-food-is-the/.

Kalkhoran, S., and Stanton A. Glantz. 2016 "E-cigarettes and Smoking Cessation in Real-World and Clinical Settings: A Systematic Review and Meta-Analysis." *The Lancet Respiratory Medicine*, 4:116–128.

Keeling, Richard P. 2002 "Binge Drinking and the College Environment." *Journal of American College Health*, 50:197–201.

Landman, Anne, and Stanton A. Glantz. 2009 "Tobacco Industry Efforts to Undermine Policy-Relevant Research." *American Journal of Public Health*, 99:45–58.

Lau, Richard R., Marilyn J. Quadrel, and Karen A. Hartman. 1990 "Development and Change of Young Adults' Preventive Health Beliefs and Behavior: Influence from Parents and Peers." *Journal of Health and Social Behavior,* 31: 240–259.

McBride, Nicole M., Blake Barrett, Kathleen A. Moore, and Lawrence Schonfeld. 2014 "The Role of Positive Alcohol Expectancies in Underage Binge Drinking among College Students." *Journal of American College Health,* 62:370–379.

McKinlay, John B. 1974 "A Case for Refocusing Upstream: The Political Economy of Illness." Pp. 502–516 in *Sociology of Health and Illness: Critical Perspectives,* Peter Conrad and Rochelle Kern (eds.). New York: St. Martin's Press.

McQuide, Pamela A., Therese Delvaux, and Pierre Buekens. 2000 "Prenatal Care Incentives in Europe." *Journal of Public Health Policy,* 19:331–349.

Martens, Matthew P., Jennifer C. Page, Emily S. Lowry, Krista M. Damann, Kari K. Taylor, and M. Delores Cimini. 2006 "Differences between Perceived Actual and Perceived Student Norms: An Examination of Alcohol Use, Drug Use, and Sexual Behavior." *Journal of American College Health,* 54:295–300.

Milio, Nancy. 1981 *Promoting Health Through Public Policy.* Philadelphia, PA: F.A. Davis.

Moore, Stephen, Sidney M. Wolfe, Deborah Lindes, and Clifford E. Douglas. 1994 "Epidemiology of Failed Tobacco Control Legislation." *Journal of the American Medical Association,* 272:1171–1175.

Mullen, Patricia D., James C. Hersey, and Donald C. Iverson. 1987 "Health Behavior Models Compared." *Social Science and Medicine,* 24:973–981.

Nasar, Jack L., and Derek Troyer. 2013 "Pedestrian Injuries Due to Mobile Phone Use in Public Places." *Accident Analysis and Prevention,* 57:91–95.

Parsons, Talcott. 1972 "Definitions of Health and Illness in Light of American Values and Social Structure." Pp. 165–187 in *Patients, Physicians and Illness* (2nd ed.), E. Gartly Jaco (ed.). New York: Free Press.

Ravert, Russell D., and Gregory D. Zimet. 2009 "College Student Invulnerability Beliefs and HIV Vaccine Acceptability." *American Journal of Health Behavior,* 33:391–399.

Roberto, Christina A., Peter D. Larsen, Henry Agnew, Jenny Baik, and Kelly D. Brownell. 2010 "Evaluating the Impact of Menu Labeling on Food Choices and Intake." *American Journal of Public Health,* 100:312–318.

Rothman, Sheila M., and David J. Rothman. 2009 "Marketing HPV Vaccine: Implications for Adolescent Health and Medical Professionalism." *Journal of the American Medical Association,* 302:781–786.

Salsbury, Helen. 2007 "The AMA and Agribusiness: The Battle over Childhood Obesity." Physicians Committee for Responsible Medicine. www. pcrm.org/news/commentary071016.html.

Schermbeck, Rebecca M., and Lisa M. Powell. 2015 "Nutrition Recommendations and the Children's Food and Beverage Advertising Initiative's 2014 Approved Food and Beverage Product List." *Preventing Chronic Disease,* 12:140–472.

Secura, Gina M., Tessa Madden, Colleen McNicholas, Jennifer Mullersman, Christina M. Buckel, Qiuhong Zhao, and Jeffrey F. Peipert. 2014 "Provision of No-Cost, Long-Acting Contraception and Teenage Pregnancy." *New England Journal of Medicine,* 371:1316–1323.

Ship, Amy N. 2010 "The Most Primary of Care— Talking About Driving and Distraction." *New England Journal of Medicine,* 362:2145–2147.

Strayer, David L., Frank A. Drews, and Dennis J. Crouch. 2006 "A Comparison of the Cell Phone Driver and the Drunk Driver." *Human Factors,* 48:381–391.

Stuber, Jennifer, Sandro Galea, and Bruce G. Link. 2008 "Smoking and the Emergence of a Stigmatized Social Status." *Social Science and Medicine,* 67:420–430.

Sutfin, Erin L., Beth A. Reboussin, Beata Debinski, Kimberly G. Wagoner, John Spangler, and Mark Wolfson. 2015 "The Impact of Trying Electronic Cigarettes on Cigarette Smoking by College Students: A Prospective Analysis." *American Journal of Public Health,* 105:e83–e89.

Turner, James J., H. Wesley Perkins, and Jennifer Bauerle. 2008 "Declining Negative Consequences Related to Alcohol Misuse Among Students Exposed to a Social Norms Marketing Intervention on a College Campus." *Journal of American College Health,* 57: 85–94.

Twaddle, Andrew. 1974 "The Concept of Health Status." *Social Science and Medicine,* 8:29–38.

United States Department of Health and Human Services. 2000 *Healthy People 2010.* Washington, DC: DHHS.

Vanlandingham, Mark J., Somboon Suprasert, Nancy Grandjean, and Werasit Sittitrai. 1995 "Two Views of Risky Sexual Practices Among Northern Thai Males: The Health Belief Model and the Theory of Reasoned Action." *Journal of Health and Social Behavior*, 36:195–212.

Virginia Tech Transportation Institute. 2009 *New Data From* VTTI *Provides Insight Into Cell Phone Use and Driving Distraction*. www.vtti.vt.edu/featured/052913-cellphone.html.

Ware, John E. 1986 "The Assessment of Health Status." Pp. 204–228 in *Applications of Social Science to Clinical Medicine and Health Policy*, Linda H. Aiken and David Mechanic (eds.). New Brunswick, NJ: Rutgers University Press.

Weber, Max. 1922/1978 *Economy and Society: An Outline of Interpretive Society.* Berkeley, CA: University of California Press.

Wechsler, Henry, and Toben F. Nelson. 2010 "Will Increasing Alcohol Availability by Lowering the Minimum Legal Drinking Age Decrease Drinking and Related Consequences Among Youths?" *American Journal of Public Health*, 100:986–992.

Weiss, Gregory L. 2006 *Grass Roots Medicine: The Story of America's Free Health Clinics.* Lanham, MD: Rowman-Littlefield.

Wolinsky, Fredric D. 1988 *The Sociology of Health—Principles, Practitioners, and Issues*, 2nd ed. Belmont, CA: Wadsworth Publishing Company.

World Health Organization. 2016 *World Health Organization Constitution.* www.who.int/governance/eb/constitution/en/.

Zimmerman, Rick S., and Catherine Conner. 1989 "Health Promotion in Context: The Effects of Significant Others on Health Behavior Change." *Health Education Quarterly*, 16:57–75.

CHAPTER 7

Experiencing Illness and Disability

Learning Objectives

- Identify and discuss Suchman's stages of illness experience.

- Identify and discuss the most important factors that influence the assessment of disease/illness symptoms.

- Explain the concepts "medicalization" and "demedicalization" and the factors that are having an impact on them.

- Identify and discuss the key social influences on the decision to seek professional medical care.

- Identify and describe the primary effects of living with a chronic illness and disability.

Medical sociologists have a natural interest in how people respond to illness. The concept **illness behavior** refers to "the way in which symptoms are perceived, evaluated, and acted upon by a person who recognizes some pain, discomfort or other signs of organic malfunction" (Mechanic and Volkart, 1961:52). On the surface, it may seem that the nature and severity of an illness would be the sole determinants of an individual's response, and for very severe illnesses this is often true. However, many people either fail to see a physician or go very late in the disease process despite the presence of serious symptoms, while many other people see physicians routinely for very minor complaints. These patterns suggest that illness behavior is influenced by social and cultural factors in addition to (and sometimes instead of) physiological condition.

STAGES OF ILLNESS EXPERIENCE

Edward Suchman (1965) devised an orderly approach for studying illness behavior with his elaboration of the five key **stages of illness experience:** (1) symptom experience, (2) assumption of the sick role, (3) medical care contact, (4) dependent-patient role, and (5) recovery and rehabilitation (see Figure 7–1). Each stage involves major decisions that must be made by the individual which determine whether the sequence of stages continues or the process is discontinued. While some elaboration of the model is necessary (e.g., see the section near the end of this chapter on living with chronic illness and disability), Suchman's schema is used for organizing the beginning part of the chapter.

STAGE 1: SYMPTOM EXPERIENCE

The illness experience is initiated when an individual first senses that something is wrong—a perception of pain, discomfort, general unease, or some disruption in bodily functioning. Suchman states that three distinct processes occur at this time: (1) the physical pain or discomfort, (2) the cognitive recognition that physical symptoms of an illness are present, and (3) an emotional response of concern about the social implications of the illness, including a possible disruption in ability to function.

Assessment of Symptoms

David Mechanic (1968) developed a **theory of help-seeking behavior** to facilitate an understanding of this assessment process and how individuals act prior to (or instead of) seeking a health care provider. Mechanic traces the extreme variations in how people respond to illness to differences in how they define the illness situation and to differences in their ability to cope with the situation. The process of definition and the ability to cope are both culturally and socially determined. As individuals mature through life stages, they are socialized within families and within communities to respond to illness in particular ways. Part of this socialization involves observing how others within the group respond to illness and noting the positive or negative reaction their behaviors elicit. Sociologists refer to this process as the **social construction of illness** (Conrad and Barker, 2010). Among the

Figure 7–1   Condensed Version of Suchman's Stages of Illness Experience

I Symptom Experience	II Assumption of the Sick Role	III Medical Care Contact
The feeling that something is wrong; the individual may self-treat (or try to ignore the problem).	The individual may surrender typical responsibilities and take on "sick role" responsibilities of trying to get better (or still be in denial).	The individual makes contact with a medical provider acknowledging that expertise is necessary and seeking illness legitimation (but may still be in denial and may get a second opinion).

IV Dependent-Patient Role	V Recovery and Rehabilitation
The individual agrees to undergo medical therapy administered by professionals (but may or may not follow medical advice).	If recovery occurs, the individual leaves the sick role and returns to customary responsibilities and activities associated with the well role (although some individuals may enjoy the benefits of the sick role and linger in that stage).

Based on Edward A. Suchman, "Stages of Illness and Medical Care," *Journal of Health and Social Behavior*, 6:114–128, 1965.

factors that Mechanic identifies as determining how individuals respond to illness are the following:

1. Perception and interpretation of symptoms: the visibility, recognizability, perceived seriousness, amount of disruption caused, and persistence of symptoms.
2. The tolerance threshold (e.g., tolerance to pain) and perceived fear of the illness by the individual.
3. Knowledge and available information about the illness.
4. Availability of and accessibility to treatment resources, the cost of taking action, and competing needs for attention and resources.

Which of these factors most influences perception of one's own health? Stewart et al. (2008) found that it was the amount of pain being experienced, limitations on ability to perform normal social roles, and feelings of having little or no energy.

The Importance of Pain as a Symptom

Although the importance of pain as a medical symptom may seem obvious, research on pain and its treatment has greatly increased only in the last 10 to 20 years. This research has found that pain is more common in the general population than was previously thought. Almost 60 percent of adults in the United States experienced chronic pain in the last year, and 40 percent said they were in pain all the time. Most say their pain is of moderate to severe intensity. Back pain is most common, followed by arthritis and joint pain, headaches and migraines, and knee and shoulder pain. A particular surprise is that adults aged 18 to 34 years are about as likely to have chronic pain as those who are older. Almost half of those in chronic pain do not consider it to be under control. Uncontrolled pain has been connected to higher rates of

depression, anxiety, sleeplessness, and suicide. About 50 percent of Americans are in pain at the time of their death.

These statistics are especially surprising because many physicians say that most pain can be safely and effectively controlled. Only in recent years has **palliative care**—treating the pain and suffering of seriously ill patients— become widespread. Palliative care programs have reached a general level of acceptance for terminally ill patients—the United States now has more than 1,600 hospital-based palliative care programs and more than 5,300 hospice programs that deal with people in the last 6 months of their life. These programs have recorded significant success in relieving pain. However, palliative care is still in its relative infancy for treating people with serious chronic (but not terminal) illnesses, who take curative medicines at the same time as pain relief medicines.

There are four major obstacles to the use of pain relief medicine for more patients. (1) Few physicians have received training in pain management, and they are ill-informed about opioids, synthetic versions of morphine, the most potent oral painkillers. (2) Insurance companies inadequately compensate physicians who can spend a very large amount of time with patients in pain. (3) The Drug Enforcement Agency has actively prosecuted physicians for a variety of offenses related to the prescription of narcotic pain relief medications. (4) Many patients are fearful that the narcotic drugs that may be used will be addictive or have significant negative side effects. Several pain relief medications have been pulled from the market. Oxycontin was found to lead to addiction and abuse, and its manufacturer was found to have lied about these risks. Vioxx, which was used to control pain for many users, was found to double the risk of heart attack and stroke. Celebrex was more likely to lead to heart problems than Vioxx. However, complicating the situation is the fact

Fed Up! (a coalition calling for an end to the epidemic of opioid addiction and overdose deaths) marches in Washington, DC. © B Christopher/Alamy Stock Photo.

that the higher risks were observed only in long-term users of high doses of the drug. Some patients said they would willingly take the risks in order to effectively control their pain. Nevertheless, prescription drug overdoses are increasing markedly in the United States. In the first decade of the twenty-first century, deaths from prescription drug overdoses exceeded deaths from heroin and cocaine combined. See the accompanying box, "America's Opioid Crisis."

Palliative care programs for non-terminally ill people are increasing in physicians' offices and hospitals. The programs are expected to evolve, mature, and become a more significant component of the health care system.

Research on Symptom Assessment

There are significant social and cultural influences on the way people interpret and respond to medical symptoms such as pain. For example, variations in response to pain are based on differing levels of pain tolerance that are culturally prescribed in different ways for women than for men, or for members of different ethnic groups.

Zborowski (1969) found that Protestants of British descent tended to respond in a matter-of-fact way to pain, which enabled them to adapt to illness more quickly than other groups. Patients of Irish heritage often repressed their suffering and tended to deny pain. Both Jewish and Italian patients responded to pain with more

IN THE FIELD

AMERICA'S OPIOID CRISIS

More than 100 million American adults experience chronic pain, and more than 25 million of them report having had pain every day for the previous 3 months. In some cases, the pain is only mild or moderate in intensity, but many people suffer from extremely painful back problems, joint problems, osteoarthritis, and other conditions. Not surprisingly, these individuals have worse overall health, use more health care resources, and have more disabilities.

In the last 25 years, pharmaceutical companies have manufactured more powerful and highly addictive opioid prescription pain medications—such as oxycodone (Vicodin), hydrocodone (Percocet), and morphine—and significantly increased their marketing to physicians and patients. More than 5 million adults in the United States now take prescription opioid medication on a regular basis, and in any given year, as many as 10 million people take the drugs. With less than 5 percent of the world's population, the United States consumes 80 percent of its opioids. The number of prescriptions for opioids has increased from around 76 million in 1991 to nearly 207 million in 2013.

Many of these individuals take the prescription opioids inappropriately. This means that they are taking the drug although it was prescribed for someone else, they are taking more than the prescribed dosage of the drug, or they are taking the drug for a recreational high rather than for pain relief, or other unintended uses. This has frequently led to or contributed to substance abuse disorders, emergency hospitalizations, and overdose deaths. Between 2000 and 2014, the rate of overdose deaths from opioids increased by 200 percent. In 2014, there were more than 47,000 drug overdose deaths in the United States, and more than 70 percent of these were from opioids. The overdose death of the legendary singer Prince in 2016 brought increased national attention to the issue.

In addition, the opioids have been shown to be a gateway drug to heroin. The development of chemical tolerance to the opioids, the greater ease of obtaining heroin than opioids in some communities, and the higher price of opioids compared with heroin have spurred increased heroin use. Largely as a result of this, the number of heroin users in the United States nearly doubled between 2005 and 2012 to about 670,000.

Adults between the ages of 45 and 85 years are at especially high risk. They are more likely than younger people to suffer from chronic pain and to be prescribed an opioid for it. As we age, the body is less able to clear drugs from our system, making overdose more likely. There is also the danger of drug interactions with medications taken for other chronic diseases, such as heart disease or diabetes.

In 2011, the well-respected Institute of Medicine published *Relieving Pain in America: A Blueprint for Transforming Prevention, Care, Education, and Research.* The document discussed the pain relief issue, care of people with pain, patient and provider education, and research needs and challenges. This was followed in 2015 with *The Prescription Opioid Epidemic: An Evidence-Based Approach* (Alexander, Frattaroli, and Gielen, 2015), published by the Johns Hopkins Bloomberg School of Public Health, which recommended seven strategies to address the problem. These strategies included stricter prescribing guidelines, required use of prescription drug-monitoring programs, more research and analysis of drug effectiveness, overdose education and treatment drug distribution programs, addiction treatment programs, and community-based prevention strategies. The federal

(Continued)

(Continued)

government committed more than US$1 billion to fighting heroin and opioid drug abuse; most of this money was focused on medication-assisted treatment.

How did the prescription opioid medication epidemic materialize in the 1990s and grow to be such a widespread problem in the next two decades? Before the 1990s, opioid pain medications were used to provide significant relief from pain from injury or after surgery as the body heals. They can be very helpful in controlling pain at the end of life. However, because they carry a high risk of overdose or addiction, they were rarely used for treating chronic pain. In the 1990s, several groups campaigned for providers to take chronic pain more seriously.

Pharmaceutical companies began a push for greater use of opioids, often through educational programs for providers. Direct marketing strategies to patients helped to build demand. Prescriptions for opioid medications for chronic pain quickly doubled. Many physicians and people who work in addiction treatment believe that the pharmaceutical companies overstated the effectiveness of the drugs and their safety, and understated the risk of addiction (Jaret, 2015). Donald Light and others have recommended a thorough analysis of the role of pharmaceutical companies in the prescription opioid drug problem (Light, Lexchin, and Darrow, 2013). A broad analysis of pharmaceutical companies is included in Chapter 14.

open emotionality. However, Jewish patients were primarily concerned about the long-term consequences of their illness, and were not much comforted by the administration of pain-killing medication, whereas Italian patients were more oriented to the current pain and were at least somewhat satisfied when the pain was relieved.

Research focusing on perceived pain when getting one's ears pierced also found significant ethnic differences. Testing both male and female volunteers between the ages of 15 and 25 years, Thomas and Rose (1991) found that Afro-West Indians reported significantly less pain than Anglo-Saxons, who reported significantly less pain than Asians—all for the same procedure.

What causes these patterns? Both role modeling within families and social conditioning are important influences. As one grows up in a family, there are countless opportunities to observe reaction to pain and alarm expressed by family members. Children's anxiety about receiving painful medical treatment has been shown to be strongly correlated with parental anxiety.

In response to the assessment of symptoms, the individual may decide to deny that the symptoms need attention, delay making a decision until the symptoms become more obvious, or acknowledge the presence of an illness. Should an illness be admitted, the person may enter stage 2—the sick role.

STAGE 2: ASSUMPTION OF THE SICK ROLE—ILLNESS AS DEVIANCE

If the individual accepts that the symptoms are a sign of illness and are sufficiently worrisome, the transition is then made to the sick role, at which time the individual begins to relinquish some or all of their normal social roles.

Background of the Sick Role Concept

The **sick role**, one of the most fundamental concepts in medical sociology, was first introduced by Talcott Parsons in a 1948 journal article, but was elaborated upon in his 1951 book, *The Social System*. Parsons emphasized that illness is not simply a biological or psychological condition, and it is not simply an unstructured state free of social norms and regulation. When one is ill, one does not simply exit normal social roles to enter a type of social vacuum. Rather, one substitutes a new role—the sick role—for the relinquished, normal roles. The sick role is "also a social role, characterized by certain exemptions, rights, and obligations, and shaped by the society, groups, and cultural tradition to which the sick person belongs" (Fox, 1989:17).

Parsons and other functionalists viewed sickness as a type of deviant behavior in that it is a violation of role expectations. Sickness is assessed as being dysfunctional for the family because when one member is sick and relinquishes normal responsibilities, other members are required to pick up the slack, and may become overburdened in doing so. In addition, sickness is dysfunctional for society. The equilibrium that society maintains can be disrupted when individual members, due to sickness, fail to fulfill routine responsibilities. The "lure" of sickness—the attraction of escaping responsibilities—requires society to exercise some control over the sick person and the sick role so that disruption is minimized.

Sickness is acknowledged to be a special form of deviant behavior; it is not equivalent to other forms of deviance such as crime or sin. Institutions (e.g., law and medicine) are created in society to deal with both behaviors, but whereas criminals are punished, the sick are provided with therapeutic care so that they become well and return to their normal roles.

Within the context of the social control responsibilities of medicine, society not only allows two explicit behavioral exemptions for the sick person, but also imposes two explicit behavioral requirements. The exemptions are as follows:

1. The sick person is temporarily excused from normal social roles. Depending on the nature and severity of the illness, a physician can legitimize the sick role status and permit the patient to forgo normal responsibilities. The physician's endorsement is required so that society can maintain some control and prevent people from lingering in the sick role.

2. The sick person is not held responsible for the illness. Society accepts that cure will require more than the best efforts of the patient, and permits the patient to be "taken care of" by health care professionals and others.

In order to be granted these role exemptions, however, the patient must be willing to accept the following two obligations:

1. The sick person must want to get well. The previous two elements of the legitimized sick role are conditional on this requirement. The patient must not get so accustomed to the sick role or so enjoy the lifting of responsibilities that motivation to get well is surrendered.

2. The sick person is expected to seek medical advice and cooperate with medical experts. This requirement introduces another means of social control. The patient who refuses to see a health care professional creates suspicion that the illness is not legitimate. Such a refusal inevitably reduces the patience and sympathy of society and those surrounding the patient.

Criticisms of the Sick Role

Sociologists today are divided on the sick role's current value as an explanatory concept. The four main criticisms of the concept are briefly described here:

1. The sick role does not account for the considerable variability in behavior among sick

people. Variation occurs not only by age, gender, and ethnicity, but also by the certainty and severity of prognosis.

2. The sick role is applicable when describing patient experience with acute illnesses only, and is less appropriate when describing people with chronic illnesses who may not have easily recognizable symptoms (e.g., a build-up of plaque in the coronary arteries) and may not get well no matter how much they want to and how vigilant they are in following the physician's instructions.

3. The sick role does not adequately account for the variety of settings in which physicians and patients interact. It is most applicable to a physician–patient relationship that occurs in the physician's office.

4. The sick role is more applicable to middle-class patients and middle-class values than it is to people in lower socioeconomic groups. Not everyone can follow this pathway—for example, lower-income persons have less freedom to curtail their normal responsibilities, especially their jobs, and thus have a more difficult time complying with the model.

Rebuttal to Sick Role Criticism

Talcott Parsons, in a 1975 journal article (he died in 1978), and others have suggested that critics have failed to capture nuances in the sick role concept and see its flexibility (Fox, 1989). For example, Parsons argued that the sick role can pertain to persons with chronic illness—even though they are not "curable," their condition is often "manageable," and they are able to return to many of their pre-illness role responsibilities—and that, as an ideal type, it is unnecessary for the concept to account for all variations.

Medicalization

While Parsons described the role of medicine as an instrument of social control, many believe that the powers of the medical institution have now expanded far beyond areas of genuine expertise. This has led to **medicalization**, a concept that has two primary meanings. First, an increasing number of behaviors and conditions that were once thought of as normal life problems (e.g., alcoholism and obesity) have come to be interpreted in medical terms, giving the medical profession increased powers in determining what is normal and desirable behavior. Second, medical practice is understood to be the proper mechanism for controlling, modifying, and eliminating these "undesirable" behaviors.

When sociologists began focusing attention on medicalization in the 1970s, it seemed clear that the medical profession was the primary force behind these efforts, although interest groups and social movements (e.g., the effort to define alcoholism as a medical problem) often played an important role. Today, however, according to Conrad (2005), the stimulus toward medicalization is coming from three other agents: (1) biotechnology [for example—as the pharmaceutical industry lobbies for medical definitions for conditions (e.g., male erectile dysfunction) in order to create a market for their drugs (e.g., Viagra)]: the new concept of **pharmaceuticalization**—"the process by which social, behavioral, or bodily conditions are treated, or deemed to be in need of treatment/ intervention with pharmaceuticals by doctors, patients, or both" (Abraham, 2010)—overlaps with medicalization, but is separate in that not all medicalized conditions require drug therapy; (2) consumers (e.g., in seeking to have procedures such as cosmetic surgery paid for by health insurance); and (3) managed care [acting either as an incentive for certain medical procedures (e.g., its willingness to pay for psychiatric medicine) or a constraint (e.g., its reluctance to pay for extensive psychotherapy)]. Other examples that illustrate medicalization are the increasing numbers of psychiatric diagnoses, menopause, obesity, baldness, anorexia, post-traumatic stress disorder, social anxiety disorder, and sleep disorders. The point is not that these are unimportant conditions. It is that medical categories and their consequent treatment have been expanded to bring more individuals and life conditions into the medical realm (Conrad and Slodden, 2013).

Freund and McGuire (1999) argue that in contemporary society the power of religious definitions of deviance has declined. Such definitions appear to lack rationality and society-wide acceptance in a religiously pluralistic country. In addition, the force of legal definitions of deviance has declined, even though they appear more rational; they often ultimately come down to the subjective decisions of a small number of people on a jury. In their place, society has turned to medical definitions of deviance that appear rational, scientifically based, and dependent upon technical expertise rather than human judgment. People may be comforted by the knowledge that "undesirable" behaviors have a nice neat medical explanation and can be eradicated when sufficient scientific knowledge is accumulated.

The consequences of this medicalization can be interpreted in various ways. Fox (1989) points out that labeling additional behaviors as sickness and extending sick role exemptions to more people may be less stigmatizing and less punitive than relying on religious definitions of sin or legal definitions of crime. Bringing behaviors such as alcoholism, drug addiction, compulsive overeating, and compulsive gambling under a medical rubric introduces a "quality of therapeutic mercy into the way that they are handled" (Fox, 1989:29).

Others argue that defining someone as being sick is ultimately a moral decision in that it requires definition of what is normal or desirable (Freidson, 1988). Medicalizing behaviors leads inevitably to social stigmatization, which has occurred today with conditions such as leprosy, AIDS, pelvic inflammatory disease, and cirrhosis of the liver (Freund and McGuire,

1999). According to this view, rather than being benevolent, the process of medicalization places a societally endorsed stamp of disapproval upon certain behaviors and extends the power of the medical profession over people's lives. An example follows.

Attention Deficit Hyperactivity Disorder (ADHD). In 1975, Peter Conrad described the medicalization of deviant behavior as it pertained to hyperkinesis (a concept that has evolved today to attention deficit hyperactivity disorder or ADHD). The term refers to a condition that has long been observed in children (about four times more common in males) and is characterized by hyperactivity, short attention span, restlessness, impulsivity, and mood swings—all typically defined as violations of social norms. Prompted by pharmaceutical developments (such as the development and marketing of Ritalin—a drug that has a depressing effect on those with ADHD) and by parents' groups (who sought medical solutions), the medicalization of ADHD occurred. Today, ADHD is the most commonly diagnosed childhood psychiatric disorder—about 9 percent of children and teens have been diagnosed with ADHD, and the number of children diagnosed each year is rapidly escalating.

By the 1990s, ADHD was increasingly being seen as an adult disease. Individuals who had never been diagnosed with ADHD as children often read about the disease in the popular or professional literature, self-diagnosed it, and presented themselves to physicians wanting pharmaceutical treatment (Conrad, 2007). Today, as much as 5 percent of the adult population has been diagnosed with ADHD, and more than 4 million adults use medication for it. Estimates are that ADHD medications globally may now be upwards of US$200 billion.

Conrad articulated the "up" side of this transition. Hyperactive children are considered to have an illness rather than to be "bad" kids (research has discovered some biochemical differences in the brains of people with ADHD), there is less condemnation of them (it is not their fault) and less social stigma, and the medical treatment may be a more humanitarian form of control than the criminal justice system. In addition, proper diagnosis increases the likelihood that ADHD kids will have access to appropriately focused educational programs.

On the "down" side, however, identifying the behavior in medical terms takes it out of the public domain where ordinary people can discuss and attempt to understand it, enables the introduction and use of new and powerful drugs (alternatives to Ritalin that have fewer negative side effects are now available and becoming more common), contributes to an "individualization of social problems" by focusing on the symptoms of the child and diverting attention from family and school and other aspects of the social structure that may be facilitating the problem, and depoliticizes deviant behavior— encouraging the view that deviant behaviors are individual problems rather than results of or challenges to the social system.

Demedicalization

Concerned that the medical profession's powers of social control have become too extensive, a countermovement toward **demedicalization** has occurred. It includes such elements as the removal of certain behaviors (e.g., homosexuality) from the American Psychiatric Association's list of mental disorders, and the deinstitutionalization of mental health patients (mental patients who can survive outside an institution and are not dangerous are mainstreamed into society). Ironically, both medicalization and demedicalization can occur simultaneously in society.

Biomedicalization

In the last few years, several medical sociologists have identified a significant new trend that they have referred to as **biomedicalization**. They use this term to refer to large technoscientific innovations occurring in molecular biology, biotechnologies, genomization, transplant medicine, and other new twenty-first century medical technologies. This is considered a continuation of medicalization, but in a much more intense way that involves highly sophisticated computer and information technologies. Examples are new clinical innovations such as improved diagnostic images and telemedicine, increased requirements for electronic patient records, networked or integrated systems of hospitals, clinics, group practices, insurance organizations, the bioscientific and medical technology and supplies industries, and the government. One aspect of this process is an expectation that patients will accept more responsibility for knowing how to use these new technologies (Bell and Figert, 2015; Clarke et al., 2003).

Symbolic Interactionism: The Labeling Approach to Illness

Whereas the biomedical approach assumes illness to be an objective state, labeling theory considers the definition of illness to be a subjective matter worked out in particular cultural contexts and within particular physician–patient encounters.

Every society has its own particular norms for identifying the behaviors and conditions that are defined and treated as illnesses. These illness definitions are not objective and are not permanently fixed in at least two important ways. First, the definitions differ from culture to culture and change over time within cultures. In the United States, alcoholism was once considered to be a voluntary, criminal act; it is now considered to be a medically treatable illness. Homosexuality used to be considered an illness; now it is more often considered to be biologically predetermined.

Second, applications of the illness label are influenced by social position. Many people might be considered mentally ill for engaging in the same kinds of behaviors for which college professors are labeled "eccentric." Cocaine addicts, alcoholics, and people who abuse Valium are all medically defined in different ways even though all of them may be experiencing chemical substance abuse. The stigma (or lack of it) is certainly influenced by the individual's social standing.

Application of the illness label is especially important because labels influence how a person is treated. Individuals who have received mental health care may always be viewed somewhat differently to people who have not received such care, even after treatment ends and mental health is restored. Likewise, someone who is diagnosed with cancer may forever be considered fragile even if the cancer is successfully combated.

The Work of Eliot Freidson

Eliot Freidson (1988) has devised a scheme to illustrate (1) that variations in the sick role do exist depending on one's illness, (2) that how sick people are treated depends upon the imputed seriousness of their disease and whether or not it is stigmatized within the society, and (3) that the illness label is not objective but rather a reflection of societal norms and cultural traditions. Freidson asserts that certain conditions are typically considered to be the responsibility of the sick person, and that society often responds negatively to these individuals, much as they would respond to one who has broken the law. Examples of these conditions would include AIDS and other sexually transmitted infections, alcohol-related diseases, and, increasingly, smoking-related diseases.

In part, the likelihood of stigma relates to the perceived seriousness of the disease—that is, the extent to which it deviates from normality.

The consequent stigma results from societal definition; diseases that are stigmatized in one society may be relatively accepted in others (e.g., leprosy is highly stigmatized in India but much less so in Sri Lanka and Nigeria) (Freund and McGuire, 1999). A person with a socially stigmatized disease is much more likely to be looked down upon or victimized by discrimination than a person with a disease not so labeled.

Freidson's typology (see Table 7–1) considers both the extent of deviation from normality created by a disease (its "imputed seriousness") and the extent of stigmatization of persons with the disease (its "imputed legitimacy"). Illness states produce one of three types of legitimacy:

1. *Illegitimate (or stigmatized illegitimacy),* which provides some exemption from role responsibilities but few additional privileges, and may carry social stigmatization. Freidson considers stammering (Cell 1) to be a minor deviation from social norms, and epilepsy (Cell 4) to be a serious deviation. Because of the stigma attached, both present challenges to people with either of the conditions. See the box "Labeling Theory and Stuttering."
2. *Conditional legitimacy,* which provides temporary exemption from role responsibilities with some new privileges—provided that the individual seeks to get well. A cold (Cell 2) and pneumonia (Cell 5) are Freidson's examples of a minor deviation and a serious deviation, respectively, from social norms, and ones that are considered legitimate.
3. *Unconditional legitimacy,* which provides permanent and unconditional exemption from role responsibilities due to the hopelessness of the condition. Pockmarks (Cell 3) are an example of a minor deviation, and cancer (Cell 6) exemplifies a serious deviation.

TABLE 7–1   Freidson's Model of Types of Illness (Deviance) for Which the Individual Is Not Held Responsible

Imputed Seriousness	Illegitimate (Stigmatized)	Conditionally Legitimate	Unconditionally Legitimate
Minor deviation	**Cell 1** "Stammer" Partial suspension of some ordinary obligations; few or no new privileges; adoption of a few new obligations	**Cell 2** "A cold" Temporary suspension of a few ordinary obligations; temporary enhancement of ordinary privileges. Obligation to get well	**Cell 3** "Pockmarks" No special change in obligations or privileges
Serious deviation	**Cell 4** "Epilepsy" Suspension of some ordinary obligations; adoption of new obligations; few or no new privileges	**Cell 5** "Pneumonia" Temporary release from ordinary obligations; addition to ordinary privileges. Obligation to cooperate and seek help in treatment	**Cell 6** "Cancer" Permanent suspension of many ordinary obligations; marked addition to privileges

Source: Eliot Freidson, *The Profession of Medicine: A Study in the Sociology of Applied Knowledge* (Chicago: University of Chicago Press, 1988).

IN THE FIELD

LABELING THEORY AND STUTTERING

Since childhood, I have had a stutter that makes a regular appearance in my oral interactions and, at one time or another, has affected nearly all facets of my life. My frustrated parents and I tried in vain to locate a solution, they hoping that years of speech therapy would pay off, me dreaming for a miracle cure that could instantly remove this painfully humiliating trait.... At the end of one school year, some of the other children in my therapy group received certificates of accomplishment. When I questioned the therapist as to why I didn't get one, she explained that, unlike me, the other children had achieved the goal of fluency and were therefore being rewarded. Most likely, she used this as a means of encouraging those of us who "failed" to try harder to succeed the next year, but to me this seemed a direct indication that my stutter was *my* fault, and that I was a less adequate person because of it.... When one is being told repeatedly that stuttering is bad and that one should attempt to eliminate it, any instance of dysfluency will contribute to the individual's sense of despair and hopelessness.... The definitive labels I received from myself and others only served to more deeply ingrain me in the role of a "stutterer." (Hottle, 1996)

STAGE 3: MEDICAL CARE CONTACT/ SELF-CARE

When Suchman's "stages of illness experience" was devised, the third stage was labeled as "medical care contact" and described as the point at which an individual sought professional medical care. Today, medical sociologists are much more aware of the variety of options available to people who have entered the sick role, the increasingly common practice of **self-care**, and the importance of the individual's social and cultural environment in shaping the action taken.

How do people decide how to behave in response to being sick? Borrowing from *rational choice theory*, one common approach has been to view sick individuals as people who have preferences and goals in life, who often meet constraints in satisfying these preferences, and who must make choices from available options. The rational individual will identify possible options, determine the advantages and disadvantages of each option, and then select the option that will maximize the opportunity to satisfy preferences. A sick individual, for example, might consider the cost, availability, and convenience of seeing a medical doctor and recall the satisfaction or dissatisfaction produced in a prior visit.

Bernice Pescosolido believes that this approach focuses on the individual too much, and that it fails to include the important influence of social relationships. She advocates for a **social organization strategy (SOS)** that emphasizes that the process of definition and the ability to cope are both culturally and socially determined.

> In the SOS approach, illness careers start with an event that sets into motion a process of attempting to cope with a physical or emotional problem, given an ongoing structured system of social relations. These attempts at coping are created in negotiation with others and constrained by social structure. (Pescosolido, 1992:1114)

The SOS approach emphasizes that responding to illness is a process—rather than making a single choice, sick people continue to talk with others, solicit advice, and possibly use a variety of professional, semiprofessional, and lay advisors until the matter is resolved or until the options are exhausted. Table 7–2, condensed from Pescosolido, identifies some of the many medical care options from which people select.

Drawing on conversations with patients in internal medicine clinics, disabilities clinics, and HIV counseling and testing sites, Maynard (2006) found strong evidence for the importance of social relationships in assessing the meaning of particular diagnoses. Frequently, the physician or the patient or a family member/ significant other of the patient suggest what the diagnosis means for the patient. Then, one of the other participants either accepts or rejects that meaning and extends the discussion. All of the participants tend to work toward alignment— that is, agreement about the short-term and long-term effects on the patient.

Emotional responses can be exhibited throughout this discussion, and these can cover a wide range, including shock, anger, sadness, threat of loss, and uncertainty. It is said that some people lose their faith and others find it. Some focus more on short-term pain and others on fear of death. Patients who have gone through this process urge that it is important to allow these emotional responses and then move attention as soon as is practicable to specific responses— learning more about the condition, considering possible treatments, contacting appropriate medical providers and other resources, and taking care of daily-life considerations such as job and family responsibilities. These responses often occur within social relationships.

Hunt, Jordan, and Irwin (1989) conducted extensive interviews with 23 women about their illness experiences just before seeing a physician and at 2, 6, 10, and 15 weeks post-consultation, and they also interviewed their physicians and

TABLE 7–2 The Range of Choices for Medical Care and Advice

Option	Advisor	Examples
Modern medical practitioners	M.D.s, osteopaths (general practitioners; specialists), and allied health professionals	Physicians, psychiatrists, podiatrists, optometrists, nurses, midwives, opticians, psychologists, druggists, technicians, and aides
Alternative medical practitioners	"Traditional" healers	Faith healers, spiritualists, shamans, curanderos, diviners, herbalists, acupuncturists, bonesetters, and granny midwives
	Modern healers	Homeopaths, chiropractors, naturopaths, nutritional consultants, and holistic practitioners
Non-medical professionals	Social workers	Police and lawyers
	Legal agents	
	Clergymen	
	Supervisors	Bosses and teachers
Lay advisors	Family	Spouse and parents
	Neighbors	
	Friends	
	Coworkers and classmates	
Other	Self-care	Non-prescription medicines, self-examination procedures, folk remedies, and health foods
None		

Source: Bernice Pescosolido, "Beyond Rational Choice: The Social Dynamics of How People Seek Help," *American Journal of Sociology*, 97:1096–1138, 1992.

collected information from their charts. All the women in the sample reported at least two non-specific symptoms, such as dizziness and fatigue.

How did these women's understanding of their illnesses evolve? The researchers discovered that each woman brought several sources of information into the process, including previous medical history, ongoing experiences, and interaction with others. Each woman had evaluated her problems prior to seeing the physician and, in part, interpreted the physician's diagnosis in the light of these prior understandings and thoughts.

In almost all the cases, the physician's diagnosis was not simply accepted or rejected by patients, but rather it was transformed and incorporated into the understanding of the illness they had prior to the consultation. The diagnoses were also filtered through previous and current observations of others, and comments and advice offered by those in the patient's social world. Over the 4-month period, the patients continually adjusted and reworked the construction of their illnesses.

The next two sections in this chapter examine two of the many options for responding to illness—seeking professional medical care and self-care.

The Decision to Seek Professional Care

In Chapter 6, we emphasized the importance of considering both macro (social-structural) and

The decision to seek formal medical care is shaped by many factors, including the patient's age and gender, the perception of the illness, and the social situation. Here, a radiologist explains the results of a set of X-rays to a patient. Photo courtesy of Janet Jonas.

micro (individual decision-making) factors as influences on participation in health behaviors. Both factors are also important influences on the decision about seeking professional medical care. Ronald Andersen and Lu Ann Aday, who have helped to guide sociological thinking about the use of medical services, developed a framework for examining access to care that includes both structural and individual factors.

They posit that access to care can best be understood by considering (1) the general physical, political, and economic environment, (2) characteristics of the health care system, including health care policy and the organization and availability of services, and (3) characteristics of the population including those that may *predispose* one to use services (age, gender, and attitudes about health care), those that *enable* one to use health services (income and health insurance coverage), and the *need* for health services (Andersen, Aday, and Lytle, 1987; Andersen, 1995, 2008).

The ability of this model to predict use of services has been affirmed in much research. McEwen (2000) has used data from a national health survey to determine the predictive ability

of the model with respect to postponement of needed medical care and to the presence of unmet medical need. She found that the best prediction of these dependent measures occurred when all three of the predisposing, enabling, and need factors were considered.

Concentrating more on the individual level, DiMatteo and Friedman (1982) have specified three factors that influence the decision to seek care:

1. *The background of the patient.* Propensity to see a physician is influenced by such factors as age, gender, race and ethnicity, and social class. For example, men are often more reluctant than women to see a physician, and many married men schedule an appointment only when pressured by their wives to do so (estimates are that women make 70 percent of all health care decisions). Many (especially older) men prefer to "tough it out" and are embarrassed to discuss such matters as sexual dysfunction, prostate enlargement, and depression.

2. *The patient's perception of the illness.* Zola (1973:677–689) has identified five *social*

triggers that influence the judgment that the symptoms need professional health care: (a) perceived interference with vocational or physical activity, especially work-related activity; (b) perceived interference with social or personal relations; (c) an interpersonal crisis; (d) a **temporalizing of symptomatology** (setting a deadline—if I'm not better by Monday, I'll call the physician); and (e) pressure from family and friends.

3. *The social situation.* Even for pain that may relate to a serious condition, situational factors matter. Symptoms that begin during the week, rather than at the weekend, are more likely to motivate prompt contact with a physician, as are symptoms that appear at work and those that appear when other people are present (DiMatteo and Friedman, 1982).

Use of Medical Care Services

Americans on average have about five or six physician contacts each year. However, this average camouflages significant differences among population subgroups. Overall, the number of contacts increases significantly with age and is higher for females than males, and is highest among people in the lowest income category.

The following section describes patterns in the utilization of health services among several important population subgroups.

The Poor and the Medically Indigent. People below the poverty level and those just above it often have difficulty gaining access to quality medical care. Since the late 1960s (and largely as a result of Medicaid and Medicare), the poor have averaged as many or more physician contacts each year as the non-poor. However, relative to their greater medical need, the poor continue to have lower access. And the lowest utilization rates relative to need are found among those just above the poverty level. These individuals—often called the *medically indigent* or the *working poor*—earn just enough money to fail to qualify for Medicaid, but not enough to afford private medical care.

In the past, most of the medically indigent lacked any form of health insurance (about 47 million Americans lacked health care coverage in 2010). Most were in households with a wage earner who worked in a job that did not offer health insurance as a benefit. The other largest groups of people without insurance were unemployed people and their families who had lost their health insurance along with their jobs, and those with major health problems who could not afford an individual insurance policy (or who had been denied insurance altogether due to their condition). These patterns have changed somewhat with the passage of the Affordable Care Act (Obamacare) in 2010 and implementation of key pieces in 2014. The Affordable Care Act is discussed at length in Chapter 14.

Even after the passage of the Affordable Care Act, use of health care services by the poor differs from that by the non-poor in at least three other important respects. First, the poor are much less likely to have a regular source of care—that is, a physician who is routinely seen for health care problems or services. Often this is due to the lack of physicians in low-income areas.

Second (as a consequence of the first), the poor are much more likely to use a hospital emergency room (ER) or outpatient department as a routine care site. While this is not an efficient use of services (care in the ER is more expensive) and may be resented by hospital staff, these may be the only available and convenient facilities (Rust et al., 2008). These public hospital and clinic sites tend to be larger, busier, colder, and more impersonal than medical offices. The waiting time to see a physician may be very long—sometimes most of a day. Staff members are often fiercely overworked and have little time for patients. The actual physician–patient encounter may be hurried and abrupt, with little warmth and little investigation of the patient's psychosocial concerns. Often this encounter is not a satisfying experience for either the patient or the physician. This "health care system barrier" reduces the likelihood of the poor receiving medical services.

Third (partially as a consequence of the first two), low-income persons are much sicker when they are admitted to a hospital, and require longer hospital stays. Due to the higher rates of disease and illness in poor communities, the lack of access to ambulatory care, and the lack of adequate financial resources or health insurance coverage to pay hospital costs, the poor often become very sick before admission occurs.

In order to study this pattern, Epstein, Stern, and Weissman (1990) interviewed almost 17,000 patients admitted to five Massachusetts hospitals. They collected information on three components of socioeconomic standing (income, occupation, and education) and several aspects of the hospital stay. Patients in the lowest socioeconomic group had hospital stays 3 to 30 percent longer than patients of higher socioeconomic status. Hospital charges were 1 to 18 percent higher, reflecting the longer stay and the greater number of services provided. These patterns were maintained even when age and severity of illness were controlled for. A separate study of a national sample of hospitals found that patients who were uninsured at the time of admission were much sicker and 1.2 to 3.2 times more likely to die while in the hospital (Hadley, Steinberg, and Feder, 1991). Studies are underway to determine the extent to which these patterns have changed since 2010.

The inability to respond to health problems occurs throughout the spectrum of health care services. For example, low-income persons and the medically indigent often forgo needed dental services (which are not covered in the ACA).

They are prevented by cost considerations from getting regular check-ups, and often they even try to get by without professional dental care when there are serious and painful dental problems. Programs that provide free dental care are often forced to concentrate on tooth extractions because the underlying problem has become extremely painful. Some organizations have been created to establish volunteer-based free dental days within communities. Recently, a 2-day dental clinic in a community of 225,000 people provided needed dental care for more than 1,000 individuals, and had to turn another 1,000 away due to having insufficient time and personnel. Many of those who received care stood in line all day for the opportunity to receive dental care. Of the patients who were seen, almost 700 had at least one tooth extracted, and the average number of teeth extracted was four.

For an international comparison, see the box "Disparities in Primary Care Experiences by Income."

The Homeless. The homeless population in the United States is in great need of mental and physical health care services, but is not receiving them. Estimates of the prevalence of psychiatric disorders among the homeless range from 25 to 50 percent, and estimates of previous psychiatric hospitalization range from 15 to 42 percent. Research has consistently found very high levels of need for physical and mental health services, but very few services received (Wood et al., 2010).

Racial and Ethnic Minorities. In recent years, the black–white disparity in utilization of health care services has almost disappeared. However, significant differences remain in other aspects of use patterns. Blacks are less likely than whites to have a regular source of health care, and are more likely to secure care in hospital outpatient clinics, ERs, or community health centers. Research has documented that

IN COMPARATIVE FOCUS

DISPARITIES IN PRIMARY CARE EXPERIENCES BY INCOME

In 2006, the Commonwealth Fund, a respected private foundation that seeks to improve the health care system, reported on a 2004 study of the use of primary care by adults in five countries—the United States, Australia, Canada, the United Kingdom, and New Zealand. The report authors summarized as follows:

> Given the strong correlation worldwide between low income and poor health—including disability, chronic disease, and acute illness—it is especially critical for people with limited incomes to have ready access to medical care. Inequities in access can contribute to and exacerbate existing disparities in health and quality of life, creating barriers to a strong and productive life. (p. xiii)

How did the United States fare in the comparison?

> Overall, the report finds a health care divide separating the U.S. from the other four countries. The U.S. stands out for income-based disparities in patient experiences—particularly for more negative primary care experiences for adults with below-average income. (p. xiii)

On 16 of the 30 specific measures of primary care experience for below-average income patients, the United States ranked last. Patients in the United States were most likely to go without care because of costs, most likely to have difficulty getting care at night, during weekends, or on holidays without going to the emergency room, most likely to report duplication of medical services (due to lack of coordination of care), and most likely to rate their encounter with the physician as being only fair or poor. The gap between above-average-income patients and below-average-income patients was by far the largest in the United States (Huynh et al., 2006).

---

racial and ethnic minorities experience more difficulty in getting initial and follow-up appointments with a physician, and wait longer during an appointment. These disparities persist even after health status and socioeconomic status are controlled for (Shi, 1999).

In addition to economic reasons, another factor accounting for these patterns is the lack of services in black communities in inner-city areas of large metropolitan cities and in rural areas, especially in the Southeast. These are the two areas of the country most underserved by physicians. This shortage makes it difficult for physicians who are located in these areas, and complicates the patients' efforts to find a physician with whom to establish a continuing relationship. Since patients with a regular source of care tend to be more satisfied with their physician, other benefits accrue, including higher compliance rates.

Despite high levels of morbidity, Hispanics have the lowest rate of utilization of medical services of any racial or ethnic group in the United States. Only about half as many Hispanics as whites have a regular source of medical care, they are twice as likely to use a hospital ER as a regular source of care, they are much more likely to be admitted to a hospital through an ER, and they are likely to be much sicker at the point of admission (indicating delay in seeking services), resulting in longer and more expensive hospital stays. Hispanics are much less likely to initiate prenatal care in the recommended first trimester, and are three times less likely to receive any prenatal care whatsoever.

Several factors are responsible for these differential utilization patterns, including lower family incomes and a lack of accessible health care services for Mexican American farm-workers and those who live in inner-city areas of large cities. Even when services are available, communication difficulties due to the absence of an interpreter and cultural differences to providers often represent important barriers.

Age. Older people are consistently the heaviest users of health care services. Persons over 65 years of age receive more preventive care than do younger people, and visit physicians more frequently in response to medical need. Although people over age 65 years comprise only about 12 percent of the United States population, they account for one-third of all personal health care expenditures.

Gender. There are consistent differences between women and men in utilization of health care services. Women use more physician services, are more likely to have a regular source of care, receive significantly more preventive care, take more medications, are more likely to visit outpatient clinics, and are more likely to be hospitalized. On the other hand, men are more likely to use ER services.

Why do women and men have such different utilization patterns? Perhaps the most obvious reason—the extra use of services by women for reproductive care—explains only part of the difference (reproduction accounts for only about 20 percent of women's physician contacts). More important factors are the greater number of illnesses reported by women (need for care being an important predictor of use) and the greater willingness of women to seek professional health care.

Gender roles are clearly implicated with the latter reason. Women are socialized to be more sensitive to medical symptoms, and once symptoms are perceived, to take them more seriously.

Once this evaluation has occurred, women find it easier to seek medical assistance; therefore they show a higher utilization rate. On the other hand, men often exhibit a reluctance to get check-ups, required screening tests, and medical attention for problems as diverse as depression, substance abuse, physical disability, and stress (Galdas, Cheater, and Marshall, 2005). Recent research has traced at least some of this pattern to the traditional gender role of men—a sense of immunity and immortality, difficulty relinquishing control, and a reluctance to seek help (Springer and Mouzon, 2011). See the accompanying box, "Gender and the Use of Medical Services in Rural India."

The Concept of Self-Care

Self-care describes the broad range of behaviors initiated by individuals to promote optimal health, prevent illness, detect symptoms of ill health, heal acute illness, and manage chronic conditions. It includes obtaining information about health and illness, doing self-screening exams, managing one's own illness (including self-medication), and formulating clear goals and preferences with regard to end-of-life treatment decisions. Although the term "self-care" implies an individual behavior, these practices occur within a social network and are very much influenced by family, friends, and cultural norms.

However self-care is defined, it is clear that self-care practices are an extremely common and routine response to illness symptoms, and are practices that are pervasive throughout the population. A national study found that more than five in six people aged 55 years or older had experienced at least one illness symptom in the previous 6 months for which they relied on self-care only. Almost 90 percent of these respondents assessed their health care efforts as being good, very good, or excellent (Kart and Engler, 1994).

IN COMPARATIVE FOCUS

GENDER AND THE USE OF MEDICAL SERVICES IN RURAL INDIA

While certain cultural norms in the United States discourage males from seeking professional medical care, the opposite pattern is evident in some parts of rural India. Even in areas where health services are readily available, certain cultural values related to gender ideology and gender-based behavior influence women to underuse medical care. To better understand this pattern, Kumar (1995) spent 9 months in a rural village in northern India conducting a general household survey and open-ended interviews with married women.

Married women in the village observe *ghungat* (veiling), which includes covering the face with a veil and complying with a set of restrictions on speech, mobility, and social relationships. The female body is associated with shame for reasons that relate to ideas about cleanliness (menstruation and childbirth add even further restrictions, due to the powerful meaning ascribed to blood as a particularly dirty substance), the necessity of maintaining pure patrilineage, and fear of uncontrolled

sexuality. Women are financially dependent on men, although men are dependent on women to manage the home and raise the children. *Ghungat* is viewed as a practice that honors both men and women because it is a visual expression of the acceptance of the greater power of males and their control over females.

When married women are sick, their access to medical care is limited by the necessity for having the husband's approval to seek care, by not having direct access to financial resources, and by the difficulty of taking time off from household chores. Limitations in movement throughout the village and a requirement not to visit the health center alone are further discouragements, as is the perceived inappropriateness of having a male physician "look at" parts of the woman's unclothed body. These cultural restraints explain the less frequent use of medical services by women than by men, and the fact that women are sometimes not seen until they have reached an advanced stage of illness.

The Self-Help Movement. Reliance on self-help is certainly not a new concept. Since the earliest civilizations, people have taken personal measures to protect their safety and well-being and deal with illnesses. However, the advent of modern scientific medicine shifted primary responsibility for managing health and illness from the individual and family to the physician. Now there is renewed interest among both the general public and many health care professionals in shifting the overall management of health care from the professional back to the individual.

At least three key factors should continue to sustain this movement:

1. The increasing amount of health-related information available on the Internet and the increasing number of people who use this information are important elements of the self-help movement.

2. An expansion of alternative medical philosophies and clinical approaches that place primary responsibility for health on the individual rather than on the professional. These include behavioral approaches, concepts of holistic health, and therapies derived from Eastern philosophies (e.g., yoga, meditation, and biofeedback).

3. Increasing health care costs have inspired potential savings from more vigorous health

promotion and disease prevention efforts. Studies indicate that people who use self-care practices reduce both the number of visits to physicians and the number of days in the hospital, and that the commonplace use of self-selected, over-the-counter drugs saves the nation millions of dollars each year in physicians' fees. One study asked a panel of physicians to evaluate the self-care practices of a random sample of people; they judged that only 2 percent of the actions of these people were medically inappropriate (Wilkinson, Darby, and Mant, 1987).

Self-Help Groups.   In recent years, there has been tremendous growth in the number of **self-help groups**—that is, groups of individuals who experience a common problem and share their personal stories, knowledge, and support to help one another. An estimated 10 to 15 million people participate in the nation's half million-plus self-help groups annually, and more than 30 million people have participated at some time. Groups have been organized around almost every conceivable disease, addiction, and disability. See the box "Selected Self-Help Groups."

Social support groups can provide significant benefits for members. One study of 232 members

An important part of the self-help movement is the self-selection of a wide variety of vitamins and herbs that are now readily available in natural food stores, grocery stores, drug stores, and other outlets. Photo courtesy of Gregory Weiss.

IN THE FIELD

SELECTED SELF-HELP GROUPS

Al-Anon and Alateen	Impotence Anonymous
Alcoholics Anonymous	Infertility Support Group
Alliance for the Mentally Ill	La Leche League
Alzheimer's Support Group	Menopause Support Group
Bereavement Support Group	Multiple Sclerosis Support Group
Breast Cancer Support Group	Narcotics Anonymous
Bulimia, Anorexia Self-Help	Overeaters Anonymous
Cocaine Anonymous	Parents Anonymous
Co-Dependents Anonymous	Parents of Children with Asthma
Compassionate Friends (Bereaved Parents)	Parents without Partners
Concerned United Birthparents	Parkinson's Support Group
Crohn's and Colitis Foundation of America	Sex Addicts Anonymous
Diabetes Support Group	Shhh (Hard-of-Hearing)
Exceptional Cancer Patients	Step-Family Association of America
Fathers United Inc.	Suddenly Single
Gamblers Anonymous	Veterans Outreach Program
Grief Support Group	Weight-Watchers

in 65 different disease-related groups revealed that most members reported many positive changes in psychosocial well-being (a reduction in emotional stress and a stronger feeling of being safe and sheltered), in feelings of competence (learning new behaviors and more self-confidence), in greater participation in social life (more social activities and more interest in helping other people), and in knowledge and understanding of their disease and its treatment. However, less than 25 percent reported improvement in physical symptoms or a reduction in physical impairment. Participants did report making more demands on professional helpers due to their ability to express their needs and their desire to play a more active role in the management of their diseases (Trojan, 1989).

A study of self-help groups for parents of children with cancer found that the group increased members' confidence and willingness to work with others for changes in the medical care system that would benefit their children or others with cancer. Thus members were inspired not only to become more active as individuals or in family units, but also to engage in social activism (Chesney and Chesler, 1993).

STAGE 4: DEPENDENT-PATIENT ROLE

The patient enters the fourth stage, the dependent-patient role, when the recommendation of the health care provider for treatment is accepted. This also creates new role expectations that include increased contact with the provider and altered personal relationships. The patient is expected to make every effort to get well. Some people, of course, enjoy the benefits of this role (e.g., increased attention and escape from work responsibilities) and attempt to malinger. Eventually, however, the acute patient will either get well and move on to stage 5 or terminate the treatment (and perhaps seek alternative treatment).

STAGE 5: RECOVERY AND REHABILITATION

The final stage of Suchman's schema for patients with most acute illnesses occurs as the treatment succeeds and recovery occurs. As that happens, the patient is expected to relinquish the sick role and move back to normal role obligations. For chronic patients, the extent to which previous role obligations may be resumed ranges from those who forsake the sick role to those who will never be able to leave it.

An interesting subfield of sociology that has developed in recent years is Animals and Society. The box "The Role of Animals in Human Therapy" describes how the animal–human bond has important implications for health and rehabilitation.

EXPERIENCING CHRONIC ILLNESS AND DISABILITY

While patients usually survive acute illnesses and recover from them, other conditions continue over time. This section of the chapter focuses on three such conditions. A **chronic illness** is one that is ongoing or recurrent, and that typically persists for as long as the person

---

IN THE FIELD

THE ROLE OF ANIMALS IN HUMAN THERAPY

Research has begun to document the health benefits for humans who interact positively with animals. Interaction with animals has been shown to have (1) *preventive benefits for health* (reduced stress, lower blood pressure, and greater happiness), (2) *therapeutic benefits* (riding horses is helpful in the physical rehabilitation of the developmentally disabled, animals can assist with the emotional recovery of battered women and their children, they assist with loneliness of groups such as the elderly or those with HIV disease, and they are valuable in working with stroke victims and those with orthopedic problems), and (3) *recovery and rehabilitation benefits* (one major study examined the influence of hundreds of physical, social, and economic factors on the long-term survival of patients released from a hospital coronary care unit—the most important influence was the extent of the damage to the heart tissue itself, but the second largest influence was living with a pet. Less than half the patients

had a pet, but those who did were four times less likely to die). In addition, service dogs and guide dogs are trained to help individuals who require physical assistance in order to maintain an independent life.

Why do these benefits occur? Research has identified that companion animals help to fulfill (1) *social-psychological needs* such as contact, comfort, a feeling of being needed, unconditional love, empathy, patience, relaxation, and coping with stress, (2) *physical needs* such as more exercise (dog owners walk much more), and (3) *help with child socialization* in that children raised with an animal have been found to be more nurturing, have a greater sense of responsibility, and have more social and less self-absorbed behavior. (Based on material from *Kindred Spirits* by Allen M. Schoen, D.V.M., M.S., copyright 2001 by Allen M. Schoen. Used with permission of Broadway Books, a division of Random House, Inc.)

Animals now assist in a variety of therapeutic procedures, and positive interaction with animals has been found to provide important benefits for human health. Photo courtesy of Gregory Weiss.

lives. Diabetes is an example of a chronic illness. While it can be treated with insulin, there is no cure for diabetes, and it never disappears. As defined in Chapter 3, a **disability** includes *impairments* (a problem in body function or structure), *activity limitations* (a difficulty in executing a task or action), and *participation restrictions* (a problem experienced in involvement in life situations). Disability is a complex phenomenon, reflecting an interaction between features of a person's body and features of the society in which he or she lives.

Relationship between Chronic Illness and Disability

Often, chronic illnesses have an insidious onset (e.g., cancer and coronary heart disease) and are characterized early on by symptoms that are not immediately detectable. Eventually, most chronic illnesses can be identified by diagnostic laboratory procedures. On the other hand, disability is more of a relational concept—it is rarely entirely present or absent in any individual, but rather its presence is often a matter of degree. It is a more subjective term in that it can

only be understood by considering an individual within the cultural context. Moreover, some individuals with chronic illness become disabled, but some do not, and disabilities may result from chronic illness but they also may be traced to trauma, accidents, injuries, and genetic disorders rather than chronic illness (Bury, 1999).

Living With Chronic Illness and Disability

Experiencing chronic illness and/or disability typically involves a period of assessment, emotional adjustment, and mental and physical accommodation. Research has identified at least five very important concerns shared by many chronically ill and disabled people:

1. *Impairment of personal cognitive functioning.* Patients may be concerned that their illness will progress to a point where their cognitive functioning ability may be impaired, or that medications will have a dulling effect on their memory, reasoning ability, and capacity for communication.
2. *Loss of personal independence.* Many people deeply value their independence and

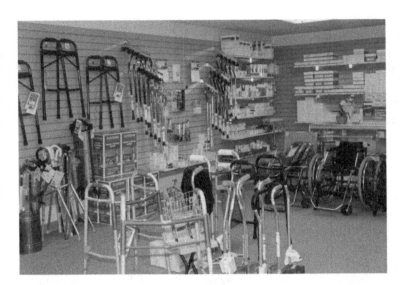

As the number of people with chronic illnesses and disabilities increases, home health care and home health equipment have become booming businesses. Photo courtesy of Gregory Weiss.

appreciate it even more when it is threatened. Reliance on others may be a devastating thought—because of the inconvenience and, in a larger sense, the idea of becoming a burden on others.

3. *Changes in body image.* For patients whose illness creates any dramatic alteration in physical image, a major readjustment may be needed. Many people view themselves as physical as much as or more than mental beings; any change in body image is significant.

4. *Withdrawal from key social roles.* Because so many people derive their identity from their work, any disruption in work pattern or work accomplishment is very threatening. If remuneration is affected, an extra emotional burden is created. The withdrawal from key family responsibilities may be of paramount concern, along with anxiety about creating more work for other family members. This withdrawal and concern about it can jeopardize family cohesiveness.

5. *The future.* Any chronic or disabling condition raises questions about the patient's future

and the extent to which there will be further incapacitation or physical or mental limitations, as well as questions about financial indebtedness and permanent losses in daily activities.

The extent of these concerns and the ability to adjust, adapt, and even resolve them occur within a social environment. A study of women living with HIV found that those with greater **social capital** (e.g., adequate financial resources, a stable housing situation, access to health care) were better able to manage the demands of their condition. They practiced better daily health habits, had greater social support, and were better able to accept the chronic nature of HIV (Webel et al., 2013).

The Impact on Sense of Self

Having a chronic illness or disability challenges the individual's sense of self. Patients may have to get accustomed to significant changes in their body, their lifestyle, and interactions, and to prolonged regimens of medication, continuing bureaucratic hassles with the medical care system, and in some cases disabling pain.

Based on more than 100 interviews with 55 people, Charmaz (1991) has described how experiencing a progressively deteriorating chronic illness can reshape a person's life and sense of self. People experience chronic illness in three ways—as an *interruption in life,* as an *intrusive illness,* and as an *immersion in illness.*

At first, a person with a chronic illness may notice the disruption in life. There is time spent hoping for the best and trying to convince oneself that things will work out. Difficult times lower hopes and increase fears that important life events will need to be sacrificed. A bargaining process may occur when the person promises to do whatever can be done to feel better. Not fully comprehending chronicity, ill people seek recovery and, in doing so, maintain the same image of self and keep the illness external, not allowing it to become an essential part of their being. Only through time and the words and actions of others do the meanings of disability, dysfunction, and impairment become real.

Chronic illness becomes intrusive when it demands continuous attention, more and more time, and significant accommodations. Intrusion happens when the illness is recognized as a permanent part of life—when symptoms and treatments are expected and planned around. The ill person loses some control over life, but may work to maintain some control and to boost their self-esteem. Limits may be placed on the illness—for example, allowing oneself a certain number of bad days. Efforts are made to prevent the illness from occupying more and more of one's time and being.

Immersion occurs as the illness begins to dominate life. Responsibilities are surrendered, and days are dominated by dealing with the illness. "No longer can people add illness to the structure of their lives; instead, they must reconstruct their lives upon illness" (Charmaz, 1991:76). They face physical and perhaps social and economic dependencies, their social world shrinks, and more and more of each day is ordered by the routines demanded by the illness. People turn inward, become more socially isolated, and begin challenging their own identity ("How can I continue to be myself while having relentless illness?") (Charmaz, 1991:101).

The trajectory of self-image for those with traumatic but stable disabilities may differ in some ways. In a study of 35 adults with traumatic spinal cord injury, Yoshiba (1993) found that patients actively sought to "reconstruct" the self, and this process swung back and forth like a pendulum between the non-disabled and the disabled aspects of self. At any one time, these adults had a "predominant identity view" that at one extreme emphasized the former non-injured self and at the other extreme emphasized the disabled identity as the total self. Between the extremes were several gradations based primarily on the extent of dependence on others. Yoshiba discovered that the primary identity view is dynamic and shifting, and can be very fluid from one day to another and/or from one situation to another.

Moreover, with the possible exception of the disabled identity as the total self, Yoshiba's respondents contradicted the popular perception that having a disability is a totally negative experience. Some shared with her examples of activities for which they had never previously had time, and several spoke of their personal maturation in dealing with the situation. These experiences are akin to observations of chronically ill and disabled patients made by Lindsay (1996). She noted a constant striving for "health within illness" among her respondents, as many sought to identify or achieve positives from their condition.

Further confirmation of this perspective comes from research by Pudrovska (2010). She compared the trajectory of personal growth among those who had had cancer and those who had not for three age cohorts (those born in the

1940s, 1950s, and 1960s, those born in the 1930s, and those born in the 1920s). For those in the oldest cohort, cancer did accelerate decline in personal growth (an impairment trajectory). However, dealing with cancer neither accelerated nor decelerated decline in personal growth for those in the middle group (a resilient trajectory), and dealing with cancer actually slowed decline in personal growth for those in the youngest age cohort (a thriving trajectory). Pudrovska referred to this as psychological growth in response to an adverse event.

The Role of Social Stigma

The adjustment of people with a chronic illness or disability can be very much influenced by the manner in which they are treated by others. When others view an illness or disability in a demeaning manner, they impose a **stigma** or deeply discrediting label on the individual. The stigmatizing attitudes of others can have a pronounced effect on an individual's sense of self.

People with AIDS in American society are stigmatized when others try to avoid or ostracize them, disparage them or their disease, and label them in negative terms. Weitz (1991) points out that stigma is a central concern during all phases of the illness, from before diagnosis (when individuals must be concerned about the consequences of being tested for HIV), to living with the illness (and being differentially treated by family, friends, and health care providers), to the time of death (and being concerned about discriminatory treatment by funeral directors).

In a study comparing perceived stigma attached to cancer patients and HIV/AIDS patients, Fife and Wright (2000) identified four dimensions of perceived stigma:

1. *Social rejection.* Feelings of being discriminated against at work and in society, including a perception that others do not respect them, want to avoid them, and feel awkward in their presence.
2. *Financial insecurity.* Inadequate job security and income that result from workplace discrimination.
3. *Internalized shame.* Feelings of being set apart from others who are well, blaming oneself for the illness, and feeling a need to maintain secrecy about the illness.
4. *Social isolation.* Feelings of loneliness, inequality with others, uselessness, and detachment.

Fife and Wright found that while stigma was a central force in the lives of both sets of patients, the HIV/AIDS patients perceived greater stigma on all four dimensions. The more negative self-perception held by both sets of patients came more from the perceived stigma attached to the disease than from the disease itself. For example, both cancer and HIV/AIDS patients had reduced self-esteem. However, this stemmed not from having the disease but from the negative stigma that had been attached to them because of the disease.

Wingood et al. (2007) found that HIV-infected women who had perceived discrimination were more likely to report high stress levels than those who had not, as well as having more symptoms of depression, lower self-esteem, a greater likelihood of considering suicide, and a greater likelihood of not seeking or continuing with medical care. Other research (Turner-Cobb et al., 2002) has confirmed that HIV/AIDS patients who are more satisfied with their relationships and are more securely engaged with others make a better adjustment. These findings well illustrate the dramatic effect of societal response on sense of self.

SUMMARY

Illness behavior refers to activity undertaken by a person who feels ill in order to define the illness and seek relief from it. As outlined by Edward Suchman, the illness experience consists of five stages: (1) symptom experience, (2) assumption of the sick role, (3) medical care contact, (4) dependent-patient role, and (5) recovery and rehabilitation. Decisions that are made during these five stages and the behaviors exhibited are culturally and socially determined.

The symptom experience stage occurs in response to physical pain or discomfort, and includes cognitive reflection and emotional response. Individuals use many types of cues to determine whether to seek help. If they decide to relinquish normal social roles in response to illness, they enter a sick role. This involves giving up normal roles and the responsibility of caring for self, but only if the individual wants to get well and takes action to do so. Labeling theorists emphasize that the definition of illness is a subjective phenomenon that is socially constructed within society and within particular physician–patient encounters.

Medicine's license to legitimize illness has extended more widely than originally envisioned—a process termed "medicalization." An increasing number of behaviors (e.g., alcoholism and infertility) have come under medicine's domain, and physicians and other health care providers are sought for guidance.

The use of professional medical services in times of illness varies among population groups. Response to symptoms is affected greatly by socioeconomic, cultural, and structural variables. Access to quality medical care is still a problem for a number of disadvantaged population groups, especially people with low income and many racial and ethnic minority groups.

Self-care is an extremely common practice that involves a number of behaviors related to promoting health, preventing illness, and restoring health if illness occurs. Millions of people are helped annually through self-help groups.

Those who experience progressively deteriorating chronic illnesses and those who experience traumatic but stable disabilities undergo transformations in self-image and sometimes experience stigmatization. While the former gradually become "immersed" in the disease, the latter often shift back and forth between a disabled and non-disabled identity.

HEALTH ON THE INTERNET

There are many health resources available online. An interesting one is *Health Knowledge*, sponsored by the Public Health Action Support Team in England (www.healthknowledge.org. uk). Why was this particular Web site created?

To sample its content, click on "Public Health Textbook," then "Medical Sociology, Policy, and Economics," then "Concepts of Health and Illness," and finally on "Section 3: Labelling and Stigma." Read the brief sections on "Labelling" and "Stigma." To test your understanding of these concepts, study Figure 1 and explain it in your own words.

DISCUSSION QUESTIONS

1. In 1997, the case of Casey Martin received considerable national publicity. Martin was a young golfer who had had some success on the professional golf tour. However, he

The case of Casey Martin (a young professional golfer with a rare circulatory disease in his right leg) raised significant questions about treatment of individuals with limiting medical conditions. Ultimately, and despite their opposition, the PGA was required by courts to allow him to use a golf cart in professional tournaments. © Andrew Redington/Getty.

suffered from Klippel–Trenaunay–Weber syndrome, a rare and painful circulatory disorder that affected his lower right leg (his right leg has only half the girth of his left) and severely limited his ability to walk a golf course.

The Professional Golf Association (PGA) mandates that participants in its tournaments walk the golf course, although they hire others to carry their golf bag. Martin requested an exemption to this rule and asked to be allowed to use a golf cart (the kind most recreational golfers use) to get around the course. The PGA refused on the grounds that walking the course is an integral part of the game.

Martin sued the PGA under the Americans with Disabilities Act (ADA). The ADA, which was passed in 1990, prohibits discrimination on the basis of disability in jobs, housing, and places of public accommodation. The law requires businesses to make reasonable modifications for people with disabilities, unless doing so would fundamentally alter the nature of the activity in question. Martin contended his being allowed to ride in a cart would not constitute such a fundamental change, but the PGA argued that it would.

The case ultimately wound its way to the U.S. Supreme Court. In May 2001, by a 7 to

2 vote, the Court ruled that walking was, at most, peripheral to the game of golf and that Martin's use of a cart would not fundamentally alter the activity. Justices Scalia and Thomas, the dissenting judges, argued that the ruling would doom all sports at all levels because anyone with any disability could insist on having the rules of a game changed to accommodate a disability. ADA advocates insisted that the "fundamental change" stipulation would prevent such interpretation.

In your judgment, did the Supreme Court rule properly or improperly in the Casey Martin case? What implications did the decision have for people with disabilities?

(As an aside, Martin gave up tournament golf in 2006, but qualified for and played in the U.S. Open in 2012. In 2013, while riding in his cart as a spectator at a U.S. Junior Amateur tournament (he is currently golf coach at the University of Oregon), the United States Golf Association pulled him off the course and told him that spectators could not ride in a cart. Despite the Supreme Court decision and despite having been given permission by the tournament chairman and rules director, the USGA disallowed him use of the cart.)

2. In June 2013, the American Medical Association formally declared obesity to be a disease. The decision was hailed by some as a long overdue action that would improve medicine's ability to treat obesity, but was denounced by others who believe it will increase the stigma experienced by obese people. Having read about medicalization issues in this chapter, identify the various ways in which this declaration will affect obese people.

GLOSSARY

biomedicalization
chronic illness
demedicalization
disability
illness behavior
medicalization
palliative care
pharmaceuticalization
self-care

self-help groups
sick role
social capital
social construction of illness
social organization strategy (SOS)
stages of illness experience
stigma
temporalizing of symptomatology
theory of help-seeking behavior

REFERENCES

Abraham, John. 2010 "The Sociological Concomitants of the Pharmaceutical Industry and Medications." Pp. 290–308 in *Handbook of Medical Sociology* (6th ed.), Chloe E. Bird, Peter Conrad, Allen M. Fremont, and Stefan Timmermans (eds.). Nashville, TN: Vanderbilt University Press.

Alexander, G.C., S. Frattaroli, and A.C. Gielen. 2015 *The Prescription Opioid Epidemic: An Evidence-Based Approach*. Baltimore, MD: Johns Hopkins Bloomberg School of Public Health.

Andersen, Ronald M. 1995 "Revisiting the Behavioral Model and Access to Medical Care: Does It Matter?" *Journal of Health and Social Behavior*, 36:1–10.

———. 2008 "National Health Surveys and the Behavioral Model of Health Services Use." *Medical Care*, 46:647–653.

Andersen, Ronald M., Lu Ann Aday, and C.S. Lytle. 1987 *Ambulatory Care and Insurance Coverage in an Era of Constraint*. Chicago, IL: Pluribus.

Bell, Susan E., and Anne E. Figert. 2015 *Reimagining (Bio)Medicalization, Pharmaceuticals and Genetics*. New York: Routledge.

Bury, Michael. 1999 "On Chronic Illness and Disability." Pp. 173–183 in *Handbook of Medical Sociology*, Chloe E. Bird, Peter Conrad, and Allen M. Fremont (eds.). Upper Saddle River, NJ: Prentice Hall.

Charmaz, Kathy. 1991 *Good Days, Bad Days: The Self in Chronic Illness and Time*. New Brunswick, NJ: Rutgers University Press.

Chesney, Barbara K., and Mark A. Chesler. 1993 "Activism through Self-Help Group Membership." *Small Group Research*, 24: 258–273.

Clarke, Adele E., Janet K. Shim, Laura Mamo, Jennifer R. Fosket, and Jennifer R. Fishman. 2003 "Biomedicalization: Technoscientific Transformations of Health, Illness, and U.S. Biomedicine." *American Sociological Review*, 68:161–194.

Conrad, Peter. 1975 "The Discovery of Hyperkinesis: Notes on the Medicalization of Deviant Behavior." *Social Problems*, 23:12–21.

———. 2005 "The Shifting Engines of Medicalization." *Journal of Health and Social Behavior*, 46:3–14.

———. 2007 *The Medicalization of Society*. Baltimore, MD: Johns Hopkins University Press.

Conrad, Peter, and Kristin K. Barker. 2010 "The Social Construction of Illness: Key Insights and Policy Implications." *Journal of Health and Social Behavior*, 51:S67–S79.

Conrad, Peter, and Caitlin Slodden. 2013 "The Medicalization of Mental Disorder." Pp. 61–173 in *Handbook of the Sociology of Mental Health* (2nd ed.), Carol S. Aneshensel, Jo C. Phelan, and Alex Bierman (eds.). New York: Springer.

DiMatteo, M. Robin, and Howard S. Friedman. 1982 *Social Psychology and Medicine*. Cambridge, MA: Oelgeschlager, Gunn, & Hain.

Epstein, Arnold M., Robert S. Stern, and Joel S. Weissman. 1990 "Do the Poor Cost More? A Multihospital Study of Patients' Socioeconomic Status and the Use of Hospital Resources." *New England Journal of Medicine*, 322:122–128.

Fife, Betsy L., and Eric R. Wright. 2000 "The Dimensionality of Stigma: A Comparison of its Impact on the Self of Persons with HIV/AIDS and Cancer." *Journal of Health and Social Behavior*, 41:50–67.

Fox, Renee. 1989 *The Sociology of Medicine*. Upper Saddle River, NJ: Prentice Hall.

Freidson, Eliot. 1988 *The Profession of Medicine: A Study in the Sociology of Applied Knowledge*. Chicago, IL: University of Chicago Press.

Freund, Peter E.S., and Meredith McGuire. 1999 *Health, Illness, and the Social Body*, 3rd ed. Upper Saddle River, NJ: Prentice Hall.

Galdas, Paul M., Francine Cheater, and Paul Marshall. 2005 "Men and Health Help-Seeking Behaviours: Literature Review." *Journal of Advanced Nursing*, 49:616–623.

Hadley, Jack, Earl P. Steinberg, and Judith Feder. 1991 "Comparison of Uninsured and Privately Insured Hospital Patients." *Journal of the American Medical Association*, 265:374–379.

Hottle, Elizabeth. 1996. "Making Myself Understood: The Labeling Theory of Deviance Applied to Stuttering." *Virginia Social Science Journal*, 31:78–85.

Hunt, Linda M., Brigitte Jordan, and Susan Irwin. 1989 "Views of What's Wrong: Diagnosis and Patients' Concepts of Illness." *Social Science and Medicine*, 28:945–956.

Huynh, Phuong T., Cathy Schoen, Robin Osborn, and Alyssa L. Holmgren. 2006 *The U.S. Health Care Divide: Disparities in Primary Care Experiences by Income*. New York: The Commonwealth Fund.

Institute of Medicine. 2011 *Relieving Pain in America: A Blueprint for Transforming Prevention, Care, Education, and Research*. Washington, DC: The National Academies Press.

Jaret, Peter. 2015 "Forty-Six Americans Die Each Day from Painkiller ODs." *AARP Bulletin*, September issue:6–8.

Kart, Cary S., and Carol A. Engler. 1994 "Predisposition to Self-Help Care: Who Does What for Themselves and Why?" *Journal of Gerontology*, 49:S301–S308.

Kumar, Anuradha. 1995 "Gender and Health: Theoretical Versus Practical Accessibility of Health Care for Women in North India." Pp. 16–32 in *Global Perspectives on Health Care*, Eugene B. Gallagher and Janardan Subedi (eds.). Upper Saddle River, NJ: Prentice Hall.

Light, Donald W., Joel Lexchin, and Jonathan J. Darrow. 2013 "Institutional Corruption of Pharmaceuticals and the Myth of Safe and Effective Drugs." *Journal of Law, Medicine and Ethics*, 14:590–610.

Lindsay, Elizabeth. 1996 "Health within Illness: Experiences of Chronically Ill/Disabled People." *Journal of Advanced Nursing*, 24: 465–472.

McEwen, Kellie J. 2000 "The Behavioral Model Applied to the Postponement of Needed Healthcare and Unmet Healthcare Need." Paper presented at the annual meeting of the Southern Sociological Society, April 2000.

Maynard, Douglas. 2006 "'Does It Mean I'm Gonna Die?': On Meaning Assessment in the Delivery of Diagnostic News." *Social Science and Medicine*, 62:1902–1916.

Mechanic, David. 1968 *Medical Sociology*. New York: The Free Press.

Mechanic, David, and Edmund H. Volkart. 1961 "Stress, Illness Behavior and the Sick Role." *American Sociological Review*, 26:51–58.

Parsons, Talcott. 1951 *The Social System*. Glencoe, IL: The Free Press.

———. 1975 "The Sick Role and Role of the Physician Reconsidered." *Milbank Memorial Fund Quarterly*, 53:257–278.

Pescosolido, Bernice A. 1992 "Beyond Rational Choice: The Social Dynamics of How People Seek Help." *American Journal of Sociology*, 97:1096–1138.

Pudrovska, Tetyana. 2010 "What Makes You Stronger: Age and Cohort Differences in Personal Growth After Cancer." *Journal of Health and Social Behavior*, 51:260–273.

Rust, George, Ye Jiali, Peter Baltrus, Elvan Daniels, Bamidele Adesunloye, and George E. Fryer. 2008 "Practical Barriers to Timely Primary Care Access." *Archives of Internal Medicine*, 168:1705–1710.

Schoen, Allen M. 2001 *Kindred Spirits*. New York: Broadway Books.

Shi, Leiyu. 1999 "Experience of Primary Care by Racial and Ethnic Groups in the United States." *Medical Care*, 37:1068–1077.

Springer, Kristen W., and Dawne M. Mouzon. 2011 "'Macho Men' and Preventive Health Care: Implications for Older Men in Different Social Classes." *Journal of Health and Social Behavior*, 52:212–227.

Stewart, Susan T., Rebecca M. Woodward, Allison B. Rosen, and David M. Cutler. 2008 "The Impact of Symptoms and Impairments on Overall Health in U.S. National Health Data." *Medical Care*, 46:954–962.

Suchman, Edward. 1965 "Social Patterns of Illness and Medical Care." *Journal of Health and Human Behavior*, 6:2–16.

Thomas, Villani J., and F.D. Rose. 1991 "Ethnic Differences in the Experience of Pain." *Social Science and Medicine*, 32:1063–1066.

Trojan, Alf. 1989 "Benefits of Self-Help Groups: A Survey of 232 Members from 65 Disease-Related Groups." *Social Science and Medicine*, 29:225–232.

Turner-Cobb, Julie M., Cheryl Gore-Felton, Feyza Marouf, Cheryl Koopman, Peea Kim, Dennis Israelski, and David Spigel. 2002 "Coping, Social Support, and Attachment Style as Psychosocial Correlates of Adjustment in Men and Women with HIV/AIDS." *Journal of Behavioral Medicine*, 25:337–353.

Webel, Allison R., Yvette Cuca, Jennifer G. Okonsky, Alice K. Asher, Alphoncina Kaihura, and Robert A. Salata. 2013 "The Impact of Social Context on Self-Management in Women Living with HIV." *Social Science and Medicine*, 87:147–154.

Weitz, Rose. 1991 *Life with AIDS*. Rutgers, NJ: Rutgers University Press.

Wilkinson, Ian F., David N. Darby, and Andrea Mant. 1987 "Self-Care and Self-Medication." *Medical Care*, 25:965–978.

Wingood, Gina M., Ralph J. DiClemente, Isis Mikhail, Donna H. McCree, Susan L. Davies, James W. Hardin, Shani H. Peterson, Edward W. Hook, and Mike Saag. 2007 "HIV Discrimination and the Health of Women Living with HIV." *Women and Health*, 46:99–112.

Wood, Michelle, Lauren Dunton, Brooke Spellman, Michelle Abbenante, and John Griffith. 2010 *Homelessness Data in Health and Human Services Mainstream Programs*. Washington, DC: U.S. Department of Health and Human Services.

Yoshiba, Karen K. 1993 "Reshaping of Self: A Pendular Reconstruction of Self and Identity Among Adults With Traumatic Spinal Cord Injury." *Sociology of Health and Illness*, 15:217–245.

Zborowski, Mark. 1969 *People in Pain*. San Francisco, CA: Jossey-Bass.

Zola, Irving K. 1973 "Pathways to the Doctor: From Person to Patient." *Social Science and Medicine*, 7:677–689.

CHAPTER 8

Physicians and the Profession of Medicine

Learning Objectives

- Define the concept "professional dominance." Identify and explain key ways in which the dominance of physicians within medicine has declined.

- Identify the key internal control mechanisms in medicine and assess their effectiveness.

- Describe how the medical malpractice system in the United States works, and identify and describe key weaknesses of the system.

- Identify and discuss key concerns related to the number, composition, and distribution of physicians in the United States.

- Identify and discuss key differences in the practice of medicine based on physician gender.

Being a physician in America in the eighteenth and nineteenth centuries was not highly regarded. Medical "knowledge" was often inaccurate and sometimes dangerous, credentials were easy to acquire or non-existent, and there was little prestige associated with the field.

Families (typically the wife and mother) were the primary locus of healing services, and information was secured from newspapers, almanacs, and domestic guides that discouraged the use of physicians. Apothecaries dispensed medical preparations, sometimes provided medical advice, and even performed amputations, midwives commonly assisted in the birthing process, and black slaves from Africa were primary healers on southern plantations.

Furthermore, a variety of countercultural health movements flourished. Most sought to disempower the dangerous techniques and drugs of the regular physicians and promote a new attitude toward health, based on the improved conditions already brought about by better nutrition and hygiene. "Every man his own doctor" was one of the slogans of the time, and the "regular" doctors were attacked as members of the "parasitic, nonproducing classes" (Ehrenreich and English, 1973).

By the early 1900s, however, medical doctors had secured virtually total domination of the health care field. They had largely eliminated many of their competitors (e.g., some of the countercultural movements), had subordinated others (e.g., women in nursing), and had obtained state-endorsed legitimation to control medical education. Few occupations in any country have ever enjoyed the dominance that was captured by professional medicine in the United States in the early part of the twentieth century—a dominance that peaked in the 1950s, 1960s, and 1970s.

THE PROFESSION OF MEDICINE

Characteristics of Professions

There have been many efforts to define the essential traits of **professions.** A classic formulation by William Goode is organized (by us) around the three common denominators of autonomy, rigorous standards, and prestige and identification (see the accompanying box "Essential Traits of a Profession").

The Dominance of the Medical Profession

In 1970, Eliot Freidson published two books, *Professional Dominance* (1970a) and *Profession of Medicine* (1970b), which dramatically influenced subsequent thinking about the medical profession. He defined a profession as "an occupation which has assumed a dominant position in a division of labor, so that it gains control over the determination of the substance of its own work" (1970a:xvii). Society gives this right

to professions on the basis of the following: (1) the profession commits to putting the interests of those whom it serves before its own interests; (2) the profession is based on technical knowledge that is not accessible to the layperson; and (3) the profession will conscientiously regulate itself (Freidson, 1970b).

In practice, dominance is achieved by convincing the public that the profession does valuable work, requires high standards for entry into the field and has rigorous educational standards, and can be trusted to perform its work ethically and to police itself. It is accepted by the public as the most knowledgeable authority on the subject matter.

If this is successful, the second requirement may be achieved—granting of legal autonomy (including the power over licensure of new members) by governing bodies. This is likely to occur only when the public is convinced that the profession is committed to a service orientation—that is, it is committed to the public good and to the welfare of clients rather than to

---

IN THE FIELD

ESSENTIAL TRAITS OF A PROFESSION

The term "profession" is used to describe occupations that have certain special traits and characteristics. Generally, professions are considered to be vocations—that is, occupations to which an individual is specially drawn and which conform to her or his talents and interests. Three traits of professions are especially noteworthy.

1. ***Rigorous standards.*** Professions carry special responsibilities, so those entering the profession must undergo a rigorous formal and informal educational and training process and must comply with stringent practice norms.

2. ***Significant autonomy***. An important aspect of professions is that they provide significant autonomy to those in the profession, and freedom from lay control. The profession maintains self-regulation—that is, it determines and enforces standards of education, licensure, and quality of practice.

3. ***Considerable prestige and identification with the profession***. In part due to the first two characteristics, professions generally are accompanied by high levels of income and prestige. Members tend to identify strongly with the profession and remain in it for their entire career (Goode, 1960).

self-interest. This legal conferral of autonomy bestows upon the profession the right to be self-regulating and to have control over other workers in the same domain—a significant departure from the status of occupations—and frees the profession from external competition, evaluation, and control (Wolinsky, 1993).

Freidson identified medicine as the epitome of professions, and introduced the term **professional dominance** to refer to the extensive control held by the medical profession over the organization, laws, training, clinical practice, and financing of medical care, and to its ability to promote its own autonomy, prestige, and income. It meant, according to Navarro (1988:59), that the medical profession was the "dominant force in medicine."

Medical credentials help to convey the amount of training and rigorous standards required to earn a medical degree. © tomas del amo/Fotolia.

The Decline of Professional Dominance

Has the medical profession remained the dominant force in the health care system? Over the last few decades, countless challenges to medicine's dominance have occurred, including the consumer movement (advocating more responsibility to patients), the women's health movement, drives for self-care, the growth of the for-profit industry in health care, increasing government efforts to regulate and bureaucratize medicine, and the managed care revolution (see Chapter 14). Has the collective weight of these and other challenges curtailed the professional dominance of medicine? Has its autonomy been eroded? Is the profession being controlled by forces outside medicine—in much the same manner as occupations experience outside controls? Two major perspectives have suggested that significant change has occurred.

Deprofessionalization.   Primarily developed by Marie Haug of Case Western Reserve University, the **deprofessionalization** theory contends that, over time, patients have become increasingly well informed about health and illness and increasingly assertive about assuming more control over their own health. Coupled with some loss of confidence in the service orientation of physicians and the medical profession, patients have sought more egalitarian relationships in medicine—more participation in decision making about their own medical treatment, and a less authoritarian demeanor in their physician. Coupled with the emergence of medical information online, this has led to a reduction in the medical profession's monopoly over medical knowledge, a reduction in the dominion of physicians over patients, and a decrease in physician autonomy—all elements of reduced professional dominance (Haug, 1973, 1988; Haug and Lavin, 1983).

Proletarianization.   John McKinlay and others concur that there has been a reduction in professional dominance, but they trace the stimulus to changes that have occurred in the health care system. For many years during the middle and latter parts of the 1900s, professional medicine was largely concerned about losing its autonomy to encroachment by the federal government. The American Medical Association (AMA) consistently opposed public health-related government programs due to fear that they would allow the government to increase its authority over medicine. Efforts to legislate some form of national health insurance were especially heatedly opposed by the AMA.

Some analysts believe that the attention of organized medicine was so strongly focused on minimizing government's involvement in health care that the increasing corporate presence in medicine was largely ignored, and its potential for reducing medical dominance was very much underestimated.

By the 1980s, however, **corporatization**—an increasing amount of corporate control of medicine—had clearly occurred and was best illustrated by the tremendous influence over the use of and payment for services by managed care companies. According to this perspective, once corporations were allowed into the medical field—in hospital construction and ownership, medical equipment supply, laboratories, and insurance companies—it was only a matter of time until they assumed greater control of medical practice itself. Their control was enhanced by other developments within medicine, such as specialization and increasingly sophisticated technologies that required more organizational complexity, greater bureaucracy, more money, and more managers to run the entire operation (Light and Levine, 1988).

This large-scale entrance of corporations into medicine created no less than a "clash of two cultures" according to McArthur and Moore (1997). They foresaw a threat to the quality and scope of medical care as the culture of medical professionalism (focusing primarily on the patient's welfare) was replaced by a commercial ethic culture that seeks profit from the clinical care of the sick. Corporatized medicine contains the paradox that physicians must increasingly rely on corporate organization and finances while simultaneously realizing that these forces intrude on their work and reduce their credibility in society (Light and Levine, 1988).

For some, this corporatization has led to a **proletarianization** of medicine—that physicians, like other workers in capitalist economies, eventually have their autonomy and self-control stripped away and replaced with control by corporate owners and managers. New medical technologies reduce the need for certain traditional skills (including diagnosis), make work more routinized (more like a trade than a profession), and create needs for capital and bureaucracy (with the potential for control by those with capital).

As examples, the government can now influence medical school admissions and curricula through the provision of grants and scholarships, and the physician–patient relationship is strongly influenced by outside parties such as insurance companies. These changes convert the physician into a worker within the system, rather than being in control of it (McKinlay and Stoeckle, 1988).

The American Medical Association

The **American Medical Association (AMA)** was first established as a national society in 1847 "to promote the science and art of medicine and the betterment of public health." It sought control over the profession by determining who entered it, how they were trained, and how they practiced medicine, and it hoped to elevate the public's opinion of the profession by driving out untrained practitioners. Although without power in the beginning, the association gained significant status as a result of the power bestowed upon it by the federal government to oversee standards for medical education and medical licensure. Over the next few decades, the AMA grew into the most powerful and effective health care lobbying group in the United States.

Today, although the AMA retains considerable power and prestige (it is one of the most well-organized, best funded, and most effective lobbying agents in Washington), its influence has declined. Almost 80 percent of licensed physicians were members in 1963, whereas only 15 percent of practicing U.S. physicians were members in 2012. As of 2012, the association had approximately 224,000 members, of whom about 22 percent were medical students and 14 percent were residents or fellows. Recent aggressive membership recruiting campaigns have largely failed to boost the membership count.

Some of the decline in membership can be attributed to increasing numbers of physicians who have joined societies within their specialty (e.g., the American College of Surgery), or a medical society based on gender (e.g., the American Medical Women's Association for female physicians) or race (e.g., the National Medical Association for black physicians), rather than the national organization. Many physicians have joined professional societies that expressly seek to offer an alternative to the traditional conservatism of the AMA, and many physicians have not joined or have dropped out due to a belief that large managed care organizations have become the most effective medical lobbying groups today. In a remarkable sign of its change in status, the AMA has recently dropped its adamant and long-standing opposition to physicians forming or joining unions. See the accompanying box "The Unionization of Physicians" about this issue.

An Alternative Theory: Countervailing Power. Donald Light and others have offered an alternative perspective from which to consider professional dominance—the theory of **countervailing power**. Light (1991) agrees that professional dominance was won by medicine

The American Medical Association is the largest professional association of physicians in the United States, although the percentage of physicians who join has decreased in the last few decades. The AMA's main office—shown here—is located in Chicago. © UniversalImagesGroup/Getty.

IN THE FIELD

THE UNIONIZATION OF PHYSICIANS

In 1999, the AMA reversed its long-standing and adamant opposition to medical unions. Responding to members' frustration with declining autonomy and stagnant incomes, the Board of Delegates voted to form a national labor union and seek federal approval for the country's private practitioners to join a union and collectively bargain.

Union activity among physicians actually began many years earlier, and at least five physicians' unions had been formed by the mid-1990s. In 1997, the largest union of physicians, namely the 9,000-member New York-based Committee of Interns and Residents, affiliated with the 475,000-member Washington-based Service Employees International Union, the country's largest union of non-physician health care workers. By the end of the year, approximately 14,000 to 20,000 physicians, about half of whom were medical residents, had joined a union. At that time, the AMA endorsed collective bargaining but steadfastly opposed unions, and encouraged members to use their state, county, and specialty medical societies for collective negotiation.

By 1999, however, the tide had turned. The AMA called its newly created labor organization *Physicians for Responsible Negotiations,* and over the next 5 years it spent more than US$3 million attempting to recruit physicians to join. Because federal antitrust laws ban collective bargaining by the self-employed (i.e., most physicians), only a minority of physicians (e.g., those employed by a hospital or a municipality) were eligible to join. In 1999, about 110,000 physicians were eligible to join a union, and about 40,000 of these individuals had already joined. Late in 1999, the National Labor Relations Board (NLRB) ruled that the nation's 90,000 medical residents in teaching hospitals were employees rather than students and had a right to join a union. Later that year, residents at Boston Medical Center became the first group to take advantage of this new right by voting 177 to 1 to join the Committee of Interns and Residents. However, a 2001 U.S. Supreme Court decision that health care workers cannot join a union if their duties include supervising other employees eliminated unionization as an option for many physicians.

Partly as a consequence of this decision and partly due to the reluctance of physicians to join organizations—especially organizations that seem political in nature and have traditionally been associated with blue-collar workers—growth in union membership never increased significantly. By mid-2004, the AMA's union had recruited only about 40 members, and the AMA discontinued it.

Meanwhile, union membership among other health care workers has increased in recent years. After a period of time during which many small unions competed feverishly against each other for members, several have now joined forces and entered into agreements with each other. In the last few years, union membership among non-physician health care workers has increased significantly, especially among the most highly skilled and highest paid workers, including registered nurses, physician assistants, and laboratory technologists. In 2014, about 14 percent of hospital workers (and more than 20 percent of nurses) held union membership, and these workers earned more than those not in a union. The Service Employees International Union (SEIU) now has more than 2 million members, with 1.2 million of these being health care workers (registered nurses, licensed practical nurses, physicians, laboratory technicians, nursing home workers, and home care workers).

To date, union membership has captured only relatively small markets of physicians—those who work in state, county, and city facilities, and medical residents and interns. However, as more physicians move from independent practice to a position of being a salaried employee (a trend described in Chapter 15), the potential for union membership and collective action increases. This will be a scenario to watch in the coming years (Blesch, 2010).

decades ago, but he does not see it as having become an entrenched part of the health care system. Rather, when any profession gains extraordinary dominance, it stimulates counter-vailing powers—that is, efforts by other agents to balance its power.

According to Light, the relationship between a profession and related institutions within a society is in a constant state of flux—sometimes an imbalance of power occurs, with one side or the other clearly gaining a dominant position. Professional dominance describes the time when the powers of the profession are great—even though that circumstance initiates efforts that will eventually diminish the profession's domi-nant position. In medicine, the use of unneces-sary procedures, the unexplained large variations in clinical practice, the lack of attention to cost-effectiveness, and the lack of technological self-restraint inevitably led to increased efforts by countervailing agents. For medicine today, these include (1) the government, (2) other providers of health care services, such as nurses and chiro-practors, (3) consumers in the form of advocacy groups such as the American Association of Retired Persons, (4) large employers ("corporate purchasers") who purchase health care for their employees, and (5) "corporate sellers" of health care services (e.g., insurance companies). Each of these agents seeks to exercise influence on health care, and thus exists in a constant inter-play with the medical profession (Hafferty and Light, 1995).

Does this mean that physicians today have been converted into corporatized workers? According to Light the answer is no. Relations between physicians and the corporate sector are very complex. Physicians sometimes own hospi-tals and facilities and laboratories, and thus are owners as well as workers. Employers, manage-ment companies, and insurance companies enter into contractual arrangements with physicians who sometimes have a voice in the companies. However, it does mean that complete physician control over any aspect of medical practice no longer exists (Light, 2000).

In recent years, many sociologists, other social scientific scholars, and policy makers have questioned the extent to which the medical profession has maintained sufficient autonomy to carry out its duty to prioritize the needs of patients, or whether professional medicine has so colluded with business philosophy and orga-nization that it is primarily focused on enhancing government protection to create and maintain a financially beneficial position (Light, 2010).

In the current climate of escalating costs, wide-spread variation in the quality of available care, a growing uninsured population, and medical errors, observers raise doubts about the physician as busi-ness entrepreneur pursuing economic opportunities at the expense of patients' best interests. At stake is whether the influx of money in health care has corrupted a professional mandate to take care of clients . . . If [medical] professionals have used their position mainly or solely to advance their own finan-cial agenda, then the professional logic would be merely another market player protected by profes-sional veneer. (Timmermans and Oh, 2010:S95)

Numerous studies have focused on the relation-ships among physicians and industry and whether these relationships have any impact on patient care. In 2009, one national survey of **primary care** physicians and specialists found that 83.8 percent of physicians had some type of relationship with the medical industry during the previous year. About two-thirds had received drug samples, more than 70 percent had received food and beverages in their workplaces, almost one in five had received reimbursements for costs associated with attending professional meetings or programs to obtain continuing education credits, and about one in seven had received payments for professional services (consulting, speaking, or enrolling patients in clinical trials) (Campbell et al., 2010).

A second line of research has been to investi-gate whether these financial incentives affect patient outcomes and health care costs. One review of dozens of empirical studies focused on (1) physicians' role in self-referring (referring patients to another medical service—such as an imaging center—in which the physician has a financial interest), (2) insurance reimbursement schemes which create incentives for certain clinical choices over others, and (3) financial relationships between physicians and the pharmaceutical industry. Researchers found that financial incentives and conflicts of interest do sometimes have an impact on clinical decisions (Robertson, Rose, and Kesselheim, 2012).

In the light of studies such as this, recent efforts have been initiated to reduce or even eliminate certain types of physician–industry relationships (especially with pharmaceutical and medical equipment supply companies). The Physician Payments Sunshine Act of 2010 seeks greater transparency by requiring manufacturers of drugs and medical supplies covered by federal programs to track and report all financial relationships with physicians. The intention is to uncover conflicts of interest. Efforts are also underway to try to use incentives to promote better health care (and not just more lucrative health care) (Madara and Burkhart, 2015).

These issues go to the very heart of the status of professionalism in medicine today. Related issues are discussed in several remaining chapters of this book, and readers are encouraged to keep this issue in mind.

THE SOCIAL CONTROL OF MEDICINE

Sociologically, the term **social control** refers both to the ability of individuals and groups to regulate themselves (internal control) and to measures taken by outsiders to regulate an individual or group (external control). One expression of the autonomy that professional groups so earnestly desire is the license to be self-regulatory and to be allowed to rely on internal control mechanisms. Perhaps more than any other profession in the United States, physicians have emphasized their autonomy and their disapproval of outside efforts at control.

This section offers a brief review of internal control mechanisms within medicine and an important external mechanism—medical malpractice litigation. Of course, in the last few decades, medicine has had to contend with two other powerful external agents—the federal government and the corporate sector. Medicine's relationship with these agents is touched upon throughout this book, but is examined in detail in Chapters 14 and 15.

Internal Control Mechanisms

Three types of internal controls are described here—peer review, hospital review committees, and the board of medicine in each state.

Peer Review. The most basic and potentially most pervasive type of control mechanism is **peer review**—the comments, questions, suggestions, and personal conversations that occur on a daily basis as physicians work with or near each other. Obviously, this does not occur for physicians working independently and with little interaction, but most physicians now work in some type of group setting and encounter other physicians while attending patients at the hospital.

Is the peer review process an effective internal control mechanism? What typically happens when one physician oversees an error or problematic behavior in a colleague? Based both on surveys of physicians and on dozens of insider accounts, the answer is clear that physicians often do not report it. An Institute of Medicine survey found that almost all physicians thought that they *should* report impaired or incompetent physicians or situations involving medical errors, but only about half actually did so (Campbell et al., 2007). Physicians express considerable reluctance about making public judgments about colleagues and provoking a hostile response. In situations like these, physicians often consider that medicine is an "art" rather than a "science," and they feel uncomfortable suggesting that they know better than the colleague being observed. Even if an obvious error occurs, many physicians express the view that everyone is fallible (there, but for the grace of God, go I).

If physicians observe a colleague making repeated errors, a personal chat may take place, patient referrals might be avoided, and a system of "grayzoning" (overseeing the physician's patient care) may be created, but there is a strong unwritten code of not making an official report. This code explains situations sometimes reported in the media of a physician practicing blatantly incompetent or negligent medicine over a period of years—with the full knowledge of others—but never being reported. Some years ago, a California physician admitted in court that he had needlessly maimed at least 30 surgical patients over a period of 7 years, and that he had performed many unnecessary procedures simply for financial gain. Despite the fact that others were aware of the situation, he was never once challenged by any other staff member.

Hospital Review Committees. A more formal mechanism occurs with a variety of review committees that now exist in all hospitals. Some of these *hospital review committees* are mandated by the federal government or other regulatory groups, and some have been created by hospital initiative. They include credentials committees (especially for new hospital employees), internal quality control committees (usually to guard against overprescribing medication or unnecessary procedures), mortality review committees (for any patient who dies in the hospital), and peer review organizations (PROs) (established to ensure that Medicare patients receive high-quality care).

Are these effective agents against poor clinical practice? Sometimes they are, but at other times not. For example, most states require all health care facilities to report to the State Board of Medicine any instance when they question the competence of a physician. However, hospitals are reluctant to do this and often do not report such cases. Imagine the terrible publicity a hospital would receive if it became known that it was questioning the performance of its own physicians. In addition, most states require that the board be advised whenever a physician loses hospital privileges (this automatically becomes public knowledge in some states). In an attempt to avoid the negative publicity, the hospital may pressure the offending physician to leave on his or her own accord. No formal action is taken, the physician often moves to another community or state, and a possibly dangerous physician is not stopped. One review of the performance of PROs determined that the committee missed two-thirds of the cases that were judged by an independent panel of physicians to have involved substandard care (Rubin et al., 1992).

A particularly egregious example occurred in 2010 when a Delaware pediatrician was charged with 471 counts of sexually abusing children over a 13-year period. It was learned that a nurse had filed a complaint against him in 1996 for inappropriately touching young girls in his care, but he was cleared. While the city police were investigating several similar complaints in 2005, the hospital was given a subpoena seeking any complaints or disciplinary actions against the physician. Because he was cleared, the hospital was not obligated to report the 1996 complaint, and they did not do so. Another police investigation in 2008 also led to no charges.

State Boards of Medicine. Ultimately, the most severe form of internal control is enacted when a physician is reported to the *State Board of Medicine.* The primary mission of State Boards of Medicine is to protect public and patient safety by ensuring that only competent and conscientious individuals are allowed to practice medicine. Although states have organized these boards in different fashions, they typically consist of several health care practitioners (sometimes also even a consumer or two) with an investigative staff who can conduct informal or formal hearings on charges against physicians. In most states the charges can be brought by anyone—the courts, hospitals, physicians, and patients. The board has various sanctions that it can levy, including reprimands, continuing education, fines, probation, suspension, and license revocation. Since 2000, disciplinary actions taken by a state medical board are automatically communicated to the medical board in all other states.

These boards work well in some states, not very well in others, and pursue wrongdoers with widely divergent levels of effort. The total number of actions taken by state medical boards is very small—in 2014, only about 4,000 disciplinary actions (involving a punitive measure such as loss of license, limitations on the license, and probation) against physicians were taken. Generally, physicians who have committed insurance fraud, abused substances, or engaged in prescribing violations receive light sanctions, whereas physicians convicted of violent crimes such as rape or assault receive very heavy sanctions.

Most agree that the number of physicians sanctioned represents only a small fraction of those guilty of wrongdoing. As an example, about 5 percent of the nation's physicians account for more than half of the medical malpractice suits. Of those physicians who have paid out more than five malpractice claims, only about one in seven has ever been professionally disciplined. Common problems among the boards are too few investigators (producing huge backlogs and long delays), failure to make actions public (in some states), and an unwillingness to impose and/or maintain penalties. Not surprisingly, therefore, there is a high recidivism rate among

physicians who have been disciplined by their state medical board (Grant and Alfred, 2007). As an example, see the accompanying box, "The Slow Disciplinary Process."

The National Practitioner Data Bank. The *National Practitioner Data Bank (NPDB)* was created in September 1990 as a federal repository for specific information on all health care practitioners. Reports of malpractice payments and adverse licensure actions must be reported to the NPDB within 30 days of final action. All health care institutions that grant clinical privileges and medical staff appointments must request information from the data bank. Ironically, the NPDB is not available to the public. In 2000, an effort in Congress to open it up so that patients could check the records of physicians received little support.

On the other hand, more than 30 states now publish lists of physicians who have been disciplined or who have been convicted of medical malpractice, and some have begun to use the Internet to post this information. National repositories of information on physicians are now springing up, although some of these are available only for payment.

Medical Errors: The Failure of Internal Control Mechanisms. The dominance that the medical profession has held carries with it the presumption that physicians will conscientiously monitor the practice of medicine. It is the most dependable method of ensuring consistently high quality of care and avoiding harmful medical errors. The failure of peer review, hospital review committees, and state medical boards to carefully protect patients from incompetent and negligent physicians and from medical care systems with inadequate quality controls is an indictment of the extent to which responsibilities have been carried out.

This failure makes likely the possibility that serious and repeated medical errors can occur, and considerable research has shown medical

IN THE FIELD

THE SLOW DISCIPLINARY PROCESS

The following is an actual account of a particular case handled before a State Board of Medicine:

April 26, Year 1: Board of Medicine informs Dr. S that it will hold a hearing on charges that he knowingly, intentionally, and unlawfully did indiscriminately prescribe amphetamines.

June 26, Year 1: Board committee concludes that Dr. S was extremely careless in the excessive prescription of amphetamine drugs and issues a reprimand, warning Dr. S not to do so in the future.

May 30, Year 2: Board committee sets up a hearing to investigate whether Dr. S has continued to improperly prescribe amphetamines.

June 11, Year 2: Committee concludes that Dr. S was extremely careless in excessive prescribing of amphetamine drugs, and restricts Dr. S's ability to prescribe controlled drugs.

April 22, Year 5: Dr. S's local medical society writes to the state board expressing concern about Dr. S's handling of two cases, indicating that Dr. S is a long-standing problem in the community and needs investigation.

May 2, Year 6: The president of the local medical society again writes to the board about Dr. S expressing fear for the safety of the general population.

May 11, Year 6: The board tells the local medical society that Dr. S is being investigated

and that the investigation will be completed in the near future.

November 26, Year 7: The board informs Dr. S that it has scheduled a formal hearing to decide whether Dr. S failed to diagnose or improperly treated 18 patients, including an 11-year-old boy who died of asthma.

January 15, Year 8: The formal hearing for Dr. S is postponed due to legal maneuvering by his attorneys.

May 27, Year 8: Dr. S's attorneys and the state's attorney general's office in consultation with a few board members reach a compromise settlement the day before the formal hearing is scheduled. Dr. S's license is suspended, and he is ordered to take continuing education courses and work under the supervision of another physician.

November 14, Year 8: The board returns Dr. S's license and puts him on probation for 2 years. He is to continue taking education courses, and his practice is monitored by a team of physicians.

August 31, Year 12: The board informs Dr. S that it will hold a formal hearing on charges that Dr. S illegally sold and prescribed weight control drugs, and failed to maintain proper records for drugs kept in his office. Dr. S retires before the hearing is held (Hite and Pardue, 1984).

---

errors to be common and devastating. In 1998, the Institute of Medicine issued a report that caught national attention. The report estimated that medical errors are responsible for the deaths of between 44,000 and 98,000 hospital patients in the United States each year.

Two types of errors were discussed. Frontline errors include such problems as failure to promptly and correctly diagnose an illness (there are an estimated 12 million diagnostic errors

each year—about 5 percent of adults who seek outpatient care—leading to 10 percent of all patient deaths), the administration of substandard or faulty treatment (leading to thousands of deaths each year), and the administration of the wrong medication or the wrong dosage of the correct medication (estimates are that 1.5 million medication errors occur in hospitals each year). Such common and obvious problems as the poor handwriting of physicians (with the result that pharmacists misread important information) and the failure of health workers to wash their hands between patients contribute to these errors. Second-line (less conspicuous) errors are those that are removed from the physician or nurse, and include inadequate staffing to offer proper care, shortcomings in practitioner licensing and credentialing, a faulty medical malpractice system, fragmented delivery systems, and a failure to implement new technologies to help physicians to avoid making errors. The *Journal of the American Medical Association* describes these medical errors as being real and common. (Medical errors are also discussed in Chapter 15.)

External Control: Medical Malpractice

Patients may attempt to exert several kinds of control over the practice of medicine. If they are sufficiently assertive and are working with a communicative physician, they may discuss desired parameters of their interaction, including the amount of communication, the right to ask questions and receive understandable answers, and how truthful they want the physician to be. If this communication does not occur or the physician is not responsive to requests, the patient may "doctor-shop" (i.e., search for a more compatible physician). Patients are always free to encourage others to see or to avoid any physician. In cases where wrongdoing is perceived, a complaint may be filed with the State Board of Medicine. In cases where an adverse event occurs as a result of physician error or negligence, the patient may file a medical malpractice legal suit. The following section of the chapter focuses on trends in the process and use of malpractice, and examines the medical malpractice system in the United States.

The Malpractice Concept.   The underlying concept of legal **medical malpractice** is straight-forward. Malpractice litigation is intended to compensate patients whose harm by the actions

(or inactions) of a physician could have been prevented, and to discourage such harms from occurring. The injured patient (the plaintiff) must prove that (1) she or he was injured or damaged, (2) the health care provider (the defendant) was negligent (i.e., failed to meet a standard of care expected in the community), and (3) the negligence caused or contributed to the injury or damage. If convicted of the malpractice, the defendant is supposed to pay the plaintiff a sum of money determined by a judge or jury. In reality, however, almost all providers carry malpractice insurance, so the insurance company is the payer in successful suits.

Malpractice Versus Actual Negligence. The malpractice system functions best when those who are injured through negligence file and win suits, and those who receive no injury or who are injured but not through negligence do not file suits and do not win if they do file. This acknowledges that some injuries occur but are not caused by negligence, and some negligence occurs but does not lead to injury. It is the negligence-caused injury that is the proper object of malpractice. See Figure 8–1.

The *Harvard Medical Practice Study* of malpractice claims and medical records of 31,429 patients hospitalized in New York State in 1984 is the most thorough study conducted on malpractice. The study identified patients who filed a malpractice claim against physicians and/or hospitals, and also examined their medical records to determine the incidence of injuries caused by medical negligence (Localio et al., 1991).

While the patients filed a total of 51 malpractice claims, the audit of medical records revealed 280 actual cases of injury caused by negligence. Were the 51 part of the 280? Not for the most part. Only 8 of the 280 cases filed a malpractice claim; 272 had a legitimate claim but did not file, and 43 did not have a legitimate claim but did file. Thus most actual cases of

Figure 8–1 The Malpractice System as Designed and as Actually Occurs

The malpractice tort system is designed to compensate victims of cases in which a medical provider's negligence causes a patient injury. Provider negligence without patient injury and patient injury without medical negligence are not situations of medical malpractice. The injury must be linked to the negligence. In the figure below, only the shaded area is medical malpractice.

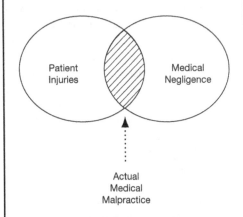

Actual
Medical
Malpractice

Unfortunately, studies show that the system does not work effectively in two ways: (1) patients who are injured by medical negligence often never file a medical malpractice suit (and therefore do not receive the compensation they are due), and (2) patients who are not actually injured or patients who are injured but not through provider negligence sometimes do file a medical malpractice suit (seeking money that they are not due). In the figure above, the sections without diagonal lines are not legitimate cases of medical malpractice, but they represent a large number of malpractice lawsuits.

number of malpractice suits being filed, and increasingly large awards being given to successful plaintiffs, and significantly larger premiums being paid by physicians for malpractice insurance, these patterns have reversed in the last decade. Measurement of malpractice is typically expressed in terms of the number of claims filed per 100 physicians. This ratio increased from only 1 per 100 physicians in 1960 to a peak of 17 per 100 physicians in the mid-1980s, and back down to 9.9 in 2013. About 1 in 14 physicians is sued for medical malpractice each year (Jena et al., 2011).

Neurosurgeons are the physicians most likely to be sued (19.1 percent annually), followed by thoracic-cardiovascular surgeons (18.9 percent) and general surgeons (15.3 percent). Pediatricians (3.1 percent) and psychiatrists (2.6 percent) were least likely to be sued. By the time they are 65 years of age, 75 percent of physicians practicing in the low-risk specialties will have been sued at least once (19 percent will have made at least one payout), and 99 percent of physicians in the high-risk specialties will have been sued (with 71 percent making at least one payout) (Jena et al., 2011).

Total malpractice payout rates per year have also increased, peaked, and are now decreasing. Payouts increased from less than US$3 billion in 1992 to US$4.8 billion in 2003, and had decreased to US$3.7 billion by 2011. Six states (New York, Pennsylvania, Illinois, New Jersey, Florida, and California) combined accounted for more than half of the payout dollars (National Practitioner Data Bank Public Use Data File, 2011). Due to the declining number of suits and declining payouts, the premiums that insurance companies charge to medical providers have also been declining in the last 10 years.

Consequences of the Malpractice Crisis. The intended consequences of the medical malpractice system represent only the tip of the iceberg with regard to the realized effects. Many

negligence-caused injury do not get filed, and a large percentage of those that are filed are not justified—the opposite of the way the system is designed to work (Localio et al., 1991). This pattern was affirmed in a similar type of study in Utah and Colorado in the early 1990s (Studdert et al., 2000).

The Incidence and Severity of Malpractice Litigation. After decades of an increasing patients who have sustained injury through medical negligence have secured compensatory damages, and many physicians who committed injuries by negligence have been found guilty. However, the health care system has been affected in other ways.

1. The AMA and individual physicians acknowledge the common practice of **defensive medicine**, whereby physicians prescribe every imaginable test for patients in order to protect themselves from liability in the case of a negative patient outcome. A study based on a survey of Massachusetts physicians found that 83 percent of the physicians reported practicing defensive medicine, and that 18 to 28 percent of tests, procedures, referrals, and consultations and 13 percent of hospitalizations were ordered for defensive reasons (Sethi and Aseltine, 2008). Estimates are that US$60 billion a year are spent for defensive medicine.
2. The premiums that physicians pay to insurance companies also add to the nation's total health care bill. Ultimately, of course, physicians pass these costs on to patients, further driving up the health care bill. On average, physicians pay about 3 or 4 percent of their revenue for malpractice insurance (as compared with about 12 percent for staff salaries, about 12 percent for office expenses, and about 2 percent for equipment). However, the premium varies widely by specialty, and obstetricians at about 7 percent pay the most. Prices tend to be higher in some states and areas than others. Rates are highest in Florida, especially southern Florida, which is sometimes called the medical malpractice capital of the United States.
3. The malpractice crisis has embittered many physicians, who are more likely to see every patient as a potential lawsuit, thus creating strain in the relationship. Many physicians believe that their profession has been subjected to criticism beyond what is

justified. Many decry the fact that there is often negative public attention when a suit is filed but little public exoneration when the complaint is unproven. (Between 70 and 80 percent of malpractice cases that make it to trial are decided in favor of the defense.) Many physicians who have been charged but not convicted of malpractice are among the most bitter because of the trauma created by the experience, as are many physicians who "settle" the case for economic reasons while perceiving themselves not to be liable (Peeples, Harris, and Metzloff, 2000).

4. The malpractice crisis has increased acrimony between the medical and legal professions, each of which accuses the other of being the root cause of the crisis. Lawyers argue that malpractice cases are caused by medical errors that physicians commit, and that the way to reduce malpractice cases is to reduce malpractice. Physicians argue that malpractice lawyers encourage patients to file suits and seek large rewards because the lawyer gets a percentage of the award. Doctors believe that the large number of cases is primarily due to attorney behavior. Some physicians have gone so far as to stop offering services to lawyers and spouses of lawyers.

Efforts to Reduce the Malpractice Crisis. Efforts that have been successful in controlling the number of suits, the number of payouts, and the cost of malpractice insurance have generally followed two approaches—efforts to improve the physician–patient relationship, and efforts to alter the malpractice system.

Research shows that negligence in physician behavior often results from poor physician–patient communication. Patients filing suits often charge that the physician did not provide sufficient information or did not clarify the risks of treatment. Moreover, patients who have rapport with a physician are much less likely to file a malpractice claim than those in a more distant relationship. In a study of sued and non-sued physicians and suing patients, Shapiro et al. (1989) found that, prior to a malpractice claim being filed, suing patients and their physicians viewed their relationship very differently. Suing patients were much less likely than the physician to believe that theirs was an honest and open relationship.

Given these findings, many physicians have enrolled in workshops and seminars to learn how to better "manage" relationships with patients. To the extent that these classes are directed at making substantive improvements, real progress may occur; to the extent that these classes are cynical efforts at manipulation, the problems are not likely to be effectively redressed.

Some states have developed *communication and resolution programs* in which medical providers discuss adverse events with patients, offer an apology, explain what happened, and possibly offer compensation. Some states have implemented *apology laws* that encourage providers to express regret or convey an apology by prohibiting those statements from being used in a malpractice case. Some states now use *dispute resolution* or *mediation* to resolve cases without a lawsuit (Mello, Studdert, and Kachalia, 2014).

Alternatively, more than 30 states have modified the malpractice system by placing a maximum cap on the dollar value of awards for "pain and suffering" and punitive damages (meaning that insurance companies would pay out less when suits are won and would therefore charge physicians lower premiums, resulting in cost savings that could be passed on to patients). The typical cap amount is US$250,000. Physicians and insurance companies strongly endorse this approach, but lawyers and patients who have been victimized strongly oppose it. Some states have set a cap at a substantially higher level, but it covers medical expenses, lost income, and pain and suffering. This creates the possibility that not even all of a victim's costs

are covered. Research has found that damage caps of US$250,000 do lead to reduced average payments (of more than US$40,000 per case), while a US$500,000 cap does not reduce average payment (Seabury, Helland, and Jena, 2014).

A *no-fault insurance system* has been considered in some states. In this case, payment could be made to a victim more quickly and in a less adversarial way without any admission of provider guilt. Another option sometimes considered is restricting the amount of money that lawyers can earn from successful malpractice suits. Typically, they receive 30 or 40 percent of the judgment in successful suits.

THE NUMBER, COMPOSITION, AND DISTRIBUTION OF PHYSICIANS IN THE UNITED STATES

Physicians in the United States have never been scrutinized as closely as they have been in the last decade. Three key areas of examination have been the number of physicians (do we have enough physicians to meet the need?), the composition of physicians (what is the representation of women and racial and ethnic minorities in American medicine?), and the distribution of physicians (are physicians sufficiently dispersed geographically and by specialty?).

The Number of Physicians

In 2010, there were 985,375 allopathic physicians in the United States (although just 794,862 were actively practicing medicine). The term "allopathic" is used to refer to the practice of scientific medicine and the basic training taught in medical schools that leads to the M.D. degree. This is an increase of about 171,000 physicians since 2000 (see Table 8–1). Growth in the number of physicians in the last 30 years has been more than four times faster than growth of the U.S. population. In 1960, there were 703 persons per physician, compared with 313 persons per physician in 2010.

It should be noted that a sizable percentage of these physicians were trained in other countries. More than 25 percent of all active physicians in the United States are international medical graduates (IMGs). Many graduated from a medical school in another country—most commonly India or Pakistan—served their residency in the United States, and then stayed in the United States to practice. Without these physicians, the United States would be in a desperate situation today.

In addition, osteopathic medicine has come to be increasingly accepted and respected in the United States. While it retains some focus on the manipulation of joints and bones, the standard training is very similar to that of allopathic physicians, and osteopathic doctors use conventional methods of diagnosis and treatment and are able to practice the full scope of medicine. Osteopathic physicians are now often integrated into medical offices with MDs. There are 31 schools of osteopathic medicine in the United States. About one in five of all medical students today, and an anticipated one in four by 2025, is enrolled in one of these schools. Osteopathic physicians need to be counted when considering the full set of medical resources available in the country (Shannon and Shannon, 2009).

Has this phenomenal growth in the number of physicians given the United States an adequate supply? There is not a single easy way to answer this question. In fact, the Council on Graduate Medical Education has reversed its position four times in the last three decades on the adequacy of physician supply. Clearly, however, the Affordable Care Act will necessitate an increase in the nation's physician supply, as will the very large cohort of physicians who will be retiring in the next two decades, and the increasing number of people in their later years.

According to the Association of American Medical Colleges, there will be 45,000 too few primary care physicians and 46,000 too few surgeons and other specialists by the year 2020. Because the education and training of a physician can take up to 10 years, it will not be possible to meet this demand by 2020, and efforts to avoid even greater shortfalls by 2025 must begin immediately (IHS Inc., 2015).

The Composition of Physicians

By Gender. The total number of female physicians in the United States increased from around 54,000 in 1980 to about 294,000 in 2010—an increase of more than 500 percent. Women accounted for only 11.6 percent of all physicians in 1980, but 32.4 percent in 2010. Significant increases in medical school applications, matriculants, and graduates in the last two decades are reflected in the age distribution of

TABLE 8–1   Number of Physicians in the United States, 1970, 1980, 1990, 2000, and 2010

Category	1970	1980	1990	2000	2010
Total	334,028	467,679	615,421	813,770	985,375
Male	92.4%	88.4%	83.1%	76.0%	67.6%
Female	7.6%	11.6%	16.9%	24.0%	32.4%
Primary care (of active, office-based physicians)	44.2%	43.0%	43.6%	44.3%	42.6%
Graduate of U.S. medical school	81.0%	77.5%	77.2%	74.5%	72.6%

Source: Data from the American Medical Association, Department of Physician Data Sources, Division of Survey and Data Resources, *Physician Characteristics and Distribution in the United States* (Chicago, IL: AMA, 2012).

male and female physicians. Older physicians in the United States are predominantly male; younger physicians are more evenly divided.

By Race and Ethnicity.   Due to extensive recruiting efforts, the number of under-represented racial and ethnic minority students in medical school increased in the 1990s, but has now leveled off or even declined slightly.

Their proportion remains low among practicing physicians and medical students. While African Americans, Hispanics, Native Americans, Alaskan and Hawaiian natives, and other Pacific Islanders comprise 35 percent of the United States population, they represent only about 7 percent of practicing physicians. The medical education of individuals from these groups is particularly important, because they are more likely than white physicians to practice

in medically underserved areas and provide medical care for underserved black, Hispanic, and Native American patients, and it is a measure of social justice (Merchant and Omary, 2010).

By Geography.   Despite the significant growth in overall physician supply, millions of Americans have inadequate access to health care. In 2012, there were more than 64 million people living in (mostly rural and inner-city) areas designated as primary care **health professional shortage areas** [which have shortages of primary medical care (5,900 areas in 2013), dental care (4,600 areas), or mental health care (3,800 areas)] and millions more in **medically underserved areas** (which are defined by the number of physicians available, the infant mortality rate, the number of people below the poverty level, and the number of people aged 65 years or older).

The number of practicing physicians per 100,000 residents is more than twice as high in urban as in rural areas. One-fourth of the U.S. population—and one-third of the elderly—live in rural areas, but only 12 percent of active physicians practice there (and many of these are nearing retirement).

Recruitment and Retention of Rural Physicians.   Why are rural areas so undersupplied? Research has discovered three key factors:

Women now account for over 30 percent of all physicians, but are approximately 50 percent of today's medical graduates. © blanche/Fotolia.

1. *Personal factors.* Preference for practice location appears to be dependent on personal desire for rural or urban living, rather than on characteristics of specific settings. Considerations include opportunity for personal time, employment opportunities for the partner, quality educational opportunities for children, and the availability of social and cultural activities.
2. *Professional considerations.* These include access to professional colleagues for consultation, medical libraries, and continuing education opportunities.

3. *Economic factors.* As more and more medical students incur large debts, economic factors influence preference for practice location. The widespread poverty in most rural areas results in lower salaries, there are many underinsured and uninsured individuals in rural areas, and Medicaid eligibility and reimbursement are often more restricted in rural states.

Have the medical profession, medical schools, and governing bodies noticed the physician shortage in rural areas? The answer is yes. Some medical schools have begun to encourage graduates to practice in rural areas, and some states and localities have devised strategies to boost recruitment of physicians in underserved areas. Research has found that the medical graduates most likely to want to practice in a rural area are those who grew up in such an area. Their desire to return to a familiar place and experience the community life offered in many small towns and rural areas draws them back. Thus, medical school admission policies can have an effect on meeting this need (Hancock et al., 2009).

In addition, the National Health Service Corps (NHSC) was created in 1972 to provide financial assistance to medical students in return for a commitment to practice in an assigned, underserved area for a specified number of years. Physicians sponsored by this program have made significant contributions to rural health care, although some studies have discovered that many were unhappy with the area where they were assigned and with the work conditions that exist in isolated areas. These programs notwithstanding, rural and inner-city areas continue to lack adequate medical resources, and significantly greater effort will be needed to correct the inequity. In 2014, President Obama's budget boosting enrollment in the NHSC from 8,900 to 15,000 for the next 5-year period was a welcome increase, but still far short of meeting the need.

International diversity of physicians in the United States has increased in recent decades, although the percentage of African American, Hispanic, and Native American doctors continues to lag behind their population percentage. © stockyimages/Fotolia.

By Specialty. At some point during the medical school years, students decide upon an area of specialization. While their choice may later change, students apply for residencies in a particular specialty. Specialization choice has been an important issue in the United States, as a large percentage of American physicians have opted for a specialty area (e.g., surgery, cardiology, radiology, ophthalmology, psychiatry, and dermatology) rather than entering a primary care field (family practice, internal medicine, and pediatrics—which are specialties themselves).

This pattern is important for two related reasons. First, primary care physicians are the logical entry point into the health care system. If primary care is unavailable, patients are forced to go to a less appropriate first stop—a specialist. Second, the cost of care from a specialist is higher than the cost of primary care, both in terms of standard fees and because of the greater number of more expensive tests conducted by specialists. Analysts estimate that we could save more than US$60 billion a year if our initial entry point into the health care system was always a primary care physician.

Early in the twentieth century, the vast majority of physicians were working in primary care, but by 2000 almost 80 percent were specialists. The percentage of medical school graduates going into primary care was low in the late 1980s and early 1990s, increased slightly in the late 1990s, and has now dropped again in the 2000s (between 1997 and 2010 the percentage of American medical school graduates going into primary care dropped by more than 50 percent).

What factors have contributed to this declining interest in primary care? Faculty in many medical schools openly encourage students to pursue specialization and explicitly discourage them from choosing primary care. Why is this? The specialties offer more prestige, higher incomes, less frantic work schedules, more research opportunities, and more opportunities to work with high-tech medicine. (See the box "Disparities in Physician Income.") As fewer physicians opt to work in primary care, a vicious cycle is created. There are more patients for fewer doctors, thus creating more time pressure and less time for each patient. The opportunity to engage in a thorough conversation with a patient—something that once attracted physicians to primary care—is

---

IN THE FIELD

DISPARITIES IN PHYSICIAN INCOME

A critical issue within the health care field is the wide variation in physician salaries. The key pattern is that specialist physicians earn considerably more than primary care physicians. Some support this pattern because it recognizes the longer period of training required in many of the specialties, and the greater expertise required with high-technology care. Others oppose this pattern because it is based on a compensation system that rewards procedures (which specialists often provide) much more than time and consultation (which are central in primary care). The divergent salaries are also an incentive for medical school graduates to enter a higher-paying specialty to help to pay off their debt, rather than primary care where the need is much greater. The following table is an example of salary divergences based on the median of several physician salary surveys in 2012.

Orthopedic surgery	US$514,000
Gastroenterology	US$450,000
Cardiology	US$449,000
Radiology	US$443,000
Dermatology	US$384,000
Anesthesiology	US$380,000
Oncology	US$377,000
Plastic surgery	US$370,000
General surgery	US$350,000
Obstetrics/gynecology	US$297,000
Emergency medicine	US$277,000
Neurology	US$260,000
Internal medicine	US$211,000
Pediatrics	US$203,000
Family medicine	US$195,000

Source: Data from Modern Healthcare, 2015, "Physician Compensation Survey," *Modern Healthcare*, July 20, 2015.

reduced. This influences even fewer physicians to choose primary care. Despite the recognized need for primary care physicians, most students have found these to be compelling reasons for opting for a specialty area. The shortage of primary care physicians is expected to grow significantly in the coming years. It is one of the key problems in the American health care system.

FEMALE PHYSICIANS

Research on physician gender has increased significantly in the last decade. Researchers have especially focused on differences between female and male physicians, and on finding explanations for those differences. Significantly less research has systematically compared black versus white physicians.

Research in a variety of settings and with a variety of samples has identified four consistent differences between female and male physicians. First, females and males tend to enter different specialties. Second, females and males have different practice patterns. Third, females and males interact differently with patients. The first two differences are examined here; the third is covered in Chapter 12. A fourth significant difference—the presence of gender-based and sexual harassment—is described in the box "Gender-Based and Sexual Harassment of Female Physicians."

Different Specializations

When female and male fourth-year students are asked about their reasons for selecting a particular specialty area for their residency, they offer similar reasons—opportunities for self-fulfillment, positive clinical experiences, and the intellectual challenge of the field. The only key differences are that financial advantage is somewhat more important to males, and type of patient is somewhat more important to females.

Despite the similarity in motivation, male and female students systematically choose different specializations (Bowman and Allen, 1985).

The clearest difference is that women are much more likely than men to train in primary care, and men are more likely than women to train in surgery. In addition to primary care, female physicians have become especially common in obstetrics and gynecology, psychiatry, and dermatology. Also, female physicians are less likely than their male counterparts to become board certified (i.e., to receive certification from a board overseeing each specialty). Over the last few decades, however, specialty choices for women and men have begun to converge. For example, internal medicine, general and family practice, and pediatrics (although in different order) are now the most common areas of medical specialization for both men and women.

This pattern is even more pronounced among black and Hispanic physicians, who are much more likely than their white counterparts to enter a primary care field.

Historically, male physicians have received higher salaries than female physicians. Most research has pointed to women's greater tendency to work in primary care and women working fewer hours as the causes. However, a study of physicians just leaving residency programs in New York State from 1999 to 2008 found a large gender gap in salaries that was unexplained by specialty choice, working hours, or other practice characteristics. During this time, newly trained male physicians earned on average US$16,000 per year more than newly trained female physicians (LoSasso et al., 2011).

Different Practice Patterns

Male and female physicians differ in several significant ways in their medical practices.

1. Women are much more likely than men to work in salaried positions in institutional

IN THE FIELD

GENDER-BASED AND SEXUAL HARASSMENT OF FEMALE PHYSICIANS

Does gender-based sexual harassment still exist in medicine? The answer is yes. Based on more than 4,500 responses in a Women Physicians' Health Study, Frank, Brogan, and Schiffman (1998) discovered that almost half of the female physicians (47.7 percent) had experienced gender-based (but not sexual) harassment, and 36.9 percent had experienced sexual harassment.

Where did harassment occur? The most common settings were in medical school and during internship, residency, and fellowship. Younger physicians reported higher rates of harassment. The authors acknowledged that this may reflect a heightened sense of awareness among younger women, but they speculated that harassment may actually be increasing,

and that female physicians continue to be trained in settings that value power and hierarchy and a legitimation of gender-based and sexual harassment.

In a 2001–2002 study of the graduating seniors at 12 U.S. medical schools (Witte, Stratton, and Nora, 2006), more than one-third of respondents reported experiences that they considered to be discriminatory or harassing. Men were more likely than women to identify experiences that they considered to involve educational inequalities. Women were more likely than men to report stereotypical comments, sexual overtures, offensive, embarrassing, or sexually explicit comments, inappropriate touching, and sexist remarks.

settings (e.g., teaching in medical school), and are more likely to practice in urban areas. They are less likely to have an office-based practice.

2. Women work fewer hours per week than men, and earn less money. While differences in both dimensions are narrowing, overall, male physicians still work about 10 to 20 percent more hours per week than female physicians (a difference of around 7–10 hours per week), and males earn considerably more in salary (not all of which can be explained by the difference in the number of working hours). Differences in the number of hours worked per week are also converging— not because women are working more, but because men are working fewer hours. (On average, physicians work 51 hours per week, which is not out of line with other professions. However, the number of hours worked has decreased by almost 10 percent in the last

15 years.) Both female and male physicians are increasingly interested in part-time work.

3. Women are more likely than men to see younger, female, and minority patients. Young black and Hispanic physicians are also much more likely to treat minority patients than are white physicians.

Reasons for the Different Specializations and Practice Patterns.   Analyses of the differences between female and male physicians have suggested two underlying causes—the fact that more non-professional demands are placed on women (number of family responsibilities relative to career), and the influences of professional socialization (especially attitudes of faculty and colleagues).

The difference in the number of hours worked per week by male and female physicians occurs almost entirely among physicians who are parents—the difference in hours worked among non-parents is insignificant. At later stages of the lifespan, when family responsibilities have largely been completed, women work about the same number of hours as men—and are even more likely to be working full-time at the age of 60 years (Zimmerman, 2000).

This pattern is explained by the different societal expectations regarding the emphasis placed on career versus family for men and women. Traditionally, few would even have thought about a male physician altering his career commitments (e.g., working fewer hours) upon the birth of a child, but that expectation is often still communicated to female physicians.

In dual-career families with a female physician, as in other dual-career families, the man's career is often still given priority. The woman has primary responsibility for family life and child rearing in addition to her career, while the man often focuses on his career. Female physicians with a family often continue to do family chores such as house cleaning with little help from their husband or an outside domestic worker. Many female physicians find full dedication to their career incompatible with full dedication to family, and compromise by temporarily dropping out of the labor force or significantly reducing the number of working hours per week—in essence, sacrificing career advancement for time to raise the children.

An alternative interpretation of this circumstance has been suggested by some analysts. Some research indicates that childcare responsibilities account for only a small part of the working hours differential. Since most female physicians (about 70 percent) are married to a professional, and about 50 percent are married to a physician, they do not have financial pressures to continue working after the birth of a child.

Upon the arrival of a child, female physicians reduce their working hours and workload to the level they most desire. However, this explanation does not account for the reason why physician-mothers desire a smaller workload than others, nor does it account for the fact that female physicians reduce their working hours after a birth but male physicians do not. Whichever explanation prevails, the woman's career is more likely to be put on hold after the birth of a child.

Some of the differences between male and female physicians are traceable to socialization processes in medical school and during internship and residency. Some female students are discouraged by male faculty members from entering into certain specialties or being so dedicated to a career that family interests are subsumed. For example, faculty often encourage women to enter specialties with limited time commitments and in which they perceive less competition; male students receive encouragement to enter more competitive specialties that require longer residencies. This problem is exacerbated by the fact that women are still very much under-represented in leadership positions in academic medicine, and are therefore less available for role models and mentoring (Yedidia and Bickel, 2001). A recent study based on in-depth interviews with 16 female physicians found that all of them could identify instances of gender bias in their educational careers (Wallace, 1998). An interesting cross-cultural example is provided in the box "Female Physicians in Mexico."

PHYSICIAN SATISFACTION AND DISSATISFACTION

Are today's physicians satisfied with their careers? Some research has found generally positive feelings. Almost 75 percent of physicians in a survey in Indianapolis reported satisfaction with their overall practice, although just 59 percent reported satisfaction with their income (Bates et al., 1998).

Most studies of physicians have found satisfaction rates with the career of around 80

IN COMPARATIVE FOCUS

FEMALE PHYSICIANS IN MEXICO

Since the 1970s, social scientists have conducted a considerable amount of research on the role of women in economic, social, and political development in developing countries. However, little of this research has focused on the small number of well-educated, middle-class professional women in these countries.

Increased access to medical education has provided many women in Mexico with the opportunity to be physicians. Today, women comprise approximately 30 percent of physicians and 50 percent of medical graduates in Mexico—both figures being about the same as in the United States. However, given the strong emphasis in Mexican culture on the family and on women's central role within family life, the question emerges about the practice patterns of female physicians. Harrison (1998) focused on the extent to which female physicians were as able as male physicians to migrate within

Mexico, especially to areas underserved by physicians. Would female physicians be more influenced by professional opportunities and responsibilities, or by expectations of responsibilities to family and home life?

Using both personal interviews and analyses of secondary data sources, Harrison found that female physicians tend to live and work in their native or adopted state (often the city in which their medical school is located) in order to be close to family and friends. This is partially influenced by constraints in the health care system, such as availability of specialist training and the medical labor market. However, at virtually every point in the life course, family and household demands strongly influence specialist choice, career development, and migration patterns. Career decisions are viewed as being subordinate to those of the husband, thus conforming to traditional Mexican sociocultural values.

percent. Physicians who work with children and those who work with the elderly report the highest satisfaction levels. Younger physicians tend to be more satisfied than older physicians. Greater satisfaction is also associated with lower educational debt at graduation.

However, there is considerable anecdotal evidence of increasing job dissatisfaction among physicians, especially in the last few years. The chief complaints relate to the expansion of bureaucratic and institutional controls that limit decision making and physician autonomy. These controls result from the many external regulations that restrict professional decision making and can reduce power and control over clinical practice. Regulations by third-party payers, the amount of paperwork, and requirements for usage of **electronic health records (EHRs)** have

been the most frequently cited sources of dissatisfaction. Physicians are clearly very frustrated by all the time that is needed to deal with the maze of regulations, and by the feeling that their clinical decisions are based more on what insurance companies will pay for than on the best interest of their patients. Those who are employees of health care facilities often feel that they have little control of or participation in practice management. These perceptions have been linked to the likelihood of feeling emotional exhaustion and a sense of burnout, or of leaving the field of medicine altogether. Primary care physicians seem to be especially frustrated with uncompensated activities (e.g., placing orders, writing prescriptions, electronic messaging, and reviewing clinical notes) that consume a significant amount of time (Dyrbye et al., 2012). Many physicians are disturbed that the mission of medicine has changed from one of service to patients to one of compliance with corporate policies.

Frustration is also expressed about declining incomes relative to purchasing power. As a result of this economic erosion, some physicians perceive a decline in their status. These concerns are accompanied by feelings of vulnerability as a result of increasing quality control mechanisms in hospitals and by insurance companies. Physicians often feel under constant scrutiny with regard to the quality of their work, and that they are easy targets for criticism and malpractice charges.

In the past, interaction among colleagues was an important source of job satisfaction among physicians. However, inter-professional communication has declined as competition among providers has increased. This lack of satisfactory contact with fellow physicians is accompanied by less satisfactory encounters with patients. Traditionally, the relationship between physician and patient was considered to be central to medical practice, both because of its importance in the diagnosis and treatment of unique individuals and because it inspired and rewarded physicians. The relationship was extremely important because physicians enabled patients to cope with their diseases, disabilities, and death. Today, tests often take the place of patient communication in diagnosis, and advanced technologies deter physicians from encouraging patients to cope with the realities of disability and death.

Physician Burnout

The perceptions of overwork combined with loss of control over practice and clinical decision making, and a perceived inability to always provide optimal care for patients, have led to increasing **physician burnout**. Burnout is typically considered to be a state of emotional and physical exhaustion, with an accompanying decrease in job identification, job satisfaction,

and confidence in work ability. In 2011, research found that there was a high rate of physician dissatisfaction with work–life balance, and that 45 percent of physicians felt burned out. When the study was repeated in 2014, satisfaction with work–life balance had declined further and the burnout rate had increased to 54 percent—that is, more than half of practicing physicians were experiencing emotional and physical exhaustion (Shanafelt et al., 2015). These findings are especially alarming given that other research has found that the quality of patient care, patient safety, and patient satisfaction decrease when physicians are experiencing burnout.

One novel response by some primary care physicians—direct care—is described in the box "Direct Care: Concierge Care for the General Public."

PHYSICIAN IMPAIRMENT: STRESSES AND STRAINS OF THE PHYSICIAN ROLE

Many people consider that physicians "have it made." They are bright, well-educated, wealthy, prestigious members of the community who typically live in exceptional houses in exceptional neighborhoods with an exceptional number of personal possessions. The image contains a lot of truth—but it misses another side to the career in medicine. Being a physician can be an extremely stressful responsibility, and physicians frequently suffer from the accumulation of stressors.

Cultural expectations for physicians are certainly high. Physicians are expected not only to be medical experts, but also to exercise this expertise without error. Every physician is expected to function at a maximum level of competence all the time. Few patients would be very understanding about a misdiagnosis that occurs because a physician's mind is temporarily diverted. Yet physicians as people experience the same personal traumas as everyone else, and

---

IN THE FIELD

DIRECT CARE: CONCIERGE CARE FOR THE GENERAL PUBLIC

In the last two decades, a small number of *concierge medical practices* have been developed in the United States. These practices typically involve a physician bypassing the health insurance system (and its requirements and paperwork) and offering direct, personalized care to patients who enroll with the physician by paying a flat monthly or annual fee. Patients then receive comprehensive primary care, including consultations, basic medications, and lab tests, and the reassurance of having a physician always on call. In the early years, concierge doctors targeted wealthy patients and charged thousands of dollars a year for their retainers. These exclusive arrangements were sometimes called "health care for billionaires." Patients often liked having a physician directly available, and those who signed up often did not have to worry about the price.

In the last few years, however, some physicians (an estimated 6,000 in 2016) have begun offering these **direct care** arrangements to the general population. It is an appealing idea to physicians who wish to avoid all of the time and costs associated with participating in the insurance system. They are able to spend more time on patient care and keep costs down. Direct care physicians have about 600 patients, as compared with the 2,500 or so patients of a typical primary care physician. Patients benefit by having close access to the physician for, in many cases, lower cost than purchasing traditional insurance. (Patients do still need insurance policies for specialist care, emergency care, and catastrophic expenses.) It is too soon to determine whether this model of care might work for larger populations, but several health care systems and employers are now experimenting with the arrangement, and others are monitoring it closely (Luthra, 2016).

---

sometimes find it difficult to block personal concerns from professional activity.

Traditionally, physicians have been expected to be assertive decision makers in the office or hospital. They have wanted and been given tremendous authority. They are often treated with considerable deference. While these qualities may not always be beneficial in a health care setting, they can be devastating within family relationships. (Many medical auxiliaries swear that physicians believe that the M.D. degree stands for medical deity.) When physicians do not make the conversion in their right to give orders from office to home, family relationships can suffer. Moreover, many physicians—especially those in primary care specialties and obstetrics/gynecology—are rarely off the job. Knowing that they are only a beep or telephone call away

from going back to work, they find it difficult to really relax. Getting out of town is the only solution for many physicians.

Stressors like these sometimes take a serious toll and produce an **impaired physician**—one who is unable to practice medicine with reasonable skill and safety due to physical or mental illness, including the loss of a motor skill due to aging, or to excessive use or abuse of drugs, including alcohol. An estimated 15 percent of physicians will be impaired at some point in their career due to alcoholism, drug dependency, or mental illness—about the same as or a slightly higher percentage than the general population. The incidence of depression is higher among practicing physicians than among members of similarly educated groups. Physicians end their own lives with greater frequency and earlier in life than other members of the general population; doctors have the highest rate of suicide of any profession. Suicide rates for female physicians are especially high relative to other occupational groupings. On average one physician commits suicide every day.

Recognizing the problem, in 1972 the AMA created an "impaired physician program" that encouraged physicians to report colleagues in trouble, and urged state and local medical societies to initiate treatment programs. Now called "physician health programs," these programs are designed to provide treatment for substance abuse and other problems while protecting confidentiality and reducing the likelihood of punitive sanctions against the impaired physician. A total of 47 states now have programs in place. Although there is limited systematic or longitudinal evidence about the success of these programs, the general feeling is that they are working well and that they have increased the willingness of physicians to report a colleague who is demonstrating worrying signs of substance abuse (Farber et al., 2005; Holtman, 2007).

SUMMARY

The medical profession in the United States evolved from a poorly regarded, poorly paid, disorganized occupation in the eighteenth and nineteenth centuries to a position of professional dominance by the mid-twentieth century. Scientific developments had given the public more confidence in medicine, and the government extended legal autonomy—the right of self-control.

However, most analysts believe that the medical profession's dominance is waning and being replaced by a variety of agents, including corporations, the federal government, and consumers. The theory of countervailing power posits that any profession's dominance is only a temporary phenomenon, existing only until other forces increase their power.

Social control of medicine refers to forces inside and outside medicine that can regulate medical practice. Internal control mechanisms have a mixed record of effectiveness as regulatory processes; patients can exercise some external control through such means as malpractice litigation. While injured patients are sometimes compensated through lawsuits, the American system has numerous problems, including many victims of malpractice who are not compensated and many non-victims who do file suits.

The number of physicians in the United States is now recognized as being inadequate. Moreover, too few physicians have been entering primary care or choosing to practice in medically underserved areas. Female, Hispanic, and black physicians are more likely than white male physicians to enter primary care, and some systematic differences between female and male physicians in terms of practice patterns remain. These are mostly attributable to family responsibilities being differentially defined, and to professional socialization. Recent research has focused on two significant problems among physicians—increasing professional dissatisfaction (including burnout), and high rates of stress-induced physician impairment.

HEALTH ON THE INTERNET

Several independent health care ratings companies have created online evaluations for individual physicians, hospitals, and other health care providers. Each is set up slightly differently, but may include background information, public liability records, and patient surveys. Surveys show that about six in ten Americans believe the information provided is very or somewhat helpful in selecting a physician. You can check out the following:

www.healthgrades.com
www.drscore.com
www.ratemds.com

What kind of information can you obtain at each of these sites? Why can't you get even more detailed information? Many physicians are unhappy with these sites, especially with those that allow any patient to add personal comments. More than 1,000 physicians now ask their patients to sign a legal form that promises not to publish any unfavorable information about the physician or care received.

How do you think the presence of Internet sites such as these will affect the practice of medicine? What advantages can you identify? What disadvantages can you identify?

DISCUSSION CASE

Source: Herbert J. Keating and Terrence F. Ackerman. 1991 "When the Doctor Is On Drugs." *Hastings Center Report*, Vol. 21 (September–October), 29.

You are both personal physician and friend to another physician, Dr. G. He has seemed withdrawn, irritable, and distracted recently. You have heard rumors through the hospital grapevine that not long ago he made a serious error in calculating a medication dosage, but that the error was caught by the pharmacist before the drug was dispensed.

Dr. G has resisted your gentle explorations and expressions of concern during casual encounters, so you are surprised when he blurts out while seeing you for a routine office visit that he is using cocaine daily. You encourage him to enter a detoxification and addiction treatment program, but he declines, saying that he can "handle it" by himself. Unfortunately, his personality changes persist, and even though he assures you that he is now drug-free, you strongly suspect that Dr. G's drug abuse is continuing. No further obvious medical errors occur, but stories are circulating in the hospital about his abusive responses to late-night telephone calls. When you directly confront him with your suspicions, he cuts off all further contact with you.

You wish to intervene, but are uncertain how to proceed. You believe you should at least raise your concerns to the quality assurance committee of the hospital medical staff or the impaired physicians' committee of the state medical society, if not to the state licensing board. (According to American Medical Association guidelines, physicians have an ethical obligation to report impaired, incompetent, and/or unethical colleagues in accordance with the legal requirements in each state.)

Are you justified in reporting your friend on the basis of your current information? Won't Dr. G just deny everything and accuse you of possessing an economic motive? Should his admission of cocaine use to you during a professional contact be kept confidential? What are the moral and legal implications of breaking confidentiality?

If you do not reveal everything that you know, you have no convincing evidence to present. You realize you have no proof that Dr. G has harmed any patient, but wonder if your social duty extends to protecting his patients from the possibility of future damage. What if you are wrong and he is no longer using drugs? If being irritable is a crime, the hospital medical staff is going to be decimated! If you intervene, there is a real chance that Dr. G will end up the victim of rumors in the community, and perhaps have his name listed in the National Practitioner Data Bank. How can you sort through your duties to him as his friend, physician, and colleague, while remembering that you have duties to society as well? Should physicians and other medical care providers be required to report suspicions of physician impairment and low-quality performance to regulatory boards?

GLOSSARY

American Medical Association (AMA)
corporatization
countervailing power
defensive medicine
deprofessionalization
direct care
electronic health records (EHRs)
health professional shortage area
impaired physician

medical malpractice
medically underserved area
peer review
physician burnout
primary care
professional dominance
professions
proletarianization
social control

REFERENCES

American Medical Association, Department of Physician Data Sources, Division of Survey and Data Resources. 2012 *Physician Characteristics and Distribution in the United States*. Chicago, IL: American Medical Association.

Bates, Ann S., Lisa E. Harris, William M. Tierney, and Frederic D. Wolinsky. 1998 "Dimensions and Correlates of Physician Work Satisfaction in a Midwestern City." *Medical Care*, 36:610–617.

Blesch, Gregg. 2010 "Labor Pains? Push for Doc Employees Could Lead to Union Growth." *Modern Healthcare*, 40:32.

Bowman, Marjorie A., and Deborah I. Allen. 1985 *Stress and Women Physicians*. New York: Springer-Verlag.

Campbell, Eric G., Susan Regan, Russell L. Gruen, Timothy G. Ferris, Sowmya R. Rao, Paul D. Cleary, and David Blumenthal. 2007 "Professionalism in Medicine: Results of a National Survey of Physicians." *Annals of Internal Medicine*, 147:795–802.

Campbell, Eric G., Sowmya R. Rao, Catherine M. DesRoches, Lisa I. Iezzoni, Christine Vogeli,

Dragana Bolcic-Jankovic, and Paola D. Miralles. 2010 "Physician Professionalism and Changes in Physician-Industry Relationships from 2004 to 2009." *Archives of Internal Medicine*, 170:1820–1826.

Dyrbye, Liselotte N., Colin P. West, Timothy C. Burriss, and Tait D. Shanafelt. 2012 "Providing Primary Care in the United States: The Work No One Sees." *Archives of Internal Medicine*, 172:1420–1421.

Ehrenreich, Barbara, and Deirdre English. 1973 *Witches, Midwives, and Nurses—A History of Women Healers*. Old Westbury, NY: The Feminist Press.

Farber, Neil J., Stephanie G. Gilbert, Brian M. Aboff, Virginia U. Collier, Joan Weiner, and E. Gil Boyer. 2005 "Physicians' Willingness to Report Impaired Colleagues." *Social Science and Medicine*, 61:1772–1775.

Frank, Erica, Donna Brogan, and Melissa Schiffman. 1998 "Prevalence and Correlates of Harassment Among U.S. Women Physicians." *Archives of Internal Medicine*, 158:352–358.

Freidson, Eliot. 1970a *Profession of Medicine: A Study in the Sociology of Applied Knowledge.* New York: Dodd, Mead.

——. 1970b *Professional Dominance: The Social Structure of Medical Care.* New York: Atherton Press.

Goode, William J. 1960 "Encroachment, Charlatanism, and the Emerging Profession: Psychology, Sociology, and Medicine." *American Sociological Review*, 25:902–914.

Grant, Darren, and Kelly C. Alfred. 2007 "Sanctions and Recidivism: An Evaluation of Physician Discipline by State Medical Boards." *Journal of Health Politics, Policy, and Law*, 32:867–885.

Hafferty, Frederic W., and Donald W. Light. 1995 "Professional Dynamics and the Changing Nature of Medical Work." *Journal of Health and Social Behavior*, Extra Issue:132–153.

Hancock, Christine, Alan Steinbach, Thomas S. Nesbitt, Shelley R. Adler, and Colette L. Auerswald. 2009 "Why Doctors Choose Small Towns: A Developmental Model of Rural Physician Recruitment and Retention." *Social Science and Medicine*, 69:1368–1376.

Harrison, Margaret E. 1998 "Female Physicians in Mexico: Migration and Mobility in the Lifecourse." *Social Science and Medicine*, 47:455–468.

Haug, Marie. 1973 "Deprofessionalization: An Alternate Hypothesis for the Future." *Sociological Review Monograph*, 20:195–211.

——. 1988 "A Re-examination of the Hypothesis of Physician Deprofessionalization." *Milbank Quarterly*, 66 (Suppl. 2):48–56.

Haug, Marie, and Bebe Lavin. 1983 *Consumerism in Medicine: Challenging Physician Authority.* Beverly Hills, CA: Sage.

Hite, Chuck, and Douglas Pardue. 1984 "Despite 'Ignorance, Carelessness,' Doctor Regains License to Practice." *Roanoke Times and World News*, October 7, pp. A1, A14.

Holtman, Matthew C. 2007 "Disciplinary Careers of Drug-Impaired Physicians." *Social Science and Medicine*, 64:543–553.

IHS Inc. 2015 *The Complexities of Physician Supply and Demand: Projections from 2013 to 2025: Final Report.* Washington, DC: Association of American Medical Colleges.

Jena, Anupam B., Seth Seabury, Darius Lakdawalla, and Amitabh Chandra. 2011 "Malpractice Risk According to Physician Specialty." *New England Journal of Medicine*, 365:629–636.

Keating, Herbert J. and Terrence F. Ackerman. 1991 "When the Doctor Is on Drugs." *Hastings Center Report* 21:29.

Light, Donald W. 1991 "Professionalism as a Countervailing Power." *Journal of Health Politics, Policy, and Law*, 16:499–506.

——. 2000 "The Medical Profession and Organizational Change: From Professional Dominance to Countervailing Power." Pp. 201–216 in *Handbook of Medical Sociology* (5th ed.), Chloe E. Bird, Peter Conrad, and Allen M. Fremont (eds.). Upper Saddle River, NJ: Prentice Hall.

——. 2010 "Health Care Professionals, Markets, and Countervailing Powers." Pp. 270–289 in *Handbook of Medical Sociology* (6th ed.), Chloe E. Bird, Peter Conrad, Allen M. Fremont, and Stefan Timmermans (eds.). Nashville, TN: Vanderbilt University Press.

Light, Donald W., and Sol Levine. 1988 "The Changing Character of the Medical Profession: A Theoretical Overview." *The Milbank Quarterly*, 66:10–32.

Localio, A. Russell, Ann G. Lawthers, Troyen A. Brennan, Nan M. Laird, Liesi E. Hebert, Lynn M. Peterson, Joseph P. Newhouse, Paul C. Weiler, and Howard H. Hiatt. 1991 "Relation between Malpractice Claims and Adverse Events Due to Negligence." *New England Journal of Medicine*, 325:245–251.

LoSasso, Anthony T., Michael R. Richards, Chiu-Fang Chou, and Susan E. Gerber. 2011 "The $16,819 Pay Gap for Newly Trained Physicians: The Unexplained Trend of Men Earning More Than Women." *Health Affairs*, 30:193–201.

Luthra, Shefali. 2016 "Fueled by Health Law, 'Concierge Medicine' Reaches New Markets." *Kaiser Health News,* January 16.

McArthur, John H., and Francis D. Moore. 1997 "The Two Cultures and the Health Care Revolution." *Journal of the American Medical Association*, 277:985–989.

McKinlay, John B., and John D. Stoeckle. 1988 "Corporatization and the Social Transformation of Doctoring." *International Journal of Health Services*, 18:191–205.

Madara, James L., and Jon Burkhart. 2015 "Professionalism, Self-Regulation, and Motivation: How Did Health Care Get This So Wrong?" *Journal of the American Medical Association,* 313:1793–1794.

Mello, Michelle M., David M. Studdert, and Allen Kachalia. 2014 "The Medical Liability Climate and Prospects for Reform." *Journal of the American Medical Association,* 312:2146–2155.

Merchant, Juanita, and M. Bishr Omary. 2010 "Clogged Up: Efforts to Train More Minority Doctors Stalled as Population Diversifies." *Modern Healthcare,* 40:24.

Modern Healthcare. 2012 "Physician Compensation Survey." *Modern Healthcare,* July 16, pp. 17–25.

National Practitioner Data Bank Public Use Data File. 2011 *2012 Medical Malpractice Payout Analysis.* Washington, DC: U.S. Department of Health and Human Services, Health Resources and Services Administration, Bureau of Health Professions, Division of Practitioner Data Banks. www.diederichhealthcare.com/medicalmalpractice-insurance/2012-medical-malpracticepayout-analysis/.

Navarro, Vicente. 1988 "Professional Dominance or Proletarianization? Neither." *The Milbank Quarterly,* 66:57–75.

Peeples, Ralph, Catherine T. Harris, and Thomas A. Metzloff. 2000 "Settlement Has Many Faces: Physicians, Attorneys, and Medical Malpractice." *Journal of Health and Social Behavior,* 41:333–346.

Robertson, Christopher, Susannah Rose, and Aaron S. Kesselheim. 2012 "Effect of Financial Relationships on the Behaviors of Health Care Professionals: A Review of the Evidence." *Journal of Law, Medicine, and Ethics,* 40:452–466.

Rubin, Haya, William H. Rogers, Katherine L. Kahn, Lisa V. Rubenstein, and Robert H. Brook. 1992 "Watching the Doctor-Watchers: How Well Do Peer Review Organization Methods Detect Hospital Care Quality Problems?" *Journal of the American Medical Association,* 267:2349–2354.

Seabury, Seth A., Eric Helland, and Anupam B. Jena. 2014 "Medical Malpractice Reform: Noneconomic Damages Caps Reduced Payments 15 Percent, With Varied Effects by Specialty." *Health Affairs,* 33:2048–2056.

Sethi, Manesh K., and Robert Aseltine. 2008 "The Investigation of Defensive Medicine in Massachusetts: Extent and Cost of Defensive Medicine." Results released at the Medical Society's Interim Meeting of House of Delegates, Waltham, MA, November 14–15. www.massmed.org.

Shanafelt, Tait D., Omar Hasan, Lotte N. Dyrbye, Christine Sinsky, Daniel Sarele, Jeff Sloan, and Colin P. West. 2015 "Changes in Burnout and Satisfaction with Work-Life Balance in Physicians and the General US Working Population Between 2011 and 2014." *Mayo Clinic Proceedings,* 90:1600–1613.

Shannon, Stephen C., and Howard S. Shannon. 2009 "The Status and Future of Osteopathic Medical Education in the United States." *Academic Medicine,* 84:707–711.

Shapiro, Robyn S., Deborah E. Simpson, Steven L. Lawrence, Anne M. Talsky, Kathleen A. Sococinski, and David L. Schiedermayer. 1989 "A Survey of Sued and Nonsued Physicians and Suing Patients." *Archives of Internal Medicine,* 149:2190–2196.

Studdert, David M., Eric J. Thomas, Helen R. Burstin, Brett W. Zbar, E. John Orav, and Troyen A. Brennan. 2000 "Negligent Care and Malpractice Claiming Behavior in Utah and Colorado." *Medical Care,* 38:250–260.

Timmermans, Stefan, and Hyeyoung Oh. 2010 "The Continued Social Transformation of the Medical Profession." *Journal of Health and Social Behavior* 51:S94–S106.

Wallace, Susan L. 1998 "Female Physicians' Perspectives on Gender Bias in Education: Negotiating Gender through Insulation." Paper presented at the Virginia Social Science Association Annual Meeting, Bridgewater, Virginia, March 27.

Witte, Florence M., Terry D. Stratton, and Lois M. Nora. 2006 "Stories from the Field: Students' Descriptions of Gender Discrimination and Sexual Harassment During Medical School." *Academic Medicine,* 81:648–654.

Wolinsky, Frederic D. 1993 "The Professional Dominance, Deprofessionalization, Proletarianization, and Corporatization Perspectives: An Overview and Synthesis." Pp. 11–24 in *The Changing Medical Profession,* Frederic W. Hafferty and John B. McKinlay (eds.). New York: Oxford University Press.

Yedidia, Michael J., and Janet Bickel. 2001 "Why Aren't There More Women Leaders in Academic Medicine? The Views of Clinical Department Chairs." *Academic Medicine,* 76:453–465.

Zimmerman, Mary K. 2000 "Women's Health and Gender Bias in Medical Education." Pp. 121–138 in *Research in the Sociology of Health Care, 2000,* Jennie J. Kronenfeld (ed.). Stamford, CT: JAI Press.

CHAPTER 9

Medical Education and the Socialization of Physicians

Learning Objectives

- Describe the Flexner Report and identify specific ways in which it altered medical education.

- Identify and discuss criticisms of today's medical school curriculum, and describe specific ways in which the curriculum is changing.

- Describe the value orientations "tolerance for uncertainty" and "detached concern,"

and explain the reasons why they are viewed as being important for medical students.

- Identify and describe the primary sources of stress for medical students.

- Identify and describe the impact of medical school on the career practice patterns of students.

Socialization is the process by which a person becomes a member of a group or society and acquires values, attitudes, beliefs, behavior patterns, and a sense of social identity. It is a lifelong process; as each new role is added, one integrates new expectations with previous behavior.

Physicians undergo both formal and informal socialization into the medical role. The medical school experience is structured to impart not only knowledge and technique but also certain attitudes and values. Through the process, medical students are consciously and subconsciously converted from laypeople to health care professionals. This chapter traces the development and organization of the formal educational system for physicians, and describes the socialization processes that occur.

THE HISTORY OF MEDICAL EDUCATION

Early Medical Education

During the colonial period, the primary mode of medical instruction was the apprenticeship system, but the quality of these apprenticeships varied enormously. A few preceptors provided meaningful experiences in active practice and close supervision of their students, but many others made little effort to provide any systematic instruction. Although a 3-year apprenticeship was considered standard, in reality a certificate was routinely issued to any student who merely registered with a physician.

By the year 1800, three formal medical schools (the University of Pennsylvania, Harvard, and King's College) had been established. These schools were eventually joined by an increasing number of proprietary (for-profit) medical schools, which became the dominant vehicle of medical education by the mid-nineteenth century. Ability to pay the fees was the only entrance requirement for white males, and few of the applicants had any college preparation. In fact, most students had completed elementary school only, and many were illiterate (Ludmerer, 1985).

Two 4-month terms of lectures made up the standard course of instruction. The curriculum focused on subjects of "practical" value, with little attention to scientific subjects. Written examinations were not required in order to graduate, but the diploma "licensed" the young physician to practice medicine anywhere in the country. Some students opted to supplement their medical education by serving as a "house pupil" in a hospital. These pupils, selected by a competitive examination, would reside in a hospital and assume responsibility for managing cases, much as medical students and house officers do today (Ludmerer, 1985).

An alternative to an apprenticeship or American medical school was European study—most often in France. Between 1820 and 1861, nearly 700 Americans studied medicine in Paris. However, few aspiring doctors had the financial means to study abroad (Ludmerer, 1985).

Medical Education for Women. Whereas the standards for admission were very lax for white males, women faced significant obstacles. By 1880, only a handful of medical schools accepted women on a regular basis. Although Elizabeth Blackwell (1821–1910) earned an M.D. degree from the Geneva College of Medicine in upstate New York in 1849 (becoming the first woman in this country to do so), most women were forced to attend independent medical schools created expressly for their training. During the second half of the nineteenth century, 14 of these women's medical colleges were established in the United States.

Some of this gender bias receded during the latter part of the nineteenth century and the first two decades of the twentieth, and numerous medical societies began admitting women. By 1900, women accounted for more than 10 percent of enrollment at almost 20 medical schools, and 12 of the women's colleges had closed or merged. However, beginning around 1920, a reversal occurred as acceptance of women into professional medicine declined.

Medical Education for Blacks. Medical education was formally denied to blacks throughout the United States prior to the Civil War. After emancipation, would-be black physicians turned to missionary or proprietary medical schools established in the South. The most common motivation for starting these schools was to train black physicians to serve the black population.

The most prestigious black medical college, Howard University, opened in 1869, and it remained the primary source for medical education of blacks for the next century. As late as 1890, however, blacks comprised less than 1 percent of physicians in the United States, and both black and female institutions engaged in constant struggles for survival.

Early Reform Efforts

Early efforts to reform medical education included raising standards for admission, lengthening the training process, revising curricula, and adding clinical instruction. One obstacle to reform was the dependence of medical professors on student fees—thus mandating that students not be discouraged from applying or persisting once admitted. In addition, American physicians distrusted the laboratory and lacked respect for experimental science, and few medical educators had any interest in research (Ludmerer, 1985).

However, by the mid-1880s, many medical schools themselves had initiated reform. The length of training expanded—eventually to

4 years—and entrance requirements were strengthened. Curricula were revised to emphasize scientific subjects, and laboratory experiences were included whenever possible. Although these changes were not instituted uniformly, and hence the quality of medical education varied greatly, momentum for reform was high (Ludmerer, 1985).

The Flexner Report. Capitalizing on this desire for improvement, the American Medical Association (AMA) made reform of medical schools a top priority in 1904 by establishing a Council on Medical Education. The council determined premedical education requirements, developed a standard training period, and constructed a licensing test. In addition, the quality of medical schools was evaluated, and many schools were judged to be inferior. The report was distributed to medical schools but was never published because it was considered politically risky for a medical organization to criticize medical schools publicly.

Instead, the council commissioned the Carnegie Foundation for the Advancement of Teaching to conduct a similar study, to be headed by Abraham Flexner. As discussed in Chapter 2, Flexner's study recognized the diversity of the American medical scene, which included some of the best and some of the worst medical schools in the world. His 1910 report, *Medical Education in the United States and Canada,* strongly attacked the weakest schools, especially the proprietaries. "The result was a classic piece of muckraking journalism that deserves to rank with the other great muckraking treatises of the era. He provided a wealth of details, named names, and devastated the bad schools with humiliating public exposure" (Ludmerer, 1985:179).

The **Flexner Report** accomplished its purpose as it aligned medical educators and the public against proprietary schools and in favor of a homogeneous, university-based system of education focused on scientific medicine and formation of a professional identity (Irby, Cooke, and O'Brien, 2010). The AMA worked closely with philanthropic foundations to provide financial assistance to help embed this model on a national level. Small proprietary schools, which could not mimic the model approach, were not funded by corporate trusts. Numerous colleges were forced to close, including five of the seven black medical schools and all but one of the women's colleges. As a result, the total number of medical graduates, and especially the number of female and black graduates, declined.

MODERN MEDICAL EDUCATION

The Foundation of a New Curriculum

By the 1920s, a new type of medical education was in place. Advocated by Flexner and embraced by the AMA and the nation's top medical schools, a revised medical school curriculum (sometimes referred to as the Johns Hopkins model) was implemented. Despite some later innovations, the basic principles of the new curriculum remain in place today. They include the following:

1. A clear separation between the basic sciences (taught in the first 2 years) and the clinical sciences (taught in the third and fourth years).
2. A heavy reliance on didactic instruction in the form of lectures to large classes (especially in teaching the basic sciences), utilizing the instructor as expert (as opposed to personal investigation).
3. Relatively independent and often uncoordinated courses taught by full-time faculty in many different departments.
4. The clerkship years (often relying on residents as instructors) as an integral part of medical education.

Academic Health Centers and Medical Schools Today

There are 145 accredited medical schools in the United States (seven more are working toward accreditation) and 17 medical schools in Canada that are accredited by the Liaison Committee on Medical Education (LCME), the official accrediting agency for programs leading to the doctor of medicine degree. The LCME is jointly sponsored by the Association of American Medical Colleges (AAMC) (the Committee on the Accreditation of Canadian medical schools in Canada) and the American Medical Association. The nation's 31 osteopathic medical schools are accredited separately by the American Osteopathic Association.

The number of medical schools in the United States represents a significant increase in just the last 10 years—a response to the perceived need for more physicians—and more will open soon. This is a major development, as no new allopathic medical schools opened in the 1980s or 1990s. U.S. medical schools employ about 160,000 full-time faculty for 86,000 medical students and 110,000 medical residents.

Each medical school is part of a large configuration of programs and services called an **academic health center (AHC)**. These centers typically consist of one or more hospitals with comprehensive medical specialties, the latest and most advanced medical technology, and sophisticated research laboratories. Often they are a dominant part of the university in which they are located, and they may be the institution's largest securer of grant money and its most prestigious component. In many cases the health centers have such extensive facilities and generate so much money that they are largely independent of university control.

Traditionally, AHCs have had a three-pronged mission—to provide cutting-edge clinical care, to conduct clinical research, and to play a key role in medical education, especially of specialists. They have proved to be very costly endeavors, sometimes mostly physician oriented, and often not clearly focused on the learning process. However, as cost-consciousness in

After two decades without the creation of any new allopathic medical schools, more than a dozen new schools have been accredited in the last few years, and several more are in various stages of establishment. Photo courtesy of Janet Jonas.

health care delivery has increased, there has been necessary belt-tightening in the AHCs, necessary restructuring, and concerns among some about their future status.

In a highly praised book, *Time to Heal: American Medical Education from the Turn of the Century to the Era of Managed Care*, Kenneth Ludmerer (1999) describes a wide range of factors that have recently put enormous pressure on the resources of the centers. These forces include the following: the managed care revolution that requires health providers to look for lowest-cost options in delivering care (such as doing more services on an outpatient basis) and collaborate in ways to be more efficient; the increasing costs of providing medical education and conducting medical research; decreased external funding for research; the substantial provision of care for those unable to pay; and sharp reductions in government reimbursement for care provided. AHCs have been hit particularly hard by these forces because of the ways in which they have traditionally been configured. Prices are typically higher in AHCs than in non-academic hospitals, staff are dominated by specialists rather than generalists, emphasis is on expensive high-tech medicine, large research expenses are incurred, and, in most schools, departments have not historically worked closely together—all patterns that are incompatible with recent changes in health care. The Affordable Care Act seeks to lower the cost of medical care in part by expanding primary care services and reducing overuse of expensive modalities. AHCs will need to adapt to this effort in order to be vital parts of the future of health care (Karpf, Lofgren, and Perman, 2009).

Ludmerer contends that part of the problem is the inability and unwillingness of the centers to reconfigure in ways that would enable them to continue providing high-quality medical education and high-quality medical care. Instead, financial cutbacks have tended to come in areas that directly compromise the quality of programs and services.

For example, new clinical faculty are hired but are often not asked to be part of the teaching program. Faculty who do teach spend less time mentoring students. Clinicians are asked to speed up each patient encounter so that more patients can be seen in the day. In this environment, Ludmerer fears that students are increasingly likely to focus on the business and bureaucratic side of medicine while neglecting medicine's core—that is, a Samaritan concern for the care, suffering, and well-being of the sick (Fox, 1999).

Not surprisingly, a negative culture within an academic medical center leaves faculty feeling dissatisfied and unfulfilled. One study of more than 4,500 medical school faculty found that most valued their work, but that one in seven had considered leaving their institution during the previous year, and an additional one in five had considered leaving academic medicine altogether. A major reason was the negative culture within the center—a feeling of unrelatedness, a lack of engagement, and low levels of institutional support were among the chief complaints (Pololi et al., 2012).

Medical Students

The number of applicants to U.S. medical schools declined significantly during the 1980s, rose sharply in the early and mid-1990s (there were about 47,000 applicants in 1996), and then dropped very sharply every year from 1997 until 2002 (when there were about 33,600 applicants). The number has risen steadily since then, to 52,550 discrete applicants in 2015 (see Table 9–1). These applicants submitted more than 781,000 applications to medical schools— an average of about 15 each. Several medical schools are currently in the process of increasing their enrollment.

At least three factors contributed to the temporary decrease: (1) many bright students became more attracted to the many opportunities and potentially larger salaries in business,

TABLE 9–1 Applications to U.S. Medical Schools During a Period of Over 35 Years

Academic Year	Number of Applicants	First-Year Enrollment
1979–1980	36,141	17,014
1989–1990	26,915	16,749
1999–2000	38,529	16,856
2009–2010	42,269	18,390
2015–2016	52,550	20,631

Source: Data from Association of American Medical Colleges, 2016a, www.aamc.org/download/321442/data/2016factstable1.pdf.

computers, and technology; (2) physician dissatisfaction with managed care dissuaded some potential medical students from applying; and (3) judicial and legislative decisions scaled back affirmative action programs, which led to a decrease in the number of racial and ethnic minority applicants.

The resurgence in applications has been stimulated by (1) increased recognition of the need for more physicians, (2) the increase in the number of medical schools and the expansion of the size of some medical school classes, (3) instability with dot.com positions, and (4) cohorts of students who have grown up with managed care and are not as discouraged from medical careers because of it.

The mean grade point average for matriculants in 2015 was 3.70. Once admitted, almost all students earn their degree (the attrition rate is only about 1 percent).

Female Medical Students. In 2015, women accounted for 42.5 percent of applicants and 47.8 percent of matriculants—both slightly lower than the highest percentages (see Table 9–2), but the percentage of women admitted by school varies widely. Given that women account for about 56 percent of all baccalaureate graduates, the numbers in medical school are still an under-representation. In 2015, male applicants had slightly higher Medical College Admission Test (MCAT) scores, and

TABLE 9–2 Women in U.S. Medical Schools During a Period of Over 35 Years

Academic Year	Number (%) of Women Applicants	Number (%) of Entering Women	Number (%) of Graduates
1979–1980	10,222 (28.3)	4,748 (27.9)	3,497 (23.1)
1989–1990	10,546 (39.2)	6,404 (38.2)	5,197 (33.9)
1999–2000	17,433 (45.2)	7,725 (45.8)	6,712 (42.4)
2009–2010	20,252 (49.9)	8,817 (47.9)	8,035 (48.8)
2015–2016	22,386 (42.5)	9,862 (47.8)	8,907 (47.6)

Source: Data from Association of American Medical Colleges, 2016b, www.aamc.org/download/321532/data/2016factstableb2-2.pdf.

TABLE 9–3 Race and Ethnic Background of Medical School Enrollees, 2015

Background	Applicants	First-Year Enrollment
White	25,094 (47.8)	10,568 (51.2)
Asian	10,121 (19.3)	4,095 (19.9)
African American	4,087 (7.8)	1,349 (6.5)
Multiple race	3,656 (7.0)	1,460 (7.1)
Hispanic/Latino	3,219 (6.1)	1,320 (6.4)
Unknown	2,434 (4.6)	937 (4.5)
Non-U.S.	2,099 (4.0)	329 (2.0)
Other	1,661 (3.2)	497 (2.4)
Native American/Alaskan Native	115 (0.2)	55 (0.3)
Native Hawaiian/Pacific Islander	50 (0.1)	17 (0.1)
Total	52,536	20,627

Source: Data from Association of American Medical Colleges, 2016c, www.aamc.org/download/321472/data/factstablea8.pdf and 2016d, www.aamc.org/download/321474/data/factstablea9.pdf.

female applicants had slightly higher grade-point averages (GPAs).

Racial and Ethnic Minority Medical Students. In 2015, just over half (51.2 percent) of medical school matriculants were white. Other racial and ethnic groups with the highest percentage of first-year medical students were Asian American (19.9 percent), students of multiple race (7.1 percent), African American (6.5 percent), and Hispanic (6.4 percent) (see Table 9–3). Acceptance of minority applicants continues to be approximately the same as for other applicants. The landmark civil rights court decisions and the legislation of the 1950s and 1960s served to open the doors of all medical schools to minority candidates. In 1969, the AAMC established an Office of Minority Affairs in an attempt to encourage more minority students to seek medical education. The AAMC has established the goal of proportional representation in medicine for all groups, and has paid special attention to minorities that have been under-represented.

However, the scaling back of affirmative action programs in the late 1990s and early 2000s led to a significant decrease in minority applicants. For example, 1,455 black students entered medical school in 1996, whereas only 1,349 did so in 2015. One of the negative consequences of this decrease is that black physicians are more likely than their white counterparts to enter primary care (a significant national need), and are more likely to practice in inner-city areas (also a national need). In addition, white medical students have less opportunity to interact with and get to know racial and ethnic minority students. This decrease in interaction has been found to decrease their confidence in being able to work with diverse populations (Saha et al., 2008).

The Medical Education Curriculum

Years 1 and 2. Most medical schools offer a similar curriculum. The first 2 years are devoted to the basic sciences (e.g., anatomy, biochemistry, microbiology, pathology, pharmacology, and physiology). Largely taught through the traditional lecture format, students are often overwhelmed by the amount of information presented.

The units are highly compact and very intense; students soon realize that they cannot possibly learn everything, so they quickly search for memorization aids. Classes are often quite

Although large lecture classes continue to be prevalent in the first 2 years of medical school, an increasing number of schools are adopting small groups as a preferred mode of teaching. © Kablonk Micro/Fotolia.

large, and medical faculty tend to be impersonal (a significant change and major disappointment for many students). Most schools require Part I of the United States Medical Licensing Examination (USMLE) (on basic science knowledge) examination to be taken and passed after the second year.

Years 3 and 4.   During the third and fourth years—the clinical years—students learn to use their basic medical science to solve actual clinical problems by working with patients (almost always in hospitals). During these 2 years, students rotate through several (typically about nine) clerkships to learn specialized applications of medical knowledge. They spend an average of about 6 weeks in family practice, 12 weeks in internal medicine, 8 weeks in general surgery, 8 weeks in pediatrics, 7 weeks in obstetrics and gynecology, and 7 weeks in psychiatry. Students often make rounds during these years—accompanied by impersonal faculty and intensive oral exams. Most schools require the passing of the two parts of Part II (on clinical knowledge and clinical skills) of the USMLE exam after the fourth year. A third part (on application of

clinical knowledge and patient management) ultimately also needs to be passed in order to receive a medical license in the United States.

The Internship and Residency.   After the fourth year, most students enter a medical residency (except for those who intend to do research or work outside medicine). A computerized matching process is used to pair residents looking for a teaching hospital with particular traits (e.g., specialization or location) and for hospitals attempting to secure the best possible residents. The number of years required in residency depends upon the specialty interests of the resident—3 years is common, but several specialties require longer. The resident (the first year of the residency is still sometimes referred to as the internship) is legally able to practice medicine under the supervision of a licensed physician.

Significant role identity change from student to physician occurs during these years. The resident has much more authority than the fourth-year student, and that often comes across in relationships with patients and ancillary staff. This is a learning period for residents, and they

IN COMPARATIVE FOCUS

MEDICAL EDUCATION IN CHINA

As the most populous country in the world and one whose population is largely rural, China faces a very difficult challenge in having a sufficient number of health care providers. In a model that is based partly on Western-style medical education and partly on its own culture and social circumstances, China provides three levels of education for physicians:

Assistant doctors are trained for 2 years and several months to be able to provide basic primary care in mostly rural villages.

Medical doctors are trained either at Level 1 (a 3-year program that includes condensed basic sciences and clinical subjects in the first 2 years and hospital practice in the third year, and prepares doctors to work in rural communities) or at Level 2 (a 5-year curriculum that includes all the basic sciences in the first 3 years, general medicine and surgery in the fourth year, and hospital practice in the fifth year, and prepares doctors to work in urban areas).

Specialists undergo 7 or 8 years of training, and essentially receive the same training as Level 2 doctors plus additional training in

specialty areas. They typically work in urban areas and provide specialty care and complex surgeries.

Medical education in China includes both a Western-style, scientifically based curriculum (including anatomy and physiology), and education in traditional Chinese healing theory and practice (including knowledge of acupuncture). Some schools focus more on Western medicine while others focus more on traditional medicine.

The Chinese system for medical education acknowledges that China does not have a sufficient number of fully trained physicians to meet the needs of the total population. By requiring fewer years of preparation for those who will solely provide basic primary care, more individuals can be medically trained and the needs of both the urban and rural populations can be addressed. In addition, health care providers can focus their education on more or less traditional healing practices, thus making both approaches available to patients (Lassey, Lassey, and Jinks, 1997).

often search for—and are most excited to work with—intriguing cases. On the other hand, medical residents are a primary source of cheap labor for hospitals, and they are expected to handle many routine responsibilities. The hours assigned are typically very long, exhaustion is not uncommon (due to medical school debts, many residents even moonlight, taking on additional paid medical responsibilities in the few off-hours they have), and it is often a frustrating and disillusioning time.

The accompanying box, "Medical Education in China," discusses a system of medical education that has been found to be more appropriate for a developing country.

Criticisms of the Medical Education Curriculum

There is considerable agreement that the traditional medical school curriculum falls short of the ideal. Critics, often from inside AHCs, have identified at least four important issues (Braunwald, 2006; Cooke et al., 2006).

First, too little priority is given to teaching by medical faculty who are hired and promoted based on their record in research, grantsmanship, and clinical practice. As the entire incentive structure focuses on non-teaching activities, dedication to working with medical students is often lacking (Regan-Smith, 1998). As an illustration, despite the fact that the number of faculty has increased more rapidly in recent years than the number of students, faculty are not spending any additional time in the classroom. In reflecting on the dominance of non-teaching activities in academic centers, David Rogers laments the passing of earlier ways:

> Gone are the leisurely laboratory sessions where students and faculty became acquainted one with another in a problem-solving mode. Gone are the informal after-hours get-togethers with faculty who knew students and vice versa, which I remember with such fondness from my own student days. Gone are the genuine, go-at-your-own-pace problem-solving sessions in which students learned to think deductively and gained experience in logical decision making. (Rogers 1987:38)

Second, an extensive amount of departmental and research specialization prevents integration of the curriculum. Many academic physicians focus on only one aspect of medical education—clinical practice, teaching, research, or administration—and have little interaction with those who have other priorities. Departments (referred to as "fiefdoms" by many faculty themselves) are locked into continuing competition for prestige and for both internal and external funding (e.g., basic science and clinical departments often struggle for power) (Ludmerer, 1985).

> The faculty members from any one discipline are usually unaware of and not interested in the material presented in other courses. As a consequence, students are presented with uncoordinated information from the various biological sciences. The content of any one course is unrelated to the content of other courses and there may be gaps or duplications. Information from the courses taken collectively is unrelated in any explicit manner to clinical application. (Bussigel, Barzansky, and Grenholm, 1988:5)

Third, most medical curricula continue to focus on the presentation of facts and on the ability of students to memorize facts. Especially in the first 2 years, lecture pedagogy and fact-based exams dominate. Much less time is devoted to the enhancement of students' analytic skills. Given the speed with which new facts become available and the nature of medicine as a question-answering, problem-solving field, the emphasis on passive rather than active learning is difficult to understand.

Moreover, crucial aspects of the actual practice of medicine are sometimes given little or no attention. Understanding the importance of sociocultural influences on patient behavior, the development of interpersonal skills (such as verbal and non-verbal communication and the development of rapport with patients), and reflection on ethical questions are rarely highlighted.

Finally, today's medical school curriculum is out of step with current realities, such as changes in disease patterns and changes in the financing of health care. Despite the fact that chronic disease accounts for approximately 75 percent of deaths in the United States, medical education continues to focus heavily on acute health problems and late-intervention therapies, and largely ignores the importance of lifestyle education, preventive health care, and the influence of social factors on disease and illness.

Curricular Reform

Over the course of the last three decades, at least four significant efforts at curriculum change have occurred.

1. **Problem-based learning (PBL)**, developed at McMaster and Michigan State Universities in the 1970s and incorporated elsewhere, attempts to overcome the fact-based approach in the traditional curriculum by emphasizing student problem solving. In contrast to traditional lecture-based learning, students using PBL are more likely to have actual patient contact from the beginning of medical school,

and to work routinely with patient case studies and simulated patients. Emphasis is placed on analytical reasoning and methods for acquiring and applying information. The instructor is not the "answer expert," but a facilitator assisting students in doing the problem solving. Students often work in small-group tutorials.

Is this an effective teaching strategy? Research indicates that it is. Several studies have found that students using PBL outperform those using lecture-based learning on tasks such as retention of factual knowledge, ability to take a history and perform a physical exam, deriving a diagnosis, and organizing and expressing information (Richards et al., 1996). Medical school faculty who have worked with PBL rate it very highly in the areas of clinical preparation, medical reasoning, and student interest, but less highly in teaching factual knowledge and efficiency of learning. Faculty most involved with PBL rate it most highly (Vernon and Hosokawa, 1996).

2. *Teaching professional skills and perspectives* has long been recommended but only recently seriously developed by a sizable number of medical schools. Although often taken only on an elective basis, courses in physician–patient communication, physical examination, health promotion and disease prevention, public health, working with diverse populations, medical ethics, and medical sociology are now widely available in medical schools, and increasingly recognized as being essential for the comprehensive training of physicians. Several schools have implemented efforts to give students a better idea of the overall health care system, health care reform, and changing organizational environments.

3. *Community-based medical education* involves the shifting of clinical training from hospital wards to outpatient settings such as physicians' offices and community health centers. While this shift may reduce the number of opportunities that medical students have to perform certain procedures (e.g., insertion of a nasogastric tube), it creates many more opportunities to interact with patients in the type of setting in which most physician–patient interaction actually occurs.

4. **Evidence-based medicine (EBM)** has become a significant curricular change. Acknowledging that wide disparities in diagnosis and standard treatment exist among and even within communities, the aim of EBM is to have physicians' selection of medical therapies rely less on intuition and anecdotal evidence and more on medical therapies that have been tested and determined to be effective in scientific research. It has evolved now to a point at which physicians are asked to integrate evidentiary knowledge with clinical experience and patient preferences. EBM allows individuals to define what "evidence" means in different ways; one study found that some pediatric residents interpreted it to mean consulting the relevant literature, while others more critically analyzed the available research. Using EBM did not remove all physician uncertainty about the proper course of action, but did strengthen use of available outcomes-based research (Timmermans and Angell, 2001; Timmermans and Mauck, 2005). Research has found that students learn well when being taught with an EBM approach (West and McDonald, 2008).

Does all of this represent significant reform in medical education? Yes, according to some; no, according to others. In 1988, Sam Bloom, himself a medical school faculty member, expressed criticism of modifications in medical curricula that left the basic teaching and learning experience unchanged. Referring to such modifications as "reform without change," Bloom said that the experience of teachers and students had changed so little "that current medical students are startled by the mirror-like familiarity of 30 year old accounts of medical student life" (Bloom, 1988:295). In the late 1990s, Bloom's analysis of the meaningfulness of reform efforts had not changed. Perhaps, however, the continued development of PBL, the teaching of professional skills and perspectives, community-based programs, and evidence-based learning offer hope of "reform with change."

Are medical schools committed to curricular change? It seems that perhaps they are. It is clear that the LCME is encouraging schools to develop more integrated curricula, promote active and PBL approaches, increase students' exposure to primary care and community settings, further develop EBM, place increased emphasis on chronic diseases, expand the focus on women's health, add emphasis on relief of pain, and introduce learning of complementary and alternative healing approaches, and health policy. In schools where these innovations have been introduced, medical students have responded favorably. Although many such programs will need to be fine-tuned, students are strong proponents of meaningful change (Khan, Long, and Brienza, 2012; Ross and Fineberg, 1998).

Recent Developments in Medical Education Reform

Recently, there have been new efforts at reform in medical education. Three of these are taking a more holistic approach in admissions decisions, revising the Medical College Admissions Test (MCAT), and further revising the medical school curriculum.

A More Holistic Admissions Process. Since the 1910 Flexner Report, the biological and physical sciences have been the core of the medical school admissions process and the medical school curriculum. Medical school admissions committees typically focused on student grades in the sciences and their performance on the science sections of the MCAT. Data support the view that these two measures predict success in medical school science courses and on Step One of the USMLE Licensing Examination. However, they are not predictors of character, behavior, interaction skills, sensitivity to patients, and values that are important ingredients of a good physician (Witzburg and Sondheimer, 2013).

Since a Supreme Court decision in 2003, the Association of American Medical Colleges (AAMC) has encouraged individual medical schools to expand the considerations they use when granting admission. The Supreme Court endorsed "highly individualized, holistic review of each applicant's file, giving serious consideration to all the ways that an applicant might contribute to a diverse educational environment," allowing each school to "seriously consider each applicant's promise of making a notable contribution to the class by way of a particular strength, attainment, or characteristic – e.g., an unusual intellectual achievement, employment experience, nonacademic performance, or personal background" (Grutter v. Bullinger, 2003) (United States Supreme Court, 2003). The Grutter case has been appealed and continues to wind its way through the courts.

The rationale is that this more holistic review allows medical schools to tap into a variety of backgrounds and experiences and interests that might contribute to becoming an excellent physician. "To the extent that these approaches attempt to determine whether applicants have a strong understanding of ethical issues, concern for underserved populations, and appropriate communication skills, they are held out as significant steps toward graduating doctors who can relate to patients" (Schwartzenstein, 2015).

A Revised MCAT. In 2011, the AAMC issued a report that emphasized the importance of the behavioral and social sciences in medical education. The next year, it was announced that the MCAT, a prerequisite for admission to almost all U.S. medical schools, would undergo significant revision in 2015. The re-formulated test consists of four sections: (1) Biological and Biochemical Foundations of Living Systems; (2) Chemical and Physical Foundations of Biological Systems; (3) Psychological, Social, and Biological Foundations of Behavior (a completely new section); and (4) Critical Analysis and Reasoning Skills.

The new Psychological, Social, and Biological Foundations of Behavior section reflects the recognition that behavioral and social factors influence health and illness and interact with biological factors to influence health outcomes. Other topics of particular interest included knowledge of the changing health care system, health care inequalities, how we think about ourselves and others, and physician stress and burnout. Fundamental knowledge about behavioral and social sciences was deemed to be critical to the practice of medicine (Kaplan, Satterfield, and Kington, 2012). In addition, medical school applicants were encouraged to take more social sciences and humanities courses as undergraduates. (About 35 percent of medical school applicants have majored in something other than biology, chemistry, or another physical science, and they are just as successful or even slightly more likely to get admitted to medical school.)

Assuming that medical schools make effective use of this new section, its inclusion on the MCAT will necessarily increase the exposure of premedical students to the behavioral and social sciences, and hopefully will pave the way for additional attention to these areas in medical school.

Further Revision of the Medical School Curriculum. In the last 10 years, several medical schools have designed and implemented major curricular innovations. Several schools have developed specializations, interest areas, or program themes in areas such as cultural competency, medical ethics, end-of-life care, family-centered care, health care leadership, changing health care delivery systems, empathy, and public health. Some schools are studying the possibility of shifting to a 3-year curriculum, and three already have for students interested in primary care.

In 2013, the American Medical Association enacted a new program to accelerate change in medical education (American Medical Association, 2016). Called "Accelerating Change in Medical Education," the program gave 11 medical schools US$1 million each in 2013 to pursue a 5-year plan to support their work on transformative medical education projects. Twenty additional schools were selected for the consortium in 2015 (more than 100 applied), with each receiving US$75,000 over 3 years for curricular reform projects. The ultimate goals are to create the medical school of the future and to transform physician training. An estimated 19,000 medical students—18% of all U.S. allopathic and osteopathic medical students—study at medical schools that are consortium members. You can learn about each school's work at www.ama-assn.org/ama/pub/about-ama/strategic-focus/accelerating-change-in-medical-education/schools.

THE MEDICAL SCHOOL EXPERIENCE: ATTITUDE AND VALUE ACQUISITION

Sociologists are keenly aware of the powerful socializing influence of the medical school experience. The length of time in medical training, the intensity of the experience, and formal and informal interaction with faculty, fellow students, other health care workers, and patients help to shape important attitudes and values of the physician-to-be. This section of the chapter summarizes research on two important attitude and value changes experienced by many medical students—a "tolerance for uncertainty" and "detached concern."

Tolerance for Uncertainty

In studies at Cornell University, researchers identified a clear and explicit effort to train medical students to be tolerant of the many kinds of uncertainties they would face as physicians. Renée Fox (1957) identified three kinds of uncertainty that confronted the students as they progressed through medical school. Early in the first year, a type of uncertainty was created when students became aware that they could not possibly master all the concepts and facts covered in their classes and textbooks. For students accustomed to mastery of course materials, the enormity of the field of medicine can be a very threatening and disheartening realization.

> In college, I didn't always do all the work, but I was good at managing my time, and I was happy with the work I was doing and satisfied with what I was achieving. But somehow here, it's Pass/Fail . . . it should be easy, [but] the pressure is so much greater . . . I think part of it is the sense that what you learn now may make the difference in someone's life. The material begins to impress you over and over again; this is serious. You need to know it to treat people. (Good and Good, 1989:304)

Second, and more gradually, students became aware that the knowledge base of medicine is incomplete. There is much about the human being—genetically, physiologically, emotionally, and socioculturally—that is yet to be fully understood, and important gaps in information exist in understanding disease and illness and their treatment. Students come to realize that, even if they could somehow know all that is known about medicine, there is still much they would not know.

The third type of uncertainty was created when students attempted to distinguish between the first two types. When they would run into a question in the process of making a patient diagnosis, students would need to determine whether it was a limitation in their own knowledge or something not yet comprehended in medicine. As clinical work increased, they were often concerned that their own lack of knowledge might jeopardize a patient's health or recovery.

Aware of this rite of passage, medical faculties and upper-level students socialized newer students to accept that some uncertainty is inevitable in medicine, that it has some fortunate consequences (e.g., stimulating new medical knowledge), and that it is best dealt with by openly acknowledging its existence (Fox, 1989).

However, students also realized the dysfunctions of being too candid about their own uncertainties. Desiring to come across as knowledgeable and competent future physicians, and not wishing to jeopardize the confidence of the patient (or their instructors) in them, they often presented themselves as more certain about a matter than they really were. Light (1979) suggests that the real socialization that occurs is "training for control." This is accomplished not only through mastery of course materials and clinical experience, but also through "psyching out instructors" (e.g., finding out what instructors want and giving it to them, and using impression management techniques) and becoming more authoritarian with patients. Katz (1984) has referred to this process not as tolerating uncertainty but as "disregarding" it.

Do these efforts to control uncertainty carry over into clinical practice? It has been suggested that some of the excessive diagnostic testing that is a concern today is due to physicians seeking diagnostic certainty and pursuing every test that might offer it (Allison, Kiefe, and Cook, 1998).

When diagnostic certainty does not exist, however, physicians often become and portray themselves to patients as being supremely confident about their conclusions ("microcertainty")—even when there is considerable dissent with other health care professionals about the diagnosis ("macro-uncertainty"). This pattern has been identified in treatment choices made by physicians working with breast cancer patients, and in the rapid decision making of nurses in an intensive care unit (Baumann, Deber, and Thompson, 1991).

Detached Concern

Concern for one's patients is certainly an accepted ideal in medical education, but students are encouraged to develop **detached concern**—that is, concern about the patient without excessive emotional involvement or over-identification. It is a "supple balance" of "objectivity and empathy" and "equanimity and compassion" that are combined to enable the "delivery of competent, sagacious, and humane patient care" (Fox, 1989:85). The danger of becoming too emotionally involved with a patient is that diagnostic proficiency or treatment recommendations might be compromised by personal involvement. The death of a patient is often difficult for physicians, but if there is extensive emotional involvement, the death may so affect the physician that the care of other patients is compromised—not a desirable circumstance. These are the reasons why many physicians prefer not to treat family members.

Students learn specific techniques to facilitate this detachment. They learn to "intellectualize" and "technicalize" the cadavers they work with in anatomy laboratory, and engage in "gallows humor" as a means of venting personal emotions. In their clinical years, they repeatedly perform certain tests (e.g., urinalyses) so that they become accustomed to them and feel less awkward about doing them. As actual patient care begins, many students feel uncomfortable about certain questions that need to be asked

(e.g., about sexual history) and certain procedures that must be performed (e.g., rectal examination). Students are often still thinking of the patient as an individual person—making these tasks more difficult. Often they consciously seek more detachment (Fox, 1989).

At some point during the third year, many students become aware that their efforts to detach have been too successful. They have made a transition by depersonalizing the patient and by focusing on diseases and procedures and tasks that are becoming second nature—rather than focusing on the person. Some refer to this as a type of "emotional numbness" (Fox, 1989). Rather than having learned to walk the fine line between concern and detachment, students often master detachment at the expense of genuine concern, become increasingly doctor centered and less patient centered (Haidet et al., 2002), and sometimes develop disinterested or even hostile attitudes toward patients.

Curing Rather Than Caring. Critics charge that these attitudes are more than an unfortunate byproduct of learning to maintain objectivity. Rather, it is posited that medical schools are so devoted to teaching students how to "cure" patients that they offer little guidance, training, or encouragement in ways to "care" for patients. Conrad (1988) analyzed four separate book-length accounts ("insider reports") of the medical school years written by medical students. The accounts portrayed an educational experience clearly oriented toward curing—understanding disease, technical procedures, and high-tech medicine—with little attempt to focus on caring for patients. An "ideology of caring" was sometimes voiced but not often demonstrated.

> Perhaps the most consistent theme that recurred in these accounts was the scarcity of humane and caring encounters between doctors and patients . . . Doctors' clinical perspectives focused almost entirely on the disease rather than on the

illness. Virtually all teaching emphasized the technical aspects of doctoring: diagnosis, treatment, and intervention. Too often this approach caused patients to become the disease: "the lymphoma in Room 304." A fascination with technological intervention pervades medicine, from neonatal intensive care to neurosurgery to cardiac catheterization. These are the frontiers of medicine . . . and are seductive to medical students. (Conrad, 1988:328)

The physician–patient interaction that is observed often devalues the importance of caring behaviors. During rounds in a hospital, physicians often talk to residents or medical students about a patient as if the patient is not even present. When talking to the patient, many doctors do not make eye contact, are not attentive, and are very abrupt—these are the behaviors that students observe.

Renée Anspach (1988) also investigated the way that physicians talk to each other about patients. She conducted a 16-month field study of life-and-death decision making in two newborn intensive care units, and spent an additional 3 months in a hospital obstetrics and gynecology department. She closely studied "case presentations"—formal and informal case histories presented at formal conferences, during daily rounds, in consultations with specialists, and at various points on the case record—made by interns, residents, and fellows. She observed that the terminology used often "de-personalized" the patient (e.g., using a very impersonal vocabulary), that the passive voice was used to omit reference to the physician, nurse, or other health care workers who attended the patient or that a technology was identified as the agent (e.g., "the arteriogram showed"), and that skepticism was often expressed about patients' self-reports.

Medical students have also developed special terms that they use among themselves to identify patients whom they perceive to be undesirable, such as "gomers" (get out of my emergency room—often used to describe patients with poor

hygiene, incontinence, habitual malingering, and a tendency to pull out intravenous lines), "crocks," "dirtballs," and "brain stem preparations" (Liederman and Grisso, 1985). Terry Mizrahi's fascinating book *Getting Rid of Patients* (published in 1986) describes a whole process of enculturation for interns and residents that often results in a GROP (getting rid of patients) perspective.

It is little wonder that when medical students begin their own interaction with patients, they are often ill-equipped to offer a caring manner. Many have yet to develop a comfort level with patients. They do not introduce themselves or do anything to try to make the patient feel more at ease. They may be very self-conscious, thinking more about how they are coming across than about the patient's pain, discomfort, or unease.

Exceptions. Are there physicians who disavow these patterns and genuinely encourage and demonstrate positive and caring interaction techniques with patients? Absolutely—and students often express admiration for them. Are there medical students, interns, and residents who are disappointed by the lack of emphasis on patients as people? Absolutely—and they often express concern that their own caring attitudes and behaviors will be threatened or lost due to the inhospitable environment. Are things changing? As described earlier in this chapter, some medical schools are now attempting to develop more humane settings for their students and to offer more encouragement for caring physician–patient interaction.

THE MEDICAL SCHOOL EXPERIENCE: STRESS

Without question, the 4 years of medical school and the 3 or more years of internship/residency are an extremely stressful time. Some have chosen to regard this stress as simply a rite of passage. Recently, however, systematic attention has been given to this issue.

Stressors in the First Four Years

Based on clinical reports (case studies of medical students who seek psychiatric or counseling support), intervention studies that measure the impact of stress-reduction programs on medical students, and social surveys that measure self-reports of stress by medical students, three primary categories of stressors in the medical school experience have been identified (Carmel and Bernstein, 1987): (1) current academic stressors—including examinations and hours required for study; (2) anticipated medical career stressors—various aspects of patient contact; and (3) social stressors—especially the limited amount of time for relationships with friends and family.

In a study of students at an Israeli medical school, the "death of a child under your care" and "death of a young adult under your care" were identified as the largest sources of stress. The other most commonly identified stressors in this study were "error in diagnosis or treatment," "lacking time for family and friends," and "death of an old person under your care." The student's gender, marital status, and year of study did not influence their perceptions, although older students were most likely to be troubled by the death of a child or young adult (Carmel and Bernstein, 1987).

Both research on medical students and anecdotal evidence have identified that medical students face considerable stress and have high levels of depression (a 15 to 30 percent higher rate than the general population), anxiety, and substance abuse. Many feel a sense of burnout, and for many this carries on past medical school. Many feel a strong sense of mistreatment in their training and from others in the learning process (Elnicki, 2013).

Stressors during Internship and Residency

Considerable research has focused on the stressful position and lifestyle of medical interns and residents. These stresses usually occur at a time in life when other stressful life events are also often happening—marriage and children, altered relationships with parents, financial worries, and post-school emotional letdown. Piled onto these activities are responsibilities that are often physically and emotionally draining. Three aspects of this role that are especially stressful are reviewed here.

1. *The grueling schedule.* The tradition of residencies calls for extended work shifts (often 36 consecutive hours on) with work weeks of 100 hours or more. The long shifts may include some time for sleep (in the hospital), but the resident remains on call and could conceivably not get any sleep during this time. The long hours are justified in various ways—as important socialization for the long hours that physicians work, an opportunity to learn more, and a way to staff hospitals—but the dangers of sleep deprivation (e.g., fatigue, lack of time for family and personal interests, and errors) are also well known.

   These dangers were dramatized in the 1984 hospital death of Libby Zion—an 18-year-old woman who was brought to the emergency room of New York Hospital at 11:30 p.m. on March 4 and died (needlessly) 7 hours later of bilateral bronchopneumonia. Although no criminal indictments were ever handed down, Zion was treated only by an intern and a junior resident, each of whom had been at work for 18 hours. The grand jury criticized five specific aspects of the care that Zion received as contributing to her death. Its report was viewed as an indictment of the traditional system of graduate medical education (Asch and Parker, 1988).

Most of the medical residents who were studied in the 1990s reported that sleep deprivation was a problem, 10 percent said that it was almost a daily problem, and 70 percent reported having observed a colleague working in an impaired state (with sleep deprivation being the most common cause) (Daugherty, Baldwin, and Rowley, 1998). In 2003 and again in 2011, the Accreditation Council for Graduate Medical Education approved national limits on the number of hours that medical residents can work (in the 2011 version, a limit of 80 hours per week, at least 10 hours of rest between shifts, not longer than 16 consecutive hours at a time for first-year residents, and not longer than 28-hour shifts for residents beyond the first year). Although these limits have been generally implemented, some hospitals have been very reluctant to comply with them.

These limits have been very controversial. Some critics contend that the longer shifts give students an opportunity to show their dedication to medicine, give them practice should they ever have to work such long hours in the future, and are an important part of resident culture, and that hospitals cannot afford to hire replacements for the hours that are lost. However, a greater number believe that the reduced hours lower the risk of medical error due to overworked and fatigued residents, and promote greater well-being among residents.

2. *Worries about medical school debts.* Although medical school tuition comprises a very small percentage of the medical school budget (4 to 5 percent on average), it has been increasing rapidly in both private and public medical schools. Approximately 90 percent of medical students receive financial assistance, but increasingly this is in the form of loans (now about 87 percent is loan assistance). Today, almost all graduating medical students accrue some debt, about four in five

owe at least US$100,000, about three in five owe at least US$150,000, and some owe more than US$300,000. The median medical school debt of 2014 graduates was US$176,000. Relative to other financial indicators, medical school is less affordable now than it has ever been. Research indicates that some qualified students forgo a career in medicine due to the anticipated level of debt. Repayment of the loan is a major worry for many medical students, and often colors their perception of the entire medical school experience.

3. *Feelings of mistreatment.* Although it is difficult for students to speak up about this, many experience feelings of being abused by the medical school process. Both empirical research and widely shared personal anecdotes are beginning to portray the extent of these feelings. A study of 431 students at a medical school discovered that almost 50 percent felt that they had received some abuse in medical school, and by the fourth year more than 80 percent reported personal abuse. The kinds of abuse reported included verbal abuse (insulting, humiliating, unjust statements), academic abuse (excessive workload, unnecessary scut work, unfair grade), sexual abuse (solicitation, harassment, sexism, discrimination), physical abuse (threatened or actual), and intentional neglect or lack of communication. Who did the abusing? For juniors and seniors, physician clinical faculty were most often cited, whereas for freshmen, Ph.D. faculty were cited most often (Silver and Glicken, 1990)— in both cases, the medical school faculty with whom they had most interaction. A recent study of female students at a New England medical school found that they became adept at dealing with inappropriate sex-based behavior from patients and female supervisors, but were more uncomfortable and less successful in handling unprofessional

behavior by male supervisors (Babaria et al., 2012).

This comes as no surprise to Howard Stein (1990), a leading critic of medical education. According to Stein, students often arrive at medical school with idealism, a concern for others, and general communication skills, but leave narrowly focused on biological factors and without the desire and ability to listen to and talk with others.

Medical students often use *excremental symbolism* to describe themselves, their work, their status, their clinical experiences, and their patients. They feel treated like "shit," they are often asked to do "shit work," they learn who is entitled to "shit on" whom, and one learns how much "shit" one must take and for how long. In effect, "one learns how to be a physician and how to occupy one of the highest of American social statuses by beginning as one of the lowest of the low" (Stein, 1990:201).

The Toll of Stress

While some medical students handle stress better than others, the high level of stressors frequently results in high levels of distress (Collier et al., 2002). Research has found that about 30 percent of interns and residents experience depressive symptoms or full-blown depression at some point in their training (Mata et al., 2015). Studies also document significant dysfunctional behaviors among medical residents. About one in eight residents increases their alcohol or other drug use during residency (although residents use fewer drugs than demographically matched non-physician groups), one in five fears that a current relationship will not survive the residency years, one in three suffers a significant depression sometime during the residency, and studies report that between 27 and 58 percent of medical students engage in some form of cheating during medical school

(Levey, 2001). Burnout is increasingly being recognized as a serious problem.

THE MEDICAL SCHOOL EXPERIENCE: CAREER CHOICES

During medical school, students make several important decisions about their medical career, including the size and type of community in which to practice, the specific type of setting desired, and the field in which to specialize. Research has attempted to understand factors that influence these choices, and especially if student preferences change (as they do for most students).

Research has shown that many students begin medical school with an interest in practicing in a small town or community, in an office-based setting, and in a primary care field. However, by graduation, they opt for a specialty located in a large city and/or connected to an academic medical center (in all cases, away from areas that are more needed to areas where physicians are well supplied). What motivates these interest changes? Exposure to (and being intrigued by) the research careers of faculty members, exposure to (and appreciation of) high-tech medicine, and the opportunity for larger salaries all play an influential role.

Reasons for Specialty Choice. Several factors influence the selection of a particular specialty. These include the content of the specialty, having a role model in a particular specialty, and the prestige, opportunities for cognitive performance, and future financial remuneration of the specialty. In recent years, medical students have begun to assign increased importance to a concept called **controllable lifestyle (CL)**—the extent to which particular specialties allow for some control over the hours worked (Newton, Grayson, and Thompson, 2005). Research has found that in the last decade

CL has become a much more powerful influence on the specialty choice of both female and male medical students (Dorsey, Jarjoura, and Rutecki, 2005). Even some young physicians practicing in primary care and surgical specialties are switching to CL specialties. Students choosing specialties with a non-controllable lifestyle (e.g., internal medicine, family practice, pediatrics, and obstetrics/gynecology) rated altruism as being a more important motivator than did those selecting CL specialties (Schwartz et al., 1990).

Choosing Primary Care.   What motivates the decision to choose primary care? In a study at eight New England medical schools, students selecting primary care rather than high-tech specialties were more likely to be motivated by opportunities to provide direct patient care and care in an ambulatory setting, and the opportunity to be involved in the psychological aspects of medical care. The opportunity to do research and to perform procedures, as well as a desire for a high income and a favorable lifestyle, were more important factors in the decisions of those of their peers who selected high-tech specialties (Kassler, Wartman, and Silliman, 1991).

Does the formal and informal structure of medical schools influence these motivations for type of practice? Yes, it does. A mission of the institution that is consistent with community service and the presence of a primary care-oriented curriculum and physician role models in primary care do influence students to pursue primary care training. A larger percentage of medical students who attend schools that promote a favorable and encouraging "primary care" culture eventually choose to pursue primary care (Erikson et al., 2013).

Are these aspects of the program the chief influence on those seeking a career in primary care? No, they are not. According to several studies, the most important factors are admissions criteria and the selection of students into the medical school. Applicants who have a high

service index reflective of a strong orientation to community service, who have taken a generous number of non-science courses as an undergraduate (and who take several non-science electives in medical school), and who come from a lower socioeconomic family background and rural areas are those who later on are most likely to pursue a career in primary care. Because all these factors are determined by the time of admission, medical schools could consciously choose those most likely to pursue primary care (Xu et al., 1999).

FUTURE DIRECTIONS IN MEDICAL EDUCATION IN THE UNITED STATES

Abraham Flexner advocated a strong scientific foundation for medicine, but not at the expense of humanism. He envisioned the ideal physician as one in whom science and humanity were united. While medical education is strongly grounded in science, many question the degree to which humanism has been maintained as a key element. This concern is highlighted by research which has found that fourth-year male medical students are much less favorably inclined than first-year students toward caring for the medically indigent (Crandall, Volk, and Loemker, 1993), that empathy and compassion decline during the medical school years (Newton et al., 2008), and that third-year students often feel it is difficult to practice patient-centered care when they are in medical sites where the opposite is role modeled (White et al., 2009).

Edmund Pellegrino (1987), a distinguished university and health center administrator, has encouraged medical education to follow a path of medical humanism by emphasizing humanitarianism—that is, humaneness and sensitivity to the patient's needs as a person. While it is possible to heal in the strictest sense without compassion, he views healing as being more complex than simply applying the correct medical method. This is true because illness and disease affect the whole life of a person and because effective clinical decisions should be "morally good" as well as technically correct. This requires the physician to have some sense of what the illness means and does to the life of a particular patient. Many of the recent curricular reforms are grounded in this orientation.

SUMMARY

Until the early 1900s, formal medical education in the United States was often poorly organized, lacking in academic rigor, and discriminatory against women and racial and ethnic minorities. The Flexner Report issued in 1910 strongly recommended a science-focused, university-based curriculum with significant clinical practice. Although several schools have been and are experimenting with innovations, the model that Flexner advocated continues to dominate medical education. However, critics contend that current circumstances prohibit medical education from achieving many of its most important objectives.

Applications to U.S. medical schools increased in the early and mid-1990s, dropped for the next several years, but are now again on the upswing. Women now account for almost 50 percent of medical students, although the percentage of traditionally under-represented minorities has dropped in recent years.

The medical school years have a profound influence on students. The structured, highly intense first 2 years in the basic sciences and the clinical experiences of the second 2 years not only are very stressful experiences but also help to mold students' attitudes, values, and career choices (especially away from interest in primary care fields in smaller towns and communities).

Among the most important value orientations to which students are socialized are a tolerance for uncertainty (learning to identify and accept what they do not know and what science does not know—and to distinguish between the two) and detached concern (learning to be concerned about the patient without being overly involved emotionally). Critics believe that formal and informal socialization often leads students to depersonalize and dehumanize patients, a problem that AHCs have recently begun to address.

HEALTH ON THE INTERNET

To find out what is happening in medical education or to learn about a particular medical school, you can gather information at the website of the American Association of Medical Colleges (AAMC) at www.aamc.org.

For insight into what medical students are working on, go to the American Medical Students Association (AMSA) at www.amsa.org. Click on "Take Action" in the top menu to identify the issues on which this group is focusing. Focus especially on "Current Campaigns" to learn about specific programs.

DISCUSSION CASE

At a recent (hypothetical) meeting of government and education leaders in your state, the usual litany of problems in medical education and health care delivery was being discussed. Those present were sensitive to the large debts that most medical students incur, and understood the pressure they felt upon graduation to enter specialties and move to locations where their earning capacity would be greater than if they practiced primary care in inner-city or rural areas, where needs are greatest. Concern was also expressed about the lack of access many people have to health care.

One of the leaders at the meeting proposed an idea to try to resolve both problems. Beginning in the next academic year, the state would initiate a mandatory program—it would pay the complete education costs for all students attending one of the state's medical schools. In return, students would be obligated to spend the first 4 years of their career in a location assigned by the state— presumably an inner-city or rural area in need of physicians. The idea is similar to the National Health Service Corps (an underfunded federal government program) and the Armed Forces Health Professions Scholarships, but differs in that it is a mandatory program.

If a state referendum were to be held on this proposal, how would you vote? Is this a creative response to the problems of large debts of medical students and the lack of health care services in certain areas? Or is the mandatory nature of the program unfair to medical students? Does the government have a right to dictate practice site to physicians even if it does pay their medical education expenses? Might other students (e.g., in law, engineering, business, education, and sociology) demand a comparable program? The state government could not afford all these programs. Is medical education and the delivery of care qualitatively different?

GLOSSARY

academic health center (AHC)
controllable lifestyle (CL)
detached concern
evidence-based medicine (EBM)

Flexner Report
problem-based learning (PBL)
socialization
tolerance for uncertainty

REFERENCES

Allison, Jeroan J., Catarine I. Kiefe, and E. Francis Cook. 1998 "The Association of Physician Attitudes About Uncertainty and Risk Taking With Resource Use in a Medicare HMO." *Medical Decision Making*, 18:320–329.

American Medical Association. 2016 *Accelerating Change in Medical Education.* www.ama-assn. org/ama/pub/about-ama/strategic-focus/ accelerating-change-in-medical-education/ schools.

Anspach, Renée. 1988 "Notes on the Sociology of Medical Discourse: The Language of Case Presentation." *Journal of Health and Social Behavior*, 29:357–375.

Asch, David A., and Ruth M. Parker. 1988 "The Libby Zion Case: One Step Forward or Two Steps Backward?" *New England Journal of Medicine*, 318:771–775.

Association of American Medical Colleges. 2016a www.aamc.org/download/ 321442/ data/2016factstable1.pdf.

——. 2016b www.aamc.org/download/321532/ data/2016factstableb2-2.pdf.

——. 2016c www.aamc.org/download/321472/data/ factstablea8.pdf.

——. 2016d www.aamc.org/download/321474/data/ factstablea9.pdf.

Babaria, Palev, Sakena Abedin, David Berg, and Marcella NunezSmith. 2012 "'I'm Too Used To It': A Longitudinal Qualitative Study of Third-Year Female Medical Students' Experiences of Gendered Encounters in Medical Education." *Social Science and Medicine*, 74:1013–1020.

Baumann, Andrea O., Raisa B. Deber, and Gail G. Thompson. 1991 "Overconfidence Among Physicians and Nurses: The 'Micro-Certainty, Macro-Uncertainty' Phenomenon." *Social Science and Medicine*, 32:167–174.

Bloom, Samuel W. 1988 "Structure and Ideology in Medical Education: An Analysis of Resistance to Change." *Journal of Health and Social Behavior*, 29:294–306.

Braunwald, Eugene. 2006 "Departments, Divisions and Centers in the Evolution of Medical Schools." *The American Journal of Medicine*, 119:457–462.

Bussigel, Margaret N., Barbara Barzansky, and Gary G. Grenholm. 1988 *Innovation Process in Medical Education*. New York: Praeger.

Carmel, Sara, and Judith Bernstein. 1987 "Perceptions of Medical School Stressors: Their Relationship to Age, Year of Study, and Trait Anxiety." *Journal of Human Stress*, 13:39–44.

Collier, Virginia U., Jack D. McCue, Allan Markus, and Lawrence Smith. 2002 "Stress in Medical Residency: Status Quo after a Decade of Reform?" *Annals of Internal Medicine*, 136: 384–390.

Conrad, Peter. 1988 "Learning to Doctor: Reflections on Recent Accounts of the Medical School Years." *Journal of Health and Social Behavior*, 29:323–332.

Cooke, Molly, David M. Irby, William Sullivan, and Kenneth M. Ludmerer. 2006 "American Medical Education 100 Years After the Flexner Report." *New England Journal of Medicine*, 355: 1339–1344.

Crandall, Sonia J.S., Robert J. Volk, and Vicki Loemker. 1993 "Medical Students' Attitudes Toward Providing Care for the Underserved." *Journal of the American Medical Association*, 269:2519–2523.

Daugherty, Steven R., DeWitt C. Baldwin, and Beverley D. Rowley. 1998 "Learning, Satisfaction, and Mistreatment during Medical Internship." *Journal of the American Medical Association*, 279:1194–1199.

Dorsey, E. Ray, David Jarjoura, and Gregory W. Rutecki. 2005 "The Influence of Controllable Lifestyle and Sex on the Specialty Choices of Graduating U.S. Medical Students, 1996–2003." *Academic Medicine*, 80:791–796.

Elnicki, D. Michael. 2013 "Cognitive Enhancement Drug Use among Medical Students and Concerns About Medical Student Well-Being." *Journal of General Internal Medicine*, 28:984–985.

Erikson, Cleese E., Sana Danish, Karen C. Jones, Shana F. Sanberg, and Adam C. Carle. 2013 "The Role of Medical School Culture in Primary Care Career Choice." *Academic Medicine*, 88: 1919–1926.

Flexner, Abraham. 1910 *Medical Education in the United States and Canada: A Report to the Carnegie Foundation for the Advancement of Teaching*. New York: The Carnegie Foundation for the Advancement in Teaching.

Fox, Renée C. 1957 "Training for Uncertainty." Pp. 207–241 in *The Student-Physician*, Robert K. Merton, George G. Reader, and Patricia Kendall (eds.). Cambridge, MA: Harvard University Press.

——. 1989 *The Sociology of Medicine: A Participant Observer's View*. Upper Saddle River, NJ: Prentice Hall.

——. 1999 "Time to Heal Medical Education?" *Academic Medicine*, 74:1072–1075.

Good, Mary-Jo D., and Byron J. Good. 1989 "Disabling Practitioners: Hazards of Learning to be a Doctor in American Medical Education." *American Journal of Orthopsychiatry*, 59:303–309.

Haidet, Paul, Joyce E. Dains, Debora A. Paterniti, Laura Hechtel, Tai Chang, Ellen Tseng, and John C. Rogers. 2002 "Medical Student Attitudes toward the Doctor–Patient Relationship." *Medical Education*, 36:568–574.

Irby, David M., Molly Cooke, and Bridget C. O'Brien. 2010 "Calls for Reform of Medical Education by the Carnegie Foundation for the Advancement of Teaching: 1910 and 2010." *Academic Medicine*, 85:220–227.

Kaplan, Robert M., Jason M. Satterfield, and Raynard S. Kington. 2012 "Building A Better Physician—The Case for the New MCAT." *New England Journal of Medicine*, 366:1265–1268.

Karpf, Michael, Richard Lofgren, and Jay Perman. 2009 "Commentary: Health Care Reform and Its Potential Impact on Academic Medical Centers." *Academic Medicine*, 84:1472–1475.

Kassler, William J., Steven A. Wartman, and Rebecca A. Silliman. 1991 "Why Medical Students Choose Primary Care Careers." *Academic Medicine*, 66:41–43.

Katz, Jay. 1984 *The Silent World of Doctor and Patient*. New York: The Free Press.

Khan, Ali M., Theodore Long, and Rebecca Brienza. 2012 "'Surely We Can Do Better': Scaling Innovation in Medical Education for Social Impact." *Academic Medicine*, 87:1645–1646.

Lassey, Marie L., William R. Lassey, and Martin J. Jinks. 1997 *Health Care Systems*

Around the World. Upper Saddle River, NJ: Prentice Hall.

Levey, Robert E. 2001 "Sources of Stress for Residents and Recommendations for Programs to Assist Them." *Academic Medicine*, 76:142–150.

Liederman, Deborah B., and Jean-Anne Grisso. 1985 "The Gomer Phenomenon." *Journal of Health and Social Behavior*, 26:222–232.

Light, Donald W. 1979 "Uncertainty and Control in Professional Training." *Journal of Health and Social Behavior*, 20:310–322.

Ludmerer, Kenneth M. 1985 *Learning to Heal: The Development of American Medical Education.* New York: Basic Books, Inc.

———. 1999 *Time to Heal: American Medical Education from the Turn of the Century to the Era of Managed Care.* New York: Oxford University Press.

Mata, Douglas A., Marco A. Ramos, Narinder Bansal, Rida Khan, Constance Guille, Emanuele Di Angelantonio, and Srijan Sen. 2015 "Prevalence of Depression and Depressive Symptoms among Resident Physicians: A Systematic Review and Meta-analysis." *Journal of the American Medical Association*, 314:2373–2383.

Mizrahi, Terry. 1986 *Getting Rid of Patients.* New Brunswick, NJ: Rutgers University Press.

Newton, Bruce W., Laurie Barber, James Clardy, Elton Cleveland, and Patricia O'Sullivan. 2008 "Is There Hardening of the Heart During Medical School?" *Academic Medicine*, 83:244–249.

Newton, Dale A., Martha S. Grayson, and Lori F. Thompson. 2005 "The Variable Influence of Lifestyle and Income on Medical Students' Career Specialty Choices: Data From Two U.S. Medical Schools, 1998–2004." *Academic Medicine*, 80:809–814.

Pellegrino, Edmund D. 1987 "The Reconciliation of Technology and Humanism: A Flexnerian Task 75 Years Later." Pp. 77–111 in *Flexner: 75 Years Later: Current Commentary on Medical Education*, Charles Vevier (ed.). Lanham, MD: University Press of America.

Pololi, Linda H., Edward Krupat, Janet T. Civian, Arlene S. Ash, and Robert T. Brennan. 2012 "Why are a Quarter of Faculty Considering Leaving Academic Medicine? A Study of Their Perceptions of Institutional Culture and Intentions to Leave at 26 Representative U.S. Medical Schools." *Academic Medicine*, 87:859–869.

Regan-Smith, Martha G. 1998 "Reform without Change: Update, 1998." *Academic Medicine*, 73:505–507.

Richards, Boyd F., K. Patrick Ober, Liza Cariaga-Lo, Martha G. Camp, James Philip, Mary McFarlane, Randall Rupp, and Daniel J. Zaccaro. 1996 "Ratings of Students' Performances in a Third-Year Internal Medicine Clerkship: A Comparison Between Problem-Based and Lecture-Based Curricula." *Academic Medicine*, 71:187–189.

Rogers, David E. 1987 "Medical Education: Its Purpose and Its Problems." Pp. 35–45 in *Flexner. 75 Years Later. Current Commentary on Medical Education*, Charles Vevier (ed.). Lanham, MD: University Press of America.

Ross, Robert H., and Harvey V. Fineberg. 1998 "Medical Students' Evaluations of Curriculum Innovations at Ten North American Medical Schools." *Academic Medicine*, 73:258–265.

Saha, Somnath, Gretchen Guiton, Paul F. Wimmers, and LuAnn Wilkerson. 2008 "Student Body Racial and Ethnic Composition and Diversity-Related Outcomes in U.S. Medical Schools." *Journal of the American Medical Association*, 300:1135–1145.

Schwartz, R.W., J.V. Haley, C. Williams, R.K. Jarecky, W.E. Strodel, A.B. Young, and W.O. Griffen. 1990 "The Controllable Lifestyle Factor and Students' Attitudes About Specialty Election." *Academic Medicine*, 65:207–210.

Schwartzenstein, Richard M. 2015 "Getting the Right Medical Students—Nature Versus Nurture." *New England Journal of Medicine*, 372:1586–1587.

Silver, Henry K., and Anita D. Glicken. 1990 "Medical Student Abuse: Incidence, Severity, and Significance." *Journal of the American Medical Association*, 263:527–532.

Stein, Howard F. 1990 *American Medicine as Culture.* Boulder, CO: Westview Press.

Timmermans, Stefan, and Alison Angell. 2001 "Evidence-Based Medicine, Clinical Uncertainty, and Learning to Doctor." *Journal of Health and Social Behavior*, 42:342–359.

Timmermans, Stefan, and Aaron Mauck. 2005 "The Promises and Pitfalls of Evidence-Based Medicine." *Health Affairs*, 24:18–28.

United States Supreme Court. 2003 *Grutter v. Bullinger,* 539 U.S. 306.

Vernon, David T.A., and Michael C. Hosokawa. 1996 "Faculty Attitudes and Opinions About

Problem-Based Learning." *Academic Medicine*, 71:1233–1238.

West, Colin P., and Furman S. McDonald. 2008 "Evaluation of a Longitudinal Medical School Evidence-Based Medicine Curriculum: A Pilot Study." *Journal of General Internal Medicine*, 23:1057–1059.

White, Casey B., Arno K. Kumagai, Paula T. Ross, and Joseph C. Fantone. 2009 "A Qualitative Exploration of How the Conflict Between the Formal and Informal Curriculum Influences Student Values and Behaviors." *Academic Medicine*, 84:597–603.

Witzburg, Robert A., and Henry M. Sondheimer. 2013 "Holistic Review—Shaping the Medical Profession One Applicant at a Time." *New England Journal of Medicine,* 368:1565–1567.

Xu, Gang, Mohammadreza Hojat, Timothy P. Brigham, and J. Jon Veloski. 1999 "Factors Associated with Changing Levels of Interest in Primary Care during Medical School." *Academic Medicine*, 74:1011–1015.

CHAPTER 10

Nurses, Advanced Practice Providers, and Allied Health Workers

Learning Objectives

- Describe the circumstances in which nursing and midwifery originated.
- Identify key orientations included in nursing socialization.
- Select any two of the key issues in nursing today and discuss the various sides of the issues.

- Compare and contrast the responsibilities of nurse practitioners and physician assistants. Discuss the extent to which they have earned patient satisfaction.
- Evaluate the extent to which physicians have positive working relationships with nurses and with allied health workers.

The shift in dominance from acute to chronic conditions and the development of increasingly sophisticated medical technologies have led to a growing array of specialized practitioners within the health care field. These practitioners play an indispensable role in the provision of health care services. This chapter focuses on nurses and the field of nursing, advanced practice providers, and allied health personnel.

EVOLUTION OF NURSES, ADVANCED PRACTICE PROVIDERS, AND ALLIED HEALTH WORKERS

Early America

Families rather than physicians were the most important health care providers in colonial America. Most families relied on their female members to provide health care, and when additional help was necessary, they employed medically knowledgeable females from other families. The duties of these formally untrained, but typically wise and benevolent "nurses" generally focused on childcare, surrogate breast-feeding, birthing, and care of the ill.

Early Midwifery. Midwives were a vital source of care for women in colonial times. Most came from England, where the Church of England granted licenses to practice. They were generally held in high esteem and often paid for their services, even though they were sometimes suspected of practicing witchcraft (e.g., in the case of an impaired baby). Many midwives served on southern plantations; some were slaves, others were white women who were paid in kind for their services. Although formal training was not available in the United States, some manuals were in print so that any woman who had borne children herself and had assisted in a few births could be designated a midwife.

With the development of the obstetric forceps and the subsequent acceptance of midwifery as a science, male physicians assumed greater responsibility for the birthing process. This transition was enabled by a belief that women were incapable of understanding and performing obstetric techniques. As formal medical education in the United States became available and was routinely restricted to men, physicians gained even further advantage over female midwives and attempted to monopolize the birthing field.

Early Nursing.   The increased dominance of men in the birthing process led many women to the field of nursing. Many became private duty nurses whose responsibilities were to tend to the sick at their bedside and provide both caring and curing services. Most of these nurses were relatively uneducated and lacked any formal nursing training, but they did provide a valuable service (Reverby, 1987).

Whereas private duty nursing was regarded as an acceptable occupation, hospital nursing—given the marginal nature of hospitals at this time—was perceived to be less desirable. Many hospital nurses both lived and worked in the hospital (and often were recovering patients themselves). Their qualifications and the quality of their work were uneven. The job was marked by long hours, physically demanding responsibilities, and frequent friction with physicians and hospital managers over the content and pace of their work.

The importance and visibility of nursing increased during the Civil War. Thousands of women on both sides of the conflict established hospitals and worked in them as volunteers and paid nurses. Many were working-class women who were accustomed to hard labor as

domestics and nurses, although others were middle-class women who had not worked previously for wages outside the home. In addition to patient care, some worked through the Sanitary Commission, which implemented several innovative public health measures, while others attempted to create a role for women in the army's medical system.

Post-Civil War to 1920: Professional Medicine and Separate Domains

Growth of Health Care Institutions.   With the end of the Civil War and the beginning of accelerated urbanization and industrialization, many families were separated geographically. Increasingly, non-family members were needed to provide care for the sick and injured and in places other than the home. It was particularly important to the growing "middling class" that the caretakers in institutions be as "reliable, respectable and clean (in all senses) as the mothers or sisters . . . formerly charged with the responsibility" (Baer, 1990:460).

As a result, a custodial role of "nurse" was established in these institutions. Religious sisters managed Roman Catholic, Lutheran, and Episcopal hospitals. Community women worked for wages in hospitals for the working poor. In big city almshouses, "the progression from inmate to keeper to assistant nurse to nurse comprised a sort of job ladder" (Baer, 1990:461). None of these "nurses" had formal training.

Advent of Nursing Education.   As more and more hospitals demanded public assistance with caring for the ill, demands for formal training of nurses accelerated. Programs were developed around the philosophy of Florence Nightingale, an upper-class British reformer who believed that the proper moral, environmental, and physical order was necessary for the restoration of health. Known as the founder of modern nursing, she made significant contributions to nursing education, nursing care, nursing research, understanding of the importance of hygiene and sanitation, and hospital design (Lee, Clark, and Thompson, 2013). She accepted a gender division of labor as given, and believed that women's characteristics made them naturally suited to creating the conditions needed for care of the ill.

Despite the fact that nursing was known for its drudgery, it attracted both white and black women who regarded it as a way to serve fellow human beings and an opportunity for personal autonomy and geographic mobility. However, employment opportunities for trained nurses were few. After completion of training, the nurse often had neither a place in the hospital (which depended upon cheap student labor) nor a position in private duty (where cheaper, untrained nurses were typically used). Many physicians and families were unconvinced that the training offered any significant benefit (Reverby, 1987).

Maternity Care.   By the late 1800s, the American medical profession had taken specific steps to ensure a place for obstetrics. In 1859, practical medicine and obstetrics was designated as one of four scientific sections of the American Medical Association (AMA), and in 1868, the *American Journal of Obstetrics* became the first specialized medical journal to be published in the United States. In 1876, the American Gynecological Society was formed, followed by establishment of the American Association of Obstetricians and Gynecologists in 1888.

Despite these developments, at least 50 percent of all births were still attended by midwives at the beginning of the twentieth century. Midwives were especially important for southern black families, immigrant families, and families living in rural areas. On the other hand, middle- and upper-class women were more likely to have physician-assisted deliveries. There was a general belief, however, that lack of adequate maternity care was a problem.

Home Nursing Care.   An important source of employment for nurses at the turn of the century was in agencies that provided home nursing care. These agencies were primarily located in northeastern cities, which had large concentrations of immigrants and were characterized by poverty, disease, and unsanitary conditions. In the beginning, a few wealthy women hired nurses to visit the poor sick in their homes, but visiting nurses soon became very popular in other settings. All types of groups began to hire these public health nurses, including Metropolitan Life, which discovered that it could reduce the number of death benefits it had to pay by offering home nursing service to policyholders.

The 1920s to the 1950s: The Advent of Scientific Medicine

Midwifery.   Debate concerning the regulation of midwifery reached its height between 1910 and 1920. In 1921, the Sheppard-Tower Maternity and Infancy Protection Act provided funds in several states for midwife education and registration. By 1930, all but ten states required midwives to be registered. These regulations were partly responsible for the decline in midwifery, but other factors such as declining birth rates, restricted immigration, an increase in the number of hospital beds available for maternity cases, and a growing anxiety about the dangers of birth also contributed to the decline. However, midwifery was sustained by the needs of the urban and rural poor (DeVries, 1985).

The first *nurse-midwives* to practice in the United States were brought from England in 1925 by Mary Breckinridge as part of her plan to provide health care for the rural people in Kentucky. As a consequence of these midwives' services, comprehensive health care services were made available to the rural population, and the maternal death rate declined dramatically. Eventually several states passed laws granting legal recognition to midwives, and several midwifery schools were established as a result.

Emergence of Staff Nursing. During the Depression years, the emphasis on nursing shifted back from private duty nursing to hospital staffing. While there was an oversupply of nurses in the 1920s and 1930s, a shortage developed during World War Two. This was due in part to the fact that women had opportunities for better-paying jobs in war-related industries. The shortage led to the creation of "practical nurses" and nursing assistants. Although these new occupations initially provided a temporary solution to a short-term problem, their contributions to health care were evident, and they eventually became permanent health care occupations.

The New Allied Health Workers. The emergence of **allied health workers** (health care workers such as physical therapists and medical technologists whose work supports that of the physician) occurred during the second quarter of the twentieth century. The development of these positions was encouraged by the complexity of new methods of diagnosis and treatment that required a specialist, and by the fact that there were not enough primary care physicians to handle the additional workload.

Beginning in the 1930s and continuing into the 1940s, the Committee on Allied Health Education and Accreditation (CAHEA) (now CAAHEP, as described later in the chapter), sponsored by the AMA, began to accredit a variety of allied health occupational areas. "Essentials" (nationally accepted minimum standards for an educational program) were first adopted for occupational therapy programs in 1935, and for most other allied health fields in the late 1930s and the 1940s.

Nursing Moves Away from Patient Care. During World War Two and its aftermath,

nursing moved away from direct patient care. Other than distributing medication, nurses spent much of the war years in the nurses' station, coordinating other staff, making notes on charts, and keeping records. In response, new categories of nurse-related workers emerged to provide direct patient care—the **licensed practical nurse (LPN)** or vocational nurse, and the nurse's aide (Reverby, 1987).

Meanwhile, nurse-midwifery struggled to establish standards for education, legal recognition, and professional identity. In 1955, the American College of Nurse-Midwifery was founded; it subsequently joined the Kentucky-based American Association of Nurse-Midwives in 1969 and formed the American College of Nurse-Midwives. However, legal recognition continued to be a problem. By 1959 only two states, New Mexico and New York, formally recognized the nurse-midwife, despite the positive impact of nurse-midwifery on maternal and infant mortality rates.

NURSES AND THE FIELD OF NURSING

Overview

In the United States, regulation of the field of nursing is a state responsibility. Under a state board of nursing, each state licenses nurses and defines the boundaries of the practice. All states require that prospective nurses attend an approved training program and take a national licensing examination. Certification in various specialty areas is administered by the American Nurses Credentialing Center, a subsidiary of the American Nurses Association (ANA).

Types of Nurses. There are three main types of nurses:

1. *Licensed practical nurses* typically are high-school graduates who have completed an

additional 1-year vocational program and have passed an examination leading to the LPN certification. There were approximately 836,000 LPNs in the United States in 2016— this figure is expected to increase to 921,000 by 2020.

2. **Registered nurses (RNs)** have obtained a diploma or degree in nursing, and are distinguished by the type of nursing education they have completed. In 2016 there were approximately 3.13 million registered nurses in the United States—this figure is expected to increase to 3.45 million by 2020.

    a. *Diploma nurses* have completed a 3-year program in a hospital-based school of nursing and earned a nursing license. Until the early 1970s, this was the dominant form of nursing education, although now only a small percentage of RNs (less than 5 percent) graduate from these programs.

    b. *Associate degree nurses* have completed a 2- to 3-year program consisting of both academic and nursing courses in a community college or junior college-based program, and earned an associate degree and a nursing license. These programs primarily offer a vocational orientation to nursing. At the time of writing, about 45 percent of nurses graduate from these programs.

    c. *Baccalaureate nurses* have completed an undergraduate curriculum of academic courses, usually with a nursing major, and have earned a Bachelor of Science in Nursing (BSN) degree. With a greater emphasis on theory and broad-based knowledge, these programs offer more of a professional orientation to nursing. Generally speaking, the more education a nurse has completed, the higher the status they enjoy. Baccalaureate programs now produce about 50 percent of nursing graduates, but are becoming more common. In

addition, many colleges that already offer the BSN degree have begun to offer "RN to BA" programs in which nurses with an associate degree can add additional courses to earn the baccalaureate degree, and "BS/BA to RN" programs for those with a baccalaureate degree in a field other than nursing.

3. **Advanced practice registered nurses (APRNs)** are registered nurses who have acquired a master's or post-master's degree and additional certification in one or more of about 20 nursing specialties. The largest categories of APRNs are nurse practitioners (NPs), clinical nurse specialists, nurse-anesthetists, and nurse-midwives. Each has a unique history and context, but they share the commonality of being APRNs, either in primary care (e.g., nurse practitioners and nurse-midwives) or in acute care (e.g., clinical nurse specialists). These nurses often have a master's degree. They must pass a certifying examination, and they take on many responsibilities that have traditionally been handled by physicians. There are now more than 240,000 APRNs in the United States—a number that is expected to grow significantly.

In 2014, the member schools affiliated with the American Association of Colleges of Nursing endorsed moving the current level of preparation necessary for advanced nursing practice from the master's degree to the doctorate level (a Doctor of Nursing Practice degree). One of the rationales was that the course credit requirements for APRNs were already equivalent to that for doctoral degrees in many other fields. The focus of the DNP curriculum was to be on evidence-based practice, quality improvement, and systems leadership, among other key areas. More than 250 schools have already made the transition to this new degree, and many more are in the process of doing so.

Key Roles of Nurses. McClure (1991) identifies the two key roles held by nurses today as being those of caregiver and integrator. As a caregiver, the nurse functions to meet patients' needs—dependency (hygiene, nutrition, safety, etc.), comfort (physical and psychological), therapy (medications and other treatments), monitoring (collecting, interpreting, and acting on patient data), and education. As an integrator, the nurse coordinates the contributions of separate medical units in the hospital or clinic to provide total and effective patient treatment and care.

Viewed from another perspective, Chambliss (1996) identifies three difficult and sometimes contradictory roles that hospital nurses must fulfill. First, nurses must be caring individuals who interact directly with patients and work with them as "whole people." Second, nurses are professionals who have an important job that requires special competence and deserves special status and respect. Finally, within the hospital hierarchy, nurses are subordinate workers who are often under the direction of physicians. The contrasting expectations created by these disparate roles place nurses in an awkward position where the practical requirements of the job may explicitly conflict with the moral expectations of the professional role.

Nurse Supply and Demand

In the last few decades of the twentieth century and the initial years of the twenty-first, there was a very significant shortage of nurses in the United States. Hospitals—where more than 50 percent of registered nurses work—routinely reported nurse vacancy rates above 10 percent, and many nursing positions in physician offices and in community-based nursing jobs such as home health care went unfilled. Projections that the demand for nurses would be growing faster than the supply of new nurses added to the concern.

What created this vast nursing shortage? Many factors were responsible, including the increased number of elderly people seeking care, the heavy time demands of patients with chronic diseases, delays in seeking treatment by the medically uninsured, thereby increasing the severity of illness, the expansion of home health care, an expansion of school nursing, increased use of a wide variety of health care technologies (for which nurses must have at least sufficient knowledge to coordinate care), and the ability of more individuals to seek medical care due to the Affordable Care Act. The fact that many nurses were reaching retirement age exacerbated the problem. Moreover, most nursing schools had a shortage of nursing faculty, and this prevented any significant expansion of nursing school classes.

Although a serious nursing shortage still exists, the situation has improved dramatically in the last decade. Hospitals have addressed the nurse shortage in several ways, including attempts to reduce demand and increase supply. In order to reduce demand, some hospitals have reorganized staff responsibilities by hiring less well-educated individuals to do traditional nursing tasks in order to downsize the number of nurses who are needed (Aiken, Sochalski, and Anderson, 1996). This effort is a very contentious issue in medicine, and is discussed in more detail later in this chapter.

Hospitals and other medical sites have tried to increase the supply of nurses in several ways, including increasing nurse salaries to draw more people into the field, and increasing recruitment of nurses from other countries. The first approach was long overdue. Nursing has been a traditionally very under-salaried career, but measurable progress has been made. In 2014, the median salary was over US$42,000 for licensed practical nurses and over US$66,000 for registered nurses. The second approach, however, has raised serious ethical concerns. Strong efforts to heavily recruit nurses from other countries,

IN THE FIELD

RECRUITING NURSES FROM ABROAD

Faced with a sizable and chronic shortage of nurses and an inability to adequately address the problem, hospitals and health care systems in the United States have begun intense recruiting of nurses from other countries. Recruitment has been most successful in the Philippines, India, Canada, Nigeria, Korea, the United Kingdom, and Russia, and is now intensifying in Mexico. In 2004, the National Council of State Boards of Nursing began to offer the mandatory U.S. licensing nursing exam in other countries to make it easier to get licensed. Hospitals frequently employ recruiting companies (and pay as much as US$15,000–20,000 per hire) to secure nurses to come to this country. About 4 percent of the nation's nurses were educated outside the United States, but this percentage is increasing by more than 10 percent per year.

The interest of nurses in other countries—especially very poor countries—is understandable. The average monthly take-home salary for nurses in Mexico is US$300 or US$400; in India it is less than US$100, compared with more than US$5,000 in the United States. However, there can be drastic consequences for the health care system in the countries from which the United States is recruiting.

There are legal, economic, cultural, social, educational, and other ramifications to be considered as the greater health care workforce, and nursing in particular, evolves globally. For example, nurses may leave their home countries because of poor working or living conditions or to provide support and resources to their families. This creates a "domino" effect in which the population health needs in one country may be negatively impacted, whereas those in another country may benefit (Jones and Sherwood, 2014:59–60).

Joyce Thompson (2003), a professor of community health nursing at Western Michigan University, says that the practice is "clearly devastating the health care infrastructure" in several of these countries, which have been forced to close hospitals due to a lack of nurses (1,000 hospitals in the Philippines alone have been forced to close). Thompson personally witnessed the exodus of nurses from Africa during her work on a program promoting women's health in Uganda and Malawi. Her reaction was that "It's always difficult (to see) a resource-rich country that hasn't planned appropriately depend on lesser-developed countries to meet their needs" (Thompson, 2003:20).

---

especially developing countries, have been successful but are accompanied by concerns for the health care system in the countries from which the nurses have departed. This issue is addressed in the accompanying box, "Recruiting Nurses from Abroad."

The issue regarding nursing school enrollment is still at the forefront. While the number of graduates from nursing schools has increased significantly (the number of RN graduates doubled between 2005 and 2014) and the number of current nursing students is at an all-time high (189,000 in 2014), there is still a problem. Nursing schools report that about 7 percent of all nurse faculty positions remain vacant, mostly due to non-competitive salaries and the limited number of doctorally prepared faculty. At the same time, many qualified applicants to baccalaureate and graduate nursing programs (an estimated 69,000 in 2014) are being turned down due to shortage of faculty and space.

Has the worst of the problem been addressed? Yes, at least for the time being, the picture is

Striking nurses march in a Detroit Labor Day parade. © Jim West/Alamy Stock Photo.

more promising than it has been in the last few decades (Auerbach, Buerhaus, and Staiger, 2011). Nevertheless, there are still thousands of unfilled nursing positions, and it is expected that demand will continue to grow. Should projections for increased demand be accurate and/or should the recent upsurge of interest in a nursing career subside, the country may again experience a severe nurse shortage (Staiger, Auerbach, and Buerhaus, 2012).

Recruitment and Socialization

Background of Nursing Students. Although the nursing field remains female dominant (90 percent of nurses are female), the number of men entering nursing is increasing. Today, men account for about 15 percent of registered nursing students and about 6 percent of advanced practice nursing students. Unlike medical students, nursing students have traditionally been drawn from working- and lower-middle-class families whose parents are less likely to be college educated than are those of comparable non-nursing students. In part, they have been drawn to nursing because of the

security of employment and the opportunity to move into the middle class.

Moreover, nursing students have traditionally reflected some value differences from other students. Over the years, several studies have found nursing students to be more likely to place value on "helping others," "altruism," and being "nurturant," and less likely than others to endorse "doing well financially" and "personal power" as important life goals.

In recent years, some important shifts have occurred. Until the surge of interest by individuals in their twenties in the 2000s, nursing students tended to be older (often in their thirties and forties) than students in the past, more likely to come from a middle-class background, frequently worked part-time in addition to going to nursing school, and many were parents (often single parents). For many, nursing is a second career—one to which they have been drawn later in life, and one which is attractive at least as much for its socioeconomic rewards as for the opportunity to enter a helping career. Research has confirmed that in the last two decades, the value of altruism as a motivating force for entering the field or being willing to change shifts has declined in

Men are occupying an increasing number of nursing positions. Today, about 10 percent of nurses are male. © Westend61/Fotolia.

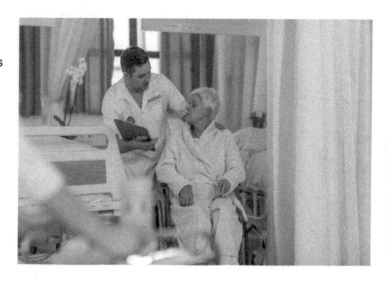

response to the different position in the life course. However, there is also a greater focus on the professional aspects and expectations of nursing, such as valuing complete honesty in communication with patients (Johnson, Haigh, and Yates-Bolton, 2007).

Socialization of Nursing Students. The socialization of nursing students has received much less systematic study than that of medical students. One of the best studies of nursing socialization was conducted at a West Coast school of nursing by Fred Davis (1972). He discovered a six-step socialization experience not unlike that experienced by medical students.

Students enter nursing school with an *initial innocence*, seeking to become mother surrogates by engaging in nurturant and helping behaviors. The failure of nursing instructors to endorse or model this image, however, creates frustration and anxiety. Students spend their time learning technical and seemingly inconsequential skills. Later during the first semester, students enter a *labeled recognition of incongruity* stage. This includes open statements of disillusionment and despair over the incongruity between their anticipated

view of nursing school and their actual experience. Many question their career choice, and many drop out of nursing school during this time.

Students who remain enter a *psyching out* the faculty stage (just as medical students do, as described in Chapter 9). They attempt to determine what part of the course materials and training the faculty thinks is most important, so that they can concentrate on that. Typically, they realize that the faculty places high value on professionalism, and like it or not, the students collectively begin to mold their behavior in that direction. This is the *role simulation stage,* which usually occurs around the end of the first year. Students engage in a type of role-playing in which they consciously attempt to exhibit toward patients the professional demeanor desired by the faculty. However, as their behaviors become more convincing, the students gain confidence in themselves.

As the students enter the second half of their training (the *provisional internalization* and *stable internalization* stages), they increasingly accept a professional identity and get accustomed to it until, by graduation, it is typically fully accepted and internalized.

However, even by the end of nursing school, substantial value differences may exist between students and their nurse instructors. Eddy et al. (1994) discovered that faculty placed significantly more value than students on freedom (e.g., honoring patients' right to refuse treatment), equality (basing care on patients' needs and not their background characteristics), and human dignity (e.g., maintaining confidentiality), whereas students placed more emphasis than faculty on aesthetics (creating a pleasing environment for patients and a pleasant work environment for self and others). The study authors suggested that these responses reflected students' idealism about work settings and their lack of experience in actual settings.

Occupational Status

Although it is common to speak of "the nursing profession," many nursing responsibilities are under the direction of physicians, and this external control is considered a primary barrier to a genuinely professional status. At the same time, however, nurses have gained greater autonomy in recent years. This is largely a result of the strengthening of nursing education and the professionalization of nursing, so that nurses have a desire to have more independence in patient care and to exercise this independence.

In addition, nursing associations and unions have developed a larger advocacy voice. Service Employees International Union (SEIU) Healthcare is the largest healthcare union in North America, with more than 1.1 million members. In addition to nurses, its members include physicians, home care and nursing home workers, laboratory technicians, environmental service workers, and dietary aides. The National Union of Healthcare Workers, a union with over 10,000 members, broke away from the SEIU in 2009 over differences in organizational structure. It has now joined forces with the 85,000 members of the politically powerful California

Nurses Association. National Nurses United (NNU), with close to 185,000 members, is the largest union and professional association of registered nurses. Its membership is largely comprised of direct care RNs. This is by far the largest nurses' association ever, and it has adopted an aggressive strategy to promote its causes. Its approaches include extensive lobbying, marches, and demonstrations in Washington and around the country. It has affiliated with the AFL-CIO.

The most prominent nursing associations are the American Nurses Association (ANA) and the National League for Nursing (NLN). The majority of ANA members are registered nurses with practice-related concerns. The ANA has experienced considerable tension in recent years over the best way to lobby for a nursing role in the changing health care system. The membership of the NLN is composed mainly of nursing educators and agencies associated with nursing education. Their primary goal is to promote quality standards for nursing education. Table 10–1 reports nurses' job satisfaction levels about specific aspects of nursing.

TABLE 10–1 Nurses' Satisfaction with 11 Job Elements, 2005

Job Element	Percentage Satisfied (%)
Interaction with other nurses	67
Professional status	65
Professional development	62
Interaction with physicians	59
Nursing management	55
Overall job enjoyment	54
Nursing administration	54
Autonomy	51
Decision making	47
Workload	47
Pay	41

Source: Data from American Nurses Association, 2005, "Survey of 76,000 Nurses Probes Elements of Job Satisfaction." www.medicalnewstoday.com/articles/21907.php.

It should be noted that these data were collected in 2005—prior to significant pay in nurse salaries. A 2015 study report found that "satisfaction with compensation" among nurses ranged from a high of 73 percent for nurse-anesthetists to a low of 43 percent for licensed practical nurses. In total, 53 percent of registered nurses reported satisfaction with compensation.

Issues in Nursing Today

Education and Image. Throughout its history, nursing has struggled internally to define its primary goals and purposes. In essence, one faction has attempted to maintain an image of a nurturer/caregiver while another faction has worked to professionalize nursing by emphasizing education and a scientifically based nursing curriculum.

This controversy over image centers on educational preparation. At one time, most practicing nurses were diploma trained, and they actively resisted increased emphasis on training in academic institutions and curricular changes that would make science rather than technique the primary focus of nursing education. Today, however, despite this resistance, nearly all training occurs in academic institutions, with science increasingly at the core of the curriculum.

Some friction remains between graduates of associate-degree and 4-year programs. Because associate-level and bachelor-level programs prepare students for the same state licensing examination, it is assumed by many that they can perform at the same skill level. Advocates of bachelor-level programs are concerned that 2-year programs do not adequately prepare students for the rapid changes in modern technology that nurses now encounter. Advocates of associate-level programs dismiss the need for an undergraduate degree and prefer the technique-focused curriculum. Because hospitals do not typically differentiate between training backgrounds when determining salary and responsibilities, advocates of baccalaureate training feel that this devalues the bachelor's degree.

Since 1965, the ANA has tried unsuccessfully to make a bachelor's degree the minimum educational requirement for licensure of registered nurses. In 1985, the ANA revised its stance to recommend two levels of nursing based on educational preparation—the professional nurse with a baccalaureate degree, and the technical nurse with an associate degree.

This is consistent with the concept of **differentiated practice**. A differentiated practice model bases the roles and functions of registered nurses on education, experience, and competence. It clarifies which type of registered nurse is appropriately accountable for which aspects of nursing by separating technical and professional practice. Proponents of the model believe that it will lead to more effective and efficient patient care, increased job satisfaction among nurses, and greater organizational viability. A sizable number of hospitals across the nation are now using some type of differentiated practice model.

In 2010, the well-respected Institute of Medicine (IOM) recommended that the percentage of nurses with a baccalaureate degree should be increased to 80 percent. Among the reasons cited was the fact that a much larger percentage of baccalaureate nurses than associate degree or diploma nurses eventually pursue an advanced practice nursing degree. Contending that the health care system desperately needs more nurse practitioners and other advanced degree nurses, the IOM advocated for increasing the percentage of nurses with an undergraduate baccalaureate degree (Aiken, 2011).

Overall, the image of nurses is very positive. A Gallup Poll in 2015 found that nursing was seen as the "most honest and ethical" occupation—an honor it has received every year except one since 1999 (see Table 10–2).

TABLE 10–2 **Rankings of Honesty and Ethical Standards of Occupations, 2015**

Occupation/Career	Percentage Ranking Very High or High (%)
Nurses	85 (highest overall ranking)
Pharmacists	68
Medical doctors	67
High-school teachers	60
Police officers	56
Clergy	45
Accountants	39
Journalists	27
Bankers	25
Lawyers	21
Business executives	17
Members of Congress	8
Lobbyists	7

Sources: Lydia Saad. December 21, 2015, "Americans' Faith in Honesty, Ethics of Police Rebounds." Gallup Poll: Princeton, NJ. www.gallup.com/poll/187874/americans-faith-honesty-ethics-police-rebounds.aspx?g_source=Socialsues&g_medium=newsfeed&g_ campaign=tiles.

Specific Job Responsibilities. Without question, nurses have taken on additional responsibilities in recent years. Some of these involve direct patient care, although others simply comply with bureaucratic requirements. In contrast to about 20 years ago, nurses are now involved in assessing patients, reading particular tests and lab results, inserting intravenous lines, checking for any abnormalities, and monitoring blood pressure. They work with electronic health records, manage chronic illness cases, transition patients to hospitals, perform health education, and work on quality improvement.

The increased responsibilities taken on by nurses have occurred simultaneously with other significant changes related to nursing practice—a dramatic increase in involvement in ethical questions (e.g., in the treatment of impaired newborns or in handling do-not-resuscitate decisions), the emotional and physical demands of working with chronically ill patients, and the ever increasing numbers of very ill geriatric patients.

Downsizing Nursing Staffs. In the mid-1990s, hospitals throughout the country began to reduce their nursing staffs. Responding to pressures to become more cost-effective, hospitals cut back on nurses and reassigned some of their job responsibilities to a new category of health care workers, variously referred to as "nurses' aides," "patient care technicians," "unlicensed assistive personnel," and "care associates." These workers, who sometimes receive only a month or two of training, typically assist with such tasks as changing linen, bathing patients, and assisting physicians with routine procedures, but they are also involved in EKG testing, drawing blood, and respiratory therapy (Norrish and Rundall, 2001). An ad that was posted on commuter trains and in bus-stop shelters in New York City, and was also carried in *New York* magazine, read as follows: "BABY CARE TECHNICIAN WANTED—Work with newborns and preemies in NY hospitals. Regulate incubators, draw blood, insert feeding tubes, give medications. On-the-job training. NO EXPERIENCE NECESSARY/NO EDUCATION NECESSARY" (Moore, 1995:3).

The ANA and other groups charged that this "reconfiguration" is threatening quality patient care (see the accompanying box, "Discontent Among Nurses: A Report on Hospital Care in Five Countries"). An impressive array of studies have found that hospitals with lower RN-to-patient ratios have higher patient mortality rates, longer hospital stays, higher rates of adverse outcomes, and higher readmission rates. To make up for a nursing shortage, hospitals often direct nurses to work extended shifts (sometimes even 12 hours or more) and extra shifts. Research now documents that the risks of making a medical error increase for nurses working these long hours (Griffiths et al., 2014).

IN COMPARATIVE FOCUS

DISCONTENT AMONG NURSES: A REPORT ON HOSPITAL CARE IN FIVE COUNTRIES

In one of the largest studies of its kind ever undertaken, a 2001 survey by Aiken and her colleagues of more than 43,000 nurses in 711 hospitals in the United States, Canada, Germany, England, and Scotland found widespread discontent. Although these countries have very different types of health care systems, nurses reported similar shortcomings in their work environment and in the quality of hospital care. Five sources of discontent emerged in the study:

1. A large majority of the nurses in all five countries indicated that there were not enough registered nurses in their hospital to provide high-quality care, that there were not enough support staff, and that hospital management was non-responsive to their needs.
2. Nurses in most countries reported that their workload increased in the last year, while nursing managerial staff were eliminated or decreased.
3. Nurses in the United States, Canada, and Germany reported that they often spent considerable time on non-nursing-skill duties

(e.g., cleaning rooms and transporting food trays), while many tasks that are markers of good patient care (e.g., oral hygiene and skin care) were left undone.
4. Nurses reported concerns about the quality of patient care being delivered. Only one in nine nurses in Germany, and one in three nurses in the other countries, rated the quality of nursing care on their unit as being excellent. Nurses in the United States and Canada were most likely to report that the quality of care provided had deteriorated in the last year.
5. Many of the nurses were dissatisfied, experiencing burnout, and intent on leaving nursing.

Interestingly, the nurses reported positive feelings about the quality of the physicians and nurses with whom they worked, and about physician–nurse interactions. Their complaints focused on problematic working conditions and the negative effects of those conditions on the quality of patient care.

A study conducted in 2004 and 2005 examined attitudes toward the nursing shortage among physicians, chief executive officers (CEOs), chief nursing officers (CNOs), and registered nurses. They substantially agreed that the nursing shortage impaired communication with patients, had a negative impact on nurse–patient relationships, reduced hospital capacity, and lowered quality of care as measured by timeliness, efficiency, and patient-centered care. There was less consensus among groups on the effect of the nursing shortage on physician workload, the closure of particular programs, and the amount of time available for team

collaboration. The key differences between the nurses/CNOs and the physicians/CEOs related to patient safety and the quality of the nurses' work environment. In both areas, nurses largely perceived a negative impact whereas physicians and CEOs did not (Buerhaus et al., 2007). This issue is likely to be at the forefront for the next several years.

Level of Political Activism.   The frustrations that many nurses feel about their working conditions have fostered increased political activism, and in recent years, union organizing has been especially fervent among nurses and other non-physician health care workers. A prime objective has been to get state legislatures to adopt nurse-staffing laws that require hospitals to maintain at least a minimum ratio of nurses to patients. California was the first state to pass such legislation. When specifying the minimum ratio, California nurses recommended that it should be one nurse per three patients, and California hospitals recommended that it should be one nurse per ten patients (it was eventually set at one nurse per six patients in medical-surgical units, one nurse per four patients in pediatric wards, and one nurse per two patients in intensive care). These efforts received a major boost in 2010 with the publication of a major study of the effect of nurse–patient ratios. The study was conducted by comparing the state of California (with minimum ratios) with Pennsylvania and New Jersey (without minimum ratios). Researchers found that the ratios required in California enabled nurses to spend more time with patients, monitor patient condition more accurately, inspire more confidence in patients and their families, lower patient mortality, and reduce nurse burnout (Aiken et al., 2010).

ADVANCED PRACTICE PROVIDERS

Two key problems in health care today are very high health care costs and a critical shortage of primary care physicians, especially in many rural and inner-city areas. One response to both of these critical problems has been the creation of several **advanced practice providers (APPs)**. These positions include several advanced practice nursing positions—the **nurse practitioner (NP)**, the **certified nurse-midwife (CNM)**, and the **certified registered nurse-anesthetist (CRNA)**—and the **physician assistant (PA)**. These APPs offer several benefits to the health care system: They provide many direct care services to patients (and are critically

important in rural and inner-city areas that have a shortage of physicians), they enable physicians with whom they work to see from 20 to 50 percent more patients, they are cost-efficient because they charge less than physicians, and many research studies have found that they offer high-quality services that are appreciated by patients.

Advanced Practice Registered Nurses

Nurse Practitioners. A nurse practitioner (NP) is a registered nurse with a graduate degree in advanced practice nursing. About 90 percent of NPs complete a 2-year master's degree beyond the RN, and some even obtain additional degrees (a doctoral degree in nursing practice is now available). NPs are able to undertake about 70–80 percent of the basic primary and preventive care offered by physicians. They take social and medical histories, conduct physical examinations (including breast and pelvic exams), perform pregnancy testing, Pap smears, and tests for sexually transmitted diseases, provide or prescribe contraceptive devices, and order laboratory tests and X-rays. They also engage in patient counseling and provide health education. In 2014 there were more than 200,000 NPs in the United States, and slightly more than 50 percent of them were working in primary care (most often in hospital inpatient and outpatient settings, private practice, primary care settings, and school settings). Expectations are that the number of NPs needed will increase rapidly in the future. In 2014, the median salary of NPs was approximately US$90,000.

Nurse practitioners are licensed by the state in which they practice, and are governed by state nurse practice acts. A national certification exam must be passed by all NPs. State policies vary, but in 21 states and the District of Columbia (DC), NPs can practice without physician supervision. Other states require some form of collaboration or supervision by a physician, but direct supervision is not required in any state. More than 50 percent of NPs in freestanding primary care settings, health maintenance organizations (HMOs), school and college health clinics, and hospital outpatient clinics reported that physicians saw less than 10 percent of their patients. All states allow some form of prescriptive privileges, although several require the prescription to be cosigned or approved by a physician. About 15 percent of all NPs have their own practice.

Professional associations of NPs advocate for fewer practice restrictions and more consistent practice regulations from state to state. The American Medical Association and the professional associations for several medical specialties have taken the position that NPs ought not to be able to practice independently, and that physician supervision is an important quality control.

Several studies have concluded that NPs typically give care that is equivalent to that provided by physicians, and that they are especially good at caring for patients with chronic health problems. Other studies have found that NPs have better communication, counseling, and interviewing skills (especially helpful with chronic patients), are more likely to be familiar with community resources such as self-help groups, are more likely than physicians to adapt medical regimens to patients' family situation and environment (Mundinger, 1994), and spend more time dealing with psychosocial issues (Campbell et al., 1990).

One study (Mundinger et al., 2000) was based on a randomized trial in which patients were randomly assigned to either a nurse practitioner or a physician, where NPs had the same authority, responsibilities, productivity, administrative requirements, and patient population as the primary care physicians. No significant differences were found in patient outcomes at either 6 months or 1 year. In part due to the extensive amount of personal interaction that

occurs, patient acceptance of NPs (and other advanced practice providers) will probably remain at a high level.

Certified Nurse-Midwives. A certified nurse-midwife (CNM) is a registered nurse who has additional nationally accredited training (usually 18 months to 2 years) in midwifery (all programs are located in a college or university), and who possesses certification by the American College of Nurse-Midwives. A national certification exam must be completed. A CNM degree is typically at the master's level. CNMs receive extensive training in gynecological care, taking histories, performing physical examinations, and monitoring care, especially as it relates to pregnancy and childbirth. Restrictive practice acts limit autonomous CNM practice in some states, but all 50 states and the DC provide at least some statutory prescriptive authority for CNMs. Most states now require private health insurers to reimburse nurse-midwives, and all states provide for reimbursement for treating Medicaid patients.

There are only approximately 7,000 CNMs who have been certified by the American College of Nurse-Midwives. Many CNMs are employed by hospitals, physicians, other CNMs, and managed care networks, or are working in private practice. They are more likely to work in inner-city areas than in any other location. In 2014, the average annual salary of CNMs was more than US$70,000.

After considerable disagreement between lay-midwives and nurse-midwives, and debate over home versus hospital deliveries, nurse-midwifery has experienced significant growth since the 1980s. In 1985, the Institute of Medicine recommended that programs serving high-risk mothers use more certified nurse-midwives, and that state laws support nurse-midwifery practice. "In 1986 the Congressional Office of Technology Assessment concluded that CNMs manage routine pregnancies safely, noting that CNMs are more likely than physicians to test for urinary tract infections and diabetes, but less inclined to prescribe drugs; that CNMs are less likely to rely on technology, but communicate and interact more with their patients; and that patients of CNMs spend less time waiting for visits, have shorter hospitalizations and are more likely to feel satisfied with their care" (Rooks, 1990:34). Despite serving mothers who are younger, more likely to be unmarried, more likely to be foreign-born, more likely to be minorities, but less likely to have received prenatal care than the average mother in the United States, midwife-attended births have better-than-average outcomes (Gabay and Wolfe, 1997) and increased satisfaction with care (Sutcliffe et al., 2012). Altogether, CNMs deliver about 10 percent (more than 300,000 babies) of U.S. births each year; worldwide, midwives deliver about 70 percent of all births.

Certified Registered Nurse-Anesthetists. A certified registered nurse-anesthetist (CRNA) is a registered nurse with an additional 2 or 3 years' training for certification, which provides a master's degree. They are fully qualified to perform anesthesiology in all 50 states. Nurse-anesthetists typically work as licensed independent practitioners.

Federal law requires physician supervision of CRNAs unless a state submits a written letter by the governor to opt out of the requirement in the best interest of state citizens. To date, 17 states have opted out, and others are considering doing so. Some states, such as California and Missouri, have passed legislation specifically stating that supervision is not required, but physician associations are seeking to overturn these laws. No state requires supervision specifically by an anesthesiologist. Studies have not detected any harm to patients when CNRAs work without physician supervision (Dulisse and Cromwell, 2010).

CRNAs administer 65 percent of all anesthetics given in the United States, and are the sole anesthesiology providers in 85 percent of rural hospitals. As of 2014, there are approximately 37,000 CRNAs in the United States (about 40,000 anesthesiologists), and their average salary is about US$160,000.

Physician Assistants. Under the direct or indirect supervision of a physician, a physician assistant (PA) can offer most of the basic care provided by the physician, including performing physical examinations, monitoring and treating minor ailments, counseling, and prescribing some medications. PAs act under laws within their state of practice, but all must pass a national certification exam. PAs must have a formal relationship with a collaborative physician supervisor. The physician supervisor must also be licensed in the state in which the PA is working, but physician supervision can be done in person, by telecommunication, or simply by being available for consultation.

The role of PA was created to handle routine patient care tasks so that physicians could spend their time on more complicated patient problems. Today, PAs work in all medical specialties, including primary care, surgery, anesthesiology, pathology, orthopedics, and radiology.

Applicants for PA programs must have completed at least 2 years of college (most have a baccalaureate degree) and have a minimum of 2 years' experience in the health care field. Programs generally require 2 years. A national certification exam must be passed before a PA can be licensed.

There are approximately 100,000 PAs licensed to practice in the United States as of the year 2014, and this number is expected to increase significantly in the coming years. More than 40 percent of PAs work in primary care, and around 50 percent in a specialty area (general surgery and emergency medicine being

There are more than 90,000 physician assistants in the United States. They work under the supervision of a physician, but are able to provide most primary care services. Photo courtesy of Janet Jonas.

the most common). Although nurse practitioners are primarily female, about 38 percent of PAs are male. The median salary of PAs in 2014 was about US$95,000.

The professional autonomy of PAs is more limited than that of NPs. Virtually all states and Washington, DC, allow PAs to provide medical services, but only under physician supervision (some states allow PAs to practice with off-site physician supervision). PAs are allowed to prescribe some medications in 48 states and Washington, DC. All government insurance programs and most private insurers pay for PA services.

Research indicates that PAs could handle more than 80 percent of all office visits with minimal physician supervision. Analysts have concluded that they are competent in taking social and medical histories and in performing physical examinations, and that quality of care is not decreased when they provide these services. Several studies have found high levels of satisfaction with the care offered by PAs. With the average cost of PA care ranging from one-quarter to one-half that of physicians, there is obvious potential for expanding PA care within the health care system.

ALLIED HEALTH WORKERS

A majority of the health care workforce is referred to as allied health personnel. Although there is some controversy about this specific term, it is generally recognized to include a wide variety of non-physician and non-nursing health care workers. These providers work in all types of care, including primary, acute, tertiary, and chronic care, and in all settings, including physicians' and dentists' offices, HMOs, laboratories, clinics, ambulance services, home care, and hospitals. Depending on the particular field, allied health practitioners require varying amounts of education and training, and they work with widely differing degrees of autonomy, dependence on technology, and regulation.

Table 10–3 lists the allied health fields that are accredited by the Commission on Accreditation of Allied Health Education Programs (CAAHEP). Many of the occupations have several levels of certification, so the prerequisites and length of training vary considerably even within some fields.

Many other health fields have developed around particular technologies or techniques that require specialized knowledge and training.

TABLE 10–3   Commission on Accreditation of Allied Health Education Programs (CAAHEP) Health Science Fields

Field
Advanced cardiovascular sonography
Anesthesia technology
Anesthesiologist assistant
Art therapy
Cardiovascular technology
Clinical research
Cytotechnology
Diagnostic medical sonography
Emergency medical services—paramedic
Exercise physiology
Exercise science
Intraoperative neurophysiological monitoring
Kinesiotherapy
Lactation consultant
Medical assisting
Medical illustration
Medical scribe specialist
Neurodiagnostic technology
Orthotic and prosthetic technician
Perfusion
Personal fitness training
Polysomnographic technology
Recreational therapy
Rehabilitative engineering and assistive technology
Specialist blood bank technology/transfusion medicine
Surgical assisting
Surgical technology

Source: Data from Commission on Accreditation of Allied Health Education Programs, *Standards and Guidelines*, 2016, Clearwater, FL. www.caahep.org.

These would include positions related to physical therapy, occupational therapy, radiological therapy, speech therapy, and the diagnostic imaging fields such as nuclear medicine technology (NMT), magnetic resonance imaging (MRI), computed axial tomography (CAT), and medical laboratory technology. Although physicians continue to do some of these procedures themselves, it is more efficient to employ specialized workers. Many of these workers (e.g., nuclear medicine technologists) perform diagnostic tests, which are then interpreted by physicians.

THE HEALTH CARE TEAM

The Concept of a Health Care Team

During the last few decades, the **health care team** approach has become commonplace in health care institutions. In practice, the concept of "team" is used in many different ways: (1) to describe a group of highly competent technical specialists, subspecialists, and supporting personnel who work together to execute some dramatic, intense, and usually short-term activity (e.g., a neurosurgery team); (2) to refer to the cooperation of technically oriented providers (e.g., physician specialists) with socially and/or behaviorally oriented providers (e.g., social workers); and (3) to simply refer to a less hierarchical and more egalitarian mode of health care organization and decision making (especially among physician and non-physician providers).

The primary objectives of team care over traditional care are to avoid duplication and fragmentation of services and to develop better and more comprehensive health plans by including more perspectives. Ideally, this occurs through a group process involving cooperation and coordination. Research has documented that the existence of a "teamwork culture" in a hospital is related to greater feelings of patient satisfaction (Meterko, Mohr, and Young, 2004).

Perceptions of the Team Approach

The team approach has only begun to develop in earnest in medicine in the last 20 years.

Health care has not always been recognized as a team sport, as we have recently come to think of it. In the "good old days," people were cared for by one all-knowing doctor who lived in the community, visited the home, and was available to attend to needs at any time of day or night. If nursing care was needed, it was often provided by family members, or in the case of a family of means, by a private-duty nurse who "lived in." Although this conveyed elements of teamwork, health care has changed enormously since then and the pace has quickened even more dramatically in the past 20 years. The rapidity of change will continue to accelerate as both clinicians and patients integrate new technologies into their management of wellness, illness, and complicated aging. The clinician operating in isolation is now seen as undesirable in health care—a lone ranger, a cowboy, an individual who works long and hard to provide the care needed, but whose dependence on solitary resources and perspective may put the patient at risk. (Mitchell et al., 2012:1–2)

Although enthusiasm for the team approach remains high among many health care workers and also among many patients, some recent re-examination of the concept has taken place. Recent studies have shown that the approach is viewed differently among different types of providers. For example, Temkin-Greener conducted interviews with 12 senior faculty who were department heads in a large medical center and teaching hospital to explore ways in which leaders in nursing and medicine understand and define the team concept, its purposes, and its goals. She found that the physicians and

nurses differed in their views of health care teams. Physicians often viewed teamwork as "a nursing concept, beneficial primarily to nursing and used to 'usurp' the traditional authority of medicine in health care provision" (Temkin-Greener, 1983:647), whereas the nurses imputed considerable value to the team approach, but believed medicine to be closed to the concept unless it was imposed from outside (e.g., by the Joint Commission for Accreditation of Hospitals).

Tempkin-Greener interprets these divergent attitudes as evidence of two different cultures—one in which medicine "emphasizes the status quo of its traditional authority and inherently hierarchical mode of organization and function," and one in which nursing "stresses a more egalitarian vision of power relations with collaboration and peer cooperation as prerequisites for team care provision" (Temkin-Greener, 1983:647). These varying perceptions indicate that the team approach is still evolving and has certain difficulties to resolve. However, it is expected to remain a part of health care delivery.

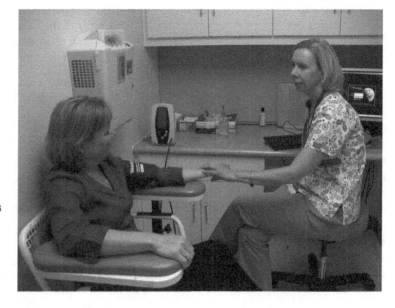

Nuclear medicine is one of several high-technology imaging fields that offer enhanced diagnostic abilities. This patient is working with a cardiac nuclear technologist. Photo by Gregory Weiss.

In many health care settings, a "team" of health care professionals works together to offer comprehensive care. "Medical homes" that are structured around physician-led teams are becoming increasingly popular. © Rawpixel.com/Fotolia.

The "Medical Home"

One approach to providing comprehensive "team-based" medical care that has recently become quite popular is the **medical home** or the patient-centered medical home. A medical home is a physician-led team that includes nurses, nurse practitioners, physician assistants, health educators, and others working together to provide comprehensive primary care. The model aims to provide better coordinated care that is more family centered and accessible. Ideally, patients would receive more time with team members than they currently do with just a primary care physician, and interaction could focus on prevention and education as well as diagnosis and treatment. The medical home philosophy also emphasizes that patients must be treated with respect, dignity, and compassion, and that strong and trusting relationships be developed between providers and patients.

Since being proposed by a variety of professional physician groups, the popularity of medical homes has increased rapidly. Within just a few years of development, by 2014 there were more than 10,000 primary care practices (7,000 of which had been certified) that created medical homes, and they involved more than 30,000 clinicians. Early assessment of clinical outcomes, costs, and patient satisfaction is very favorable. The Affordable Care Act provides funding for pilot programs for several types of medical home configurations. With the current shortage of primary care physicians, the medical home may have added utility.

Accountable Care Organizations

The Affordable Care Act has also encouraged the formation of accountable care organizations (ACOs). ACOs are similar in many ways to medical homes. They involve a variety of medical providers coming together to offer well-coordinated and high-quality care and to lower costs by reducing unnecessary tests and treatment. The intention is to accomplish this by changing the method by which providers are compensated. Rather than being paid for each office visit, test, and procedure—that is, most of the current system—an ACO is rewarded for keeping patients healthy and for working with patients to avoid unnecessary services. This gives the medical providers and the patients an incentive to be cost-conscious. By 2015, about 24 million Americans were participating in an ACO.

RELATIONSHIPS AMONG HEALTH CARE WORKERS

The delivery of health care services involves an extensive and interdependent network of personnel. Each position carries with it certain expectations for the practitioners themselves as well as for those with whom they interact. Furthermore, these positions are arranged in a hierarchy of status based on prestige and power. These occupational expectations and status arrangements significantly affect the dynamics of interaction among personnel throughout health care. The following section examines the relationship among physicians and other medical providers discussed earlier in this chapter.

The Relationship between Physicians and Nurses

Of all the interactions among health care workers, the relationship between the nurse and the physician has received the most attention (Gordon, 2005). To better understand this relationship historically, Keddy et al. (1986) interviewed 34 older nurses who had worked and/or trained in the 1920s and 1930s about their interactions with physicians. They recalled that 50 years ago, physicians were primarily in control of nursing education, giving many of the lectures and examinations, serving on registration boards, and controlling the hiring of nurses. The role of the nurse was defined in terms of efficient compliance with the physician's orders, rather than patient care responsibilities. Early in training, student nurses were taught the hierarchy of the hospital personnel and proper conduct in the presence of physicians. They were expected to show respect to physicians by standing at attention when physicians were

present, and they were taught never to make direct recommendations regarding patient care and never to suggest diagnoses to the physician. Although nurses had ideas, they did not voice them. For carrying out this role, these nurses believed that the doctors admired and respected them. One interviewee recalled that "The physician signs and he'd write this long order, and then he'd look at you over his glasses and say 'Now it's up to you whether she gets better or not.' They didn't all say it, but . . . it was implied" (Keddy et al., 1986:749).

Dynamics such as these persisted, and in 1967, Leonard Stein coined the phrase "the doctor–nurse game" to describe these relationships. According to this game, physicians and nurses agree that their relationship is hierarchical, that physicians are superordinate, and that this structure must be maintained. While nurses can make recommendations to physicians, the suggestions must appear to be initiated by the physician, and open disagreements are to be avoided at all costs.

In 1990, Stein and two colleagues revisited the doctor–nurse game in an article in the *New England Journal of Medicine*. They described a changing milieu that encouraged a new type of physician–nurse relationship. Changes that had occurred included a decline in public esteem for physicians, increased questioning of the profession's devotion to altruistic concerns, and a greater recognition of physicians' fallibility. By 1990, physicians were increasingly likely to be female, and although female medical graduates are trained to play the same game as their male counterparts, "the elements of the game that reflect stereotypical roles of male dominance and female submissiveness are missing" (Stein et al., 1990:546). The critical nursing shortage at the time also restructured nurse–physician interaction by focusing attention on the value of nurses, especially as they became more highly trained and specialized. They perceived the possibility that a feeling of colleagueship between the two might replace the typical hierarchical relationship between superior and subordinate.

For all these reasons, and partly in response to the women's movement, nurses now seek greater equality with physicians as well as autonomy in defining their own roles. In addition, nursing education, which is increasingly located in academic settings, is socializing nursing students to relate to physicians differently to how they did in the past. Most nurses are no longer willing to stand aside as subordinates. This has provoked a mixed reaction among physicians—while some physicians are supportive of nurses' attempts to become more professional and autonomous, others believe that nurses are no longer doing their jobs.

The "Revisited" piece aroused considerable discussion in the editorial section of the *New England Journal of Medicine* (Lewis, 1990). Much resistance was expressed by physicians who tended to defend an ongoing status differential between themselves and nurses. The letter writers stated that nurses are not equal partners with physicians because they are less well educated and less technically proficient, and they are not autonomous because they lack ultimate responsibility for patient treatment.

Two nurses responded that as physicians' control over medical practice shrinks, physicians "are beginning to appreciate what it is like to provide care for patients when one has little or no control over one's work" (Lewis, 1990:201), and that nurses are still unappreciated for what they offer to health care.

Campbell-Heider and Pollock caution that nurses' expectations that their status will be enhanced through increased knowledge and skills fail to consider the deeply rooted gender hierarchy in medical care: "It is clear that the social control of nurses (and women) has enabled physicians to increase their own status and that the maintenance of female stereotypes has increased the power differentials between gender groups" (Campbell-Heider and Pollock, 1987:423).

One of the most extensive studies on the dynamics within the physician–nurse relationship was conducted by Prescott and Bowen (1985). In contrast to a number of studies documenting significant problems in the relationship between nurses and physicians, they found considerable satisfaction among both groups, although they differed in their descriptions of the elements of a good relationship and in the factors that contribute to positive relationships.

In total, 69 percent of nurses and 70 percent of physicians described their relationships as essentially positive. Nurses emphasized mutual respect and trust as the most important elements of a good relationship, and considered it important that physicians regard them as intelligent resources who should be involved in the planning and decision making related to patient care. For physicians, the most important elements of a good relationship with nurses were how well the nurse communicated with the physician, the nurse's willingness to help the physician, and the nurse's competency.

Areas of disagreement between physicians and nurses were also examined. Nurses disagreed most often with physicians about the general plan of care, specific orders, and patient movement (from unit to unit, and the timing of discharge). On the other hand, physicians were concerned about nurses' taking actions which they considered to be outside the nursing domain, making poor clinical decisions, and not following specific physician orders. Approximately half of the physicians and a third of the nurses reported that disagreements were handled in the organization through the medical chain of command, but final authority almost always rested with the physician.

More recently, McGrail et al. (2009) studied episodes of physician–nurse collaboration by asking physicians, nurses, nurse faculty, and medical residents to write narratives about successful collaborations that they had experienced. The themes that they identified and the affective component of the collaboration were not affected by gender, ethnicity, or profession. Physicians and nurses, especially novice members of both fields, wrote that they often entered a care episode feeling worried, inadequate, or uncertain, but that the interaction led to feelings of satisfaction, being understood, and appreciation for their colleagues. One theme that emerged from the narratives was the importance of "collaborative competence"—that is, skills in interacting with and relating to others in a collaborative episode. This suggests that the kinds of orientations and demeanors that have been off-putting in physician–nurse collaboration might be at least somewhat amenable to education and training.

Despite the benefits of meaningful collaboration among physicians and nurses, Leape et al. (2012) are skeptical as to whether things will really change until the underlying problem is addressed. They describe a too often dysfunctional medical culture in which there is widespread disrespectful conduct of physicians toward nurses, residents, and students. They see this culture being caused by and reflected in physicians' belief in individual privilege and their own autonomy. This disrespectful organizational culture sometimes exists despite its negative effect on patient care. It may impair open communication with nurses and with other members of the care team, and it may create distance from patients. It may also help to explain resistance to the following of safety protocols. Lack of respect certainly undermines morale and prevents collegial and collaborative patient care (Leape et al., 2012).

The Relationship between Physicians and Advanced Practice Providers

There are many situations in which physicians and advanced practice providers work cooperatively and with mutual respect. There are also many situations in which the interests and goals of the groups differ and conflict prevails. In general, physicians are most comfortable with practitioners who clearly supplement their own work and who are restricted from practicing without physician supervision. For this reason, physicians have had more amicable relationships with physician assistants (who typically work for physicians and under their supervision) than with nurse practitioners (who are sometimes seen as more of a competitor for patients seeking primary care) and with CRNAs and CNMs who work independently and are reimbursed directly.

The most heated point of contention today is the extent to which APRNs should be able to practice independently. For years now, nurse practitioners have been playing an ever larger role in the health care system. In recent years, many states have considered and passed legislation to enable NPs to take on an even larger share of primary care responsibility. Nurses' associations contend that the 2 to 4 years of training beyond the nurses' degree should qualify APRNs to serve as primary care providers without physician supervision. In addition, the associations believe that, where necessary, state laws should be changed to enable APRNs to receive direct reimbursement from public and private insurance programs and to have extensive—if not complete—legal authority to write prescriptions.

The AMA vehemently opposes these changes. It contends that the additional training required of physicians makes them the most effective providers of health care services, and the only group sufficiently knowledgeable about pharmacology to have full prescription-writing authority. An AMA report issued in late 1993 stated that "Substitution for, rather than extension of, physician care by non-physicians raises questions of patient safety, competence of therapeutic decision, fragmentation of care and delays to patients in need of medical care" (Burda, 1993:6).

Several studies have documented communication problems between physicians and advanced practice providers. An intriguing study by Susan B. Graham, an anthropologist and physician, analyzed interaction patterns of physicians and midwives working in an obstetrical training program at a major medical center (Graham, 1991). Midwives were added to the Department of Obstetrics and Gynecology at the center to help to provide additional coverage for an increased workload. All the 20 midwives were CNMs, and all the physicians were residents in obstetrics/gynecology.

The CNMs were to provide prenatal care to low-risk patients and perform normal vaginal deliveries of those patients. Residents would have responsibility for high-risk patients and difficult labors and deliveries. The faculty and administration envisioned two separate but equal services, and they expected little friction between the two groups of providers. In fact, what emerged were competing and often conflicting systems that potentially jeopardized patient care.

Because 70 percent of the residents and all the CNMs were female, Graham concluded that differences between the two groups could not be attributed to gender. Instead, the primary problems were the absence of a formally articulated structure for interaction and differing perceptions concerning group status. The CNMs saw themselves as

professionals who had already completed their training and had acquired many years of experience. They regarded residents as inexperienced apprentices.

On the other hand, residents regarded themselves as "doctors" and the midwives as "nurses," stressing their own extended training, abilities to perform procedures that the CNMs could not, and longer working hours. Differing treatment philosophies also contributed to the problem. The midwives considered their emphasis on the individual and the use of non-interventionism to be superior to what they regarded as the impersonal, interventionist philosophy of the residents.

THE CHANGING ENVIRONMENT AMONG HEALTH CARE WORKERS

Relationships among physicians, nurses, advanced practice providers, and allied health personnel must be viewed as a constantly evolving and dynamic process. This process is governed not only by factors internal to each field—such as changing education requirements and a search for autonomy—but also by changes in the wider health care system (such as the Affordable Care Act), the economy, and society (Hartley, 1999).

SUMMARY

The numbers and types of health care workers in the United States have changed significantly in the past 200 years. With these changes has come a complex bureaucracy to regulate and control millions of providers working in numerous health care settings.

The field of nursing is undergoing significant change. No longer content to be silent and obedient assistants to physicians, nurses have sought to professionalize the field through

increased educational requirements and greater assertiveness. While in most cases nursing does not offer genuine autonomy—an important prerequisite for a profession—the field does have much in common with professions. Nurses have become more centrally involved in the direct provision of health care.

Several important advanced practice providers—nurse practitioners, physician assistants, certified nurse-midwives, and certified registered nurse-anesthetists—now occupy important roles in the health care system. While their ability to practice independent of physician supervision varies, all perform services once provided by physicians, and at lower cost. Research confirms that these practitioners offer high-quality services with which patients are satisfied. Relationships with physicians vary, but physicians' attitudes are more positive when the advanced practice provider has less autonomy.

Extremely important scientific developments during the 1920s, 1930s, and 1940s led to the development of a wide variety of allied health positions that have become essential parts of the overall health care system. These personnel perform diagnostic work that is interpreted by physicians, and they provide certain therapeutic modalities and types of rehabilitative care.

HEALTH ON THE INTERNET

The National Institute of Nursing Research (NINR) is the home base of nursing research within the National Institutes of Health (NIH)—the medical research center of the federal government. The NINR website contains a wealth of information on nursing, including nursing case studies and other trends and issues related to nursing. A particularly fascinating document prepared by NINR is "Changing Practice, Changing Lives: 10 Landmark Nursing Research Studies." You can access this document by visiting www.ninr.nih.gov/NewsandInformation/ NINRPublications/ and then scrolling down until you reach the document. Click on it, look through these ten studies, and then answer the following two sets of questions about them. (1) What is the focus of each study? Is it on national or state policy or nursing practice? Who might benefit from this knowledge? (2) What research methods were used? Was a survey conducted, or an experiment? Was observational research conducted? Was there analysis of existing data?

DISCUSSION QUESTION

As described in this chapter, some groups of health care workers (most often nurses and allied health workers) have unionized. Ostensibly, the unions will help to provide a bargaining force for increased salaries and benefits, job security, and a greater say in management decisions. However, these unions very often threaten to strike or go on strike regarding patient safety and quality of patient care issues. Unions derive much of their power from the willingness of members to go on strike if they feel that they have not been treated fairly by management.

Suppose you heard that all the hospital-based nurses in your community had presented a list of grievances (lower-than-average salaries, inadequate benefits, little workplace autonomy, reduction in staff, and patient care being compromised) to the administrative officers of the hospitals, who have refused to consider them. In response, efforts are under way to form a nurses' union to establish stronger bargaining power. The nurses have indicated that they will consider a general strike if their requests (demands?) are not met.

Should health care workers have the same rights as other workers to unionize, and, if they deem it necessary, to go on strike? Are health care occupations qualitatively "different" from other occupations because of their role in working in life-and-death situations? If nurses cannot unionize and go on strike, what options do they have in terms of bargaining for better conditions?

Is your position the same or different with regard to the right of physicians to unionize, to collectively bargain, and, if deemed necessary, to go on strike? What are the conditions, if any, in which you think that a physicians' strike would be justifiable?

GLOSSARY

advanced practice providers (APPs)
advanced practice registered nurses (APRNs)
allied health workers
certified nurse-midwife (CNM)
certified registered nurse-anesthetist (CRNA)
differentiated practice

health care team
licensed practical nurse (LPN)
medical home
nurse practitioner (NP)
physician assistant (PA)
registered nurse (RN)

REFERENCES

Aiken, Linda H. 2011 "Nurses for the Future." *New England Journal of Medicine*, 364:196–198.

Aiken, Linda H., Julie Sochalski, and Gerard F. Anderson. 1996 "Downsizing the Hospital Nursing Workforce." *Health Affairs*, 15:88–92.

Aiken, Linda H., Sean P. Clarke, Douglas M. Stoane, Julie A. Stochalski, Reinhard Busse, Heath Clarke, Phyllis Giovannetti, Jennifer Hunt, Anne Marie Rafferty, and Judith Shamian. 2001 "Nurses' Reports on Hospital Care in Five Countries." *Health Affairs*, 20:43–53.

Aiken, Linda H., Douglas M. Sloane, Jeannie P. Cimiotti, Sean P. Clarke, Linda Flynn, Jean A. Seago, Joanne Spetz, and Herbert L. Smith. 2010 "Implications of the California Nurse Staffing Mandate for Other States." *Health Services Research*, 45:904–921.

American Nurses Association. 2005 "Survey of 76,000 Nurses Probes Elements of Job Satisfaction." www.medicalnewstoday.com/articles/21907.php.

Auerbach, David L., Peter I. Buerhaus, and Douglas O. Staiger. 2011 "Registered Nurse Supply Grows Faster Than Projected Amid Surge in New Entrants Ages 23–26." *Health Affairs*, 30:2286–2292.

Baer, Ellen D. 1990 "Nurses." Pp. 459–475 in *Women, Health, and Medicine in America: A Historical Handbook*, Rima D. Apple (ed.). New York: Garland Publishing, Inc.

Buerhaus, Peter I., Karen Donelan, Beth T. Ulrich, Linda Norman, Catherine DesRoches, and Robert Dittus. 2007 "Impact of the Nurse Shortage on Hospital Patient Care: Comparative Perspectives." *Health Affairs*, 26:853–862.

Burda, David. 1993 "AMA Report Slams Practice of Using Nurses, Not Doctors, as Primary Care Providers." *Modern Healthcare*, 23:6.

Campbell, James D., Hans O. Mauksch, Helen J. Neikirk, and Michael C. Hosokawa. 1990 "Collaborative Practice and Provider Styles of Delivering Health Care." *Social Science and Medicine*, 30:1359–1365.

Campbell-Heider, Nancy, and Donald Pollock. 1987 "Barriers to Physician-Nurse Collegiality: An Anthropological Perspective." *Social Science and Medicine*, 25:421–425.

Chambliss, Daniel. 1996 *Beyond Caring: Hospitals, Nurses, and the Social Organization of Ethics.* Chicago, IL: University of Chicago Press.

Commission on Accreditation of Allied Health Education Programs. 2016 *Standards and Guidelines.* www.caahep.org.

Davis, Fred. 1972 *Illness, Interaction, and the Self.* Belmont, CA: Wadsworth.

DeVries, Raymond G. 1985 *Regulating Birth: Midwives, Medicine, and the Law.* Philadelphia, PA: Temple University Press.

Dulisse, Brian, and Jerry Cromwell. 2010 "No Harm Found When Nurse Anesthetists Work without

Supervision by Physicians." *Health Affairs*, 29:1469–1475.

Eddy, Diane M., Victoria Elfrink, Darlene Weis, and Mary J. Schank. 1994 "Importance of Professional Nursing Values: A National Study of Baccalaureate Programs." *Journal of Nursing Education*, 33:257–262.

Gabay, Mary, and Sidney M. Wolfe. 1997 "Nurse-Midwifery: The Beneficial Alternative." *Public Health Reports*, 112:386–394.

Gordon, Suzanne. 2005 *Nursing Against the Odds: How Health Care Cost Cutting, Media Stereotypes, and Medical Hubris Undermine Nurses and Patient Care.* Ithaca, NY: Cornell University Press.

Graham, Susan B. 1991 "A Structural Analysis of Physician–Midwife Interaction in an Obstetrical Training Program." *Social Science and Medicine*, 32:931–942.

Griffiths, Peter, Chiara Dall'Ora, Michael Simon, Jane Ball, Rikard Lindqvist, Anne-Marie Rafferty, Lisette Schoonhoven, Carol Tishelman, and Linda H. Aiken. 2014 "Nurses' Shift Length and Overtime Working in 12 European Countries: The Association with Perceived Quality of Care and Patient Safety." *Medical Care,* 52:975–981.

Hartley, Heather. 1999 "The Influence of Managed Care on Supply of Certified Nurse-Midwives: An Evaluation of the Physician Dominance Thesis." *Journal of Health and Social Behavior*, 40:87–101.

Johnson, Martin, Carol Haigh, and Natalie Yates-Bolton. 2007 "Valuing of Altruism and Honesty in Nursing Students: A Two-Decade Replication Study." *Journal of Advanced Nursing*, 57:366–374.

Jones, Cheryl B., and Gwen Sherwood. 2014. "The Globalization of the Nursing Workforce: Pulling the Pieces Together." *Nursing Outlook*, 62:59–63.

Keddy, Barbara, Margaret J. Gillis, Pat Jacobs, Heather Burton, and Maureen Rogers. 1986 "The Doctor–Nurse Relationship: An Historical Perspective." *Journal of Advanced Nursing*, 11:745–753.

Leape, Lucian L., Miles F. Shore, Jules L. Dienstag, Robert J. Mayer, Susan Edgman-Levitan, Gregg S. Meyer, and Gerald B. Healy. 2012 "Perspective: A Culture of Respect, Part I: The Nature and Causes of Disrespectful Behavior by Physicians." *Academic Medicine*, 87:845–852.

Lee, Geraldine, Alexander M. Clark, and David R. Thompson. 2013 "Florence Nightingale – Never More Relevant Than Today." *Journal of Advanced Nursing*, 69:245–246.

Lewis, Mary Ann. 1990 "Correspondence: The Doctor–Nurse Game Revisited." *New England Journal of Medicine*, 323:201–203.

McClure, Margaret L. 1991 "Differentiated Nursing Practice: Concepts and Considerations." *Nursing Outlook*, 39:106–110.

McGrail, Kathleen A., Diane S. Morse, Theresa Glessner, and Kathryn Gardner. 2009 " 'What is Found There': Qualitative Analysis of Physician-Nurse Collaboration Stories." *Journal of General Internal Medicine*, 24:198–204.

Meterko, Mark, David C. Mohr, and Gary J. Young. 2004 "Teamwork Culture and Patient Satisfaction in Hospitals." *Medical Care*, 42:492–498.

Mitchell, Pamela, Matthew Wynia, Robyn Golden, Bob McNellis, Sally Okun, C. Edwin Webb, Valerie Rohrbach, and Isabelle V. Kohorn. 2012 *Core Principles and Values of Effective Team-Based Health Care.* Washington, DC: Institute of Medicine. www.iom.edu/tbc.

Moore, J. Duncan. 1995 "Nurses Nationwide Air Gripes Against Hospitals." *Modern Healthcare*, 25:3.

Mundinger, Mary O. 1994 "Advanced Practice Nursing—Good Medicine for Physicians?" *New England Journal of Medicine*, 330:211–214.

Mundinger, Mary O., Robert L. Kane, Elizabeth R. Lenz, Annette M. Totten, Wei-Yann Tsai, Paul D. Cleary, William T. Friedewald, Albert L. Siu, and Michael L. Shelanski. 2000 "Primary Care Outcomes in Patients Treated by Nurse Practitioners or Physicians." *Journal of the American Medical Association*, 283:59–68.

Norrish, Barbara R., and Thomas G. Rundall. 2001 "Hospital Restructuring and the Work of Registered Nurses." *The Milbank Quarterly*, 79:55–79.

Prescott, Patricia A., and Sally A. Bowen. 1985 "Physician–Nurse Relationships." *Annals of Internal Medicine*, 103:127–133.

Reverby, Susan M. 1987 *Ordered to Care: The Dilemma of American Nursing, 1850–1945.* Cambridge, UK: Cambridge University Press.

Rooks, Judith P. 1990 "Nurse-Midwifery: The Window is Wide Open." *American Journal of Nursing*, 90:30–36.

Saad, Lydia. 2015 "Americans' Faith in Honesty, Ethics of Police Rebounds." www.gallup.com/poll/187874/americans-faith-honesty-ethics-police-rebounds.aspx?g_source=SocialIssues&g_medium=newsfeed&g_campaign=tiles.

Staiger, David O., David I. Auerbach, and Peter I. Buerhaus. 2012 "Registered Nurse Labor Supply and the Recession—Are We in a Bubble?" *New England Journal of Medicine*, 366:1463–1465.

Stein, Leonard I. 1967 "The Doctor–Nurse Game." *Archives of General Psychiatry*, 16:699–703.

Stein, Leonard I., David T. Watts, and Timothy Howell. 1990 "The Doctor–Nurse Game Revisited." *New England Journal of Medicine*, 322:546–549.

Sutcliffe, Katy, Jenny Caird, Josephine Kavanagh, Rebecca Rees, Kathryn Oliver, Kelly Dickson, Jenny Woodman, Elaine Barnett-Paige, and James Thomas. 2012 "Comparing Midwife-Led and Doctor-Led Maternity Care: A Systematic Review of Reviews." *Journal of Advanced Nursing*, 68:2376–2386.

Temkin-Greener, Helena. 1983 "Interprofessional Perspectives on Teamwork in Health Care: A Case Study." *Milbank Memorial Fund Quarterly*, 61:641–657.

Thompson, Joyce. 2003 Quoted in Patrick Reilly, "Importing Controversy." *Modern Healthcare*, 33:20–24.

CHAPTER 11

Complementary and Alternative Medicine

Learning Objectives

- Define "complementary and alternative medicine," and identify and describe the key characteristics that they have in common.

- Discuss the extent to which CAM has become institutionalized in the United States.

- Compare and contrast the origins and historical development of the four CAM approaches examined in this chapter.

- Compare and contrast the relationship with organized medicine of the four CAM approaches examined in this chapter.

Through much of the twentieth century, the scientific medicine paradigm (as described in Chapter 2) was so dominant in the United States that it was referred to as *orthodox* or *conventional* medicine. While alternatives to medical doctors—everything from home remedies to prayer to chiropractors—were frequently used, they were considered to be unorthodox or unconventional medicine. Scientific medicine has been taught almost exclusively in health courses in schools, has been the subject of public health campaigns, and has been the dominant perspective in the medical school curriculum.

THE MEANING OF COMPLEMENTARY AND ALTERNATIVE MEDICINE (CAM)

Because scientific medicine has been given this societal endorsement, it is rather remarkable that *complementary and alternative medicine (CAM)*—"an array of health care approaches with a history of use or origins outside of mainstream medicine" (National Center for Complementary

and Integrative Health (NCCIH), 2016d:1)—has flourished and is now more popular than ever before. The NCCIH (as of 2014, the new name for the original National Center for Complementary and Alternative Medicine) (2016d) makes the following distinctions between the key terms:

1. **Complementary medicine** is a non-mainstream practice that is used *together with* conventional medicine.
2. **Alternative medicine** is a non-mainstream practice that is used *instead of* conventional medicine.
3. **Integrative medicine** consists of practices that attempt to *integrate* mainstream and non-mainstream approaches in medicine.

Generally, CAM techniques fall into one of the other of two categories:

1. Natural products including herbs, vitamins and minerals, and probiotics [foods or supplements that contain living microorganisms (such as yogurt) that can change the bacterial

balance in the human body]. They are widely marketed, readily available to consumers, and often sold as dietary supplements.

2. Mind and body practices, including acupuncture, massage therapy, meditation, movement therapies, relaxation techniques, chiropractic and osteopathic manipulation, and yoga.

In addition to these two categories, there are some whole medical systems that would be complementary or alternative to conventional American medicine. These "whole systems" include traditional Chinese healing, Ayurveda (an Indian approach emphasizing herbal medicines, mediation, and yoga), folk healing, homeopathy, and naturopathy.

Goldstein (1999) has extracted five core elements from this wide variety of CAM healing practices:

1. *Holism.* This practice involves treating the patient holistically—that is, considering the entire physical, mental, spiritual, and social makeup of the patient when diagnosing illness and providing therapeutic care.

2. *The interpenetration of mind, body, and spirit.* While most physicians today recognize the importance of the mind–body connection, CAM places great emphasis on their relationship, and generally never treats one without the other.

3. *The possibility of high-level wellness.* Health is viewed as being a very positive physical–emotional state, and not just as the absence of symptoms or clinical disease.

4. *Vitalism: life suffused by the flow of energy.* Life is viewed as a type of ecosystem in which the various elements of mind, body, and spirit are united by a force or flow of energy throughout the body. (An amusing overview of the evolution of CAM is provided in the accompanying box, "A Short History of Medicine.")

5. *The healing process.* In most forms of CAM, unlike much of conventional medicine, healing is viewed as a cooperative, active process that involves both healer and patient. The healer is a caring and nurturant individual who works "with" instead of "on" patients.

Given the disdain that organized medicine has historically had for CAM (and in many cases the disdain that CAM has had for scientific medicine), the popularity of the alternatives makes an important statement about many people's understanding of health and healing. In fact, Goldner (1999) argues that one of the reasons why many patients choose a CAM technique is precisely because they feel alienated from the impersonality of conventional medicine, and they prefer a more holistic approach.

IN THE FIELD

A SHORT HISTORY OF MEDICINE

"Doctor, I have an earache."		A.D. 1940	"That potion is snake oil, swallow this pill."
2000 B.C.	"Here, eat this root."		
1000 B.C.	"That root is heathen, say this prayer."	A.D. 1985	"That pill is ineffective, take this antibiotic."
A.D. 1850	"That prayer is superstition, drink this potion."	A.D. 2000	"That antibiotic is artificial. Here, eat this root."

SCIENTIFIC MEDICINE AND ALTERNATIVE HEALING

Orthodox Medicine's View of Alternative Healers

Historically, physicians justified their opposition to complementary and alternative healing practices in two ways. First, many medical doctors have considered any form of "non-scientific" healing to be quackery (a medically worthless practice) or a danger to public health (if a harmful substance is administered or if people delay seeking conventional care). Their criticism of CAM was viewed as being part of a duty to protect the public's health. Physician-critics acknowledge that some alternative healers seem to have a professional manner and appear to base their practice on well-articulated (although non-scientific) principles. However, on account of offering a healing practice that has not undergone rigorous scientific testing, they are viewed as deluding the public and risking people's health (Angell and Kassirer, 1998).

Second, physicians have expressed concern that some people are fooled into believing the claims of complementary and alternative healers. Whether it is due to effective advertising or to appeals made to people who have not been helped by orthodox medicine, users of CAM have sometimes been seen as being unable to distinguish between legitimate and illegitimate medical care (Beyerstein, 2001).

An alternative view suggests that organized medicine's opposition to complementary and alternative healers has been based on perceived self-interest. By persuading the public (and politicians) that scientific medicine is the only legitimate healing practice, its cultural authority (as described in Chapter 2) is protected. This in turn restricts competition for patients and for private and public money spent on health care. How has this been done?

One way to do so was through an educational campaign, using the vast public relations resources of the AMA and other organizations to expose the dangers and errors of these cults. Another approach was to employ political leverage and legal muscle. Organized medicine excluded from its ranks those who espoused such systems; denied such practitioners the privilege of consultation; refused to see patients when such healers were assisting in the case; prevented such practitioners from working in or otherwise using public hospitals; went to court to prosecute them for violating existing medical practice acts; and actively opposed legislative protection for them or, when that failed, opposed allowing them any additional privileges. (Gevitz, 1988:16–17)

CAM's View of Conventional Healers

Practitioners and proponents of complementary and alternative healing practices view their work in a completely different way. Many have argued that their goal is the same as that of conventional medicine—to offer effective healing therapies. Their belief is that orthodox medicine has helped some people but has failed to help many others, and in fact often harms them (e.g., due to negative drug reactions or drug dependency).

CAM healers contend that the many people who have been helped by their practices, the high levels of satisfaction in their patients, and the high percentage of people who see them on a continuing basis testify to the efficacy of their treatments. They believe that patients should have an unencumbered right to choose their healing practice from a variety of options, just as they have a right to choose their religion. If a particular type of healing practice is worthless, patients will soon discover that, and the demand for that service will diminish. Complementary and alternative healers have often asked for the right to practice without attack from organized medicine. See the box "The Ability of Teenagers to Choose a CAM."

IN THE FIELD

THE ABILITY OF TEENAGERS TO CHOOSE A CAM

In 2005, a 15-year-old Virginia teenager, Abraham Cherrix, underwent 3 months of chemotherapy for Hodgkin's disease, a type of cancer. The treatment left him so weak and so nauseated that at times he had to be carried by his father because he couldn't walk. In February 2006, when he learned that the cancer had become active once again, he refused to undergo another round of chemotherapy and radiation. He said that he did not think he could live through it. Hodgkin's is generally considered a treatable condition, and has a 5-year survival rate of about 80 percent. However, with the recurrence, Abraham's survival probability was estimated at 50 percent.

Instead, after doing significant reading, he chose a sugar-free organic diet that included large amounts of fruits and vegetables, herbs, and visits to a clinic in Mexico. This raised the issue of the age at which an individual is able to make lawful decisions for him- or herself. Abraham's parents supported him in his choice, saying that they believed he was a mature and thoughtful young man. In May, a judge issued a temporary order finding Abraham's parents neglectful for supporting his choice. They were ordered to give partial custody of Abraham to the County Department of Social Services, so that the chemotherapy and radiation could be continued. The parents were told that if they refused to comply they would lose all custody of Abraham.

In August 2006, a Circuit Court judge cleared the family of all charges of medical neglect, and allowed them to follow their treatment course of choice as long as Abraham would be periodically examined by a specific board-certified oncologist in Mississippi who was experienced in alternative cancer treatments. This resolution was acceptable to Abraham and his parents. On his 18th birthday in 2008, Abraham was doing well, but the Hodgkin's returned in 2009. In the succeeding years, Abraham has had recurrent bouts of Hodgkin's separated by times in which he has felt well. At the last report, Abraham was being treated with infrared saunas, herbs, nutritional supplements, and heated needle therapy.

The case of Abraham Cherrix—shown here—raised the important question of whether mature individuals under the age of consent may choose to follow CAM rather than conventional medicine. © Steve Helber/AP.

COMPLEMENTARY AND ALTERNATIVE HEALERS

Use of Complementary and Alternative Healers

It is now recognized that millions of people use complementary and alternative healers every year. According to the National Center for Complementary and Alternative Medicine (NCCAM), more than 30 percent of American adults and about 12 percent of American children use at least one form of complementary and alternative medicine. When broader definitions of CAM are used, about half of all Americans use it. Annually, Americans pay more visits to CAM healers than to primary care physicians. When Oxford Health Plans included use of CAM in its benefit package, between 40 and 50 percent of members saw a CAM provider in the first year (Kilgore, 1998). Many health maintenance organizations around the country have now begun to include coverage for CAM. CAM has become a US$34 billion a year industry.

CAM is commonly used by both men and women (women are slightly more likely to use it), by both blacks and whites (whites are somewhat more likely to use it), among people of all ages (with especially high rates of use by middle-aged persons), among people at all levels of education (with highest rates of use by the most well educated), and in all socioeconomic groups (with highest rates of use among those with the largest income) (Barnes, Bloom, and Nahin, 2008; Grzywacz et al., 2007). A recent study of more than 2,500 undergraduate and graduate students at Columbia University found that nearly 82 percent reported using at least one form of CAM in the last 12 months.

Figure 11–1   CAM Use by Age, 2007

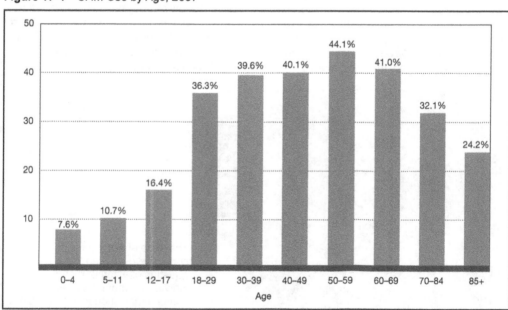

Source: Patricia M. Barnes, Barbara Bloom, and Richard L. Nahin, "Complementary and Alternative Medicine Use among Adults and Children: United States, 2007," *National Health Statistics Report*, Number 12 (Hyattsville, MD: National Center for Health Statistics, 2008).

Figure 11–2   CAM Use by Race/Ethnicity among Adults, 2007

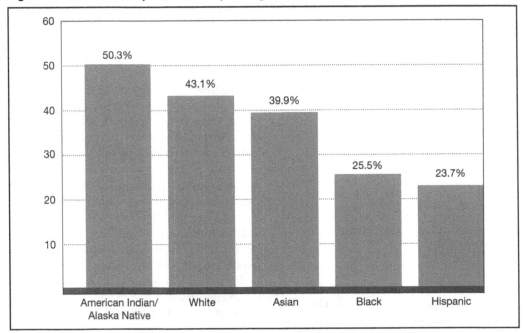

Source: Patricia M. Barnes, Barbara Bloom, and Richard L. Nahin, "Complementary and Alternative Medicine Use among Adults and Children: United States, 2007." *National Health Statistics Report*, Number 12 (Hyattsville, MD: National Center for Health Statistics, 2008).

Among the commonly used practices were non-vitamin, non-mineral products (green tea, herbal tea, aloe, ginger, and chamomile), yoga, deep breathing exercises, massage therapy, and meditation (Versnik et al., 2015). Research has also shown that many people who do not have the financial resources to access the health care system often turn to CAM because it is more affordable (Pagan and Pauly, 2005). Figures 11–1 and 11–2 illustrate additional patterns of use of CAM services in the United States.

The most common problems for which CAM therapies are used are back pain, neck pain, and joint pain. Table 11–1 lists the ten most frequently cited reasons for using a CAM practitioner. The most commonly used CAM therapies are listed in Table 11–2, and the most commonly used natural products are listed in Table 11–3.

TABLE 11–1   The Ten Most Common Reasons Why Adults See a CAM Practitioner

Condition	Used Alternative Healer in the Last Year (%)
Back pain	17.1
Neck pain	5.9
Joint pain	5.2
Arthritis	3.5
Anxiety	2.8
Cholesterol levels	2.1
Head or chest cold	2.0
Other musculoskeletal pain	1.8
Severe headache/migraine	1.6
Insomnia	1.4

Source: Patricia M. Barnes, Barbara Bloom, and Richard L. Nahin, "Complementary and Alternative Medicine Use among Adults and Children: United States, 2007." *National Health Statistics Report*, Number 12 (Hyattsville, MD: National Center for Health Statistics, 2008).

TABLE 11–2   The Ten Most Common CAM Therapies Used by Adults, 2012

Therapy	Used in the Last Year (%)
Natural products	17.7
Deep breathing	10.9
Yoga, Tai Chi, Oi Gong	10.1
Chiropractic/osteopathy	8.4
Meditation	8.0
Massage	6.9
Diet-based therapies	3.0
Homeopathy	2.2
Progressive relaxation	2.1
Guided imagery	2.1

Source: Tainya C. Clarke et al., "Trends in the Use of Complementary Health Approaches among Adults: United States, 2002–2012," *National Health Statistics Report*, Number 79 (Hyattsville, MD: National Center for Health Statistics, 2015).

TABLE 11–3   The Ten Most Common Natural Products Used by Adults, 2007

Therapy	Used in the Last Year (Of Those Using a Natural Product) (%)
Fish oil/omega 3	37.4
Glucosamine	19.9
Echinacea	19.8
Flaxseed oil pills	15.9
Ginseng	14.1
Combination herb pills	13.0
Gingko biloba	11.3
Chondroitin	11.2
Garlic supplements	11.0
Coenzyme Q-10	8.7

Source: Patricia M. Barnes, Barbara Bloom, and Richard L. Nahin, "Complementary and Alternative Medicine Use among Adults and Children: United States, 2007," *National Health Statistics Report*, Number 12 (Hyattsville, MD: National Center for Health Statistics, 2008).

The Dual Model of Care

Are all or most of the people who use CAM completely dissatisfied with conventional medical care? No. Researchers have discovered that many people follow a "dual model of medical care," making use of an alternative healer at the same time as they receive care from a medical doctor.

While some people have become disillusioned with conventional care and have made a cognitive commitment to complementary and alternative practices, the more common pattern is that individuals use different healers for different problems. For example, many patients consult with chiropractors about chronic low back pain but continue to rely on medical doctors for other problems. Their selection of a healer is made on very pragmatic grounds. They continue to see medical doctors for most ailments because that has been helpful in the past, but if their back pain has received little relief from the family doctor, they will seek relief from a chiropractor. If that works, they will maintain allegiance to both practitioners—each in a specified domain (Kronenfeld and Wasner, 1982; Shim, Schneider, and Curlin, 2014).

In a 1985 study of asthma patients using an alternative healer, more than 75 percent reported that they were satisfied with *both* their medical doctor and the alternative healer (Donnelly, Spykerboer, and Thong, 1985). However, several studies have discovered that most people who follow the dual model of care do not inform their medical doctor that they are also seeing a CAM healer, even if it is for the same complaint. One survey found that almost 75 percent of Americans aged 50 years or older have not talked to their physicians about non-traditional treatments being received simultaneously (National Center for Complementary and Integrative Health, 2016c).

Other common reasons for using a CAM approach include a belief that products obtained from nature are more pure or safe than prescriptive medicines, and appreciation of the more holistic approach taken by many CAM providers.

The Efficacy of Complementary and Alternative Healers

Is this information a valid and reliable indication that at least some CAM healers offer efficacious treatment? Possibly it is, but not necessarily. Determining the efficacy of any medical treatment—conventional or unconventional—is more complicated than it might seem at first. Rodney Coe (1970) identified three reasons why the use of magic in primitive medicine is (or seems to be) effective. These reasons can be generalized to any form of medical treatment, whatever the level of scientific sophistication in the society.

First, in all societies, most patients most of the time will recover regardless of the form of treatment received or even whether any treatment is provided. The amazing recuperative powers of the human body are only now being recognized. The same point is made by the old adage about seeing a physician for a cold—if you do, you'll be well in a week; if you don't, it will take 7 days. Thus, whether one receives muscle relaxants from a medical doctor or spinal manipulation from a chiropractor, one's back pain will usually diminish eventually. Typically, we give credit to whatever treatment was received, although we would often have healed without treatment.

Second, when patients believe strongly in the medical care they receive, it has great psychotherapeutic value, whatever its direct effects. The determination to get well and the confidence that recovery will occur are relevant factors in the healing process. Believing in the cure offered by your family physician can contribute to its success, just as believing in the efficacy of being needled by an acupuncturist or sharing prayer with a Christian Science practitioner can.

Finally, some medical practices are empirically correct, even though there is not a clear explanation. Coe uses the example of a medicine man treating a snakebite victim. He might open the wound further and suck out the evil spirit that had entered. In so doing, he is actually sucking out the poisonous venom from the wound, thus accomplishing what orthodox medicine would recommend, but basing it on an entirely different underlying theory.

Furthermore, every medical treatment must be considered within the context of the practitioner–patient relationship. It is now well recognized that the quality of this relationship may influence the course of treatment and the healing process.

Treatments offered by alternative healers are often enhanced by the greater rapport they develop with patients. Alternative healers are often more sympathetic than medical doctors to minor but nagging conditions that can trouble an individual. Most of the alternative healing practices involve more talking and more touching—both tremendously reassuring processes—than are often involved in treatment by the medical doctor. Alternative healers are also viewed as giving more time (more than four times as much time as M.D.s give per patient), doing a better job of avoiding medical jargon, and providing warmer, more relaxed treatment settings. One study found that individuals who use CAM are more likely than those who do not to report their own health as being excellent and their health to have improved in the last year (although the study was not done in such a way as to determine causality) (Nguyen et al., 2011).

All this is not to say that we do not make individual judgments about the efficacy of medical care received. We do. And it is not to say that patterns of efficacy cannot be studied. They can. But it is to say that drawing firm conclusions about the efficacy of any form of medical care must be done very carefully.

Mainstream Interest in Complementary and Alternative Healing Practices

In recent years, interest in complementary and alternative healing practices has increased among policy makers. In 1992, the U.S. Senate established the Office of Alternative Medicine

(OAM) within the National Institutes of Health, with a budget of US$2 million to evaluate the effectiveness of unconventional medical practices. The budget for the now-renamed National Center for Complementary and Integrative Health in 2015 was US$124 million, most of which was allocated to research projects on various practices and to public education.

Many medical schools have started or are developing courses on complementary and alternative therapies—more than 75 percent of medical schools in the United States now offer at least one CAM course. Many hospitals now offer selected CAM techniques such as massage therapy and acupuncture. Health insurance policies now routinely cover care from at least some types of alternative healers, and Washington has become the first state to pass an "any-willing-provider" law that requires insurers to cover the services of every licensed or certified health care provider in the state.

The general attitude of medical doctors toward CAM practices has certainly softened. While some remain skeptical about approaches that have not undergone rigorous scientific testing, many physicians now accept the value of at least some of the practices, and routinely refer patients whom they are unable to help to CAM practitioners. Efforts are also underway to better disseminate to physicians the results of clinical trials of CAM healing practices (Tilburt et al., 2009). Many nurse practitioners also see value in certain CAM approaches, and sometimes refer their patients to them (Geisler et al., 2015).

In this chapter, we examine four CAM practices—chiropractic, acupuncture, religious healing (particularly Christian Science), and ethnic folk healing (curanderismos and Navajo healers).

CHIROPRACTIC

The field of **chiropractic** contains many contradictions. Millions of people in the United States

enthusiastically support chiropractic, while many continue to see it as nothing more than successful quackery. (A former president of the American Chiropractic Association was fond of saying "People either swear by us or at us.") Without altering its basic philosophy or practice, it has achieved increased acceptance by many M.D.s, yet is condemned by others. There is even dissensus among chiropractors themselves as to the appropriate boundaries of the field.

Nevertheless, certain facts are clear. Chiropractic is a licensed health profession in all 50 states, and chiropractors are recognized and reimbursed by federal, state, and most commercial insurance companies. There are more than 80,000 licensed doctors of chiropractic in the United States, and there are currently about 10,000 students in a nationally accredited chiropractic school. Doctors of Chiropractic (DCs) must complete a 4-year doctoral graduate school program in a curriculum that includes a minimum of 4,200 hours of classroom, laboratory, and clinical internship (which is equivalent to MD and DO schools). An estimated 27 million people are treated by chiropractors each year.

Origin

The field of chiropractic was founded by Canadian-born Daniel David Palmer (1845–1913), a healer living in Davenport, Iowa. Palmer credited his vision of the field to two successful experiences he had in 1895. By realigning displaced vertebrae, he restored hearing to one man who had become deaf 17 years earlier when something had "given way" in his back and he relieved another patient's heart problems. He reasoned that if two such disparate conditions could be treated through manipulation of the vertebrae, potential existed for curing all ailments in this fashion. His research findings, published in 1910, served as the foundation for this new healing practice and the basis for a chiropractic school, which he established in 1897 (Wardwell, 1992).

Basic Principles

The National Center for Complementary and Integrative Health (2016b) identifies three basic tenets of chiropractic:

1. The body has a powerful self-healing ability. Illness results from a failure to maintain homeostasis—the positive bodily drive toward health. Maintenance of homeostasis occurs through good nutrition, good posture, exercise, stress management, creative meditation, and natural (non-pharmacological) healing. Serious disease is viewed as the end result of a process that could have been avoided through this holistic approach.
2. The body's structure (primarily that of the spine) and its function are closely related, and this relationship affects health. Vital energy flows throughout the body's nerves during a homeostatic state. However, this energy can be blocked by subtle malalignments of the vertebrae called subluxations. These subluxations are the origin of most human illness.
3. Therapy aims to normalize this relationship between structure and function and assists the body as it heals. By correcting the spinal malfunction, the chiropractor expects the specific problem to disappear and the patient's general health to improve.

Caplan (1984) explicates the three main ways in which this philosophy of healing contrasts with orthodox medicine:

1. Medical doctors typically equate symptoms with particular diseases and often identify health as the absence of symptoms. Disease is discovered when symptoms appear and is usually judged to have ended when the symptoms disappear. Chiropractic does not make this equation. A body is assumed to be diseased for some period of time before symptoms appear. Rather than focusing on symptoms, chiropractors focus on the subluxation.
2. Orthodox medicine considers germs to be the underlying cause of many disorders. The medical profession considers this to have been scientifically proven and disdains any healing philosophy that does not subscribe to it. The task of the physician is to diagnose what germs are present and offer treatment to

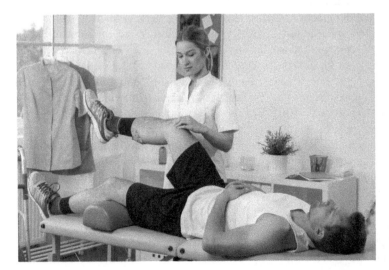

Chiropractors believe that health problems are expressions of underlying problems, including blockages of the flow of vital energy caused by malalignments of the vertebrae. © photographee.eu/Fotolia

reduce their presence in order to restore health.

Chiropractic's adherence to the belief that subluxations cause disease is in seeming contradiction to scientific medicine. Chiropractors believe that germs are a necessary condition for many diseases, but not a sufficient one. For a disease to occur, the host must have been made susceptible to the disease by factors such as poor nutrition, stress, heredity, and vertebral subluxations.

3. While chiropractors see themselves as holistic healers specializing in preventive care, some physicians believe the field should be restricted to musculoskeletal conditions or eliminated altogether.

Historical Developments

Early on, the field of chiropractic split into camps. The first camp, which included many M.D.s who were also chiropractors, maintained that chiropractors ought to offer a wide variety of treatment techniques in addition to spinal adjustment. This group created a national association—the American Chiropractors Association (ACA)—in 1922, and is today the far larger of the groups. An alternative philosophy—that chiropractic was not the practice of medicine and ought to offer solely spinal adjustment as a therapeutic modality—emerged and in 1938 created the International Chiropractic Association (ICA).

The field of chiropractic struggled through its early years. The Flexner Report of 1910 condemned existing chiropractic schools for failure to develop ties with universities and for the absence of demanding training programs. The Great Depression significantly reduced philanthropic contributions and cut back applications for schooling.

However, the most important early objective for chiropractic was to gain state-sanctioned licensure. It was not an easy battle, as

chiropractors were often jailed for practicing medicine without a license. Ultimately, being jailed became a successful strategy used to win public support for the field as a reaction to its persecution. Kansas passed the first chiropractic licensing law in 1913, 39 states gave some form of legal recognition by 1931, and in 1974, when Louisiana began licensure for chiropractors, acceptance had been won in every state.

Wardwell (1992) has suggested that 1974 was the turning point for chiropractic. In addition to Louisiana's accepting licensure, the U.S. Office of Education gave the Chiropractic Commission on Education the right to accredit schools of chiropractic, the federal government determined that chiropractors' fees were reimbursable under Medicare, and Congress authorized the spending of US$2 million on a study of the merits and efficacy of chiropractic treatment by the National Institute of Neurological Disorders and Stroke (NINDS) of the National Institutes of Health. The NINDS Conference concluded that spinal manipulation does provide relief from pain, particularly back pain, and sometimes even cures.

Organized Medicine and Chiropractic

For decades, the American Medical Association (AMA) attempted to drive chiropractic out of existence. As early as 1922, AMA officials adopted the slogan "Chiropractic Must Die" (Reed, 1932). In 1963, the AMA's Committee on Quackery referred to the elimination of chiropractic as its ultimate mission, and engaged in such activities as "producing and distributing anti-chiropractic literature, communicating with medical boards and other medical associations, fighting chiropractic-sponsored legislation, and seeking to discourage colleges, universities, and faculty members from cooperating with chiropractic schools" (Gevitz, 1989:292).

In 1965, the AMA declared it a violation of medical ethics for M.D.s to have any professional association with chiropractors. Presumably, this proscription included making or accepting referrals of patients, providing diagnostic, laboratory, or radiology services, teaching in chiropractic schools, and practicing jointly in any form.

What was the motivation for such strong action? Organized medicine defended its actions on the grounds that it was attempting to eliminate a practice it considered to be detrimental to patient welfare. Believing the vertebral subluxation concept to be grossly inaccurate and denigrating the low standards of chiropractic education, orthodox medicine defined chiropractic as having little or no therapeutic value and as being potentially dangerous. The AMA viewed these efforts as being consistent with its responsibility for guarding the public against medical quacks and charlatans.

On the other hand, chiropractic contended that the AMA's actions were motivated by professional elitism (i.e., not wanting to share the prestige of the medical profession) and an effort to restrict economic competition. In fact, these contentions became part of a lawsuit brought by chiropractors in 1976 against the AMA for violating the Sherman Antitrust Act.

Whether motivated by sincere change in ideology or fear of an expensive defeat in the courts, the AMA instituted changes in policy during the decade or more for which the case was bogged down in court. In 1978, the AMA adopted the position that medical doctors could accept referrals from and make referrals to chiropractors, and in 1980 the Principles of Medical Ethics were revised to eliminate the professional association prohibition.

Nevertheless, in August 1987, U.S. District Judge Susan Getzendanner found the AMA, the American College of Radiology, and the American College of Surgeons guilty of violating the Sherman Antitrust Act. She judged that the three associations had acted conspiratorially in instituting a boycott of chiropractic, and

had failed to justify it by its "patient care defense." She required that the actions cease.

Current and Future Status

Chiropractic clearly has established a very important place in the health care system. The educational preparation for chiropractors has continued to be upgraded. The curriculum is now comparable to that in medical schools with respect to study of the basic sciences. The major difference is that chiropractic students take courses in spinal analysis and manipulation and nutrition rather than in surgery and pharmacology (chiropractors are prohibited from performing surgery or prescribing drugs). Chiropractors must pass a national examination administered by the National Board of Chiropractic Examiners, and must be licensed by a state board. Unlike many medical doctors, chiropractors are required to continue their education in order to retain their license (Wardwell, 1992). Both the ACA and the ICA promote the field of chiropractic and view the field as being patient oriented and wellness focused.

Unquestionably, many people believe strongly in the value of chiropractic treatment. Several studies have reported benefits of chiropractic care. A New York study conducted in 1982 (discussed by Meeker and Haldeman, 2002) found that almost three in ten (28 percent) people had been examined by a chiropractor at some time, that 72 percent of recent users found chiropractic to be very effective, and that 92 percent would definitely or probably see a chiropractor again should the need arise. Numerous other studies confirm that an increasing percentage and genuine cross section of the population visits chiropractors, that levels of patient satisfaction are quite high, and that the general prestige of the field is on the upswing (Meeker and Haldeman, 2002).

Has all this changed the attitudes of physicians toward chiropractic? Apparently it has to some extent. An increased number of medical doctors now recognize the benefit that chiropractic has for some patients, and medical doctors and chiropractors are increasingly likely to make and accept referrals from each other.

What will be the future status of chiropractic in American society? Apart from a continuation of the status quo, Wardwell (1988) suggests four possibilities:

1. Chiropractic could be absorbed by orthodox medicine as a routine part of medical practice, and it could be taught to all medical doctors (especially those in appropriate specialties) as part of their medical education. Although chiropractors fear this eventuality, it is unlikely that orthodox medicine could easily absorb the practice, or that there would be sufficient M.D.s to provide all the required treatments.

2. Chiropractic could become a profession but be subordinate to physician supervision. Although organized medicine may prefer that manipulative therapy be undertaken by physical therapists (or chiropractors serving as physical therapists), this option is not appealing to chiropractors, who would have to surrender the autonomy of having patients come directly to them.

3. Chiropractic could practice in a limited domain but be independent of supervision or regulation by organized medicine. This would require chiropractic to modify its underlying theory.

4. Chiropractic could become a parallel profession (like osteopathic medicine) by elevating its standards of medical training, reducing the gulf in underlying theory, and continuing to gain greater acceptance in the eyes of the public and organized medicine. Clearly, many young chiropractors prefer this possibility and would like to be seen as appropriate family care providers. However, some skepticism in organized medicine remains, and

many chiropractors are determined not to compromise their basic practice modality. Nevertheless, this seems to be the current direction.

ACUPUNCTURE

Chinese understanding of health and illness has evolved over nearly 3,000 years, and is recorded in more than 6,000 texts. Traditional Chinese medicine is a holistic system in which health is understood only in the context of the relationship between the human body and nature.

Medical theory rests on the belief that each object in nature is both a unified whole and a whole comprised of two parts with opposing qualities—*yin* and *yang*—that are constantly in a dynamic interplay, shifting from being opposites to becoming each other. Yin represents the cold, slow, and passive principle, while yang represents the hot, excited, and active principle. Health is achieved and maintained by maintaining a balanced state within the body, and disease occurs when the yin and yang forces become imbalanced (National Center for Complementary and Integrative Health, 2016a).

An imbalance leads to a blockage that disrupts the flow of *chi* (vital energy) within the body. Chi is considered to be the primary force of nourishment and bodily protection. Although there is nothing exactly comparable in Western thought, it is sometimes viewed as the "will to live." Chi flows through the body through 12 (or 14 or 20; sources vary) main channels (or meridians), activating energy in the circulatory system as it flows. The exact location of these channels has been charted and diagrammed, and each is thought to represent (and be connected with) an internal organ. Some of the exercises and martial arts performed by Chinese people stimulate the flow of this vital energy in the channels.

The harmony and balance within the body may be disrupted either by endogenous factors, which originate from some serious internal imbalance, or by exogenous factors, which come from the external environment and may be physical (e.g., climatic conditions) or biological (e.g., bacteria and viruses). In performing diagnosis, traditional Chinese medicine follows the principle that "anything inside is bound to manifest outwardly." An implication of this principle is that even localized symptoms (e.g., a headache) are not viewed as local disturbances, but rather as a sign of abnormality within bodily organs and the body's channel system. Therefore a headache does not necessarily mean an imbalance in or near the head.

The primary goal of Chinese medicine is to restore the internal balance of the body and the harmony between the environment and the human being. Since the body's internal balance is constantly fluctuating, specific treatment must be tailored to the situation at the time.

While much of Western attention has focused on acupuncture as a treatment technique, it is actually only one of many options in traditional Chinese medicine. Other important treatment techniques include acupressure (significant pressure applied to the body via the fingertips), herbology (the use of natural herbs), moxibustion (placing ignited moxa wool on certain points of the body to create heat), various breathing exercises, physical activity, massage, and cupping (placing a small jar with a partial vacuum created by a flame over a selected part of the body producing an inflammatory response). Due to acupuncture's unique history in the United States, this section will focus on it as a healing practice.

Origin of Acupuncture in the United States

Even though it has been used in China for almost 3,000 years, and was often practiced by Chinese immigrants in the states, acupuncture gained broad popular attention in the United States only in the early 1970s. This discovery of acupuncture can be traced to two events that occurred in 1971: first, the lifting of the "bamboo curtain" with China, which opened relations between the countries, and second, an attack of appendicitis suffered by famed *New York Times* columnist James Reston while he was visiting China—acupuncture was used the day after surgery to eliminate significant pain. Reston wrote of his experience in the *Times,* thus attracting widespread interest in the subject. A select group of American physicians (including a delegation from the AMA) visited China in the ensuing months, and their glowing reports of the efficacy of acupuncture ensured further popular and professional attention (Wolpe, 1985).

Basic Principles

Acupuncture is the insertion of fine needles into one or more acupuncture "points" charted on the body. To date more than 700 points have been identified, although only 40 or 50 are commonly used. The needles used vary in length, width, and type of metal, and treatments vary with regard to the depth to which needles are inserted, the duration of insertion, and the needle rotation.

The insertion of the needles is performed to stimulate chi in the body and to redirect it so that imbalances are corrected. The needles are inserted in those points that correspond to the particular internal organs where the imbalance exists.

Historical Developments

Although American physicians largely focused on the anesthetic value of acupuncture, and ignored its therapeutic utility, the popular press offered vivid descriptions of acupuncture as a miracle process. The federal government encouraged research into acupuncture, and scientific journals published scores of articles. The Internal

Revenue Service decided that payments for acupuncture service qualified as a medical expense, and the Food and Drug Administration developed quality control regulations for acupuncture needles. An American Society of Chinese Medicine was formed (Wolpe, 1985).

In July 1972, the first acupuncture clinic opened in New York City. When it was shut down a week later for practicing medicine without a license, it had already served 500 patients and was booked solid for several months. Acupuncture had captured America by storm. Although the manner in which it would be incorporated remained to be determined, acupuncture seemed on the verge of becoming a major healing practice in the United States.

Organized Medicine and Acupuncture

The medical establishment, however, quickly reigned in the enthusiasm. One can understand the professional embarrassment caused by a healing practice based on a theory that seemed completely contradictory to "scientific" medicine. The tremendous media and lay interest in acupuncture

> quickly became anathema to most of organized medicine. Physicians had no expertise in acupuncture and no knowledge of physiological mechanisms that could account for it. Indeed, it seemed to violate laws of anatomy and neurophysiology. Acupuncture was an alien treatment with an alien philosophical basis imported as a package from the East; it was not an indigenous alternative modality that reacted to (and thus was informed by) the biomedical model. (Wolpe, 1985:413)

Negative and often hostile physician reactions escalated. The therapeutic effects of acupuncture were dismissed as being nothing more than placebo, and its effectiveness as an anesthetic was dismissed as being a type of hypnosis or form of suggestibility, or it was even suggested that "Chinese stoicism" or patriotic zeal enabled patients to undergo excruciatingly painful surgery without other anesthetics (Wolpe, 1985). One physician referred to acupuncturists as "nonscientific weirdos," and attempted to portray the entire acupuncture practice as modern-day quackery (Goldstein, 1972).

Wolpe (1985) contends that in order to protect its cultural authority over medicine, the medical establishment employed two additional strategies. The first was to sponsor and conduct research that would explain acupuncture in terms of the traditional biomedical model. While Chinese practitioners strongly believe that the practice cannot be separated from its underlying theory, and therefore cannot be studied by traditional scientific methods, much research has been conducted to find a conventional explanation for its anesthetic effects.

For example, Melzack and Wall (1965) developed the "gate control theory" based on research which shows that the insertion of needles excites certain nerve fibers that enter the spinal column and inhibit the onward transmission of pain to the brain. Stimulating these nerve fibers effectively "closes the gate" to pain. An alternative theory, also consistent with traditional neurophysiology, is that the needle insertion stimulates the release of certain pain-reducing hormones (endorphins and enkephalins), which create the anesthetic or analgesic effects. Some recent research has found that needle insertion reduces the flow of blood to the areas of the brain that control pain.

The second strategy was to arrange for the practice of acupuncture to be placed under the jurisdiction of medical doctors. After all, if acupuncture was beneficial only for pain relief, and if the explanation for that could be provided in conventional terms, then it could be argued that Oriental practitioners were not as able as Western practitioners to provide safe and effective treatment. Regulations governing the practice of acupuncture were quickly established in many states (either by the legislature or by the State Medical Board).

Current and Future Status

There are now more than 60 accredited schools of Oriental Medicine in the country, and more than 27,000 licensed (by the National Certification Commission for Acupuncture and Oriental Medicine, or NCCAOM) practitioners. The NCCAOM offers certification in oriental medicine, acupuncture, Chinese herbology, and Asian bodywork therapy. The additional designation of licensed acupuncturist (L.Ac.) is awarded by a state regulatory board. Currently, 44 states plus the District of Columbia require NCCAOM certification or the passing of the NCCAOM examinations as a requirement for licensure to practice acupuncture. Each state board has a unique set of requirements for licensure. It is estimated that more than 3 million adults in the United States use acupuncture each year. Many private insurers and the Medicaid programs in some states now cover the cost of acupuncture treatment.

Is acupuncture an effective anesthetic or therapeutic healing practice? Considerable research has reported favorable findings. In late 1997, a panel of scientists at the National Institutes of Health (including some who practice acupuncture and some skeptics) concluded that acupuncture is clearly effective in treating many conditions, including nausea and vomiting after chemotherapy and surgery, the nausea of pregnancy, and postoperative dental pain. Although fewer data were available, they concluded that acupuncture may help stroke rehabilitation and relieve addictions, headaches, menstrual cramps, a variety of muscle pains, carpal tunnel syndrome, insomnia, arthritis, and asthma. They acknowledged that these benefits occur while acupuncture has fewer side effects and is less invasive. The World Health Organization now recognizes more than 40 conditions as being effectively treatable by acupuncture. Acupuncture is a fully accepted and practiced therapy in countries around the world.

The accompanying box, "Legalizing Medical Marijuana?", discusses a CAM technique that is currently in the news.

Most states require traditional Chinese medicine practitioners to have a Master of Acupuncture or Oriental Medicine degree or its equivalent, and national certification. Photo by Gregory Weiss.

IN THE FIELD

LEGALIZING MEDICAL MARIJUANA?

In 1996, California voters approved Proposition 215, which permitted physicians to *recommend* marijuana for their patients. Because it would violate federal law, physicians were prohibited from *prescribing* it. In 1997, the *New England Journal of Medicine* endorsed the legalization of medical marijuana, arguing that it has clearly brought relief from pain for many people. Later that year, the AMA, although rejecting endorsement of legalization, called for the right of physicians to discuss any treatment alternatives with patients without possibility of criminal sanction. By early 2016, 23 states plus D.C. allowed cannabis to be cultivated and used for medical purposes, and several now allow retail pot dispensaries (although some of the dispensaries have been accused of selling marijuana to anyone). Oregon permits medical marijuana cardholders to socialize at designated cafes and to use free, over-the-counter cannabis. Many more states are considering similar legislation. Four states (Colorado, Washington, Oregon, and Alaska) plus D.C. have voted to legalize recreational use of marijuana.

Until 2009, the U.S. Justice Department maintained that federal law prohibits any use of marijuana, and indicated that it would use its authority under the Controlled Substances Act to revoke the license to prescribe drugs of any physician who *recommended* marijuana to a patient. In May 2001, the U.S. Supreme Court had ruled that the federal law prohibiting the manufacture and distribution of marijuana means that it cannot be sold or used for medicinal purposes. Although medical marijuana users are typically not prosecuted, they are in the awkward position of engaging in a behavior that has been expressly approved by their state but disapproved by the federal government. In 2009, the Attorney General of the United States, Eric Holder, indicated that President Obama would follow his campaign promise to stop raids on state-approved marijuana dispensaries (Hoffman and Weber, 2010). However, the federal government has not recognized or approved marijuana as medicine.

Can marijuana be medicinal? Yes it can. Research has shown four beneficial medical

A patient identification card that can be used to legally obtain marijuana through the Arizona Medical Marijuana Program. © Norma Jean Gargasz/Alamy Stock Photo.

effects. (1) It reduces the nausea associated with cancer chemotherapy. (2) It reduces "wasting syndrome"—the deadly loss of appetite and consequent weight loss that many AIDS patients feel near the end of life. (3) It reduces the painful muscle spasms and tremors experienced by many people with spinal cord injuries and multiple sclerosis. (4) It reduces pressure inside the eye for people with glaucoma (although another drug is now more effective). There is experimental evidence that it may also be helpful in treating other conditions, such as depression, Crohn's disease, hepatitis C, and multiple sclerosis.

Are there any demonstrated negative side effects of marijuana use? Yes there are. Two such effects are (1) that it impairs cognitive functioning, negatively affecting coordination and short-term memory (studies have been inconsistent on whether there is any long-term cognitive impairment), and (2) that it leads to respiratory damage (studies have found that smoking marijuana is even more harmful to the lungs than smoking tobacco).

Proponents of medical marijuana argue that individuals should have the right to decide for themselves whether the benefits outweigh the harms. Because many of the users are and would be light users, and would be using it only on a temporary basis, they argue that the harms are overstated. Besides, it is well known that many people with cancer or AIDS have long been using marijuana for relief, but have been forced to do so surreptitiously. Opponents argue that liberalizing use of the drug might lead to increased use of marijuana and/or other drugs, and that the harms of the drug justify its continued ban. In addition, pharmaceutical companies, anticipating the possibility of patenting (potentially very profitable) drugs that include tetrahydrocannabinol (THC), which is the active ingredient of marijuana, have opposed legalization of medical marijuana.

SPIRITUAL HEALING AND CHRISTIAN SCIENCE

A belief in "psychic healing" has been present in both early and modern times and in both Western and non-Western cultures. Psychic healing "refers to the beneficial influence of a person on another living thing by mechanisms which are beyond those recognized by conventional medicine. These mechanisms may include focused wishes, meditation, prayers, ritual practices, and the laying-on-of-hands" (Benor, 1984:166).

Psychic healers use one of four approaches: (1) activating innate recuperative forces within the patient; (2) transferring their own healing energy to the patient; (3) serving as a conduit through which universally available cosmic energy is transferred to the patient; or (4) serving as a conduit through which the healing powers of spirits or God are transferred to the patient. The final channel is also referred to as **spiritual healing** or "faith healing" (Benor, 1984). Spiritual healers do not claim any personal ability to heal, but rather an ability to convey the power of some transcendent being to the sick. Spiritual healers may or may not be affiliated with a particular church and may or may not be full-time healers.

Efficacy of Spiritual Healing

Determining the efficacy of spiritual healing is difficult. Most of the evidence supporting positive effects is anecdotal and comes from people strongly predisposed to its benefits. Other more systematic research has been conducted, but in ways that allow alternative explanations of the findings.

Many people accept that there are at least some cases where a subject's health status has improved following a spiritual healing encounter. These cases are interpreted in different ways. Those involved in the healing process typically contend that God has intervened and in a miraculous way effected a cure. Others believe that the health improvement or cure has occurred through psychological processes—for example, marshaling the patient's mental powers and determination to combat the ailment and/or convincing the patient that a cure will occur (akin to the placebo effect).

In a study of spiritual healing groups in Baltimore in the early 1980s, Glik (1988) discovered that most of the reported illnesses were chronic and mild to moderate in severity, with a "non-specific" diagnosis (but related to psychosomatic, stress, or mental health problems). Less than 10 percent of the reported conditions were life-threatening or serious. Many of the symbols and rituals used in the groups (as well as the supportive social context) would be likely to affect the psyche of those present.

In the largest study ever undertaken on the topic, researchers from six hospitals throughout the United States examined the effects of intercessory prayer—that is, someone praying for therapeutic improvement for another (Benson et al., 2006). Previous well-controlled clinical tests had not supported such benefits, but they had not addressed whether any outcomes were due to prayer itself or to the knowledge that prayer was being offered by someone. Patients in the study were divided into three groups: (1) 604 individuals who received prayer after being informed that they might or might not receive it, (2) 597 individuals who did not receive prayer after being told they might or might not receive it, and (3) 601 individuals who received prayer after being told that they would receive it. All of the patients were recovering from coronary artery bypass graft surgery.

The researchers focused on whether or not there were any complications from the surgery, any secondary major events, and mortality. Complications occurred for 52 percent of those

who received prayer and 51 percent of those who did not (a statistically non-significant difference). Of the patients who were certain of receiving intercessory prayer, 59 percent had complications, compared with 52 percent of those who were uncertain (a statistically significant difference).

Public Perceptions of Spiritual Healing

Many people do relate religion and illness experience. The perception that disease and illness are caused by God declined through the 1900s, but has increased in the last two decades. Many people continue to rely on religion as a coping mechanism when they are sick.

A recent study of older adults discovered many who were unclear about God's role in health and illness, but nevertheless turned to prayer when sick. For most of these illnesses, care had also been sought from a medical doctor. Rather than viewing prayer and conventional medical treatment as being mutually exclusive, most of these respondents saw them as being complementary (Bearon and Koenig, 1990).

Most of the increasing numbers of studies that are being conducted have found that religion has a positive influence on health. Compelling evidence has accumulated that individuals who attend a religious service on a regular basis have a longer life expectancy than non-churchgoers. Other research has found that regular churchgoers on average have lower blood pressure and cope better with illness. The findings may be interpreted in different ways. One national survey found that about one-third of Americans use prayer for health concerns, and that about seven in ten of these individuals considered it to be very helpful (McCaffrey et al., 2004).

Several studies have found that individuals who regularly attend church are less likely to engage in unhealthy lifestyles. Some research has found that prayer or meditation has a calming effect on individuals, which would help to explain patterns such as lower blood pressure (Koenig, McCullough, and Larson, 2001). Many analysts are concerned that these studies might be misinterpreted as providing evidence that faith-based practices may be used in lieu of medical treatment. All agree that more research is needed in order to understand the basis for these patterns.

The high level of religious commitment among many patients and the potentially positive effects of religious participation on health are acknowledged by most physicians. Even physicians who are themselves religiously skeptical must walk a thin line on this issue for fear of alienating devout patients. Koenig, Bearon, and Dayringer (1989) found that about two-thirds of a sample of family physicians and general practitioners believe that strong religious beliefs and frequent involvement in religious activities have a positive impact on mental health, and four in ten believe that there is a positive effect on physical health. Many of the physicians were unclear about the extent to which they should become involved in religious discussions with patients. Most would in some circumstances, but few preferred this as a standard course of action. Almost 25 percent expressed a belief that faith healers can divinely heal some people whom physicians cannot help.

However, skepticism about spiritual healing remains at a high level. Spiritual healers do not have (nor have they created) any licensure process, there are no formal associations per se, and they may even be arrested for practicing medicine without a license. Even though it is careful in its language, the AMA is disdainful of spiritual healing and sees the practice as an attempt to take advantage of vulnerable people.

Public opinion surveys reveal that many in the general public share this suspicion of spiritual healing. A survey in rural North Carolina, an area where one might expect to find above-average participation in spiritual healing, found that 58 percent of respondents considered faith healers to be quacks (King, Sobol, and DeForge, 1988).

Christian Science as an Example of Spiritual Healing

Of the specific spiritual healing philosophies, that of **Christian Science healing** has received the most professional study.

Origin. In order to understand the many dimensions of Christian Science, it is necessary to understand its founder, Mary Baker Eddy (1821–1910). During her youth, Mary Baker suffered frequent bouts of illness that prompted her to devote her life to finding a cure for disease. Failing to be helped by medical doctors, she experimented with a variety of alternative healing philosophies.

At the age of 45 years, Mary slipped on an icy street, causing very painful head, neck, and back problems. When she received little help from local physicians, she turned to the Bible for comfort. While reading the account of the healings of Jesus, she discovered the "Healing Truth" and experienced a complete recovery. She initiated work as a healer, and in 1875 wrote *Science and Health,* which became the textbook of Christian Science.

The next few years were not easy. While alternately gaining followers and losing them (because of charges of temper tantrums, love of money, and hypocrisy), Mary Baker, her third husband, Asa Eddy, and a small group of devotees moved to Boston and founded the First Church of Christ, Scientist, in 1879. Although criticized by some, the church grew rapidly, branching out to additional churches, local societies, and schools. However, concerned about the bureaucratization of the church, Mary dismantled much of its organizational structure and substituted a highly centralized structure with herself and the mother church in key positions.

Basic Principles. Gottschalk summarizes the basic principle of Christian Science healing as follows:

> Christian Scientists hold that behind all diseases are mental factors rooted in the human mind's blindness to God's presence and our authentic relation to God, revealed in the life of Christ. They hold that treatment is a form of prayer or communion with God in which God's reality and power, admitted and witnessed to, become so real as to eclipse the temporal "reality" of disease and pain. (1988:603)

In other words, illness and pain are not real, but only illusions of the mind. Since people are reflections of God, and God cannot be sick, people cannot be sick. A person feels ill only when the underlying spiritual condition is in disrepair. This causes the mind to think illness is present.

The only appropriate curative techniques are prayer and spiritual rediscovery. Through prayer, a deeper understanding of one's own spirituality is achieved. Christian Scientists believe that they have the power within to heal themselves, although the assistance of a Christian Science practitioner is frequently used.

Unlike many alternative healing practices, Christian Science healing is believed to be incompatible with orthodox medicine. Medical doctors are viewed as adding pain and illness to the world as a consequence of their lack of understanding of the role of the mind. In fact, even obtaining a medical diagnosis is considered to be likely to worsen any condition.

Historical Developments. The key issues in the last century have pertained to the standardization of Scientist-healing practices and external negotiation regarding their legality. Issues such as the appropriateness of Christian Science healing for emotional disorders and the extent to which Scientists should be commanded to live a "healthy lifestyle" have been debated.

Organized Medicine and Christian Science. Two chief points of contention continue to exist between the medical establishment and Christian Scientists. The first is the extent to which Christian Science healing should be acknowledged by the government and commercial health insurance companies as a legitimate form of health care. While this issue continues to be debated, it is clear that Christian Science has largely prevailed.

Several states have written legislation that provides recognition for Christian Science healing as the equivalent of conventional medical care (e.g., Christian Science practitioners can sign certificates for sick leave and disability claims). Hundreds of commercial insurance companies reimburse charges for Christian Science practitioners as they would for medical doctors. Christian Science prayer treatment is typically covered by insurance plans for government employees, and Medicaid and Medicare also provide coverage.

The second continuing issue is the status of **religious exemption laws,** which permit legal violation of other laws based on religious grounds. For example, some states have religious exemptions for premarital blood tests for adults, prophylactic eyedrops for newborns, required physical examinations for schoolchildren, and instruction about diseases and health in school. Some states provide for exemption from required immunizations such as that for measles.

Following a widely reported case in Massachusetts in 1967, in which a Christian Scientist was convicted of manslaughter after her 5-year-old daughter died of medically untreated pneumonia, Christian Scientists have conducted a massive lobbying campaign for exemption from child neglect laws. Today, almost every state provides some type of exemption for religious groups relative to these laws. Still in dispute, however, is whether these laws extend to situations where forgoing orthodox medical treatment that is likely to be effective results in the death of a child.

Christian Scientists argue that religious exemption laws are required to enable adherents to practice their religion. What meaning is there in "freedom of religion," they ask, if society compels its members to violate important tenets of the faith? Christian Science healing "is part of a whole religious way of life and is, in fact, the natural outcome of the theology that underlies it. This theology ... is both biblically based and deeply reasoned" (Talbot, 1983:1641).

In addition, a second line of reasoning has been adopted, namely that Christian Science treatment is at least as efficacious as orthodox medicine. In a widely quoted passage, Nathan Talbot, a senior official in the First Church of Christ, Scientist, said:

> Christian Scientists are caring and responsible people who love their children and want only the best possible care for them. They would not have relied on Christian Science for healing—sometimes over four and even five generations in the same family—if this healing were only a myth. (Talbot, 1983:1641)

The church now disseminates data from research it has conducted to demonstrate that Christian Science children are healthier than their peers and that there are lifetime health benefits in relying solely on Christian Science treatment. This line of reasoning has recently been incorporated in statutes in some states that permit reliance on healing practices that have a "proven record of success" or a "generally accepted record of efficacy" (Skolnick, 1990a).

Opponents of religious exemption laws contend that they violate the anti-establishment clause of the First Amendment, which prohibits special privileges for any religious group. Since Christian Science is singled out in some of these statutes, it is argued that they are given special license or endorsement by the government. For instance, in several states, Christian Science nursing homes do not have to meet required minimum standards for staffing or daily care provided to patients.

Religious exemptions to health laws are said to have harmful public health consequences. For example, a schoolteacher in Van Nuys, California, died in 1954 of tuberculosis after exposing hundreds of children to the disease. As a Christian Scientist, she had been exempted from the routinely required chest examination. Other reported disease epidemics include 11 children paralyzed by polio at a Christian Science boarding school in 1972, an outbreak of measles at an Illinois college for Christian Scientists in 1985, a second outbreak of measles in 1985 at a Colorado camp attended by Christian Scientists, and a small outbreak of polio in a Minnesota Amish community in 2005.

Opponents of these laws are especially critical when the care provided for children is affected. The argument is that children are unable to make fully informed and competent decisions about their religious preference, and should not be placed in a life-threatening situation by the religious beliefs of their parents. An analogy often cited is the medical treatment given to Jehovah's Witness children. While most courts today routinely allow adult Jehovah's Witnesses to forgo blood transfusions (an important proscription of the faith), children are routinely transfused despite the wishes of the parents. Only at the age of competence does the scale tip in favor of the patient's wishes. The American Academy of Pediatricians has recently been leading an effort to remove religious exemptions to child neglect laws, and a couple of states have already made this change in the law.

Current and Future Status. The number of Christian Scientists in the United States reached a peak of 270,000 in the 1930s, dwindled to 106,000 in 1990, and is estimated to have decreased since then. There were more than 9,700 Christian Science churches in the 1930s, but only an estimated 778 in 2016. There were just under 1,000 Christian Science healers in 2016.

Specialized training for Christian Science practitioners remains minimal. Typically, people who have demonstrated special interest and knowledge in Christian Science healing are selected for training. The primary course lasts only about 2 weeks, and focuses on Christian Science theology. At the conclusion of the class, one is listed as a practitioner in the *Christian Science Journal*. After 3 years of full-time successful healing, practitioners may apply to the Board of Education to take a 6-day course. Graduates of the class are given a CSB (Bachelor of Christian Science) degree.

Is Christian Science healing efficacious? Apart from the highly favorable data published by the church itself, two scientific studies by researchers outside the church have been conducted. An early study (based on data from 1935 to 1955 in the state of Washington) found lower life expectancy among Christian Scientists, a much higher than average rate of cancer, and about 6 percent of deaths that would have been medically preventable (Skolnick, 1990b).

A second study (Simpson, 1989), which compared the longevity of graduates of a Christian Science college with those of a neighboring university, found a much higher death rate among Christian Scientists. This pattern was discovered despite the fact that Christian Scientists neither smoke nor drink—factors that should have prompted a lower death rate.

The efficacy of Christian Science treatment is at least somewhat amenable to scientific study. In order to resolve the contradictory patterns reported by the church and the two studies cited above, Christian Science practitioners and patients may need to make themselves available for study by impartial outsiders.

ETHNIC FOLK HEALING

Folk understandings of disease and illness are typically interwoven into the beliefs and practices of cultural groups. In the United States, folk understandings of the causes and cures of disease occur most often in low-income racial and ethnic minority groups. Some of the common denominators in folk healing systems have been identified and illustrated by Snow (1993) in her studies of black folk healers and their patients in Chicago. She found that her subjects' views of disease and illness were part and parcel of their religious beliefs— that illness may result from natural factors but might also be the result of sorcery, a temptation from Satan, or a punishment from God. Although traditional herbal remedies and prayer might be sufficient for some conditions, others were perceived to be beyond the scope of either self-care or care by medical doctors, and required a special healer from within the group. The folk healers practiced holistic medicine— that is, they treated the whole person rather than just the particular malady, and were more concerned about the cause of the illness than its symptoms.

These patterns also appear in the two most widely studied systems of folk healing—curanderismo (the Mexican and Mexican American form of folk healing) and traditional Native American folk healing—which are covered in this section.

Curanderismo

Although many people use the term **curanderismo** to refer only to Mexican American folk healing, the term is used throughout the Hispanic world (especially in Mexico, Latin America, and the southwestern United States) to describe a unique system of health care beliefs and practices that differ significantly from modern scientific medicine.

Origin and Historical Developments. Curanderismo developed from three primary sources: (1) the theory of bodily humors; (2) herbal medicine as practiced by the Aztecs, Mayans, and other Native American groups; and (3) religious belief systems, including both Spanish Catholicism and various witchcraft belief systems (Kiev, 1968). Over time in Hispanic communities, curanderismo has taken on important cultural meaning above and beyond its therapeutic value.

Basic Principles. First, good health is associated with "a strong body, the ability to maintain a high level of normal physical activity, and the absence of persistent pain and discomfort" (Krajewski-Jaime, 1991:160–161). Good health is viewed as a reward for those who have kept God's commandments:

> Even when a curandero uncovers specific causes of illness, he is still likely to focus on sin and the will of God as critical factors which have affected the susceptibility of the patient and predisposed him to illness. When illness occurs in a religious and pious person, it is rationalized by the belief that God allows men to suffer in order to learn. (Kiev, 1968:34)

Second, diseases are classified according to their underlying cause. Krajewski-Jaime (1991) traces disease etiology along three lines: (1) natural and supernatural forces (diseases believed to be caused by natural forces, such as moonlight, eclipses, cold, heat, air, wind, sun, and water, or traced to the supernatural and magic); (2) imbalances of heat and cold (drawing directly from the ancient humoral theory, which identified positive health as occurring when the hot and cold forces within the body are in balance); and (3) emotion-based diseases (often resulting from a frightening or traumatic experience).

Third, like all other healing systems, curanderismo healing logically follows the nature of disease etiology. Because disease is traced through several lines, the curandero (or curandera) must have several types of healing treatments available, including prayer, herbal medicine, healing rituals, spiritualism, massage, and psychic healing. Two examples (the first pertaining to hot–cold diseases and the second to emotion-based diseases) are used to illustrate this. First:

> Some diseases are hot and some are cold. Foods and herbs are also classified into hot or cold for treatments. Sickness that enhances the cold within the body requires a hot treatment to restore the balance, and vice versa. To avoid a hot sickness, the person must not become cold; therefore, the individual must not walk barefoot on cold tiles for fear of catching tonsillitis. . . . People are given chili, a hot food, or chicken soup, for a cold disease such as pneumonia or a common cold, and lard, having cold properties, is used on burns. (Krajewski-Jaime, 1991:162)

The second example is a healing treatment used for a person suffering from *espanto*—a form of fright thought to be caused by the spirit being so frightened that it leaves the body:

> Treatment by the folk healer includes having the patient lie down on the floor with arms outstretched in the position of a cross. Sweeping the body with branches, herbs, and prayers, she coaxes the lost spirit to re-enter the victim's body. (Krajewski-Jaime, 1991:162)

Finally, the curandero–patient relationship is very close. Curanderos typically live in the same community as their patients, share the same basic values, and recognize the importance of personal involvement and rapport. Patients expect, and receive, extensive time with the curandero. The culture within which this relationship occurs supports the therapeutic value of the curandero's healing practices.

Organized Medicine and Curanderismo. Due to the cultural importance of folk healing in the Chicano community, the extent to which it is intertwined with religious beliefs, and its location primarily in just one region of the United States (although it exists in Hispanic communities around the country), organized medicine has been reluctant to aggressively comment on or act against curanderos. Research indicates that they are paid very little (sometimes with food or other goods) and are not viewed as representing a generalized or serious threat to the medical establishment. While there is evidence that use of curanderos has declined during the last few decades, curanderismo remains an important part of many Hispanic communities.

Current and Future Status.   Research has found that many Hispanic people follow the "dual model of medical care" in that they seek care from both medical doctors and curanderos. Padilla et al. (2001) found that almost all the Hispanic patients receiving conventional care at a public hospital in Denver knew what a curandero is, and 29 percent had been to a curandero at some time in their life. Visits were most commonly for treatment for Mexican folk illnesses such as espanto and *empacho* (gastrointestinal obstruction). Research on Hispanic patients with diabetes found two-thirds who used some form of alternative medicine (mostly herbs and prayer), but none who used a curandero (Hunt, Arar, and Akana, 2000).

Native American Healing

Traditional Native American healing continues to be commonly used among the 5 million Native Americans and Alaskan natives in the United States. While a general understanding of the causes of health and illness and healing practices is shared by all Native American peoples, there are in effect as many different healing systems as there are tribes. This section focuses on healers and healing among the Dineh—the Navajo people—the largest full-blooded tribe (with about 286,000 members),

and the second-largest Native American group (after the Cherokee) when both full-bloods and mixed bloods are counted (with about 330,000 members).

Origin and Historical Developments. Navajo healing practices can only be appreciated within the context of Navajo culture. Understandings of disease and illness emanate from and are consistent with Navajo beliefs about the creation of earth and how the Navajo people came to be located where they are—on Dinetah (mostly northern Arizona).

Navajo healing is completely intermeshed with the religious belief system. Many of the Navajo religious rituals are focused on maintaining good health—or on wellness—and eliminating the root causes of illness. To maintain good health, one must live according to prescribed lifeways that were identified at the time of creation.

Basic Principles.   Navajo philosophy is based on the belief that "everything in the world has life; all things breathe and live and have a spirit and power . . . all of these beings are interrelated and influence the workings of the universe; each has a role and responsibility for maintaining order in the universe" (Avery, 1991:2271). This philosophy contributes to a love and respect for "Mother Earth" and "Father Sky" and the wonders of the natural environment, and a feeling of "oneness" with animals. Navajos do not attempt to "master" nature, but to be one with it.

Wellness exists when one is in harmony with nature. Ursula Knoki-Wilson, a Navajo nurse-midwife, interpreter, and teacher, defines health holistically as "the synergistic interaction of all the dimensions (physical, mental, and spiritual) of a person at full potential," and wellness as the "way that positive thought influences feeling so that the nature of a person's life experience includes growth, renewal, and miracles" (Knoki-Wilson, 1992).

Second, when imbalances or disharmony develop, illness results. Illness occurs "when the free flow of spiritual energy to the mind, body, and soul is decreased by factors inside or outside the person" (Knoki-Wilson, 1992). Internal factors include such things as violence, destructiveness, anger, stubbornness, guilt, shame, and participation in any Navajo taboos (e.g., wasting natural resources). External factors include being a victim of witchcraft, disease, or object intrusion (i.e., invasion of the body by a worm, snake, or insect) and soul loss (which usually occurs during a dream when the soul departs the body). All these occurrences may have a supernatural origin (Knoki-Wilson, 1983).

Third, restoration to health occurs when the disharmony or imbalances are resolved or eliminated. Healing is enacted in physical, mental, and spiritual dimensions. Practitioners of Western medicine often emphasize the mental and spiritual dimensions of Navajo healing, but only because these are often given so little prominence in their own techniques. Navajos emphasize that healing can only occur when all three dimensions are involved. The ultimate goal of the healing practice is a return to oneness or harmony with nature. Figure 11–3 summarizes the ingredients necessary for successful Navajo healing.

Finally, at least four separate medical persons (all of whom can be female or male) are used in Navajo healing. One sees a *diagnostician* to learn the cause of illness and to obtain a prescription for the appropriate healing practice. The diagnostician, who is believed to have a special gift, may be a hand trembler (who diagnoses by passing their hands over the patient's body and receiving messages from the spirits), a stargazer (who reads messages in the stars), or a crystal gazer (who looks through crystals to "X-ray" the body in order to locate problems).

The primary healer is called a *medicine person* or *singer*, and has received a divine calling as someone with special qualities through whom the spirits can work: "Medicine persons are gifted with extrasensory perception that allows them to make mythological associations and identify the causes and remedies for illnesses" (Knoki-Wilson, 1983:279). Healing practices include prayer, participation in rituals, use of herbal medicines, chants, physical manipulations, and ceremonial observances (Avery, 1991). Elaborate ceremonies lasting from a few hours to 9 days (with only brief respites)—for example, the Yeibeichei Dance—are used to effect cures. Because the ceremonies are very structured and elaborate and must be followed precisely, medicine persons often study and apprentice for years in order to be able to conduct just one or two types.

The *herbalist* has practical knowledge about treatment of minor illnesses, and has expertise in the preparation and use of herbal remedies.

Figure 11–3 Ingredients of Navajo Healing

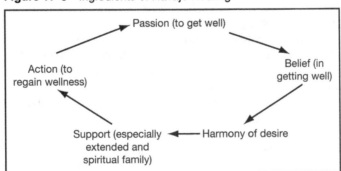

Rather than utilizing the complex traditional healing ceremonies, some Navajos will use religious rituals of the Native American Church and practitioners known as *roadmen*. These ceremonies typically use peyote as the healing herb and last only a single night, but they combine elements of the philosophy of the Navajos, the Plains Indians, and Christianity.

Organized Medicine and Native American Healing. Today, scientific medicine and Native American healing practices largely coexist peacefully on the Navajo reservation. Although scientific medicine is practiced in the hospitals and clinics of the Indian Health Service, provisions are made within the hospitals for patients to bring in medicine persons, and space is provided for traditional healing ceremonies. Many Navajos, including those who live on the reservation and those who live in urban areas, use both conventional and traditional types of medicine (Buchwald, Beals, and Manson, 2000; Kim and Kwok, 1998). Navajos often use scientific medicine to treat the symptoms of illness, but rely on traditional healing practices to treat the cause of illness. This enables access to modern medical knowledge and technology without sacrificing the many benefits of the holistic approach and the community support provided by traditional healing practices.

Current and Future Status. It is hoped that the beauty of the Navajo culture and the benefits of traditional Native American healing practices will be preserved. A major challenge will be to continue to find young Navajo women and men who have been called to be healers and who are willing to make the commitment to learn the healing ceremonies.

SUMMARY

Although scientific medicine is firmly established in the United States, millions of people use, are satisfied with, and even prefer complementary and alternative healing practices. Organized medicine contends that many CAM practices are ineffective and potentially harmful to users' health (if only because they divert contact from conventional healers). CAM healers argue that, like conventional healers, they seek to provide effective care, and they counter that orthodox healing practices have proved ineffective or even harmful for some. Many people follow a "dual model of medical care," using both orthodox and CAM healers.

Although chiropractic may still be a "marginal" profession, it has also gained significant legitimacy. It is licensed in all 50 states, accepted by insurance companies, and is increasingly being accepted by many medical doctors.

In the early 1970s, acupuncture took America by storm. Although it quickly became very popular with patients, orthodox medicine did not accept its theoretical foundation and acted to restrict its practice. Recently, however, there has been substantial scientific endorsement of acupuncture, as a result of which its use has become more common.

Many physicians and laypeople perceive religious practices to have beneficial effects on health, but much skepticism exists about the general efficacy of spiritual healing. While the relative health of the Christian Science population is in dispute, Christian Scientists have achieved much recent success in having their healers recognized as legitimate and in getting religious exemption laws passed in states.

Curanderismo and Native American healing represent two types of folk healing practices.

Both are very much a part of their respective cultures and religious belief systems. Although there are differences between the systems, both are more holistic than orthodox medicine and more concerned with the causes of illness than with merely treating symptoms.

HEALTH ON THE INTERNET

You can learn more about complementary and alternative medicine by visiting the website of the National Center for Complementary and Integrative Health at

www.nccih.nih.gov

What is the purpose of this site? Click on "Health Info" and then click on "What is Complimentary, Alternative, and Integrative Health?" Read through all the information provided. How many of the CAM practices identified here have been used by you, members of your family, or your friends?

In order to find out about two other popular CAM healing practices, visit www.homeopathic.org (National Center for Homeopathy) to learn about homeopathy and www.naturopathic.org (American Association of Naturopathic Physicians) to learn about naturopathy. How are these two practices alike, and how are they different?

DISCUSSION CASE

In June 1990, a jury in Boston, Massachusetts, found David and Ginger Twitchell guilty of the negligent homicide (involuntary manslaughter) of their 2½-year-old son Robyn. The Twitchells were sentenced to 10 years probation for failing to provide medical care that could have saved the life of their son, who died of an untreated bowel obstruction. The parents had contacted a Christian Science practitioner, but not a medical doctor. Massachusetts law does recognize spiritual healing as a form of medicine, but it requires parents to seek orthodox medical care for seriously ill children.

Testimony at their trial revealed that Robyn had suffered excruciating pain during the last 5 days of his life. A large section of his colon, scrotum, and other tissues had become necrotic, and even the pressure of a diaper on his abdomen caused him to scream in pain. Before becoming comatose, he began vomiting fecal material. The Twitchells consulted a Christian Science practitioner and nurse whose treatment consisted of "heartfelt yet disciplined prayer." A medical doctor was not consulted. The Twitchells' defense contended that the couple were within their First Amendment rights to treat their son's illness with prayer, and that Massachusetts had recognized this right in an exemption to the statute outlawing child neglect.

The jury was said to be affected by testimony that, while forbidding medical care for children with critical illnesses, Christian Science does permit orthodox obstetric care (Mrs. Twitchell had received anesthesia when Robyn was born) and orthodox dental care (Mr. Twitchell had received treatment from a dentist for a root canal and impacted wisdom teeth).

What should be the legal responsibility of parents with critically ill children? Should society legally obligate all parents, regardless of their religious convictions, to utilize orthodox medical care? Would this, as Christian Scientists claim, interfere with the First Amendment right to religious freedom? Do judges and juries have a right to state that prayer is inadequate medical treatment? Based on the histories of alternative healing practices presented in this chapter, what dangers would there be from this type of regulation?

On the other hand, there are many laws in the United States governing parental behavior toward children and prohibiting child abuse and neglect. Shouldn't the failure to obtain medical care that would probably have eliminated their son's pain and saved his life be considered the ultimate act of child abuse? Even if adults have a right to use whatever type of healing practice they choose, shouldn't society require orthodox

medical care for children (after all, wasn't Robyn too young to adopt Christian Science as his own religious philosophy)?

In this particular case, the Twitchells were convicted of involuntary manslaughter. They were sentenced to 10 years probation and required to take their remaining children for regular visits to a pediatrician. In 1993, the conviction was overturned on a legal technicality. However, a spokesperson for the prosecutor's office stated that the law now clearly stated that parents could not sacrifice the lives of their children in the name of religious freedom.

GLOSSARY

acupuncture
alternative medicine
chiropractic
Christian Science healing
complementary medicine

curanderismo
dual model of care
integrative medicine
religious exemption laws
spiritual healing

REFERENCES

Angell, Marcia, and Jerome P. Kassirer. 1998 "Alternative Medicine: The Risks of Untested and Unregulated Remedies." *New England Journal of Medicine*, 339:839–841.

Avery, Charlene. 1991 "Native American Medicine: Traditional Healing." *Journal of the American Medical Association*, 265:2271, 2273.

Barnes, Patricia M., Barbara Bloom, and Richard L. Nahin. 2008 "Complementary and Alternative Medicine Use among Adults and Children: United States, 2007." *National Health Statistics Report*, Number 12. Hyattsville, MD: National Center for Health Statistics.

Bearon, Lucille B., and Harold G. Koenig. 1990 "Religious Cognitions and Use of Prayer in Health and Illness." *The Gerontologist*, 30:249–253.

Benor, Daniel J. 1984 "Psychic Healing." Pp. 165–190 in *Alternative Medicines: Popular and Policy Perspectives*, J. Warren Salmon (ed.). New York: Tavistock.

Benson, Herbert, Jeffery A. Dusek, Jane B. Sherwood, Peter Lam, Charles F. Bethea, William

Carpenter, Sidney Levitsky, Peter C. Hill, Donald W. Clem, Manoj K. Jain, David Drumel, Stephen L. Kopecky, Paul S. Mueller, Dean Marek, Sue Rollins, and Patricia L. Hibberd. 2006 "Study of the Therapeutic Effects of Intercessory Prayer (STEP) in Cardiac Bypass Patients: A Multicenter Randomized Trial of Uncertainty and Certainty of Receiving Intercessory Prayer." *American Heart Journal*, 151:934–942.

Beyerstein, Barry L. 2001 "Alternative Medicine and Common Errors of Reasoning." *Academic Medicine*, 76:230–237.

Buchwald, Dedra, Janette Beals, and Spero M. Manson. 2000 "Use of Traditional Health Practices among Native Americans in a Primary Care Setting." *Medical Care*, 38:1191–1199.

Caplan, Ronald L. 1984 "Chiropractic." Pp. 80–113 in *Alternative Medicines: Popular and Policy Perspectives*, J. Warren Salmon (ed.). New York: Tavistock.

Clarke, Tainya C., Lindsey I. Black, Barbara J. Stussman, Patricia M. Barnes, and Richard L.

Nahin. 2015 *Trends in the Use of Complementary Health Approaches among Adults: United States, 2002–2012*. National Health Statistics Reports, Number 79. Hyattsville, MD: National Center for Health Statistics.

Coe, Rodney M. 1970 *Sociology of Medicine*. New York: McGraw-Hill.

Donnelly, William J., J. Elisabeth Spykerboer, and Y.H. Thong. 1985 "Are Patients Who Use Alternative Medicine Dissatisfied with Orthodox Medicine?" *The Medical Journal of Australia*, 142:539–541.

Geisler, Carol, Corjena Cheung, Stasia J. Steinhagen, Peggy Neubeck, and Alvina D. Brueggemann. 2015 "Nurse Practitioner Knowledge, Use, and Referral of Complementary/Alternative Therapies." *Journal of the American Association of Nurse Practitioners*, 27:380–388.

Gevitz, Norman. 1988 *Other Healers: Unorthodox Medicine in America*. Baltimore, MD: The Johns Hopkins University Press.

———. 1989 "The Chiropractors and the AMA: Reflections on the History of the Consultation Clause." *Perspectives in Biology and Medicine*, 32:281–299.

Glik, Deborah C. 1988 "Symbolic, Ritual, and Social Dynamics of Spiritual Healing." *Social Science and Medicine*, 27:1197–1206.

Goldner, Melinda. 1999 "How Alternative Medicine is Changing the Way Consumers and Practitioners Look at Quality, Planning of Services, and Access in the United States." *Research in the Sociology of Health Care*, 16:55–74.

Goldstein, David N. 1972 "The Cult of Acupuncture." *Wisconsin Medical Journal*, 71:14–16.

Goldstein, Michael S. 1999 *Alternative Health Care*. Philadelphia, PA: Temple University Press.

Gottschalk, Stephen. 1988 "Spiritual Healing on Trial: A Christian Scientist Reports." *The Christian Century*, 105:602–605.

Grzywacz, Joseph G., Cynthia K. Swerken, Rebecca H. Neiberg, Wei Lang, Ronny A. Bell, Sara A. Quandt, and Thomas A. Arcury. 2007 "Age, Ethnicity, and Use of Complementary and Alternative Medicine in Health Self-Management." *Journal of Health and Social Behavior*, 48:84–98.

Hoffman, Diane E., and Ellen Weber. 2010 "Medical Marijuana and the Law." *New England Journal of Medicine*, 362:1453–1457.

Hunt, Linda M., Nedal H. Arar, and Laurie L. Akana. 2000 "Herbs, Prayer, and Insulin: Use of Medical and Alternative Treatments by a Group of Mexican American Diabetes Patients." *Journal of Family Practice*, 49:216–223.

Kiev, Ari. 1968 *Curanderismo: Mexican-American Folk Psychiatry*. New York: Free Press.

Kilgore, Christine. 1998 "Alternative Medicine: Probing Its Core." *Health Measures*, 3:26–30.

Kim, Catherine, and Yeong Kwok. 1998 "Navajo Use of Native Healers." *Archives of Internal Medicine*, 158:2245–2249.

King, Dara E., Jeffrey Sobol, and Bruce R. DeForge. 1988 "Family Practice Patients' Experiences and Beliefs in Faith Healing." *Journal of Family Practice*, 27:505–508.

Knoki-Wilson, Ursula M. 1983 "Nursing Care of American Indian Patients." Pp. 271–295 in *Ethnic Nursing Care*, Modesta S. Orque, Bobbie Bloch, and Lidia S. Monroy (eds.). St. Louis, MO: C.V. Mosby.

———. 1992 Lecture: "Navajo Traditional Healing," Chinle, AZ, June 23.

Koenig, Harold G., Lucille B. Bearon, and Richard Dayringer. 1989 "Physician Perspectives on the Role of Religion in the Physician–Older Patient Relationship." *Journal of Family Practice*, 28:441–448.

Koenig, Harold G., Michael E. McCullough, and David B. Larson. 2001 *Handbook of Religion and Health*. New York: Oxford University Press.

Krajewski-Jaime, Elvia R. 1991 "Folk-Healing Among Mexican American Families as a Consideration in the Delivery of Child Welfare and Child Health Care Services." *Child Welfare*, 70:157–167.

Kronenfeld, Jennie J., and Cody Wasner. 1982 "The Use of Unorthodox Therapies and Marginal Practitioners." *Social Science and Medicine*, 16:1119–1125.

McCaffrey, Anne M., David M. Eisenberg, Anna T.R. Legedza, Roger B. Davis, and Russell S. Phillips. 2004 "Prayer for Health Concerns." *Archives of Internal Medicine*, 164:858–862.

Meeker, William C., and Scott Haldeman. 2002 "Chiropractic: A Profession at the Crossroads of Mainstream and Alternative Medicine." *Annals of Internal Medicine*, 136:216–227.

Melzack, Ronald, and Patrick Wall. 1965 "Pain Mechanisms: A New Theory." *Science*, 150: 971–979.

National Center for Complementary and Integrative Health. 2016a "Acupuncture." www. nccih.nih.gov/health/acupuncture/introduction. htm.

———. 2016b "Chiropractic." www.nccih.nih.gov/health/chiropractic/introduction.htm.

———. 2016c "Health Information." www.nccih.nih.gov/health/.

———. 2016d "What Is CAM?" www.nccih.nih.gov/health/whatiscam.

Nguyen, Long T, Roger B. Davis, Ted J. Kaptchuk, and Russell S. Phillips. 2011 "Use of Complementary and Alternative Medicine and Self-Rated Health Status: Results from a National Survey." *Journal of General Internal Medicine*, 26:399–404.

Padilla, Ricardo, Veronica Gomez, Stacy L. Biggerstaff, and Phillip S. Mehler. 2001 "Use of Curanderismo in a Public Health Care System." *Archives of Internal Medicine*, 161:1336–1340.

Pagan, Jose, and Mark V. Pauly. 2005 "Access to Conventional Medical Care and the Use of Complementary and Alternative Medicine." *Health Affairs*, 24:255–262.

Reed, Louis. 1932 *The Healing Cults*. Chicago, IL: University of Chicago Press.

Shim, Jae-Mahn, John Schneider, and Farr A. Curlin. 2014 "Patterns of User Disclosure of Complementary and Alternative Medicine (CAM) Use." *Medical Care,* 52:704–708.

Simpson, William F. 1989 "Comparative Longevity in a College Cohort of Christian Scientists." *Journal of the American Medical Association*, 262:1657–1658.

Skolnick, Andrew. 1990a "Religious Exemptions to Child Neglect Laws Still Being Passed Despite Convictions of Parents." *Journal of the American Medical Association*, 264:1226, 1229, 1233.

———. 1990b "Christian Scientists Claim Healing Efficacy Equal if Not Superior to That of Medicine." *Journal of the American Medical Association*, 264:1379–1381.

Snow, Loudell F. 1993 *Walkin' Over Medicine: Traditional Health Practices in African-American Life*. Boulder, CO: Westview Press.

Talbot, Nathan A. 1983 "The Position of the Christian Science Church." *New England Journal of Medicine*, 309:1641–1644.

Tilburt, Jon C., Farr A. Curlin, Ted J. Kaptchuk, Brian Clarridge, Dragana Blocic-Jankovic, Ezekiel J. Emanuel, and Franklin G. Miller. 2009 "Alternative Medicine Research in Clinical Practice." *Archives of Internal Medicine*, 169:670–677.

Versnik Nowak, Amy L., Joe DeGise, Amanda Daugherty, Richard O'Keefe, Samuel Sweard, Suma Setty, and Fanny Tang. 2015 "Prevalence and Predictors of Complementary and Alternative Medicine (CAM) Use among Ivy League College Students: Implications for Student Health Services." *Journal of American College Health*, 63:362–372.

Wardwell, Walter I. 1988 "Chiropractors: Evolution to Acceptance." Pp. 157–191 in *Other Healers: Unorthodox Medicine in America*, Norman Gevitz (ed.). Baltimore, MD: The Johns Hopkins University Press.

———. 1992 *Chiropractic: History and Evolution of a New Profession*. St. Louis, MO: Mosby Year Book.

Wolpe, Paul R. 1985 "The Maintenance of Professional Authority: Acupuncture and the American Physician." *Social Problems*, 32:409–424.

CHAPTER 12

The Physician–Patient Relationship: Background and Models

Learning Objectives

- Identify and explain each of the three key dimensions of the physician–patient relationship.

- Discuss the extent to which patients want to be fully informed about their health and be active participants in their health care. Identify and discuss the key reasons why patient expectations are often not met.

- Discuss the impact of race on physician attitudes and patient care.

- Identify and discuss ways in which the gender of the physician and the gender of the patient influence patient care.

- Discuss the issue of patient compliance with medical regimens from a sociological perspective.

Despite the increasing complexity of the health care system and the wide variety of healers and healing techniques that exist, the actual encounter between physician and patient remains a key element. In the United States, patients make about one billion visits to physicians' offices each year. These visits are typically the gateway to services throughout the health care system. Many people have an idealized picture of this relationship—a sick patient seeks comfort from a benevolent physician, the sincere and helpful patient places trust in the concerned and caring physician, and both do whatever is necessary to restore health to the patient.

In fact, neither patients nor physicians are so uncomplicated or behave in such a uniform manner, and the relationship between the two can be an elusive phenomenon to diagram. As sociologists, our goal is to help to clarify the relationships that actually develop between physicians and patients and to identify important influences on the relationship.

MODELS OF THE PHYSICIAN–PATIENT RELATIONSHIP

The Parsonian Model

Nature of the Relationship. Within sociology, Talcott Parsons (1951) pioneered efforts at explaining the sociocultural foundation of health care. He viewed the physician–patient relationship as a subsystem of the larger social system. The key values in this subsystem reflected key values in society; they were shared by physicians and patients as they entered a relationship.

According to Parsons, the physician–patient relationship is inevitably (and fortunately) an asymmetrical one. Parsons believed that three circumstances dictated that physicians play the key, powerful role within the dyad and govern the relationship with patients.

1. **Professional prestige.** This is based on the physician's medical expertise, years of training, and the societal legitimation of the physician as the ultimate authority on health matters.
2. **Situational authority.** It is the physician who has established the medical practice and is offering her or his services to patients who have admitted their own inadequacies by soliciting the physician.
3. **Situational dependency.** It is the patient who has assumed the role of supplicant by seeking out service, scheduling an appointment, often waiting past the scheduled time, answering the physician's questions, and allowing an examination to occur.

Throughout each encounter, the "competency gap" between physician and patient is highlighted as the patient is dependent on the physician and the resources of the physician's office. However, Parsons expected that physicians would use their power wisely in promoting patients' best interests, and that patients would accept this arrangement as being the most efficient means to enact cure.

Freidson's Criticisms of the Parsonian Model. Perhaps the most important criticism of Parsons' model is that it overstates the "mutuality of interests" between physician and patient and does not provide for the considerable variation that now exists in physician–patient encounters. Conflict theorists dispute the notion that physicians and patients interact harmoniously and develop mutually satisfactory relationships through cooperation and consensus. Eliot Freidson (1970) was a leading critic of the

Parsonian model and an advocate for a conflict approach. He contended that conflict and dissensus are inevitable in any relationship in which the parties have such different backgrounds and power is so unequally distributed.

The Szasz–Hollender Model

An early (and now classic) effort to modify the Parsonian model was developed by two M.D.s, Thomas Szasz and Marc Hollender (1956). Arguing that Parsons paid too little attention to the important influence of physiological symptoms, they developed their own typology of the physician–patient relationship, which includes three models.

The Activity–Passivity Model. This model closely parallels the asymmetrical relationship described by Parsons. The physician represents medical expertise, controls the communication flow between the two parties, and makes all important decisions. The patient is the supplicant, regarded as lacking in important information and necessarily relying on the knowledge and judgment of the physician. The relationship is akin to that of a parent and infant, in which the parent takes actions without need of explanation.

The Guidance–Cooperation Model. Szasz and Hollender view this form of interaction as typical of most medical encounters. The patient is acknowledged to have feelings, may be alarmed by the medical problem, and has certain hopes and aspirations for the outcome of the medical encounter. Compared with the activity–passivity model, the patient has increased involvement in providing information and making decisions with regard to treatment. While the physician is still in charge and has responsibility for guiding the encounter, the cooperation of the patient is sought. The physician is less autocratic in the sense that some explanation is provided to the patient, and the patient's assent to decisions is desired, but the physician retains the dominant position. Szasz and Hollender describe this relationship as being similar to that between a parent and an adolescent.

The Mutual Participation Model. Based on a view that egalitarian relationships are to be preferred in medicine, this model elevates the patient to the level of full participant. In this case, both physician and patient acknowledge that the patient must be a central player for the medical encounter to be successful. The patient knows more about her or his own situation—medical history, symptoms, and other relevant events—than does the physician. While the physician attempts to ask the proper questions to elicit key information, it is assumed that the patient also has an obligation to ensure that relevant information is disclosed.

In order for this type of relationship to work, Szasz and Hollender identify three essential traits that must be present. First, both participants must have approximately equal power (it is similar to a relationship between two adults); second, there must be some feeling of mutual interdependence (i.e., a need for each other); and finally, they must engage in interaction that will in some ways be satisfying to both parties.

Because this model "requires" more from the patient, Szasz and Hollender suggest that it may be less appropriate for children or those who are mentally deficient, poorly educated, or very immature. On the other hand, those who are more intelligent or sophisticated, who have broader experiences, and who are more eager to take care of themselves may find this to be the only satisfying relationship.

KEY DIMENSIONS OF THE PHYSICIAN–PATIENT RELATIONSHIP

An appropriate model of the physician–patient relationship must acknowledge the considerable differences that exist among physicians and patients about what should occur within the relationship. The following three dimensions of the relationship are key:

1. The appropriate model of health (a belief in the biomedical or biopsychosocial model of health) as viewed by physician and patient.
2. The primary ethical obligation of the physician (patient autonomy or beneficence) as viewed by physician and patient.
3. The extent of commitment to and realization of genuine therapeutic communication.

The actual relationship that develops between a given physician and a given patient is determined by the orientations held by both parties. This is not to deny that the physician is in a very powerful position. For the reasons enumerated by Parsons and elaborated upon by many others, physicians have the potential to command the decisive voice. However, many physicians now reject this position, and many patients have been socialized not to let them assume it.

The Appropriate Model of Health

The Biomedical Model. As scientific discoveries produced meaningful explanations of diseases and effective medical treatments, the **biomedical model** of health became the dominant therapeutic orientation—a position that it held for most of the last century. Biomedical medicine is essentially disease oriented or illness oriented rather than patient oriented. The key to effective medical care is believed to be correct diagnosis of some physiological aberration followed by proper application of the curative agent. Physicians seek to learn all they can about symptoms and abnormalities so that they can provide the appropriate "magic bullet."

Consideration of social, psychological, and behavioral dimensions of illness has little place in this framework because it appears unnecessary.

Engel (1977:129) cited one health authority speaking at a Rockefeller Foundation seminar who urged that "medicine concentrate on the 'real' diseases and not get lost in the psychosociological underbrush. The physician should not be saddled with problems that have arisen from the abdication of the theologian and the philosopher." Another speaker had advocated "a disentanglement of the organic elements of disease from the psychosocial elements of human malfunction."

This biomedical focus has been reflected in medical education, which has surely helped to sustain it. Both coursework and clinical experience have emphasized the biological basis of disease and illness, while psychological and social factors have traditionally received little attention.

The Biopsychosocial Model. While there have always been individuals who lobbied for a broader-based approach to health care (George Engel, a professor of psychiatry and medicine at the University of Rochester Medical School, was a key figure during his career), it was not until the 1970s that the campaign flourished. Engel argued that the benefits of the biomedical approach need not be sacrificed while incorporating psychosocial matters, and that both are needed to provide optimal health care.

To provide a basis for understanding the determinants of disease and arriving at rational treatments and patterns of health care, a medical model must also take into account the patient, the social context in which he or she lives, and the complementary system devised by society to deal with the disruptive effects of illness—that is, the physician role and the health care system. This requires a **biopsychosocial model** (Engel, 1977:132).

While discussing the development of primary care as a medical specialty, Quill (1982) emphasized its potential for applying the biopsychosocial approach. He suggested that the following four principles distinguish broad-based primary

care from the traditional disease-dependent care. In primary care:

1. The patient is addressed as a whole person, whether or not he or she has a disease.
2. The doctor–patient relationship is continuous, at all stages of the patient's life, through sickness and health, until either the physician or the patient dies, moves, or decides to terminate the relationship.
3. The physician utilizes both biotechnical skills and interpersonal skills to help the patient.
4. Both the patient and the physician make explicit, and then negotiate, their respective needs and expectations (Quill, 1982).

Current Assessment. The extent to which physicians employ the biomedical or biopsychosocial approach can be analyzed by their efforts to identify psychosocial concerns of patients. Three empirical questions can be posed. First, do many patients have specific psychosocial concerns? Second, do patients want their physicians to consider these concerns? Third, do physicians attempt to do so?

Many researchers have formulated a specific list of social or psychological matters that may affect health status, and then ask patients and/or physicians if these matters have been discussed with individual patients. For example, the "Psychosocial Concern Index Taxonomy for Provider Behavior" developed by Campbell, Neikirk, and Hosokawa (1990) identifies matters such as family and interpersonal relationships, socioeconomic status, work environment and activities, sexual activity, nutritional patterns, and self-care practices—all topics that may influence health, but topics that many physicians do not routinely discuss.

Research shows that as many as half of patient visits to primary care providers include psychosocial complaints (Robinson and Roter,

1999). Most patients presenting themselves to a physician do not have a serious physical disorder; in general medical practice, estimates are that two-thirds or more are without a serious physical ailment.

What then is the motivation for so many physician contacts being initiated for non-biomedical reasons? Barsky (1981) summarized the major reasons as being life stress and emotional distress (normal anxiety, grief, frustration, and fear), diagnosable psychiatric disorders (for which general medical physicians are seen more often than specialists), social isolation (people seeking advice, interpersonal stimulation, and a sense of belonging and sustenance that can be provided by a social support system), and informational needs (which are perhaps even greater than the need for treatment of symptoms).

Are patients genuinely interested in discussing these psychosocial concerns with their physician? Do these discussions actually occur? In one study, questionnaires were administered to 530 patients of a family practice medical center. A total of 281 questionnaires solicited information on what psychosocial concerns respondents would want their physician to address, whereas the remaining 249 questionnaires asked which concerns the respondents would expect their physician to address. Overall, the results showed that patients do want involvement across a wide range of psychosocial issues, but typically do not expect it to happen (Frowick et al., 1986).

A study conducted in 23 primary care practices found that more than 70 percent of the patients believed it was appropriate to seek help from primary care physicians for psychosocial problems, but less than one-third of those who had experienced such problems had discussed them with their physician. Providers frequently failed to recognize emotional distress and family difficulties (Good, Good, and Cleary, 1987).

These results are consistent with studies which have found that family physicians are unaware of most of what is happening in their patients' lives, and that less than 10 percent of the conversation during average medical visits centered on patient psychosocial concerns (Roter, Hall, and Katz, 1988). Medical students and residents often report ineffective training in handling psychosocial concerns, and many remain unconvinced that knowledge of these concerns will ultimately lead to better health outcomes (Astin et al., 2008). Some reasons that physicians commonly cite to explain their avoidance of psychosocial issues are detailed in the accompanying box, "Physician Avoidance of Psychosocial Aspects of Health Care."

Primary Ethical Obligation

Perhaps the most important ethical orientation of physicians relative to patient care is whether they give priority to patient autonomy or beneficence.

The Principle of Autonomy. Autonomy is a term derived from the Greek words for "self" and "rule, governance, or law." When applied to individuals, it refers to the concept of self-determination. Autonomous individuals are able to make their own choices and decisions and have them respected by others. The concept of autonomy makes three key assumptions:

1. An autonomous person is able to make rational and competent decisions following contemplative thought. People who are incapable of acting autonomously include those who are too young, or who are severely mentally retarded or have some significant mental disability, or who are coerced or unduly pressured into a decision by physicians or other health care professionals—or, more commonly, by family members ("You

IN THE FIELD

PHYSICIAN AVOIDANCE OF PSYCHOSOCIAL ASPECTS OF HEALTH CARE

Given the importance of attending to psychosocial concerns, why don't more physicians do this? Inadequate exposure in medical school to its importance is one answer, but there are more. Williamson, Beitman, and Katon (1981) wrote about their experience of teaching the biopsychosocial approach to family practice residents. They were confronted with three types of beliefs that inhibited the residents from thinking psychosocially about their patients.

First, some of the residents held the belief that the physician's primary role was to focus on organic disease, and that attending to psychosocial issues was either unrelated to illness, beyond their expertise, or more than they were able to handle. Second, some of the residents believed that patients wanted them to deal only with organic issues, and that they would

consider questions about psychosocial issues to be an invasion of privacy. Finally, some residents lacked confidence in their own ability to treat patients as people and to genuinely help patients through these kinds of problems.

Recent research has found that medical schools are now placing more emphasis on teaching communication skills and the psychosocial dimensions of patient care. Kern et al. (2005) have developed a set of initial questions and follow-up questions for a range of psychosocial issues (e.g., alcoholism, depression, low health literacy, and post-traumatic stress disorder). However, evidence suggests that these efforts to investigate psychosocial dimensions are frequently not modeled in the clinical setting, and may become extinguished because of this.

have the surgery or the kids and I are leaving").

2. A second assumption is that an action does not cause harm to others. The freedom of any individual to act stops short of causing harm to another; a decision to harm another incurs no obligation of respect.

3. Patients do not have the right to demand that physicians or other health care professionals violate a personal or professional moral code. For example, patients cannot make an unrestricted claim on some scarce resource (e.g., by demanding a liver transplant). This assumption was clearly expressed in the Elizabeth Bouvia case described in the accompanying box, "The Case of Elizabeth Bouvia."

Application of the principle of autonomy involves physicians ensuring that patients are

able to make fully informed decisions, and that those decisions are then respected. This does not limit professional expertise in diagnosis, developing a prognosis, making recommendations for treatment, or carrying out agreed-upon treatment. However, it does limit physicians in selection and pursuit of treatment without the patient's fully informed consent.

Informed Consent.   The **informed consent** requirement is a key mechanism to protect patient autonomy. Legally and ethically, patients who are able to exercise autonomy must be given all relevant information regarding their condition and alternative treatments, including the possible benefits, risks, costs, and other consequences and implications. For a genuine informed consent to be obtained, the patient must be competent, be given all of the

IN THE FIELD

THE CASE OF ELIZABETH BOUVIA

In the summer of 1983, Elizabeth Bouvia, a 26-year-old woman with physically incapacitating cerebral palsy, checked into Riverside (California) Hospital and stated her intention to starve herself to death. She said that her deteriorating condition (an inability to feed or care for herself in any way, increasingly painful arthritis, and physical incontinence) made life not worth living. She said that she was unable to take her own life and wished the hospital to provide hygienic care and pain relief while she starved herself to death.

The hospital refused her request and made plans to force-feed her should she not eat of her own volition. The chief of psychiatry at the hospital was quoted as saying "The court cannot order me to be a murderer nor to conspire with my staff and employees to murder Elizabeth." The story became public, and the American Civil Liberties Union decided to represent Elizabeth's wishes in court.

Eventually, the court ruled against Elizabeth Bouvia. The judge acknowledged prior court decisions (and the ethical principle) that competent, informed patients have the right to refuse medical care, even if their refusal contradicts medical advice or might shorten their life. However, he concluded that Elizabeth's plan not to take food and water in the hospital involved more than a refusal of treatment. Because she desired care while she died of malnutrition and dehydration, she was, in essence, asking hospital staff to assist in a suicide or direct killing that was morally and professionally unacceptable to them.

While the *Bouvia* decision carried several ramifications, and was later overturned, it has been interpreted as supporting the principle that neither physicians nor hospital staff may be forced to act in ways that they interpret as violating a professional or personal moral code.

---

information that might affect their decision making, comprehend this information, and make a voluntary choice. For surgery, other invasive procedures, or procedures with any significant risk, patients are typically required to sign an official informed consent form. However, the spirit of informed consent is no less applicable—although often less followed—in the medical office.

The Principle of Beneficence. An alternative guiding principle for physicians is **beneficence**—that is, doing good for the patient. While the general meaning of the concept is to promote goodness, kindness, or charity, in the medical context it refers to physicians taking whatever

actions (e.g., surgery or prescribing a medication) are considered to be in the patient's best interest.

Prioritizing Autonomy and Beneficence. An ethical dilemma arises when doing good for the patient (beneficence) conflicts with an informed patient's wishes (patient autonomy). It often happens that a rational and competent patient chooses to take an action that a physician believes is not in the patient's best interest. At this point, physicians decide whether it is more important to allow the patient to make her or his own choice or to act in a manner believed to be in the patient's best interest. A physician is said to be showing **paternalism** when she or he overrides a patient's wishes and takes action that is presumed to be in the patient's best interest but is unwanted by the patient. This situation also creates a choice for the patient. If a patient desires self-determination, and the physician refuses to grant it, the patient can try to be persuasive, accede to the physician's wishes, or shop for another physician. Of course, in many cases the patient would not be aware of physician behavior that is molding or limiting their choices.

The accompanying box, "Autonomy and Paternalism in Israel," describes how the tension between these orientations is worked out in another country.

Current Assessment. Traditionally, most physicians have automatically made decisions for patients, and neither physicians nor patients gave much thought to the importance of patient self-determination. However, the principle of autonomy has gained significant stature in the last 60 years. Today, most physicians express positive attitudes about patient participation in medical decision making based on the principle of autonomy, although many still see themselves as the ultimate decision maker (McGuire et al., 2005).

Researchers have attempted to study desire for autonomy by studying patients' requests for information from physicians and their desired

---

IN COMPARATIVE FOCUS

AUTONOMY AND PATERNALISM IN ISRAEL

In 1991, the U.S. Congress passed the Patient Self-Determination Act (PSDA) as a means to protect and highlight patient autonomy. The PSDA requires hospitals and other institutional providers to inform patients that they have a legal right to make their own health care decisions (through the process of informed consent), to prepare an advance directive to indicate how they would like to be treated if they are unable to make their own decisions at some future time, and to refuse unwanted medical treatment. It is a clear expression of the importance of patient autonomy in the United States.

In 1996, Israel passed the Israeli Patient Rights Act (IPRA) to address some of the same issues. The IPRA guarantees that Israel will provide universal health care coverage (which, of course, is not provided in the United States) and embraces the concept of informed consent. However, Israelis were not provided with a right to refuse unwanted medical treatment, and physicians were not obligated to respect the

wishes of any patient making an informed refusal of treatment. In those cases, the matter is submitted to an ethics committee, which typically requires that the treatment be given for as long as it is expected to help the patient's condition, and there is some expectation that the patient will give consent *after* the procedure.

The U.S. law is rooted in the importance of the individual and in the right of individuals to determine their own course of action without paternalistic intervention by the health care provider. Israel is a communitarian society with a high level of collective consciousness, mutual concern, and interdependence. In communitarian societies, individual rights are often subservient to collectively defined ideals and goals. Ensuring that health care is available to all citizens is one aspect of the collective ideal, and ensuring that individuals receive lifesaving treatment, with or without their consent, is another aspect (Gross, 1999).

participation in actual decision making. In a study of 106 rehabilitation medicine patients, Beisecker and Beisecker (1990) found that patients overwhelmingly want as much information as possible. However, there is ambivalence regarding the proper decision maker. While few subjects believe that the patient should make decisions by him- or herself, excluding the physician, many believe that it should be a shared process, and many are most comfortable with the physician being the primary decision maker.

This pattern was affirmed in research on participation in medical decision making by more than 600 patients at a Boston hospital. Based on responses to a series of questions, the authors placed each patient in one of four categories: (1) pre-contemplation (do not participate and do not intend to), 17.2 percent of patients; (2) contemplation (do not participate but contemplating doing so), 6.9 percent of patients; (3) preparation (participate to some degree), 36.1 percent of patients; and (4) action (participate fully), 39.8 percent of patients. What predicted the patients' level of participation? Patients who were older, less educated, had greater severity of illness, and were most trusting of the physician had the lowest level of participation and the least interest in participating. Younger patients, the well-educated, those with less severe illnesses, and those with the most self-efficacy (confidence in their own decision making) wanted to be and were the most involved (Arora, Ayanian, and Guadagnoli, 2005).

The percentage of patients who want to participate in actual decision making has increased significantly during the last three decades. Research has found that when patients are provided with instruction in ways to be more effective participants in their own care and are given encouragement by physicians to participate, their desire for detailed information and participation in decision making increases (Fraenkel and McGraw, 2007). The situation

today with regard to living wills (see Chapter 16) illustrates this pattern. Research has shown that the vast majority of people want to have candid discussions with their physician about their options and preferences regarding end-of-life treatments, and want to have their wishes followed. However, many physicians do not engage their patients in conversations about this subject, they are sometimes unaware that particular patients have written a living will, and they are often unable to accurately predict the end-of-life treatment wishes of their patients.

Braddock et al. (1999) audiotaped more than 1,000 encounters between patients and primary care physicians or orthopedists in order to determine the extent to which the patients were genuinely informed decision makers. The criteria that they used included discussion of the nature of the decision and asking the patient to voice a preference. They judged that only 9 percent of all decisions made fulfilled their criteria for informed decision making. Routinely, the physicians failed to appropriately inform and involve the patient. Other studies have found the same pattern in other medical settings.

When patients do fully participate, it is often because they have been assertive and initiated their participation. In one study of patients at three clinical sites, most (84 percent) of the active participation of patients was initiated by the patients rather than being prompted by physician partnership building or supportive talk (Street et al., 2005). A study of women receiving care in an ultrasound clinic for reasons other than pregnancy found that those who were more assertive—repeating information when they thought the physician had not heard them, asking the physician to clarify information that they did not understand, and reminding the physician about screening tests—were in fact more likely to receive a mammogram than the patients who were less assertive (Andersen, Abullarade, and Urban, 2005).

Moreover, even on occasions when it may appear that physicians are seeking to involve the patient in decision making, they sometimes conduct themselves in such a way as to offer patients only an illusion of choice. In these situations, the physicians have essentially predetermined a course of action and then present the options in such a way as to steer the patient toward the physician's preferred course (Zussman, 1992).

Establishment of Therapeutic Communication

It may seem obvious that effective and meaningful communication between physician and patient is to be desired. However, this common-sense understanding understates the therapeutic importance of good communication, and would certainly not predict its lack of attention in medical education. This section addresses four questions. (1) What is meant by "therapeutic communication?" (2) Does it routinely develop?

(3) What barriers prevent it from developing more often? (4) How can it be facilitated?

Therapeutic Communication. There are three components of **therapeutic communication**. (1) The physician engages in full and open communication with the patient and feels free to ask questions about psychosocial as well as physical conditions. (2) The patient provides full and open information to the physician and feels free to ask questions and seek clarifications. (3) A genuine rapport develops between physician and patient.

The Frequent Absence of Therapeutic Communication. Although many physicians place a high value on developing therapeutic communication with patients, and routinely do so, therapeutic communication does not exist in many physician–patient dyads. This is because patients do not feel comfortable with the physician, do not feel free to talk openly about their worries and concerns (and sometimes even

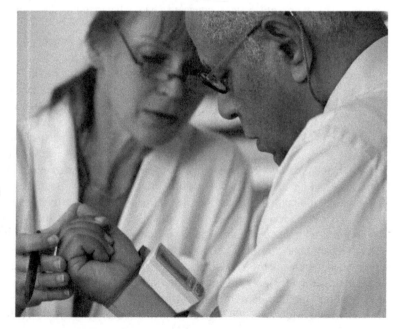

Providing ample time for patients, engaging in full and open communication, and establishing rapport are all ways in which physicians encourage therapeutic communication.
© iStock @ Thomas_EyeDesign

symptoms), have questions that go unasked or unanswered, and do not understand information that is provided. These are not satisfying encounters for most patients.

Barriers to Therapeutic Communication. Development of genuine therapeutic communication requires considerable effort, even for those committed to it as an ideal. This is due to the fact that there are several inherent obstacles to open communication in the medical setting.

1. *Setting of the medical encounter.* Most physician–patient contacts occur in the physician's office or in a hospital—settings that are not conducive to making the patient feel at ease. The unpleasant odors, the many sick people who seem to be invading each other's space, and the paperwork requirements all contribute to discomfort. There are few ways to relax except by reading current editions of esoteric magazines or news magazines that were timely in some previous year.

2. *Length of the medical encounter.* Genuine therapeutic communication cannot be developed in brief abbreviated segments of time. The average length of an office visit with a primary care physician is about 15 minutes. Because some patients require more than 15 minutes, some receive less time. Of course, only a fraction of this time is spent discussing the patient's illness.

3. *The mental state of the patient.* It would be a rare person who could communicate best when feeling worst. Most patients are feeling ill, are uncomfortable, may be anxious about their health and fearful of what will be learned, and are in awe of the physician. Not surprisingly, many do not think, speak, or hear clearly.

4. *Mismatched expectations of physicians and patients.* Patients go to a physician with symptoms, feelings of discomfort, and an inability to carry on normal activities. They seek clarification and information, and they want to know what they need to do to get better. Physicians, on the other hand, have been trained to convert patient complaints into medical diagnoses. Sometimes uncomfortable dealing with psychosocial issues, they evade discussions of anxieties and fears, and focus on the "medical facts." What the patient may need most is what the physician is least prepared to offer. These contrary expectations make therapeutic communication unlikely. One recent small study found that physician and patient priorities in an encounter were aligned in 69 percent of encounters studied. Although this is an impressive figure, it still allowed only partially aligned priorities in 19 percent of cases, and totally unaligned priorities in 12 percent of cases (Tomsik et al., 2014).

5. *Language barriers.* The increasing diversification of the U.S. population has brought with it an increasing number of people with limited proficiency in the English language. In 2015, it was estimated that more than 60 million Americans (about 21 percent of the population) spoke a language other than English at home, and that many of these individuals understood little or no English. Although an increasing number of health care sites offer interpreters in Spanish or whatever other language is most familiar to their patients, many sites do not do this. In these cases there is little likelihood of therapeutic communication taking place (Jacobs et al., 2006), and less favorable outcomes occur as a result.

6. *Physician communication style.* Research on physician–patient communication conducted over the last three decades has demonstrated remarkable consistency regarding two key patterns. First, physicians often "talk down" to patients, are abrupt with them, and discourage open communication. Some physicians offer little greeting to patients as they enter the room. Going after "just the

facts," they provide no opening for patients to talk about their concerns or how they perceive current problems relate to other events in their life. These physicians may interrupt patients or otherwise signal a lack of interest in what is being said. They maintain spatial distance when not conducting a physical examination, and do everything possible to reinforce social distance. Buller and Buller (1987) refer to this as the *control* style of communication, and the net result is predictable—almost no therapeutic communication occurs. Often physicians who adopt this style do not allow patients to complete their opening statement, and also they often do not respond directly to patient questions. The second or alternative style, *affiliation,* includes such behaviors as friendliness, empathy, genuineness, candor, openness to conversation, and a nonjudgmental attitude, and is designed to establish a positive relationship with the patient.

Candace West, in an intriguing book entitled *Routine Complications: Troubles with Talk Between Doctors and Patients* (1984), confirmed this asymmetrical communication process. West transcribed 532 pages of physician–patient encounters in a family practice center in the southern United States. She examined such factors as the number of times each party interrupted the other (male physicians were most likely to interrupt), who asked the questions and who answered (physicians asked almost all the questions), and who invoked laughter (patients invited laughter more often, but there was often no response). However, some encounters did display a symmetrical communication pattern.

Second, patients often do not understand the terminology used by physicians. People who have learned the jargon of a particular subject or profession often forget that most others have not done so. Even terms that are familiar to most college students, such as "eating disorder" and "depression," are not understood by many patients. These are commonly used terms in the medical setting, yet when they are used, many patients misunderstand the message being communicated. Recent studies have confirmed the continuing use of medical jargon that is not clarified for the patient (Castro et al., 2007). Not surprisingly, many physicians underestimate their own use of medical jargon.

Physician Frustration with the Communication Process. Physicians also report frequent feelings of frustration with patient interaction. Recent research identified that the most common sources of frustration reported by physicians were (1) patients' lack of adherence (not accepting responsibility for their own health and not following through on recommended therapies), (2) patients with a large number of complaints requiring an extensive amount of time, (3) patients being demanding, controlling, and complaining, and (4) patients with problems associated with alcohol, other drugs, and chronic pain. In more than half of the self-identified frustrating patient visits, the physician perceived the patient to be the source of the problem (Levinson et al., 1993).

These feelings of frustration may be perceived by patients and further inhibit effective communication. A recent study (Frosch et al., 2012) in San Francisco found that even relatively affluent and well-educated patients often perceive their physician to be authoritarian, feel compelled to defer to the physician in a clinical encounter, and consciously fear being categorized as a difficult patient. These feelings prevented them from participating more fully in their own care.

THE CURRENT MOVE TO PATIENT-CENTERED CARE

In the last few years, clinical and social science analysts have initiated a major move toward patient-centered care—that is, the provision "of care that is respectful of and responsive to individual patient preferences, needs, and values, and ensuring that patient values guide all clinical decisions" (Institute of Medicine, 2001). In one sense it is a statement of advocacy regarding the three principal components of the physician–patient relationship, because it endorses a biopsychosocial model of medicine that values patient autonomy and the development of therapeutic communication. It goes beyond the simple education of patients about healthy behaviors, diagnoses, treatments, and prognoses, but it does not mean simply acceding altogether to patient wants and desires.

Rather, it is a fully fledged effort in designing the delivery of health care to fully consider the patient's cultural traditions, personal values, family situation, and social circumstances. The emphasis is on providing ready access to coordinated care for all people, treating the whole person, developing effective communication, empowering patients, and developing physical spaces to facilitate effective care. The intent is to shift health care's orientation from the physician as centerpiece to the patient as centerpiece. If accomplished, the health care system would be modified to fit and prioritize the patient rather than having the patient adapt to the system.

The key to enhancing patient participation and involvement is now referred to as patient activation. **Patient activation** describes "the skills and confidence that equip patients to become actively engaged in their health care" (Hibbard and Greene, 2013:207). This entails having individuals assume greater responsibility for managing their own health and their own health care. It would include making good decisions about lifestyle—for example, about diet, exercise, and tobacco use—and knowledgably using health care resources available to them. It would be a cultural shift toward individuals being more responsible, but also a shift in creating environments in which positive and appropriate health actions are encouraged.

An important pathway to achieving patient activation is increasing every person's **health literacy**—a term which is often focused on the individual level, but is increasingly being viewed more globally as "the degree to which individuals, organizations, and communities obtain, process, understand, and share health information and services needed to make appropriate health decisions" (Seubert, 2009). Typical estimates are that only 12 or 13 percent of adults in the United States are at a proficient health literacy level, while more than a third have difficulty with tasks such as understanding patient handouts, following medication instructions, or reading nutrition labels. Thus health literacy not only has an important individual dimension, but it also has an important dimension of health care professionals and organizations working together to empower and enable patients to make informed health care decisions and choices.

What is the reason for the current push toward patient activation and health literacy? It is because there is accumulating research evidence that they lead to significant benefits to individuals, patients, and the health care system. Research has revealed that patients with lower patient activation levels:

- Are more likely to report unmet medical needs
- Are more likely to have unmet prescription drug needs
- Are more likely to delay care
- Have lower levels of preventive health behaviors and preventive care
- Are less likely to engage in self-management of health conditions
- Are less likely to seek and use health care information from available health sources
- Appear to get less support from their providers in managing their health

- Are less likely to report that their provider helped them to set goals and taught them how to self-manage their condition
- Are less likely to follow through on lifestyle changes and comply with treatment plans
- Are less likely to ask questions (Seubert, 2009).

Research has also shown that those with lower levels of health literacy:

- Are more likely to report poor health status
- Are less likely to obtain preventive health services
- Are twice as likely to be hospitalized
- Remain in the hospital for more days during each admission
- Are less likely to comply with recommended treatment
- Are more likely to make medication errors
- Incur higher health care costs

- Are less likely to ask health care questions (Seubert, 2009).

Advocates for strengthening the emphasis on patient activation and health literacy will need to be careful not to slip into a "blaming the victim" mentality. However, as long as the emphasis remains on the important contributions made by health care providers and the health care system in addition to individuals, many see this movement as having significant potential for health care reform. For example, Koh et al. (2013) recommend that health literacy should become an organizational value of health care organizations that is part of all aspects of planning and design, including self-management support, delivery system design, shared decision-making support, clinical information systems to track and plan patient care, and helping patients to access community resources.

IN THE FIELD

CHANGING THE PHYSICIAN–PATIENT RELATIONSHIP

In addition to the "patient-centered care" movement, at least four other recent developments are changing the physician–patient relationship:

1. The use of comparative effectiveness research. Historically, health care providers have used a variety of techniques to develop treatment recommendations. These have included information learned in medical school and in continuing education, personal experience with previous patients, peer consultation, personal intuition, and reading medical journals. The fact that there is considerable variety among physicians in formulating treatment plans for similar diagnoses stems in part from differences in these learning experiences. Recently, a major drive

has been underway to conduct comparative effectiveness research—that is, research comparing active treatments, and also on which treatments overall have worked best for particular diagnoses—and to encourage physicians to follow what has been learned. If it was to be widely implemented, variation among physicians would decrease.

2. The increased use of patient satisfaction surveys in physician reimbursement. There is some inconsistency in the results of research that has examined the consequences of patients being satisfied or dissatisfied with their health care providers. Nevertheless, some research has found that satisfied patients are more likely to maintain

a continuing relationship with their provider and are more likely to comply with medical instructions. Hospitals are looking more closely at patient satisfaction data in an effort to boost community reputation. Beginning in 2013, part of physicians' reimbursement from Medicare has been based on patient satisfaction data, thus giving physicians a financial incentive to establish more satisfied patients.

3. The increased public availability of health information. Through both the Internet and direct-to-consumer advertising, medical knowledge is increasingly available to the general public (Boyer and Lutfey, 2010). The number of health-related apps is increasing every day, and enables users to monitor their health in previously unavailable ways. Various consumer groups—including the influential American Association of Retired Persons—are encouraging individuals to procure and use this information to their health benefit. Although many physicians have yet to be convinced of the utility of the widespread availability of all this information, it is highly improbable that it will decrease in popularity.

4. The increasing incorporation of and financial incentives to use electronic health records (EHRs). EHRs are an electronic version of a patient's medical record, including background information, medical history, medications, vital signs, immunizations, laboratory data, radiology reports, and billing information. EHRs are designed to eliminate the need to track down a patient's previous paper medical records, and hopefully assist in ensuring accurate and legible data. The federal government offers incentives to medical providers to make meaningful use of EHRs (DeAngelis, 2014).

EHRs are increasingly being used as part of the patient activation process. They can be useful in electronic messaging, facilitating patient access to personal medical records and test results, tracking chronic illness management, and providing health education (White and Danis, 2013).

> The fundamental change between past and present medicine is access to information. There used to be a steep inequality between doctor and patient. No longer. As people understand the risks as well as the benefits of modern medicine, we increasingly desire more information before we are willing to rely on trust to see us through. This need to be transparent about what doctors know (and what they do not), to engage in a consultation on closer to equal terms with patients, has changed the way medicine is practiced. (Horton, 2003:40)

In a 2013 Institute of Medicine workshop, discussion of patient-centeredness had shifted somewhat from 2001, and referred more to education of patients to work effectively with physicians in using clinical data and available information on health and disease (Millenson, 2014). The three changes listed in this box all illustrate the new emphasis.

THE INFLUENCE OF RACE, SEXUAL ORIENTATION AND GENDER IDENTITY, AND GENDER ON THE PHYSICIAN–PATIENT RELATIONSHIP

Ideally, physicians offer their best professional efforts to every patient. This does not mean that every patient will be treated in exactly the same manner—that is unrealistic. College professors do not treat all students the same, clergy do not treat all parishioners the same, and physicians do not treat all patients the same. However, a reasonable objective is that physicians will impartially deliver their best efforts to every patient. Yet considerable empirical research and anecdotal evidence document that physicians have a more difficult time working with some patients than with others. This causes less effective interactions with, for example, patients from lower socioeconomic groups, or patients with a specific gender identity, or patients who are of a different gender, race, or ethnic group to the medical provider.

The existence of cultural stereotypes, prejudice, and discrimination has been and remains a powerful force in the United States. When explicit biases and personal discrimination (unjust treatment of members of a particular group that are committed by an individual) are enacted, inequities in life circumstances naturally result. When institutional discrimination (unjust treatment of members of a particular group by practices that are embedded in large organizations such as governments and corporations) exists, the oppressive forces on entire groups of people can be enormous. These forces have certainly existed in health care.

Recently, considerable attention in the provision of health care services has been focused on the concept of **implicit bias**. An implicit bias is one that may not be consciously endorsed, intended, or even recognized, but which nevertheless exists. Research suggests that such implicit biases do contribute to health care inequities by shaping provider behavior and generating differences in medical treatment based on factors such as socioeconomic status, gender, gender identity, and race. For example, research has discovered that physicians experience higher levels of anxiety and frustration when working with lower-class patients, are less interested in the patient encounter, and spend less time with the patient. Because implicit biases are unrecognized, they can be especially difficult to monitor and control, but they can exert a very strong influence on behavior (Chapman, Kaatz, and Carnes, 2013; Hall et al., 2015).

Why does this discomfort or anxiety exist in some provider–patient relationships? Shim has proposed that these patterns are grounded in the perceived **cultural health capital** of the patient. Following on from the work of French sociologist, anthropologist, and philosopher Pierre Bourdieu, she conceives of cultural capital as referring to the "repertoire of cultural skills, verbal and nonverbal competencies, attitudes and behaviors, and interactional styles" that people have to one degree or another and that may be prized or not at certain historical moments. Shim (2010:4), like Bourdieu, sees cultural capital as being context-specific, so she uses the term "cultural health capital" to denote:

- Knowledge of medical topics and vocabulary, which in turn depends upon an understanding of scientific rationality and health literacy
- Knowledge of what information is relevant to health care personnel
- The skills to communicate health-related information to providers in a medically intelligible and efficient manner
- An enterprising disposition and a proactive stance toward health, both of which presuppose a sense of mastery and self-efficacy
- The ability to take an instrumental attitude toward one's body
- Belief in the value of, and the resources to practice, self-discipline
- An orientation toward the future and its control through calculation and action
- A sensitivity to interpersonal dynamics and the ability to adapt one's interactional styles
- The ability to communicate social privilege and resources that can act as cues of favorable social and economic status and consumer savvy.

These traits are especially valued in American culture, and are traits which embody many medical providers. They have become especially important at this juncture of history.

Over the course of the past four decades, this shifting health care landscape has intensified the demands placed on patients to be knowledgeable about how to maneuver through the health care bureaucracy and to be self-directive about their own care in a time of shortened appointments and heightened gate-keeping . . . Patients who possess or acquire and display an enterprising and proactive disposition, a fluency in biomedical concepts and language, bureaucratic know-how, and an interactional agility with authoritative experts are more able to successfully navigate such organizational complexity. The cultural expectations and responsibilities of contemporary patienthood—in terms of self-knowledge, self-surveillance, health promotion, disease management, and the like—have also escalated, at least in the United States. (Shim, 2010:6)

Thus provider–patient interactions are shaped in part by the cultural health capital brought to an interaction by the patient, and in part by the receptiveness of the provider and their willingness to work with the patient to develop cultural health capital. This is very much a micro perspective. However, Shim also advocates for understanding how broader social forces—including explicit biases and personal and institutional discrimination—confer advantages of social status, education, and power on some rather than others, and thus enable some to develop more cultural health capital. This adds a more macro-institutional perspective to her analysis.

Race

An expansive list of research studies has found that people of color in the United States experience disparities across the health care system (Feagin and Bennefield, 2014). They have less access to health care, less satisfactory interactions with medical providers, slower and less referral to a variety of medical procedures, and worse health outcomes. An increasing number of studies have found that many white physicians feel some discomfort in working with black patients. One study of 139 first-year medical students found that they expected to be significantly less comfortable when working with black patients, and they believed that black and Latino patients would be less likely to comply with medical regimens (Gregory, Wells, and Leake, 1987).

Recently, Hall et al. (2015) examined 15 studies of health care bias that met methodologically rigid criteria. They discovered that 14 of the studies found low to moderate levels of implicit racial and ethnic bias among health care professionals. Implicit bias towards black, Hispanic, Latino, Latina, and dark-skinned people was held by most of the providers, and was at about the same level as that found in the general population.

Does this implicit bias make any difference to provider–patient interactions and health outcomes? It seems that it does, according to many studies (Chapman, Kaatz, and Carnes, 2013; Sabin et al., 2009). African American patients rate their visits to physicians as being less participatory than do whites (Cooper-Patrick et al., 1999), they receive less supportive talk from physicians (Street et al., 2005), have lower levels of trust in their physician (Armstrong et al., 2013), receive less pain management control in emergency rooms (Shah et al., 2015), wait longer for medical care (Ray et al., 2015), are more likely to have felt discriminated against in the health care system (Cuffee et al., 2013), have a greater concern about harmful medical experimentation (Boulware et al., 2003), and have a lower survival rate from early-stage lung cancer, which is largely explained by lower rates of surgery (Bach et al., 1999).

Several studies have reported evidence of disparities in treatment for heart disease received by blacks and whites. For example, data from the National Hospital Discharge Survey showed that blacks were less likely than whites to receive cardiac catheterization, coronary angioplasty, and coronary artery bypass surgery even after controlling for age, health insurance, hospital, and condition. The authors concluded that the race of the patient influenced the likelihood of receiving these procedures (Giles et al., 1995). In a study of more than 5,000 Medicare recipients, Epstein et al. (2003) found that whites were more likely than blacks to receive clinically indicated revascularization procedures, and that the underuse by black patients was linked to higher mortality rates. Key documents published by the Institute of Medicine in 2003 and within the American Sociological Association's Series on How Race and Ethnicity Matter (Spalter-Roth, Lowenthal, and Rubio, 2005) have concluded that systematic racial bias in the provision of health care contributes to the unequal health outcomes among racial and ethnic groups.

Sexual Orientation and Gender Identity

Implicit and explicit biases have also been revealed in studies of the health care treatment of lesbian, gay, bisexual, and transgender individuals. In a study that lasted from 2006 to 2012 and included more than 2,300 medical doctors, more than 5,300 nurses, more than 8,500 mental health providers, and more than 2,700 other treatment providers, heterosexual providers had implicit preferences for treating heterosexual people over lesbian and gay people. Heterosexual nurses—both male and female—had the strongest implicit preference for treating heterosexual men as opposed to gay men. Among all groups of providers, implicit preferences were stronger than explicit preferences (Sabin, Riskind, and Nosek, 2015).

Transgender individuals sometime encounter the same kinds of negative response in the health care field. A recent study of transgender individuals discovered that many had experienced gender insensitivity, displays of discomfort, and verbal abuse by medical providers, and some

had received substandard care or been denied care altogether (Kosenko et al., 2013). This discrimination and associated stigma influence many transgender individuals to postpone seeking health care even when it is needed (Cruz, 2014).

Gender

More research has been conducted on the role of gender in the physician–patient relationship than on other background characteristics. This section focuses on both gender of the physician and gender of the patient.

Gender of the Physician. Weisman and Teitelbaum (1985) have suggested that physician gender could influence the physician–patient relationship in three ways:

1. *Systematic differences between male and female physicians in personality, attitudes, or interpersonal skills.* Weisman and Teitelbaum speculated that early gender-role socialization might result in female physicians being more nurturant and expressive while male physicians might be more reserved and less able to develop empathic relationships. On the other hand, females who have been sufficiently assertive to break through the traditional male stranglehold in medicine might be less likely to have been socialized to traditional gender roles, and/or the professional socialization that occurs in medical school might dissipate earlier socialization experiences.

2. *Alteration of the expectations that patients bring to the encounter.* This influence could occur in two ways. Patients who are expecting female physicians to be more nurturant and empathic may convey more information to them, allowing them greater opportunity to actually engage in a more caring relationship (a self-fulfilling prophecy), or patients may

simply see what they expect to see—a more nurturant and empathic female physician—even if actual practice style does not differ by gender.

3. *Alteration of the "status relationship" between physician and patient.* The key to this is the match or lack of match in gender between physician and patient. For example, a female patient seeing a female physician is more likely to have status congruence than a female patient seeing a male physician. This status congruence could contribute to openness in the relationship, extended rapport, and increased patient participation. This pattern was partially demonstrated in one study which found that female patients tended to be more satisfied with female than with male physicians, but that satisfaction of male patients was unrelated to physician gender (Derose et al., 2001).

The following sections examine the first two of these mechanisms of influence in the light of recent research.

Systematic Differences Between Female and Male Physicians. Several studies have identified aspects of practice style that are unaffected by physician gender. Female and male family practice physicians evaluate common medical problems in a similar manner; there are few differences in diagnoses, prescriptions of psychotropic medications, or frequency in hospitalizing patients among female and male psychiatrists; and female and male physicians react to patient deaths similarly and offer similar amounts of personal contact, availability, and follow-up with families after a loved one's death.

These similar practice styles are influenced by the professional socialization process. First-year female medical students do differ from their male counterparts in being more patient oriented and placing higher value on patient contact. However, these differences dissipate during medical school and the residency processes. The increased interest that first-year female medical students have compared with males in valuing the interpersonal, psychosocial, and preventive aspects of medicine diminishes by the end of medical school.

However, consistent differences between female and male physicians have been documented in two areas. First, female physicians demonstrate superior communication skills. Research indicates that female physicians spend more time with each patient, provide more opportunities for patients to talk, make more empathic statements, ask more questions, smile and nod more frequently, are more egalitarian in the patient relationship (Hall, Blanch-Hartigan, and Roter, 2011), and demonstrate a greater orientation to preventive services (Flocke and Gilchrist, 2005).

Second, female physicians express more sensitivity than male physicians to health-related "women's issues," including contraception, abortion, and discrimination against female physicians and patients. These gender differences exist in medical school, throughout residency, and into practice, and may be a key indicator to women of overall physician sensitivity. Moreover, research has shown that female physicians are more likely than male physicians to perform mammograms and Pap smears, and that this difference persists even when health status and background characteristics are controlled for (Lurie et al., 1997).

This finding is consistent with that of several studies which have found that women's strongest preference for a female physician occurs in relation to women's health problems, including cervical screening, breast screening by physical examination, breast screening by mammography, and instruction in breast self-examination. Moreover, while female physicians spend more time than male physicians with each patient, the greatest differential is in obstetrics and gynecology. This is also the medical field in which the superior communication skills of female physicians are especially noted (Christen, Alder, and Bitzer, 2008).

Gender of the Patient.   Although there is considerable anecdotal evidence of sexist ideology among physicians, research has produced an inconclusive picture of the extent to which gender stereotyping of patients still occurs. Among the frequently cited health-related stereotypes of women are that they express higher levels of emotional illness and emotional instability, exaggerate claims of the severity of medical symptoms, and are more demanding patients. Research has found that these views are still held by some physicians.

Does gender stereotyping lead to differential treatment? In one widely cited study conducted in San Diego, the answer was yes. Five medical complaints (back pain, headache, dizziness, chest pain, and fatigue) were studied in married couples who had been seen for at least 5 years by one or more male family practice physicians. The researchers found that the physicians had conducted more extensive workups for the male patients, and concluded that gender stereotyping had affected care (Armitage, Schneiderman, and Bass, 1979).

However, other studies have failed to detect treatment differences. Greer et al. (1986) attempted to replicate the Armitage study (using the same five medical complaints) when examining the medical charts of 100 married couples who had been seen for a minimum of 2 years by one or more of 20 physicians (10 male and 10 female) in a prepaid health maintenance organization. They found no significant differences in the extent of the workup based on the gender of the patient. The different organizational circumstances (prepaid setting, and 50 percent of the physicians being female) might help to explain the different findings.

The largest study conducted utilized data on 46,000 adults collected in the 1975 National Ambulatory Medical Care Survey. Verbrugge and Steiner (1981) focused on the extent to which significant differences in care occurred between male and female patients and whether or not these were attributable to medically relevant factors. They considered diagnostic services, therapeutic services, and dispositions for follow-up in all visits, visits associated with 15 major groups of complaints, and five specific complaints (the same ones as those used in the previously mentioned studies).

The data indicated that health care was often similar for female and male patients, but that significant gender differences occurred in 30 to 40 percent of the services and dispositions studied, with women receiving more services (including laboratory tests, blood pressure checks, drug prescriptions, and return appointments). These differences persisted even after controlling for medically relevant factors (e.g., patient age, seriousness of problem, and reasons for visit) (Verbrugge and Steiner, 1981). The additional services provided for women could be interpreted in either a favorable or unfavorable light, but they are not consistent with the view that female patients are generally deprived of services offered to male patients.

Yet another study (Waitzkin, 1984) attempted to identify biases that occur in the actual communication process between female patients and their physicians. Using audiotapes of 336 interactions between male internists and their male and female patients, evidence of withholding information from or "talking down" to female patients more often than in the case of male patients was sought. Contrary to expectations, female patients received more physician time, asked more questions, and received more technical explanations and more clarifications of the technical explanations.

On the other hand, there now seems to be conclusive research evidence that gender bias does exist in the management of coronary heart disease. Chakkalakal et al. (2013) studied the application of five specific aspects of the physical examination given by medical residents to patients presenting with chest pains. The residents were more likely to correctly perform each of the five aspects of the examination on male patients than on female patients. In addition, male residents were less likely to perform each of the five aspects of the examination on female patients.

A separate study of adults presenting to an emergency room with acute chest pain found that female patients were less likely to be admitted to the hospital, undergo a stress test in the next month, and undergo cardiac catheterization, even after controlling for clinical and non-clinical factors (Johnson et al., 1996). Other studies have found that women receive less aggressive treatment than men following a heart attack, even after controlling for relevant factors.

Researchers have been trying to explain exactly how this happens. Welch et al. (2012) have found that physicians tend to treat heart disease symptoms less aggressively—that is, they order fewer diagnostic tests and delay prescribing appropriate medication—when they are uncertain about the diagnosis. Because so much heart disease research has been conducted on men, and because the prevailing understanding is that women are more likely to have atypical heart disease symptoms, physicians have greater diagnostic uncertainty when considering heart disease for female patients than for male patients. This is one avenue that leads to slower and less aggressive treatment. More needs to be learned about gender differences in clinical decision making, but the significant evidence of gender bias in the treatment of heart disease requires immediate attention and remediation.

Cultural Competency

In recent years, efforts have begun to produce "culturally competent" physicians. **Cultural competence** is an ability to work effectively with members of different cultures. It includes awareness of one's own cultural background, knowledge about other cultures, an openness to working with diverse individuals, and effective communication skills to do so (Office of Minority Health, 2010). The Society of General Internal Medicine Health Disparities Task Force has developed guidelines for cultural competence training that include (1) examining and understanding attitudes such as mistrust, subconscious bias, and stereotyping, (2) gaining knowledge of health disparities and the measures needed to reduce them, and (3) acquiring the skills to communicate effectively with members of diverse cultures (Smith et al., 2007).

In 2005, New Jersey became the first state to require cultural competence in order to obtain a medical license. Several states now require culture competence training for medical students, and for physicians to take continuing medical education credits in cultural diversity. Research has found some success as a result of these efforts, as members of all cultures express positive feelings for physicians undergoing this training and report improved interaction (Paez et al., 2009). Broader studies have also found that positive physician affect, rapport-building behaviors, and longer visits have reduced racial disparities in level of physician trust for minority patients (Martin et al., 2013). However, for programs aimed at reducing racial disparities to be genuinely effective, Malat (2013) cautions that they must go beyond efforts to understand "cultural differences" and squarely address the existence and effects of the racial bias and discrimination discussed earlier in this chapter.

PATIENT SATISFACTION WITH PHYSICIANS

Even if there was no instrumental value attached to patient satisfaction, it would be a highly desirable end product of the physician–patient encounter. However, research has confirmed that patient satisfaction is linked to several other desirable outcomes. Satisfied patients are more likely to comply fully with medical regimens, more likely to return for scheduled follow-up visits and to maintain continuity of care (seeing the same physician), more likely to seek physician care when sick, and less likely to initiate a medical malpractice suit. There is increasing recognition that positive health outcomes are more likely to occur when the patient is satisfied with the care received.

Level of Satisfaction

Are most patients satisfied with the primary health care they receive from a physician? The answer is yes. Research over the last few decades shows a consistent pattern—patients have significant misgivings about the health care system in general and about physicians in general, but they are very satisfied with their own physician. On most surveys, satisfaction level is quite high, although not as high as in many other countries.

Do patients make distinctions between various aspects of physician–patient interaction? Yes, they do. Most researchers have concluded that patients distinguish between the technical competence of the physician (which they have difficulty judging) and the socioemotional aspects of the encounter (which therefore become more important in their evaluation, and are the basis for much of the rating of their own physician).

Factors Related to Patient Satisfaction

Based on dozens of studies, four conclusions can be drawn about factors that influence patient satisfaction.

1. When other relevant factors are controlled for, most patient background characteristics

have little effect on satisfaction. As discussed earlier, race is a clear exception. In a systematic review of the literature on this subject, Malat (2001a) concluded that satisfaction with medical care is lower among blacks than among whites, and identified both structural factors (e.g., lower incomes, less likelihood of health insurance, and less likelihood of continuity of care) and micro-level factors (e.g., racial discrimination and social distance) as contributing to the pattern.

Several studies have found that, among all racial and ethnic groups, patient satisfaction is higher when the race of the provider and the patient is the same (LaVeist and Nuru-Jeter, 2002). Audiotaped physician–patient encounters have documented that race-concordant visits are longer and are characterized by more positive patient affect (Cooper et al., 2003), and that African American patients perceive that they are treated more respectfully by black than by white physicians (Malat, 2001b). However, few studies have found clear clinical benefits from race-concordant relationships (Jerant et al., 2011; Strumpf, 2011).

2. Most patients feel ill equipped to assess the technical competence of their physician. In most cases, patients simply assume that the physician is competent and base their evaluation on other factors. However, patients are now more knowledgeable than ever before about health matters, and many actively solicit second opinions. This may provide patients with more information with which to make informed assessments of the technical competence of their physician.

3. The level of satisfaction or dissatisfaction that patients have with their health care is significantly influenced by the quality of the communication process that occurs. Patients are much more likely to be satisfied with their health care when they establish an ongoing

relationship with a physician (Rodriguez et al., 2007), when they establish rapport with the physician, when the physician conveys empathy (Epstein et al., 2007), when they are given (and retain) more information about their symptoms and participate more in possible treatments (Chen et al., 2008), and when they are able to ask questions and discuss their ideas and the ideas of the physician. Not surprisingly, patient satisfaction is lower in situations where there are language differences between physician and patient (Morales et al., 1999).

4. Patient satisfaction is significantly affected by efforts of the physician to talk about psychosocial concerns and preventive health care. Despite the reluctance of some physicians to delve into these areas, or their belief that patients might prefer not to talk about them, patients want these matters discussed and are more satisfied with the care received when they are (Bertakis, Callahan, and Helms, 1998).

PATIENT COMPLIANCE WITH MEDICAL REGIMENS

Compliance with medical regimens refers to the extent to which patients follow the instructions given to them by physicians. These instructions include requests for follow-up visits, the taking of medications, and changes in lifestyle—either temporary (e.g., get plenty of rest this week) or long term (e.g., stop smoking cigarettes). Research shows that about 25 percent of prescriptions are never filled, and about 50 percent of all patients fail to take their medications as instructed and fail to comply with other regimens. Understanding the reasons for this non-compliance has become an important area of research as compliance has been associated with improved patient outcomes, reduced number of hospital visits, and lower out-of-pocket expenses (Roebuck et al., 2011).

Studies show that physicians tend to view **non-compliance** in terms of non-cooperative patients. Most physicians believe that they provide sufficient information and rationale for

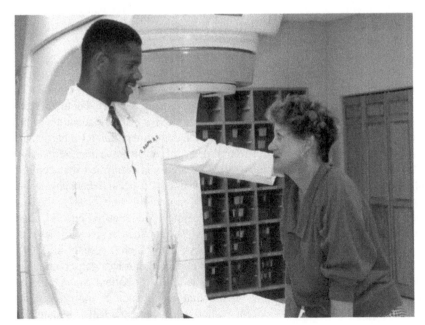

Research indicates that patients want and appreciate physicians who take time with them and establish genuine rapport. Photo by Janet Jonas.

patients to fully comply with their instructions, and regard non-compliance as an irrational response centered in the patient. Physicians also tend to underestimate the percentage of their patients who are non-compliers.

Factors Related to Compliance

Research on factors related to compliance behavior has identified several clear patterns:

1. Sociodemographic characteristics of patients such as age, gender, level of education, and social class are not reliable predictors of compliance behavior.
2. Patient knowledge of the disease or illness that has prompted the instructions does not accurately predict compliance. For many years, clinicians and social scientists believed that compliance rates could be increased by creating better-informed, more knowledgeable patients. However, many non-compliers are very knowledgeable about their condition but still choose not to follow instructions.
3. The seriousness of the patient's disease or illness is not strongly related to compliance behavior—that is, more seriously ill patients are not more likely to be compliers.
4. The complexity of the medical regimen does influence compliance behavior. More complex regimens (e.g., medications that must be taken several times per day in restricted situations for a long period of time) are less likely to be fully followed than simpler, more short-term medication orders.
5. The most important factor affecting compliance is the extent of change required in the patient's life. Regimens that require significant life change (e.g., a major change in diet, a significant increase in exercise, or a significant reduction or elimination of alcohol or tobacco products)—especially those that require giving something up as opposed to adding something—are least likely to be followed.

The top eight reasons (Rees, 2015) that patients cite for failing to take medications as prescribed are as follows:

1. Fear of potential *side effects*, including inability to perform other life responsibilities
2. Inability to afford the *cost* of the medication
3. *Misunderstanding* the need for the medication, the nature of the side effects, or the length of time for which the medication needed to be taken
4. *Difficulty remembering the schedule* due to taking a large number of medications with varying dosing frequencies
5. *Lack of noticeable improvement*
6. *Worry* about becoming dependent on a medication
7. *Depression* that causes lack of commitment to getting well
8. *Mistrust* of the physician.

Sociological Explanations for Compliance Behavior

Sociologists have tested three plausible explanations for non-compliance, and each of these explanations has received some empirical support. One explanation locates the problem within the communication process between physician and patient—that is, non-compliance results from inadequate or poorly communicated information from physician to patient about the nature or rationale of the regimen (in particular) or from the lack of physician–patient rapport (in general). Research has confirmed that compliance is more likely to occur when physicians communicate thoroughly and clearly about a proposed treatment regimen (Zolnierek and DiMatteo, 2009), and when the patient's level of trust in the physician is high (Lee and Lin, 2009).

A second explanation traces non-compliance to the health beliefs of the patient. Some research has found that compliance is more likely to occur when the patient feels heightened susceptibility to the disease or illness, when the condition is believed to have a negative effect on daily functioning, and when the medical regimen is considered to be an efficacious method of deterring or eliminating the health problem. When the views of physician and patient on these beliefs match, compliance is higher (Christensen et al., 2010).

Third, Peter Conrad (1987) has suggested that non-compliance should be regarded as a matter of patient self-regulation. Rather than viewing non-compliance as a matter of deviance that needs correction, this explanation sees non-compliance as a matter of patients tailoring their medical regimens to their lifestyles and life responsibilities. An in-depth study of 19 women who had been assigned one or more regimens found that they assigned greater priority to normal life routines, and modified treatment regimens to fit into their pre-existing lifestyles. Rather than seeing themselves as being non-compliant, they perceived that they were complying as much as possible, given their other life responsibilities (Hunt et al., 1989).

SUMMARY

Talcott Parsons laid the foundation for understanding physician–patient interaction. Writing in the mid-nineteenth century, he perceived that the physician–patient relationship is asymmetrical, with power residing in the physician. He believed that this asymmetry was inherent in the relationship due to the professional prestige of the physician, the authority of the physician on health matters, and the situational dependency of the patient. Physician–patient relationships have evolved since then and are now much more complex.

Three key dimensions define the physician–patient relationship—the patient treatment approach (biomedical or biopsychosocial), the primary ethical obligation of physicians (patient autonomy or beneficence), and the extent to which genuine therapeutic communication develops within the relationship. Patients do go to physicians with many psychosocial concerns that they want the physicians to address, but many physicians do not do this. Patients want to be well informed, but many still prefer the physician to be the chief decision maker. Research shows that many physicians talk down to patients and use terminology with which patients are not familiar.

Despite the existence of many similarities between female and male physicians, female physicians have better communication skills and convey more interest to patients with regard to "women's issues." Approximately one-third to one-half of patients have a preference with regard to gender of their physician, but the clearest difference is that many female patients prefer a female obstetrician-gynecologist. Patients are more likely to reveal personal information to or discuss mental health issues with a physician of the same gender.

Most patients are satisfied with primary health care received. The quality of communication between physician and patient and the physician's interest in patient psychosocial concerns are the major determinants of patient satisfaction level. About 50 percent of all patients fail to comply fully with medical regimens. The more complex the regimen and the more invasive its effect on the patient's lifestyle, the lower is the likelihood of compliance. Non-compliance can occur when there is a breakdown in physician–patient communication, when the patient does not feel especially alarmed by the condition or confident in the regimen, and when the patient modifies the regimen to fit with their other life responsibilities.

HEALTH ON THE INTERNET

An interesting medical school-based website that deals with issues in the physician–patient relationship is sponsored by the University of Washington. Connect to this site at

www.depts.washington.edu/bioethx/topics/index.html.

What kinds of topics are covered? Click on "The Physician–Patient Relationship." Which of the three key dimensions in the physician–patient relationship—the patient treatment approach (biomedical or biopsychosocial), the primary ethical obligation of physicians (patient autonomy or beneficence), and the extent to which genuine therapeutic communication develops within the relationship—are encouraged in these sections? Click on Case #1. How would you respond in this circumstance? What values would underlie your responses?

DISCUSSION CASE

A complex situation occurs in medicine when a patient's religious beliefs dictate a medical decision that could be life-threatening. Attending physicians are caught between respect for the patient's personal religious values and the First Amendment right to privacy on the one hand, and their commitment to engaging in all reasonable medical efforts to save the lives of patients on the other.

A specific illustration of this dilemma occurs when a member of the Jehovah's Witnesses sect needs a blood transfusion in order to survive. Jehovah's Witnesses adamantly refuse this procedure based on their interpretation of biblical scripture forbidding the "eating" or "taking in" of blood. They believe that voluntary or involuntary receipt of blood results in the loss of eternal life, and blood transfusions both for adults and for children are rejected. For discussion purposes, three cases involving Jehovah's Witnesses (modified from Tierney et al., 1984) are presented here.

Scenario 1: A 45-year-old bachelor visits his private physician after regurgitating large quantities of blood in the preceding 2 hours. He is taken to the hospital where examination reveals a continued slow oozing of blood in the patient's stomach. He is fully alert and informs his physician that, as a Jehovah's Witness, he will not accept a blood transfusion. His condition worsens, and the physician determines that a transfusion may be necessary to save his life.

Scenario 2: A 26-year-old married woman with two small children is involved in an automobile accident. It is determined that immediate removal of the spleen and a blood transfusion are necessary to save her life. The woman protests that she is a devout Jehovah's Witness and would sacrifice the chance to be with her family for eternity if she is transfused.

Scenario 3: An otherwise healthy infant is suffering from Rh incompatibility and is in need of an immediate life-saving blood transfusion. However, the parents are Jehovah's Witnesses, and refuse transfusion of any blood products to their child. The parents consult with the deacon at their church and then state that they would rather have their child die (and be granted eternal life) than be transfused and continue life on earth but sacrifice eternal life.

What do you think should be done in each of these three situations? Should the blood transfusions be given? What are the implications of your position for the medical profession and for the rights of patients?

GLOSSARY

autonomy	implicit bias
beneficence	informed consent
biomedical model	non-compliance
biopsychosocial model	paternalism
cultural competence	patient activation
cultural health capital	patient-centered care
health literacy	therapeutic communication

REFERENCES

Andersen, M. Robyn, Janne Abullarade, and Nicole Urban. 2005 "Assertiveness with Physicians is Related to Women's Perceived Roles in the Medical Encounter." *Women and Health*, 42:15–33.

Armitage, Karen J., Lawrence J. Schneiderman, and Robert A. Bass. 1979 "Response of Physicians to Medical Complaints in Men and Women." *Journal of the American Medical Association*, 241:2186–2187.

Armstrong, Katrina, Mary Putt, Chanita H. Halbert, David Grande, Jerome S. Schwartz, Kaijun Liao, Noora Marcus, Mirar B. Demeter, and Judy B. Shea. 2013 "Prior Experiences of Racial Discrimination and Racial Differences in Health Care Systems Distrust." *Medical Care*, 51:151–157.

Arora, Neeraj, John Z. Ayanian, and Edward Guadagnoli. 2005 "Examining the Relationship of Patients' Attitudes and Beliefs with Their Self-Reported Level of Participation in Medical Decision-Making." *Medical Care*, 43:865–872.

Astin, John A., Victor S. Sierpina, Kelly Forys, and Brian Clarridge. 2008 "Integration of the Biopsychosocial Model: Perspectives of Medical Students and Residents." *Academic Medicine*, 83:20–27.

Bach, Peter B., Laura D. Cramer, Joan L. Warren, and Colin B. Begg. 1999 "Racial Differences in the Treatment of Early-Stage Lung Cancer." *New England Journal of Medicine*, 341:1198–1205.

Barsky, Arthur J. 1981 "Hidden Reasons Some Patients Visit Doctors." *Annals of Internal Medicine*, 94:492–498.

Beisecker, Analee E., and Thomas D. Beisecker. 1990 "Patient Information-Seeking Behaviors When Communicating with Doctors." *Medical Care*, 28:19–28.

Bertakis, Klea D., Edward J. Callahan, and L. Jay Helms. 1998 "Physician Practice Styles and Patient Outcomes: Differences between Family Practice and General Internal Medicine." *Medical Care*, 36:879–891.

Boulware, L. Ebony, Lisa A. Cooper, Lloyd E. Ratner, Thomas A. LaVeist, and Neil R. Powe. 2003 "Race and Trust in the Health Care System." *Public Health Reports*, 118:358–365.

Boyer, Carol A., and Karen E. Lutfey. 2010 "Examining Critical Health Policy Issues Within and Beyond the Clinical Encounter: Patient–Provider Relationships and Help-Seeking Behaviors." *Journal of Health and Social Behaviors*, 51:S80–S93.

Braddock, Clarence H., Kelly A. Edwards, Nicole M. Hasenberg, Tracy L. Laidley, and Wendy Levinson. 1999 "Informed Decision Making in Outpatient Practice." *Journal of the American Medical Association*, 282:2313–2320.

Buller, Mary K., and David B. Buller. 1987 "Physicians' Communication Style and Patient Satisfaction." *Journal of Health and Social Behavior*, 28:375–388.

Campbell, James D., Helen J. Neikirk, and Michael C. Hosokawa. 1990 "Development of a Psychosocial Concern Index from Videotaped Interviews of Nurse Practitioners and Family Physicians." *Journal of Family Practice*, 30: 321–326.

Castro, Cesar M., Clifford Wilson, Frances Wang, and Dean Schillinger. 2007 "Babel Babble: Physicians' Use of Unclarified Medical Jargon with Patients." *American Journal of Health Behavior*, 31(Suppl. 1):S85–S95.

Chakkalakal, Rosette J., Stacy M. Higgins, Lisa B. Bernstein, Kristina L. Lundberg, Victor Wu, Jacqueline Green, Qi Long, and Joyce P. Doyle. 2013 "Does Patient Gender Impact Resident Physicians' Approach to the Cardiac Exam?" *Journal of General Internal Medicine,* 28:561–566.

Chapman, Elizabeth N., Anna Kaatz, and Molly Carnes. 2013 "Physicians and Implicit Bias: How Doctors May Unwittingly Perpetuate Health Care Disparities." *Journal of General Internal Medicine,* 28:1504–1510.

Chen, Judy Y., May L. Tao, Diana Tisnado, Jennifer Malin, Clifford Ko, Martha Timmer, John L. Adams, Patricia A. Ganz, and Katherine L. Kahn. 2008 "Impact of Physician–Patient Discussions on Patient Satisfaction." *Medical Care,* 46: 1157–1162.

Christen, Regula N., Judith Alder, and Johannes Bitzer. 2008 "Gender Differences in Physicians' Communicative Skills and Their Influence on Patient Satisfaction in Gynaecological Outpatient Consultations." *Social Science and Medicine,* 66:1474–1483.

Christensen, Alan J., M. Bryant Howren, Stephen Hillis, Peter Kaboli, Barry Carter, Jamie Cvengros, Kenneth Wallston, and Gary E. Rosenthal. 2010 "Patient and Physician Beliefs About Control Over Health: Association of Symmetrical Beliefs with Medication Regimen Adherence." *Journal of General Internal Medicine,* 25:397–402.

Conrad, Peter. 1987 "The Noncompliant Patient in Search of Autonomy." *Hastings Center Report,* 17:15–17.

Cooper, Lisa A., Debra L. Roter, Rachel L. Johnson, Daniel E. Ford, Donald M. Steinwachs, and Neil R. Powe. 2003 "Patient-Centered Communication, Ratings of Care, and Concordance of Patient and Physician Race." *Annals of Internal Medicine,* 139:907–915.

Cooper-Patrick, Lisa, Joseph J. Gallo, Junius J. Gonzales, Vu H. Thi, Neil R. Powe, Christine Nelson, and Daniel E. Ford. 1999 "Race, Gender, and Partnership in the Physician-Patient Relationship." *Journal of the American Medical Association,* 282:583–589.

Cruz, Taylor M. 2014 "Assessing Access to Care for Transgender and Gender Nonconforming People: A Consideration of Diversity in Combating Discrimination." *Social Science and Medicine,* 110:65–73.

Cuffee, Yendelela L., J. Lee Hargraves, Milagros Rosal, Becky A. Briesacher, Antoinette Schoenthaler, Sharina Person, Sandral Hullett, and Jeroan Allison. 2013 "Reported Racial Discrimination, Trust in Physicians, and Medication Adherence among Inner-City African Americans with Hypertension." *American Journal of Public Health,* 103:e55–e62.

DeAngelis, Catherine D. 2014 "The Electronic Health Record: Boon or Bust for Good Patient Care?" *The Milbank Quarterly,* 92:442–445.

Derose, Kathryn P., Ron D. Hays, Daniel F. McCaffrey, and David W. Baker. 2001 "Does Physician Gender Affect Satisfaction of Men and Women Visiting the Emergency Department?" *Journal of General Internal Medicine,* 16:218–226.

Engel, George L. 1977 "The Need for a New Medical Model: A Challenge for Biomedicine." *Science,* 196:129–136.

Epstein, Arnold M., Joel S. Weissman, Eric C. Schneider, Constantine Gatsonis, Lucian L. Leape, and Robert N. Piana. 2003 "Race and Gender Disparities in Rates of Cardiac Revascularization." *Medical Care,* 41: 1240–1255.

Epstein, Ronald M., Taj Hadee, Jennifer Carroll, Sean C. Meldrum, Judi Lardner, and Cleveland G. Shields. 2007 " 'Could This Be Something Serious?': Reassurance, Uncertainty, and Empathy in Response to Patients' Expressions of Worry." *Journal of General Internal Medicine,* 22:1731–1739.

Feagin, Joe, and Zinobia Bennefield. 2014 "Systematic Racism and U.S. Health Care." *Social Science and Medicine,* 103:7–14.

Flocke, Susan A., and Valerie Gilchrist. 2005 "Physician and Patient Gender Concordance and the Delivery of Comprehensive Clinical Preventive Services." *Medical Care,* 43:486–492.

Fraenkel, Liana, and Sarah McGraw. 2007 "What are the Essential Elements to Enable Patient Participation in Medical Decision Making?" *Journal of General Internal Medicine,* 22: 614–619.

Freidson, Eliot. 1970 *Professional Dominance: The Social Structure of Medical Care.* New York: Atherton Press.

Frosch, Dominick L., Suepattra G. May, Katherine A.S. Rendle, Caroline Tietbohl, and Glyn Elwyn. 2012 "Authoritarian Physicians and Patients' Fear of Being Labeled 'Difficult' Among Key

Obstacles to Shared Decision Making." *Health Affairs*, 31:1030–1038.

Frowick, Bonnie, J. Christopher Shank, William J. Doherty, and Tracy A. Powell. 1986 "What Do Patients Really Want? Redefining a Behavioral Science Curriculum for Family Physicians." *Journal of Family Practice*, 23:141–146.

Giles, Wayne H., Robert F. Anda, Michele L. Casper, Luis G. Escobedo, and Herman A. Taylor. 1995 "Race and Sex Differences in Rates of Invasive Cardiac Procedures in United States Hospitals." *Archives of Internal Medicine*, 155:318–324.

Good, Mary-Jo D., Byron J. Good, and Paul D. Cleary. 1987 "Do Patient Attitudes Influence Physician Recognition of Psychosocial Problems in Primary Care?" *Journal of Family Practice*, 25:53–59.

Greer, Steven, Vivian Dickerson, Lawrence J. Schneiderman, Cathie Atkins, and Robert Bass. 1986 "Responses of Male and Female Physicians to Medical Complaints in Male and Female Patients." *Journal of Family Practice*, 23:49–53.

Gregory, Kimberly, Kenneth B. Wells, and Barbara Leake. 1987 "Medical Students' Expectations for Encounters with Minority and Nonminority Students." *Journal of the National Medical Association*, 79:403–408.

Gross, Michael L. 1999 "Autonomy and Paternalism in Communitarian Society: Patient Rights in Israel." *Hastings Center Report*, 29:13–20.

Hall, Judith A., Danielle Blanch-Hartigan, and Debra L. Roter. 2011 "Patients' Satisfaction with Male versus Female Physicians: A Meta-Analysis." *Medical Care*, 49:611–617.

Hall, William J., Mimi V. Chapman, Kent M. Lee, Yesenia M. Merino, Tainayah W. Thomas, B. Keith Payne, Eugenia Eng, Steven H. Day, and Tamera Coyne-Beasley. 2015 "Implicit Racial/Ethnic Bias among Health Care Professionals and Its Influence on Health Care Outcomes: A Systematic Review." *American Journal of Public Health*, 105:e60–e76.

Hibbard, Judith H., and Jessica Greene. 2013 "What the Evidence Shows About Patient Activation: Better Health Outcomes and Care Experiences: Fewer Data on Costs." *Health Affairs*, 32: 207–214.

Horton, Richard. 2003 *Second Opinion: Doctors, Diseases and Decisions in Modern Medicine*. London: Granta Books.

Hunt, Linda M., Brigitte Jordan, Susan Irwin, and C.H. Browner. 1989 "Compliance and the Patient's Perspective: Controlling Symptoms in Everyday Life." *Culture, Medicine and Psychiatry*, 13:315–334.

Institute of Medicine. 2001 *Crossing the Quality Chasm: A New Health System for the 21st Century*. Washington, DC: National Academies Press.

Jacobs, Elizabeth, Alice H. Chen, Leah S. Karliner, Niels Agger-Gupta, and Sunita Mutha. 2006 "The Need for More Research on Language Barriers in Health Care: A Proposed Research Agenda." *The Milbank Quarterly*, 84:111–133.

Jerant, Anthony, Klea D. Bertakis, Joshua J. Fenton, Daniel J. Tancredi, and Peter Franks. 2011 "Patient-Provider Sex and Race/Ethnicity Concordance: A National Study of Healthcare and Outcomes." *Medical Care*, 49:1012–1020.

Johnson, Paula A., Lee Goldman, E. John Orav, Li Zhou, Tomas Garcia, Steven D. Pearson, and Thomas H. Lee. 1996 "Gender Differences in the Management of Acute Chest Pain." *Journal of General Internal Medicine*, 11:209–217.

Kern, David E., William T. Branch, Jeffrey L. Jackson, Donald W. Brady, Mitchell D. Feldman, Wendy Levinson, and Mack Lipkin. 2005 "Teaching the Psychosocial Aspects of Care in the Clinical Setting: Practical Recommendations." *Academic Medicine*, 80:8–20.

Koh, Howard K., Cindy Brach, Linda M. Harris, and Michael L. Oarchman. 2013 "A Proposed 'Health Literate Care Model' Would Constitute a Systems Approach to Improving Patients' Engagement in Care." *Health Affairs*, 32:357–367.

Kosenko, Kami, Lance Rintamaki, Stephanie Ramey, and Kathleen Maness. 2013 "Transgender Patient Perceptions of Stigma in Health Care Contexts." *Medical Care*, 51:819–822.

LaVeist, Thomas A., and Amani Nuru-Jeter. 2002 "Is Doctor–Patient Race Concordance Associated with Greater Satisfaction with Care?" *Journal of Health and Social Behavior*, 43:296–306.

Lee, Yin Yang, and Julia L. Lin. 2009 "The Effects of Trust in Physician on Self-Efficacy, Adherence, and Diabetes Outcomes." *Social Science and Medicine*, 68:1060–1068.

Levinson, Wendy, William B. Stiles, Thomas S. Inui, and Robert Engle. 1993 "Physician Frustration in Communicating with Patients." *Medical Care*, 31:285–295.

Lurie, Nicole, Karen L. Margolis, Paul G. McGovern, Pamela J. Mink, and Jonathan S. Slater. 1997 "Why Do Patients of Female Physicians Have Higher Rates of Breast and

Cervical Cancer Screening?" *Journal of General Internal Medicine*, 12:34–43.

McGuire, Amy L., Laurence B. McCullough, Susan C. Weller, and Simon N. Whitney. 2005 "Missed Expectations? Physicians' Views of Patients' Participation in Medical Decision Making." *Medical Care*, 43:466–470.

Malat, Jennifer. 2001a "Race and Satisfaction with Medical Care: What Do We Know?" Paper presented at the Annual Meeting of the Southern Sociological Society, Atlanta, GA.

———. 2001b "Social Distance and Patients' Rating of Healthcare Providers." *Journal of Health and Social Behavior*, 42:360–372.

———. 2013 "The Appeal and Problems of a Cultural Competence Approach to Reducing Racial Disparities." *Journal of General Internal Medicine*, 28:605–607.

Martin, Kimberly D., Debra L. Roter, Mary C. Beach, Kathryn A. Carson, and Lisa A. Cooper. 2013 "Physician Communication Behaviors and Trust among Black and White Patients with Hypertension." *Medical Care*, 51:151–157.

Millenson, Michael L. 2014 "New Roles and Rules for Patient-Centered Care." *Journal of General Internal Medicine*, 29:979–980.

Morales, Leo S., William E. Cunningham, Julie A. Brown, Honghu Liu, and Ron D. Hays. 1999 "Are Latinos Less Satisfied with Communication by Health Care Providers?" *Journal of General Internal Medicine*, 14:409–417.

Office of Minority Health. 2010 *Cultural Competency*. www.minorityhealth.hhs.gov.

Paez, Kathryn A., Jerilyn K. Allen, Mary C. Beach, Kathryn A. Carson, and Lisa A. Cooper. 2009 "Physician Cultural Competence and Patient Ratings of the Patient-Physician Relationship." *Journal of General Internal Medicine*, 24:495–498.

Parsons, Talcott. 1951 *The Social System*. Glencoe, IL: Free Press.

Quill, Timothy E. 1982 "How Special Is Medicine's Nonspecialty?" *The Pharos*, 45:25–30.

Ray, Kristin N., Amalavoyal V. Chari, John Engberg, Marnie Bertolet, and Ateev Mehrotra. 2015 "Disparities in Time Spent Seeking Medical Care in the United States." *Journal of the American Medical Association*, 175:1983–1986.

Rees, Lauren. 2015 *Eight Reasons Patients Don't Take Their Medications*. www.ama-assn.org/ama/ama-wire/post/8-reasons-patients-dont-their-medications.

Robinson, John W., and Debra L. Roter. 1999 "Psychosocial Problem Disclosure by Primary Care Patients." *Social Science and Medicine*, 48:1353–1362.

Rodriguez, Hector P., William H. Rogers, Richard E. Marshall, and Dana Safran. 2007 "The Effects of Primary Care Physician Visit Continuity on Patients' Experiences with Care." *Journal of General Internal Medicine*, 22:787–793.

Roebuck, M. Christopher, Joshua N. Liberman, Marin Gemmill-Toyama, and Troyen A. Brennan. 2011 "Medication Adherence Leads to Lower Health Care Use and Costs Despite Drug Spending." *Health Affairs*, 30:91–99.

Roter, Debra L., Judith K. Hall, and Nancy R. Katz. 1988 "Patient-Physician Communication: A Descriptive Summary of the Literature." *Patient Education and Counseling*, 12:99–119.

Sabin, Janice A., Brian A. Nosek, Anthony G. Greenwalk, and Frederick P. Rivara. 2009 "Physicians' Implicit and Explicit Attitudes about Race by MD Race, Ethnicity, and Gender." *Journal of Health Care for the Poor and Underserved*, 20:896–913.

Sabin, Janice A., Rachel G. Riskind, and Brian A. Nosek. 2015 "Health Care Providers' Implicit and Explicit Attitudes toward Lesbian Women and Gay Men." *American Journal of Public Health*, 105:1831–1841.

Seubert, Doug. 2009 *The Connection between Health Literacy and Patient Activation.* Marshfield, WI: Marshfield Clinic. www.wisconsin-literacy.org/documents/HealthLiteracy_Patient-Activation.pdf.

Shah, Adil A., Cheryl K. Zogg, Syed N. Zafar, Eric B. Schneider, Lisa A. Cooper, Alyssa B. Chapital, Susan M. Peterson, Joaquim M. Havens, Roland J. Thorpe, Debra L. Roter, Renan C. Castillo, Ali Salim, and Adil H. Haider, 2015 "Analgesic Access for Acute Abdominal Pain in the Emergency Department Among Racial/Ethnic Minority Patients: A Nationwide Examination." *Medical Care*, 53:1000–1009.

Shim, Janet K. 2010 "Cultural Health Capital: A Theoretical Approach to Understanding Health Care Interactions and the Dynamics of Unequal Treatment." *Journal of Health and Social Behavior*, 51:1–15.

Smith, Wally R., Joseph R. Betancourt, Matthew K. Wynia, Jada Bussey-Jones, Valerie E. Stone, Christopher O. Phillips, Alicia Fernandez, Elizabeth Jacobs, and Jacqueline Bowles. 2007 "Recommendations for Teaching about Racial and

Ethnic Disparities in Health and Health Care." *Annals of Internal Medicine*, 147:654–665.

Spalter-Roth, Roberta, Terri A. Lowenthal, and Mercedes Rubio. 2005 *Race, Ethnicity, and the Health of Americans*. ASA Series on How Race and Ethnicity Matter. Washington, DC: American Sociological Association.

Street, Richard L., Howard S. Gordon, Michael M. Ward, Edward Krupat, and Richard L. Kravitz. 2005 "Patient Participation in Medical Consultations: Why Some Patients Are More Involved Than Others." *Medical Care*, 43:960–969.

Strumpf, Eric C. 2011 "Racial/Ethnic Disparities in Primary Care: The Role of Physician–Patient Concordance." *Medical Care*, 49:496–503.

Szasz, Thomas S., and Marc H. Hollender. 1956 "The Basic Models of the Doctor–Patient Relationship." *Archives of Internal Medicine*, 97:585–592.

Tierney, William M., Morris Weinberger, James Y. Greene, and P. Albert Studdard. 1984 "Jehovah's Witnesses and Blood Transfusion: Physicians' Attitudes and Legal Precedents." *Southern Medical Journal*, 77:473–478.

Tomsik, Philip E., Ann M. Witt, Michael L. Raddock, Peter DeGolia, James J. Werner, Stephen J. Zyzanski, Kurt C. Stange, Peter J. Lawson, Mary Jane Mason, Samantha Smith, and Susan A. Flocke. 2014 "How Well Do Physician and Patient Visit Priorities Align?" *Journal of Family Practice*, 63:E8–E13.

Verbrugge, Lois M., and Richard P. Steiner. 1981 "Physician Treatment of Men and Women Patients: Sex Bias or Appropriate Care?" *Medical Care*, 19:609–632.

Waitzkin, Howard. 1984 "Doctor-Patient Communication: Clinical Implications of Social Scientific Research." *Journal of the American Medical Association*, 252:2441–2446.

Weisman, Carol S., and Martha A. Teitelbaum. 1985 "Physician Gender and the Physician-Patient Relationship: Recent Evidence and Relevant Questions." *Social Science and Medicine*, 20:1119–1127.

Welch, Lisa C., Karen E. Lutfey, Eric Gerstenberger, and Matthew Grace. 2012 "Gendered Uncertainty and Variation in Physicians' Decisions for Coronary Heart Disease: The Double-Edged Sword of 'Atypical Symptoms.'" *Journal of Health and Social Behavior*, 53:313–328.

West, Candace. 1984 *Routine Complications: Troubles with Talk between Doctors and Patients*. Bloomington, IN: Indiana University Press.

White, Amina, and Marion Danis. 2013 "Enhancing Patient-Centered Communication and Collaboration by Using the Electronic Health Record in the Examination Room." *Journal of the American Medical Association*, 309: 2327–2328.

Williamson, Penny, Bernard D. Beitman, and Wayne Katon. 1981 "Beliefs That Foster Physician Avoidance of Psychosocial Aspects of Health Care." *Journal of Family Practice*, 13:999–1003.

Zolnierek, Kelly B., and M. Robin DiMatteo. 2009 "Physician Communication and Patient Adherence to Treatment: A Meta-Analysis." *Medical Care*, 47:826–834.

Zussman, Robert. 1992 *Intensive Care: Medical Ethics and the Medical Profession*. Chicago, IL: The University of Chicago Press.

CHAPTER 13

Professional and Ethical Obligations of Physicians in the Physician–Patient Relationship

Learning Objectives

- Distinguish between principlism, casuistry, and the sociology of bio-knowledge as approaches for determining moral rules of behavior.

- Compare and contrast the relevant moral codes regarding physicians' obligations always to tell patients the truth, always to protect confidentiality, and always to treat patients who have highly contagious diseases.

- Identify and discuss the major arguments on both sides of the three issues discussed in this chapter.

- Discuss patient preferences regarding physician behavior relevant to these three issues.

- Discuss physician preferences and actual behavior relevant to these three issues.

An important strategy for delving into the dynamics of the physician–patient relationship is consideration of the "rights" of patients versus the professional obligations of physicians. Three such issues (truth-telling, confidentiality, and the obligation to treat patients with highly contagious diseases) have received significant attention from social scientists, clinicians, and medical ethicists.

For sociologists, these issues are important for many reasons. They are closely related to the nature of the medical profession, the status of patients, and interactions between physicians and patients, they are creating new role demands for physicians and patients, and they are now a part of the formal and informal socialization process for health care professionals.

Moreover, the sociological perspective is essential for understanding the social context of these issues. In the preface to *Bioethics and Society*, DeVries and Subedi (1998:xiv) articulate sociology's contribution to understanding these issues as "getting the whole picture," "looking beyond the taken for granted," scrutinizing "existing arrangements of power," and raising "questions about the social bases of morality"—"classic sociological concerns."

THE APPROACH OF MEDICAL ETHICS

The term **ethics** is derived from the Greek word "ethos" (meaning "character") and the Latin word "mores" (meaning "customs"). Ethics is a field of study that helps to "define what is good for the individual and for society and establishes the nature of duties that people owe themselves and one another" (Legal Information Institute, 2016). As such, ethics leads us to rules of moral conduct. **Medical ethics** is one of many applied areas of ethics. It focuses on rules of moral conduct as they apply to the practice of medicine. While traditionally a branch of moral philosophy, medical ethics is most informative when it draws from history, sociology, anthropology, theology, philosophy, and the clinical sciences.

As described in Chapter 2, thinking about medical ethics began in ancient times and is most associated in early history with Hippocrates in the fourth and fifth centuries B.C. As an academic discipline, medical ethics really began to emerge in the 1970s. Certainly, discovery of the gruesome medical experiments conducted by clinicians and others in Nazi Germany without, of course, any consent from the subjects stimulated the focus of more academic attention on the field. So did magazine reports of so-called "God Committees" in Seattle in 1962 deciding who would and who would not receive kidney dialysis and a chance to live, reports (also in 1962) of seriously questionable medical research projects in the United States, and the first human heart transplant in 1967. The social activism of the 1960s and the emphases on civil rights for African Americans, Native Americans, women, and lesbian, gay, bisexual, and transgender individuals led naturally to greater consideration of the rights of patients.

Approaches to Determining Moral Rules of Conduct Relative to Medicine

Principlism.   Stemming in part from criticism of the Nazi medical experiments, many medical ethicists, clinicians, and others adopted an approach called **principlism** that based morality of conduct on its consistency with well-considered moral principles. This approach was given a substantial boost with the publication of Tom Beauchamp's and James Childress' *The Principles of Biomedical Ethics* in 1979. (It is now in its seventh edition, published in 2012.) Beauchamp and Childress carefully and thoroughly laid out four moral principles relevant to medicine:

- Autonomy—the right of competent individuals to be self-determining
- Beneficence—the commitment to doing good for others
- Non-maleficence—the commitment not to harm others
- Justice—fair distribution of social benefits and burdens.

Principlists believe that the appropriateness of each of these principles should be considered, and thought given to their relative priority. When a question of moral duty occurs in the medical field, one can determine the moral action by applying and following the principles.

Casuistry.   While there is some variation in how this term is used, it is generally an approach that emphasizes the value of beginning with analysis of particular cases, extracting moral rules from them, and applying these rules to new cases. It may be seen as a contrast to principlism, which starts with consideration of moral principles and then moves to particular cases. Casuistrists are more likely than principlists to consider specific aspects of cases in determining whether particular actions are moral.

A Sociology of Bio-Knowledge.   Some critics of the emphasis on principlism in medical ethics contend that a new approach that gives much more attention to social context is needed.

Alan Petersen, a medical sociologist at Monash University in Australia, commends the idea of developing a **sociology of bio-knowledge** that focuses on human rights in determining what is moral and what is not. He envisions contributions to this field from various fields of scholarship, including the sociology of human rights, science and technology studies, feminist bioethics, and the work of Michel Foucault. Foucault was a French social theorist and social critic, philosopher, and historian of ideas whose intellectual contributions included efforts to understand the ideas that shape our present society and how power and knowledge exert social control. Petersen is especially interested in emerging biotechnologies and our need for more useful tools in considering them (Petersen, 2013).

As you read through the three issues in this chapter, think about both the moral principles involved in each, and the influence of social context, social outcomes, and human rights in determining the professional and ethical obligations of physicians.

TRUTH-TELLING AS AN ISSUE

An important gauge of the relative status of patients in the physician–patient relationship is the discretion felt by physicians to lie to or in some manner intentionally deceive patients. This issue occurs in various ways, but is common when a physician learns some distressing news about a patient, such as a diagnosis of terminal cancer or some other life-threatening or chronic disease. The following brief case study illustrates one kind of situation in which the issue of truth-telling might arise:

> A physician determines that a male patient is suffering from an advanced stage of lung cancer. It is too late for benefit from surgery, chemotherapy, or radiation. She feels that communicating this diagnosis to the patient will so depress and traumatize him that he will simply give up and die. In order to try to provide even a few weeks of additional time, she tells him the tests are inconclusive and asks him to return in a couple of weeks for the tests to be performed again.

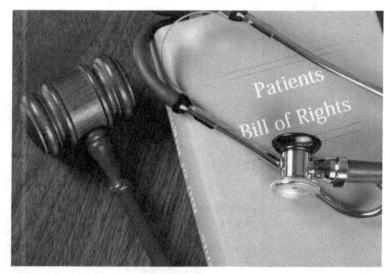

Many medical associations and organizations have now formally expressed the "rights" of patients in medical settings and in medical research. © ericsphotography/Getty

Are Lying and Deception Acceptable Professional Behaviors?

Medical Codes. Historically, most codes of ethical behavior for physicians were silent about the issue of lying and deception. While the Hippocratic Oath includes numerous pledges by physicians to patients, including confidentiality, nothing is said about truth-telling. There is no reference to truth-telling in the Declaration of Geneva, written in 1948 by the World Medical Association as a response to Nazi atrocities performed in World War Two under the name of medical science, or in the AMA's Code of Ethics until 1980.

Other prominent ethical codes in medicine have addressed truth-telling and have occasionally made a strong statement on its behalf. Both the "Patient's Bill of Rights" and the AMA's Code of Medical Ethics (American Medical Association, 2016c) now clearly state that patients have a right to complete current information regarding diagnosis, treatment options, and prognosis. Recent Presidential Commissions for the Study of Bioethical Issues have also supported full disclosure of information to patients as a way of increasing patient participation in actual decision making.

Arguments Used to Justify Lying and Deception. The most often cited justification for lying and deception by physicians is referred to as **benevolent deception**. Traditionally, some physicians have believed that they have a professional duty to lie to patients if this is perceived to be in the patient's best interest. This argument is supported by the rationale that physicians are employed by patients to provide the best possible diagnosis and treatment. Since physicians are not automatons, they cannot and should not be expected simply to report the "facts." Instead, as persons with extensive training in the practice of medicine, they should be given license to make judgments about what information would be beneficial for a patient to have and what information would do harm to the patient, and to act on these perceptions.

Guiora (1980) suggests that too much has been made of "freedom of information" while too little consideration has been given to the idea of "freedom from information":

> Information is medicine, very potent medicine indeed, that has to be titrated, properly dosaged based on proper diagnosis. Diagnosis, of course, in this context means an assessment of how information will affect the course of illness, how much and what kind of information is the most therapeutic in face of the patient's preferred modes of coping. (Guiora, 1980:32)

A second argument used to justify lying is that patients are typically unable to comprehend the "whole truth" of a matter, and physicians therefore cannot be expected to try to provide it. This situation is said to occur because most patients have limited medical knowledge and may incorrectly (or at least incompletely) interpret terminology used by the physician. Conveying a diagnosis of cancer exemplifies the point. Despite the tremendous progress made in the treatment of cancer and the steadily increasing rate of cure for many cancers, the "C" word continues to carry frightening implications. Since patients lack understanding of the disease and its treatment, the argument goes, it would make little sense to obligate physicians to communicate this diagnosis fully.

Finally, many physicians believe that some patients prefer not to hear the whole truth. Discounting surveys that show that a large majority of patients want full information, some physicians believe patients subtly communicate otherwise to them. They contend that some patients explicitly state their desire to have the truth couched in gentle language or withheld altogether, and others communicate this preference implicitly through body language, tone of voice, or a message that requires the physician to "read between the lines." If this is the message being communicated, some physicians argue, it would be unethical for them to reveal the truth.

Arguments Used to Oppose Lying and Deception. An alternative view is that truth-telling is an unconditional duty of medical professionals—that physicians are morally required always to provide full information to patients and never to lie or attempt to deceive them. Four primary arguments buttress this position. The first is that telling the truth is part of the respect owed to all people. To lie to or intentionally deceive another is to denigrate that person's worthiness and treat that person as undeserving of a full and honest account. The legal requirement for informed consent from patients or research subjects implies a decision maker who is fully informed and has complete access to the truth. A physician who fails to provide honest information to a patient has usurped the possibility that a genuine informed consent can occur.

Second, veracity is consistent with the ideas of fidelity and keeping promises. When a patient solicits a physician, he or she is entering into an implied contract. In exchange for payment, the patient seeks the best possible diagnosis, recommendations for treatment, and (if agreed upon) the provision of treatment. Accordingly, any information learned by the physician about the patient should be provided to the patient. After all, who can be said to "own" that information? Does the physician own it and have a right to parcel it out according to his or her discretion? Or does the patient own this information? Those arguing from this position believe that the contract established between the patient and the physician requires that a full and honest account always be provided.

A third argument used to support unconditional truth-telling is that lying or deception undermines a trusting relationship between patient and physician. If it is assumed that patient trust in a physician is a desirable goal, and that this trust facilitates a therapeutic relationship, then physicians must act in such a way as to maintain this trust. A patient who learns that he or she has been intentionally deceived by a physician may never again be able to fully trust information provided by that physician.

Finally, those taking this position claim that it offers certain clear benefits to the patient. It is argued that no one, including the physician, knows a patient better than the patient him- or herself. For a physician to determine that a given patient would be better off being deceived than hearing the truth would, at the very least, require intimate familiarity with the patient's life history, important values, perceived obligations to self and significant others, and the decisions the patient would make in the light of truthful information. Rarely, if ever, could a physician claim to have access to such matters or to know more about patients than they know about themselves.

Sissela Bok, a prominent medical ethicist at Brandeis University, summarizes this point:

> The damages associated with the disclosure of sad news or risks are rarer than physicians believe; and the benefits which result from being informed are more substantial, even measurably so. Pain is tolerated more easily, recovery from surgery is quicker, and cooperation with therapy is greatly improved. The attitude that "what you don't know won't hurt you" is proving unrealistic; it is what patients do not know but vaguely suspect that causes them corrosive worry. (Bok, 1991:78)

A recent study of 590 terminally ill cancer patients (median survival time was just 5.4 months) revealed that 71 percent wanted to be told their life expectancy, but only 17.6 percent recalled a prognostic disclosure by their physician. Those who had received a prognostic disclosure had a much more realistic idea of their likely life expectancy. Those who had an overly optimistic view about their survival chances were much more likely to choose aggressive therapies that made them sick but did not extend their life. Those with realistic views were more likely to opt for treatments designed simply to make them comfortable. Patients who were given an accurate prognostic disclosure did not experience more sadness, more anxiety, or a deterioration in the physician–patient relationship (Enzinger et al., 2015).

The Current Situation Regarding Truth-Telling

Do Patients Want to Know the Truth?   Social science surveys have found that most respondents express a desire for truthfulness from physicians. As early as 1950, 89 percent of cancer patients, 82 percent of patients without cancer, and 98 percent of patients participating in a cancer detection program expressed a desire for honesty in a cancer diagnosis (Kelly and Friesen, 1950). Surveys conducted since that time have routinely found that eight or nine out of every ten respondents want all of the available information about a medical condition and treatment, even if it is unfavorable. This preference for candor crosses all population subgroups—it is not specific to any age, gender, race, or socioeconomic group.

Are Physicians Truthful with Patients?   In the middle of the twentieth century, the large majority of physicians reported that they sometimes withheld the truth from patients. As attention to ethical issues in medicine increased in the 1960s and 1970s, more physicians adopted a truth-telling perspective. By the late twentieth century and early twenty-first century, most physicians reported a propensity to tell the truth but also a continued willingness to deceive. Physicians typically acknowledge that most patients want accurate information about the diagnosis and prognosis, and that they typically provide it. However, they also sometimes indicate a reluctance to communicate as

straightforwardly as possible with patients who have a very negative prognosis. Many physicians place greater emphasis on the consequences (or outcomes) of a medical encounter than on adherence to a principle of unconditional truth-telling (Novack et al., 1989).

The most recent large-scale study of the propensity of physicians to give complete information to patients was conducted in 2003. This study of more than 1,000 practicing physicians found that 86 percent believed that physicians are obligated to present all information and medical options to patients. This does not mean that one should discount all physician discretion, and 63 percent of the physicians believed that it is ethically permissible to explain to patients their moral objections about certain possible actions. This research also identified what may be a developing trend. One physician in seven (14 percent) did not believe they had any obligation to present information about procedures with which they disagreed, or to refer the patients to other physicians who did not have the same moral outlook as themselves. These physicians tended to be very religious, and justified the withholding of medical options from patients based on their own religious beliefs (Curlin et al., 2007).

The findings of these studies are consistent with important research conducted by Naoko Miyaji (1993), who discovered that American physicians seem to value ethical principles that support disclosure of information to patients— through both truth-telling and informed consent—and these physicians give the impression that patients have control over obtaining information. However, in reality, physicians continue to manage the information-giving process. They interpret the principle of disclosure selectively and in such a way that they share with patients only as much information as they wish them to have. In the case of a patient with a newly diagnosed terminal illness, physicians emphasize possible treatments and decision-making options and give extensive information about them, but give much less information about and play down grim prognosis information, citing uncertainty and lack of relevance to future actions.

This communication pattern is justified by physicians as showing compassion and respect for the patient *and* the principle of disclosure while preserving as much hope as possible. These physicians could well respond to survey questions that they provide truthful diagnoses to patients; this may explain some of the very high percentage of physicians who now report themselves to be unconditional truth-tellers. However, on closer examination, it is clear that they still control the information-giving process and may not share complete information about the patient's condition. Miyaji concludes that this pattern

shows the ambiguity and tension which define the doctor's new role as a partner of the patient.

Preservation of their image (and self-image) as compassionate and caring physicians helps them to manage patient care in emotionally-laden situations like truth-telling as a healer. However, this humanistic model of the physician serves also to maintain the power of the profession, enhancing its "cultural authority" over patients. (Miyaji, 1993:250)

The manner in which medical truth-telling is handled in Japan is described in the accompanying box, "Truth-Telling and Cancer Patients in Japan."

CONFIDENTIALITY AS AN ISSUE

The *Tarasoff* Case

On July 1, 1976, the California Supreme Court handed down a decision in the case of *Tarasoff v. Regents of the University of California*, one of

---

IN COMPARATIVE FOCUS

TRUTH-TELLING AND CANCER PATIENTS IN JAPAN

Most countries in the world continue to struggle with the moral issues involved in disclosing or failing to disclose a terminal prognosis. Japan is a country in which physicians have traditionally refused to disclose terminal illness. In the United States, the right of autonomous individuals to be informed is now commonly respected (at least to a degree). In Japan, however, individuals are viewed primarily as being a part of a family and a community. The Confucian emphases on *kyokan* (the feeling of togetherness) and *ningen* (the human person in relationship to others) are prioritized over individual autonomy.

Given these emphases, Japanese physicians have traditionally lied to or deceived patients who are terminally ill (e.g., pretending the cancer is just an ulcer) and instead revealed

the prognosis to family members and consulted with them. Family members were strongly encouraged not to inform the patient of the real circumstances. Consultation with members occurred both in face-to-face interaction and through written communication.

In recent years, the tradition has begun to give way to greater respect for the autonomy of the individual. While young people still respect the role of the family in decision making and medical care, there is now a greater call for open disclosure to the patient. While the likelihood of medical truth-telling in Japan is still less than in the United States, today more and more Japanese physicians are providing full disclosure of a terminal illness (Brannigan and Boss, 2001; Elwyn et al., 1998).

the most important judicial cases to affect medical practice in our country's history. The facts of the case were basically undisputed. In 1969, a student at the University of California at Berkeley, Prosenjit Poddar, confided to his psychologist, Dr. Lawrence Moore, who was on the staff at Cowell Memorial Hospital on the Berkeley campus, that he intended to kill Tatiana Tarasoff, a young woman who lived in Berkeley but was at that time on a trip to Brazil.

Dr. Moore, with the concurrence of a colleague and the assistant director of the Department of Psychiatry, reported the threat to the campus police and asked them to detain Poddar and commit him to a mental hospital for observation. The campus police questioned Poddar, but satisfied that he was rational and based on his promise to stay away from Tarasoff, they released him. They reported their action to Dr. Harvey Powelson, the director of the Psychiatry Department.

Dr. Powelson requested no further action to detain Poddar or to follow up on the threats. Two months later, shortly after Tarasoff returned from her Brazil visit, Poddar went to her home and killed her. Later, when Tatiana's parents learned that university officials had known about the threat to their daughter's life but had failed to detain Poddar or warn them or their daughter, they brought a negligence suit against the therapists involved, the campus police, and the university, and sought additional punitive damages.

The original court hearing of the case dismissed all charges against all defendants. However, the California Supreme Court partially reversed the lower court's judgment when a majority ruled that general damages against the therapists and the university were in order for their failure to warn the girl or her family (punitive damages were dismissed) (Tobriner, 1976). (Due to a technical error, Poddar's second-degree murder conviction was overturned; since more than 5 years had elapsed since the murder,

he was not retried under an agreement that he would return to his native India, which he did.)

What are the implications of this ruling? Should the therapists have been morally and legally required to warn Tatiana Tarasoff? If so, what other circumstances would justify breaching confidentiality? Or should physicians maintain absolute confidentiality regarding information shared with them by all patients in all circumstances?

The Meaning of Confidentiality

The term **confidentiality** is often used interchangeably with "privacy" and with the concept of "privileged communication." However, the terms mean different things. **Privacy** refers to freedom from unauthorized intrusions into one's life. As applied to medical matters, it largely refers to the control that an individual has over information about him- or herself (Wasserstrom, 1986).

Clearly, there are some things—a person's thoughts, hopes, or fears—which no one else will know about unless that individual chooses to disclose them. As individuals, we are permitted to retain full custody of our private thoughts, and we cannot be compelled to compromise this sense of privacy. There are some occasions when we reveal our private thoughts to others but still hold dominion over them. For example, when we share information with certain professionals, such as physicians or the clergy, we do so with an understanding that this other person will respect our privacy and not reveal what has been said. This is the notion of "professional secrecy" (Wasserstrom, 1986).

Once information has been revealed to another person, it is never again as private. At this point, the individual must rely on the professionalism or goodwill of the other person not to reveal the information. This is the meaning of confidentiality. In the medical encounter, an individual patient who reveals information to a physician must now rely on the physician not to share the information with others. Maintaining confidentiality means that the information goes no further.

The idea of **privileged communication** comes from the legal system, which operates on the basis of *testimonial compulsion*—that is, individuals with pertinent information can be required to present that information in a court of law. However, our legal system recognizes the value of professional secrecy. In order to foster a close and trusting relationship between individuals and selected professionals, information shared with these professionals may be exempt from testimonial compulsion. The information or communication is said to be "privileged" in this sense.

The Laws Pertaining to Confidentiality

Contrary to common perception, there are no constitutional provisions covering confidentiality of information shared with a physician. Although the Fourth Amendment deals with the issue of privacy, its relevance to medical confidentiality has been left up to judicial interpretation. There is no common law that obliges physicians to hold confidential information shared by a patient. Such law does exist between lawyers and clients and between the clergy and parishioners.

In order to fill this void, individual states have developed privileged communication statutes. About two-thirds of the states now have these statutes, which specify that physicians cannot be compelled to reveal in a court of law information that has been received from a patient. However, states have also identified certain types of information that physicians are legally obligated to share with proper authorities. This information includes certain health conditions (primarily communicable diseases such as tuberculosis and sexually transmitted infections), gunshot wounds, and suspected or clear physical or sexual abuse of children. Some states now require physicians to report patients who may be unfit drivers (e.g., older individuals with certain illnesses), and some states recently tried unsuccessfully to require physicians to notify authorities if they treat undocumented immigrants.

Does a patient who feels that their physician has wrongfully breached confidentiality have any recourse in the law? Yes, they do. Physicians may be sued for malpractice for wrongfully disclosing patient information under one or more of three legal theories: (1) an unauthorized disclosure of confidential information, (2) an invasion of privacy, and (3) a violation of an implied contract between the physician and the patient.

The most significant legislation ever passed in the United States regarding medical confidentiality is the **Health Insurance Portability and Accountability Act 1996 (HIPAA)**. It includes several measures to protect the privacy of patients and their medical records and to establish security of electronic health information. This legislation has led to significant changes in protocol in medical facilities and with regard to the sharing of information about patients (United States Department of Health and Human Services, 2010).

Medical Codes

The principle of confidentiality has been firmly rooted in codes of medical ethics. The classic reference to the importance of confidentiality occurs in the Hippocratic Oath (see Chapter 2): "What I may see or hear in the course of the treatment or even outside of the treatment in regard to the life of men, which on no account one must spread abroad, I will keep to myself holding such things shameful to be spoken about."

This statement is credited with influencing all subsequent efforts to note the ethical

Health Care for
America's Families

The most important bill
ever passed in the United
States regarding medical
privacy was the Health
Insurance Portability and
Accountability Act 1996.
© J. SCOTT
APPLEWHITE/AP.

responsibilities of physicians. Today, the ethical code for nearly every medical group includes some reference to confidentiality, such as the Code of Medical Ethics (American Medical Association, 2016a).

When Confidentiality Becomes an Issue

Today, we generally think of four kinds of situations in which medical confidentiality may be an issue. The first are accidental or not so accidental "slips of the tongue" that physicians commit when chatting with family, friends, or colleagues. Fortunately, most health care professionals are careful not to let information about patients slip, although these "irresponsible" breaches do occur—often when inhibitions have been lowered by exhaustion or alcohol.

In addition, as the use of social networking sites such as Facebook and Twitter by the general population has increased in recent years, so has their use by medical professionals. Although there are restrictions on clearly unethical online behavior by medical professionals, there are also cases of communications which technically do not violate the HIPAA but are ethically questionable. Often these are situations in which medical students reveal important details about a patient or medical situation without revealing the patient's name. The purpose may be benign (e.g., reflecting on a difficult situation or seeking out social support), but such cases could inadvertently disclose a patient's identity, violate a patient's desire for privacy, or undermine trust in the health care system (Wells, Lehavot, and Isaac, 2015).

The second type of situation results from the increasingly large number of people who have access to patient information and data. With the advent of **electronic health records (EHRs)**, more and more physicians, nurses, and allied health workers have access to patients and patient records, and more and more agencies, including public health agencies, third-party payers, medical peer review committees, employers, credit investigation agencies, social welfare agencies, and medical researchers have a legal right to obtain patient data. There are some legal restrictions. However, there are volumes of people even beyond the obvious who are legally able to view patient information. For example, when an individual applies for life insurance, disability insurance, or long-term care insurance, the insurance companies are legally permitted to hire specialty firms to analyze the applicant's medication records. Thus employees of the specialty firm are given access to medical records. Etzioni (1999) has referred to these breaches of confidentiality as "authorized abuse." They occur on a daily basis and are perfectly legal, but they raise serious ethical questions.

The third area of concern is the increasing level of cyberattacks against physicians, clinics, and hospitals in efforts to steal medical records and personal patient information. The sensitive data that are stolen can be used by identity thieves to facilitate such matters as taking out a loan, getting a passport, blackmail, and making fraudulent income tax returns. An estimated 29 million health records in the United States were breached between 2010 and 2013. Not all of these were cases of cyberattacks, but many were. In 2015, Anthem, one of the nation's largest health insurance companies, announced that hackers had breached a database containing 80 million patient records. One month later, Premera Blue Cross reported that 11 million of its patient records had been hacked (Gosk, 2015). In 2015 a total of 100 million medical records were hacked. Cyberattacks now cost the health care system an estimated US$6 billion a year. Addenda to the HIPAA were provided in 2009 that require public reporting of breaches of personal health data, and in 2013 that encourage medical facilities to strengthen data-security measures against breaches, and penalize them if they do not, but progress has been slow.

Finally, an intriguing set of ethical questions occur in situations in which physicians must make a conscious decision as to whether or not to violate confidentiality. Examples like the *Tarasoff* case dramatize the issue. The remainder of this section of the chapter focuses on this subject.

Justifications for the Principle of Confidentiality

Philosopher Sissela Bok (1989) summarizes four justifications for physicians to protect the privacy of information shared by patients: (1) protection of the patient's autonomy over personal information; (2) enhancement of the physician–patient relationship; (3) respect for the patient; and (4) the opportunity for individuals to communicate more freely with the physician.

This final rationale was used by the justices writing the dissenting opinion in the *Tarasoff* case. Writing for the minority, Justice William P. Clark (1976) described three specific reasons why confidentiality ought not be broken. First, individuals who need treatment will be more likely to seek help if they have trust in physician confidentiality. Second, individuals seeking assistance will be more likely to provide full disclosure. Third, trust in the psychotherapist will be enhanced. Although distressed by situations like the *Tarasoff* case, the justices contended that maintaining confidentiality, rather than breaking it, will minimize tragedies in the long run because those needing help will not be dissuaded from seeking it.

Grounds for Breaking Confidentiality

Few people would dismiss the importance of confidentiality. However, whereas some individuals see confidentiality as an unconditional duty (never to be broken), others believe it to be a prima facie responsibility—that is, it can justifiably be broken if there are compelling reasons for doing so. Three such reasons are cited.

The first is benefit to the patient him- or herself—the principle of beneficence. An example where this rationale might apply would be a temporarily depressed or traumatized individual who threatens to commit suicide or engage in some disreputable, out-of-character behavior. In order to secure assistance to prevent the action, the physician may need to break confidentiality and disclose the stated intention of the person. However, physicians must be sure that an action contemplated by a patient really is a product of an irrational mind. Many people are too quick to assume that any decision made by another that is inconsistent with one's own values is not a rational decision.

A second possible justification for violating medical confidentiality is that it may conflict with the rights of an innocent third party. As a society, we must determine whether we prefer that innocent third parties be warned of impending danger, even though that means a breach of confidentiality, or that confidentiality not be broken.

The *Tarasoff* case is an example of this justification, but it may occur in less extreme circumstances. For example, suppose that a physician has as a patient a young man engaged to be married. He knows that the young man is concealing his permanent impotence from his fiancée. The question arises as to whether the physician should break confidentiality with this young male patient and reveal the information to the fiancée, or place priority on maintaining confidentiality and letting the chips fall where they may.

A third possible rationale for violating the principle of confidentiality is danger or threat to the rights or interests of society in general. As previously mentioned, various states require physicians to report certain specified diseases or conditions to proper authorities. However, not all such situations are governed by law. For example, how should a physician respond when he or she detects a serious medical problem in a patient whose occupation influences the safety

or lives of countless other people? What should be done in the case of a railroad signaler who is discovered to be subject to attacks of epilepsy, or an airline pilot with failing eyesight? Cases such as these force physicians to determine their primary obligation. Is it to protect the confidentiality of the diagnosis, recognizing all the accompanying benefits, or is there a greater obligation to the unknown others whose lives may be jeopardized by the medical condition of the patient (Allmark, 1995)?

Right Versus Duty to Breach Confidentiality

If, in certain situations, society decides that physicians have a "right" to break confidentiality, would we advocate a policy that says they have a "duty" to do so? That is, does the physician who diagnoses the epileptic railroad signaler not only have a right to disclose the information but also have a moral responsibility to do so? Or a legal responsibility? Should society morally and legally insist that the proper authorities be notified?

Where serious harm is likely to occur, Bok (1991) argues that the duty to warn is overriding. She contends that patients have no right to entrust information of this type to physicians and expect them to remain silent, and physicians have no right to promise confidentiality about such information. Of course, this is also the position taken by the majority in the *Tarasoff* case when the judges argued that the university psychotherapists had a duty to warn Tatiana of the threat that had been made.

Others, including many psychotherapists, were unhappy (to say the least) with the *Tarasoff* decision. Even those who could abide the idea that physicians *may* disclose a threat objected to the requirement that physicians *must* disclose it. For many, that compromised professional autonomy. The difficulties in determining which patients are serious about stated threats and the questions about the required severity of threat (e.g., is a broken arm sufficiently serious?) make this requirement an impossibility for them. Some research has shown that predictions of dangerousness are unreliable, and that mental health professionals are more likely to be incorrect than correct when making such predictions, and usually err on the side of over-predicting dangerousness (Oppenheimer and Swanson, 1990).

The manner in which personal characteristics of the patient might influence physician behavior regarding confidentiality is addressed in the box "The Influence of Patient Gender, Race, and Sexual Orientation on Maintenance of Confidentiality."

OBLIGATION TO TREAT PATIENTS WITH HIGHLY CONTAGIOUS DISEASES

An intriguing question related to the responsibilities of medical professionals concerns their duties with regard to treatment of patients with contagious diseases. The manner in which their responsibilities are defined makes an important statement about professional obligations, duty to individual patients and society, and duty to self. Any disease epidemic can raise these issues (as has occurred recently with the Ebola virus, SARS, and several recent influenza outbreaks), although the discovery of the HIV/AIDS virus in the early 1980s dramatically raised these issues and led to serious conflicts of perspective. This section summarizes the key arguments in this debate about professional obligation to treat patients with highly contagious diseases by focusing on HIV/AIDS in the years after it was discovered and before any treatments were available.

Physicians' Perceptions Regarding the Obligation to Treat

In the decade after AIDS came to public attention, much research showed that a sizable

---

IN THE FIELD

THE INFLUENCE OF PATIENT GENDER, RACE, AND SEXUAL ORIENTATION ON MAINTENANCE OF CONFIDENTIALITY

Physicians may consider a variety of factors in determining whether to break a confidence with a patient. Schwartzbaum, Wheat, and Norton (1990) attempted to determine whether physician behavior was at all influenced by the gender, race, or sexual orientation of the patient—factors that would not seem relevant. A sample of white male primary care physicians was given a case study in which an HIV-infected patient presented a risk to a third party. Eight different descriptions of the gender, race, and sexual orientation of the patient were distributed randomly among the physicians, one description to each of them. Each physician was asked to select his own likely behavior from a list of five choices reflecting a range of confidentiality breaches.

Findings showed that the physician respondents were more likely to report black homosexual and heterosexual men to the health department and black heterosexual men to their partners than hypothetical patients in other categories. Were these physicians influenced by the greater use that blacks make of public health departments (so that informing the health department seemed logical)? Were they influenced by the perception that black HIV-positive men are more likely to be intravenous drug users and thus possibly less likely to be conscientious about informing their partners? Were these physicians reflecting an explicit or implicit racial bias that influenced behavior?

percentage of physicians did not wish to treat AIDS patients and did not believe that they had a professional obligation to do so. For example, Link et al. (1988) surveyed medical and pediatric interns and residents in seven New York City hospitals with large AIDS patient populations. While only 11 percent of respondents were moderately or extremely resentful of having to care for AIDS patients, 25 percent stated that they would not continue to care for them if given a choice. Moreover, 24 percent believed that refusing to care for AIDS patients was not unethical, 34 percent believed that house officers should be allowed to decide for themselves whether to treat AIDS patients, and 53 percent believed that medical students should be offered treatment choice. In a national survey of family physicians, 62.9 percent stated that physicians have a right to refuse to care for a patient solely because he or she is infected with the AIDS virus (Bredfeldt et al., 1991).

Historical Perspectives on the Obligation to Treat

Does history offer a clear picture as to how physicians in earlier times viewed the issue of obligation to treat contagious diseases? Yes, but a consistent tradition does not exist. Zuger and Miles (1987) found no such tradition in earlier epidemics such as the Black Death (in Europe in the thirteenth century), the Great Plague (in London in the seventeenth century), and yellow fever (in the United States in the eighteenth century). Many physicians fled from patients with contagious disease and cities with a large disease population, but many others, often at considerable personal risk, remained to care for these patients.

Laws Pertaining to the Obligation to Treat

Several legal principles do pertain to the issue of treatment obligation. George Annas summarizes the basic concept of legal obligation to treat:

American common law is firmly grounded on notions of individual liberty and economic freedom that support the proposition that absent some special relationship, no citizen owes any other citizen anything. As applied to the practice of medicine, the general rule, sometimes denoted the "no duty rule," is that a physician is not obligated to treat any particular patient in the absence of a consensual doctor-patient relationship. In the absence of a prior agreement or a statutory or regulatory prohibition, physicians (like other citizens) can, in deciding whether to accept patients, discriminate among them on the basis of all sorts of irrelevant and invidious criteria; from race to religion, to personal appearance and wealth, or by specific disease, like AIDS. (Annas, 1988:26)

The "special relationship" referred to in the quotation pertains to the obligation to treat of emergency room physicians, physicians in an ongoing doctor–patient relationship, and physicians with a contractual obligation (e.g., through a health care institution or insurance plan).

Medical Codes

Hippocratic Oath. It is unclear as to whether the **Hippocratic Oath** specifies any legal obligation to treat. A line in the oath, "into whatsoever houses I enter, I will enter to help the sick," has been interpreted by many to be stating a prescribed duty of physicians, one "neither abrogated or attenuated by incapacitating or terminal disease, nor by the assumption of personal risk" (Kim and Perfect, 1988:136). On the other hand, some contend that the line attaches only very loosely to "obligation to treat," and does not offer sufficient detail to clarify a complex matter such as treating AIDS patients.

The AMA's Code of Medical Ethics. The official position of the AMA on obligation to treat has evolved through the years and has undergone important transformations. In constructing its first code of medical ethics in 1847, the AMA broke from existing medical codes by establishing a duty to treat: ". . . and when pestilence prevails, it is the [physician's] duty to face the danger, and to continue their labors for the alleviation of the suffering, even at the jeopardy of their own lives" (Jonsen, 1990:161).

This phrase notwithstanding, a revision of the Code of Ethics in 1912 included the addition of the statement that "A physician shall, in the provision of appropriate patient care, except in emergencies, be free to choose whom to serve" (Judicial Council of the American Medical Association, 1986).

Over the last 50 years, the AMA code has been revised on several occasions, sometimes emphasizing the "duty to face danger" phrase and sometimes the "free to choose" phrase. An attempt in 1986 to reaffirm the profession's longstanding role in treating contagious patients while simultaneously offering physicians a method of exemption (e.g., if they were not emotionally able to care for AIDS patients) satisfied some, but also engendered some backlash. In critical response, the American College of Physicians and the Infectious Diseases Society of America issued a joint statement which proclaimed that "denying appropriate care to sick and dying patients for any reason is unethical" (Health and Public Policy Committee of the American College of Physicians and the Infectious Diseases Society of America, 1986). Public opinion strongly supported the "duty to treat" position (Wallis, 2011). A year later, in December 1987, the AMA issued another position paper, clearly shifting its emphasis toward the duty to treat AIDS patients.

The AMA leadership appears to be caught in a dilemma. On the one hand, there seems to be recognition that it is inappropriate for physicians to refuse treatment to AIDS patients or patients with other contagious diseases simply on the basis of that diagnosis, and that an obligation to treat represents a more respectable professional standard. Criticism, especially from inside medicine,

has not gone unnoticed. On the other hand, the free-to-choose tenet also has a long tradition in medicine and is clearly very important to many physician members of the AMA.

This dilemma may explain the frequency of revised statements and even the current situation. For although the current statement offers emphatic support for treatment, AMA leaders have made it clear that any physician who wishes not to treat AIDS patients can label him- or herself incompetent to treat, and the AMA will pro forma accept the excuse (American Medical Association, 2016b).

George Annas, a professor of health law, concluded that "In effect, this reduces the AMA's position to a statement that a doctor *must* treat an AIDS patient if the doctor *wants* to treat an AIDS patient" (Annas, 1988:S30).

Rationale for No Obligation to Treat

A key aspect of the philosophical underpinning of the "no-obligation" position is that physicians ought to be free to select their patients. Part of the traditional autonomy of a career in medicine lies in not being told which patients must be seen. In the early years after the discovery of HIV/AIDS, many physicians explicitly stated that they wished to exercise this freedom of selection by excluding AIDS patients.

On what grounds could AIDS patients be excluded? Ezekiel Emanuel (1988), an M.D. in Harvard's Program in Ethics and the Professions, has identified four factors that were used as specific justifications for having no obligation to AIDS patients.

Excessive Risks. Unquestionably, many physicians were fearful of contracting HIV from patients. Studies in the 1980s routinely found that between one-third and one-half of medical residents reported moderate to major concern about treating HIV/AIDS patients. Almost half of the physicians surveyed by Taylor et al.

(1990) said that they were more frightened of contracting AIDS than any other disease. Those who perceived the greatest risk were most likely to believe in the no-obligation position. Response to treating AIDS patients was influenced by the physician's stage of career and setting. Medical residents—who then provided a significant amount of care for AIDS patients, but without having any choice in the matter—were more likely than medical faculty and medical students to report fear of exposure to AIDS and an unwillingness to treat AIDS patients (Yedidia, Barr, and Berry, 1993).

These results assess subjective state—the fear of or concern about contracting AIDS. These perceptions are crucial because physicians, as well as others, behave on the basis of what they perceive to be real. Based on experimental studies, the Centers for Disease Control and Prevention estimates that the risk of becoming infected with HIV and developing AIDS after a single accidental exposure to HIV at work (most likely through an accidental puncture wound) is 0.5 percent (1 in 200) or less.

Were the concerns and fears expressed by physicians unreasonable, given these documented levels of risk? Many suggest that physicians overreacted to the possibility of risk and should have recognized that their own behavior (e.g., extreme carefulness in avoiding punctures) would reduce the likelihood of transmission. However, a commentary in the *Journal of the American Medical Association* took the opposite point of view, and condemned efforts to reduce the perceived risks of infection by emphasizing "low" transmission rates. Gerbert et al. (1988) asked what is meant by "low" when discussing a condition that is always fatal, and one that can be contracted regardless of the physician's carefulness and other infection control measures. Among their recommendations for dealing with the fear felt by many health care professionals was acknowledgment that risk does exist and that concern is warranted.

Questionable Benefits. A second rationale for no obligation pertained to the lack of long-term benefits in treating AIDS patients that was perceived at the time ("After all, he (or she) is going to die anyway, so why bother?"). Physicians are not obligated to provide unnecessary useless care, and some procedures (e.g., cosmetic surgery on a dying patient) could hardly be said to be ethically obligatory. (Recall that the advances in drug therapy for those with HIV/AIDS did not start to occur until the very late 1990s and early 2000s.)

Obligations to Other Patients. Obligation to other patients was used as a rationale for the no-obligation position. The argument was that, by treating AIDS patients, physicians risked contracting AIDS, which would make it impossible for them to care for their other patients. Moreover, other patients might discontinue their relationship with the physician when they learned he or she was seeing AIDS patients. One survey reported that 40 percent of a sample of family practice physicians feared that they would lose some patients if they found out that AIDS patients were also being seen in the office (Bredfeldt et al., 1991).

Obligations to Self and Family. Refusing to treat an AIDS patient on the grounds that his or her medical care cannot justify the jeopardizing of the physician's life or health is a perception that was held by some physicians. Some critics have asked whether this position was bolstered by an implicit (or explicit) judgmental process about the relative value of the individuals involved—that is, were physicians more likely to feel this way because many of their patients were gay, or intravenous drug users?

Later research indicated that the answer was yes. A study of matriculating medical students in Chicago found that 92 percent would welcome HIV patients into their practice, but that homophobia and fear of infection were the most common explanations for those who would not (Carter, Lantos, and Hughes, 1996). A research study of preclinical medical students also found largely favorable attitudes toward treatment, but that students who were uncomfortable with homosexual behavior and felt awkward about taking a sexual history from gay people were least willing to treat (McDaniel et al., 1995). Finally, a study that compared the attitudes of students in their fourth year of medical school and again as third-year residents found that the strongest predictors of change in attitudes for those whose willingness to treat declined were homophobic attitudes and aversion to intravenous drug users (Yedidia, Berry, and Barr, 1996).

Two other considerations emerged from research studies. First, some physicians were concerned that treating AIDS patients carried financial liability. Physicians who were not treating AIDS patients were more likely to believe that these patients were a financial risk to a practice, that they would drive away other patients, and that they created considerable legal liability. Second, some physicians expressed considerable fear that they might unknowingly contract HIV and transmit it to their own partner and/or children. Consideration of this rationale may come down to two questions. First, do physicians' partners and families need to expect to share in some risks of the profession? Second, are the risks so great as to overcome whatever professional rationale exists for treating AIDS patients?

Rationale for Obligation to Treat

While historical traditions, laws, and medical codes offer a perspective on the obligation-to-treat position, often they do not articulate the underlying philosophical principles on which it is based. Recently, medical practitioners, philosophers and ethicists, lawmakers, and social scientists have reflected on reasons why there may be an obligation to treat. Three such principles are described here.

The Nature of the Profession.   Perhaps the firmest principle on which to base an obligation to treat is the inherent nature of the profession of medicine. Professions represent special statuses; typically, they involve more training and greater commitment than other careers, and are rooted in a special ideal of service to others. Emanuel traces a duty to treat to the nature of the profession:

> The objective of the medical profession is devotion to a moral ideal—in particular, healing the sick and rendering the ill healthy and well. The physician is committed to the help and betterment of other people—"selflessly caring for the sick," as the president of the American College of Physicians has put it. When a person joins the profession, he or she professes a commitment to these ideals and accepts the obligation to serve the sick. It is the profession that is chosen. The obligation is neither chosen nor transferable: it is constitutive of the professional activity. (Emanuel, 1988:1686)

According to this viewpoint, making distinctions among the sick based on the type or nature of the disease is contrary to the ideal of the profession. The noble dimension of this professional duty is treatment of all patients—especially the most vulnerable—without making these distinctions.

It is largely this factor that led the U.S. Supreme Court to rule that health care workers cannot refuse treatment to individuals with HIV/AIDS. The justices contended that the objective and reasonable view of health care professionals is that there is minimal risk in treating AIDS patients, and that a contrasting judgment of an individual physician is not sufficient to override the obligation not to discriminate by non-treatment.

The Social Contract.   The second principle used to support obligatory treatment rests on the implicit *social contract* made between society and the medical profession. This rationale states that physicians have an obligation to treat the sick and vulnerable in exchange for the discretionary powers they have been given over the clinical practice of medicine. Potential danger in doing so does not exempt the physician from fulfilling this obligation any more than it exempts a police officer or firefighter (Arras, 1988).

Fulfillment of this reciprocal obligation, however, can be viewed in two ways. One interpretation is that it creates an obligation on the part of each physician to treat those in medical need and not to shun those with particular diseases. After all, the argument goes, every physician benefits from the control that physicians have over medical practice. For any physician to treat only those individuals whom he or she has selected would be a failure to perform the expected reciprocal obligation.

A second view posits that the obligation to care for the sick is attached to physicians in general, but not necessarily to individual physicians. According to this view, the reciprocal obligation is fulfilled as long as there are a sufficient number of physicians to care for the sick—specifically, here, to treat AIDS patients—even if not every individual physician participates (Arras, 1988).

This latter interpretation is consistent with a voluntaristic system in which only willing physicians treat people with AIDS. The idea was appealing in the sense that AIDS patients might expect the most compassionate care from those freely choosing to offer treatment. However, the downside was that it could place an unfair burden (in terms of risk, stress, etc.) on those willing to offer treatment (Arras, 1988).

The Dependent Patient.   A third justification is that physicians are linked to patients in ways that extend beyond an explicit or implicit contract. According to this view, there is something unique about the physician–patient relationship. It takes on a moral dimension, especially in cases of a "dependent" patient in need of the professional's services.

This responsibility is even more compelling given the physical and emotional suffering endured by AIDS patients. Peter Conrad (1990) and others have written about the "marginal" place in which society often places AIDS patients, and the severe stigma attached to the disease. Although it is now clear that AIDS knows no sexual orientation boundaries, the fact that the disease was first reported to be a disease of homosexuals (it was called the "gay plague") created a lack of empathy, and sometimes even blatant hostility and disregard, for those with the virus.

Siegel and Krauss (1991) studied the major challenges of daily living experienced by 55 HIV-positive gay men. One of the three major adaptive challenges they reported was dealing with reactions to a stigmatizing illness. They talked openly in focused interviews of their feelings of shame and contamination based on the way that others interacted with them. Even deciding whom to tell of their infected status was a difficult decision, as they knew that many would respond negatively. Those who speak of a special relationship between physician and "dependent" patient find no better example than that of a physician working with AIDS patients. Many physicians who care for HIV-infected individuals do find their work rewarding and stimulating. In one study, 60 percent of physician respondents noted patient gratitude for their work, 57 percent mentioned the intellectual challenge of dealing with the disease and well-informed patients, and 30 percent identified a desire to serve the underserved (Epstein, Christie, and Frankel, 1993).

SUMMARY

Much can be learned about the dynamics of the physician–patient relationship by examining the manner in which the issues of truth-telling, confidentiality, and the obligation to treat patients with highly contagious diseases are handled. Surveys consistently show that the vast majority of people want physicians to unconditionally tell the truth, but many physicians (although fewer than in the past) still use their discretion when deciding whether or not to tell the whole truth (including a clear statement of prognosis) to individual patients.

Those who support unconditional truth-telling justify their position by stating that only truth-telling displays real respect for the patient, that it is necessary to keep promises, that lying would undermine the patient's trust in the physician, and that patients need to know the truth in order to be able to make decisions on an informed basis. Those who believe that physicians should use their discretion argue that it might be in the patient's best interest, that it is impossible to communicate the "full truth" to a medical layperson, and that many patients really do not want to know the truth about a serious illness.

While most medical codes emphasize the importance of protecting confidentiality, some justify breaking confidentiality in order to protect the patient, an innocent third party (e.g., in the case of Tatiana Tarasoff), or society in general. Others believe that confidentiality should always be maintained in order to protect the patient's autonomy, legitimate secrets, keep faith with a patient, and encourage people who need help to feel free to seek it.

Research has shown that, at least in the early years of AIDS, many physicians preferred not to treat AIDS patients. While neither history nor medical codes offer a decisive position on the existence of a "duty to treat," many believe that physicians should not have been compelled to offer care to AIDS patients for four reasons: (1) excessive risks, (2) questionable benefits of treatment, (3) obligations to other patients, and (4) obligations to self and family.

Those who believe that there is a duty to treat cite three reasons. First, it is an inherent part of the nature of the profession; second, it is part of a social contract between society and medicine; and third, the "special" physician–patient relationship calls for physicians to offer care to dependent patients.

HEALTH ON THE INTERNET

You can research the latest ethical policies of the AMA on issues covered in this chapter by accessing the Code of Medical Ethics at:

www.ama-assn.org/ama/pub/physician-resources/medical-ethics/code-medical-ethics.page

Click on "Principles of Medical Ethics." What are the emphases of these nine principles? What rights are patients given in these principles?

Go back to the "Principles." Click on "Opinions of the Physician–Patient Relationship." Read Opinion 10.01 (Fundamental Elements of the Patient–Physician Relationship) and Opinion 10.015 (The Patient–Physician Relationship. What responsibilities are assigned to physicians within these opinions?).

Go back to the "Principles." Click on "Opinions on Professional Rights and Responsibilities." Click on Opinion 9.121 (Racial and Ethnic Health Care Disparities)

and Opinion 9.122 (Gender Disparities in Health Care). What are the important messages being communicated to physicians in these items?

DISCUSSION CASES

Case 1. *Scenario 1:* A 35-year-old woman who is unmarried and without children, but has parents and three sisters in a neighboring state, is diagnosed as having cancer. By the time of diagnosis, the cancer has already spread throughout her body. It is too late to perform surgery, and her physician determines that neither chemotherapy nor radiation can be successful at this advanced stage. Patients diagnosed with cancer at this stage rarely live more than a year.

The physician knows that the patient has been working on her first novel for 2 years, and that it has been the major interest in her life. The patient expects to have it completed in the next 3 or 4 months. The physician believes that he can stall giving the correct diagnosis and prognosis, through deception and evasive answers, until the patient has completed her novel. He fears that providing the honest diagnosis at this point will so depress the patient that she will not be able to finish the book. The physician and patient have never discussed how a situation like this should be handled.

How would the physician–patient relationship be affected by a general expectation of unconditional truth-telling versus an expectation that physicians ought to use their discretion in revealing information to patients? How do these two expectations affect the physician's role in the encounter, and how do they affect the patient's role? In this case, do you believe the physician ought to provide this patient with the correct diagnosis and prognosis or attempt to deceive her until her novel is completed?

Scenario 2: Alter the preceding scenario as follows. On the day before the patient is to return to the office to hear her test results, her parents call the physician long distance. They explain that they are calling out of love and concern for their daughter and due to a fear that she has cancer or some other life-threatening disease. If that is the case, they plead for the physician not to reveal the diagnosis. Their understanding of their daughter leads them to believe that hearing the correct diagnosis will so traumatize her that she would quickly give up the will to live.

Should the physician be influenced by the wishes of the family and attempt to deceive the patient, or should he be sympathetic with the family but make it clear that he must be honest with their daughter? What does his decision imply about the role of significant others in the care of patients?

Scenario 3: Add the following circumstance to scenario 1, and omit the information in scenario 2. On the day of her return visit, the patient initiates conversation with the physician. She expresses her fear that she has a life-threatening disease. If that is the case, she says, she would rather not know it. She states that she would rather avoid hard-and-fast reality, believing that this would give her the best opportunity to complete her novel and carry on as normally as possible for as long as possible.

What should the physician do? Do patients have a right to make this request of physicians? If they do, should physicians comply with the expressed wishes of the patient or explain that the physician's responsibility is to convey as accurately as possible what has been learned?

Case 2. The State Medical Board in your home state is considering a new regulation that would strictly forbid any physician to refuse to accept a patient or to refuse to continue seeing a patient (whom he or she is qualified to treat) solely on the basis that the patient has a highly contagious disease. Suspected violations of this policy would be investigated by the State Medical Board, and a hearing would be held. If convicted of violating this regulation, a physician would lose their medical license for 6 months for a first offense, 1 year for a second offense, and permanently for a third offense.

Knowing that you have taken a course in medical sociology and have a keen interest in this subject, the board has called you to testify about this proposed regulation. Would you testify in favor of or against this proposal? What is the rationale for your testimony?

GLOSSARY

benevolent deception
casuistry
confidentiality
electronic health records
ethics
Health Insurance Portability and Accountability Act 1996 (HIPAA)

Hippocratic Oath
medical ethics
principlism
privacy
privileged communication
sociology of bio-knowledge

REFERENCES

Allmark, Peter. 1995 "HIV and the Bounds of Confidentiality." *Journal of Advanced Nursing*, 21:158–163.

American Medical Association. 2016a "Opinion 5.05: Confidentiality." *Code of Medical Ethics*. Chicago, IL: American Medical Association.

———. 2016b "Opinion 9.131: HIV-Infected Patients and Physicians." *Code of Medical Ethics*. Chicago, IL: American Medical Association.

———. 2016c "Opinion 8.082: Withholding Information from a Patient." *Code of Medical Ethics*. Chicago, IL: American Medical Association.

Annas, George J. 1988 "Legal Risks and Responsibilities of Physicians in the AIDS Epidemic." *Hastings Center Report*, 18:S26–S32.

Arras, John D. 1988 "The Fragile Web of Responsibility: AIDS and the Duty to Treat." *Hastings Center Report*, 18:S10–S20.

Beauchamp, Tom L., and James F. Childress. 2012 *The Principles of Biomedical Ethics*, 7th ed. New York: Oxford University Press.

Bok, Sissela. 1989 *Secrets: On the Ethics of Concealment and Revelation*. New York: Vintage.

———. 1991 "Lies to the Sick and Dying." Pp. 74–81 in *Biomedical Ethics* (3rd ed.), Thomas A. Mappes and Jane S. Zembaty (eds.). New York: McGraw-Hill.

Brannigan, Michael C., and Judith A. Boss. 2001 *Healthcare Ethics in a Diverse Society*. Mountain View, CA: Mayfield Publishing Company.

Bredfeldt, Raymond C., Felicia M. Dardeau, Robert M. Wesley, Beth C. Vaughn-Wrobel, and Linda Markland. 1991 "AIDS: Family Physicians' Attitudes and Experiences." *The Journal of Family Practice*, 32:71–75.

Carter, Darren, John Lantos, and J. Hughes. 1996 "Reassessing Medical Students' Willingness to Treat HIV-Infected Patients." *Academic Medicine*, 71:1250–1252.

Clark, William P. 1976 "Dissenting Opinion in *Tarasoff v. Regents of the University of California.*" Pp. 160–162 in *Taking Sides: Clashing Views on Controversial Bioethical Issues* (2nd ed.), Carol Levine (ed.). Guilford, CT: The Dushkin Publishing Group.

Conrad, Peter. 1990 "The Social Meaning of AIDS." Pp. 285–294 in *The Sociology of Health and Illness: Critical Perspectives* (3rd ed.), Peter

Conrad and Rochelle Kern (eds.). New York: St. Martin's Press.

Curlin, Farr A., Ryan E. Lawrence, Marshall H. Chin, and John D. Lantos. 2007 "Religion, Conscience, and Controversial Clinical Practices." *New England Journal of Medicine*, 356:593–600.

DeVries, Raymond, and Janardan Subedi. 1998 *Bioethics and Society*. Upper Saddle River, NJ: Prentice Hall.

Elwyn, Todd S., Michael D. Fetters, Daniel W. Gorenflo, and Tsukasa Tsuda. 1998 "Cancer Disclosure in Japan: Historical Comparisons, Current Practices." *Social Science and Medicine*, 46:1151–1163.

Emanuel, Ezekiel J. 1988 "Do Physicians Have an Obligation to Treat Patients with AIDS?" *New England Journal of Medicine*, 318:1686–1690.

Enzinger, Andrea C., Baohui Zhang, Deborah Schrag, and Holly G. Prigerson. 2015 "Outcomes of Prognostic Disclosure: Associations with Prognostic Understanding, Distress, and Relationship with Physician among Patients with Advanced Cancer." *Journal of Clinical Oncology*, 33:3809–3816.

Epstein, Ronald M., Michael Christie, and Richard Frankel. 1993 "Primary Care of Patients with Human Immunodeficiency Virus Infection: The Physician's Perspective." *Archives of Family Medicine*, 2:159–167.

Etzioni, Amitai. 1999 "Medical Records: Enhancing Privacy, Preserving the Common Good." *Hastings Center Report*, 29:14–23.

Gerbert, Barbara, Bryan Maguire, Victor Badner, David Altman, and George Stone. 1988 "Why Fear Persists: Health Care Professionals and AIDS." *Journal of the American Medical Association*, 260:3481–3483.

Gosk, Stephanie. 2015 "Electronic Medical Records Are Latest Target for Identity Thieves." www.nbcnews.com/us-news/electronic-medical-records-latest-target-identity-thieves-n365591.

Guiora, Alexander Z. 1980 "Freedom of Information Versus Freedom From Information." Pp. 31–34 in *Ethics, Humanism, and Medicine*, Marc D. Basson (ed.). New York: Alan R. Liss.

Health and Public Policy Committee, American College of Physicians, and the Infectious Diseases Society of America. 1986 "Position Paper: Acquired Immunodeficiency Syndrome." *Annals of Internal Medicine*, 104:575–581.

Jonsen, Albert R. 1990 "The Duty to Treat Patients with AIDS and HIV Infection." Pp. 155–168 in

AIDS and the Health Care System, Lawrence O. Gostin (ed.). New Haven, CT: Yale University Press.

Judicial Council of the American Medical Association. 1986 *Current Opinions—1986*. Chicago, IL: American Medical Association.

Kelly, William D., and Stanley R. Friesen. 1950 "Do Cancer Patients Want to Be Told?" *Surgery*, 27:822–826.

Kim, Jerome H., and John R. Perfect. 1988 "To Help the Sick: An Historical and Ethical Essay Concerning the Refusal to Care for Patients with AIDS." *American Journal of Medicine*, 84:135–137.

Legal Information Institute. 2016 *Ethics: An Overview*. Ithaca, NY: Legal Information Institute. www.law.cornell.edu/wex/ethics.

Link, Nathan R., Anat R. Feingold, Mitchell H. Charap, Katherine Freeman, and Steven P. Shelov. 1988 "Concerns of Medical and Pediatric House Officers about Acquiring AIDS from Their Patients." *American Journal of Public Health*, 78:455–459.

McDaniel, J. Stephen, Lisa M. Carlson, Nancy J. Thompson, and David W. Purcell. 1995 "A Survey of Knowledge and Attitudes about HIV and AIDS among Medical Students." *Journal of American College Health*, 44:11–14.

Miyaji, Naoko. 1993 "The Power of Compassion: Truth-Telling among American Doctors in the Care of Dying Patients." *Social Science and Medicine*, 36:249–264.

Novack, Dennis H., Barbara J. Deterling, Robert Arnold, Lachlan Forrow, Morissa Ladinsky, and John C. Pezzullo. 1989 "Physicians' Attitudes Toward Using Deception to Resolve Difficult Problems." *Journal of the American Medical Association*, 261:2980–2985.

Oppenheimer, Kim, and Greg Swanson. 1990 "Duty to Warn: When Should Confidentiality Be Breached?" *Journal of Family Practice*, 30:179–184.

Petersen, Alan. 2013 "From Bioethics to a Sociology of Bio-Knowledge." *Social Science and Medicine*, 98:264–270.

Schwartzbaum, Judith A., John R. Wheat, and Robert W. Norton. 1990 "Physician Breach of Patient Confidentiality Among Individuals with HIV Infection: Patterns of Decision." *American Journal of Public Health*, 80:829–834.

Siegel, Karolynn, and Beatrice J. Krauss. 1991 "Living with HIV Infection: Adaptive Tasks of

Seropositive Gay Men." *Journal of Health and Social Behavior*, 32:17–32.

Taylor, Kathryn M., Joan M. Eakin, Harvey A. Skinner, Merrijoy Kelner, and Marla Shapiro. 1990 "Physicians' Perception of Personal Risk of HIV Infection and AIDS Through Occupational Exposure." *Canadian Medical Association Journal*, 143:493–500.

Tobriner, Mathew O. 1976 "Majority Opinion in *Tarasoff v. Regents of the University of California.*" Pp. 154–159 in *Taking Sides: Clashing Views on Controversial Bioethical Issues* (2nd ed.), Carol Levine (ed.). Guilford, CT: The Dushkin Publishing Group.

United States Department of Health and Human Services. 2010 *The Health Insurance Portability and Accountability Act of 1996 (HIPAA) Privacy and Security Rules.* www.hhs.gov/ocr/privacy/.

Wallis, Patrick. 2011 "Debating a Duty to Treat: AIDS and the Professional Ethics of American Medicine." *Bulletin of the History of Medicine*, 85:620–649.

Wasserstrom, Richard. 1986 "The Legal and Philosophical Foundations of the Right to Privacy." Pp. 140–147 in *Biomedical Ethics* (2nd ed.), Thomas A. Mappes and Jane S. Zembaty (eds.). New York: McGraw-Hill.

Wells, Deva M., Karen Lehavot, and Margaret L. Isaac. 2015 "Sounding Off on Social Media: The Ethics of Patient Storytelling in the Modern Era." *Academic Medicine,* 90: 1015–1019.

Yedidia, Michael J., Judith K. Barr, and Carolyn A. Berry. 1993 "Physicians' Attitudes Toward AIDS at Different Career Stages: A Comparison of Internists and Surgeons." *Journal of Health and Social Behavior*, 34:272–284.

Yedidia, Michael J., Carolyn A. Berry, and Judith K. Barr. 1996 "Changes in Physicians' Attitudes toward AIDS During Residency Training: A Longitudinal Study of Medical School Graduates." *Journal of Health and Social Behavior*, 37:179–191.

Zuger, Abigail, and Steven H. Miles. 1987 "Physicians, AIDS, and Occupational Risk: Historical Traditions and Ethical Obligations." *Journal of the American Medical Association*, 258:1924–1928.

CHAPTER 14

The Health Care System of the United States

Learning Objectives

- Describe and discuss evaluative ratings of the pre-Affordable Care Act health care system in the United States.

- Describe the foundation and origin of the private nature of the health care system in the United States, and the entry of public programs such as Medicare and Medicaid.

- Describe and evaluate the managed care approach that was developed to control rapidly increasing health care costs.

- Identify and explain five key reasons for the high cost of health care in the United States.

- Describe the pre-Affordable Care Act "uninsured" problem in the United States and the extent to which it has or has not been improved. Discuss the problems associated with not having health insurance.

- Thoroughly analyze the Affordable Care Act. Describe how it changes the U.S. health care system, who benefits most from it, and political perspectives about the law.

America's health care system is undergoing one of the most significant transformations in its history. After extensive health care policy debates in the 1990s and 2000s, significant health care reform legislation—the Patient Protection and Affordable Care Act, now routinely identified as the Affordable Care Act (ACA) or Obamacare—was passed in 2010. Almost all of the legislation has survived ongoing constitutional challenges in the years since then. Both implementation of the Act and efforts by congressional Republicans to overturn passage or strike down parts of the Act continue.

Prior to the Affordable Care Act, almost all knowledgeable analysts agreed that the U.S.

health care system, at its best, was an innovative system that provides effective, high-technology care that is among the world's finest. At the same time, the health care system was generally recognized as being extremely expensive, inefficient and wasteful, grounded in profit making, and leaving tens of millions of Americans lacking the resources to obtain basic health care. This chapter describes the health care system of the United States up until reform legislation was passed in 2010, including the serious fiscal crisis of the system and its inability to provide care for all in need, and it examines the health care reform process, passage of the Affordable Care Act, and the early outcomes of the legislation.

RATING THE HEALTH CARE SYSTEM OF THE UNITED STATES

Based on Systematic Analysis

In the first decade of the 2000s, a major research effort was undertaken to systematically evaluate the overall quality of the U.S. health care system (Schoen et al., 2006). The Commonwealth Fund (CF) is a respected private non-partisan foundation that seeks to promote a higher-quality medical care system. In 2006, the CF initiated an annual review of 37 important indicators of the functioning of the health care system. The five general focus areas were health outcomes, quality, access, efficiency, and equity. Specific indicators included items such as number of deaths from preventable disease, number of school days children miss due to illness, life expectancy, percentage of physicians who use electronic records, and percentage of national health expenditures that go for administrative costs. Performance of the U.S. system was compared with benchmarks from within the country and with health care systems in other countries.

Ultimately, based on a 100-point scale, the performance of the U.S. health care system was calculated as being 66 (by 2011 the score had dropped to 64). On no indicator did the U.S. system function as well as the top performers, and in some cases its performance was far behind that of the leaders. It was calculated that by improving its performance on key indicators, the United States could annually save as many as 150,000 lives and up to US$100 billion. Study leaders summarized the situation as follows:

> The overall picture that emerges from the scorecard is one of missed opportunities and room for improvement. Despite high expenditures, the United States lags behind other countries on indicators of mortality and healthy life expectancy. Within the United States, there is often a substantial spread between the top and bottom groups of states, hospitals, or health plans as well as wide gaps between the national average and top rates. . . . On multiple indicators, the United States would need to improve its performance by 50 percent or more to reach benchmark countries, regions, states, hospitals, health plans, or targets. (Schoen et al., 2006:472)

Based on Consumer Attitudes

Prior to reform, were Americans generally satisfied or dissatisfied with the health care system? Was there a propensity to defend the system or had conditions reached a point where there was significant unhappiness? Many surveys have been conducted during the last few decades, and they have consistently pointed to increased consumer dissatisfaction with the U.S. health care system.

One consistent finding has been that most Americans made a distinction between the quality of the personal care that they receive and the quality of the health care *system*. Whereas most have been satisfied with their own care, they have been frustrated, angry, and disappointed with the functioning of the health care system. Fewer than four in ten respondents in surveys expressed a great deal of confidence in the nation's medical care system, and most had higher regard for other social institutions (e.g., the legal system and the education system) (Blendon et al., 2006).

In a 2006 survey, only 13 percent of Americans agreed with the statement that the health care system works pretty well and only minor changes are needed to make it work better, 49 percent saw the system as having some good features but believed fundamental changes were needed, and 37 percent believed that the system had so much wrong with it that it needed to be completely rebuilt (Harris Interactive Poll, 2006). This negative assessment of the health care system has been found consistently for more than two decades.

The question then is how and why the United States developed a health care system that is fundamentally different to those in all other countries, and that is by far the world's most expensive system, yet one that is both objectively and subjectively rated so unfavorably.

THE HEALTH CARE SYSTEM OF THE UNITED STATES

The Foundation of the Health Care System

The foundation of today's U.S. health care system largely originated in a series of events that occurred between 1850 and the early 1900s. Advances in the scientific understanding of disease and illness and in the effectiveness of medical procedures, the expansion and elaboration of hospitals, and the growth of commercial health insurance companies contributed to an increasingly complex system of health care delivery and financing. The professionalization of medicine, the establishment of high standards for medical education, and the institution of medical licensure contributed to significant autonomy for medical providers, increasing medical fees, and greater difficulty for those with fewer financial resources to access needed care.

Since those early years, America's health care system has been based on a "private market" approach. This means that the system is allowed to function based on private decisions made by medical facilities, medical providers, and patients without government involvement or intervention. The rationale for the private market approach is that the competition for resources—profit—would be the strongest possible motivator for individuals and companies to work their hardest and to do their best. The laws of supply and demand that functioned in other areas of the economy were also considered appropriate for the health care system.

This approach assumes that the most equitable means of allocating health care is through the private market. Health care is to be viewed as an economic good or a privilege that would be most accessible by those with the greatest resources. Proponents contend that this competitive basis has stimulated the drive for the development of superior medical schools, new medical technologies, and the highest quality of health care possible.

Many countries around the world used a similar approach early on, but later converted from it. While the United States maintained strong belief in the principle of individualism, other countries showed a greater collective orientation and stronger commitment to the general welfare of the people. Over time, other countries determined that a private market approach was unsuccessful with regard to health. They observed that the health care system did not follow basic rules of supply and demand, that many people were unable to access health care services, and that the health care system was not functioning as effectively or justly as was desirable.

In fact, every other modern country in the world today emphasizes a "social justice" approach to its health care system rather than a private market approach. Other countries identify health care as a "right" that should be made available to everyone, rather than an economic good or privilege. They believe that the government is more effective than the private market in allocating health care equitably and ensuring that no one goes without needed health care services.

The Development of Private Health Insurance

Although private health insurance companies began appearing in the mid-1800s, they really became the cornerstone of health care financing in the United States in the early 1900s. Initially, they provided compensation for workers who were losing wages because they had been injured on the job or had become sick. During the early 1900s—the time when medicine was professionalizing and hospital care was growing in importance—private insurers saw potential in selling health insurance policies. These quickly became a crucial element in paying for health care.

Today, there are almost 1,300 *private* (commercial) health insurance companies in the United States. Some of these companies offer only health insurance, while others also offer life, homeowners, renter, automobile, and other types of insurance. These are profit-making companies whose intention is to set premiums at a level that will allow them to pay out all claims, pay for all administrative, salary, and overhead expenses, and have money left over for profit for investors.

Health insurance policies are sold to individuals, families, and groups (usually businesses). It is often said that no two health insurance policies are exactly alike—they cover whatever the buyer negotiates. They may include basic health benefits, benefits for very large bills, income replacement during disability, and benefits for dental care, eye care, drugs, and so forth. In addition to the basic premium, policies usually have a *deductible* provision (the policy owner pays a set amount of money before the insurance kicks in) and *coinsurance* provision (the policy owner pays a set percentage of all costs beyond the deductible) and *co-payments* (specific fees paid out of pocket for particular services, such as US$20 for each visit to a primary care physician beyond what the insurance pays).

In the United States, health insurance became a benefit provided by employers for workers and their families. This arrangement was considered to be consistent with the private market approach. It gave individuals an additional incentive to have a job and work hard, and it gave employers an extra mechanism for recruiting and retaining good workers. Because they represented large numbers of workers and families, employers could purchase sizable policies which gave them leverage to negotiate a good rate. Insurance companies competed with each other for sales, and this gave them an incentive to be efficient.

Thus was the advent of a private-market, employer-based health insurance system. Individuals and families without employer-sponsored health insurance, but with sufficient wealth, could purchase their own policies. Those without health insurance coverage and without adequate financial resources could not afford to access the system, but this was seen as an acceptable result for people who had not successfully competed in the job world. Health insurance companies, pharmaceutical companies, medical equipment companies, some hospitals, and a variety of other health services became part of the private market designed to be profit making.

The Development of a Non-Profit Health Insurance Alternative

By the late 1920s and the Depression, it was apparent that millions of individuals were not in the labor force through no fault of their own, and they certainly were unable to afford private health insurance. Their need for health care services was high, but they were unable to pay for the services. Hospitals sometimes provided their care, but did not get paid. To offer a more affordable alternative than the for-profit companies, Blue Cross—later to become Blue Cross-Blue Shield (BC-BS)—a non-profit health insurance company, was created in 1929. In exchange for its non-profit status (and exemption from paying taxes), the BC-BS plans offered comprehensive policies to a wide range of individuals at prices often measurably below those of commercial companies. This approach was enormously successful, and throughout much of the twentieth century the health insurance field was dominated by BC-BS. However, in the 1990s the "Blues" determined that their non-profit status did not serve them well in the changed health care system, and most BC-BS plans (now with a variety of company names) around the country converted to a for-profit basis.

The Entry of Public (Government-Sponsored) Health Insurance

In the 1960s, the United States experienced considerably heightened awareness about the extent of poverty and the fact that many individuals—adults and children alike—were in very poor health yet unable to afford medical care. Many analysts believed that the private market had failed to function effectively with regard to health care, and advocated for increased public (government) involvement in the health care system. They pointed out that public programs are often created to serve those whose needs are not being met by the private sector. Among the many health programs that were already supported by public dollars even before the passing of the Affordable Care Act were those for members of the armed forces, veterans, mothers and children, Native Americans, schoolchildren, and the disabled.

By the 1960s, the two groups who seemed most unable to access services in the private market were (1) older people who were retired and trying to live on Social Security and perhaps a small pension, and (2) people on a very low income, who frequently worked at jobs that did not offer employer-sponsored health insurance. Presidents Kennedy and Johnson formulated legislation that led to the passage of Medicare (largely for those aged 65 years or older) and Medicaid (largely for those on a very low income) in 1965. These have become by far the largest government-sponsored health insurance programs.

Medicare. **Medicare** is a federal insurance program originally designed to protect people aged 65 years or older from the rising costs of health care. In 1972, permanently disabled workers, their dependents, and people with end-stage renal disease were added to the program.

The two key long-standing parts of the program are Part A (the hospital insurance program, which covers inpatient hospital services, skilled nursing services, home health services, and hospice care) and Part B (the physician services program, which covers physician services, outpatient hospital services, and therapy). All people aged 65 years or older are eligible for Part A simply by enrolling, although there are deductible and coinsurance provisions. A premium must be paid for participation in Part B, which also includes a deductible and coinsurance. Medicare is financed by a combination of general tax revenues and payroll taxes levied on employers and employees in addition to the enrollee payments.

Historically, Medicare has not contained any coverage for prescription drugs—a very serious omission. That led many seniors (perhaps as many as 25 percent of those aged 65 years or older) to forgo getting needed prescriptions filled. As the price of medications skyrocketed, the problem became more severe. In 2003, Congress added a hotly debated and very narrowly passed prescription drug benefit (Part D) to Medicare. Using a complex formula, enrollees in the drug benefit paid a monthly premium, had a deductible, had co-payments, paid all costs between designated amounts, and paid a different, smaller co-payment after that. The opponents of the bill were primarily those who felt that the bill did not go far enough and did nothing to control drug price increases. For example, Congressional Democrats wanted Medicare to be able to use its size to negotiate lower drug prices from pharmaceutical companies, but Congressional Republicans opposed this as being too great an interference with the private market. The payment formula was so complex that the bill was widely regarded (even by most Medicare enrollees) as a bad law, and it has now been modified. Analyses consistently find that Medicare enrollees still pay a substantial amount for health care and for their medications, but that the program contributes significantly to the health and wellness needs of those aged 65 years or older.

In 2014, Medicare covered more than 55 million people (more than 17 percent of the U.S. population) at an annual cost of more than US$618 billion. Medicare alone accounts for one-fifth (20 percent) of all health dollars spent in the United States.

Medicaid.   **Medicaid** is a jointly funded federal-state program designed to make health care more available to the very poor. Eligibility requirements and program benefits vary from state to state, even though the federal government requires that people receiving certain types of public assistance (as well as pregnant women, children under the age of 6 years, Medicare enrollees, and recipients of foster care and adoption assistance not covered by other programs) be eligible for the program.

Federal and state funds paid through Medicaid for health care amounted to more than US$495 billion for more than 65 million recipients (about 20 percent of the U.S. population) in 2014. Medicaid accounts for 16 percent of all health dollars spent in the United States. (It is possible to receive Medicare and Medicaid simultaneously, so the total number of recipients is less than the combination of the two sets of enrollment.) Together, in 2014, Medicare and Medicaid paid for 37 percent of national spending on health care and generated more than 40 percent of hospital revenues.

The elderly, blind, and disabled account for more than 50 percent of Medicaid funds, even though they represent less than 25 percent of recipients. On the other hand, more than two-thirds of Medicaid recipients are members of a family receiving public assistance, but they receive only 25 percent of program benefits.

The Medicare and Medicaid programs are examples of "entitlement" programs. This means that people receive benefits automatically when they qualify for the programs (in the case of Medicare Part B, qualifying includes payment of a premium). The number of people covered is determined primarily by the number of people aged 65 years or older for Medicare and by the number of people below a designated income/assets line for Medicaid. Because the government has little control over the number of participants, it has limited ways to control costs. Eligibility requirements for Medicaid can be tightened, but more than half of all people under the age of 65 years and below the poverty level are already ineligible for Medicaid. Benefits can be reduced, but they are already at meager levels. The reimbursement to providers can be reduced, but compensation from both programs has already been cut. Medicaid reimbursement for primary care physicians is now less than two-thirds of prevailing market rates. In addition, both Medicare and Medicaid are in financial difficulty. Prior to the 2010 reform legislation, it was anticipated that Medicare would go bankrupt within a few years. Most states are having a difficult time balancing their budgets due in part to their Medicaid expenditures.

Children's Health Insurance Program (CHIP).   A third large public program, although much smaller than Medicare and Medicaid, is the **Children's Health Insurance Program (CHIP,** formerly known as SCHIP). CHIP was created in 1997 with the objective of reducing the number of children without health insurance. CHIP serves uninsured children up to the age of 19 years in families with incomes too high to qualify them for Medicaid. States have broad discretion in setting their income eligibility standards, and eligibility varies greatly across states. The federal government gives grants to states that pay for about two-thirds of the program, and the state pays for the remainder. In the first 10 years of CHIP's existence, the percentage of children in the United States without any health insurance decreased from 23 percent to 15 percent, and by 2012 it was down to 7 percent. However, the more successful the program has become in covering children (about 8 million children are now enrolled), the more the program costs have increased. Analyses of CHIP have uniformly found it to be a very effective program (Oberlander and Jones, 2015).

Despite the program's success, in 2006 some states stopped enrolling additional children in the program. The fact that many children still went without needed medical care was undisputed, but states argued that they could not afford to pay for more. By 2007, about one-third of the states stopped new enrollment, and several threatened to begin dis-enrolling children already in the program. Congress voted to authorize additional funds so that children already enrolled could stay in the program and additional children in need could be added to it. At this time, about 9 million children in the United States lacked health insurance. President Bush countered with a proposal that would add only 40 or 50 percent as much money as Congress had sought. This laid the groundwork for a very contentious debate.

Most congressional Democrats wanted to significantly increase the allocation to CHIP (adding US$75 billion over 5 years). A bipartisan group recommended adding US$35 billion over 5 years. President Bush threatened to veto either approach as being too expensive. Ultimately, Congress voted for the US$35 billion—enough to add 4 million children. Public opinion surveys showed overwhelming support for the bill, but President Bush vetoed it. Congress passed a revised bill, keeping it at US$35 billion but making other revisions. President Bush again vetoed it. In February 2009, less than a month after the election of President Obama, Congress passed a US$33 billion addition to CHIP allowing enrollment of 4 million additional children, and President Obama signed it (Oberlander and Lyons, 2009).

Incentives to Overuse Services

The creation of the Medicare and Medicaid programs (and later CHIP) has been of tremendous help to those who are covered by them. In many cases the programs mean the difference between receiving and not receiving health care, and between life and death. They have also pumped billions of dollars into the health care system and ensured that many providers would be compensated for services delivered. However, the programs also highlighted a problem with the traditional way that insurers compensated providers.

In the traditional reimbursement method, patients covered by any form of health insurance would see a medical provider and receive a set of medical services. The medical provider would determine the amount to be charged and send a bill to the insurance company, which would remit the amount of the charge. This system lacks cost control mechanisms, as no one has an incentive to be cost conscious. Patients often paid nothing for services received and willingly accepted all of the suggested services. Physicians could charge whatever they wanted and receive full reimbursement. Insurers could pass on higher premiums to those they insured. After the passage of Medicare and Medicaid, both the number of people able to receive services and the number of services provided to each patient increased and the charges for services rapidly escalated. The period of tremendous growth of the health care system had arrived.

Provision of Unnecessary Services. By the early 1980s, compelling evidence had been uncovered that the lack of cost-consciousness had led to many unnecessary health care services being provided. Academic researchers and policy analysts had determined that as many as one-sixth to one-fifth of all operations were unnecessary, that the annual cost for these unnecessary operations was of the order of billions of dollars, and that as many as 12,000 patients per year died in the course of an unnecessary procedure. Table 14–1 shows the increase in overall health expenditures since 1960.

TABLE 14–1   National Health Expenditures

Year	Total Amount (US$)	Domestic Product (%)	Amount per Capita (US$)
1960	26.9 billion	5.1	141
1970	73.2 billion	7.1	341
1980	247.2 billion	8.9	1,051
1990	699.5 billion	12.2	2,689
2000	1.3 trillion	13.3	4,670
2010	2.6 trillion	17.4	8,428
2014	3.0 trillion	17.5	9,523

Note: The average medical cost for a family of four in 2014 was US$23,215.

Source: National Center for Health Statistics, *FastStats,* Centers for Disease Control and Prevention, Atlanta, GA, 2016.

The most intensive study of surgical necessity was conducted by the Rand Corporation, a think tank in Santa Monica, California. Based on input from medical experts, they developed a list of indicators of the need for four specific procedures. Then they applied this list to the records of 5,000 recent Medicare patients. They found that 65 percent of carotid endarterectomies (removal of blockages from one or both arteries carrying blood to the brain) were unnecessary, as were 17 percent of coronary angiographies (an X-ray technique in which dye is injected into the coronary arteries to diagnose blockages), 17 percent of upper gastrointestinal tract endoscopies (examination of the digestive organs with a fiber-optic tube), and 14 percent of coronary bypass surgeries (relieving or replacing blocked arteries by adding or rerouting other blood vessels). Other studies with other population groups found very high rates of unnecessary surgery for procedures such as Caesarean section, hysterectomy, laminectomy, tonsillectomy, colonoscopy, spinal fusion, prostate removal, gall-bladder removal, hip replacement, and knee replacement.

In response, policy makers sought ways to restructure the health care system to discourage unnecessary procedures and to create some cost control incentives. Cost containment strategies and the managed care approach were developed with this in mind.

Cost Containment and the Development of Managed Care

Cost containment strategies are an effort to give financial incentives to provide only necessary services and to do so in a cost-efficient manner. Until the Affordable Care Act was passed, the most significant cost containment event within health care financing in the last 30 years was the movement toward **managed care**. Managed care plans attempt to realize cost containment by combining the traditional insurance function of private insurance companies and the government with a delivery system of health care providers. They are and will remain (at least in the near future) a central part of the health care system.

The rationale underlying managed care is that these plans can control health care cost increases because they oversee and monitor patient behavior, provider behavior, and insurer behavior. Controls are designed to manage or guide the patient care process, attempting to ensure that appropriate and cost-efficient care is provided and that inappropriate and unnecessarily expensive care is not. Originally, managed care provisions were incorporated within traditional health insurance plans, but they have now almost completely replaced traditional plans. Table 14–2 shows the distribution of insured people across types of insurance plans in 1990,

TABLE 14–2 Distribution of Employees across Health Benefit Plans in the Years Prior to Passage of the Affordable Care Act

Type of Plan	1990 (%)	2000 (%)	2009 (%)
Conventional	62	8	1
Health maintenance organization	20	29	20
Preferred provider organization	13	42	60
Point of service	5	21	10
High deductible	0	0	8
Total managed care	38	92	99

Source: Reprinted with permission from the Henry J. Kaiser Family Foundation, 2016. The Kaiser Family Foundation based in Menlo Park, California, is a non-profit, private operating foundation focusing on the major health care issues facing the nation, and is not associated with Kaiser Permanente or Kaiser Industries.

2000, and 2009 (the year prior to passage of the Affordable Care Act).

How does this control work? There are three essential components. First, a **managed care organization (MCO)** (ownership today is often held by a traditional private health insurance company) recruits medical providers in an area to be part of the MCO. Typically, a physician who joins continues to practice in the same location but understands that some of their patients will now be insured by the MCO and that there will be special regulations when treating these patients. The physician must also agree to a lower-than-usual reimbursement amount. Why would physicians or hospitals sign up? The reason is because the MCO is promising large numbers of patients and warning that these patients will go elsewhere unless the provider agrees to join.

Second, the MCO recruits patients. Very often this means contracting with local employers to cover all of their employees. If the employer signs on, patients will be given financial incentives to see only providers who are part of the MCO, and they also agree to abide by special regulations. Why would an employer contract with a particular MCO? The reason is because the MCO is guaranteeing the best deal—the most services covered for the least amount of money (the facts that providers are accepting a lower reimbursement amount and that patient behavior will be regulated enable a good deal to be offered).

Third, the MCO will construct the list of providers, the cost per service, and the "special regulations." What might these regulations be? They can include a requirement to see a primary care physician before a specialist for a care episode (because primary care physicians are less expensive), pre-admission review for all elective hospital admissions (because some may not be necessary), mandatory second opinions before surgery (because less expensive options might be identified), continued review of patient care during hospital stays, discharge planning, and alternative benefit coverage (e.g., outpatient surgery, home health care, and skilled nursing facility care). In the case of pre-admission and continued review of hospital stays, a physician (or their nurse or assistant) will call the MCO to have a nurse reviewer verify the admission and report the expectations (e.g., length of stay) of the insurance company. Failure of the physician or hospital to stay within the limits jeopardizes full reimbursement. Renegotiation can occur while the patient is in the hospital. In addition, almost every service covered will include a coinsurance or co-payment. This is to give patients an added incentive not to overuse services.

Types of Managed Care Organizations. There are four main types of MCOs—health maintenance organizations (HMOs), preferred provider organizations (PPOs), point-of-service plans (POS), and the fast-growing exclusive provider organizations (EPOs).

Health maintenance organizations (HMOs) are *prepaid* plans in which a group of physicians and hospitals provide health care in return for a fixed premium from enrollees. HMOs are responsible for providing a stated range of health care services (typically a minimum of ambulatory and hospital care, dental care, medications, and laboratory tests) that must be available 24 hours a day. These services are typically provided by a subset of a community's providers who contract with the HMO and accept a lower reimbursement level and some guidelines to follow in exchange for a promise of patients.

There are three primary differences between HMOs and traditional private insurance plans. First, in a traditional plan, the provider is reimbursed after a service is provided. The more services that are provided, the more the provider makes. In HMOs, physicians are typically compensated on a "capitation" basis—that is, based on the number of patients they are willing to see and not on the number of services provided. Thus traditional financing arrangements have built-in incentives for providers to do more tests and procedures in order to maximize income, while HMOs have incentives to reduce the use of services. HMOs maximize profit by keeping people healthy (they emphasize wellness and prevention) and by discouraging inappropriate use of costly physician and hospital services.

Second, with private health insurance, the patient has complete freedom to select any available provider. HMO enrollees must select from the list of providers who have contracted with the HMO, so there is less freedom to choose one's provider.

Third, both providers and patients agree to all of the HMO's regulations for each care episode.

While there are other differences, many patients view enrollment in an HMO as entailing willingness to accept some regulations on care and sacrifice some choice of provider in order to pay lower health care costs. Although numbers vary considerably from community to community, on average, HMOs save patients approximately 10 to 20 percent in expenditures.

Ownership of HMOs remains highly diversified, but the clear trend is toward for-profit models. Growth in ownership has been fastest among commercial health insurance companies such as CIGNA, Aetna, and Prudential. More than two-thirds of HMOs are now controlled by for-profit companies, and some predict that the figure will eventually be 100 percent.

Do HMOs offer high-quality care? Are patients and physicians satisfied with their experiences? The answer to both questions is that it depends on the particular HMO. Much research has found that, in general, HMO enrollees receive more preventive care, have the same or slightly more physician visits, receive fewer expensive tests and procedures, have lower hospital admission rates, have a shorter length of stay when hospitalized, have less use of costly technology, and have mixed but generally better health outcomes. However, significant variations in the provision of services exist among HMOs.

The most heated controversy surrounds the issue of whether HMOs are apt to deny needed services in order to maximize short-term profit. Recall that in managed care, profit is maximized (at least in the short term) when expensive services are *not* performed, and some HMOs have developed explicit incentive systems that could easily discourage physicians from ordering services. For example, some HMOs have given telephone clerks (people typically with little or no medical training who answer phone calls from patients wanting to make an appointment) cash bonuses for keeping calls short and limiting the number of appointments that they make. Many HMO enrollees have publicized cases in which they were denied care that they considered to be necessary.

In some HMOs, most patients express satisfaction with the care they receive, but in other HMOs most patients express dissatisfaction. Reported satisfaction levels range from as high as 75 percent to as low as 35 percent. These differences have led some of the best HMOs to adopt marketing plans that attempt to distinguish them from more lowly rated plans. Many physicians express frustration with HMOs for overly interfering in the care of patients, and for all of the paperwork involved in securing compensation/reimbursement.

Preferred provider organizations (PPOs) are networks of physicians and hospitals that agree to give price discounts to groups who enroll in their program, use their services, and agree to follow specified regulations (e.g., pre-admission hospital review). PPOs allow members to receive care outside the network, although the co-payments are higher. Though patients typically pay for care received on a fee-for-service basis (unlike HMOs) as members of a PPO, they pay lower fees than do other patients. In exchange for discounting fees, PPO providers are likely to see more patients. On average, cost savings for PPOs relative to traditional fee-for-service arrangements are in the range of 5 to 15 percent. More than 80 percent of PPOs are run on a for-profit basis, with commercial insurance companies accounting for most PPO ownership.

Over time, HMOs and PPOs have come to more closely resemble each other. The four key differences are that (1) HMOs do more regulation of patient care, (2) HMOs have smaller rosters of available medical providers from which to choose, (3) HMOs cost less than PPOs, and (4) providers are typically paid by the capitation method in HMOs but by discounted fees in PPOs. When given a choice between the two, patients decide whether to accept the greater restrictions and smaller roster of providers in HMOs in order to achieve greater cost savings, or to pay more for PPO membership to get fewer regulations and a larger list of providers from which to choose.

Point-of-service (POS) plans are a hybrid of HMOs and PPOs. Typically, they offer more choice of providers (like PPOs) while retaining more care management regulations (like HMOs). Providers are reimbursed by the capitation method. Members are able to receive care outside the system (i.e., use a provider who is not part of the plan) by paying a higher premium or absorbing a larger share of the cost. Some have described POS plans as having the benefits of the network discount of PPOs and the gatekeeper process of HMOs, but with the possibility that the participant can receive partially subsidized care outside the network. Because they add flexibility for participants, POS plans have become quite popular.

Exclusive provider organizations (EPOs) have recently become more commonly used in an attempt to save more money. They are structured in the same way as PPOs, with the important exception that EPOs do not pay anything to enrollees for services received from a provider who is not in the plan's network (and they do not count toward the deductible). EPOs had quickly grown to about 10 to 15 percent of all plans in 2015, but it is predicted that they will become the most common plan within just a few years. Because HMOs already have tighter regulations, they are largely replacing PPOs and POS plans.

High Deductible Health Plans. A second type of cost-containment approach is the *High Deductible Health Plan (HDHP)*—a type of health insurance plan that costs less because it incorporates a very high deductible (at least US$1,000 for individuals and US$2,000 for families, although it is often much higher). Typically, this type of plan is linked to a personal (or health) savings account and goes by the name *consumer-driven health plan (CDHP)*. Health savings accounts allow individuals and families to set aside pretax dollars to pay for health care costs as they arise (and to have this backed up by an insurance policy that covers catastrophic situations). Money not used for deductibles and other health care costs in one year can be rolled over until the next year. The cost-containment rationale is based on the fact that individuals and families will be paying a large amount out of pocket for their health care before insurance kicks in, and therefore they will only do so when absolutely necessary. These plans have become increasingly popular, and more and more employers are offering them to employees—sometimes as the only health insurance option. However, many analysts believe that these programs have only a limited effect on the problem of lack of access in the United States, and are especially unsuitable for low-income individuals and families.

THE FINANCING OF HEALTH CARE IN THE UNITED STATES

How Much Money Does the United States Spend on Health Care?

The United States has the most expensive health care system in the world (by far), and costs have been escalating rapidly. During the last five decades, health care spending has grown more rapidly than any other sector of the economy. **National health expenditures (NHEs)**—that is, the total amount of spending for personal health care and for administration, construction, research, and other expenses not directly related to patient care—reached US$3.0 trillion (i.e., US$3,000 billion) in 2014—or more than 12 times the amount spent in 1980 and almost 4 times that spent in 1990. Notice the tremendous increase in all three items in Table 14–1.

The 2014 figure accounts for almost 18 percent of the gross domestic product (GDP)—the nation's total economic output. That is to say that health care represents about 18 percent of the U.S. economy, and about US$1 in US$6 spent in the United States is on health care. The percentage of GDP spent on health care is much higher in the United States than in any other modern country, and, unlike the United States, all other modern countries provide universal health care coverage. Americans spent an average of US$9,523 per person on health care in 2014—more than twice as much as people in any other country. By 2024, it is estimated that health care will occupy about 20 percent of the United States economy.

The annual rates of increase in NHE in the 1980s and early 1990s were among the highest ever—sometimes more than 10 percent per year. In the late 1990s, the rate of increase was lower—about 4 to 6 percent per year—but still higher than the increase in the overall consumer price index. By the early 2000s, however, annual increases were back in the 7 to 10 percent range, and analysts believed that is where they would remain. The economic downturn starting in 2008 depressed spending throughout the economy, including in health care, but spending growth has been back at 4 and 5 percent per year since then.

Personal health expenditures (PHEs) include all spending on such health services as hospital care, physician, dental, and other professional medical services, home health care, nursing home care, and drugs and over-the-counter products purchased in retail outlets, but not money for things such as medical research. It is by far the largest component (about 85 percent) of NHE. In 2013, PHE amounted to approximately US$2.5 trillion. The next section focuses on PHE.

Who Receives the Dollars Spent on Personal Health?

Who receives the dollars that are spent by Americans on health? What are we buying with the health care dollar? The five largest items (listed by dollars spent in 2013 and rounded off) are as follows:

1. *Hospital care* (US$937 billion—38 percent of PHE). Hospitals remain the largest recipient of health care dollars. More than one-third of all personal health care dollars are in payments to hospitals. Over the last few years this percentage has remained largely unchanged.

2. *Physician services* (US$587 billion—24 percent of PHE). Physicians are the second largest recipient of health care dollars. After many years of increases, this percentage has actually dropped or held steady in recent years due to more tightly controlled reimbursement levels used by the government and MCOs, and sharp increases in spending in other categories.

3. *Drugs and medical supplies* (US$370 billion—15 percent of PHE). Prescription drugs and durable (e.g., wheelchairs, sleep-assistance machines) and non-durable (e.g., over-the-counter medications) medical products are the fastest increasing category of PHE. This category includes only those drugs and over-the-counter products that are purchased from retail outlets, and excludes drugs dispensed in hospitals, nursing homes, and physicians' offices. Retail sales of prescription drugs account for 75 percent of this category. If all drugs are included, this percentage increases to around 18 percent.

4. *Nursing home care and home health care* (US$236 billion—10 percent of PHE). While the growth rate for nursing home care dollars is decelerating, the increasing number of elderly people and the high charges per day make this the fourth largest category of expenditures. The home health care industry continues to expand, and now accounts for almost US$80 billion per year.

5. *Dental care* (US$111 billion—5 percent of PHE). This is the fifth largest recipient of PHE, and the only other one over US$100 billion in 2013.

Who Spends the Dollars for Personal Health Care?

How is money channeled into the health care system? Health care in the United States is financed by a complex mix of private purchasers (employers, families, and individuals) and public purchasers (the federal and state governments) who pay health care providers directly for services and products or channel payment through private or public health insurance.

Private Sources

In 2013, over half (57 percent) of all personal health care services were paid for by private sources. The fact that this percentage is close to 50 reflects both the private market foundation of the U.S. health care system *and* the fact that the system has become a public–private mix. It also reflects the fact that even prior to health reform, public dollars accounted for almost half of those spent on health care. Most of these private payments—and the single largest source of payments for health care—came from private health insurance companies, and most of the remainder was paid out of pocket by individual patients and their families (see Table 14–3). Over the last 50 years, the relative contribution of private insurance within this category has increased while the relative contribution paid out of pocket has decreased, but passage of the

TABLE 14–3   Source of Payments for Health Services, 2013

Item	Amount (%) of Expenditures (in US$ billion) (rounded)
Personal health expenditures	2,468.6
Paid by private sources	1,406.6 (57% of PHE)
Private insurance	786.1 (35% of PHE)
Out of pocket	846.0 (14% of PHE)
Other	221.2 (8% of PHE)
Paid by the government	1,061.9 (43% of PHE)
Medicare	550.5 (22% of PHE)
Medicaid	410.8 (17% of PHE)
Other	100.6 (4% of PHE)

Source: Centers for Medicare and Medicaid Services, Office of the Actuary, Office of National Health Statistics, Baltimore, MD, 2016.

Affordable Care Act will increase the number of dollars coming from the public sector.

Payment for health insurance policies comes both from employers (who pay for all or part of a policy for employees and their families as a job benefit) and from individuals and families (who typically pay for part of the employer-provided policy or purchase a policy directly from a private health insurance company and must pay the entire premium).

Employers.   Health insurance policies are expensive regardless of who pays. In 2015, employers paid more than US$17,000 per worker to provide the company's share of health insurance for the worker and covered dependents (and employees contributed about US$5,000). Employers paid more than US$6,000 as their share for a policy to cover a single employee (and the employee contributed more than US$1,000). Businesses derive funds to pay for these policies largely by increasing the price of goods or services that they sell.

Rapid increases in insurance premiums in the last two decades have prodded many companies to revise the health insurance benefit provided to employees. Four changes have been especially dramatic:

- Some small businesses (which are hardest hit by providing insurance) have discontinued employee coverage. Only about three in five workers today are covered by an employer-provided plan—the lowest percentage in several decades, and still decreasing. In 2015, just under half (47 percent) of firms with three to nine employees offered a health insurance benefit to employees, while 98 percent of businesses with 200 or more employees did so.
- Most employers have increased the percentage of the health insurance plan that must be paid by employees. Whereas many companies formerly paid 100 percent of the

costs, the average today has dropped to about 74 percent. In addition, employer contributions for coverage for dependents (many of whom had been largely subsidized) have been decreased.
- Employers have reduced the types and amount of health care covered by the policy.
- Policies have increased the deductible, increased the coinsurance, and increased the co-payment for those covered.

Employers feel pressure to pay for a reasonable share of employee health insurance cost. For large companies, this is a huge amount. In 2012, General Electric paid US$2.5 billion for health care premiums. The dollar value is smaller for small firms, but the percentage of operating costs is higher. Given the changes that have occurred, employees and dependents now pay more out of pocket for health care than ever.

Individuals and Families.   These changes in the provision of employer-provided health insurance mean that individuals and families pay for health care in a variety of ways: (1) by paying a portion of the cost of a health insurance policy that is largely paid for by the employer or by paying the entire cost if the employer does not provide insurance coverage; (2) by paying out-of-pocket health care expenses not covered by an insurance policy (deductibles, coinsurance, co-payments, and uncovered services); and (3) through various taxes such as the Medicare tax (employees have 1.45 percent of salary or wages deducted to subsidize Medicare; employers match this amount).

For many workers, the decreasing percentage that employers pay for worker health care insurance and the changing structure of health care benefits make paying for health care extremely difficult or impossible. In 2005, workers paid an average of US$584 for health care before insurance kicked in; in 2015, the figure was US$1,318. In 2005, only 55 percent of workers had a deductible on their plan; in 2015, 81 percent did so, and many of these were high-deductible plans that require workers to pay a first amount anywhere from US$1,300 to US$6,000–10,000. Once the deductibles were fulfilled, in 2015, on average, workers had a co-payment of US$24 to see a primary care physician, US$37 to see a specialist, and US$308 for a hospital admission (Brandeisky, 2015). Research has found that nearly 30 percent of adults with deductibles of at least US$1,500 per person per year forgo needed medical care because they cannot afford it (Sutherly, 2015).

Public Sources (Government)

Over the last 40 years, one of the most important changes in the way that we pay for health care has been a shift from a reliance on private sources to increased government funding. Between 1960 and 2013, the percentage of health care financing that came from the government increased from 24.9 to 43 percent.

In order to see health care spending in perspective, it is helpful to consider the overall budget for the United States. The 2015 budget called for overall expenditures of about US$3.9 trillion—that is, US$3,900,000,000,000, or US$3,900 billion. Of that sum, approximately US$1.1 trillion was designated for health-related purposes (including Medicare, Medicaid, CHIP, veterans' health care, the Indian Health Service, etc.). Added to this amount is that paid by state governments (Medicaid expenditures are the largest health-related item for states).

EXPLANATIONS FOR THE HIGH COST OF AMERICAN MEDICINE

How does the United States manage to spend more money and a higher percentage of its GDP on health care than any other modern country, while being the only one that fails to provide universal health care coverage? In reality, the high cost of health care can be traced to several complex interrelated changes that have occurred in society and within the health care system. This section examines three of the most important factors.

The Aging of the Population

The most important factor *external* to the health care system (but *not* the largest overall factor) that is contributing to increases in health care costs is the aging of the population and the accompanying increase in the experience of chronic diseases.

In 2015, the United States surpassed the 320 million population figure. The U.S. is the fastest growing developed country in the world, and much of this growth is based on immigration and a high birth rate among Hispanics—the largest immigrant group by far. However, the demographic trend that most contributes to increased health care spending is the fact that more Americans are living to older ages. Between 2000 and 2040, the number of people in the United States aged 65 years or older will increase from 34.8 million to 77.2 million, and the number of people aged 85 years or older will increase from 4.3 million to 14.3 million.

The increasing number of older Americans contributes to increased health care costs in several ways. As people age, they are more likely to experience one or more chronic degenerative diseases such as heart disease, cancer, and diabetes. These diseases are often manageable, but they are resource intensive in terms of the number of health care workers, health care facilities, and medications that are necessitated—all of which are very expensive. (It is estimated that 86 percent of all health care dollars spent are for chronic diseases.) The very high and rapidly increasing cost of drugs is especially problematic. These individuals may require home health care, assisted living, or nursing home care—all of which are very expensive. Data show that health care costs escalate rapidly after the age of 65 years, and people older than 75 years incur health care expenditures about five times greater than those between the ages of 25 and 34 years. (It is estimated that a 65-year-old couple who retired in 2013 will need US$240,000 of their own money for health care costs in their lifetime.)

As one nears the end of life, extremely expensive high-technology care is often used to prolong life—sometimes for a matter of only days or weeks, and often in a painful or uncomfortable condition. Studies show that the last year of one's life tends to incur far more health care costs than any other year, and sometimes more than in the rest of one's whole lifetime.

Having an increasing number of older people in the population is certainly not unique to the United States. Most countries in the world are experiencing the same trend. What is different is the fact that medical services—especially drugs—are far more expensive in the United States, and the fact that the United States is much more likely to use expensive, high-technology care during the final days of life. At this stage, other countries put more emphasis on pain relief and allowing death to occur. This largely explains why just 1 percent of Americans now account annually for more than 20 percent of health care costs.

Given the significance of factors within the health care system, this factor is probably responsible for only 6 or 7 percent of health care cost increases. Nevertheless, in a health care system as expensive as that in the United States, it represents very significant dollar amounts (Reinhardt, 2003).

The High Cost of New Medical Technologies

Many social scientists and health care policy analysts believe that this is the most important factor driving up health care costs.

Clearly there is more emphasis in the United States than in any other country on quickly incorporating new medical technologies. This occurs for several reasons. Medical providers want to offer the best possible care to patients, and high-technology innovations are often viewed as the highest-quality treatments. Hospitals often engage in fierce competition

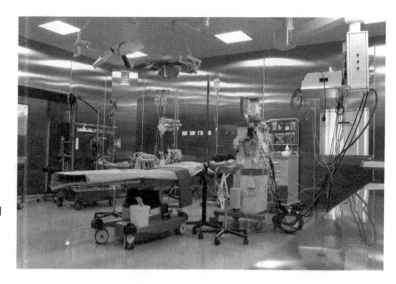

Advances in high-technology forms of medical diagnosis and treatment have improved patient treatments but have also driven up the cost of medical care. © sudok1/Fotolia.

with each other and want to attract top physicians and other providers. Having the latest equipment (whether or not it substantially improves patient outcomes) can be an effective marketing device both to the community and to medical providers (Bodenheimer, 2005).

High-technology medical equipment comes with a very high price tag (e.g., most diagnostic cameras cost at least several hundred thousand dollars, plus the cost of maintaining the equipment and having people trained to use it). Makers of the equipment heavily promote it. Once it has been purchased, hospitals and medical providers have a strong financial incentive to use the equipment and to have it bring in revenue. Studies show that greater availability leads to greater per-capita use. Greater per-capita use leads to higher expenditure on these procedures, but rarely to lower expenditure on other procedures. The overall contribution to cost increases is substantial. For example, throughout the last decade of the twentieth century and the first decade of the twenty-first, the number of diagnostic imaging procedures (including MRIs, CTs, PETs, and nuclear medicine) increased dramatically every year, tripling or quadrupling over a 10-year period. For example, there were 3 million CT scans performed in the United States in 1980, 80 million in 2010, and the number is increasing by about 10 percent each year.

Defensive Medicine. Two other factors contribute to the increasing use of expensive, high-technology medical care, sometimes in situations where it is unnecessary. Chapter 8 examined the medical malpractice situation in the United States and the fact that malpractice suits are much more common in the United States than in any other country. Most physicians readily admit to practicing **defensive medicine**—that is, undertaking medical tests more in an attempt to protect against a malpractice suit than to afford genuine benefit to the patient. Often these extra services are

high-technology diagnostic services or surgical procedures. To the extent that they are motivated primarily or solely in order to protect against a lawsuit, unnecessary medical costs occur.

Physician Self-Referral. In the last 20 years, a major controversy has developed over **physician self-referral**—that is, physicians referring patients to other health care facilities in which the physician has a financial interest—a practice that became very common in the 1980s and 1990s. A 1991 Florida study discovered that 40 percent of the physicians in Florida had investments in medical businesses to which they could refer patients. At that time, 40 percent of physical therapy centers, 60 percent of clinical laboratories, 80 percent of radiation therapy centers, and 93 percent of diagnostic imaging centers in Florida were owned by physicians. The physician-owned facilities did more procedures per patient and charged higher fees. Eventually, the Florida legislature halted self-referrals.

Other studies have affirmed this pattern. Hillman et al. (1990) studied the use of diagnostic imaging tests among primary physicians who performed the tests in their own office (with financial benefit) and primary physicians who referred patients to radiologists (with no financial benefit). They analyzed more than 65,000 insurance claims for patients with acute upper respiratory symptoms, pregnancy, low back pain, and difficulty in urinating (for men). For all four conditions, self-referring physicians obtained 4 to 4.5 times more imaging examinations than the radiologist-referring physicians, and the charges were higher per examination for those self-referring. Other studies have affirmed that self-referral is associated with higher costs but not with improved outcomes (Hughes, Bhargavan, and Sunshine, 2010).

Defenders of self-referring practices counter that these studies do not prove that the higher use of services is inappropriate. They argue that having physician-owned facilities increases the likelihood of needed services being available in communities, and that the ease of self-referring may enable physicians to get more appropriate tests performed for their patients. Nevertheless, the American Medical Association (AMA) has declared self-referring to be unethical and has encouraged physicians to abstain from it, and Congress passed sweeping new anti-self-referral legislation in 2009 that with some exceptions bans referral of Medicare and Medicaid patients to laboratories and facilities in which the referring physician has a financial stake.

Medical Entrepreneurialism

The Medical–Industrial Complex. In 1980, Arnold Relman, then editor of the *New England Journal of Medicine*, used the term the **medical–industrial complex** to describe the huge and rapidly growing industry that supplied health care services for profit. It included "proprietary hospitals and nursing homes, diagnostic laboratories, home care and emergency room services, renal dialysis units, and a wide variety of other medical care services that had formerly been provided largely by public or private not-for-profit community based institutions or by private physicians in their offices" (Relman, 1991:854). He referred to this effort to invest in health as a means to profit as being **medical entrepreneurialism.**

At that time, the medical–industrial complex accounted for between 17 and 19 percent of health care expenditures. What was the problem? Relman expressed concern that the marketing and advertising techniques of the companies and their drive for profit would encourage unnecessary use, inappropriate use, and overuse of health care resources that would push up health care costs, that expensive technologies and procedures would be preferred to less costly efforts, that attention would become riveted on patients able to pay, leaving the poor and uninsured to an overburdened not-for-profit sector,

and that physicians' allegiance to patients would be usurped by their involvement in health-related profit-making ventures (Relman, 1980).

Four specific concerns about the medical–industrial complex are linked to the issue of the high cost of medical care: (1) corporate profit, (2) high administrative costs, (3) exorbitant salaries and compensation packages for management, and (4) medical fraud.

Corporate Profit. Data clearly show that pharmaceutical and medical products companies are among the most profitable industries in the United States. Even in down years, they tend to outperform the rest of the economy by a wide margin. The profitability of health insurance companies is on a smaller scale, with annual profit margins of about 6 or 7 percent over time—far less than drug or medical products companies, but still a very healthy return. The accompanying box, "Growing Criticism of the Pharmaceutical Industry," describes this issue in more detail.

A key trend recently has been the merger of health insurance companies. Between 1995 and 2008 more than 400 corporate mergers involving health insurers occurred. This increased the market share of the largest firms and decreased competition. In 2008, the AMA reported that 94 percent of insurance markets in the United States were highly concentrated, with only one or a few insurers controlling the market. In 2009, the percentage of markets that were highly concentrated bumped up to 99 percent. In these markets, insurers do not have to compete with each other and have reduced need to seriously negotiate with providers because they will simply pass on increases to consumers. Not long after the AMA issued its report, Anthem in California announced that it would be increasing rates by 39 percent for the next year (Berry, 2010).

High Administrative Costs. The United States spends a much greater percentage of its health care dollars on administrative activities

IN THE FIELD

GROWING CRITICISM OF THE PHARMACEUTICAL INDUSTRY

The pharmaceutical industry has become a global force dominated by several huge multinational companies ("Big Pharma"). The largest companies are Novartis (US$57 billion annual sales), Pfizer (US$50 billion), Merck & Company (US$42 billion), Sanofi (US$41 billion), and Roche Holding (US$39 billion) (Modern Healthcare, 2015). Together with the next five largest companies, they control more than half of the pharmaceutical market. All of these companies are highly commercial, make a significant profit, and are major contributors to the economy of the nation in which they are based (most but not all of the largest companies are based in the United States). The companies all enter into alliances with smaller biotechnology firms, which contribute to the research on new drugs. They make most of their revenue on patent drugs (Busfield, 2006).

The pharmaceutical industry was once a very widely respected industry, but it has been the subject of significant criticism over the last few years. Among the most common criticisms are the following:

- The price of medications is extremely high and increasing very rapidly. Prescription drugs account for 10 percent of national health care expenditures in the United States, more than that if drugs administered in hospitals and nursing homes are included, and even more if over-the-counter medications are counted. In most recent years, prescription drug payments have increased more than twice as fast as any other type of health expenditure, and sometimes much more than that. For example, in 2000 the average annual cost for cancer drugs was approximately US$18,000; in 2014, the average price was US$120,000. Before 2000, the cost of a cancer drug was US$52,000 for each additional year lived; by 2014, it was more than US$210,000.

In 2015, two price-raising cases received widespread publicity in the United States. In early 2015, Canada-based Valeant Pharmaceutical raised the price of a drug used to treat high blood pressure from US$257.80 per vial to US$805.61 (an increase of 312 percent), and increased the price of a drug used to treat cardiac arrest from US$215 per vial to US$1,346 (an increase of 626 percent). The company said that both drugs had been underpriced. In a second case, Martin Shkreli, a "drug entrepreneur" and CEO of Turing Pharmaceuticals and KaloBios Pharmaceuticals, purchased rights to a drug that is used to treat a parasitic disease which affects AIDS sufferers and others with weakened immune systems, such as organ transplant recipients. He immediately hiked the price from US$13.50 a pill to US$750 (a 5,000 percent increase), and wrote in a memo that almost all of the windfall (perhaps US$375 million in the first year) would be profit. He was called in to Congress to testify, but he refused to answer any questions, asserting his constitutional protection against self-incrimination. At the time of writing he is under indictment for unrelated securities fraud charges.

While generic medications (i.e., those no longer under patent and therefore able to be produced by multiple manufacturers—about 80 percent of the drug market) are typically very much less expensive than medications that are still under patent, even their price is increasing rapidly. Because they make less money for the drug manufacturers per dosage, some manufacturers are decreasing their production of generics. This has reduced the competition that has kept the price of generics lower, and has now led to rapidly escalating prices even for generics. One generic drug used for hypertension and heart failure increased in price from 1.4 cents per capsule in November 2012 to 39.6 cents per capsule in November 2013 (an

(Continued)

(Continued)

increase of more than 2,800 percent). The price of an antidepressant that is also used for obsessive–compulsive disorder increased in the same time period from 22 cents per pill to US$8.32, and the cost of an antibiotic that has been used since 1967 increased from 6.3 cents per pill to US$3.36 (Alpern, Stauffer, and Kesselheim, 2014).

Among the most expensive prescriptive medicines are new specialty drugs, which are in a class called biologics (Lotvin et al., 2014). They are very complex medicines that are made from organic materials. They are being increasingly used to treat relatively uncommon and/or very serious chronic ailments, including some forms of cancer, rheumatoid arthritis, hepatitis C and multiple sclerosis. Research is finding that these drugs are more effective than conventional drugs and have fewer negative side effects. However, they are far more expensive than conventional medicines (on average, biologics cost about 20 times more) because they have little or no competition, they require special handling (e.g., refrigeration), and they often need to be administered intravenously.

Prices for specialty drugs range up to US$100,000 or more per year. A 12-week treatment with one specialty drug for the hepatitis C virus (which if untreated can cause serious liver damage and even death) cost US$84,000 in 2014. (While some specialty drugs improve treatment only modestly, many—like this drug—are significantly more effective than their predecessor.) A new specialty drug that treats two life-threatening blood diseases costs US$440,000 per year. In 2014, every new drug approved by the Food and Drug Administration was priced at more than US$120,000 per year. In 2014, specialty drugs represented only 1 percent of all prescribed medications, but represented one-third of spending on pharmaceuticals. It is predicted that they will account for half of all pharmaceutical spending by 2019. It is not impossible that the first million-dollar-a-year drug is on the way. Not surprisingly, many patients do not have access to these drugs.

- The pharmaceutical industry is a US$300 billion-plus-a-year market and is extremely profitable. In recent years, pharmaceuticals have been the most profitable industry in the United States (with an average annual return on investments of 20 to 25 percent in the last decade). Most drugs cost significantly more in the United States than in other countries—typically between 3 and 16 times higher). While overall health care costs have been growing faster than the rate of inflation, drug costs have been growing faster than overall health care costs.

- The pharmaceutical industry spends far too much on marketing and far too little on research and development. Part of the reason why drugs cost so much is that drug-makers spend billions of dollars each year (in 2015, more than US$5 billion) on advertising in attempts to persuade physicians and patients to use their products rather than those of a competitor. Pharmaceutical companies spend about 20 percent of their budgets on research and development but about 40 percent on advertising.

- Part of the marketing budget goes to provide physicians with all-expenses-paid trips ("educational symposia") to plush resorts for themselves and their partner (sometimes an honorarium is thrown in). In the first 5 years of the 2000s, more than 90 percent of physicians reported some type of relationship with the pharmaceutical industry (e.g., receiving food or beverages in the workplace, drug samples, payments for speaking, tickets to cultural or sporting events, reimbursements for travel, and financial incentives for prescribing specified levels of certain drugs) (Campbell et al., 2007). In 2007, the pharmaceutical industry spent more than US$1 billion to provide "continuing education" for physicians and more than US$30 billion overall on promotion of its products. In 2013, about 25 percent of Medicare's top medication-prescribing physicians (more than one million dollars' worth of drugs prescribed a year) received consulting fees and/or other benefits from the manufacturers of the drugs that they prescribed. (Herman, 2015).

Research has also found significant payments being extended from pharmaceutical companies to individuals serving on FDA Advisory Committees for drug approvals. A study of the time period between 1997 and 2011 found that FDA advisory board members with financial interests solely in one drug manufacturer were more likely to vote to approve their drugs than were members with ties to more than one manufacturer (Pham-Kanter, 2014). Now there is a growing movement for medical providers to no longer accept gifts from pharmaceutical companies because they represent an ethical conflict of interest. The medical profession and the pharmaceutical industry are attempting self-regulation on the issue, and several states now require public disclosure of such practices (Grande, 2010).

• The pharmaceutical industry has provided inaccurate and/or inadequate information in its drug advertising. This can happen in several ways. For example, about 25 percent of biomedical researchers in the United States who study drugs and may speak favorably about them have financial ties to the companies whose products they are studying—although not illegal, this represents a clear conflict of interest. Researchers receiving industry funding are more than 3.5 times more likely to report a result that is favorable to the company (Bekelman, Li, and Gross, 2003). An especially egregious example came to light in 2009 when it was learned that an anesthesiologist-researcher in Massachusetts had fabricated results in 21 painkiller studies and published bogus findings in top journals. Two of the drugs about which he had published favorable findings were made by Pfizer, which had given him undisclosed amounts of speaker fees and five research grants during the same time period. One of the drugs has been linked to heart attacks in patients taking it, and has been recalled. Pfizer settled for US$2.3 billion in fines for illegally marketing the drug.

• Pharmaceutical companies have been fined for promoting use of their drugs for purposes other than that for which they have been approved. Television commercials for prescription drugs have been found to omit any mention of causes of or risk factors for the condition involved, fail to mention non-drug alternatives for the condition, and unrealistically portray the medication's role in improving health (Frosch et al., 2007). Like many industries, drug manufacturers have created front groups—such as United Seniors Association and the Seniors Coalition—which ostensibly are groups of seniors advocating for health benefits, but are really just supporting drug company positions on issues. Virtually all of the funding of some of these groups has come from the pharmaceutical industry. In recent years, some of the largest companies have paid fines for such crimes as overcharging the Medicaid program and for inducing physicians to bill the government for some drugs that the company gave them for free (fraud).

• Pharmaceutical companies have strongly lobbied to prevent the importation of less expensive drugs from other countries. Most countries have placed price controls on drugs to ensure that they do not bankrupt the government, insurers, or patients. In Canada, which is one such country, drug prices are 50 to 80 percent lower than those in the United States. So why don't Americans just buy their drugs online from Canadian pharmacies? U.S. pharmaceutical companies strongly oppose this, for fear that it would undercut exorbitant prices in the United States, so they have warned Canadian wholesalers and pharmacies not to do this or to risk losing business with United States industry. Through much of the first decade of the 2000s, the U.S. government argued that Canadian drugs might be counterfeit or adulterated (despite the fact that this had never happened). Laws were passed to prevent Americans from engaging in large-scale drug buying from other countries, although several states and cities ignored the warnings and established purchase arrangements (Kesselheim and Choudhry, 2008).

(Continued)

(Continued)

• Pharmaceutical companies have taken advantage of patients in developing countries in several ways. First, they test drugs on patients in developing countries because it is less expensive to do so there. This occurs even when the drug may be for a condition that is more likely to be found in developed countries. Second, the drug companies do not focus research on or market drugs for conditions that are common in developing countries but not developed countries, because the anticipated profits are less. Third, the pharmaceutical industry has lobbied intensively to prevent poor countries from manufacturing their own generic equivalent of patented medicines. Big Pharma has pressured to levy trade sanctions on countries such as India and Egypt for producing generic drugs (Petryna, Lakoff, and Kleinman, 2006).

• In the last decade the medical care system has experienced frequent shortages of certain drugs, especially drugs that are effective against cancer and heart disease. Hospitals and physicians have complained that treatment is being delayed for some patients. In 2007, the FDA listed 154 drugs that were in short supply or no longer available; 5 years later, the number had increased to 456. While the explanation for these shortages seems to be multifactorial, a key reason is that the drugs are generic and do not make as much money for pharmaceutical companies as do drugs that are still under patent. Physician professional associations and the Food and Drug Administration have complained and are attempting to address the problem (Chabner, 2011).

The pharmaceutical industry strongly defends its practices. The industry contends that its profit motivation is necessary to encourage investment in the companies and to attract top management. Significant price increases are justified by overall price inflation in society and by the costs involved in drug research. A high advertising budget and extensive marketing techniques are necessary to capture the attention of physicians and patients. They contend that they have a right to defend themselves and to conduct successful businesses.

However, Marcia Angell, a physician, former editor of the *New England Journal of Medicine*, and now a senior lecturer at Harvard University Medical School, wrote the following in the preface to her book, *The Truth About the Drug Companies: How They Deceive Us and What to Do About It*:

> Sadly, there is little sign that the pharmaceutical industry is responding to its current difficulties by changing its behavior. It continues ... to use its massive marketing muscle to promote them [non-innovative drugs] relentlessly, to charge prices as high as it can get away with, and to act as if it puts short-term profits ahead of everything. It doesn't have to be that way. Drug companies could be what they once were—businesses that were quite profitable, yes, but also sources of cutting edge research that produced real medical miracles. (Angell, 2005:xv)

than does any other country. Most countries spend around 10 percent of their total health expenditure on administration, but the United States spends 25 to 30 percent. That means that between one-fourth and one-third of the money spent on health is used for running the health care system, regulatory reporting, billing patients, and clerical matters.

How much does this chaotic system cost in unnecessary administrative expenditures? Woolhandler, Campbell, and Himmelstein (2003) examined 1999 fiscal expenses for 5,220 U.S. hospitals. They determined that hospital administrative costs in the United States averaged 24.3 percent. This percentage was almost double the hospital administrative costs in Canada (12.9 percent). While this comparison may be influenced by several variables, they concluded that if the United States trimmed its hospital bureaucracy to the Canadian level, tens of billions of dollars could be saved annually. In addition, a similar amount could be saved on overhead expenses of insurance companies and physicians' paperwork. (The AMA estimates that physicians spend an average of 17 hours per week on administrative duties—completing patient charts, ordering tests, justifying procedures to insurers, and seeking reimbursement.)

A key part of the problem is billing. Consider the difference between a hospital located in a country where everyone carries an identical health card and is governed by the same regulations, and a hospital in the United States in which patients may or may not have insurance, and if they do, it could come from any one of 1,300 private companies or the government, each of which has a wide configuration of benefits. A medium-sized hospital in most countries will have a couple of people who work in billing; in the United States, it would have dozens and dozens of billing agents. No wonder that an estimated one in five medical bills contains at least one error.

The Institute of Medicine estimates that the United States spends more than US$360 billion annually on health care administration—more than twice what is spent on heart disease and three times what is spent on cancer (Cutler, Wikler, and Basch, 2012).

Exorbitant CEO Salaries and Compensation Packages. Extraordinarily large salaries and compensation packages occur throughout the nation's economy. Corporate executives of health insurance companies, pharmaceutical companies, medical equipment companies, hospitals, and health associations who receive noticeably large salaries have come under special criticism given that health care is so expensive. The total annual compensation packages received by the CEOs of some health care organizations in 2015 were as follows: Masimo Corporation (medical equipment), US$119 million; Horizon Pharma, US$93 million; Medtronic, US$40 million; CVS Health, US$29 million; Alexion Pharmaceuticals, US$25 million. Given all of the health care

organizations in the country, compensation packages just for CEOs represent a sizable sum.

Medical Fraud. There is a massive amount of **medical fraud** occurring on a regular basis in the United States. Pharmaceutical companies have frequently been the target of fraud charges. Among those paying settlements in 2011 alone were Abbott Laboratories (US$421 million for knowingly reporting false and inflated prices for a variety of pharmaceutical products), Par Pharmaceuticals (US$154 million for overcharging Medicare and Medicaid), Watson Pharmaceuticals (US$79 million for defrauding Medicaid), and Serono Laboratories (US$44 million for illegal kickbacks to healthcare providers). In 2012 the Department of Justice announced the largest ever settlement in a healthcare fraud case, with GlaxoSmithKline (pharmaceutical company) pleading guilty to three criminal counts plus civil charges and paying US$3 billion to the federal government and participating state governments. Among the many cases in 2013 was Johnson & Johnson paying US$2.2 billion to settle claims for promoting drugs for uses not approved by the FDA, and for paying kickbacks to physicians. Five medical companies (an owner of dialysis clinics, a home care company, a skilled nursing company, and two pharmaceutical companies) paid settlements of more than US$100 million in 2014. In June 2015 the federal government arrested more than 240 health care professionals in 17 cities for hundreds of millions of dollars' worth of false claims.

In addition, the parent company of a chain of dental clinics agreed to a US$24 million settlement after insiders reported that they were performing medically unnecessary and substandard procedures on children to bilk Medicaid. A Miami man submitted US$61 million in false Medicare claims for the treatment of patients with HIV/AIDS, cancer, and other ailments. A Miami physician cheated Medicare out of

US$40 million by dishonestly describing home care patients as being blind and diabetic in order to bill for extra nursing visits. A Massachusetts dentist used paper clips instead of stainless steel posts inside the teeth of root canal patients and charged Medicaid for the more expensive parts. An owner of a wheelchair company paid Medicare recipients to state wrongly that they had received an expensive wheelchair, which he billed to Medicare. A Missouri pharmacist diluted chemotherapy drugs given to thousands of cancer patients. Scam artists have sent bills to Medicare using the ID numbers of deceased physicians. A hospital executive in California was arrested for heading a scheme to recruit homeless people as phony patients and then bill the government for millions of dollars. The nation's largest rehabilitation hospital was found guilty of massive fraud. Conservative estimates are that medical fraud costs the United States about US$70 billion each year. Florida—with its very large number of Medicare beneficiaries—has consistently led the nation in its very high rates of medical fraud.

AMERICA'S UNINSURED POPULATION

While government programs have offered substantial help to millions of people, they have never become an effective safety net. By 2010 (the year in which the Affordable Care Act was passed), approximately 47 million Americans (almost 25 percent of them under the age of 18 years) did not have any private *or* public health insurance coverage. This equates to about one person in eight in the United States. In any 2-year period, more than 80 million Americans spent at least some time without health insurance, and about two-thirds of these individuals lacked insurance for at least 6 months. In addition, millions more Americans have been *under-insured*—they have an insurance policy that either contains major loopholes (important

services that are not covered) or requires large out-of-pocket payments for services, or both.

The Uninsured

Many people have not understood that becoming uninsured is something that can happen to anyone. For example, most people who lack insurance are employed. In 2010, more than 60 percent of uninsured Americans were in families with a worker who was employed full-time year round, and an additional 20 percent or more were in families with a year-round part-time worker or a partial-year full-time worker.

People of all ages were uninsured. The uninsured included people in the early years of their careers, just beginning to get financially settled, and often still moving from job to job, as well as people throughout the age spectrum all the way up to the age of 65 years, when Medicare eligibility occurs. Although two-thirds of the uninsured were white, people of all races and nationalities dealt with this problem—about one-seventh being Hispanic and about one-eighth being black. However, members of racial and ethnic groups were more likely than whites to be uncovered. About 30 percent of Hispanics were uninsured, as were just under 20 percent of blacks and Asians, and about 12 percent of whites.

People at almost any income level can be uninsured. Many are below the federally established poverty level. Others are just above the poverty level—often referred to as the *medically indigent* or the *working poor*—and are sometimes in greatest need of health care. The cost of purchasing health insurance had increasingly become a problem even for people in the middle class. The percentage of people earning incomes of US$50,000 or more who lacked insurance had risen over the last few years, reflecting just how expensive policies had become. "Many of these families have children to support, home mortgages to pay, and college loans to reimburse, in addition to other basic expenses. Many are self-employed; many have been working only a few years and do not have large financial savings; and many are taking care of elderly relatives" (Weiss, 2006:63). In such circumstances, paying US$10,000 a year or more for a family health insurance policy is just not possible. While some argue that many uninsured persons can actually afford health insurance, much research has found this not to be true (Bernard, Banthin, and Encinosa, 2009).

The Role of the Employment-Based Health Insurance System

As described earlier, health insurance provision in the United States largely relies on voluntary, employer-provided programs. Most large businesses offer health insurance to their employees as a benefit of employment. Typically, the employer pays for most of the cost of the policy (the average today is about 74 percent) for employees. Employees pay the remaining amount of the premium, pay attached deductibles, coinsurances, and co-payments, and pay for whatever services are not covered in the policy. This system worked well for many, but it was a complete failure for millions more. In 2010, 160 million Americans had health insurance through employer-provided policies, more than 100 million people were covered by Medicare, Medicaid, and other public programs, 16 million people purchased their own health insurance, and more than 47 million people (about 17 percent of the entire population) lacked any form of health insurance.

Prior to the Affordable Care Act, the public/private, employment-based system in the United States failed to make health insurance available to at least seven primary groups (and of course their dependents were affected as a result) (Weiss, 2006):

1. *Individuals who were unemployed.* Because the primary way in which health insurance is provided is through employment, people without a job were automatically cut off from this benefit. These individuals could purchase a health insurance policy directly from a health insurance company, but that can be a very expensive option fraught with difficulties. Coverage for existing medical problems was often excluded, and if the problems were serious, an individual might not have been able to purchase insurance at all (i.e., those who needed it most were least likely to get it).

2. *Individuals after retirement but before Medicare.* Some individuals are fortunate enough to have worked for an employer who continues to subsidize their health insurance even after retirement. However, many companies had discontinued this benefit, and most companies had significantly raised the percentage of the cost that must be borne by the retiree. Two-thirds of companies offered retiree health benefits in 1990, but only one-third did so in 2005, and the percentage decreased in later years. Of the companies that did offer it, the percentage of cost that the retiree was responsible for had jumped from 0, 10, or 20 percent to 50 or 60 percent or more. For wealthy retirees, this was not a problem. However, for low-income retirees, who had just entered a time of significantly reduced income, increased expense for health insurance was a heavy burden.

3. *Individuals during any transition period from one job to another.* Millions of Americans change jobs each year. Until the 1980s, when an individual left a job, employer-provided health insurance ended completely. Coverage by health insurance provided by the new employer did not begin until the individual started their new job, and often not for another 6 or 12 months. This created a dangerous gap between coverage periods during which the individual and their dependents lacked health insurance. In 1986, Congress passed the Consolidated Omnibus

Budget Reconciliation Act (COBRA), which enables specified workers who have lost their jobs to continue their health insurance coverage for themselves and their dependents for up to 18, and sometimes 36, months. To do this, however, the displaced worker is required to pay the portion of the insurance cost that they were paying plus the amount that was being paid by the employer plus an additional amount. This is often too expensive for displaced workers to afford. In the years leading up to the Affordable Care Act, only 20 to 25 percent of those eligible to purchase insurance through COBRA did so.

4. *Individuals working part-time, including those who are working simultaneously at two or more part-time jobs.* Many workers are not able to secure a full-time position and work only part-time. In order to try and make ends meet, many take on a second part-time job and may work a total of more than 40 hours per week. However, employer-provided health insurance is typically a benefit given only to full-time workers (defined as working at least 30 hours per week). Therefore even though an individual may be working at a combination of part-time positions that total more hours than many full-time positions, no health insurance is provided. Furthermore, some employers—fast-food restaurants are a common example—intentionally hire workers at just under the number of hours per week that would make them full time and eligible for a health insurance benefit.

5. *Individuals who work for small businesses.* Small businesses are in a very difficult position with regard to health insurance, and employees of small businesses suffer the consequences. Large employers have a distinct advantage in negotiating for health insurance coverage. Insurance providers recognize that especially costly procedures received by one or a few individuals in a large employee group can be spread across the entire group. Because many will use few services, part of the difference can be used to cover the higher costs incurred for others. Small businesses do not have this luxury. If one or a small number of employees in a small business has exceptionally high costs, there are not enough fellow employees to cover it. Therefore health insurance companies routinely charge higher fees for policies—an average of almost 20 percent more—for small businesses, and raise their rates more sharply when high expenses occur. The result of this pattern is that small businesses are much less likely to provide health insurance coverage for their employees.

6. *Individuals who cannot afford the employee share of employer-provided health insurance.* Few employers continue to pay for the total cost of a health insurance policy for employees. In 2010, only 2 percent of large companies, and virtually no small companies, still paid the full health insurance premium for employees. Many had decided that they could not afford to provide this extensive coverage, and so they began making employees absorb a greater share of the cost. This has been achieved in several ways. First, the services provided by the policy have been reduced, so that employees have to pay for some services that were formerly covered. Coverage for mental health services is often the first to go. Second, the amount of deductibles and co-payments has increased because this reduces the cost of the policy. Third, the percentage of the policy premiums paid by employees has been increasing. Fourth, even in situations in which the company continues to pay a high percentage of the premiums for the employee, the amount contributed to cover the employee's family has begun to decrease. Only about two-thirds of employees today are covered by health insurance plans offered by their employer.

7. *Individuals who are in this country illegally.* More than 11 million individuals in the United States have entered the country illegally. Many employers knowingly hire these individuals because they are willing to do jobs that others will not do, and because they are willing to work for less than the minimum wage. Often they are paid under the table, so that their illegal status is not discovered. Typically they are not provided with any health benefits. Working at a low wage and without health insurance means that it is very difficult for these people to afford medical care regardless of the seriousness of any disease or illness they may have.

The Consequences of Being Uninsured

The lack of personal financial resources to pay for private medical care and the lack of health insurance have a profound effect on the health of individuals and families, and this was one of the driving forces that led to the passage of the Affordable Care Act. People without health insurance are less likely to seek preventive medical care such as medical checkups (especially Pap smears and mammograms for women, and prostate cancer screening for men) and immunizations. They are more likely to try to get through illnesses on their own without seeking a medical provider. If they do see a medical provider, often they will have waited until they have become very sick, their health is more threatened, and in some cases, such as patients with cancer or diabetes, the benefits of early detection are lost. They are less likely to have a regular source of medical care and more likely to see a different provider on each visit. They are also less likely to receive mental health care, dental care, eye care, and care from primary care physicians, and are especially unlikely to receive care from specialists (Freeman et al., 2008).

They are less likely to be admitted to a hospital, but are more ill when they are admitted.

They receive fewer expensive medical treatments while in the hospital, and are often deprived of the benefits of medical technology (even when controlling for need, the uninsured are less likely to receive clearly beneficial procedures such as heart bypass surgery, cataract surgery, and treatment for depression). When they analyzed discharge abstracts for almost 600,000 patients who were hospitalized in 1987, Hadley, Steinberg, and Feder (1991) found that the uninsured had, at the time of admission, a 44 to 124 percent higher risk of in-hospital mortality and, after controlling for this difference, a 1.2 to 3.2 times greater likelihood of dying in hospital.

These negative health patterns occur among children as well as adults. Uninsured children are only one-sixth as likely as insured children to have a usual site where they receive health care. Uninsured children are more than five times more likely as the insured to have at least one unmet medical need each year, more than three times more likely to forgo a needed prescription, and 70 percent more likely to go without needed medical care for childhood conditions such as sore throats, ear infections, and asthma.

Not surprisingly, people without health insurance end up in poorer health and with earlier death than those with insurance. A 2003 study that compared mortality rates of the insured and uninsured in Kentucky found significant disparities. The 3-year survival rate for patients with prostate cancer was 98 percent for the insured but only 83 percent for the uninsured. For patients with breast cancer, the survival rate was 91 percent for insured patients and 78 percent for the uninsured. The comparable figures for those with colorectal cancer were 71 percent and 53 percent, respectively, and for those with lung cancer, 23 percent and 13 percent, respectively (McDavid et al., 2003). In 2009, the Institute of Medicine determined that 18,000 deaths each year could be blamed on the lack of health insurance and the resulting absence of preventive services, timely diagnoses, and appropriate care (Institute of Medicine, 2009).

One's risk of a health care catastrophe does not end even when one is insured. As many as half of all Americans have trouble paying for medical care each year, and most of these people have some form of health insurance. Prior to the passage of the Affordable Care Act, there were approximately 25 million such underinsured people in the United States. Their insurance often did not cover the types of care that were needed, may have had a low limit on the total amount that would be paid, or had such high premiums, deductibles, and co-payments that care could not be afforded. Research found that many insured people went without needed medical treatment due to the cost. In 2008, 34 percent of Americans skipped dental care, 27 percent put off getting needed medical care, 23 percent skipped a recommended medical test, 21 percent failed to get a prescription filled, 15 percent cut their pills in half or skipped doses, and 7 percent had trouble getting mental health care (Kaiser Family Foundation, 2009).

HISTORICAL EFFORTS TO REFORM THE HEALTH CARE SYSTEM

Efforts to enact health care reform have a long history. Initiatives began in 1926 when the privately funded Committee on the Costs of Medical Care (CCMC) considered policy changes to address the high costs of and inadequate access to health care services. The CCMC proposed that health care should be delivered primarily by physicians organized in group practices, and that funding should come from voluntary insurance plans and subsidies from local governments for low-income persons. However, the AMA and many other groups inside and outside medicine strongly opposed these ideas as threats to private practice and physician autonomy (Waitzkin, 1989).

The Roosevelt administration pushed for National Health Program (NHP) legislation in 1938, as did the Truman administration in 1945, but Congress supported neither. Despite widespread popular support, the AMA along with the American Hospital Association and the U.S. Chamber of Commerce led campaigns against what they labeled "socialized medicine." Coupled with the general anticommunist sentiment of the 1950s, no proposal was ever passed (Waitzkin, 1989).

The turmoil of the 1960s revitalized support for health care reform. As a consequence, Congress considered a number of proposals for an NHP, leading to the eventual establishment of Medicaid and Medicare in 1965. These programs brought major changes in public funding for health care, but did not create a comprehensive program with universal coverage.

The 1990s and the Clinton Health Initiative

By the late 1980s and early 1990s, public sentiment seemed to be running strongly in favor of a national health program. A 1989 Lou Harris poll of consumers in Great Britain, Canada, and the United States found that U.S. consumers were the *least* satisfied with their own health care system. Only 10 percent of U.S. respondents assessed the health system as working even fairly well, and nine out of ten respondents thought that the system was in need of fundamental change in direction and structure (Coddington et al., 1990). Several surveys found that a large plurality, or even a majority, of Americans had a preference for a Canadian-style, single-payer system with universal coverage.

Moreover, a broader cross-section of the population expressed support for health care reform than in earlier years, and it included many business leaders and health care providers who had formerly been opposed to significant change. Popular support for a comprehensive program appeared to be so pervasive that a bipartisan effort in Congress seemed possible.

Against this backdrop, Bill Clinton made health care reform a major issue in the 1992 presidential campaign and, after his election, a major commitment of his administration. After many months of fact-finding and deliberation by a task force led by Hillary Clinton, the Clinton proposal—termed *managed competition*—was introduced in November 1993. This proposal attempted to address both the problems of access and cost in a way that would be politically acceptable to Congress, key health care constituencies, and the American people. It called for a system that would guarantee a comprehensive set of health care services for all Americans (universal coverage). Large health alliances (groups of employers) would be created to negotiate for the best financial arrangements with MCOs. The plan would largely be funded through taxes applied to employers, with small employers being subsidized. Other cost-control mechanisms, such as capping insurance premiums and malpractice reform, were included. The complete proposal—all 1,342 pages of it—contained an enormous amount of detail.

Opposition to the plan emerged within weeks. The Health Insurance Association of America (HIAA), an organization that represented many small- and medium-sized insurance companies, led lobbying efforts to oppose health care reform. Small business owners felt that they could not afford to provide health care coverage for their workers. Small insurance companies were alarmed that they would not survive in the new system. Liquor, beer, and cigarette companies decried the extra taxes that would be placed on their products to help to pay for the system. The AMA and the AHA opposed limits being placed on physicians' fees and hospital charges. Drug companies opposed mandatory cost controls on drugs. Trial lawyers opposed malpractice reform. Many people expressed reservations about new forms of bureaucracy

(e.g., the health alliances) being created. Some analysts charged that the Clinton administration had failed to work sufficiently closely with congressional leaders in developing the plan, while others cited the continual difficulty of passing any broad-based reforms within the American political system (Quadagno, 2005).

In the ensuing months, when the Congressional Budget Office (CBO) declared that the proposal would cost significantly more than Clinton had estimated, many middle-class families became frightened about the necessity for tax increases. While public opinion polls continued to show support for many of the basic values guiding the proposal (e.g., guaranteeing health care for everyone), controlling costs had become a more important objective for most people than universal coverage. In September 1993, almost six in ten Americans supported the proposal; by July 1994, almost six in ten opposed it. By fall of 1994, it was clear that the proposal lacked majority support in either house of Congress, and it was essentially dropped.

Health Care Reform at the State Level

While the executive and legislative branches of the federal government were debating health care reform, several of the individual states initiated their own statewide efforts. These reforms typically aimed both to increase the number of people covered by health insurance and to create effective cost-containment provisions.

The momentum began in Hawaii, where since 1974 all employers have been required to provide their employees with comprehensive health care benefits. Employees also make a contribution. Combined with Medicare and Medicaid (which is set at the most generous eligibility level in the country), 98 percent of Hawaiians have basic health care coverage. Between 1974 and 2010, more than half of the states considered legislation to make health insurance more affordable. In recent years, Massachusetts passed a plan based on a requirement that everyone purchase health insurance with the state government assisting individuals, families, and small businesses in finding an affordable plan and helping to subsidize those who could not afford it. Vermont and Maine passed voluntary programs intended to make health insurance more affordable. However, fiscal problems being experienced in many states curbed legislative enthusiasm and caused states to back off their stated goals. Several states even reduced Medicaid funding or enacted other restrictions. Thus although there was more commitment to assisting the uninsured in some of the states than in the federal government, until 2010 there were severe limits on what they could accomplish (McDonough, Miller, and Barber, 2008).

HEALTH CARE REFORM OF 2010: THE PATIENT PROTECTION AND AFFORDABLE CARE ACT

After the unsuccessful attempt of President Clinton to enact health care reform legislation in the early 1990s, the issue moved off the front burner in the national political arena. Although President Bush supported the enactment of the very significant Part D of Medicare—the prescription drug benefit—he was not an advocate for sweeping health care reform. However, the presidential campaign of 2008 brought health care issues back to the surface. Plans for reform were a hot issue in the Democratic primary. Although both Senator Clinton and Senator Obama supported large-scale health care reform, their individual proposals differed in important details. With Senator Obama's nomination, he made health care reform a major issue in the presidential campaign running against Senator McCain. The campaign seemed to indicate that a majority of people were in favor of significant health care reform, but also that many people strongly opposed it.

Positions on Health Care Reform

Within the Congress as within the country, positions on health care reform cover a wide spectrum. As of 2010, however, three broad categories encapsulated most specific positions.

Advocates for a Private Market Approach. Private market approaches are based on preserving the largest possible role for the private sector and the smallest possible role for the federal government. This approach is favored by all or almost all Republican politicians and, in earlier debates on health care reform, by the health insurance, pharmaceutical, and other for-profit health care businesses. The U.S. Chamber of Commerce is also a strong supporter. These groups have consistently opposed any significant intervention by the federal government in health care.

Advocates for an Incremental Social Justice Approach. *Incremental social justice approaches* are based on the belief that the best or only way to achieve universal health care coverage is to make as many changes as possible on a one-at-a-time basis. For example, on an individual basis, they have promoted instituting a uniform insurance billing form, prohibiting the denial of insurance because of pre-existing conditions, and working to guarantee coverage for all children as soon as possible. Many Democrats and Independents had come to support this approach.

Advocates for a Social Justice Approach. Proponents of this approach contended that significant health care reform was necessary, that the private market approach had failed, and that federal government intervention was essential. Some advocated for a single-payer system (as in Canada) where the government is the only entity that pays for health care. Others advocated for a public–private mix (as in many

European countries) in which both the government and a for-profit or not-for-profit private sector play a large role and are involved in financing health care. This approach was also favored by many Democrats and Independents, and won endorsement from groups such as the Institute of Medicine, the American Public Health Association, and the Catholic Health Association.

The Political Process of Reform

Within weeks of his election, President Obama began engaging the country and both political parties with ideas for health care reform. There were many possibilities about specific details, but the overarching goals were to guarantee coverage for most or all people and to do it in such a way as to contain costs—the two overarching problems of the health care system. President Obama hoped for passage of a bill in the summer of 2009; there seemed to be strong support, and there were reasonably cooperative relations between the parties (or at least an absence of hostility). For a time it seemed that significant reform was inevitable.

Then things quickly began to fall apart. Some Republican politicians decided to test the commitment of Americans to health care reform. They called the plan "socialism" and "socialized medicine," and characterized it as a "government takeover" of health care. These arguments had always been successful in the past, and they took hold again. In July 2009, the cost of the proposed reform was estimated to be over US$1 trillion, and that also stirred much opposition. The Congressional Budget Office, a carefully non-partisan agency that attempts to base its conclusions only on available evidence, declared that the proposed legislation would not slow health care cost increases. Polls began to show declining support for reform, and Republicans, now encouraged that they could defeat the bill and not allow the opposition party a significant

political accomplishment, became more forceful opponents.

The declaration of the CBO caused Democrats to revisit an idea for controlling costs that had been discussed earlier but not pursued—creation of a "public option." This would be a public-sponsored health insurance program like Medicare that would compete with private insurers and force them to better control costs and premiums. Two-thirds of the public expressed support, but health insurance companies argued that they would not be able to successfully compete. Republicans argued that the plan would force the private sector out of health care. It became obvious that health care reform was not close to smooth sailing.

Summer 2009: Opponents of Large-Scale Reform Go on the Attack. When Congress convened for the summer, many politicians set up sessions ("town hall meetings") with constituents to hear their views about the reform proposals. Opponents of reform attended these sessions en masse and often behaved in an unruly fashion. Angry and hostile comments were made, and supporters of reform were shouted down by opponents and called "un-American." Supporters began yelling back, and the meetings became even more contentious. Conservative television talk-show host Rush Limbaugh put on his website an image of an Obama health care logo that morphed into a Swastika. Interestingly, public opinion polls at the time found that many people considered angry attacks on the bill a "sign of democracy" rather than an "abuse of democracy."

At about the same time, Sarah Palin, 2008 Republican vice presidential candidate, began targeting one of the components of reform legislation—encouragement of physicians to genuinely talk to people near the end of their life about what treatments they wanted and did not want. This idea was based on much research which has found that people really want this

Many people strongly desired the creation of a "public option"—a government-run health insurance program that would compete with commercial companies and hopefully force them to moderate price increases. © MARK RALSTON/Getty

conversation, and often are happier in their remaining days when they have this chance to knowledgeably participate in this way. However, Palin and others portrayed these sessions as "death panels." House Republican leader John Boehner said that they were a precursor to "government-encouraged euthanasia." Some contended that it was Obama's way of trying "to kill granny." This became a common attack, frightened many senior citizens, and clearly riled those who believed these characterizations. Although seniors would have benefited most from the provision, their fears caused the item to be dropped from the proposal. The Republican National Committee quickly switched gears and mailed a fundraising letter suggesting that Democrats might use health care reform to deny medical treatments to Republicans. Prospects for reform looked dim.

September and October 2009: Supporters of Large-Scale Reform Strike Back. By September and October, supporters of reform began to fight back. The American Medical Association, the American Nurses Association, the American Association of Retired Persons,

and columnists in a wide variety of magazines and newspapers challenged the accuracy of what opponents were saying. They referred to their arguments as "myths," "falsehoods," "an assault on truth," and "lies," and they tried to calm public fears about reform. The Department of Health and Human Services published carefully prepared state-by-state analyses showing that residents of every state would benefit from reform. Congressional Democrats continued to tinker with reform bills, trying to find an approach that would be acceptable to all 60 Democrats and Independents in the Senate and perhaps capture some Republican support. Sixty was the magic number of votes needed to avoid a Republican filibuster and to secure passage. There was tremendous pressure placed on Democrats to support and on Republicans to oppose.

Then another argument against the proposal surfaced. Democratic and Republican legislators who oppose abortion argued that the bill did not include any absolute assurance that public dollars could not be given to insurance plans that cover abortions. Supporters contended that the bill did not make any changes with regard to reimbursement for abortion, but conservative Democrats threatened to withdraw their support from the entire proposal unless changes were made.

November 2009: House Passes Reform Bill, But It Stalls in the Senate. In early November, the House passed an amendment to put tight restrictions on abortions for those receiving services paid by federal dollars. This mollified conservative Democrats, and the House approved a health reform bill by a vote of 220 to 215 (Democrats supported it by 219 to 39; Republicans opposed it by 176 to 1). The bill was 1,990 pages long and made changes costing US$1.06 trillion over 10 years. The bill went on to the Senate.

The Senate first had to vote to bring the bill to the floor, and assuming no Republican support, the vote of all 60 Democrats and Independents was needed. A roadblock occurred when Democratic Senator Ben Nelson of Nebraska and Independent Senator Joe Lieberman of Connecticut said that they would not allow a plan with a public option to be voted upon. Although the public option was a critical piece to contain costs and had been a point of emphasis by President Obama from the beginning, Democrats had no choice but to drop it. Recognizing that each Democrat and Independent had leverage to make demands for changes in the proposed bill in order to keep that person's vote, the demands rolled in. Among them, Senator Mary Landrieu of Louisiana wanted US$300 million in extra Medicaid support for her state, Senator Nelson wanted to retain an antitrust exemption for the insurance industry, and Vermont Senator Bernie Sanders wanted US$10 billion more for community health centers. They all got what they wanted, and the bill passed with just the 60 necessary votes.

December 2009: Senate Passes Reform Bill. The health reform bill came to the Senate in early December. As expected, the debate was rancorous, with accusations flowing both ways. Once again, Democrats needed 60 votes to cut any Republican filibuster and pass the bill. Once again, demands were made by some of the 60. Senator Nelson wanted more restrictive language on abortion and said that he would not vote for the bill unless he got it. He got it. Senator Liebermann (again) and Senator Nelson (again) said that they would not vote for the bill unless the public option plan was eliminated (it remained in the version of the bill being debated in the Senate). They got it. Senator Nelson (again) wanted the federal government to pay for all of his state's Medicaid expansion in perpetuity. He got it. Massachusetts and Vermont also got extra money for Medicaid. Connecticut got a medical school. Florida's elderly were exempted from certain Medicare cuts. Many Senate Democrats expressed their disappointment about these "me first" tactics, but they had no choice but to accept them. The bill—2,074 pages plus 383 pages of last-minute revisions totaling US$871 billion over 10 years—was passed on December 24 by a vote of 60 to 39 (all Democrats and Independents voting yes and all Republicans voting no).

January 2010: The Importance of a Single Vote. What remained? Because the House bill and Senate bill had hundreds of differences with regard to details, a joint committee needed to be formed to make the two bills identical for a final passage. Some of these differences concerned critical matters on which one body or the other did not want to compromise. President Obama entered the negotiations. Progress was being made. A hybrid bill that would need to go back to the House and Senate for final passage seemed close. Then something unexpected occurred. In a vote to replace Senator Ted Kennedy, who had died in August, Massachusetts elected Scott Brown, another Republican opponent. Suddenly the 60 supporters had shrunk to 59. A crucial piece of the puzzle had changed, and the future of health care reform was in serious doubt. Democrats halted their deliberations on a reform bill.

February 2010: A Democrat–Republican Summit But No Change.   In early February, President Obama called for a new round of bipartisan talks on health care reform as a way of trying to salvage the bill. Republicans begrudgingly said they would participate, but clearly the power had shifted to their side. Public opinion polls showed a slight majority of Americans still wanting immediate health care reform, although they were almost evenly divided on the best approach. Three days before the summit, President Obama introduced a new proposal with some changes that he hoped would make conservative Democrats and Republicans more comfortable about voting for a bill.

The bipartisan summit did occur—a 7½-hour televised event—and it was a detailed, deeply felt discussion of two completely contrary positions regarding health care reform. Neither Democrats nor Republicans wanted to compromise on their basic positions.

March 2010: Congressional Passage of Large-Scale Health Care Reform—but Not an End to Partisan Politics.   In mid-March, President Obama put forward a revised proposal (US$940 billion over 10 years) that included ideas from both the Senate and House bills (but getting rid of all of the pet projects from individual Democratic and Independent legislators), and asked for a straight up-or-down vote on it. The hope seemed to be that in this situation one or two Senate Republicans would vote for the bill, although that was considered to be extremely unlikely.

At about this time, the process changed again. Democrats identified a way to pass the Obama proposal without having to go back to the Senate where their 59 votes would dictate defeat. The process called "reconciliation" would (1) have the House pass the Senate bill without making any changes to it (so the Senate would not have to vote on it again), (2) have the House pass a newly written second bill that makes changes to the Senate bill to bring the composite in line with President Obama's proposal, and (3) have the Senate pass the second bill (by parliamentary rules, this "reconciliation" procedure required only 51 votes for passage). Republicans lashed out at the procedure as being unethical, although they themselves had used the same procedure on several occasions in similar circumstances. Enormous political pressure was placed on House and Senate members to vote in favor or against the bill.

On March 21, the House passed the Senate bill by 219 to 212 and the package of changes by 220 to 211. On March 22, the Senate passed the package of changes by 56 to 43 (one of the three Democrats who voted no was Nebraska Senator Nelson). The House then passed the complete bill by 220 to 207. No Republicans in the House or Senate voted in favor of any of the bills. On March 23, President Obama signed into law the Patient Protection and Affordable Care Act.

Was the battle ended? It was not. Even before the bill was passed, some state legislatures in conservative states voted that their citizens could not be required to buy health insurance (one component of the bill—a so-called "individual mandate"—required everyone to have some form of health insurance). On the day of the signing, the attorney generals in 14 states (all conservative Republicans plus the conservative Democratic attorney general in Louisiana) filed legal challenges to the bill on this "no requirement to buy" rationale. Most legal scholars thought that the lawsuits had little chance—that federal laws routinely trump state laws. However, when Republicans gained control of the House of Representatives in the November 2010 elections, they initiated immediate

On March 23, 2010, before a group of supporters, President Obama signed into law the Patient Protection and Affordable Care Act. © Bloomberg/Getty

conversation about the possibility of repealing the entire health reform bill.

Basic Benefits of Health Care Reform

The health reform plan was designed to be implemented over a period of several years. Some provisions began as early as 2010, most were in place by 2014, and all others will be in effect by 2019 (Barry, 2010). The basic benefits of health care reform are as follows:

1. Approximately 32 million additional Americans receive health care insurance.
2. Everyone is required to have health insurance (the individual mandate). Subsidies to enable this purchase are provided for those with moderate or low income, and more people become eligible for Medicaid. Financial penalties are assessed to anyone not having health insurance.
3. States are encouraged to expand their Medicaid programs, and the federal government will pay all the costs for doing so in the first few years and most of the costs in ensuing years.
4. Health insurance companies are prevented from denying insurance on the basis of any pre-existing conditions, or placing a lifetime maximum on insurance benefits.
5. Several new health insurance benefits are required to be provided, such as coverage for adult children until the age of 26 years, and required coverage for preventive

services such as childhood immunizations, cancer screenings, and contraceptives.

6. State-run **health insurance exchanges** are created to offer a choice of private health insurance plans for people who are not covered by an employer. If a state chooses not to set up its own exchange, the federal government does so for it. (Since 2010, two additional options have been created. Both involve partnerships of the federal and state government.)

7. Employers with at least 50 employees are required to offer health insurance plan options to their employees.

8. Tax credits are offered to small businesses to assist them in buying insurance for their employees.

9. Several changes are made in Medicare to keep it financially sound for at least 10 more years, to guarantee basic benefits for everyone in Medicare, to make preventive care services free for most, and to make drug coverage more affordable.

10. Incentives are offered to physicians to encourage them to go into primary care practice, including higher reimbursement levels (although there is general agreement that more needs to be done to ensure there will be sufficient physicians to treat the much larger number of insured persons).

11. There are many additional provisions, including the following:

- Requiring members of Congress to buy plans through the exchanges
- Taxing tanning parlor salons
- Providing new long-term care options
- Increasing funding for community health centers
- Providing bonus payments to primary care physicians practicing in underserved areas
- Denying use of the health insurance exchanges or receipt of subsidies to undocumented immigrants.

Who Pays for Health Care Reform?

The health care reform plan is estimated to cost US$940 billion over its first 10 years. It will be paid for in the following ways:

1. An annual fee on health insurance companies of US$8 billion starting in 2014; the fee increased to US$11.3 billion in 2015, and will rise to US$13.9 billion in 2017, and US$14.3 billion in 2018.

2. An annual fee on pharmaceutical manufacturers of US$2.5 billion starting in 2011; the fee increased to US$3 billion in 2012, and will rise to US$3.5 billion in 2017, and US$4.2 billion in 2018.

3. A Medicare tax rate increase from 1.45 to 2.35 percent on earnings over US$200,000 for an individual and US$250,000 for a family, and a new Medicare tax imposed on unearned income for the same groups.

4. Penalty payments from those not obtaining health insurance and from businesses with at least 50 employees that are not offering health insurance benefit.

5. A tax on high-cost insurance plans (this is referred to as the "Cadillac" tax).

6. Individuals and families with any form of health insurance. The ACA insurance plans require a premium, have very high deductibles, and include both co-insurance and co-payments. This mirrors what is happening with private insurance plans. These costs raise funds but are also designed to have patients with "more skin in the game," in the hope that the financial requirements will motivate them to lead healthier lives and to use health care services more thriftily, by avoiding unnecessary services and shopping around for the lowest prices.

7. Anticipated cost savings from efficiencies such as greater use of primary care physicians (with reduced reliance on more expensive specialists), more preventive care, many fewer people using the emergency room for

non-emergency care, and increased use of information technology.

Who Benefits the Most from Health Care Reform?

1. The uninsured, who will obtain health insurance through one provision or another. This will include the part-time employed, unemployed, self-employed, and people between jobs.
2. People with health problems, who will no longer be disallowed or have a lifetime maximum on benefits.
3. Young adults, who will be covered on family insurance plans until the age of 26 years.
4. Medicare beneficiaries, who will receive added services and more complete coverage of drugs.
5. People who already have good, employer-sponsored health insurance, who will be able to keep their insurance and get some added benefits.
6. Private health insurance companies, pharmaceutical companies, and other for-profit companies, which will be part of the system, will continue to be run for profit, and will have additional members.
7. Primary care physicians, whose compensation levels will increase.

What Are the Key Criticisms of the Plan?

Conservative criticism of the plan centers on three key points:

• There is too much government involvement. As we have discussed in this chapter, congressional Republicans prefer a private-market approach in all or almost all matters, and minimal involvement of government. Even when Medicare was passed in 1965, a majority of Senate Republicans voted against it. In a 2004 survey, access to health care coverage was the top health care priority for Democrats and Independents, but was not among the top four selections for Republicans (Public Opinion Strategies, 2004). The Affordable Care Act extensively utilizes both the public and private sectors, but certainly increases government responsibility for paying for increased access to health care.

• The plan costs too much. Proponents of the plan acknowledge the high cost but argue that new revenues and cost savings will largely pay for the program. Opponents argue that those approaches together will fall far short, and that middle-income taxpayers will be called upon to make up the difference. Ironically, the public option that conservatives forced out of the bill was a primary mechanism to control cost increases by health insurers.

• Medical malpractice reform is not addressed. Conservative critics (and some from the left) criticize the reform package for not addressing tort (medical malpractice) reform. To the extent that the practice of defensive medicine in response to the threat of lawsuits is a contributor to the high cost of care, the reform plan misses an opportunity to reduce these wasted dollars.

Liberal criticism of the plan centers on two key points:

• The plan does not provide health insurance coverage for everyone. There were 47 million uninsured people at the time when the Act was passed, and that number was expected to increase to about 53 million by 2016. The reform package is expected to cover an additional 32 million people by that time, leaving about 21 million uncovered. About 50 percent of the remaining uninsured will be undocumented immigrants. Young people who are not covered on their family's plan and who would rather pay the financial penalty than purchase insurance will probably be the second largest group. The Congressional Budget Office predicts that around 4 million people will opt for the penalty payment. That number is an issue for those who want this system to cover everyone—an important priority for Democrats and Independents.

• There is too much private for-profit company involvement. If indeed the complexity of the plan and the retention of a strong private sector lead to or maintain high profit, administrative waste, exorbitant salaries, and continuing medical fraud, then an opportunity has been missed to make the system more efficient by spending fewer dollars on items other than health care.

What Was the Successful Strategy in Getting Health Care Reform Legislation Passed?

How did the situation change from the lack of success of the Clinton proposal to the enacted legislation in 2010? Some analysts have suggested that a key was that Obama proposal leaders were more effective in dealing with key stakeholders in the reform debate. While political opposition from Republicans was intense, many stakeholders saw reasons to support in 2010 what they had opposed in 1993.

Physicians. While there were differences of opinion among physicians in 2010, surveys found that most physicians supported the reform proposal. For the first time, the AMA went on record in support. Many physicians expressed unhappiness about the lack of social justice in the health care system, and appreciated that many formerly uninsured patients would now have their medical bills paid. (Nursing groups were strong supporters both in 1993 and in 2010.)

Hospitals. Hospitals have been trapped between the demands of paying bills (and making a profit in for-profit hospitals) and providing charity care. The conversion of 32 million people to insured status means that the number of people unable to afford their hospital bills should decrease. This won over some support from hospital groups.

Health Insurers. The health insurance industry was divided about health care reform, but ended up agreeing to provide funds to help to support the system. When health care reform looked inevitable, the greatest fear of the insurance industry was that either for-profit insurance would be banned or a competing public non-profit insurance company would be created that would drive down industry profits. In return for allowing current companies to continue to dominate the market and creating the insurance mandate, they agreed to abide with new regulations, contribute funds annually to help to support the system, and not to strongly oppose it. America's Health Insurance Plans, a major insurer lobbyist, advocated for much of the plan.

Pharmaceutical Companies. Like health insurers, pharmaceutical companies feared the worst from health care reform—that caps would be placed on the cost of drugs (as has been done in other countries), thus lowering company profits. In return for not creating these caps, for further subsidizing the purchase of drugs for Medicare beneficiaries, and for not including provisions that would help generic drug-makers, pharmaceutical companies also agreed to help to fund health care reform and not to speak strongly against it.

Business Groups. Although many business owners continued to oppose health care reform, and the U.S. Chamber of Commerce was a leading opponent, many large and small businesses supported reform and appreciated the subsidies that will help them to offer health insurance to employees. (Most labor unions endorsed health care reform in 1993 and 2010.)

The support of these stakeholders is especially important because they have powerful lobbying voices and large amounts of money to support lobbying. In 2009, health care interests spent US$652 million lobbying Congress, and they spent an additional US$160 million in the first 3 months of 2010. Which health groups spent the most? The U.S. Chamber of Congress was by far the biggest spender, but the Pharmaceutical Research and Manufacturers of America, Pfizer, AARP, the AMA, the American Dental Association, Blue Cross-Blue Shield, and the American Hospital Association were all very large spenders. Lobbying efforts can influence public opinion, but most funds are spent directly lobbying congressional members.

Constitutional Challenges

Opponents of the Affordable Care Act began almost immediately to attempt to overturn it, and their efforts have not ceased. Some Republican-controlled states announced that they would refuse to obey aspects of the law. Lawsuits were filed in Circuit Courts, with some courts ruling that the ACA was constitutional and some ruling that features of it were not constitutional. One judge ruled that the entire act was unconstitutional.

These conflicting decisions enabled both the Obama administration and proponents of the act and the opposing states and other opponents to appeal to the United States Supreme Court to decide on the constitutionality of the act.

The months leading up to the case and to its ultimate decision were filled with drama and conjecture about how individual justices would decide and how a majority of the court would rule. In March 2012 the judges heard 5½ hours of arguments—an unprecedented amount of time in recent history—in favor of and opposed to the constitutionality of the law. The most important issue was whether Congress had constitutional authority to require private citizens to purchase

health insurance. Should the Court rule no on this issue, many believed the entire act would collapse. The second most important issue was whether the law unconstitutionally coerced states into expanding their Medicaid programs. (The law required states to expand Medicaid or lose all federal funds for the program.)

On June 28, 2012 a highly divided court ruled 5 to 4 to uphold most of the features of the Affordable Care Act. The very conservative Chief Justice of the Court, John Roberts, surprisingly joined the court's four liberal justices in approving the constitutionality of the individual mandate. That decision meant that the ACA would go forward. However, the court also ruled that requiring Medicaid expansion was unconstitutional and would need to be changed or eliminated. The court's four other conservative justices voted to scrap the entire act.

In the ensuing years, the ACA as planned has been gradually implemented. The features of the plan that were rolled out first have largely succeeded in accomplishing their objectives. For the first time in history, the percentage of Americans who are uninsured has dropped below 10 percent. The number of adults in their early and mid-twenties with health insurance has sharply increased. Much preventive care is now provided without charge, and more people are receiving preventive services. The cost of prescriptive medications for Medicare enrollees has declined. Individuals with pre-existing conditions are able to access health insurance. More low-income individuals and families have been accepted by Medicaid. Efforts to identify and stop medical fraud in relation to Medicare and Medicaid have significantly increased. Hospital readmissions have declined.

Nevertheless, Republican efforts to repeal the law or to defund it have persisted. By the end of 2015, the House of Representatives had voted more than 50 times to repeal the ACA (each time the effort failed in the Senate or was vetoed by the President). The Senate has voted more

Supporters of the Affordable Care Act cheer after the Supreme Court ruled that ACA tax credits can go to residents of any state—a major victory in 2015 for President Barack Obama's health care reforms. © AP

than three dozen times on bills to repeal or defund. Of course, none had a chance of being signed by President Obama.

In 2015, the U.S. Supreme Court heard another case that could have had devastating effects on the ACA. This case challenged the constitutionality of granting insurance subsidies in the states with a federally run exchange. This time the Court voted 6 to 3 that the subsidies were constitutional, thus once again protecting the law and program.

By 2015, public support for the Affordable Care Act and for specific provisions of it had reached a high level. An overwhelming majority of Americans believe that access to health care is a moral issue, and that if other developed nations can afford to do it, so should the United States (87 percent of Democrats and 33 percent of Republicans support universal health care). Although slightly more than half disapprove of the individual coverage mandate, a substantial plurality support Medicaid expansion, and wide majorities support the employer mandate, guaranteed issuance of insurance, including to people with pre-existing conditions, keeping the exchanges, and keeping the subsidies for low-income people. Overall, 26 percent want to keep the ACA as it is, 30 percent want to keep the ACA but change some parts of it, and 33 percent want to repeal the ACA. Ten percent of Democrats and 65 percent of Republicans favor repeal (Thompson, 2015).

Key Issues to Watch

Five issues in particular will be important to watch over the next few years.

- What option will individual states and D.C. choose for their health insurance exchanges? As of December 2015, 13 states have created their own exchange, 11 states have created a partnership with the federal government exchange, and 27 states have opted to use the federal exchange. Most (but not all) states with Democratic-controlled legislatures have set up their own exchange or use the partnership model. Most (but not all) states with a Republican-controlled legislature use the federal government exchange. Selecting the type of exchange used has been a very contentious issue in many states. About 12 million people received their health insurance through an exchange in 2015.

- Will states expand their Medicaid programs to accept more low-income individuals and families? Even with the federal government funding the total cost of expansion for 3 years and 90 percent thereafter, many states have thus far been unwilling to participate. As of 2015, 29 states plus D.C. have expanded their Medicaid and CHIP programs to include more low-income individuals and families. These expansions have brought health insurance to an additional 14 million people, and save an estimated 5,200 lives each year. These states

The Tea Party Coalition protests Medicaid expansion in Tucson, Arizona. © Norma Jean Gargasz/ Alamy Stock Photo.

almost all have Democratic-controlled legislatures or a Republican governor who has supported Medicaid/CHIP expansion. Almost all Republican-controlled legislatures have rejected expansion. Had they expanded, an additional 4 million people would be covered by health insurance.

States that have expanded have sharply reduced their number of uninsured, with concomitant increases in the percentage of people with chronic conditions accessing care and in the percentage of people able to fill their prescriptions, and a reduction in unpaid medical bills.

- What will be the status of contraception as a required preventive service under the ACA? The ACA mandates that employers offer coverage of certain essential health benefits, including coverage of preventive services without any payment cost sharing. Contraception is one of the included services. It is included on most lists of preventive services, has been required in insurance coverage by the Pregnancy Discrimination Act, and was already in force in 28 states. As an accommodation, churches are exempt from the requirement, and non-profit religious organizations may apply for an "accommodation" that passes responsibility to the insurance company. However, no special provisions were made for for-profit secular businesses with religious owners.

One such company is Hobby Lobby, a craft store chain with more than 14,000 employees. It is owned by a Protestant family that operates the business in accordance with its Christian principles. For example, it donates a portion of its sales to Christian missions and it is closed on Sundays. The owners did not object to covering certain types of contraceptives for its employees, but objected to those that prevent implantation of a fertilized egg

(believing this to be a type of abortion). The Mennonite owners of Conestoga Wood Specialties also objected. Both filed suit, and the consolidated cases went all the way to the United States Supreme Court. In June 2014, the Court ruled 5 to 4 in favor of the stores (Cohen, Lynch, and Curfman, 2014). The justices in the majority argued that employers such as these should be able to participate in the "accommodation" process described above.

However, an additional argument occurred as some of the non-profit religious organizations who could participate in the "accommodation" process believed that even having to request such an accommodation was unjust and could be interpreted as making them complicit in the act of contraception. This issue also ended up in the U.S. Supreme Court. It is based on the complaints of six groups, including the Little Sisters of the Poor Home for the Aged—the group by which the case has become known. Arguments were heard in March 2016. At the time of writing of this book, the case is pending.

- Ultimately, how many people will be covered by some form of health insurance and how many will still be uninsured even after full implementation of the Affordable Care Act? Recall that approximately 47 million people (over 15 percent of the population) lacked health insurance in 2010, and that the population had increased by about 15 million people by 2015. In 2015, nearly 32 million Americans (just under 10 percent) were still uncovered. Estimates are that about 10.5 million of those people are eligible for subsidized insurance coverage on an exchange, and several million more are eligible for Medicaid.

Who are these individuals? Analysts are still working to answer this question, but two groups are most apparent.

1. *The working poor.* These individuals either work for small businesses (which are still having difficulty providing health insurance for employees) or they have a job (in areas such as food service, construction, sales, cleaning and maintenance, office and administrative support, transportation, and personal care) but are classified either as part-time workers or as independent contractors, so their employers are not obligated to provide employer-sponsored health insurance. These people often live in states that have refused to expand Medicaid, but they live throughout the country. Surveys show that many do not understand the insurance exchange process or the available subsidies, and many of these individuals are eligible for assistance.

   However, more often they earn slightly too much to qualify for Medicaid or for exchange subsidies, but too little to afford ACA health insurance that requires a premium, a high deductible, co-insurance, and co-payments. With the very high deductibles for exchange insurance (US$3,000 on average, but they can be up to US$10,000 for the plans with the lowest premiums), many families would be responsible for paying for most or all of their own care. They recognize the value of the cap that the ACA puts on annual health expenditures (US$6,600 per year per person), but the outlay for the insurance premium combined with the deductible, co-insurance, and co-payments is prohibitive. Studies have found that people in this group with ACA insurance could still end up spending 20 or 25 percent of their income on health care.

   To encourage these individuals to purchase insurance, the ACA penalizes those who do not get it. In 2016, the financial penalty was set at US$695 per person or 2.5 percent of household income, whichever is higher. (The amount of this penalty increases each year.) So far, these individuals have chosen to pay the penalty, but the pressure to join an exchange will increase as the amount of the penalty does.

2. *Undocumented immigrants.* Recall that the nation's approximately 11 million undocumented immigrants are excluded from the various health insurance programs. Advocates for providing health care benefits to them contend that reimbursement to physicians, hospitals, and other medical providers would improve, that the younger and healthier immigrants would lower insurance costs, and that the goal of everyone in the country having access to health care would be achieved. California, New York, Massachusetts, Illinois, and D.C. have agreed to provide health care insurance for undocumented children up to the age of 19 years, and some states are considering expanding coverage to adults (California has led the way on this). Opponents disapprove of granting any benefits to people who are in this country illegally, and of increased health care costs. Republicans have insisted on this exclusion, so the sizable number of undocumented immigrants remains without health insurance.

- Ultimately, what will Affordable Care Act programs cost? Everyone acknowledges that the cost of health care will continue to increase. Affordable Care Act proponents contend that the law includes many features that will slow the rate at which these cost increases will occur and result in billions less being spent over time. Opponents of ACA contend that the law will accelerate cost increases and result in billions more being spent over time. This question will be answered only as the many features of the law are implemented.

SUMMARY

Despite the fact that the United States health care system has many positive qualities, it has been rated unfavorably relative to the systems in other countries. The system has been very inefficient, fragmented, and very expensive. It has been inaccessible to many people, especially the uninsured and underinsured. America spent almost 18 percent of its GDP on health care in 2010—more than any other country in the world—yet had more than 47 million people without health insurance.

The financing of health care is provided by a complex mix of employers, individuals and families, and the government. Over time, third-party payers have paid a greater share of health care costs. The implementation of Medicaid and Medicare has made the federal government the largest single purchaser of health care services.

Several factors have contributed to the rapidly escalating costs of health care, including the aging of the U.S. population, expensive new medical technologies, and medical entrepreneurialism (including high profits, high administrative costs, exorbitant CEO salaries, and medical waste). In response, cost-containment strategies such as managed care have been implemented.

Managed care organizations—such as HMOs, PPOs, and ELOs—combine health insurance and a health care delivery mechanism into a single package. They attempt to provide cost-efficient care by securing lower provider reimbursements, regulating patient care, and rewarding physicians for keeping patients healthy.

In 2010, after very contentious debate, the United States passed significant health care reform legislation—the Patient Protection and Affordable Care Act. This legislation has brought health insurance to an additional 32 million people and has modified the health care system in several important respects.

HEALTH ON THE INTERNET

The Centers for Medicare and Medicaid Services (CMS) is responsible for collecting data about Medicare, Medicaid, and other government-sponsored health care programs. Connect to the CMS website at

www.cms.gov.

By clicking on "Medicare" and "Medicaid," you can connect to links with information about each of these programs. How does Medicare work? What are the basic programs offered through Medicare? How does Medicaid work? What are the basic services offered through Medicaid?

Both Medicare and Medicaid will undergo change based on the Affordable Care Act. Find information about these changes on the website. What are the most important ways in which each program will change?

DISCUSSION CASE

As this book was nearing completion of the production process, Republican Donald Trump was elected president, and Republicans maintained majority control of both the Senate and the House of Representatives. One of Trump's emphases during the campaign was a promise, if elected, to repeal and replace Obamacare (The Affordable Care Act). His stated objectives were to use free market principles to (1) broaden access to health care, (2) make health care more affordable, and (3) improve the quality of health care available to all Americans. Consider the following questions about the handling of health insurance by President Trump's administration:

1. Who have become President Trump's key advisers regarding health insurance? What is their background? Are any Democrats included among the advisers?

2. What has occurred regarding the repeal of The Affordable Care Act?

3. What are the key provisions in the replacement plan? What are the major changes between this plan and The Affordable Care Act?

4. Is the new plan broadening access to health care? making health care more affordable? improving the quality of health care available to all Americans?

5. In your judgment is the Trump plan superior to the Affordable Care Act? Why or why not? Is the Trump plan superior to a universal health insurance program? Why or why not?

GLOSSARY

Children's Health Insurance Program (CHIP)
cost containment
defensive medicine
exclusive provider organizations (EPOs)
health insurance exchanges
health maintenance organizations (HMOs)
managed care
managed care organizations (MCOs)
Medicaid

medical entrepreneurialism
medical fraud
medical–industrial complex
Medicare
national health expenditures (NHEs)
personal health expenditures (PHEs)
point-of-service (POS) plan
preferred provider organizations (PPOs)
physician self-referral

REFERENCES

Alpern, J.D., William M. Stauffer, and Aaron S. Kesselheim. 2014 "High-Cost Generic Drugs — Implications for Patients and Policymakers." *New England Journal of Medicine,* 371:1859–1862.

Angell, Marcia. 2005 *The Truth About the Drug Companies: How They Deceive Us and What to Do About It.* New York: Random House.

Barry, Patrica. 2010 "Health Care Reform." *AARP Bulletin,* May:19–26.

Bekelman Justin E., Y. Li, and Cary P. Gross. 2003 "Scope and Impact of Financial Conflicts of Interest in Biomedical Research: A Systematic Review." *Journal of the American Medical Association,* 289:454–465.

Bernard, Didem M., Jessica S. Banthin, and William E. Encinosa. 2009 "Wealth, Income, and the Affordability of Health Insurance." *Health Affairs,* 28:887–896.

Berry, Emily. 2010 "Health Plans Extend Their Market Dominance." *American Medical News,* www.amednews.com/article/20100308/business/303089976/2/.

Blendon, Robert J., Mollyann Brodie, John M. Benson, Drew E. Altman, and Tami Buhr. 2006 "Americans' Views of Health Care Costs, Access, and Quality." *The Milbank Quarterly,* 84:623–657.

Bodenheimer, Thomas. 2005 "High and Rising Health Care Costs: Part 2." *Annals of Internal Medicine,* 142:932–937.

Brandeisky, Kara. 2015 "Here's How Much the Average American Worker Has to Pay for Health Care." *Time,* September 22.

Busfield, Joan. 2006 "Pills, Power, People: Sociological Understandings of the Pharmaceutical Industry." *Sociology*, 40:297–314.

Campbell, Eric G., Russell L. Gruen, James Mountford, Lawrence G. Miller, Paul D. Cleary, and David Blumenthal. 2007 "A National Survey of Physician–Industry Relationships." *New England Journal of Medicine*, 356:1742–1750.

Centers for Medicare and Medicaid Services. 2016 *Office of the Actuary*. Baltimore, MD: Office of National Health Statistics.

Chabner, Bruce A. 2011 "Drug Shortages—A Critical Challenge for the Generic Drug Market." *New England Journal of Medicine*, 365:2147–2149.

Coddington, Dean C., David J. Keen, Keith D. Moore, and Richard L. Clarke. 1990 *The Crisis in Health Care: Costs, Choices, and Strategies*. San Francisco, CA: Jossey-Bass Publishers.

Cohen, I. Glenn, Holly F. Lynch, and Gregory D. Curfman. 2014 "When Religious Freedom Clashes with Access to Care." *New England Journal of Medicine*, 371:596–599.

Cutler, David, Elizabeth Wikler, and Peter Basch. 2012 "Reducing Administrative Costs and Improving the Health Care System." *New England Journal of Medicine*, 367:1875–1878.

Family Foundation. 2016 "Employer Health Benefits." kff.org/report-section/ehbs-2016-section-five-market-shares-of-health-plans/.

———. 2009 "Trends in Health Care Costs and Spending." www.kff.org/insurance/7692.cfm.

Freeman, Joseph D., Srikanth Kadiyala, Janice F. Bell, and Diane P. Martin. 2008 "The Causal Effect of Health Insurance on Utilization and Outcomes in Adults: A Systematic Review of U.S. Studies." *Medical Care*, 46:1023–1032.

Frosch, Dominick L., Patrick M. Krueger, Robert C. Hornik, Peter F. Cronholm, and Frances K. Barg. 2007 "Creating Demand for Prescription Drugs: A Content Analysis of Television Direct-to-Consumer Advertising." *Annals of Family Medicine*, 5:6–13.

Grande, David. 2010 "Limiting the Influence of Pharmaceutical Gifts on Physicians: Self-Regulation or Government Intervention." *Journal of General Internal Medicine*, 25:79–83.

Hadley, Jack, Earl P. Steinberg, and Judith Feder. 1991 "Comparison of Uninsured and Privately Insured Hospital Patients." *Journal of the American Medical Association*, 265:374–379.

Harris Interactive Poll. 2006 *Trend Data*. Storrs, CT: Roper Center for Public Opinion Research.

Herman, Bob. 2015 "Drugmakers Funnel Payments to High-Prescribing Doctors." *Modern Healthcare*, September 21:7.

Hillman, Bruce J., Catherine A. Joseph, Michael R. Mabry, Jonathan H. Sunshine, Stephen D. Kennedy, and Monica Noether. 1990 "Frequency and Costs of Diagnostic Imaging in Office Practice—A Comparison of Self-Referring and Radiologist-Referring Physicians." *New England Journal of Medicine*, 323:1604–1608.

Hughes, Danny R., Mythreyi Bhargavan, and Jonathan H. Sunshine. 2010 "Imaging Self-Referral Associated with Higher Costs and Limited Impact on Duration of Illness." *Health Affairs*, 29:2244–2251.

Institute of Medicine. 2009 *America's Uninsured Crisis: Consequences for Health and Health Care*. Washington, D.C.: Institute of Medicine.

Kesselheim, Aaron S., and Niteesh K. Choudhry. 2008 "The International Pharmaceutical Market as a Source of Low-Cost Prescription Drugs for U.S. Patients." *Annals of Internal Medicine*, 148:614–619.

Lotvin, Alan M., William H. Shrank, Surya C. Singh, Benjamin P. Falit, and Troyen A. Brennan. 2014 "Specialty Medications: Traditional and Novel Tools Can Address Rising Spending on These Costly Drugs." *Health Affairs*, 33:1736–1744.

McDavid, Kathleen, Thomas C. Tucker, Andrew Sloggett, and Michel P. Coleman. 2003 "Cancer Survival in Kentucky and Health Insurance Coverage." *Archives of Internal Medicine*, 163:2135–2144.

McDonough, John E., Michael Miller, and Christine Barber. 2008 "A Progress Report on State Health Access Reform." *Health Affairs*, 27:105–115.

National Center for Health Statistics. 2016 *FastStats*. Atlanta, GA: Centers for Disease Control and Prevention.

Oberlander, Jonathan B., and Barbara Lyons. 2009 "Beyond Incrementalism: SCHIP and the Politics of Health Reform." *Health Affairs*, 28:399–410.

Oberlander, Jonathan, and David K. Jones. 2015 "The Children's Cliff — Extending CHIP." *New England Journal of Medicine*, 372:1979–1981.

Petryna, Adriana, Andrew Lakoff, and Arthur Kleinman. 2006 *Global Pharmaceuticals: Ethics, Markets, and Practices*. Durham, NC: Duke University Press.

Pham-Kanter, Genevieve. 2014 "Revisiting Financial Conflicts of Interest in FDA Advisory Committees." *Milbank Quarterly,* 92:446–470.

Public Opinion Strategies. 2004 "Survey on Top Health Care Priorities." *Modern Healthcare,* November 29, 26.

Quadagno, Jill. 2005 *One Nation Uninsured: Why the U.S. Has No National Health Insurance.* New York: Oxford University Press.

Reinhardt, Uwe E. 2003 "Does the Aging of the Population Really Drive the Demand for Health Care?" *Health Affairs,* 22:27–39.

Relman, Arnold S. 1980 "The New Medical–Industrial Complex." *New England Journal of Medicine,* 303:963–970.

———. 1991 "The Health Care Industry: Where Is It Taking Us?" *New England Journal of Medicine,* 325:854–859.

Schoen, Cathy, Karen Davis, Sabrina K.H. How, and Stephen C. Schoenbaum. 2006 "U.S. Health System Performance: A National Scorecard." *Health Affairs,* 25:457–475.

Sutherly, Ben. 2015 "Pinched by Deductibles, Some Forgo Medical Care." *The Columbus Dispatch,* November 22. www.dispatch.com/content/stories/local/2015/11/22/pinched-by-deductibles-some-forgo-medical-care.html.

Thompson, Dennis. 2015 "Most Americans View Access to Health Care as a Moral Issue. . ." *Health Day/Harris Poll,* September 8. www.ncpa.org/media/most-americans-view-access-to-health-care-as-a-moral-issue.

Waitzkin, Howard. 1989 "Health Policy in the United States: Problems and Alternatives." Pp. 475–491 in *Handbook of Medical Sociology* (4th ed.), Howard E. Freeman and Sol Levine (eds.). Upper Saddle River, NJ: Prentice Hall.

Weiss, Gregory L. 2006 *Grass Roots Medicine: The Story of America's Free Health Clinics.* Lanham, MD: Rowman and Littlefield.

Woolhandler, Steffie, Terry Campbell, and David U. Himmelstein. 2003 "Costs of Health Care Administration in the United States and Canada." *New England Journal of Medicine,* 349:768–775.

CHAPTER 15

Health Care Delivery

Learning Objectives

- Describe the key events in the origin and development of hospitals.

- Discuss three important issues facing hospitals today.

- Discuss two of the freestanding ambulatory and surgical sites. Identify and describe key reasons why non-hospital delivery sites have increased in importance.

- Describe what is meant by "hospice." Describe the primary benefits of hospice care facilities and the primary concerns about their future.

- Compare and contrast informal and formal home health care.

Throughout much of the twentieth century, the private physician's office (for primary care) and the hospital (for emergency, life-threatening, and surgical care) were almost the only medical treatment sites. However, in the last few decades, the health care delivery system has undergone a significant transformation, and now a wide array of care sites is available. This chapter describes and analyzes changes in five important components of the health care delivery system: (1) hospitals; (2) freestanding primary care, urgent care, and surgical sites; (3) nursing homes; (4) hospices; and (5) home health care.

HOSPITALS

History

Although the first American "hospital" was founded by William Penn in Philadelphia in 1713, it was primarily created to provide shelter for the poor. The first hospital designed primarily

to serve the sick was Pennsylvania Hospital, founded in Philadelphia in 1751 by Thomas Bond, a local physician, and Benjamin Franklin. The hospital began in a small rented house that was capable of holding no more than 20 patients, but grew in stages until the early 1800s. The hospital was always crowded, as the average length of stay was weeks or months long, but its main problem was a large influx of mentally ill people who occupied most of the beds. These patients were eventually moved to a new facility in 1835.

Most of the general hospitals that were built in the late 1700s and the 1800s provided care primarily for people without family and without the financial means to acquire housing. Most were financed by charitable contributions, and many physicians volunteered their time. A steward or matron generally controlled the small staff and the patients, and a small number of women, assisted by a few volunteers, performed "nursing" duties. Most of the care focused on making the patients comfortable and preparing them for death.

With advances in science and the development of medical technologies, hospitals underwent significant transformation. By 1900, hospitals mostly admitted only sick but curable patients, while other resources were sought for the elderly and the homeless. Religious appeals for funding gave way to a more secular approach that emphasized the value of hospitals in treating illness and protecting the community against epidemics. As a result, cities of all sizes began to build community hospitals.

By 1920, the hospital had become the primary center of acute care treatment. Surgery was the key to both the growth and the increased status of hospitals, along with the development of a skilled nursing force and the introduction of ancillary services such as X-ray facilities and laboratories. As the size of the hospital and the scope of its services increased, administrators were added to coordinate this work, and the complex bureaucratic hospital of today emerged (Rosenberg, 1987). Expansion in the number of community hospitals was spurred by the Hill-Burton Hospital Construction Act of 1946. This massive program committed nearly US$4 billion of federal monies and over US$9 billion of state and local government monies for the construction of new hospitals and the renovation of existing ones.

During the middle years of the twentieth century, the hospital became the primary acute health care organization and the center for the distribution of modern medical technologies. Advances in life expectancy and shifts in morbidity patterns from acute infectious diseases to chronic degenerative diseases resulted in a greater number of older patients who were chronically ill. This led to an enlargement of diagnostic services, an increased number of surgical procedures, and the development of rehabilitation units. In the remaining part of this section of the chapter, we will discuss developments in hospitals in the last few decades and especially in the last few years.

Organizational Structure

Today's hospitals are highly bureaucratic and hierarchical social organizations that exemplify the key characteristics of bureaucracies explicated by Max Weber. They typically contain an authority hierarchy (although not pyramidal in shape), extensive rules and regulations, fixed areas of responsibility based on competence, recruitment based on merit, regular remuneration, promotion based on objective criteria, and separation between the power of a position and of the incumbent. However, superimposed upon these bureaucratic traits are twin lines of authority that run throughout hospital decision making.

Dual Line of Authority.   These twin lines are referred to as the **dual line of authority**. Figure 15–1 provides one model of hospital organizational structure. Most hospital departments report either to the first line of authority, namely the hospital administrator (generally a person trained in hospital or health administration and with a strong background in business), or to the second line of authority, namely the medical director or other person who is medically trained. Both the hospital administrator and the medical director are ultimately responsible to the hospital's governing body—generally a board of trustees.

This dual system of authority frequently results in tension between the business orientation of the administrator and the clinical orientation of the medical director. Although both the administrative and medical staff share the primary goal of patient care, they do not always agree on related goals and the methods by which to achieve quality and efficient patient care. Fundamental to this conflict is that the administrator is responsible for the fiscal survival of the institution, and the medical staff is most concerned with clinical efficacy.

Related to this dispute is the struggle between professional autonomy and bureaucratic control.

Given their medical expertise, physicians maintain that only they are competent to make decisions regarding patient care and to issue instructions to the medical staff. However, many issues related to patient care also involve administrative decisions, and thus physicians may perceive an impingement on their clinical autonomy.

Nurses and other ancillary health care providers can be placed in an awkward situation by this structure. They are expected to carry out physicians' orders at the same time that they are obligated to follow hospital protocol. Being responsible to both can lead to stressful and conflicting responsibilities.

Relations among physicians and hospitals involve more tension today than perhaps ever before. The fact that many physicians are establishing freestanding sites that offer services once found only in the hospital and the fact that some hospitals have hired more physicians from the community to work on staff and have bought out local physician practices have led to some erosion of cooperation between the two groups (Berenson, Ginsburg, and May, 2007; Goldsmith, 2007).

Personnel and Division of Labor. In 2015, more than 18 million people worked in the health care field in the United States. More than 7 million of these individuals (about 40 percent) worked in hospitals, and this number has increased almost every year. About 80 percent of the people who work in hospitals are female.

As medical science has become more technologically sophisticated, health care practitioners have become increasingly specialized and numerous new allied health occupations have emerged. In the last three decades, most hospitals have added new technologies to their roster of services. For example, magnetic resonance imaging (MRI) did not exist in the early 1980s, but today there are more than 9,000 MRI units in the United States.

The Number of Hospitals and Hospital Beds

Interestingly, as the American population continues to increase, the number of hospitals and hospital beds is decreasing. The number of hospitals in the United States increased each year from the mid-1940s to 1979, when the number began to decline, resulting in a total of 5,686 hospitals in 2013 (see Table 15–1). Of these, 4,974 are short-term general hospitals. Since 1980, the number of hospitals has declined by more than 20 percent due primarily to the closing of rural and inner-city facilities.

The total number of hospital beds began to decline earlier than the number of hospitals, peaking in the mid-1960s at about 1.7 million and declining to just slightly more than 910,000 in 2013. The total number of hospital admissions increased each year until the mid-1980s (nearly 40 million per year), but has since dropped to 35.2 million. However, given the increase in population in the last two decades, the likelihood of any one person being hospitalized continues to decline.

Why are the number of hospitals and the number of hospital beds decreasing? There are two main answers—changing insurance reimbursement rates and an increase in the number of outpatient surgery centers. Hospital care is the most expensive form of health care. In order to keep their prices as low as possible, private insurance companies and managed care organizations have applied pressure, where feasible, to substitute other forms of care (e.g., outpatient surgery) for hospital care and to keep the number of days of hospitalization as low as possible. In addition, levels of reimbursement for hospitalized care, including that from Medicare and Medicaid, are being controlled more tightly. These efforts have led to a reduction in hospital admissions and a decline in average length of stay. They have also led to an increase in the number of surgical settings outside the hospital. With demand down, fewer hospitals and fewer hospital beds are needed.

Figure 15–1 Typical Hospital Structure

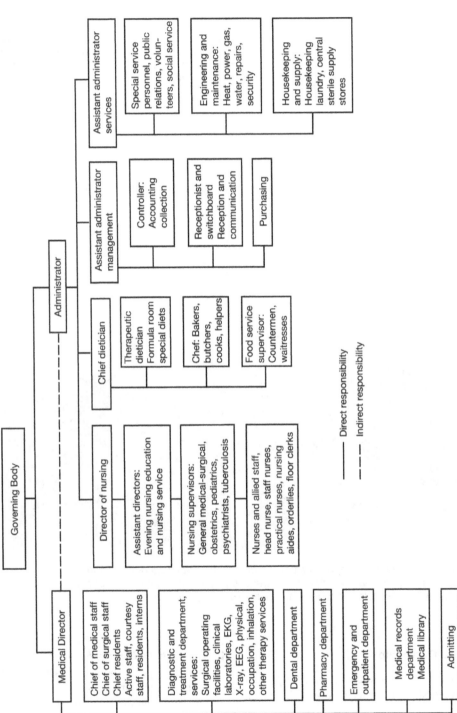

Source: Department of Labor, *Technology and Manpower in the Health Service Industry* (Washington, DC: Government Printing Office, 1967).

TABLE 15–1　Trends among U.S. Hospitals

Year	Hospitals	Beds (million)	Admissions (million)
1950	6,788	1.46	18.48
1960	6,876	1.66	25.03
1970	7,123	1.62	31.76
1980	6,965	1.37	38.89
1990	6,649	1.21	33.77
2000	5,810	0.98	34.89
2010	5,754	0.94	36.92
2013	5,686	0.91	35.42

Source: National Center for Health Statistics. *Health, United States, 2015* (Hyattsville, MD: United States Department of Health and Human Services, 2016).

The United States has approximately 5,700 hospitals employing more than 7 million workers. Physician-owned clinics (like the one pictured to the left in the photo) often locate adjacent to hospitals (pictured on the right). Photo by Janet Jonas.

Hospital Ownership

Each of the 4,974 short-term general hospitals in the United States is owned by one of three main entities:

1. *Non-profit (voluntary) hospitals* are the most common type of short-term general hospital in the United States. In 2013, there were 2,904 non-profit hospitals in the United

TABLE 15–2   Number of Community (Short-Term) Hospitals

Ownership Type	1980	1990	2000	2010	2013
Total	5,830	5,384	4,915	4,985	4,974
Non-profit	3,322	3,191	3,003	2,904	2,904
For-profit	730	749	749	1,013	1,060
Government	1,778	1,444	1,163	1,068	1,010

Source: National Center for Health Statistics. *Health, United States, 2015* (Hyattsville, MD: United States Department of Health and Human Services, 2016).

States—58 percent of all short-term community hospitals. As non–profit-making facilities, they answer to a board of directors that is typically comprised of community leaders, and end-of-year financial surpluses are reinvested in the hospital (as opposed to being paid to investors).

2. *For-profit (proprietary) hospitals* accounted for approximately 21 percent of all short-term hospitals. In 2013, there were 1,060 for-profit hospitals, an increase in the last decade. These hospitals are created by individual or corporate entrepreneurs; they are sometimes "public" in the sense that shares in the hospital (or controlling agent) are bought and sold on the stock market and are sometimes simply privately owned. These hospitals are expected to have greater revenues than expenses each year so that the difference can be returned to investors as profit.

3. *State and local government (public) hospitals* represent the third type of ownership. There were 1,010 public hospitals in 2013, which accounted for approximately 20 percent of all short-term hospitals in that year. The number of public hospitals is declining. Most state-funded hospitals are part of the mental health system, and locally funded hospitals are typically designed to serve the general population but end up being the primary care site for the poor and medically indigent. Public hospitals have charity caseloads about four times larger than those of other hospitals. All public hospitals rely on funding from the sponsoring government. Table 15–2 shows the changing number of hospitals from 1980 to 2013.

Until the beginning of the twentieth century, the majority of American hospitals were small for-profit institutions owned primarily by physicians. Gradually these were replaced by larger and more sophisticated community or church-owned non-profit hospitals. Beginning in the 1970s, considerable (and often very heated) debate about the role of profit-making hospitals was inspired by the growth of large conglomerates that purchased and ran multiple for-profit hospitals.

For several years, experts predicted that the for-profit hospitals would again assume control of the market. During the 1980s, however, cost-containment efforts reduced the profitability of hospitals and discouraged significant expansion of the profit-making sector. Since that time, the operating profit margin for hospitals (based on what is left of operating income after paying expenses) has been up and down. This helps to explain the fact that the percentage of hospitals that are for-profit has increased, but only by a small amount.

Multihospital Chains

The year 1968 is often cited as the key point in the development of large **multihospital chains** in the United States. In that year, two men—one a physician and the other an entrepreneur—joined forces to create the Hospital Corporation of America (HCA) to provide funds for capital expansion for the physician's hospital and to acquire additional hospitals. At that time, few of the nation's short-term general hospitals were part of a chain (Light, 1986). Since then, there has been a significant growth of hospital chains, which are now the dominant form of hospital ownership.

Megamergers

Perhaps the most significant trend of the 1990s was the hospital **megamerger**—the merger of hospital chains. For example, in 1993, the second largest chain, Columbia Healthcare (94 hospitals), acquired the largest chain, Hospital Corporation of America (96 hospitals), for US$5.7 billion, creating a gigantic Columbia/HCA Healthcare company. Two months later, Healthtrust and Epic Holdings, two other large chains, merged to create a new company with 116 hospitals (a US$1 billion deal); this became the second largest chain. Tenet Healthcare Corporation was created from the merger of two other large firms—National Medical Enterprises and American Medical International. In most years there are hundreds of mergers and acquisitions, although the economic downturn in 2008 and 2009 decreased merger activity. As of 2014, HCA was the largest for-profit chain (with 162 hospitals and US$37 billion in operating revenue), followed by Community Health Systems (193 hospitals and US$19 billion in operating revenue) and Tenet (80 hospitals and US$17 billion in operating revenue).

Many analysts now believe that the standalone hospital will soon disappear. Why is this occurring? Hospitals are under intense pressure to lower costs, the number of patients is decreasing, and fewer patients are spending nights in the hospital (decreasing that revenue stream).

In the last two decades, several of these large corporations have been under federal investigation, criminal indictments have been filed, and a mega-corporate shakeup has occurred. For example, in 2003, HCA agreed to pay US$871 million to settle allegations of health care fraud (filing false claims for Medicare and Medicaid and paying kickbacks to doctors so that they would refer patients to its hospitals). This settlement brought to more than US$1.7 billion the amount that HCA has paid in recent years in civil fines and criminal penalties. In 2005, Tennessee senator and senate majority leader at the time, William Frist, whose family had helped to create HCA, agreed to pay shareholders US$20 million to settle a lawsuit that he had personally benefited financially from false reporting of company profits (he had sold all his HCA stock 2 weeks before it dropped significantly). In 2006, the Frist family and other personal investors bought the company for US$33 billion and converted it from a public company (with shares sold on the stock market) to a privately held company. In 2010, they announced that the company would again go public.

Key Issues in Hospitals

The Relative Contributions of Not-For-Profit and For-Profit Hospitals. Advocates of not-for-profit hospitals contend that it is inappropriate to make a profit from patients' ill health. Through the first decade of the 2000s, for-profit hospitals made a profit of 4 to 7 percent each year except during the economic problems of 2008 and 2009. Non-profit advocates posit that their managers are able to focus on the needs of patients and the resources necessary to meet those needs without having to consider the profitability of choices made. Because they do not need to earn a profit, their fees reflect only enough money to cover all expenses plus the additional money necessary for capital and service improvements. Generally, non-profits are less expensive than for-profits.

Because they have non-profit status, these hospitals do not have to pay federal, state, or local taxes. The exemption from taxation saves non-profit hospitals approximately US$25 billion each year. In exchange for this benefit, these hospitals agree to provide some community benefits, including accepting many patients who are non-paying (this is referred to as "uncompensated care"). Uncompensated care is the total amount of care provided to patients who are unable or unwilling to pay. It is comprised of three types: (1) **charity care**—the value of care provided to patients who have been deemed by the hospital to be unable to pay (usually determined prior to admission), (2) bad debt—the value of care provided to patients who are unable or unwilling to pay (but who have not requested charity care), and (3) payments from Medicaid that are less than the hospital's costs. The total annual value of uncompensated hospital care is approximately US$40 billion—holding relatively steady at about 6 percent of expenses. The non-profits do spend much more money than the for-profits to provide services for patients who are unable to pay.

Recently, however, many local, state, and federal government officials have expressed concern that some non-profit hospitals have failed to invest enough of the difference between their income and expenses to provide services for the community's indigent. For some community hospitals in recent years, this margin (even after deductions for depreciation, overhead expenses, and community service projects) has approximated that of for-profit hospitals. Some non-profits dedicate as much as 20 percent of their operating expenses to charity care, whereas for others the figure is only 1 percent. The average is about 8 percent (Young et al., 2013). Ironically, in 2013, seven of the ten most profitable hospitals were not-for-profit (Bai and Anderson, 2016).

Community hospital administrators report that much of this money has been placed in reserve accounts that may be needed should an increasing number of people lack the ability to pay for care. However, the tax exemption for non-profit hospitals is in jeopardy in a few states. Both for-profits and not-for-profits are devising more sophisticated means of calculating the value of service rendered to the community.

On the other hand, advocates of for-profit hospitals contend that the business approach that they bring to health care leads to both the highest quality of care (because they must attract enough patients to earn a profit) and greater efficiencies (because eliminating waste maximizes profit). For-profit advocates also emphasize that the considerable taxes they pay make an important contribution to their communities, a contribution that is not made by the tax-exempt non-profit hospitals.

Most for-profit hospitals do provide some charity care, but they are much more likely to turn away those who cannot pay or to look for the money somewhere else. One technique is **cost shifting** to other payers—usually those covered by personal health insurance, and especially the uninsured who are paying out of pocket. Thus uninsured payers are helping to pay for the charity care and bad debt of the hospitals (Anderson, 2007). In 2015, research identified 50 hospitals (all but one of which were for-profit) that were charging uninsured patients more than 10 times the actual cost of patient care. (If a patient's care cost US$100, the hospital charged US$1,000) (Bai and Anderson, 2015). Only two states—Maryland and West Virginia—set hospital rates, so this practice has been legal. The typical American hospital charges 3.4 times the cost of patient care. The Affordable Care Act now makes it illegal to charge uninsured patients more than others, but there are reports of this still occurring.

A 2009 case in California illustrates the pattern. Emergency-room physicians spent 5 minutes trying to revive a college student who had been severely beaten in his dorm room. Everyone acknowledged that the effort to save him was heroic, but the young man died. The hospital, incorrectly thinking he was uninsured, sent a bill for US$29,000 to his parents. Had the hospital known that he was insured, it would have sent the bill to the insurer, who would have paid a considerably lesser amount based on what they had negotiated.

Proponents of not-for-profit hospitals have charged that the for-profits use a variety of techniques to discourage access by poor patients. One way that this is done is by for-profit hospitals locating in more affluent suburban areas where many patients have private insurance and where they can target marketing campaigns to these middle- and upper-class people (a process called **cream skimming**). In the early and mid-2000s, there was a boom in hospital construction in the United States, and it largely consisted of new high-tech high-amenities hospitals being built in suburban areas to replace older downtown facilities. This relocation contrasts with the area where need is greatest.

A second way in which for-profit hospitals discourage poor patients is by conducting "wallet biopsies" in order to refuse uninsured patients access to the hospital. If the patient needs to be seen, the for-profit arranges a transfer to a non-profit or public hospital, assuming it will accept the patient (a process called **patient dumping**), which some analysts believe happens frequently. Prompted by reports that hospitals sometimes turned away even emergency patients because they would be unable to pay for medical care, the federal government passed legislation in 1986 to stop this patient dumping. The law requires hospitals to medically screen all emergency patients, and prohibits them from transferring patients with unstable medical conditions or women in labor to other facilities for economic reasons. The maximum penalty for each violation is US$50,000 and the possible loss of Medicare funding. Occasionally, however, patient dumping stories are still reported.

Both for-profit and not-for-profit hospital administrators acknowledge that the large number of uninsured people unable to pay for hospital care is a significant problem within the health care system. For example, in the late 1980s, a young man in Georgia, without medical insurance, suffered burns over 95 percent of his body and was taken to the closest medical center (which did not have a burns unit). The medical center contacted more than 40 hospitals with burns units—both within the state and in neighboring states, and both for-profit and non-profit—asking each to accept the patient. All of them refused, mainly due to the anticipated high costs associated with treatment and the likelihood of not being paid. Finally, a hospital in Baltimore, Maryland, accepted the patient, and he was flown there.

A case with some similarity occurred in 1998 at a California hospital. A woman who was having painful contractions and breathing problems due to asthma, and was about to give birth, requested an epidural (which allows a woman to remain awake during labor while blocking pain in the lower part of the body). The anesthesiologist demanded US$400 in cash on the spot, and refused the woman's offer of a credit card, check, or Western Union number for cash confirmation. The epidural was not given.

The Effect of Multihospital Chains on Independent Hospitals. Hospitals that are members of multihospital chains have several advantages over independent hospitals. Among the most important advantages are (1) economies of scale in purchasing (the chains buy more products and get a lower per-unit cost), (2) greater negotiating leverage with managed care networks and health insurance companies (they can offer more favorable rates due to the larger number of people being covered), (3) greater ability to share the costs of new technologies across many hospitals, and (4) elimination of some duplication of services.

Lacking these benefits, independent hospitals have been put in a squeeze. Especially hard hit have been black-owned hospitals and rural hospitals. Between 1961 and 1988, 57 of the country's 83 black-owned hospitals closed and an additional 14 others either merged, converted, or consolidated. Today there are only a few black-owned hospitals in the United States, and some of these are in a serious financial condition. Traditionally, these hospitals have served the uninsured who could not receive care elsewhere. Their demise has left a significant gap in hospital services for the poor and medically indigent.

In addition, many of the nation's 2,000 hospitals in rural areas are struggling to survive. Many of these hospitals are small, but they are the only hospital and perhaps the only urgent care site within 100 miles. Inpatient admissions to many of these hospitals have declined in recent years—as they have in most hospitals—but the effect of this can be more overwhelming for a small facility. Between 2010 and 2015, a total of 51 rural hospitals closed, and 283 more are in danger of going under. The vast majority of these hospitals are in the South, and most have a Republican governor and Republican-controlled state legislature. They opted not to expand Medicaid (about 75 percent of the closures were in the 20 states not expanding Medicaid) under the rubric of the Affordable Care Act, and a greater percentage of their low-income residents experience health care access problems. New hospital quality regulations have also been more difficult for smaller rural hospitals to meet.

Recognizing the problem, many of the nation's independent hospitals have responded with a strategy that includes both horizontal and vertical integration of services. In order to capture some of the same economies of scale and other advantages of the hospital chains, many independent hospitals have themselves consolidated—a process referred to as **horizontal integration**. Theoretically, this creates the same bargaining and powers of leverage that exist in the for-profit chains. Many not-for-profit hospitals have also engaged in **vertical integration** activities. A common procedure is the creation of a corporation (often a holding company) that owns both non–profit-making (including the hospital) and profit-making enterprises. Sometimes the profit-making companies are health related (e.g., hospital supply companies), which gives the conglomerate control over various levels of health care, and sometimes they are unrelated to health care (e.g., real estate companies). These arrangements allow the hospital to retain its non-profit, tax-exempt status while it secures access to the funds raised by the profit-making companies (although taxes are paid on these profits).

In the last decade, many not-for-profit hospitals have been acquired by for-profit chains and converted to profit-making status. With many non-profits struggling financially to compete, and with "acquisition fever" running at a high level, several non-profit hospitals have chosen to sell. This has resulted in some very bitter debates between profit-making companies and community representatives who wish to retain the hospital's not-for-profit basis, and also between the companies and groups of physicians affiliated with the hospital, who do not wish ownership of the hospital to change (Claxton et al., 1997). Physicians in New York City, Los Angeles, and other cities have gone to court in attempts to halt these mergers and acquisitions.

The Survival of Public Hospitals. While many independent hospitals have found means to compete with the multihospital chains, public-supported hospitals have fared less well. Public hospitals have been confronted with twin problems: (1) a rapidly increasing number of patients who are unable to pay their hospital bills (more than one-third being unable to pay), and (2) more competition for patients who are able to pay (and whose payments traditionally have helped to subsidize the charity cases). Fewer paying patients and more non-paying patients have placed many public hospitals—which often provide the only available hospital care for the medically indigent—in a desperate situation.

In order to help to take up the slack, public hospitals have postponed needed capital improvements and service developments, and thus they have become a less desirable care option for insured patients. They tend to do less well on quality assessment and have a more difficult time improving performance (Werner, Goldman, and Dudley, 2008). Even at that, many public hospitals lose money year after year. Can this situation continue indefinitely? It cannot, as the survivability of public hospitals is at stake. The Affordable Care Act is intended to enable more patients to be paying, but it is not a guarantee that they will use public hospitals. This is an issue that will play out in the coming years.

For a view of the role of public hospitals in a special situation, see the accompanying box, "Hurricane Katrina and the Resulting Health Care Crisis."

Reconfiguration of Patient Care Services. Today's economic marketplace for hospitals is very different from that which existed only a decade ago. The days of rapid expansion of facilities, services, staffing, and prices are rapidly disappearing. In order to compete in the new managed care environment, hospitals realize that they need to become leaner, more efficient, and more diversified than they have been in the past. In what ways is this happening?

First, most hospitals are attempting to significantly *reduce expenditures*. They are doing this by eliminating inefficiencies (e.g., reusing

supplies that formerly would have been discarded) and downsizing staffs. Studies show not only that the positions of hourly wage workers have been cut, but also that the positions of nurses, senior and middle managers, and medical technicians have been cut back. This downsizing has been controversial, but hospitals have determined that labor costs had to be reduced. In addition, hospitals are beginning fewer construction projects and purchasing less large equipment. By the turn of the twenty-first century, however, much of the downsizing had already occurred, and most hospitals now anticipate steady staffing levels at the new lower level.

In recent years, a new medical specialist—the hospitalist—has emerged. Hospitalists are physicians who work in and for a hospital and focus just on hospitalized patients. Most have a background in primary care. Currently, there are more than 45,000 hospitalists in the United States, and that number is expected to increase. Hospitals hope that these specialists will help to closely manage the care of each hospitalized patient, improve patient outcomes, and be economically efficient. Importantly, they also release office-based physicians from the need to check in personally each day with their hospitalized patients—a benefit given the shortage of primary care physicians in the United States (Lopez et al., 2009; Williams, 2008).

Second, many hospitals are *diversifying patient care services*. Prompted by the cost-containment environment and the increased willingness of Medicare, Medicaid, and private insurance companies to pay for low-tech out-of-hospital services, hospitals are offering a wider variety of non-acute care services. The best illustration of this shift is the increasing number of outpatient primary care departments in hospitals, and the increasing propensity of hospitals to perform outpatient surgery. In 2015, about two-thirds of all surgeries undertaken in hospitals were done on an outpatient basis, and they

IN THE FIELD

HURRICANE KATRINA AND THE RESULTING HEALTH CARE CRISIS

On August 29, 2005, Hurricane Katrina landed in the Gulf Coast states of the country and created massive destruction throughout the region. Louisiana, Mississippi, Alabama, and Florida experienced significant destruction. The city of New Orleans, long feared to be vulnerable should a hurricane strike, was especially hard hit. Two flood walls and a levee collapsed, unleashing torrents of water that covered 80 percent of the city. Residents of the city without the means to have evacuated prior to the arrival of Katrina were housed at the Superdome. The city and rescue workers "faced oppressive heat, darkness from downed power lines, difficulties communicating by telephone, little fuel for their cars, and widespread devastation" (Wilson, 2006:153).

A 2006 survey of the effects of Katrina estimated that 1,500 lives were lost, 780,000 people were displaced, 850 schools were damaged, 200,000 homes destroyed, 18,700 businesses destroyed, and 220,000 jobs lost (Louisiana Recovery Authority, 2006). As much of a public health emergency as was created during and in the immediate aftermath of the hurricane, the longer-term picture was also a reflection of serious problems.

> Threats existed in the mountainous debris; faulty sewage treatment; toxic chemical and oil spills; contaminated water; swirling dust; pesky insects and vermin; and mold, mold, and more mold. (Wilson, 2006:153)

Moreover, New Orleans had one of the nation's highest rates of poverty and lack of health insurance. These residents bore the brunt of the hurricane damage. They relied on a system of state-run public hospitals and a network of more than 350 clinics that primarily served the poor and uninsured. Altogether, the city lost 7 of its 22 hospitals and more than 50 percent of its hospital beds. The Medical Center of Louisiana at New Orleans consisted of two hospitals that were the safety net for the uninsured. Both were severely damaged. An interim and much smaller version of University Hospital opened in 2006. Charity Hospital, which had been plagued by overcrowding, budget shortfalls, and an inconvenient location, but was the only option for many low-income residents, never reopened. Long-term care facilities and mental health services and emergency-room resources were especially hard hit. Many health care providers who evacuated from New Orleans just prior to the hurricane decided not to return after the disasters (Rudowitz, Rowland, and Shartzer, 2006).

Post hurricane, some policy analysts hoped that the catastrophe would be a stimulus to rebuild a stronger and more accessible health care system than that which existed prior to Katrina. And that is what has occurred. With a US$100 million grant from the federal government and additional support from the state government and foundations, a system of more than 60 community health centers based on the medical home model were established. Most of these centers have same-day appointments, and all serve everyone who comes in. The expanded use of electronic health records was extremely helpful. Area medical schools and their faculty and students provided significant help. A US$1.1 billion medical center has recently opened. Although many challenges remain—especially in the city's mental health care system—some observers now call New Orleans' efforts a model for big city downtown health care renewal (Todd, 2015).

accounted for about 60 percent of total hospital revenues—the highest ever percentage.

Hospitals have also become major purchasers of freestanding surgical centers, and frequently partner with existing clinics. There are now more than 9,000 freestanding urgent care centers in the United States, and they see up to 160 million patients annually. While the reimbursement for outpatient procedures performed outside the hospital is less, the costs to the hospital are far lower, so the hospital profit margin is greater.

More Efficient Use of the Emergency Room. Almost all acute care hospitals (95 percent) in the United States have emergency units open 24 hours a day. Designed to provide care for acutely ill and injured patients, the emergency room (ER) has become something of a family physician for many people. In 2015, more than 136 million visits were made to emergency rooms—in almost 50 percent of these cases, urgent care was *not* needed. Nearly as many patients complained of coughs and sore throats as complained of chest pain. Approximately 25 percent of all acute care outpatient visits occur in the ER. Use of the emergency room had increased sharply in the years leading up to the Affordable Care Act even as use of other hospital services had leveled off. Because ER visits cost two to three times more than office visits to a primary care physician, they add significantly to health care costs (Schuur and Venkatesh, 2012).

What motivates so many individuals to seek primary care services from the ER? Hospital emergency rooms appeal to people for several reasons. Access is relatively easy because it does not depend on affiliation with a physician, an appointment, or time of day; the availability of advanced technology leads to a public perception of high-quality care; third-party payers have historically covered emergency room visits; and hospitals are obligated to provide emergency care even if the patient is not insured.

Not surprisingly, lack of access to primary care—either financially or in available hours—has been viewed as the main reason. Non-emergency visits to the ER are highest in areas where physicians are least willing to provide primary care to uninsured and Medicaid patients, and where there are the fewest providers and facilities open outside regular business hours (O'Malley, 2013). In recent years there has been a significant increase in the number of patients experiencing dental pain. Because government programs do not cover adult dental care, many with dental pain go to the ER for pain medication even though dentists do not staff ER rooms and patients cannot get a genuine resolution of their problem. Overall, people receiving Medicaid are the most common users of the emergency room.

The expectation has been that the Affordable Care Act would reduce use of the emergency room for individuals seeking non-emergency care. As more of the uninsured have gained health care coverage, it seemed reasonable to assume that they would seek out primary care physicians in their offices. However, during the first few years of the Affordable Care Act, use of the emergency room actually increased. This suggests that other factors are at play in preventing access to private care, such as physicians refusing to see Medicaid patients, or patients being unable or unwilling to pay co-payments, or not having another care site, or just being accustomed to visiting the emergency department for their care. It will be interesting to see whether patterns of use change in the future.

Medicare Patient Readmissions. In Chapter 14 we discussed the efforts of hospitals to save money on costs by discharging Medicare patients as early as possible. In the last few years this has become a major firestorm as records indicate that many Medicare patients (more than 1 million per year) have to be quickly readmitted for the same or a related condition. The reasons for this could range from the healing process being insufficiently completed to not being able to get a prompt follow-up appointment, to at-home issues such as an inability to get prescriptions filled. The estimated total cost of these readmissions is US$17 billion per year.

Readmission rates vary significantly from hospital to hospital and from region to region of the country. In 2010, by region, surgical patients had a 7 percent to 18 percent risk of being readmitted within 30 days. Nearly 20 percent of Medicare beneficiaries discharged from the hospital are re-hospitalized within 30 days. In two hospitals in New York, more than one-third of discharged Medicare patients were readmitted within 30 days. Furthermore, readmission rates have remained basically unchanged since 2004, when data on this were first collected and published.

In 2013, Medicare began levying heavy fines on hospitals that had too many readmissions. Fines for hospitals that do not reduce their number of readmissions could reach US$125,000 per hospital.

Medical Errors.   Errors happen in medicine as they do everywhere else. However, in the space of just a few months in 1995, an alarming

---

IN THE FIELD

PROBLEMS IN THE MILITARY MEDICAL CARE SYSTEM

The Veterans Health Administration (VHA) is one of the largest single-target health care systems in the United States. In 2015, the VHA had a US$60 billion budget (provided by the federal government) to run 1,600 facilities (largely hospitals and outpatient clinics). It has 288,000 employees—including 20,000 physicians—and serves more than 9 million enrollees. In total, 13 million veterans opt not to receive their medical care from VA facilities.

Over the years, VA medical facilities have faced several criticisms relating to their less than top-notch quality, low accessibility (long patient wait times for an appointment), and unnecessary inefficiencies. In 2014, these controversies once again became a major issue when it was discovered that the VA hospital in Phoenix, Arizona had average wait times for an appointment of nearly 4 months to see a physician, and that schedulers were using a variety of subterfuges to conceal this fact from regulators. This information led investigators to expand their study, and they found similar problems throughout other facilities.

How could such devastating problems occur in the military medical care system? The VA stated that they had been overrun with the high care needs of aging Vietnam War veterans and seriously wounded veterans—many with brain injuries and post-traumatic stress disorder—from the wars in Iraq and Afghanistan. Moreover, the VA facilities—like the nation as a whole—have a shortage of primary care physicians. They argued that they needed more funds to offer competitive salaries.

New legislation was passed in 2014 and this has provided additional funding. A new program that subsidizes care at private providers for veterans living more than 40 miles from a VA medical center is being implemented. The overall system average for wait times has been reduced to about 40 days—a significant improvement, but still considerably more than the target goal of 30 days. Most analysts believe that an antiquated administrative structure in the VA needs to be addressed in order for more progress to be made (Giroir and Wilensky, 2015) and embarrassing series of very serious errors occurred in hospitals around the country. At one hospital in Tampa, Florida, in the space of 3 weeks, arthroscopic surgery was performed on the wrong knee of a female patient, the wrong leg was amputated on a 51-year-old male patient, and a 77-year-old man died after a hospital employee mistakenly removed his respirator. Around the same time, the wrong breast was removed from a mastectomy patient in Michigan, the prostate gland was removed from the wrong patient in Maryland, a drug overdose killed an award-winning health columnist in Massachusetts, and oxygen was accidentally shut off to dozens of patients for up to 15 minutes in a Florida hospital.

The number and severity of these cases raised the issue of the adequacy of precautions and safeguards taken by hospitals to minimize the risk of error. Investigators immediately promised to determine whether particular kinds of hospitals or hospitals with particular structures or formal and informal protocols have a greater likelihood of being the site of serious error. However, in early 1998, another flurry of reports was published. The Centers for Disease Control and Prevention reported that 2 million people each year contract an infection while in hospital, and nearly 90,000 of them die from it. Several studies reported increasing evidence of drug errors in anesthesia and medications administered to patients.

In 1999, the Institute of Medicine published the first large-scale systematic study on medical errors and their consequences. It reported that as many as 98,000 Americans die each year as a result of medical errors, and that millions more are injured. About one-third of these deaths occur in hospitals, and the remainder occur in physicians' offices, nursing homes, and other care sites. This study received massive publicity and renewed calls for medical providers to take steps to at least significantly reduce the problem. In 2005, researchers at Harvard's School of Public Health repeated the study. They found that some hospitals and other providers had made significant improvements (although the pace of change was very slow), but many had not. They reported that the number of fatalities annually was still about 98,000 (Leape and Berwick, 2005).

What have we learned since then? About 1,300 times each year, surgeons operate on the wrong person or the wrong body part. Once in every 5,000 surgeries, a medical instrument is left inside a patient's body. Medication errors are not uncommon—there are an estimated 400,000 drug-related injuries each year. A study conducted in 2013–2014 by researchers in the anesthesiology department at Massachusetts General Hospital found that about 50 percent of all surgeries involved some kind of medication error or unintended drug side effects, and that harm to the patient occurred in one-third of these cases (Nanji et al., 2016). About 650,000 patients a year contract an infection (e.g., pneumonia, or infections at the surgical site) while in hospital, between 5 and 8 percent of intensive-care patients on ventilators get pneumonia, and 100 patients a day wake during the middle of surgery. A 2008 study found more progress, but most hospitals were still unwilling to install the recommended safety procedures and checks published by the Centers for Disease Control and Prevention, due to the amount of time required and the costs involved. However, some of the checks require little time and no money. For example, studies continually show that medical providers do not always wash their hands between patients, and the lowest washing frequency is by physicians.

In 2016, researchers from Johns Hopkins Medical School reported that medical errors in hospitals and other health care facilities were still incredibly common, and claim 251,000 lives each year in the United States. This would make medical errors the third leading cause of death after heart disease and cancer. The estimate was based on an analysis of four impressive large studies that were conducted between 2000 and 2008 (Makary and Daniel, 2016).

Many analysts contend that the errors are a symptom of a larger systemic problem—medical culture. Lucian Leape, a pioneer in patient safety, says that the health care culture in almost all hospitals is incredibly dysfunctional. Hospitals remain very hierarchical, and those lower in the hierarchy are very reluctant to call out those who are higher. Thus a nurse may observe a physician breaking a protocol—for example, not washing his or her hands between patients—but not say anything about it for fear of personal consequences (Leape et al., 2012). Peter Pronovost and Eric Vohr, co-authors of *Safe Patients, Smart Hospitals* (Pronovost and Vohr, 2010), identify physician overconfidence and reluctance to admit errors or limitations as being part of this culture that endangers patients. In order to put dollars behind the campaign to improve patient safety, some private insurers and Medicare now refuse to pay any costs associated with medical errors and/or hospital-acquired illnesses.

One interesting suggestion for improvement that is now being implemented in some hospitals is increased *transparency*. This involves hospitals reporting data that would allow consumers to compare patient treatment, outcomes, and cost. For example, the Dartmouth-Hitchcock Medical Center in New Hampshire has developed a website that provides these kinds of data. Go to www.dartmouth-hitchcock.org, click on "Quality Reports" in the menu at the bottom of the page, then click on "Dartmouth-Hitchcock Medical Center: Quality Reports," and check out each of the following: "Heart Attack," "Pneumonia," "Overall DHMC Performance Results," and "What Our Patients Say about Us."

In addition, the Patient Protection and Affordable Care Act introduced several mechanisms for care sites that had high rates of medical errors and were refusing to take the necessary steps to address the problem. These include Medicare penalties, wider use of electronic records, and grants to medical providers attempting to find ways to improve the situation. Although it is too early to draw definitive conclusions, research has detected more progress in reducing certain types of medical errors, including hospital-acquired infections, adverse drug events, unnecessary use of antibiotics, and bed sores. Despite this progress, medical errors remain a very serious problem.

FREESTANDING AMBULATORY AND SURGICAL SITES

Ambulatory care is personal health care provided to an individual who is not an inpatient in a health care facility. Ambulatory care services include preventive care, acute primary care, minor emergencies, and many surgical procedures, and they are provided today in an increasing variety of facilities.

The Traditional Setting

The traditional and still most common means of delivering ambulatory care is by a private physician (working alone, with a partner, or in a group) in an office or clinic setting. About nine in ten active U.S. physicians are involved in patient care, and 75 percent of these physicians have an office-based practice (the other 25 percent are full-time staff, residents, or clinical fellows in hospitals). However, today, of more than 350 million annual visits for newly arising health problems, only 42 percent are made to patients' personal physicians. Visits to emergency rooms, outpatient departments, and specialists are in aggregate more common (Pitts et al., 2010).

Of physicians working in patient care, the long-term shift has been from solo practice (i.e., a physician practicing alone) to group practice (i.e., three or more physicians formally organized and practicing together). About one-third of physicians in private practice now work alone or with just one other colleague, and the remainder work in group practice. Group practice began in the late nineteenth century in the United States with the establishment of the Mayo Clinic. The clinic started in the 1880s as a small but busy for-profit surgery practice involving a father and his two sons, and grew into a mammoth clinic (that was converted to not-for-profit status) with enough staff to handle not only surgery but also extensive diagnostic and preventive services (Starr, 1982).

With the growing awareness of the successful Mayo Clinic, the increasing specialization of medicine, and the positive experience that physicians had with group practice during World War One, interest grew rapidly. By the 1930s, approximately 300 group practices existed, with a median size of five or six physicians (Starr, 1982).

However, many physicians expressed reservations about group practice. Some considered groups to be a threat to physician autonomy and to the sanctity of the physician–patient relationship. Many solo practitioners considered group practices to be a threat to their very existence, and many objected that the group format opened the door to corporate control of medical practice and erosion of clinical autonomy. Nevertheless, expansion of group practices has continued.

Freestanding Sites

The number of both independently owned and hospital-affiliated freestanding ambulatory care centers has increased dramatically in the last few years. Services offered in these settings include primary and urgent care, diagnostic imaging, rehabilitation, sports medicine, dialysis, and minor surgery. Some of the most important of these care sites are described in this section of the chapter.

Urgent-Care Centers (Walk-In Centers). *Urgent-care (or walk-in) centers* provide services without an appointment for minor medical problems such as a sore throat or a cut needing stitches. Developed in the early 1980s to attract patients who need acute episodic care, they are now often viewed as an alternative to the family physician because they offer a stable professional staff, and many are open for extended hours 7 days a week. In 2015, there were more than 7,000 of these clinics. About 50 percent are owned by physicians and about one-third by hospitals.

Patients of walk-in centers tend to be young to middle-aged adults who are attracted to these facilities by their convenience and flexibility. This group of patients experiences a higher incidence of acute episodic rather than chronic health problems, so continuity of care may be of less importance, and they are less likely to have established a relationship with a regular health care provider.

Retail Store Clinics. In the first decade of the twenty-first century, a new treatment site emerged inside retail chain stores and pharmacies. CVS and Walgreens were among the first to establish clinics, and Target stores and Krogers are increasing their presence in the field. Walmart anticipates having 1,000 of its own sites within a couple of years. By 2015, there were approximately 1,900 of these clinics around the country (double the number that existed in 2006).

The typical retail clinic is a small thin-walled structure built into an existing store. Nurse practitioners and physician assistants rather than physicians are the providers. At first they offered a limited set of services, including screening tests, adult vaccinations, written prescriptions, and treatment for straightforward and simple medical problems such as sinusitis. However, almost all of the clinics now engage in diagnosis and treatment of patients for chronic conditions such as asthma, hypertension, diabetes, impaired kidney function, and high cholesterol.

The clinics emphasize their convenience to the many shoppers in these stores, and also that a patient can be seen without an appointment, that many of the clinics are open in the evenings and at weekends when many physicians' offices are closed, the ease of filling a prescription at the care site, and the lower charges for services. About 50 percent of the patients at retail clinics do not have a regular source of care. Charges are typically about one-third less than in doctors' offices, extended hours are offered, and typically there is much available parking. It was hoped that this model might be used to address the shortage of physicians in low-income areas, but these clinics have largely been established in more advantaged neighborhoods.

The lower charges and easy availability appeal to many patients and insurance companies. Many nurse practitioners see opportunities for them to become front-line providers. Many entrepreneurs see what could be a very profitable business model. However, some physicians have raised concerns, such as the lack of continuity and comprehensiveness of care, and the fact that the clinics typically see only the uncomplicated and least intensive conditions, which puts more pressure on office and clinic physicians who will see only the more serious conditions.

Ambulatory Surgical Centers (Surgicenters or ASCs). *Surgicenters* offer minor low-risk outpatient surgery. Only a few years ago, the vast majority of surgical procedures were performed in hospital operating rooms on an inpatient basis. Today, however, an increasing proportion of surgery is performed on an outpatient basis, and much of it in facilities other than the hospital.

Studies have found that outpatient surgery for appropriate procedures is cost-effective and has equivalent or lower rates of complications

and mortality. Approximately 65 percent of all surgical procedures today are performed on an outpatient basis, and two-thirds of these (more than 40 percent of all surgeries) are undertaken in a freestanding facility. The most common outpatient surgeries are cataract surgery, removal of benign tumors, gynecological diagnostic procedures, and minor ear, nose, and throat procedures.

Outpatient surgery performed in offices and clinics and in freestanding facilities is typically less expensive and more convenient than that undertaken in hospitals, and takes place in an atmosphere where a higher priority is given to the physician–patient relationship. However, hospital-affiliated services have a more readily available emergency backup system and, if necessary, easier transfer to an inpatient unit.

The cost-efficiency of outpatient surgery is traceable to several factors. First, hospital stays are extremely expensive. Therefore, when recovery can occur at home or in a recovery center with minimal staff, less capital investment, and lower overheads than a hospital, substantial savings result. A surgicenter can also be more cost-effective because it is designed to accommodate only the less complex and low-risk surgical procedures, and thus can avoid the need to purchase some of the most sophisticated and expensive equipment. Moreover, ASCs operate with fewer legal regulations, thus eliminating associated costs.

Federally Qualified Health Centers. These are comprehensive health care programs that are funded by Section 330 of the Public Health Service Act and provide care for medically underserved populations. The 1,200 clinics operate at about 8,000 sites, serve more than 20 million patients annually, and are comprised of the following:

- *Community health centers* provide primary care for Americans who are uninsured.

They are community based and led by boards of community residents.

- *Migrant health centers* provide health care services for migrant and seasonal agricultural workers.
- *Health care for the homeless programs* provide services for homeless individuals.
- *Public housing primary care programs* are located in and provide services to residents of public housing.

Originally conceived in 1965 as part of the War on Poverty, these centers are located in underserved areas, usually in inner-city neighborhoods and in rural areas, and primarily serve uninsured or publicly insured (especially Medicaid) racial and ethnic minorities. Individuals who have purchased a high-deductible health insurance plan (which is the most affordable plan for low-income individuals and families) under the Affordable Care Act have become frequent users of these clinics. Because they have to pay for all of their care until the deductible is reached, they would typically go without care were it not for these clinics.

Care is often provided by nurse practitioners and physician assistants. Seventy percent of the patients live below the poverty line, two-thirds are racial and ethnic minority group members, and 40 percent (prior to the Affordable Care Act) had no health insurance. Services are offered on a sliding-scale fee (i.e., the amount you pay is determined by your income). Studies show that a large majority of the 22 million users each year (at about 9,000 clinics) consider the centers to be their primary (and sometimes only) source of care. The Affordable Care Act included a significant amount of money to establish new community health centers, and by 2016 almost 1,000 new clinics had been created.

Free Health Clinics. A *free health clinic* movement emerged in the United States in the late 1960s to establish free clinics for people unable to afford private care and/or for those estranged from the conventional medical system. The early clinics were targeted to people experiencing drug-related illnesses, problem pregnancies, and sexually transmitted infections. They were very much countercultural organizations that highly valued their independence—many

Free clinics emerged in the 1960s, but their numbers have increased rapidly in the last two decades as a community-based means of providing health care for the working poor. Photo by Gregory Weiss.

even being reluctant to work with each other. They were genuine grassroots clinics started within communities, and they typically worked beside local medical care systems rather than with them.

The clinics have evolved in several ways from the 1960s and 1970s until today. The focus of the clinics has shifted more and more to serving either the very poor or the working poor (i.e., those who are working and are just above the poverty level, but who do not have private health insurance or qualify for Medicaid). Since the inception of the Affordable Care Act, many have modified their eligibility requirements to include those who have high-deductible health insurance. Undocumented immigrants, unable to participate in the health insurance exchanges, often rely on free clinics. In most communities the free clinics are a well-accepted and well-regarded component of the medical system, and they work closely with other medical providers (Weiss, 2006). There are now strong state and regional associations of free clinics, and even a national association (the National Association of Free and Charitable Clinics). The free clinic in Hilton Head, South Carolina, which was formed in the early 1990s by Dr. Jack McConnell, has created a related organization—Volunteers in Medicine—to assist other communities in establishing a free clinic. By 2016, they had helped to establish 95 free clinics around the country.

Although there are many variations in the more than 1,200 free clinics nationally, most of them (1) offer primary health care services, (2) are staffed largely by volunteer physicians, other health care providers, and laypeople (about 90 percent of services are provided by volunteers), (3) serve people who are unable to afford private medical care, and (4) provide an atmosphere that emphasizes treating each patient with dignity and a supportive, non-judgmental attitude. They have become a very important component of the health care system in the communities where they are located, and often receive tremendous support from the professional medical community.

Free clinics provide care to approximately 4 million patients each year. In addition, many free clinics have helped to set up networks of local physicians who, rather than volunteering at a free clinic, accept free patient referrals from a free clinic in their own office. Financial support comes from several sources, including local and state governments, United Way, corporate donations, church groups, private donations, contributions (often in kind) from the medical community, and patient donations (Weiss, 2006). The accompanying box, "Focus on a Free Health Clinic," describes the evolution of one particular free clinic.

Reasons for the Emergence of New Ambulatory Care Sites. The emergence of these ambulatory care sites is rooted in several changes within society and the medical profession. Like so many other changes, these new sites represent efforts to offer health care at a lower cost (walk-in clinics, retail clinics, and surgicenters) or to deter the medically indigent from using the very expensive care of the hospital emergency room as a primary care provider [Federally Qualified Health Centers (FQHCs) and free health clinics]. Lowell-Smith links the development of walk-in clinics and surgicenters (and now retail clinics) to other factors:

> Patient-consumers have become more mobile and thus less likely to establish a long term relationship with a physician. Patient-consumers have also become more knowledgeable in terms of their health needs and thus less likely to rely solely on the advice of a physician. In addition, there is the rise of convenience as a "cultural value." This desire for health care when the patient wants it rather than when the physician is available has aided the growth of walk-in clinics and outpatient surgery centers... [Also] improvements in medical technology have made it possible for many tests and procedures to be performed outside the hospital and in ambulatory settings. (Lowell-Smith, 1994:277)

IN THE FIELD

FOCUS ON A FREE HEALTH CLINIC

The Bradley Free Clinic in Roanoke, Virginia, was established in 1974 with US$250 in seed money, one volunteer physician, one volunteer nurse, and the free rental of the first floor of an old house (donated by the adjacent church). With the dedication of a small group of concerned citizens and the energy and enthusiasm of a barely paid director, the clinic was able to offer free health services to the local medically indigent two nights per week. The commitment of the director and volunteers was noticed in the medical community, by other lay volunteers, and by local governments—important factors in the clinic's subsequent support.

Each year the clinic provides more than 14,000 patient visits at no charge, prescribes more than 25,000 medications (almost all of which are given at no charge out of the clinic's own pharmacy, which is filled mostly with drugs donated by pharmaceutical companies and local physicians), offers extensive dental services (mostly out of its own fully modern dental operatories, supplied by donations from dental equipment companies and local

dentists), provides countless hours of mental health counseling (by local professionals volunteering their time), and performs basic laboratory tests (in its own small laboratory of mostly donated equipment). The clinic now sits in its own medical building (purchased with funds from a US$1 million donation by a local philanthropist). The estimated value of annual services provided is more than US$4 million (Weiss, 2006). For every dollar contributed to the clinic, it is able to provide US$4 worth of medical care.

Supplementing a small paid staff are a host of volunteers—more than 100 primary care physicians, dentists, nurses, pharmacists, laboratory technicians, pharmacy and dental assistants, and mental health counselors who volunteer some time at the clinic, plus 50 specialists who accept free referrals of clinic patients, and scores of lay volunteers. Care is provided at no charge in an atmosphere of respect for the dignity of each patient. By 2015 the Bradley Free Clinic had provided care valued at more than US$60 million.

The Federally Qualified Health Centers and free health clinics are founded primarily on the desire to provide accessible health care (both financially and geographically) for people who are unable to afford private medical care. Patients typically opt for these clinics not out of convenience, but out of need, and without programs of these types, even more people would go without needed care.

NURSING HOMES

Although the term is used in many different ways, a *nursing home* is a long-term residential facility that provides nursing and other therapeutic and rehabilitation care services. Nursing homes serve mainly incapacitated elderly residents, but also some younger adults with significant physical or mental health problems. About 6 percent of older adults in the United States live in nursing homes. Few residents are under the age of 65 years. Around 75 percent of residents are women, and 70 percent of them are widowed, divorced, or never married. Dementia is a common problem, with between 50 and 75 percent of residents exhibiting signs of dementia.

Residential care facilities like nursing homes were first developed in the early 1800s. Prior to this time, communities offered only almshouses in which the incapacitated elderly were placed with the homeless, the mentally ill, and the chronically inebriated. However, women's and church groups, concerned that some elderly members of their own social class, ethnicity, or religion might end up in the almshouses, began to establish benevolent care centers. These early nursing homes often required a substantial entrance fee and credentials showing good character, and thus were limited to a rather small number (Foundation Aiding the Elderly, 2016).

Throughout the 1800s, communities established a variety of residential facilities such as orphanages, hospitals for the acutely ill, and mental health hospitals, and many residents of the almshouses were moved to more specialized facilities. In this way, the incapacitated elderly became a much larger percentage of the almshouses. By the 1930s, society recognized that many elderly people were permanently unable to care for themselves, and that an improved system of residential care facilities was necessary. Nursing homes, as we think of them today, grew in number through the middle years of the 1900s and received a significant boost with the passage of Medicare and Medicaid in the 1960s. As the number of homes continued to increase, so did government concern about their quality, and the last 20 years have been marked by increased inspection and required compliance with safety and quality guidelines (Foundation Aiding the Elderly, 2016).

Types of Nursing Homes

The two main types of nursing homes are "skilled nursing facilities" and "intermediate care facilities." Skilled nursing centers are for residents who require ongoing medical care, such as respiratory therapy, physical therapy, occupational therapy, a feeding tube, or dialysis. These centers are staffed by registered nurses or licensed practical nurses who are available 24

hours a day. Intermediate care facilities basically provide residents with assistance in performing life's daily activities, such as feeding, personal hygiene, toileting, and bathing. These facilities are staffed primarily by certified nursing assistants. The term "nursing home" may also include "assisted living centers," in which seniors live on their own but receive assistance with meals, housekeeping, and medication, and "independent living centers," in which seniors basically live on their own and care for themselves but have someone to check in on them periodically and provide them with transportation.

Benefits of Nursing Homes

High-quality nursing homes provide a safe, healthy, and stimulating environment for seniors who are not able to live a fully independent life. In addition to basic necessities, they offer programs to try to help residents to avoid loneliness, boredom, and helplessness. The availability of various types of nursing homes means that seniors can receive whatever services are necessary to maximize their independence.

Concerns about Nursing Homes

When nursing homes are of less than high quality, they create living conditions that may be unsafe, unhealthy, and without the desired mental simulation. The Centers for Medicare and Medicaid Services, which conducts periodic evaluations of nursing home quality, rates each home from 1 star (lowest quality) to 5 stars (highest quality). In 2011, 15 percent of nursing homes received just one star and 20 percent received just two stars. Only 16 percent received five stars. Among the factors associated with low quality is the financial basis of the home. For-profit nursing homes represent 40 percent of the total number, but account for 67 percent of the consistently lowest performers. There are many references to low-quality nursing home care in America, and these address genuine concerns that are held by many seniors. These concerns include:

1. *Neglect.* When the number of staff members is insufficient, staff are not properly trained, or there is an absence of commitment to high-quality care, residents can end up with problems ranging from medication errors to bedsores, dehydration, and intense boredom.
2. *Abuse.* Periodically, social scientific or clinical research or journalistic exposés uncover cases in which nursing home residents have been physically, mentally, or pharmaceutically (e.g., by overuse of antipsychotic medication) abused.
3. *Accidents.* Especially in understaffed homes, residents can be vulnerable to serious accidents (e.g., falls and burns).
4. *The high price of care.* In 2016 it was estimated that the median daily cost of a private room in a nursing home had reached over US\$250—that is, about US\$7,700 a month or more than US\$92,000 per year. Assisted living care averaged about US\$44,000 per year. Few individuals or families can afford such extraordinary costs. It has become quite common for individuals to intentionally deplete almost all of their financial resources in order to qualify for Medicaid, because Medicaid pays for long-term care. Medicaid is the largest payer for long-term care, and paying for long-term care consumes nearly a third of Medicaid expenditures. This pattern sharply drives up the cost of Medicaid, which, as described in Chapter 14, is a major financial issue for state governments and the federal government.

HOSPICES

The term *hospice* refers to a philosophy of providing care and comfort to people during the dying process. As far back as the eleventh century, the word was used to identify guest-houses and places of shelter for sick and weary travelers. During the 1960s, British physician Dr. Cicely Saunders developed a modern approach to hospice that emphasized professional caregiving and the use of modern pain management techniques to compassionately care for the dying. She worked with others in establishing St. Christopher's Hospice near London, a hospice that significantly influenced the creation of other hospices around the world. The first hospice in the United States was established in New Haven, Connecticut, in 1974.

During the years of its development, hospice has evolved from offering services only in its own locations to offering services within hospitals, nursing homes, and especially in the patient's own home. Surveys indicate that a very large percentage of Americans would prefer to die in their own home. Nationally, only about 25 percent of deaths occur in the home, but about 60 percent of hospice patients die there. There are approximately 6,100 hospice providers in the United States today, and they are located in every state. Hospices range in size from small all-volunteer staffs who provide services for fewer than 50 patients per year to large multi-hospice providers that serve several thousand people each day. In 2014, an estimated 1.7 million patients received hospice care, including around 1.2 million who died during that year. Others were still in hospice care at the end of the year or had returned to curative care (National Hospice and Palliative Care Organization, 2016). About 50 percent of all people who died in 2014 were under the care of a hospice at the time of their death.

Benefits of Hospice.   Hospice services are available only to patients who have been attested by two physicians to be in the last 6 months of life. Hospices regard the dying process as being a normal part of life. They attempt to make patients as comfortable and pain free as possible during these months, and they do not do anything to hasten or postpone death. The median length of time under hospice care in 2014 was 17 days, and the mean amount of time was 71 days. Contrary to popular perception, hospice patients on average live 1 month longer than comparable patients who do not receive hospice care.

Hospice staff may include physicians, nurses, social workers, counselors, home health care aides, clergy, therapists (physical, occupational, massage, recreational, music, art, pet, etc.), dietitians, and volunteers. The services offered to patients and their families include the following (The Hospice Foundation, 2016):

- Knowledge about medical care and the dying process offered by specially trained professionals, volunteers, and families working in a team approach
- Addressing all symptoms of disease, but with a special emphasis on controlling the patient's pain and discomfort (i.e.,

palliative care) and treating the patient with concern and dignity
- Dealing with the emotional, social, and spiritual needs of patients and their families
- Offering bereavement and counseling services to families before and after a patient's death.

Payment for hospice services is covered by Medicare, Medicaid, and many private health insurance policies. Hospices work with uninsured patients to determine whether they might qualify for any insurance or financial assistance. Often patients do qualify for this, and if they do not, many hospices will accept them anyway. The Medicare and Medicaid Hospice Benefit has been available for individuals whose condition requires reasonable medical and support services but would no longer benefit from curative services. If a patient lives longer than 6 months, payment continues as long as the attending physician still considers the patient to be terminally ill.

Hospices provide many services for terminally ill patients and their families, including care and comfort, pain management, physical and emotional support, and grief counseling. Photo by Janet Jonas.

Beginning in the 1980s, some hospices converted to an "open-access" model in which terminally ill patients could continue to receive chemotherapy and other curative treatments even while being under hospice care. In part this model was inspired by some AIDS patients who wanted to receive hospice care but also wanted to continue trying other medical options. The Affordable Care Act passed in 2010 directed the Children's Health Insurance Program and Medicaid to immediately cover simultaneous medical care and hospice care for children with terminal illnesses (O'Reilly, 2010).

Several factors have contributed to the growth of hospices in the United States. These include the increasing number of older people who are experiencing and dying from chronic and painful illnesses, the difficulties of patients and their families having to contemplate death through a long dying process, the increasing cultural value of "death with dignity," and popular support for the humaneness of the hospice philosophy.

Concerns about the Future of Hospice. Although hospice has become an increasingly popular concept and program in the United States, there are pockets of resistance. Some individuals are uncomfortable with any approach that conflicts with doing everything possible to prolong the life of a patient. The acceptance of death and the dying process that is part of hospice is objectionable to them.

Some hospice enthusiasts strongly prefer the original model of hospice as "an antiestablishment, largely volunteer movement advocating a gentle death as an alternative to the medicalized death many people had come to dread" (Henig, 2005:3). The open-access model in which patients may be receiving various forms of high-technology care concurrently with hospice care seems to be a contradiction to the kind of serene environment on which hospice was grounded.

This concern is amplified by the fact that ownership of hospice is shifting rapidly from the non-profit to the for-profit sector. The hospice movement was entirely non-profit in its origin, and as late as 1983 all U.S. hospices were non-profit or government owned. However, by 2001, one-third of U.S. hospices were owned by individuals or companies seeking to make a profit (often hospitals or home health care companies). In 2014, about 60 percent of all hospice ownership was for profit (34 percent non-profit and 6 percent government). The shift toward for-profit ownership has stimulated higher costs and significantly increased Medicare spending for hospice. In 2011, the nation's fastest-growing for-profit hospice owner agreed to pay US$12.5 million to settle Medicare fraud claims, and in 2013 the nation's largest for-profit hospice owner was sued by the Department of Justice for tens of millions of dollars in Medicare fraud (billing for ineligible patients and inflated services). Discussion of profit margins, productivity adjustments, and market efficiencies seems to many to clash with the original ideals of hospice.

Finally, there is some controversy as to whether or not hospice eliminates any need for euthanasia. Some supporters contend that the pain management and emotional support offered in hospice mean that no one should have to suffer through the dying process and that euthanasia should never be necessary. Other supporters of hospice care argue that, in some cases, relieving significant pain can be very difficult and can only be accomplished through heavy sedation, and some dying patients also experience other unpleasant emotions such as frustration with confinement and psychic pain accompanying the loss of independence and body control. They contend that some of these patients may still prefer euthanasia (Burns, 1995). This issue, like the others discussed, will be very interesting to watch in the next decade.

HOME HEALTH CARE

Informal Home Health Care

Prior to the widespread development of hospitals and nursing homes, most people with illness and disability were cared for at home by family members. As formal organizations developed for taking care of those needing assistance with basic daily tasks, the family and family setting became somewhat less important. However, *home health care* has always been relied upon by many individuals, and it has once again become more common. About one in five U.S. households provides informal caregiving for a person aged 18 years or older.

Almost all care for minor illnesses is provided without formal entry into the health care system. Symptoms are monitored, activity may be restricted, medications are taken, and special attention may be given to eating nutritious foods and taking in fluids. These situations may involve temporary and even meaningful inconvenience to family caregivers, but they are typically very short term. More intensive home care is provided for people with chronic illnesses, disabilities, and mental retardation, and for those who are dying.

Informal home care offers many important benefits. It can be very personal and nurturing, there is continuity of care, and it is usually not as isolating as institutional care. The very high cost of care in hospitals and nursing homes also makes home care advantageous.

However, there can be disadvantages. Some families are not able to provide the necessary medical assistance, assistance with daily living tasks, or nurturance. Some family members may be resentful about giving their time, energy, and resources to caring for another. Because this resentment may be difficult or awkward to express, inner tensions may develop that are ultimately vented by verbal or physical abuse.

Even when the caregiving is provided without resentment, the emotional burden can be great.

Caregivers often become very stressed, develop health problems of their own, and many are not aware of effective coping and social support techniques. Many communities do have caregiver support groups, but some caregivers are unaware of them or are too physically and emotionally tired to participate. About one-third of caregivers describe their own health as being fair to poor.

In addition, family caregiving tends not to be evenly distributed among family members. The obligation to care for ill members tends to fall disproportionately upon females in the family, especially the wife and/or mother. Women provide about two-thirds of informal caregiving, and about 60 percent of caregivers are also employed outside the home. Studies confirm that in most families the adult female assumes the caring/nursing role, and this is true regardless of their work and other commitments outside the home. Employed mothers report three times as many hours missed from work due to family illness as are reported by employed fathers.

The federal and some state governments have taken notice of this situation. Legislation has been passed to give family caregivers paid leave from work. Through the National Family Caregiver Support Program, the federal government now gives state and local governments funding to pass on to families in the form of services and support. Some states have created programs to work with patients as they prepare for discharge from the hospital, to plan for home health care.

Formal Home Health Care

Formal home health care services began 100 years ago with the Visiting Nurse Society of New York. Other home care agencies developed over the years, but by the mid-1960s there were just 1,300 such agencies in the whole of the United States. The enactment of Medicare in 1965 spurred phenomenal growth in the home care industry—to more than 9,000 Medicare-certified agencies today, which provide about US$60 billion annually of formal home health care. More than 8 million individuals currently receive home care services because of acute illness, chronic health conditions, permanent disability, or terminal illness. About two-thirds of these patients are female, and about two-thirds are aged 65 years or older.

More than 50 percent of the nation's 2 million home care workers are home care aides. Registered nurses comprise the second largest group of home health care workers—about 20 percent of the total—but the field also includes many licensed practical nurses, physical therapists, occupational therapists, social workers, and others. Employment in home care is expected to increase by 50 percent between 2014 and 2024. To date, physician involvement in home health care has been minimal. However, physicians are being called upon more frequently to participate in the planning and management of elderly patients at home, and many hospitals have initiated home care departments.

The largest payer for home health care is Medicare (about 37 percent of total payments), but Medicaid and state and local governments (both 19 percent of the total) are also significant payers. About 12 percent of payments are made by private insurers. Over the last 10 years, home health care has become extraordinarily profitable, in part because wages for entry-level home care aides are among the lowest in the health care field, leading to high job turn-over. Home care companies have averaged 12 to 15 percent annual profit in the last few years.

Several factors are responsible for the growth of this industry, including the increased number of elderly people with chronic conditions, the lower costs associated with home health care compared with institutional care, and cost-containment efforts by private insurers and the government that have led to earlier hospital discharges of sicker patients.

SUMMARY

The sites in which health care services are delivered continue to change with the development of modern medical technology and in response to economic conditions. Although hospitals continue to be a central part of the system, the numbers of hospitals and hospital beds have decreased as cost-containment efforts and managed care have stimulated efforts to deliver care at lower cost. Hospitals today face several critical issues—the relative contributions of for-profit versus not-for-profit hospitals, the effect of large chains of hospitals on independent hospitals, the survival of public hospitals, the reconfiguring of patient services to maximize marketability, making more efficient use of the emergency room, new penalties for Medicare readmissions, and the curbing of medical errors.

Ambulatory care is still most often delivered through physicians' offices or clinics, but also increasingly through group practices. However, the number of freestanding ambulatory care and surgical facilities has increased dramatically in recent years, especially walk-in centers, retail store sites, and surgicenters that appeal to young and middle-aged adults and to people without a regular source of care. The number of Federally Qualified Health Centers and free health clinics, which are designed to serve the poor and medically indigent, has also increased in recent years.

The importance of nursing homes within the health care delivery system has increased significantly. When they perform with high quality, they provide a safe, healthy, and mentally stimulating environment for seniors. However, many nursing homes are consistently low-quality performers, and there are serious concerns about neglect, abuse, accidents, and their very high cost.

Hospice care offers comfort, concern, and efforts to reduce the pain of terminally ill patients. The concept has been very positively received, and many people now enter hospice care during the last days or months of life. Nevertheless, there are concerns about how the large-scale entry of for-profit companies into hospice ownership will affect this model of care.

Home health care is experiencing a revitalization as the population continues to age and the demands for lower-cost services increase. Home care is much less expensive than hospital and nursing home services. It offers many benefits to patients and their families, but also carries with it some important concerns.

HEALTH CARE ON THE INTERNET

The American Hospital Association (AHA) is the professional association of hospitals in the United States. Log on to its website at www.aha.org. What is the "vision and mission" (see menu at bottom of page) of the AHA? Under "Advocacy Issues" and "Key Issues," click on "Eliminating Racial and Ethnic Disparities in Health Outcomes." Check out any two of the recent efforts. What rights are emphasized in the AHA's "Patient Care Partnership"? (Click on "Advocacy Issues," then look under "Key Initiatives.")

Make sure that you understand the difference between a "federally qualified health center" and a "free health clinic." What are their key similarities and key differences?

DISCUSSION CASE

An important issue within health care systems and one that is discussed both in Chapter 14 and in this chapter relates to the relative benefits of for-profit versus not-for-profit facilities and services. Identify what you consider to be the major advantages of for-profit facilities and the major advantages of not-for-profit facilities. This chapter discusses the fact that hospices are increasingly being owned by for-profit companies. Would you expect hospices to change based on the type of ownership? If so, how and why? If not, why not?

GLOSSARY

ambulatory care
charity care
cost shifting
cream skimming
dual line of authority
horizontal integration

megamerger
multihospital chains
palliative care
patient dumping
vertical integration

REFERENCES

Anderson, Gerard F. 2007 "From 'Soak the Rich' to 'Soak the Poor': Recent Trends in Hospital Pricing." *Health Affairs*, 26:780–789.

Bai, Ge, and Gerard F. Anderson. 2015 "Extreme Markup: The Fifty U.S. Hospitals with the Highest Charge-to-Cost Ratios." *Health Affairs*, 34:922–928.

———. 2016 "A More Detailed Understanding of Factors Associated with Hospital Profitability." *Health Affairs*, 35:889–897.

Berenson, Robert A., Paul B. Ginsburg, and Jessica H. May. 2007 "Hospital–Physicians Relations: Cooperation, Competition, or Separation?" *Health Affairs*, 26:31–43.

Burns, John. 1995 "Hospices Play Bigger Role in Care Continuum." *Modern Healthcare*, 25:96.

Claxton, Gary, Judith Feder, David Schactman, and Stuart Altman. 1997 "Public Policy Issues in Nonprofit Conversions: An Overview." *Health Affairs*, 16:9–28.

Department of Labor. 1967 *Technology and Manpower in the Health Service Industry.* Washington, D.C.: Government Printing Office.

Foundation Aiding the Elderly. 2016 "The History of Nursing Homes." www.4fate.org/history.pdf.

Giroir, Brett P., and Gail R. Wilensky. 2015 "Reforming the Veterans Administration Hospital — Beyond Palliation of Symptoms." *New England Journal of Medicine*, 373:1693–1695.

Goldsmith, Jeff. 2007 "Hospitals and Physicians: Not a Pretty Picture." *Health Affairs*, 26:72–75.

Henig, Robin M. 2005 "Will We Ever Arrive at the Good Death?" *New York Times Magazine*, August 7. www.nytimes.com/2005/08/07/magazine/07DYINGL.html.

Institute of Medicine. 1999 *To Err is Human: Building a Safer Health Care System.* Washington, D.C.: National Academy of Sciences.

Leape, Lucian L., and Donald M. Berwick. 2005 "Five Years After to Err Is Human." *Journal of the American Medical Association*, 293:2384–2390.

Leape, Lucian L., Miles F. Shore, Jules L. Dienstag, Robert J. Mayer, Susan Edgman-Levitan, Gregg S. Meyer, and Gerald B. Healy. 2012 "Perspective: A Culture of Respect, Part 1: The Nature and Causes of Disrespectful Behavior by Physicians." *Academic Medicine*, 87:845–852.

Light, Donald W. 1986 "Corporate Medicine for Profit." *Scientific American*, 255:38–45.

Lopez, Lenny, Leroi S. Hicks, Amy P. Cohen, Sylvia McKean, and Joel S. Weissman. 2009 "Hospitalists and the Quality of Care in Hospitals." *Archives of Internal Medicine*, 169:1389–1394.

Louisiana Recovery Authority. 2006 *Hurricane Katrina Anniversary Data for Louisiana.* Baton Rouge, LA: Louisiana Recovery Authority.

Lowell-Smith, Elizabeth G. 1994 "Alternative Forms of Ambulatory Care: Implications for Patients and Physicians." *Social Science and Medicine*, 38:275–283.

Makary, Martin A., and Michael Daniel. 2016 "Medical Error—The Third Leading Cause of Death in the U.S." *British Medical Journal*, 2016;353:i2139.

Nanji, Karen C., Amit Patel, Sofia Shaikh, Diane L. Seger, and David W. Bates. 2016 "Evaluation of Perioperative Medication Errors and Adverse Drug Events." *Anesthesiology*, 124:25–34.

National Center for Health Statistics. 2016 *Health, United States, 2015.* Hyattsville, MD: United States Department of Health and Human Services.

National Hospice and Palliative Care Organization. 2016 *NHPCO's Facts and Figures: Hospice Care in America.* Alexandria, VA: NHPCO.

O'Malley, Ann S. 2013 "After-Hours Access to Primary Care Practices Linked with Lower Emergency Department Use and Less Unmet Medical Need." *Health Affairs*, 32:175–183.

O'Reilly, Kevin B. 2010 "Medicare to Test Allowing More than Palliative Care in Hospice." *American Medical News.* www.ama-assn.org/amednews/2010/05/24/prsb0524.htm.

Pitts, Stephen R., Emily R. Carrier, Eugene C. Rich, and Arthur L. Kellermann. 2010 "Where Americans Get Acute Care: Increasingly, It's Not at Their Doctor's Office." *Health Affairs*, 29:1620–1629.

Pronovost, Peter and Eric Vohr. 2010 *Safe Patients, Smart Hospitals: How One Doctor's Checklist Can Help Us Save Health Care from the Inside Out.* New York: Hudson Street Press.

Rosenberg, Charles E. 1987 *The Care of Strangers: The Rise of America's Hospital System.* New York: Basic Books.

Rudowitz, Robin, Diana Rowland, and Adele Shartzer. 2006 "Health Care in New Orleans before and After Hurricane Katrina." *Health Affairs*, 25:393–406.

Schuur, Jeremiah D., and Arjun K. Venkatesh. 2012 "The Growing Role of Emergency Departments in Hospital Admissions." *New England Journal of Medicine*, 367:391–393.

Starr, Paul. 1982 *The Social Transformation of American Medicine*. New York: Basic Books.

The Hospice Foundation. 2016 "What Is Hospice?" www.hospicefoundation.org/whatishospice.

Todd, Susan. 2015 "10 Years After Katrina, New Orleans Has Transformed Primary Care, Behavioral Health." *Modern Healthcare*, 45:27.

Weiss, Gregory L. 2006 *Grass Roots Medicine: The Story of America's Free Health Clinics*. Lanham, MD: Rowman and Littlefield.

Werner, Rachel M., L. Elizabeth Goldman, and R. Adams Dudley. 2008 "Comparison of Change in Quality of Care between Safety-Net and Non-Safety-Net Hospitals." *Journal of the American Medical Association*, 299: 2180–2187.

Williams, Mark V. 2008 "Hospitalists and the Hospital Medicine System of Care are Good for Patient Care." *Archives of Internal Medicine*, 168:1254–1256.

Wilson, Jennifer F. 2006 "Health and the Environment after Hurricane Katrina." *Annals of Internal Medicine*, 144:153–156.

Young, Gary Y., Chia-Hung Chou, Jeffrey Alexander, Shoou-Yih D. Lee, and Eli Raver. 2013 "Provision of Community Benefits by Tax-Exempt U.S. Hospitals." *New England Journal of Medicine*, 368:1519–1527.

CHAPTER 16

The Social Implications of Advanced Health Care Technology

Learning Objectives

- Identify seven key recent advancements in medical technology.

- Identify and discuss five important social implications of rapidly developing medical technology.

- Explain the key arguments for and against patients being able to demand and refuse medical treatment. Identify and explain the key arguments for and

against the legality of physician-assisted suicide.

- Discuss the important issues related to organ donation. Discuss the important issues related to organ donation policy.

- Identify and describe four modern assisted procreative techniques. Identify and explain the key arguments for and against the legality of surrogate motherhood.

The development of **technology**—the practical application of scientific or other forms of knowledge—is a major stimulus for social change in most modern societies. Western cultures subscribe to a belief system that prioritizes "technical rationality"—a mind-set in which "essentially all problems are seen as manageable with technical solutions, and rationality (reasonableness, plausibility, proof) can be established only through scientific means using scientific criteria" (Barger-Lux and Heaney, 1986:1314). However, many social scientists believe that technology is not only influenced by cultural values but also in return has a powerful and deterministic effect on culture and social structure—a theory known as **technological determinism.**

Today's health care system reflects the rapid rate of technological innovation in the last few

decades. Hospitals and medical clinics contain sophisticated pieces of equipment and specially trained personnel to operate them. The benefits of advanced health care technologies are apparent, including more accurate and quicker diagnoses, effective treatment modalities, and increased life expectancy. However, there are also negative consequences of technological innovations, including increased costs, inequities of access, technological "advancements" that fail (e.g., the artificial heart and thalidomide), and troubling ethical issues (Chang and Lauderdale, 2009).

SOCIETAL CONTROL OF TECHNOLOGY

Advocates view technological development as a means for society to fulfill its needs and to create a better life for its citizens. The need for more powerful means of information storage and processing produced the computer revolution. The need for faster food preparation techniques for on-the-go families led to the microwave oven. Automobile air bags are a safety innovation in a society where thousands lose their lives each year in traffic accidents. According to this view (sometimes referred to as a *utopian* view), society controls the introduction of new technologies, and technological advancements continue because they are beneficial to society.

Others, however, are concerned that technologies also create problems (sometimes referred to as a *dystopian* view). They critique modern societies (especially the United States) for a failure to systematically assess potential technologies in order to determine whether or not they should be pursued. Instead, American society is said to be controlled by a **technological imperative**—the idea that "if we have the technological capability to do something, then we should do it. . . . [it] implies that action in the form of the use of an available technology is always preferable to inaction" (Freund and McGuire, 1999:243).

Critics charge that this technological imperative is clearly demonstrated in medicine—in the desire of individual physicians to perform the newest and most sophisticated procedures (even if more conservative treatment would be just as appropriate), in health insurance companies' greater willingness to pay for high-tech medicine rather than low-tech or non-tech care, and in the march of hospitals to create (and thus be forced to use) high-tech wards (e.g., coronary intensive care units), even when they are shown not to offer any consistent advantage over more conservative, low-tech, and less expensive forms of treatment (Barger-Lux and Heaney, 1986; Freund and McGuire, 1999). Historian David Rothman argues that the insistence of the middle class that they have unfettered access to medical technologies has been the most

important influence on America's health policy for at least the last 60 years (Rothman, 1997).

HEALTH CARE TECHNOLOGY

Advancements in health care technology occurred throughout the twentieth century and the first part of this one, but the pace of development in the last few decades has been phenomenal. Key advancements during these years include the following:

1. *Critical care medicine.* Significant advances have been made in handling intensive care unit (ICU) cardiopulmonary patients (those with insufficient heart and lung capacity). An estimated 20 percent of all hospital patients require some form of respiratory therapy or support, including administration of oxygen to patients who cannot maintain adequate oxygen levels in their blood with their own breathing, performance of physical therapy to break up secretions and mucus in the lungs, and mechanical ventilation for patients who are unable to breathe on their own.

2. *Cardiac care medicine.* Important innovations include the cardiac pacemaker (which senses the heart's own electrical activity and paces it appropriately), the defibrillator (which maintains the rhythmic contractions of the heart to avoid a "heart attack"), increasingly successful heart bypass surgery, and heart transplants.

3. *Cancer care medicine.* Important advances are occurring in the use of blood tests to identify hard-to-find cancers, and new immunotherapy cancer vaccines that trigger the body's immune system to fight off cancer cells.

4. *Genomic medicine.* Whereas genetics examines single genes and their function, **genomic medicine** examines the interaction of multiple genes with each other and with the environment. Many diseases, including

breast and colorectal cancers, HIV/AIDS, Parkinson's disease, and Alzheimer's disease, can best be understood and addressed using this multifactorial approach.

5. **Personalized medicine.** Based on genetic information (a test that does personal genetic sequencing), medications will be developed for each individual, rather than using today's one-size-fits-all approach. These are expected to be extremely expensive but more effective.

6. **Medical imaging.** Non-invasive techniques such as nuclear medicine, ultrasound, computer tomography (CT; also called computerized axial tomography, or CAT), and magnetic resonance imaging (MRI) allow pictures to be taken of internal bodily organs. Recent advances provide even more information about bodily tissues.

7. **Health care computers (information technology).** New powerful computers are now used throughout the modern health care facility—in the clinical laboratory, in instrumentation, in building patient databases, and in diagnostic support systems. Some analysts believe that in the near future tens of millions of Americans will wear wireless monitoring devices that automatically send vital signs to medical professionals—an extension of devices that now provide automatic fall detection. See the accompanying box, "Telemedicine."

IN THE FIELD

TELEMEDICINE

The information superhighway has created many new opportunities for sharing, obtaining, and discussing information. Although the development and use of this technology in medicine (as in other fields) is still in its infancy, already some of the potential is evident. Research has found that more than 85 percent of physicians and 72 percent of adults in the United States use the Internet for health-related information retrieval (Pew Internet Health Tracking Survey, 2014). A dozen states have passed legislation that requires private insurers to cover services that are provided through **telemedicine**. Medicaid already compensates for telemedicine services in most states, and will soon do so in all 50 states. More than one-third of physicians now email patients, although 90 percent of patients would like them to do so. Listed below are some of the ways in which the Internet is affecting health care.

- Patients can make "virtual" visits to their own physician via a smartphone or online video connection. Many patients find this much more convenient than going to a clinic, less expensive, and just as effective for minor health problems. It also enables physicians to see more patients, although quality issues remain a concern. If one's own physician does not provide virtual visits, a patient can contact a dot-com physician ("cyberdoc") who has established a website or signed on with a virtual medical company. The physician does need to be licensed in the state of residence of the patient.

- Home health care nurses can "virtually" visit patients through monitors that enable the two to see each other while talking on the telephone, and can even check the patient's heart rate (the patient uses a stethoscope, and the nurse uses a headset attached to the computer). This is being referred to as "telehealth." More than 30 states now allow doctors to treat patients and to prescribe drugs online without any personal contact. More than 50 percent of U.S. hospitals now use some form of telehealth. It is also being adopted successfully with nursing home patients in several areas.

- Anyone with Internet access can retrieve information about any health care condition and treatment from a variety of Web sources. This reduces the traditional dominance of the physician as gatekeeper to medical knowledge and enables individuals to directly access information. However, because well-educated middle- and upper-income individuals have the most Internet access, they will continue to obtain the most information. Medical journals can place abstracts or full text of articles on the Internet.

- An estimated 50,000 smartphone health care applications (mHealth) are now available, and they were downloaded an estimated 247 million times in 2012—a year in which the number of health app users doubled. "mHealth generally refers to any use of mobile telecommunication technologies for the delivery of health care and in support of wellness" (Steinhubl, Muse, and Topol, 2013). The Food and Drug Administration estimated that there were 500 million users worldwide in 2015. Especially popular is Epocrates, a drug reference tool that has been consulted by about 50 percent of U.S. physicians, followed by UpToDate and Medscape, both of which are clinical decision support reference tools. Some of the apps now come with medical devices, such as an ultrasound wand, in anticipation that eventually a physical examination could be performed virtually.

- The reading of diagnostic tests is now sometimes "outsourced"—that is, it is read and interpreted by a physician in another country. For example, if a patient in the United States undergoes an emergency brain scan in the middle of the night, the scan will be electronically sent to a physician—perhaps in India or Australia, for example—for interpretation, rather than calling a radiologist into the hospital. This is referred to as "teleradiology."

- Health education online games are being created for children and adolescents to teach them about such things as healthy lifestyles and the importance of taking prescribed medications. Public health departments are using tools such as Facebook, texting, and Twitter to provide easily available information to young people.

- Electronic support groups ("e-health") and Internet Support Groups (ISGs) are now available for thousands of diseases and conditions and millions of Americans. Research has identified benefits for users, especially for those who create health information through blogging and contributing to social networking on health topics (Ziebland and Wyke, 2012). Various studies have found beneficial results from the use of text messaging about nutrition with college students, the use of Facebook and Twitter by public health departments, text messaging in smoking cessation programs, the use of Twitter to recruit health research volunteers, and text messaging to remind patients to take medications.

- Electronic mail can be used to enhance communication, especially among those located in rural areas without a wide support network. In 2014, there were about 200 telemedicine networks in the U.S. connecting to around 3,000 largely rural sites for medical education and consultations.

- Online physician "report cards" are now available enabling patient evaluations of medical care providers.

- Educational courses can be offered on the Internet—as is already occurring in efforts to bring more public health information to health professionals and patients in developing countries.

Assessment of these interventions is still in the early stages, but promising results have been obtained. However, it is clear that the accuracy and quality of online health information vary widely, so consumers must always be very careful when selecting reputable sites.

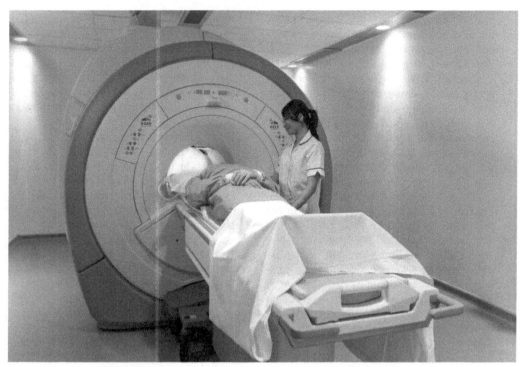

Magnetic resonance imaging (MRI), which uses magnetic fields, radio-wave energy, and sophisticated computer software, has enabled clearer and more detailed pictures of internal organs to be obtained. MRI machines can cost up to US$3 million, and the average price per MRI exceeds US$2,700. © Juice Images/Fotolia.

The Social Implications of Advanced Health Care Technology

Sociologists and other social scientists have identified at least five specific social implications of advanced health care technologies.

First, advanced health care technologies create options for people and society. These include using today's sophisticated emergency personnel and equipment to sustain a life that once would have expired, cardiac bypass surgery (where blocked cardiac arteries can be replaced by veins taken from the leg), and assisted procreation.

Second, advanced health care technologies alter human relationships. The existence of technological apparatuses that are able to sustain life after consciousness has been permanently lost has caused families throughout the country to discuss their personal wishes, and has created difficult decisions for family members of patients whose wishes are unknown. Physicians and other health care professionals consider the option of "DNR" ("do not resuscitate") or "no code," and engage family members in discussions about it.

Many people are concerned that the continuing introduction of advanced health care technologies has led to a dehumanization of patient care. Patients complain that physicians concentrate so much on the disease (in anticipation of selecting and using the appropriate technology) that they lose sight of the patient as a person. Feeling that they are being treated more like an object than a person, patients despair that the warmth and empathy demonstrated by many physicians in the pre-high-tech era are being lost (Barger-Lux and Heaney, 1986). Discussion today of "cyber-docs," "robodocs," and "virtual doctors" indicates the increasing use of modern computer wizardry in medicine, but also suggests to many an increasingly distant physician–patient relationship.

Renée Anspach's ethnographic work *Deciding Who Lives: Fateful Choices in the Intensive-Care Nursery* (Anspach, 1993) illustrates this concern. Anspach discovered that the different ways in which physicians and nurses relate to infants in an intensive care (IC) nursery affect their medical interpretations. Physicians, who have more limited contact with the infants and whose interaction is primarily technologically focused, rely on diagnostic technology to develop prognoses. Nurses, whose contact with the infants is more continuous, long-term, and emotional, develop prognoses more on the basis of their interaction and observations. While Anspach does not suggest that either prognostic technique is superior, her analysis demonstrates that one's position in the social structure of the nursery influences one's perceptions and that, to a certain extent, technology may "distance" the physician from the patient.

Third, advanced health care technologies affect the entire health care system. For example, technology has been the most important stimulus for the rapid increase in health care costs. An estimated 50 percent of recent health care inflation is due to new technologies. Much of the problem relates to increasingly expensive equipment such as CT scanners and nuclear medicine cameras, which can cost upward of US$1 million. The overall price tag for medical technologies in the world's developed countries in 2010 approached US$1 trillion.

The United States is now confronting the realization that it cannot afford every potentially helpful medical procedure for every patient. Increasing the amount of funds spent on health care (already considered by many to be at an unacceptably high level) would mean reducing the amount of money spent on education, the environment, and/or other areas of government funding. When the country (i.e., the government or health insurance companies) chooses to subsidize new technologies, it is explicitly or implicitly choosing not to subsidize other health care programs.

These macro-allocation decisions have led to increasingly sophisticated means of **technology assessment** and cost–benefit analysis. Efforts have been made to quantify the outcomes of implementing specific technologies and to compare these outcomes with those expected from other health care programs. For example, should the government fund 50 organ transplant procedures or offer prenatal care to 5,000 low-income women? The accompanying box, "Technology Assessment in Medicine," discusses this process.

These decisions also include value questions related to such issues as the amount of money spent on preventive care versus curative measures, the amount of money spent on people near the end of their lives, the amount of money spent on newborns who will require extensive lifetime care, the amount of money spent on diseases related to "voluntary lifestyles," and mechanisms to provide equal access to available programs.

Fourth, advanced health care technologies stimulate value clarification thinking. Medicine continues to raise issues that force individuals to confront provocative value questions about life and death.

As discussed in Chapter 4, the United States and other countries have recently mapped and sequenced the human genome (i.e., the complete set of human genes). The knowledge gained has dramatically increased our understanding of

IN THE FIELD

TECHNOLOGY ASSESSMENT IN MEDICINE

What is health technology assessment (HTA)? According to Lehoux and Blume (2000:1063), it is "a field of applied research that seeks to gather and synthesize the *best available evidence* on the costs, efficacy, and safety of health technology." Littenberg (1992:425–427) recommends that any proposed medical technology be assessed on the following five levels:

1. *Biological plausibility* assesses whether "the current understanding of the biology and pathology of the disease in question can support the technology."

2. *Technical feasibility* assesses whether "we can safely and reliably deliver the technology to the target patients."

3. *Intermediate outcomes* assess the immediate and specific "biological, physiologic, or clinical effects of the technology."

4. *Patient outcomes* assess "overall and ultimate outcomes for the health of the patient."

5. *Societal outcomes* assess the external effects of the technology on society, including the ethical and fiscal consequences.

A recent example demonstrating assessment of the impact of technology is the use of surgical robots. These have received significant attention in the popular press, and have become very popular in hospital operating rooms and among hospital marketing staffs. By 2012 more than 1,500 surgical robots were in use in the United States. However, a recent research study discovered that 144 deaths, 1,391 injuries, and 8,061 device malfunctions were recorded out of a total of more than 1.7 million robotic procedures carried out between 2000 and 2013 (Alemzadeh, 2016). These robots are, of course, very expensive. The typical cost of a surgical robot is US$2.3 million, with an additional annual requirement of US$135,000 for service fees. Using surgical robots adds an estimated US$3,000–6,000 to each surgery.

However, assessment has demonstrated that there is no clear benefit of surgical robots over traditional human hands-on surgery with regard to patient outcome (robotic surgery does require smaller incisions). Perhaps additional benefit will occur as the devices evolve, but so far they seem to be mostly driven by the technological imperative. As cost-consciousness within the health care system becomes more ingrained, it will be necessary for medical technology firms to offer more systematic assessment and to price products at a more affordable level (Robinson, 2015).

---

human evolution and humans' genetic relatedness with other organisms, the connection between genes and human behavior, and the relationship between specific genes and particular diseases. It is conceivable that this knowledge will eventually enable the elimination or control of all genetic diseases.

However, this process also raises value questions. For example, if all genetic diseases can someday be diagnosed and eliminated during fetal development, will such action be required? Would broad genetic screening programs with mandatory participation for all prospective parents or pregnant women be established? Would it be illegal or immoral to produce a child with an unnecessary genetic disease? Could such a child file a "wrongful life" suit against their parents?

Who should (or probably would) have access to genetic information about individuals? Would an employer have a right to a genetics background check of prospective employees? Would health insurance companies be able to require a genetic check-up when deciding whether or not to offer insurance to someone, or when calculating the cost of the insurance policy? How would discrimination in hiring or insuring be proved and handled?

In addition to using prenatal therapy to correct defective genes, will it be permissible to use therapy to provide genetic enhancements? For example, would it be legal to attempt to "boost" the intelligence gene(s), or would it be ethical to abort any (or even all?) fetuses with low intellectual potential? Should the government subsidize prospective parents who want therapy to produce a taller offspring or a shorter one? What are the long-term implications for altering the gene pool? These questions exemplify the difficult value questions that are created by this new knowledge.

Finally, advanced health care technologies create social policy questions. Of course, issues that raise difficult value questions for individuals often raise complicated social policy questions for societies. Critics have charged that legislatures and courts have shaped policy regarding ethical issues in medicine prior to adequate public debate. This situation is beginning to change as these issues are now receiving greater public scrutiny.

An example of an advanced medical technology forcing social policy consideration occurs with fetal tissue transplants. The vast majority of abortions are performed in the first trimester by the suction curettage method in which the fetus is removed by suction through a vacuum cannula. While the fetus is fragmented in this procedure, cells within tissue fragments can be collected. In about 10 percent of abortions using suction curettage (about 75,000 per year), the fragment containing the fetal midbrain can be identified and retrieved.

Research has demonstrated that transplantation of an aborted fetus's midbrain can relieve or even cure certain diseases, including diabetes, Parkinson's disease, and Alzheimer's disease. A high rate of successful transfer is due partially to the fact that this very immature tissue is unlikely to be rejected by the recipient. In the early 2000s the issue became focused on stem cell retrieval. The stem cell is a universal cell that resides in embryos and fetuses, where it is called upon to construct hearts, lungs, brains, and other vital organs and tissues. When retrieved, stem cells can be transformed or molded into any type of organ or tissue. The created organ or tissue would potentially be a cure for a wide range of diseases.

However, fetal tissue and stem cell transplants are opposed by most of those who believe that personhood begins at the instant of conception. Because the fetus or embryo is destroyed in the process of obtaining the tissue or stem cells, it is believed that the procedure (even for the purpose of a beneficial result) is an act of complicity in the ending of a human life. Presidents Ronald Reagan and George H.W. Bush placed a moratorium on publicly sponsored research on fetal tissue transplants. President Clinton overturned this ban. President George W. Bush enacted a policy that allowed research on a relatively small number of stem cell lines already in existence, but prohibited public support for research on additional lines, thus restricting and reducing research in this area. President Obama issued an executive order restoring publicly funded research.

In addition, it is conceivable that this issue will become moot, as very recent research is exploring the possibility of converting adult cells (which could easily be obtained by scraping cells off a person's arm) into stem cells, and in turn shaping the stem cells to become a specific kind of cell. For example, a person with a damaged heart could have cells taken and ultimately converted into healthy heart cells and inserted to replace the damaged heart cells. This work is in the very early stages of testing.

Social Issues Raised by Advancing Health Care Technology

The remainder of this chapter examines three issues that raise questions about the rights of individuals and patients versus the force of technology. Each issue has led to serious discussion of the rights of individuals to access or refuse to access modern medical technology, and of the responsibilities of society to control and regulate use of the technology. These questions involving individual choice versus public good and the means by which medical resources are allocated have become increasingly common as sophisticated high-technology care continues to be developed and made available.

Do patients have a legal right to refuse medical treatment, including artificial means of nourishment? Can patients demand a particular medical treatment even if physicians judge it to be futile? Can physicians participate in patient suicides? Should organ donation policies be revised in order to obtain more organs for transplantation? Should there be more investigation of the ways in which human relationships are altered by decisions to give and receive an organ? Should assisted procreative techniques be made available to anyone who wants them? Is it proper for society to regulate these techniques and/or even to prohibit them?

THE RIGHT TO REFUSE OR DEMAND ADVANCED HEALTH CARE TECHNOLOGY

Health care technology is at a stage of development in which it is often able to keep people alive but without being able to cure their disease, relieve their pain, or, at times, even restore consciousness. As this critical care technology (especially the artificial ventilator) has been developed and incorporated in hospitals, the traditional practice has been to use it whenever possible.

Gradually, however, patients and their families have begun to challenge the unquestioned use of technology and have asked (in the words of the book, play, and film) "Whose life is it anyway?" Patients and/or their proxies have become more assertive in requesting, and sometimes demanding, that the technology be withheld or withdrawn. In some circumstances, physicians and hospitals have complied, but, in other circumstances, requests have been refused. These situations have often ended in court hearings, and it has been the court system rather than legislators that has primarily dealt with the rights of patients and their families versus the rights of hospitals and physicians to determine the use of, or refusal to use, advanced health care technologies.

Do Patients Have a Legal Right to Refuse Medical Treatment?

Do competent patients, and incompetent patients through their representatives, have a right to refuse medical treatment? Or are physicians and hospitals required (or, at least, lawfully able) to use all forms of medical treatment, including high-tech medicine, whenever they deem this to be appropriate? Although this issue has been discussed for many years, three landmark court cases have addressed this issue of "fundamental rights."

Karen Ann Quinlan. In April 1975, 21-year-old Karen Ann Quinlan was brought to a hospital emergency room. She had passed out at a party and temporarily stopped breathing (during which time part of her brain died from lack of oxygen). Blood and urine tests showed that she had had only a couple of drinks and a small amount of aspirin and Valium, but that significant brain damage had occurred. Karen was connected to an artificial respirator to enable respiration (see the accompanying box, "Defining Death").

IN THE FIELD

DEFINING DEATH

The brain consists of three divisions:

1. The *cerebrum* (with the outer shell called the cortex; also called the "higher brain") is the primary center of consciousness, thought, memory, and feeling; many people believe it is the key to what makes us human—that is, it establishes "personhood."

2. The *brainstem* (also called the "lower brain") is the center of respiration and controls spontaneous vegetative functions such as swallowing, yawning, and sleep–wake cycles.

3. The *cerebellum* coordinates muscular movement.

Historically, death was defined as the total cessation of respiration and pulsation. Any destruction of the brainstem would stop respiration, preventing the supply of oxygen to the heart, which would stop pulsation, and death would typically occur within 20 minutes.

This definition was rendered inappropriate by the artificial respirator, which in essence replaces the brainstem. It enables breathing and therefore heartbeat.

In 1968, the "brain death" definition of death was developed at Harvard Medical School. It defines death as a permanently non-functioning whole brain (cerebrum and brainstem), including no reflexes, no spontaneous breathing, no cerebral function, and no awareness of externally applied stimuli. Thus if breathing persists, but only through the use of an artificial respirator, the person is officially dead. Many people today would prefer a higher-brain-oriented definition of death such as that suggested by Robert Veatch (1993:23), namely "an irreversible cessation of the capacity for consciousness." One effect of this definition would be that patients in a persistent (or "permanent") vegetative state would be declared to be dead.

After 4 months, the Quinlans acknowledged that Karen was unlikely ever to regain consciousness, and that she would be severely brain damaged if she did. Their priest assured them that the Catholic Church did not require continuation of extraordinary measures to support a hopeless life. The family requested that the artificial ventilator be disconnected. The hospital refused, arguing that Karen was alive and that it was their moral and legal obligation to act to sustain her life. The Quinlans went to court asking to be designated as Karen's legal guardians in order that the ventilator could be disconnected. Part of the rationale offered by their attorney was that the Constitution contains an implicit right to privacy which guarantees that individuals (or people acting on their behalf) can terminate extraordinary medical measures even if death results.

The Superior Court ruled against the Quinlan family, but the case was appealed to the New Jersey Supreme Court, which overruled the prior decision and granted guardianship to Mr. Quinlan. The court ruled that patients have a constitutionally derived right to privacy that includes the right to refuse medical treatment, and this right extends to competent and incompetent persons.

After a protracted series of events, the respirator was disconnected. When this occurred, surprisingly, Karen began to breathe on her own. It was determined that she was in a **persistent vegetative state (PVS).** In PVS, the patient is not conscious, is irretrievably comatose, is nourished artificially, *but* is respiring on their own. This happens when the brainstem is functioning, but the cerebrum is not. The eyes are open at times, there are sleep–wake cycles, the pupils respond to light, and gag and cough reflexes are normal. However, the person is completely unconscious and totally unaware of their surroundings, and will remain in this state until their death (which may not occur for many years). At any one time, about 10,000 people in the United States are in PVS. It is not the same as **brain death**, in which neither the cerebrum nor the brainstem is functioning. To be sustained, patients in PVS require artificial nutrition and hydration but no other forms of medical treatment. To be clear, the court ruled about medical treatment in the Quinlan case—not about nutrition and hydration. Karen was moved to a chronic care institution, where she continued breathing for 10 years before expiring.

Nancy Cruzan.   Does this right to privacy extend to the refusal to accept artificial means of nourishment? (This is typically administered through a nasogastric tube that delivers fluids through the nose and esophagus, or a gastrostomy in which fluids are delivered by tube through a surgical incision directly into the stomach, or intravenous feeding and hydration in which fluids are delivered through a needle directly into the bloodstream.) Or is the provision of nutrition and hydration so basic that it is not considered to be "medical treatment"?

In a poignant and lengthy travail through the court system, the case of Nancy Cruzan provided a judicial answer to the question. In January 1983, Nancy was in an automobile accident and suffered irreversible brain damage. She entered a PVS. After 4 years, Nancy's parents asked the Missouri Rehabilitation Center to withdraw the feeding tube. The center refused, and the Cruzans filed suit. They informed the court that Nancy had indicated that she would not want to be kept alive unless she could live "halfway normally." The Circuit Court ruled in favor of the Cruzans, but under appeal the Missouri Supreme Court overruled, disallowing the feeding tube from being disconnected. The court

concluded that there was not "clear and convincing evidence" that Nancy would not have wanted to be maintained as she was. Missouri law required such evidence for the withdrawal of artificial life-support systems.

The Cruzans appealed to the U.S. Supreme Court, and, for the first time, the Court agreed to hear a "right to die" case. On June 25, 1990, the Court handed down a 5–4 decision in favor of the state of Missouri. States were given latitude to require "clear and convincing evidence" that the individual would not wish to be sustained in PVS—meaning that families could not use their own judgment to decide to discontinue feeding.

However, the Court did acknowledge a constitutional basis for **advance directives** (see the accompanying box, "Advance Directives") and the legitimacy of surrogate decision making. Its rationale cited the Fourteenth Amendment's "liberty interest" as enabling individuals to reject unwanted medical treatment. Because the decision did not distinguish between the provision of nutrition and other forms of medical treatment, the feeding tubes could have been removed had the qualifications of the Missouri law been met.

Ultimately, another hearing occurred in the Circuit Court. Friends of Nancy came forward to offer additional evidence that she would not have wanted to be maintained in a PVS, and the judge again ruled for the Cruzans. No appeal was filed, and the feeding tubes were removed on December 14, 1990. Nancy died 12 days later.

Terri Schiavo.   In 2004 and 2005, the nation's attention was riveted by a Florida case that once again raised issues regarding persistent vegetative states, the role of proxy decision makers, and the power of the media and politicians to dramatize complex medical issues. On February 25, 1990, 26-year-old Terri Schiavo suffered a cardiac arrest that was, at least in part, brought on by an eating disorder. The disruption

IN THE FIELD

ADVANCE DIRECTIVES

A **living will** is a document signed by a competent person that provides explicit instructions about desired end-of-life treatment if the person is unconscious or unable to express his or her wishes. Legal in all 50 states and the District of Columbia, the living will is commonly used to authorize the withholding or withdrawal of life-sustaining technology, and provides immunity for health care professionals who comply with the stated wishes. Approximately 35 percent of adult Americans have completed a living will. Ironically, in most situations, physicians and hospitals ignore the living will if family members request medical treatment.

A *health care power of attorney* can be signed by a competent person to designate someone who will make all health care decisions should the person become legally incompetent. It requires the person to be available in the needed situation, but allows the person to consider the particulars of the situation before making a decision. Most experts agree that both types of advance directives have some benefit, and encourage people to do both.

The *Patient Self-Determination Act* (sometimes called the "medical Miranda warning") went into effect on December 1, 1991. It requires all health care providers who receive federal funding to inform incoming patients of their rights under state laws to refuse medical treatment and to prepare an advance directive. The law is intended to ensure that people are aware of their rights vis-à-vis life-sustaining medical technology.

to the oxygen supply caused permanent brain damage. Like Nancy Cruzan (and, ultimately, Karen Ann Quinlan), Terri entered a PVS and was kept alive by artificial nutrition and hydration.

For several years her case was not unlike that of thousands of other PVS patients as both her husband, Michael, and her birth family did all they could to provide support. In 1994, the relationship between Michael and her parents and siblings broke down over the manner in which a medical malpractice judgment would be spent. Four years later, in 1998, having become resigned to the fact that Terri's brain damage was permanent, Michael asked that the feeding tubes be withdrawn. Like Nancy Cruzan, Terri did not have any form of advance directive, and Michael was the legal guardian and proxy.

Her family opposed this decision and filed a series of court cases over the next few years to

remove Michael as guardian. All of these found that Michael was acting within his legal rights. In the early 2000s, the media picked up on the case, and details of the situation were reported on a routine basis. Governor Jeb Bush, the Florida state legislature, and eventually President Bush and the Republican leadership in Congress became involved in the case and sought all available means to overturn the several court rulings in the case and to prevent the withdrawal of the feeding tube. Twice the feeding tube was withdrawn and then reinserted. Congressional Republicans passed a bill that pertained just to Terri, but federal judges immediately found it to be unconstitutional. Ultimately, every court involved in the case ruled in favor of Michael's right to decide. The feeding tube was once again removed, and Terri died (Hampson and Emanuel, 2005; Werth, 2006). Political involvement and partisan wrangling in the case was at such a high level, according to the results of one study conducted in the aftermath of *Schiavo*, that college students began seeing this issue more from a political viewpoint than from an ethical one (Weiss and Lupkin, 2009–2010).

Can Patients Demand a Particular Medical Treatment?

The cases of Karen Ann Quinlan, Nancy Cruzan, and Terri Schiavo illustrate circumstances in which a patient or their proxy wishes to refuse medical treatment. In 1991 and in 2013, an unusual twist occurred in the Helga Wanglie and Jahi McMath cases. The hospital wished to stop medical treatment, and the family demanded that it continue. This created the reverse of the usual question: Does a patient or their representative(s) have the right to demand medical treatment?

Helga Wanglie and Jahi McGrath

In December 1989, Helga Wanglie, an active, well-educated 85-year-old woman, tripped over a rug and broke her hip. During the next few months she experienced several cardiopulmonary arrests. In May 1990, she suffered severe anoxia and slipped into a PVS. Her breathing was reinforced by a respirator, and she was fed through a feeding tube. By the year's end, her medical bills were approaching US$500,000.

In December, the medical staff recommended to Oliver Wanglie, her husband of 53 years, that the respirator be disconnected. He refused on the grounds that he and his wife believed in the sanctity of life and that, in good conscience, he could never agree to have the respirator disconnected.

The hospital petitioned the court to have Mr. Wanglie replaced as Helga's legal guardian. The rationale was that Mr. Wanglie had made some statements which indicated that Helga had never voiced an opinion about being sustained in PVS,

and that he was not legally competent to serve as her guardian. The hospital justified its request to disconnect by stating that it did not feel it should be obligated to provide "medically futile" medical treatment.

On July 1, 1991, the judge issued a narrow ruling that the hospital had not demonstrated that Mr. Wanglie was incompetent, and therefore he was the most appropriate legal guardian. Without the tubes being removed, Helga died 3 days later.

In December 2013, 13-year-old Jahi McMath underwent surgery for sleep apnea. Surgeons removed her tonsils and other parts of her nose and throat to widen her air passages. While recovering in the ICU, Jahi experienced severe bleeding and went into cardiac arrest. She was placed on a respirator. Three days later she was declared brain dead, and the hospital expressed its intention to remove the respirator.

Her mother, Nailah Winkfield, said that she believed her daughter was alive as long as her heart was beating. She went to court twice to secure injunctions that would prohibit the hospital from disconnecting the respirator. However, she refused to order the hospital to fit Jahi with the breathing and feeding tubes that she would need for longer-term care. A few days later, Nailah and the hospital reached an agreement to have Jahi transferred to a facility that would agree to keep her on a respirator. In January that transfer was made. As of March 2016, Jahi was still alive and her condition was unchanged.

Medical Futility. Although the judges in these cases did not directly address the "medical futility" issue, the concept caught the attention of social scientists, medical ethicists, health care practitioners, and the lay public, and significant attention is now being given to it. It has proved to be an elusive concept to define. Schneiderman, Jecker, and Jonsen (1990:950) have defined **medical futility** as "an expectation of success that is either predictably or empirically so unlikely that its exact probability is often incalculable." In a quantitative sense, "when physicians conclude . . . that in the last 100 cases, a medical treatment has been useless, they should regard the treatment as futile" (Schneiderman et al., 1990:951). In a qualitative sense, "any treatment that merely preserves permanent unconsciousness or that fails to end total dependence on intensive medical care should be regarded as non-beneficial and, therefore, futile" (Schneiderman et al., 1990:952). If a treatment fails to appreciably improve the person as a whole, they argue, physicians are entitled to withhold the treatment without the consent of family or friends.

While courts have supported patients' "negative rights" to refuse medical treatment, the issue of a "positive right" (the request for a particular intervention) is very different. It raises two issues: (1) a resource allocation issue—the more dollars that are spent on non-beneficial treatment, the fewer dollars there will be available to spend on those who would benefit, and (2) the reasonableness of requiring health care practitioners to engage in actions they consider to be unwarranted (and possibly harmful). Some believe that unless some benefit is anticipated, specific measures cannot be demanded.

However, successful intervention may be defined differently by different people. Families may be satisfied as long as everything possible is done—even if the patient dies. Their values may rest more on effort than on outcome, and they may never define effort as being futile. Some view the issue as showing respect for the autonomy of patients and their families by honoring these value differences but working together to avoid futile treatments (Quill, Arnold, and Back, 2009).

Physician-Assisted Suicide

Physician-assisted suicide occurs when a physician provides a means of death (e.g., a particular drug) and instructions (e.g., how much of the drug would need to be taken for it to be lethal) to a patient but does not actually administer the cause of death. This is different to **active euthanasia**, in which the physician directly administers the cause of death. Some now support the term "aid in dying" rather than "physician-assisted suicide."

Active euthanasia is legal in the Netherlands, Ireland, Luxembourg, and Columbia. Physician-assisted suicide is legal in Canada, Switzerland, Japan, Germany, Albania, and Belgium. It has become a very controversial issue in the United States, where five states—Oregon, Washington, Vermont, Montana, and, in 2015, California—have legalized the practice. In 1997, the U.S. Supreme Court ruled unanimously that terminally ill persons do not have a constitutional right to physician-assisted suicide, but that states could enact legislation consistent with their own constitution that permits it. Thus far, only the five states mentioned here have legalized physician-assisted suicide, while 39 states have laws prohibiting it. To date, the number of people using physician-assisted suicide has been small. Oregon, the first state to legalize, had a total of 859 deaths in its first 17 legalized years. People who engaged in physician-assisted suicide were overwhelmingly white and highly educated, and most of them had cancer. They mainly feared losing their autonomy, losing the ability to participate in enjoyable activities, and the loss of dignity (O'Reilly, 2010). The accompanying box, "Advance Directives and Navajo Culture," describes how this concept is considered in a Native American culture.

Two situations originally drew considerable attention to the issue of physician-assisted suicide in the United States.

Dr. Timothy Quill. In 1991, Dr. Timothy Quill, a 41-year-old general internist in Rochester, New York, published an article in the

IN COMPARATIVE FOCUS

ADVANCE DIRECTIVES AND NAVAJO CULTURE

Discussion of ethical issues outside the context of particular cultures means that vital information is not considered. On a broad level in the medical context, it increases the likelihood of social policies that conflict with important values of particular groups. On an individual level, it creates potential for misunderstandings and frustration between health care providers and their patients, and may lead to suboptimal care.

This is the case with regard to discussions about advance directives with Navajo patients. An important Navajo cultural norm is avoidance of discussion of negative information. In the Navajo belief system, talking about an event increases the likelihood of that event occurring. This belief obviously comes into conflict with several norms in medical settings—for example, discussing risks as well as benefits of intended procedures, telling patients the truth about a negative diagnosis or prognosis, and preparing an advance directive. Ignoring the cultural values of a Navajo patient almost inevitably means that care and treatment will be interrupted and perhaps discontinued.

On the other hand, acting with cultural sensitivity can enable the values of the patient to be respected while medical responsibilities are discharged. Health care providers who work with the Navajo have been encouraged to pursue situations of this type in four ways: (1) determining whether the patient is or is not willing to discuss negative information; (2) preparing the patient by building rapport and trust, involving the family, giving an advance warning that bad news is coming, and involving traditional Navajo healers in the encounter; (3) communicating in a kind caring manner that is respectful of traditional beliefs (e.g., referring to the patient in third-party language rather than directly); and (4) following through in a manner that fosters reasonable hope (Carrese and Rhodes, 2000).

New England Journal of Medicine in which he described how he assisted "Diane," a 45-year-old woman with leukemia, who had been his patient for 8 years, to end her life. Diane had rejected the option of chemotherapy and bone-marrow transplantation, which had a one-in-four chance of success, due to the certain negative side effects. After they had had a thorough discussion and Quill was convinced of her full mental competence, he prescribed barbiturates and made sure that Diane knew how much to take for sleep and how much to take to end her life. They continued to meet regularly, and she promised to meet with him before taking her life— which she ultimately did. While reaction was mixed, Dr. Quill received considerable praise for his action with Diane and his courage in describing the events in print.

Dr. Jack Kevorkian. By far the key figure in this debate has been Dr. Jack Kevorkian, a retired Michigan pathologist who assisted more than 100 people to end their lives by providing a painless means to do so and by being present at the time of death. Each of these individuals contacted Kevorkian (none of them were patients of his) and convinced him that they had made a rational choice to die. The particular means used varied from case to case. Although two juries refused to convict Kevorkian of a crime, ultimately he engaged in an act of active euthanasia in which he did cause the death to occur. A Michigan jury convicted him in 1999 on this charge and sentenced him to 10 to 25 years in prison. He was released in 2007 after 8 years with a promise that he would no longer assist in suicides, but that he could continue to

Dr. Jack Kevorkian, a retired Michigan pathologist, repeatedly and successfully challenged prohibitions against physician-assisted suicide. Eventually he was convicted of second-degree homicide for directly causing the death of an individual who was in the late stages of amyotrophic lateral sclerosis (ALS) and had requested Kevorkian's assistance with his death. © Carlos Osorio/AP.

advocate for physician-assisted suicide. He died in 2011.

Arguments in Favor of Physician-Assisted Suicide. Proponents of the legalization of physician-assisted suicide offer the following rationale:

1. It is perfectly appropriate to have physicians and other health care professionals create a comfortable and peaceful environment in which death occurs.
2. People have a right to self-determination; if a person has reflected on their life circumstances and made a rational and competent decision to die, the assistance of physicians in the act is appropriate. People should not be required to undergo mental and physical decline, endure emotional and physical pain, and incur sizable medical expenses for treatment that is not desired.
3. In order to prevent abuse, laws could require certain safeguards (e.g., there is intolerable suffering, the patient is mentally competent, a written witnessed request is provided, the patient requests death consistently and repeatedly over time, and two physicians— one of whom has not participated in the patient's care—agree that death is appropriate).
4. An extremely high rate of suicide already exists. In addition to that which occurs without medical contact, it is clear that many deaths in hospitals occur with some "assistance." An estimated 70 percent of the 1.3 million deaths that occur in American hospitals each year involve some agreement not to take aggressive action to sustain the patient.
5. Public opinion polls show that a majority of Americans (recent polls indicate 70 percent) favor the legalization of physician-assisted suicide, and that in certain circumstances as many as 50 percent would consider it for themselves. Derek Humphry (1991), founder of the Hemlock Society, a national organization in favor of legalized euthanasia, and past president of the World Federation of Right to Die Societies, wrote *Final Exit: The Practicalities of Self-Deliverance and*

Assisted Suicide for the Dying. It is a how-to-commit-suicide guidebook, and it became an overwhelming bestseller.

Arguments Opposing Physician-Assisted Suicide. Opponents of physician-assisted suicide offer the following rationale:

1. Traditionally, we have considered the physician's responsibility to be to sustain life and relieve suffering. While actions taken by physicians may sometimes have the opposite effects, their intention is to do good. The primary purpose of physician-assisted suicide, however, is to cause death. The American Medical Association, the American Bar Association, and some medical ethicists believe this to be inconsistent with the physician's professional obligations.

2. Patients considering physician-assisted suicide may be sufficiently ill or so worried that they are not capable of genuine contemplative thought or the exercise of a true informed consent. The depression that might lead to consideration of this act might itself be treatable.

3. The legal possibility of physician-assisted suicide may interfere with a good physician–patient relationship. A physician's willingness to participate may be interpreted by the patient as confirmation that society (and the physician) would prefer that suicide occurs. This interpretation may place implicit pressure on the patient to request the act. Elderly and dying patients may be especially vulnerable psychologically. On a broader scale, a climate may be created in the country in which terminally ill people are expected to end their lives.

4. There could be a slippery-slope argument—that by legalizing physician-assisted suicide for patients with terminal illnesses, we increase the likelihood that suicide will become acceptable for other people, such as the mentally retarded, those with physical disabilities, and the very old.

5. Significant progress has been made in dealing with the pain that often accompanies late-stage diseases. An increasing number of hospitals have developed palliative care programs to manage and control patients' pain, and an increasing number of health care providers are receiving training in palliative care (although there are still far too few programs and trained providers). Hospices are increasingly successful in reducing the amount of pain their clients experience.

Reaction to the two cases mentioned earlier in the general population and among clinicians was divided. The primary point of distinction in the cases is that Dr. Quill assisted in the suicide of a patient whom he had known for many years and with whom he had long and engaging discussions about life and death. In that context, he agreed to participate. On the other hand, although Dr. Kevorkian spoke at some length with all his suicides, he did not have long-standing physician–patient interaction with any of them. Many physicians, medical ethicists, and laypeople believe that the lack of a personal relationship with the patients is the most troubling aspect of Kevorkian's behavior, although many others believe that he had adequate assurance of the competent desires of each person. He has been both widely praised and widely condemned.

ORGAN DONATION AND TRANSPLANTATION

The ability to successfully transplant organs from a cadaver or a living related donor began with a successful transplant in Boston in 1954, when a 23-year-old man received a kidney from his genetically identical twin brother. The

IN THE FIELD

THE BROKEN END-OF-LIFE CARE SYSTEM

A 2015 report by the well-respected Institute of Medicine (IOM) concluded that end-of-life care in the United States is largely broken and in need of significant transformation (Institute of Medicine, 2015). Most people want to die at home, but most die in hospitals. Most want a peaceful setting at death and not to be tethered to countless pieces of high-tech medical care, but the final stage of life for many is in an intensive care unit with every effort being made to delay the moment of death. The number of days that patients spend on average receiving aggressive treatment in the ICU is actually increasing.

Almost one-third of all Medicare dollars are spent on people in the last 6 months of life, and much of it not only has little benefit but actually makes the patient feel worse. Despite the availability of advance directives, many have not contemplated their own care at the end of life and have not discussed their wishes with family members or physicians. Increasing numbers of people are using hospice services, but many come to hospice only at the very end, and only after probably futile efforts have been made to extend their survival (Volandes, 2015).

The IOM panel that published the report included physicians, nurses, insurers, lawyers, religious leaders, and experts on aging, The panel's co-chair, David Walker, stated that "The bottom line is the health care system is poorly designed to meet the needs of patients near the end of life. The current system is geared towards doing more, more, more, and that system by definition is not necessarily consistent with what patients want, and is also more costly."

Some of the recommendations of the panel would require legislative changes. For example, they recommended that Medicare dollars would emphasize home health services and pain management rather than expensive high-tech hospital services, and that Medicaid would provide better coverage of the long-term health care needs of those who are covered by it. Other recommendations could be accomplished without new laws. Increased efforts need to be undertaken in education, by civic leaders and religious groups and employers and others to encourage individuals to take more responsibility for their own health and for end-of-life planning. Insurers could begin reimbursing health care providers for conversations they have with patients about advance health care planning, advance directives, and end-of-life care (this idea is now being enacted). Experimental efforts are also underway to provide more training for medical students, residents, and physicians in discussing end-of-life care with patients, and some groups are developing online and written materials to assist both doctors and patients. Physicians, other health care providers, medical associations, and hospitals need to re-commit to treating patients near the end of life with dignity, including consideration for their physical comfort, autonomy, sense of meaningfulness, preparedness, and interpersonal connection (Cook and Rocker, 2014). In short, a major cultural and organizational change is needed to fix the end-of-life care system.

recipient recovered completely and lived another 8 years before dying of an unrelated cause. Bone marrow was first successfully transplanted in 1963 (in Paris), the same year as the first liver transplant (in Denver); the first pancreas was transplanted in 1966 (in Minneapolis), the first heart in 1967 (in Cape Town, South Africa), the first heart–lung in 1981 (in Palo Alto, California), the first partial pancreas in 1998 (in Minneapolis), the first hand in 1998 (in Paris), the first partial face in 2005 (in Paris), and the first windpipe in 2008 (in Barcelona).

Social Policy Issues Related to Organ Transplantation

The success of these sophisticated medical technologies has prolonged the life of many recipients, but has also created several complex ethical and social policy issues. Nancy Kutner (1987) and Renée Fox and Judith Swazey (1992) have identified the following key issues:

1. Do the medical and quality-of-life outcomes for organ recipients (and donors) justify organ transplantation procedures? The question to be asked before all other questions is whether organ transplants have been shown to have sufficient therapeutic value for them to be continued. If the answer to the first question is affirmative, then at least the four following additional questions need to be addressed.

2. Given that the demand for transplant organs exceeds the supply, how should recipients be selected? Should a complex formula be devised to prioritize potential recipients, or would a "first come first served" (or random) policy be more consistent with democratic principles?

3. How can the supply of organs be increased? Organ donation policy has evolved during the last four decades, but demand continues to exceed supply. What policy might increase motivation to donate while maintaining a voluntary nature?

4. How much money should be allocated to organ transplant procedures? Given the finite amount of money available to be spent on health care, how much should be directed to these very expensive procedures (most cost between US$100,000 and US$200,000) that

benefit a relatively small number of people versus less dramatic, less costly procedures that might benefit a much larger number?

5. Who should pay for organ transplant procedures? Should (or can) the government be willing to pick up the tab because these procedures are so expensive? Should health insurance companies guarantee coverage? At the time of writing, the federal government's Medicare program pays for kidney, heart, and some liver transplants, and some health insurance policies cover transplants. People not covered in these ways are on their own, and those unable to pay are turned away.

This section focuses on the evolution of organ donation policy in the United States, assesses the current and alternative donation policies, and discusses the psychosocial dimension of organ donation.

Organ Donation Policy in the United States

The success of the early transplant efforts in the 1950s and 1960s forced the United States to establish a formal organ donation policy. The initial policy was one of *pure voluntarism*— donation was made legal, and it was hoped that volunteers would come forward. Courts ruled that competent adults could voluntarily donate organs to relatives, which at first seemed like the only possibility. Organs could be donated by minors only with parental and judicial consent.

Donations did increase, but as the supply was increasing, so was the demand. The success rate for transplants improved with the development of the artificial respirator and the heart–lung machine, and with the discovery of effective immunosuppressive drugs to suppress the body's immune system, thereby making the recipient's body less likely to reject a transplanted organ.

In 1968, the United States adopted "brain death" as the legal standard for death determination. This definition enabled organs to be taken from those who had suffered irreversible loss of brain function (and who therefore were legally dead) but were being sustained on artificial respirators. Death could be pronounced, the organs taken, and then the respirator disconnected.

These changes forced the United States to develop a more assertive organ donation policy—*encouraged voluntarism*. This occurred in 1968 with the passage of the Uniform Anatomical Gift Act (UAGA), which was adopted in every state and in Washington, D.C. by 1971. The UAGA permitted adults to donate all or part of their body after death through donor cards and living wills, and gave next of kin authority to donate after an individual's death, as long as no contrary instructions had been given. The UAGA was praised for maintaining the country's allegiance to a voluntary approach, and was successful in increasing the number of donors. However, about 90 percent of the 20,000–25,000 people who were potential donors each year in the United States still failed to donate, there was no centralized system for identifying those needing and those willing to make a donation, and hospitals had little involvement in the program.

A dramatic change in organ donation policy occurred in 1987 with the establishment of a *weak required request policy*. In order to receive essential Medicare and Medicaid reimbursements, each of the nation's more than 5,000 hospitals must make patients and their families aware of the organ donation option, and must notify a federally certified organ procurement organization (OPO) when there is consent to donation.

In addition, a national central registry, now called the *United Network for Organ Sharing (UNOS)*, was created in Richmond, Virginia, to maintain a national list of potential donors and recipients. In order to receive Medicare and Medicaid funding, all the country's nearly 250 transplant centers and 58 procurement organizations are required to affiliate with UNOS. When an organ for transplant becomes available, UNOS engages in a matching process, taking into consideration medical need, medical compatibility (size and blood type), and geographic proximity. Much of the physical work is performed by the OPOs, which encourage donation, contact UNOS when an organ becomes available, send teams to collect and process the organ, and deliver it to its designee.

The weak required request policy maintains the voluntary and altruistic nature of organ donation, but seeks to ensure that potential donors are aware of the donation option. The request is sometimes handled very sensitively but sometimes with little enthusiasm and little tactfulness.

Studies indicate that few physicians and nurses have received any education or training in how to make a request for organ donation, and many feel uncomfortable doing so. Many physicians have been unwilling to be the one who asks, citing such reasons as uncertainty about their own attitudes regarding organ donation, lack of knowledge about organ donation criteria and processes, reluctance to bother a family during a time of grief, not knowing how to make the request, and lack of time and reimbursement for the donation request (May, Aulisio, and DeVita, 2000).

Yet studies indicate that more than 90 percent of health care professionals approve of organ donation, and many are willing to donate their own organs. A study of more than 700 physicians in a variety of specialties suggested that organ donation information programs for physicians would alleviate some of their concerns and make them more willing to make the request (McGough and Chopek, 1990).

These attitudes are extremely important because the comfort level of the requestor has

IN THE FIELD

CHALLENGING UNOS

While UNOS has generally been praised for its commitment to a fair allocation system, there are occasions when the anguish of a particular individual on the waiting list creates a challenge for the organization's protocols. Such was the situation in 2013 with the simultaneous cases of 10-year-old Sarah Murnaghan of Newtown Square, Pennsylvania and 11-year-old Javier Acosta of New York City. Both children had end-stage cystic fibrosis, were terminally ill, and required a lung transplant to extend their life. More than 80 percent of cystic fibrosis patients who receive a lung transplant survive for at least 1 year, and 50 percent survive for at least 5 years.

However, UNOS policy requires that patients under the age of 12 years receive a lung only from another adolescent. The policy was developed because lungs from an adult, which become available much more often, would be too large for a child-size body. As Sarah's prognosis grew worse, her parents made public pleas for reconsideration of the policy. Politicians became involved and requested that the Secretary of Health and Human Services, Kathleen Sebelius (whose cabinet department oversees UNOS) mandate a lung transplant for Sarah. She declined with the reasoning that the protocols were set up in the fairest way possible

and were time-tested. A lawsuit was filed, and the judge ruled the next day that Sarah should be moved to the front of the queue until a formal court hearing could take place a few days later.

This prompted a special review board at UNOS to consider the case. They recommended no change in the policy, saying that it would be wrong to hastily make a change based on one or two cases, and that any policy which grants an organ to one person necessarily deprives another from receiving the organ. However, they did advise that a special appeals process be created for situations like Sarah's. Before that hearing could take place, an adult lung became available, Sarah was first on the list, and she received a double-lung transplant. Almost immediately, Sarah had problems, and doctors had a difficult time weaning her from the respirator. Several days later the double-lungs were removed, but a new double-lung set was transplanted. During the second procedure her diaphragm was perforated, and a breathing tube was necessitated. Later she had surgery on her diaphragm and, after a bout of pneumonia, seemed to be doing well. Javier Acosta also received a lung transplant from which at last reporting he recovered well.

---

been shown to have a significant impact on the likelihood of donation. When families are approached with lines such as "I don't suppose you want to donate, do you?" or "The law says I have to ask if you want to donate," a refusal is very likely.

Has the 1987 legislation succeeded? The level of criticism directed at UNOS has been minimal; it seems to be well run. (See the accompanying box, "Challenging UNOS.")

The number of organ donors did increase after the policy was implemented—but only to a 25 to 30 percent consent level (it has now increased to 41 percent). There are now about 28,000 organ transplants (including the heart, liver, kidney, heart–lung, lung, and partial pancreas) annually. Moreover, organ transplants are more likely to be successful than ever before, and recipients are living longer. Yet more than 50 percent of the families that are asked to consider donation after a relative has died do not give their consent.

There are now more than 120,000 people on the waiting lists in Richmond who have been medically and financially approved for transplants. It is likely that two-thirds of these individuals will eventually receive a transplant (half within 5 years), but one-third will die before receiving a transplant. (About 18 people die each day while awaiting a transplant.) The American Council on Transplantation estimates that an additional 100,000 people would benefit from some type of organ transplant but are not on the list because they are unable to demonstrate the means to pay for a transplant. Ironically, research shows that people without health insurance often donate organs but rarely receive them (Herring, Woolhandler, and Himmelstein, 2008).

Alternative Directions for Organ Donation Policy

There is some support in the United States for adopting a different or enhanced policy regarding organ donation. A recent study of transplant surgeons, coordinators, and nurses found that the current policy of altruistic donation was rated as being the most morally appropriate policy, but that several alternative, more aggressive policies were also considered to be morally appropriate (Jasper et al., 2004). If the United States should choose to revise its organ donation policy again, there are five main alternatives.

1. *Strong required request.* Every citizen would be asked to indicate their willingness to participate in organ donation—either on income tax returns or through a mandatory check-off on the driver's license. This policy retains the voluntary and altruistic nature of the system but is more aggressive in forcing people to consider organ donation and to take a formal position. Some states already do this, and many of these have more than a 50

percent donor rate (the rates in Montana and Alaska are highest, at 82 and 80 percent, respectively, followed by Washington, Oregon, and Iowa, all in the range of 70–79 percent. Most states do not, and several of these have a donor rate of less than 30 percent (Vermont is lowest at 5 percent, followed by Texas at 17 percent, New York at 20 percent, Mississippi at 24 percent, and South Carolina at 29 percent).

2. *Weak presumed consent.* Hospitals would be required by law to remove and use all suitable cadaver organs for donation unless the deceased had expressly objected through a central registry or a non-donor card, or if family members objected. Sometimes called "routine salvaging of organs," this remains a voluntary and altruistic system but with a very significant change—the presumption or default position is that donation will occur. In presumed consent, the person must take an action to prevent donation. Several European countries, including Spain, Belgium, and Norway, have this policy. Spain is considered to be the country with the world's highest donation rate—between 80 and 85 percent.

3. *Strong presumed consent.* Physicians would be given complete authorization to remove usable organs regardless of the wishes of the deceased or family members. Also referred to as "expropriation," it is the only alternative that eliminates the voluntary dimension of organ donation policy, but it is also the policy that retrieves the largest number of transplantable organs. This policy is also in effect in several European countries.

4. *Weak market approach.* Individuals or next of kin for deceased donors would receive a tax benefit for the donation of organs (perhaps a 1-year deduction from federal and state taxes) or a cash payment of sufficient size to offset some funeral expenses. This approach adds financial incentive to a volunteer-based system, thus reducing the role of altruism.

Proponents argue that offering financial benefit is fair and sensitive, but opponents prefer altruistic motivation. They worry that some likely donors would be so offended by the suggestion of payment that they would choose not to donate. Pennsylvania became the first state to incorporate this technique in 2000, when it began offering US$300 to help families of organ donors to cover their funeral expenses.

5. *Strong market approach.* Individuals or next of kin would be able to auction organs to the highest bidder. Like the weak market approach, this system places greater emphasis on increasing the number of organs donated than on retaining altruistic motivation for donation. Critics of the strong market approach worry that the financial incentive may place undue pressure on individuals on low income and on people in developing countries to donate. Once organs are on the market, the wealthy clearly would have easier access.

The buying and selling of organs is unlawful in the United States and in all other countries except Iran. The selling of a kidney in Iran is legal and regulated by the government. While many are critical of this approach, Iran does not have a waiting list for kidneys. While no other country openly permits the selling of organs, there is an ongoing black market for organs in several countries. A former company in Germany routinely sent a form letter to all people listed in the newspaper as having declared bankruptcy. The individual was offered US$45,000 (plus expenses) for a kidney, which was then sold for US$85,000. This is no longer legal.

The Psychosocial Dimension of Organ Transplantation and Donation

Some of the most insightful work done in medical sociology and medical anthropology

has pertained to attitudes, motivations, and consequent feelings related to organ donation. Anthropologist Lesley Sharp (2006) has recently written about not only the illuminated side of organ transplantation—the medical successes and altruistic motivations—but also the less studied complicated relationships and social injustices related to the gap between supply and demand. Renée Fox and Judith Swazey (1978, 1992), leaders for many years in this field of study in medical sociology, have written forcefully that the organ donation decision needs to be placed within a social-structural context. Based on years of systematic observation in transplantation settings and countless interviews with physicians, patients, donors, and families, they have raised three important concerns about donation and transplantation.

1. There is still some "uncertainty" about the therapeutic value of organ transplantation. Although significant progress has been made, there continue to be concerns. For example, there are still cases of long-term (5 or 10 years post-transplant) or chronic rejection of transplanted organs, many organ recipients are prone to redeveloping the same life-threatening medical conditions that led to the transplant, and there have been repeated failures with certain transplant modalities (e.g., animal-to-human transplants and the totally implantable artificial heart). Fox and Swazey argue that these types of questions have not been adequately and genuinely reflected upon.

2. There has been too little consideration of the psychosocial dimensions of organ donation and receipt. The focus of attention has been so fixed on the "organ shortage problem" and the "allocation of scarce resources" that the human dimensions of the process have seemed inconsequential. The concept of the "gift-exchange" relationship between donor and recipient has given way to discussions of

"supply and demand" and compensation for donors. Fox and Swazey contend that this way of thinking commodifies body parts and re-conceptualizes the "gift of life" idea.

3. The high price of transplant procedures and the fact that more people seek an organ than have been willing to donate one have created real, and not yet fully answered, questions of distributive justice and public good.

The Donor–Recipient Relationship

Although research has shown that the decision to donate a kidney to a relative is typically made very quickly and with little regret, the decision to donate and the decision to receive an organ are governed by often unspoken but powerful social norms. Family members may express an "intense desire" to make a potentially lifesaving gift to someone close, and they sometimes feel that donating is part of a family obligation (even sensing some family pressures). With this "gift of life," an incredible bond can be established between the giver and the receiver. In addition, some cases of "black sheep donors" have surfaced, in which individuals who felt remorse for previous wrongs against the family wished to make amends through donation of an organ (Fox, 1989). For those who donate to strangers, there is often enhancement of self-image—a feeling of having actualized traits of helpfulness and generosity to others and having demonstrated their own altruistic nature.

Just as prevailing norms may motivate organ donation, they also motivate accepting it. Rejection of an offer to donate constitutes a form of rejection of the donor. When the donation and transplant occur, a type of "obligation to repay" is incurred by the recipient. Having received something so profoundly important, the recipient becomes, in a sense, a debtor—owing something back to the donor (Shaw, 2010). Fox and Swazey (1978) referred to this as the **tyranny of the gift**.

Similar considerations occur in family members' decisions to offer cadaver organs. These decisions are almost always made in traumatic situations, such as automobile accidents, in which the death is sudden and there has been no preparation for it. Family members often consent to donation as a way of bringing meaning or some sense of value to a senseless tragedy. The altruistic and humanitarian aspects of organ donation become powerful motivating forces (Fox and Swazey, 1978).

Fox and Swazey's *Spare Parts: Organ Replacement in American Society* (1992) is a powerful critique of organ donation and organ transplantation in American society. They indict society for the extent to which it has become obsessed with rebuilding people and sustaining life at all costs, and for doing so while failing to fully consider quality-of-life considerations and the psychosocial aspects of donation and transplantation.

ASSISTED PROCREATION

Infertility

The reported incidence of **infertility**, defined as the absence of pregnancy after 1 year of regular sexual intercourse without contraception, is increasing in the United States. An estimated 10 to 15 percent of American couples of child-bearing age are defined as being infertile. However, this percentage may give an exaggerated picture; up to 50 percent of the couples who are not pregnant after 1 year become pregnant on their own in the second year. The increased incidence of infertility is due to several factors, including an actual increase in infertility (probably due to increased exposure to radiation and pollution, ingestion of certain drugs, and higher levels of sexually transmitted infections), the number of older women now trying to get pregnant (peak fertility occurs between 20 and

29 years of age), and more couples seeking assistance with lack of fertility.

The specific reason for a couple's infertility is traceable to the female partner in approximately 40 percent of cases. The most common specific causes are inability to produce eggs for fertilization, blocked Fallopian tubes (so the eggs cannot travel to meet the sperm), and a sufficiently high level of acidity in the vagina to kill deposited sperm. In another 40 percent of infertility cases, the specific cause is traceable to the male partner—typically it is low sperm count and/or low sperm motility. The specific cause of the remaining 20 percent of infertility cases is either undeterminable or traceable to both partners.

The Development of Assisted Procreative Techniques

In order to enable infertile couples to produce children that are biologically related to at least one of the partners, several assisted procreative techniques have been developed. These techniques have in common the fact that at least one of the four traditionally essential steps of procreation—sexual intercourse, tubal fertilization, uterine implantation, and uterine gestation—is eliminated. About 1.5 million assisted procreative techniques are attempted worldwide each year, resulting in the birth of 350,000 babies. As of 2015, more than 5 million births had occurred in total using assisted procreation. This section discusses four techniques—intrauterine insemination, *in vitro* fertilization, ovum donation (surrogate embryo transfer), and surrogate motherhood. The main focus is on surrogate motherhood—the most controversial of the four techniques.

Intrauterine Insemination. Technologically, the least complicated technique is *intrauterine insemination (IUI)*. During the time of the month when the woman is ovulating, she receives three inseminations of sperm though a

catheter inserted into the uterus. The sperm may have been provided by her partner, an anonymous donor, or a mixture of the two. The overall success rate is reported to be 85 percent (15 to 20 percent for each attempt), although success on the first attempt is rare.

Intrauterine insemination is typically used in the following circumstances: (1) when the male partner cannot produce a sufficient number of healthy sperm to fertilize an egg (it takes only one, but the higher the concentration of sperm, the more likely is fertilization to occur); (2) when the female partner's vaginal environment is biochemically inhospitable to sperm, or the position of the uterus is such or the size of the opening to the uterus is sufficiently small that fertilization is unlikely; (3) if both partners are carriers of a recessive gene for a genetic disorder (e.g., Tay–Sachs disease) or the male partner is a carrier of a dominant gene (e.g., Huntington's chorea); or (4) increasingly, for single women.

Fertility centers—also called "infertility and reproduction centers"—assist individuals and couples in producing offspring through a wide variety of techniques. © creative soul/Fotolia.

Precise records are not kept, but approximately 100,000 births per year in the United States occur to women who have been inseminated. The cost of an insemination is in the range of US$300–700, but there are additional costs for initial evaluation and fertility tests, so the total price is typically US$1,500–4,000. As many as three, four, or more cycles may be necessary (if the technique is going to work, it typically does so by the fourth cycle). All states deal with paternity by statute; in most states, insemination by donor sperm for married couples is legal with the husband's consent, and the offspring is considered his legal responsibility.

In Vitro Fertilization (Embryo Transfer). When infertility is due to the female partner's blocked Fallopian tubes or to the low motility or low count of the male partner's sperm, *in vitro fertilization (IVF)* may be used. In this process, the woman is given a reproductive hormone to stimulate her ovaries to produce multiple eggs. A few hours before ovulation is expected, a small incision is made in the abdomen. A laparoscope (an instrument with a lens and a light source) is inserted to examine the ovaries. Mature eggs are located and removed by a vacuum aspirator and transferred to a petri dish (the so-called "test tube") with the male partner's sperm and a nutrient solution, where fertilization occurs about 80 to 90 percent of the time. About 2 days later, at an appropriate stage of cell development, the fertilized egg is introduced through the vagina into the uterus. If the cell continues to divide naturally, it will attach itself to the uterine wall.

For women under 35 years of age, about one attempt in two now results in a pregnancy, but some women try several times before achieving pregnancy. Each attempt may cost US$12,000–15,000. To increase the likelihood of a pregnancy, many fertility clinics implant multiple eggs. However, this has led to a sharp increase in multiple births. In the United States, about

3 percent of births are twins, but about 45 percent of IVF babies are multiples (twins or higher). The concern is that multiple births increase the incidence of life-threatening prematurity (12 percent of U.S. births are preterm, but 37 percent of IVF babies are), low birth weight, and birth defects. More than 60,000 IVF babies are born in the United States each year.

Among the modifications of IVF is gamete intrafallopian transfer (GIFT), whereby eggs are retrieved from the woman's ovary and implanted with a sample of the male partner's sperm in her Fallopian tube where fertilization may occur. This technique may be helpful for couples who have not had success with IVF, but unlike IVF it involves a surgical procedure.

Ovum Donation (Embryo Transfer). Some female infertility is traceable to the absence of ovaries or to non-functional ovaries. Since eggs are not produced, there can be no genetic offspring. However, if the uterus is functional, there is no biological obstacle to gestating a fetus and giving birth. If the couple wishes to have the offspring genetically related to the male partner, *ovum donation* can be used. This procedure can occur in any one of three ways: (1) transfer of a donor's egg to the woman's Fallopian tube, followed by sexual intercourse, (2) *in vitro* fertilization of a donor's egg with the male partner's sperm, followed by insertion in the woman, and (3) artificial insemination of an egg donor with the male's sperm, resulting in fertilization, and then washing the embryo out of the donor and transferring it to the woman's uterus.

Embryo transfer is the most recently developed technique (early 1980s), the most expensive (approximately US$25,000 per attempt), and the least commonly used, but it has a higher rate of success than IVF. Approximately 14,000 births each year in the United States occur with donated eggs. In most cases, the woman donating the egg(s) receives reimbursement for expenses and some compensation. The average payment is about US$6,000, but some couples who wish to have donor eggs from a woman with a particular background offer several times that amount.

Surrogate Motherhood. While all the assisted procreative techniques carry some controversy, *surrogate motherhood* has been the most controversial of all. In this process, a woman who is not capable or desirous of carrying a pregnancy and her male partner contract with another woman (the surrogate) to carry the pregnancy, and the surrogate is artificially inseminated with the male partner's sperm. If fertilization occurs, the surrogate gestates the fetus, bringing it to term, and then gives it to the couple. The woman receiving the baby must adopt it.

The process usually occurs with the assistance of a lawyer/broker who develops an extensive contract. Early in the history of the technique, a payment of US$10,000 to the surrogate was typical (today the payment is typically in the range of US$30,000–55,000, but the total cost may be two or three times that). Many experts distinguish between surrogate motherhood which is "commercialized" (done for payment) and that which is "altruistic" (most commonly done for a sister or other relative, or a close friend). There are an estimated 1,200 to 1,500 surrogate births annually in the United States.

Considerable public attention was brought to the surrogate motherhood technique in the mid- to late 1980s in the *Baby M* case. A New Jersey couple (the Sterns) contracted through a broker with another New Jersey woman (Mary Beth Whitehead) to be a surrogate. Whitehead had registered to be a surrogate with the Infertility Center of New York, saying that she wanted to help another couple. A contract was signed. The Sterns accepted all responsibilities for the baby even if there were birth defects. Amniocentesis was required, an abortion was agreed to if problems were detected, US$10,000 for Whitehead were put in escrow, and the baby would be given to the Sterns. IUI was performed, and a pregnancy resulted.

After the baby's birth, Whitehead changed her mind about surrendering the baby and refused the payment. When the authorities came to collect the baby, she took her and fled to Florida. This prompted a 3-month search by the FBI, police, and private detectives. When they were caught, the baby was returned to the Sterns, and the legal battle began. Ultimately, the New Jersey Supreme Court ruled that surrogate motherhood contracts are illegal, that both the Sterns and Whitehead had claim to the baby but that it would be awarded to the Sterns based on the perceived best interests of the baby, and that Whitehead would get visitation rights.

Gestational Surrogacy. A modification of surrogate motherhood occurs when a woman is hired only to gestate an embryo created from the sperm and egg of a contracting couple. In other words, the egg is not contributed by the surrogate, who agrees only to have the embryo implanted, to provide gestation, and to give the resulting baby to the contracting couple. In the United States about 750 births per year occur to gestational surrogates.

Analyzing Surrogate Motherhood

The Case for Surrogate Motherhood. Proponents of surrogate motherhood base their position on two primary points. First, there is a constitutionally protected right to **procreative liberty**. While some recent Supreme Court decisions have limited full access to abortion services, there is a tradition of judicial and legislative action that suggests a fundamental right not to procreate. The right *to* procreate has not received the same explicit judicial endorsement because states have not challenged married couples' efforts to give birth. Nevertheless, the Supreme Court has on several occasions indicated strong support for procreative liberty—especially for married persons.

Proponents of surrogate motherhood and the other assisted procreative techniques contend that this right to procreate extends to non-coital as well as coital reproduction, and extends to the use of donors and surrogates. Non-coital assisted procreation would be supported by the same values and interests that have always supported coital reproduction (e.g., a right to privacy and a belief that families provide emotional and physical support). Infertility ought not to be allowed to unnecessarily restrict a couple from procreation.

Second, the use of surrogate motherhood is an expression of the involved parties' autonomy and may directly benefit everyone involved. Couples who are unable to procreate without such technology are given the expanded option of producing an offspring genetically related to at least one of the parents. The offspring will be born into a situation where he or she is very much desired, given that the parents have gone to considerable lengths to have the child. The surrogate mother has the opportunity to make a contribution to others' happiness and to earn a not insignificant sum of money (although paltry if considered by the hour). All assisted procreative techniques are freedom-enhancing procedures (Robertson, 1994).

The Case Against Surrogate Motherhood. Opponents of surrogate motherhood level three main criticisms. First, surrogate motherhood is not in the best interests of the surrogate mother, the baby, and even the contracting couple. The deliberate separation of genetic, gestational, and social parentage places everyone involved in an awkward and improper position. Reproductive arrangements are negotiated between non-spouses; the surrogate mother conceives without

the intention of raising the baby, who could foreseeably be denied important medical information about their lineage and could be psychologically harmed when told about the circumstances surrounding the birth. Both families could experience tension due to the unusual status of the surrogate offspring.

The legal and ethical requirement for an informed consent (see Chapter 13) may inherently be violated in the surrogate motherhood contract. Critics charge that it is impossible for a woman to know at the time when a contract is being signed how she will feel about surrendering the offspring once he or she has been born. Moreover, the requirement for voluntariness may be violated by the lure of a payment, especially for low-income women. If so, surrogate motherhood creates the possibility of exploitation of poor women.

Second, surrogate motherhood has a negative effect on the status of women within society. Woliver (1989) is critical of the extent to which discussions of assisted procreative techniques focus on questions of individual rights and are presented as expanding options for women. She contends that they may expand options for individual women, but they restrict choices for women as a group.

Women's freedom to make parenting choices must be understood to occur within a culture that remains, in many respects, patriarchal. The zeal with which some women desire children and the vestiges of stigma attached to those who do not are culturally influenced. The growing movement to consider the individual rights of the fetus relative to the mother could restrict women's autonomy over their own bodies. In this environment, technologies have significant potential for abuse and oppression (Rothman, 1989).

Third, surrogate motherhood devalues people and creates a "**commodification of life**—treating people and parts of people as marketable commodities" (Rothman, 1988:95):

This commodification process is very clearly seen in the notion of "surrogate" motherhood. There we talk openly about buying services and renting body parts—as if body parts were rented without the people who surround the part, as if you could rent a woman's uterus without renting the woman. We ignore our knowledge that women are pregnant with our whole bodies, from the changes in our hair to our swollen feet, with all of our bodies and perhaps with our souls as well. (1988:96–97)

According to this line of reasoning, the child—the contracted-for baby—is also commodified in that it is the subject of a contract and, in the end, will be surrendered in exchange for a cash payment. The transaction is tantamount to "baby selling" as the potential baby is "ordered precisely as one orders a car or buys pork futures" (Holder, 1988:55).

Surrogate Motherhood and Public Policy. Laws pertaining to surrogate motherhood are the responsibility of each state. There are three main options: (1) to legalize without restriction, (2) to legalize with restriction, and (3) to prohibit.

Strong proponents of surrogate motherhood believe that it is inappropriate to place any greater restriction on this technique than on coital reproductive methods. If (at the least) married couples have a constitutionally based right to reproduce coitally, and if that right extends to non-coital techniques, then the case is made that these techniques ought to have the same lack of restrictions. However, few states have adopted this approach.

Most advocates of surrogate motherhood acknowledge that one or the other (or both) of two restrictions may be appropriate. The first is that states may restrict the ability of the contracting couple to demand specified behaviors during pregnancy, and (more significantly)

may insist that the surrogate has the right to change her mind by some specified point in time and retain maternal claim to the baby.

The second is that states may prohibit surrogacy for cash payment. The commercial dimension of the technique is the most objectionable part to many people. Macklin (1988) does not believe that surrogacy violates any fundamental moral principle, but believes that commercialism in the process does. Rothman (1989) would prohibit the surrogate from selling or trading the offspring, although she would be able to give it to a couple in an arrangement that would be tantamount to an adoption. In this case, all parties would be governed by the traditional rights and responsibilities of an adoption proceeding. Many states are following this policy direction that makes surrogacy legal but only without financial payment. In the United Kingdom, commercial surrogacy is banned, but the surrogate may receive expenses (usually in the range of US$15,000–30,000) for time, lost earnings, and costs associated with the pregnancy.

Finally, many states have banned surrogacy altogether and have established a fine or imprisonment for anyone participating in a surrogacy arrangement.

In order to evade the strict regulations regarding surrogacy in some countries and to reduce the amount of payment to surrogates, an international surrogacy market has been created in the last decade. This multimillion-dollar global industry matches women or couples in wealthy nations with potential surrogates in developing countries. In most cases the contracting woman or couple and surrogate mother never meet. India, with more than 350 surrogacy clinics across the country, has developed the largest industry.

SUMMARY

The myriad of new health care technologies has several social consequences. It creates new options for people, it can alter human relationships, it can affect the entire health care system, it stimulates reflection on important value questions, and it raises social policy questions that must be resolved.

Advances in critical care medicine enable us to keep people alive even though we cannot cure them, relieve all their pain, or sometimes even restore them to consciousness. The cases of Karen Ann Quinlan, Nancy Cruzan, and Terri Schiavo have clarified the judicial right for competent and incompetent persons to refuse medical treatment, and even food and hydration. Despite the reluctance of many health care professionals to provide medically futile treatment—even when this is demanded by patients' families—the courts refused to allow a hospital to stop treatment for Helga Wanglie and Jahli McMath.

The ability to successfully transplant organs and the demand for transplants have raised several complex questions regarding the nation's organ donation policy and the consequences for individuals who are involved. The United States now has a policy of weak required request, whereby patients or their families must be notified about the option of organ donation, and a request for donation is to be made. Because many people die before an organ becomes available, there is discussion about shifting to a more aggressive policy that presumes people wish to donate, or even shifting to a policy that enables donors to benefit financially.

Many American couples who are infertile seek to use one of the assisted procreative techniques. The most controversial of these techniques is surrogate motherhood. Its proponents argue that there is and should be procreative liberty, and that patient autonomy demands that couples have access to this technique. Its opponents argue that surrogacy is not in the best interest of the surrogate, the child, or even the contracting couple, that the process demeans women and reduces them to their reproductive capacity, and that it leads to a commodification and cheapening of life. Some states have retained the legality of surrogacy, but outlawed payment to the surrogate; other states have banned the practice.

HEALTH ON THE INTERNET

1. The United Network for Organ Sharing (UNOS) makes available to the public updated information about transplant programs and services. Visit their website at www.unos.org.

   Click on "Data Reports and Policies," then click on "Data" in the top menu, and then click on "National Data" under "View Data Reports" in the left-hand menu. Answer the following questions by clicking on "Donor," "Transplant," and "Waiting List" in "Choose Category." How many transplants have been performed in this calendar year? How many donors were used? Of the donors, how many were deceased and how many were living? How many individuals are currently on the waiting list for a transplant? Go back to "Data" and click on the link to specific organs. Select an organ and determine the kinds of information that are available about the transplantation of this organ.

2. In 2014, Brittany Maynard, a 29-year-old California woman, was diagnosed with a malignant brain tumor and told that she had between 3 and 10 years to live. Two months later, new tests found an even more

aggressive cancer, and she was given less than 6 months. At the time, California did not have legal physician-assisted suicide, so she and her family moved to Oregon, a state where she could legally be prescribed life-ending medications. Before she died, she taped a message to California legislators and put it on YouTube. Access it at "Brittany Maynard Legislative Testimony." It has received more than 100,000 hits. What are the main arguments that she makes in favor of aid in dying?

DISCUSSION CASES

1. In 1993, the Dutch Supreme Court officially acted to decriminalize active euthanasia, a practice that had been occurring for more than 25 years. The 1993 ruling protects physicians who engage in physician-assisted suicide or in any form of active euthanasia as long as basic guidelines are followed. The guidelines include the following:

   a. The patient's request is the result of sound informed consent (the patient is competent and the request is voluntary and made without undue pressure) and is reviewed, discussed, and repeated.
   b. The patient's suffering, both physical and mental, is severe and cannot be relieved by any other means.
   c. The attending physician must consult with a colleague regarding the patient's condition and the genuineness and appropriateness of the request for euthanasia.
   d. Only physicians may engage in euthanasia.

   Requests for active euthanasia performed by physicians come mainly from patients with incurable cancer (70 percent), chronic degenerative neurological disorders (10 percent), and chronic obstructive pulmonary disease. Patients seeking active euthanasia report being in both physical and psychological pain. Although Dutch law requires physicians to report the causes of death, some critics charge that active euthanasia is under-reported. Estimates are that approximately 4,000 cases of death by active euthanasia or assisted suicide occur each year. Public opinion polls have found that more than 90 percent of Dutch citizens favor the legalization of physician-assisted suicide and more than 60 percent favor the legalization of active euthanasia performed by physicians.

   What arguments favor active euthanasia by physicians, and what arguments oppose the practice? How do these compare and contrast with the arguments cited in the text regarding physician-assisted suicide? Should the United States adopt the Dutch policy? What would be the social ramifications of adopting this policy?

2. In the United States, many people who support organ donation do not themselves register to become organ donors. One suggested idea—referred to as a "reciprocity system"—is to give registered organ donors who need a transplant priority over non-donors. Surveys indicate that many people think this policy would increase the number of donors, but that they are unsure about its fairness. How would you assess this proposal?

GLOSSARY

active euthanasia
advance directives
brain death
commodification of life
genomic medicine
infertility
living will
medical futility
persistent vegetative state

personalized medicine
physician-assisted suicide
procreative liberty
technological determinism
technological imperative
technology
technology assessment
telemedicine
tyranny of the gift

REFERENCES

Alemzadeh, Homa, Ravishankar K. Iyer, Zbigniew Kalbarczyk, Nancy Leveson, and Jaishankar Raman. 2016 "Adverse Events in Robotic Surgery: A Retrospective Study of 14 Years of FDA Data." *PLoS ONE*, 11(4) e0151470. doi:10.1371/journal.pone. 0151470.

Anspach, Renee. 1993 *Deciding Who Lives: Fateful Choices in the Intensive-Care Nursery*. Berkeley, CA: University of California Press.

Barger-Lux, M. Janet, and Robert P. Heaney. 1986 "For Better and Worse: The Technological Imperative in Health Care." *Social Science and Medicine*, 22:1313–1320.

Carrese, Joseph A., and Lorna A. Rhodes. 2000 "Bridging Cultural Differences in Medical Practice." *Journal of General Internal Medicine*, 15:92–96.

Chang, Virginia W., and Diane S. Lauderdale. 2009 "Fundamental Cause Theory, Technological Innovation, and Health Disparities: The Case of Cholesterol in the Era of Statins." *Journal of Health and Social Behavior*, 50:245–260.

Cook, Deborah, and Rocker, Graeme. 2014 "Dying with Dignity in the Intensive Care Unit." *New England Journal of Medicine*, 370:2506–2514.

Fox, Renée C. 1989 *The Sociology of Medicine: A Participant Observer's View*. Upper Saddle River, NJ: Prentice Hall.

Fox, Renée C., and Judith P. Swazey. 1978 *The Courage to Fail: A Social View of Organ Transplants and Dialysis*, 2nd ed. Chicago, IL: University of Chicago Press.

Fox, Renée C., and Judith P. Swazey. 1992 *Spare Parts: Organ Replacement in American Society*. New York: Oxford University Press.

Freund, Peter E.S., and Meredith B. McGuire. 1999 *Health, Illness, and the Social Body*, 3rd ed. Upper Saddle River, NJ: Prentice Hall.

Hampson, Lindsay A., and Ezekiel Emanuel. 2005 "The Prognosis for Changes in End-of-Life Care After the Schiavo Case." *Health Affairs*, 24:972–975.

Herring, Andrew, Steffie Woolhandler, and David U. Himmelstein. 2008 "Insurance Status of U.S. Organ Donors and Transplant Recipients: The Uninsured Give But Rarely Receive." *International Journal of Health Services*, 38:641–652.

Holder, Angela R. 1988 "Surrogate Motherhood and the Best Interests of Children." *Law, Medicine, & Health Care*, 16:51–56.

Humphry, Derek. 1991 *Final Exit: The Practicalities of Self-Deliverance and Assisted Suicide for the Dying*. Los Angeles, CA: The Hemlock Society.

Institute of Medicine. 2015 *Dying in America: Improving Quality and Honoring Individual Preferences Near the End of Life*. Washington, D.C.: The National Academies Press.

Jasper, John D., Carol A.E. Nickerson, Peter A. Ubel, and David A. Asch. 2004 "Altruism, Incentives, and Organ Donation: Attitudes of the Transplant Community." *Medical Care*, 42:378–386.

Kutner, Nancy G. 1987 "Issues in the Application of High Cost Medical Technology: The Case of Organ Transplantation." *Journal of Health and Social Behavior*, 28:23–36.

Lehoux, Pascale, and Stuart Blume. 2000 "Technology Assessment and the Sociopolitics of Health Technologies." *Journal of Health Politics, Policy, and Law*, 25:1063–1120.

Littenberg, Benjamin. 1992 "Technology Assessment in Medicine." *Academic Medicine*, 67:424–428.

McGough, E.A., and M.W. Chopek. 1990 "The Physician's Role as Asker in Obtaining Organ Donations." *Transplantation Proceedings*, 22:267–272.

Macklin, Ruth. 1988 "Is There Anything Wrong with Surrogate Motherhood? An Ethical Analysis." *Law, Medicine, & Health Care*, 16:57–64.

May, Thomas, Mark P. Aulisio, and Michael A. DeVita. 2000 "Patients, Families, and Organ Donation: Who Should Decide?" *The Milbank Quarterly*, 78:323–336.

O'Reilly, Kevin B. 2010 "Assisted Suicide Laws Cited in 95 Deaths in Washington, Oregon." Amednews.com. www.amednews.com/article/20100325/profession/303259996/8/.

Pew Internet Health Tracking Survey. 2014 "The Social Life of Health Information." www.pewresearch.org/fact-tank/2014/01/15/the-social-life-of-health-information/.

Quill, Timothy E. 1991 "Death and Dignity: A Case of Individualized Decision Making." *New England Journal of Medicine*, 324:691–694.

Quill, Timothy E., Robert Arnold, and Anthony L. Back. 2009 "Discussing Treatment Preferences with Patients Who Want 'Everything.'" *Annals of Internal Medicine*, 151:345–349.

Robertson, John A. 1994 *Children of Choice: Freedom and the New Reproductive Technologies*. Princeton, NJ: Princeton University Press.

Robinson, James C. 2015 "Biomedical Innovation in the Era of Health Care Spending Constraints." *Health Affairs,* 34:203–209.

Rothman, Barbara K. 1988 "Reproductive Technology and the Commodification of Life." *Women and Health*, 13:95–100.

———. 1989 *Recreating Motherhood: Ideology and Technology in a Patriarchal Society*. New York: W.W. Norton.

Rothman, David J. 1997 *Beginnings Count: The Technological Imperative in American Health Care*. New York: Oxford University Press.

Schneiderman, Lawrence J., Nancy S. Jecker, and Albert R. Jonsen. 1990 "Medical Futility: Its Meaning and Ethical Implications." *Annals of Internal Medicine*, 112:949–954.

Sharp, Lesley A. 2006 *Strange Harvest: Organ Transplants, Denatured Bodies, and the Transformed Self.* Berkeley, CA: University of California Press.

Shaw, Rhonda. 2010 "Perceptions of the Gift Relationship in Organ and Tissue Donation: Views of Intensivists and Donor and Recipient Coordinators." *Social Science and Medicine*, 70:609–615.

Steinhubl, Steven R., Evan D. Muse, and Eric J. Topol. 2013 "Can Mobile Health Technologies Transform Health Care?" *Journal of the American Medical Association,* 310:2395–2396.

Veatch, Robert M. 1993 "The Impending Collapse of the Whole-Brain Definition of Death." *Hastings Center Report*, 23:18–24.

Volandes, Angelo. 2015 *The Conversation: A Revolutionary Plan for End-of-Life Care*. New York: Bloomsbury USA.

Weiss, Gregory L., and Lea N. Lupkin. 2009–2010 "First-Year College Students' Attitudes About End-of-Life Decision Making." *Omega*, 60:143–163.

Werth, James I. 2006 "The Implications of the Theresa Schiavo Case for End-of-Life Care and Decisions." *Death Studies*, 30:99–100.

Woliver, Laura R. 1989 "The Deflective Power of Reproductive Technologies: The Impact on Women." *Women & Politics*, 9:17–47.

Ziebland, Sue, and Sally Wyke. 2012 "Health and Illness in a Connected World: How Might Sharing Experiences on the Internet Affect People's Health?" *Milbank Quarterly*, 90: 219–249.

CHAPTER 17

Comparative Health Care Systems

Learning Objectives

- Identify and describe the major factors that influence the structure of the health care system within countries.

- Discuss the most important issues for health care systems in developing countries.

- Identify and discuss the concept of "global health."

- Identify and describe the four broad categories of health care systems in the world.

- Compare and contrast the effectiveness of the health care systems of China, Canada, England, and Russia.

Studying the health care systems of other countries offers at least three valuable benefits: (1) an understanding of the diversity of approaches that exist to meet health care needs; (2) an understanding of the variety of factors that have shaped the development of these approaches; and (3) an understanding of how the health care system in the United States compares and contrasts with those in other countries. Donald Light, who has written extensively on health care systems around the world, has said that the health care system in the United States "is so unusual that only by comparing it with other systems can those of us who live inside it gain the perspective we need to understand how it works" (Light, 1990:429). See the accompanying box, "Comparing the World's Health Care Systems."

MAJOR INFLUENCES ON HEALTH CARE SYSTEMS

Comparative studies of public policy have taught us at least one clear principle—every public policy in every country at any given point in time is shaped by a wide and complex configuration of forces. Whether the subject is policy as it relates to education, the environment, or health care, and whether the focus is the United States, China, or Canada, a host of factors are important determinants.

The range and number of factors that influence or determine what governments do or, for that matter, what they choose not to do, are virtually infinite. Public policy may be influenced by prior policy commitments, international tension, a nation's climate, economic wealth, degree of ethnic conflict, historical traditions, the personality of its leadership, the level of literacy of its people, the nature of its party system, and whether it is governed by civilian or military leaders. . . . Virtually anything can influence or determine what governments do. (Leichter, 1979:38)

However, social scientists are able to see patterns among these forces and have identified four key influences on the health care and other social systems (Leichter, 1979; Lassey, Lassey, and Jinks, 1997):

1. *The physical environment* (e.g., the presence of environmental pollutants and the resources needed to combat them).
2. *Historical and situational events* that influence health care policy (e.g., America's Depression in the 1920s and 1930s).
3. *Cultural norms and values*—for example, Lynn Payer (1989) relates the propensity of American physicians to order more drugs, perform more diagnostic procedures, and undertake more surgery than their European counterparts to the aggressive "can do" spirit that is part of the cultural makeup of the United States.
4. *The structure of society*, including political factors (the extent of government centralization), economic factors (the level of national wealth), demographic factors (age structure and degree of urbanization), and social factors (reliance on family versus social organizations).

Of course, not all social scientists assign the same weight to each of these factors in public policy formation. For example, in the United States, many economists hold a *popular choice* position—that is, that we have the type of health care system we do because it is the type of system people want. People's preferences are expressed through individual decisions in the marketplace and through voting behavior. Others, including many sociologists and political scientists, favor a *power group* explanation—that health policies have largely been shaped by the power and influence of certain groups (e.g., the AMA, hospitals, and insurance companies). Some analysts emphasize the influence of economic development and demographic makeup (e.g., the influence of available resources and the percentage of elderly within the society). Marxist analysis focuses on the role of class formation, class interests, and the political behavior of the classes, and explains America's lack of universal health care coverage as being due to the weakness of labor unions and the absence of an influential and broadly based socialist party.

HEALTH CARE SERVICES IN DEVELOPING COUNTRIES

The world's developing countries experience a doubly difficult situation with regard to providing for public health—more health problems, and considerably fewer resources to invest in the health care system (see Tables 17–1 and 17–2 for illustrations of this pattern). Developing countries today still have high rates of many communicable diseases, increasingly high rates of chronic degenerative diseases, and much less money to invest in the health care system.

Over the next few decades, developing countries are expected to undergo an epidemiological transition as their disease and illness pattern comes to more closely resemble that of developed countries. Expected improvements in the prevention of acute infectious diseases should lead to a reduction in mortality in children under the age of 5 years, and an overall decline in mortality from communicable diseases, but higher rates of diseases like heart disease and cancer. Wide variations will probably continue to exist among low-income countries. Today, adult mortality in sub-Saharan Africa is more than twice that found in Latin America and the Caribbean.

IN THE FIELD

COMPARING THE WORLD'S HEALTH CARE SYSTEMS

Can the United States learn anything about health care systems by studying other countries?

In recent years there have been several impressive efforts by well-respected groups to evaluate, rate, and compare the world's health care systems. Study after study has concluded that the U.S. health care system is poorly rated and compares unfavorably with the health care systems in other modern countries.

In 2000, the World Health Organization evaluated the health care systems of 191 nations on health care delivery. The report took into consideration the overall health of each country, health inequities in the population, how nations respond to problems in their health care systems, how well people of varying economic status within a country are served by their system, and how costs are distributed. Which country earned the highest score? The top scorer was France, followed in the rankings by Italy, San Marino, Andorra, Malta, Singapore, Spain, Oman, Austria, and Japan. Despite spending much more money on health care than any other nation—in both absolute and relative terms—the United States finished 37th (World Health Organization, 2000).

A joint study by the Organization for Economic Cooperation and Development and the World Health Organization, conducted at around the same time, compared the current performance of the health care systems in 29 modern industrialized nations in 2000 with that in studies conducted in 1960 and 1980. The evaluation focused on six categories of performance: (1) preventive health care (e.g., immunization and promotion of healthy lifestyles); (2) health care use and services (e.g., number of physician visits per year); (3) sophisticated technology (e.g., availability of high-tech equipment); (4) mortality; (5) health system responsiveness; and (6) stability of per capita health spending relative to national income. On most indicators, the United States fared poorly. The overall relative performance of the United States and its relative performance on most individual categories had declined since 1960, and the United States did not improve its relative ranking in a single category (Anderson and Hussey, 2001).

In a study of hospital administrative costs in 2011 in eight wealthy nations, the United States was found to spend a much higher percentage of the health care dollar on administration and bureaucracy (Himmelstein et al., 2014). In 2014, Bloomberg News studied 51 nations with respect to health spending per person, life expectancy, and health care cost as a percentage of the economy. The U.S. health care system ranked only 44th, trailing Serbia, Turkey, China, and many others (Edney, 2014). In 2015, the Commonwealth Fund compared health care spending, supply, utilization, prices, and health outcomes in 13 high-income countries (Australia, Canada, Denmark, France, Germany, Japan, Netherlands, New Zealand, Norway, Sweden, Switzerland, the United Kingdom, and the United States). The United States spent far more on health care than any other country (driven mostly by greater use of medical technology and higher prices), but had poorer health outcomes, including lower life expectancy and a higher incidence of chronic conditions (Squires and Anderson, 2015).

It will be a major challenge for developing countries to inject sufficient money into the health care system to keep apace of already existing problems and those created by the transition. Today, low-income countries spend only about 4 or 5 percent of their income on health care—about 50 percent of what most developed countries spend. High-income

TABLE 17–1   Wealth of Country, Per Capita Gross Domestic Product, and Per Capita Health Expenditures, 2014

	Per Capita GDP (US$)	Per Capita Health Expenditures (US$)
High-Income Countries (Exs.)		
United States	54,630	9,403
United States	50,231	5,292
United Kingdom	46,297	3,935
Upper-Middle-Income Countries (Exs.)		
Brazil	11,727	947
Romania	10,000	557
China	7,590	420
Lower-Middle-Income Countries (Exs.)		
Egypt	3,366	178
Vietnam	2,052	142
Pakistan	1,317	36
Low-Income Countries (Exs.)		
Haiti	824	108
Afghanistan	634	57
Central African Republic	359	16

Source: World Bank. *World Development Indicators.* 2014a and 2014b. www.data.worldbank.org/indicator/SH.XPD.PCAP/countries and www.data.worldbank.org/indicator/NY.GDP.PCAP.CD/countries.

TABLE 17–2   Wealth of Country, Life Expectancy, and Infant Mortality Rate, 2014

	Life Expectancy (Years)	Infant Mortality Rate (%)
High-Income Countries (Exs.)		
United States	79.7	5.9
Canada	81.8	4.7
United Kingdom	80.5	4.4
Upper-Middle-Income Countries (Exs.)		
Brazil	73.5	18.6
Romania	74.9	9.9
China	75.4	12.4
Lower-Middle-Income Countries (Exs.)		
Egypt	73.7	21.6
Vietnam	73.2	18.4
Pakistan	67.4	55.7
Low-Income Countries (Exs.)		
Haiti	63.5	48.8
Afghanistan	50.9	115.1
Central African Republic	51.8	90.6

Source: Data from Central Intelligence Agency, *World Factbook*, 2016a and 2016b. www.cia.gov/library/publications/resources/the-world-factbook/rankorder/2102rank.html. www.cia.gov/library/publications/resources/the-world-factbook/rankorder/2091rank.html.

countries have four times more hospital beds per capita than low-income countries, and about seven times more physicians per capita (World Health Organization, 2010).

Health system reform movements in developing countries are already facing some of the same problems as are developed countries, namely access to care, quality of care, and system

---

IN COMPARATIVE FOCUS

THE GLOBALIZATION OF HEALTH CARE

When many people think about **global health**, they think only of health problems in developing countries. While that is certainly part of the issue, the concept has a much broader focus and includes (1) health problems that transcend national borders (e.g., the Zika virus), (2) health problems of such magnitude that they have an impact on economic and political systems around the world (e.g., HIV/AIDS), and (3) health problems that require cooperative action and solutions by more than one country (e.g., Ebola) (FamiliesUSA, 2010).

These health problems require significant attention to a variety of issues related to health:

1. Health and climate change and other changes in the ecosystem (the countries that will be most negatively affected are those that have contributed the least to the problem).
2. Food security (the world had an estimated 795 million chronically hungry people in 2015, with devastating health consequences).
3. Acute infectious diseases such as malaria and diarrheal diseases that are continuing problems in many areas of the world.
4. Chronic degenerative diseases such as cancer and heart disease that are common causes of death in the developed world and are increasingly common in developing countries.
5. Maternal and child health as maternal mortality rate and infant mortality rate in particular continue at unnecessarily high levels.
6. Inadequate, ineffective, and inequitable health care systems that do not offer the necessary health support to people.

7. Shortages of health care workers—with the accompanying problem that wealthy countries sometimes recruit trained health care workers from developing countries—and shortages of medical equipment and supplies.

Commentators sometimes ask why people in modern countries like the United States should have any concern about worldwide health problems or problems that occur primarily in developing countries. FamiliesUSA (2010), an organization that promotes global health programs, offers four reasons:

1. Humanitarian reasons—hundreds of millions or more people continue to suffer needlessly.
2. Equity reasons—roughly 90 percent of the world's health care resources are spent on 10 percent of the world's people.
3. Direct impact reasons—in the increasingly connected world, diseases can more easily than ever migrate from nation to nation.
4. Indirect impact reasons—countries with significant health problems often experience economic and political instability that has worldwide consequences.

Are global health problems so immense that there is little hope of having any significant impact on them? The answer is no. All of the discussions that have occurred in the World Health Organization, FamiliesUSA, Global Health Initiative, and many, many other groups are a needed step in genuinely addressing these problems. Representatives from disciplines such as public health (which has always had a strong global component), medicine, law, international relations, sociology, anthropology,

(Continued)

(*Continued*)

economics, political science, management, environmental science and policy, and others are combining their expertise to combat global health problems. **Global health partnerships (GHPs)** are being developed in other countries by many American and European universities, by private foundations such as the Bill and Melinda Gates Foundation, and by public health/epidemiological groups such as the World Health Organization and the Centers for Disease Control and Prevention. Some schools and programs are affiliating with hospitals, schools, and programs in Africa, Asia, and South America. For example, Harvard University has established partnerships in Dubai, Turkey, and India, and the University of Virginia is working with a program in Lesotho. The Global Health Service Partnership sends U.S. physicians and nurses to serve as faculty at medical and nursing schools in low-resource countries. In 2013 these individuals went to Malawi, Tanzania, and Uganda. Among other benefits, these programs will improve the medical infrastructure in these countries and hopefully entice more trained health workers to stay in their home country (Crone, 2008; Ngoasong, 2009).

efficiency. More resources need to be invested in the public health infrastructure, especially in rural areas. Given the government's smaller revenue-raising ability, pressures mount to turn more of the system over to the private market. This may work to the benefit of the middle and upper classes, but it forces many in the lower classes out of the health care system just as it did in the United States prior to the Affordable Care Act. The accompanying box, "The Globalization of Health Care," describes the very significant efforts occurring today in the globalization of health care.

Nevertheless, there are some significant success stories in the efforts of low- and middle-income countries to create and maintain effective health care systems. As recently as 1970, Mexico's health care system was in disarray, and health indicators were similar to those in many developing countries. However, significant improvements were made in the final decades of the 1900s, and in 2003, Mexico approved landmark health reform legislation that created a government-funded system (*Seguro Popular*) to deliver medical care to all citizens regardless of ability to pay. Approximately 50 million previously uninsured people received health care insurance with this new system, while health care costs in the country were maintained at 5.6 percent of total spending—a very manageable level. Until this time, the only insurance available was through one's employer or through expensive private insurance.

Since this time, Mexico has experienced marked improvement in health indicators for both children and adults. Although much remains to be done to close disparity gaps and to make services available to those living in rural areas, Mexico has thoughtfully reformed its health care system by using scientific assessments of the quality and outcomes of each aspect of its system. It is a good example of a country that is using a public–private mix of health care services.

TYPES OF HEALTH CARE SYSTEMS

The world's health care systems can roughly be organized into four categories:

1. *Private and public insurance with private entrepreneurial services.* The United States has been the only modern nation in the world to emphasize the private market in the health care system. Health insurance companies, pharmaceutical companies, medical equipment companies, and many hospitals are run to make

a profit. Of course, as we learned in Chapter 14, there has also been a large public (government) sector in the U.S. health care system. Prior to recent health care reform, 47 million people in the United States lacked health care insurance. All other modern countries believe that health care is a right, and everyone in these countries receives health care at no or minimal cost.

2. *National health insurance with private regulated services.* With some variations, the health care system in these countries is private as it is in the United States. However, the federal government has established a plan (plans differ from country to country) whereby everyone is covered by health insurance and receives health care at no or minimal cost at the point of service. Canada is an example of this type of system, and is one of the countries described in detail later in this chapter.

Germany has a model that is similar in many respects to that found in several European countries, and is a highly respected approach. The system is based on a belief that people's health care needs should be met regardless of their income. Everyone pays a type of income tax into the system, and everyone can count on their health care being covered when they are sick or injured.

The federal government requires all individuals to have health insurance (like the individual mandate under the Affordable Care Act), but it does not directly provide the insurance. Most German people (about 89 percent) buy heavily regulated non-profit insurance from one of 160 "sickness funds." The government requires these plans to be comprehensive, not to turn anyone away due to a pre-existing condition, and to have premiums based on ability to pay. There are no deductibles, only very small co-payments, and ready access to all health care services. These funds compete with each other for survival rather than for profit. About 11 percent of Germans opt out of these funds

and purchase private (for-profit) insurance. Premiums in these plans depend on age and health (older and sicker enrollees pay more).

Most hospitals are government owned (50 percent of all hospital beds) or have non-profit ownership (about 35 percent of beds). Most physicians work in private practices or work in a hospital for a salary. Physician compensation is negotiated by professional medical associations (so that there is a uniform fee schedule), and the government establishes limits on what hospitals can charge.

The German health care system is widely respected around the world, and, within the country, health indicators are very good, access to services is prompt, and there is much public satisfaction with the system. Health care prices are much lower in Germany, but the quality of services is excellent.

3. *National health insurance with public regulated services.* Countries that adopt this approach have public ownership of the health care system and publicly provided health insurance. The government owns health care facilities, employs health care workers, and collects taxes to pay for health care. Patients receive health care at no or minimal cost at the point of service. General practitioners must be seen in order to receive a referral to a specialist. Many of these countries now allow a small private sector for wealthier patients who desire quicker or enhanced service (e.g., a private hospital bed). England is an example of this type of system, and is one of the countries described in detail later in this chapter.

Norway offers a government-owned and government-run health care system with publicly provided health insurance. Health funding is provided to localities which in turn allocate funds to particular services. After completing payment of a deductible, all individuals receive comprehensive health care services at no or minimal cost at the point of service. Private insurance is also available, but is rarely used because the public system is so good. Individuals would typically buy private insurance to avoid a hospital waiting list or for services like plastic surgery.

Most physicians are salaried, although some exceptions exist. The government pays for the program from general tax revenues rather than a specially designated tax. General practitioners must be seen in order to receive a referral to a specialist. Patients are admitted to a hospital either through its emergency department or through a referral by their physician. The quality of all hospitals is excellent. While there may be lengthy waiting lists for non-emergency care, receipt of emergency care is prompt. If a physician refers an individual to the hospital, the care is free. The Norwegian health care system is widely respected around the world and within the country, health indicators are very good, and there is much public satisfaction with the system.

4. *National health insurance state-run system (socialized medicine).* Countries that adopt this approach have an entirely government-owned and government-funded health care system. All health care workers are employees of the government. Theoretically, at least, there is no private health care sector. The government typically conducts extensive health care planning, budgeting, organization, and regulation. For example, in the former Soviet Union, a country covered in detail later in this chapter, patients were assigned to a particular neighborhood physician, and physicians were assigned a particular roster of patients. Patients receive health care at no or minimal cost at the point of service. Patient waiting times vary, but typically are not long.

Cuba represents an excellent example of **socialized medicine**. The government operates a national health system in which all medical facilities are owned by the government and all medical providers are employed by the government. There are no private facilities or private providers. All medical care is free, and there are no deductibles, co-insurance, or co-payments. The emphasis throughout the system is on prevention.

In part because medical providers are not well paid (although medical education is free), there are more physicians per capita in Cuba than in the United States. They not only spend more time with each patient, but every patient also receives a home visit once a year. Health providers live in the same community as their patients. Despite it being a low-income country, life expectancy is virtually the same as in the United States, the infant mortality rate is lower, and vaccination rates are the highest in the world (Campion and Morrissey, 2013). Moreover, Cuba sends out more than 30,000 medical providers each year to more than 70 developing countries to contribute to health care delivery.

The United States health care system having already been examined, the four countries selected for review in this chapter represent a cross section of other approaches. Many Chinese people are still extremely poor, although there is increasing wealth in the cities. Canada illustrates the national health insurance with private regulated services approach. England illustrates the national health insurance with public regulated services model. Russia, when it was part of the Soviet Union, illustrated the national health insurance state-run system (socialized medicine) model.

The health care system of each of these countries is described in terms of (1) its historical, political, and philosophical foundation, (2) the organization of the health care system, (3) the extent to which health services are accessible to the people, (4) indicators of the performance of the health care system, and (5) recent developments in the system. Table 17–3 compares the level of advancement in health care of technology, resources, and access in these countries with that in the United States.

TABLE 17–3   Comparative Analysis of the Health Care System in Five Countries

Country	Level of Advancement of Health Care System		
	Technology	Resources	Access
China	Low	Low	Moderate
Russia	Low	Low	Moderate
Canada	High	High	High
England	High	Moderate	High
United States	High	High	Moderate

Source: Marie L. Lassey, William R. Lassey, and Martin J. Jinks, *Health Care Systems Around the World* (Upper Saddle River, NJ: Prentice Hall, 1997).

As you are reading about the individual countries, note how each is affected by the same key forces (e.g., rapidly escalating health care costs), and note the similarities and differences in the types of responses that are being made. For each country, consider how its health care system has been influenced by environmental, situational-historical, and cultural norms and values, and the structural factors described earlier.

CHINA

The Historical, Political, and Philosophical Foundation

With a population of 1.4 billion people, China has almost 20 percent of all the people in the world, and more than any other country. These people live on a landmass that is similar in size to the mainland United States. Only recently has a majority of China's population been urban based. China is undergoing rapid modernization, but many Chinese people continue to remain very poor.

With regard to health care, three distinct phases are apparent in China's recent history: (1) the focus on improving health care from the time that Mao Zedong came to power in 1949 until 1965; (2) the radical restructuring of the health care system during the Cultural Revolution from 1965 to 1977; and (3) the

initiation of reform efforts and movement toward free-market entrepreneuralism in the late 1970s and increasing up to the present day.

Mao inherited a China in desperate condition. Plagued by years of both civil war and war with Japan, the economy was in a shambles, with both agricultural and industrial productivity at low levels. Food shortages were common, as were epidemics of disease. About one baby in five died in the first year of life, and almost one in three before the age of 5 years. Hospitals and other health facilities were in desperately short supply in urban areas, with even fewer in rural areas. Most physicians practiced only traditional Chinese medicine that had been learned through apprenticeships.

At the very first National Health Congress, Mao presented four precepts as the ideological basis for health services:

1. Health care must be directed to the working people.
2. Preventive medicine must be given priority over curative medicine. By the mid-1960s, the government had conducted several Patriotic Health Movements in which millions of Chinese worked at getting rid of the "four pests" (flies, mosquitoes, bed bugs, and rats), improving general sanitation, preventing parasitic diseases, and eliminating sexually transmitted disease.

3. Modern health care needed to be added to traditional Chinese approaches. The Chinese adage that "China walks on two legs: one traditional and one modern" is nowhere more true than in medicine.
4. Health workers must be involved with mass movements. An example is the family planning movement in China with the mandatory "one child per family" objective (which has now been discontinued).

Considerable efforts were directed to increasing access to medical care for the massive rural population. Rural areas were divided into *communes* (which averaged between 15,000 and 50,000 people), which were subdivided into *production brigades* (with 1,000–3,000 people), each of which had its own health station. These health stations were staffed by public health workers, midwives, and barefoot doctors. **Barefoot doctors** (later called *countryside doctors*) were peasants who had received a few months of medical training and then returned to their commune to treat minor illnesses (including colds, gastrointestinal ailments, and minor injuries), provide immunizations and birth control, and improve sanitation. Their existence compensated for the critical shortage of physicians in rural areas.

Within a decade and a half, substantial progress had been made. However, in 1966, frustrated and angered that his ideas were being incorporated too slowly, and mistrustful of various societal institutions, including medicine, Mao launched the Cultural Revolution—a violent campaign of political and social repression. Those who were suspected of having ideological differences with Mao were imprisoned, tortured, and sometimes murdered. Schools and medical colleges were closed, medical research was halted, and health expenditures declined. Mao proclaimed that the health care system was not sufficiently directed toward rural areas, that medical education had become too Westernized

and not sufficiently practical, and that many physicians were shunning traditional Chinese medicine in favor of Western approaches.

Following the death of Mao in 1976, China maintained its commitment to a socialist economic system with extensive government control of all areas of the economy. This system was believed to offer the most effective strategy for ensuring that the basic needs of the people were met. Access to health care was deemed a right of all people, and there was a strong moral commitment to providing health care free or at very little charge. Emphasis was placed on preventive care, the use of minimally trained health care personnel, and the combining of traditional Chinese and Western-style medicines. The Chinese health care system became the envy of developing countries around the world.

However, Chinese leaders became frustrated at the slow pace of modernization. Since 1980, leaders have insisted that, while China remains a socialist country politically, efforts to accelerate economic development should occur by shifting from a planned economy with extensive control by the national government to a market-oriented economy with private ownership of enterprises and private investments in all sectors. This created a dramatic transformation for the country—with rapid industrialization and considerable economic growth—but it had dire consequences for health care delivery and health outcomes.

Local governments cut subsidies to rural hospitals and clinics. The decreased funding led to many countryside doctors entering farming and other occupations where they could make more money, or entering the private practice of medicine, so that they could charge fees. Rural peasants, who had been able to receive services for no payment or only a small payment, became subject to a fee-for-service system in which they paid the village doctor out of pocket. By the year 2000, China's health care system had transitioned from one in which affordable preventive and curative services were accessible to everyone to a system in which most people could not afford basic health care and no government or private health insurance existed (Yip and Hsiao, 2008).

Since that time, China has embarked on a series of modifications to its health care system. Although major changes were introduced in 2003 and 2005, in 2008 Chinese leaders concluded that the private market system had completely failed for health care. Major initiatives were introduced in 2009, 2013, and 2014 to create more affordable, quality medical care through a government-sponsored insurance system.

Organization of the Health Care System

China is comprised of five autonomous regions, 22 provinces, four direct-controlled municipalities (Beijing, Shanghai, Tianjin, and Chongqing), and two largely self-governing regions (Hong Kong and Macau). It is a one-party state (the Communist Party). Since 2013, the National Health and Family Planning Commission has overseen formulation of health care policies, established prices that physicians can charge, and supervised medical research for the entire country. The health department in each province oversees the actual distribution of health resources, and works with local governments in the financing and delivery of health care services according to local needs.

Primary care is now delivered primarily by village doctors and other health workers in rural (village) clinics, and by general practitioners in rural (township) hospitals, small urban community hospitals, and multipurpose urban hospitals. Village doctors are not licensed general practitioners and can work only in village clinics. The rural population typically uses the village clinics and township hospitals, and the urban population typically uses the community hospitals.

Anyone can see a GP in the multipurpose hospitals. Specialists primarily work out of hospitals. Most township and community hospitals are public, but multipurpose hospitals can be public or private.

With the recent health care reforms, about 95 percent of Chinese people have health insurance through one of three plans: (1) a compulsory urban employees insurance program, (2) a voluntary but subsidized insurance program for all rural residents, or (3) a voluntary but subsidized program for unemployed urban residents, including students, young children, and the elderly. Combined with other recent changes in the system (e.g., the addition of private insurance plans, greater availability of needed drugs, and the establishment of primary care-based community health centers), significant improvements have occurred.

The government does continue to set the prices that providers can charge, and for all services except drugs and high-technology care these are set at below cost. Therefore, in order to make money, physicians tend to overprescribe drugs and overuse high-tech care—both of which have a steep markup.

Accessibility of Health Care

The government continues to affirm its belief that every citizen is entitled to receive basic health care services that are provided by local governments. Its stated intention is to have 100 percent health insurance coverage by 2020 (when it is anticipated that China will spend US$1 trillion annually on health care). Those with insurance are covered for primary, specialist, emergency, hospital, and mental health care, prescription drugs, and traditional Chinese medicine. A few dental and optometry services are provided, but are mostly paid out of pocket, as are home-based and hospice services. Subsidies are available for people with low incomes. Efforts are underway to increase the number of medical facilities and to enhance care coordination and integration among facilities (Fang, 2016).

Performance of the Health Care System

Despite these recent changes, disease patterns in China vary considerably between urban and rural areas and between wealthy and poor people. In urban China, the major health concerns are the same as in the industrialized world—heart disease and cancer. Lung cancer has become a particular problem in China. About 300 million Chinese people smoke cigarettes (70 percent of adult males but just 7 percent of adult females are smokers), 750 million are affected directly by second-hand smoke, and death and illness from smoking-related causes have become a paramount health concern. Smog is a huge problem in cities. In addition, the typical diet contains an increasingly high percentage of fat (there are many fast-food restaurants), lifestyles are becoming much more sedentary, once unheard-of obesity is increasing (20 to 30 percent of Chinese people are overweight or obese), and excessive alcohol consumption is becoming more of a problem. HIV/AIDS, long ignored by the government, is now acknowledged as a significant problem. The recent SARS epidemic brought worldwide attention to the lack of adequate health preparation in China. In rural areas, environmental pollution and the absence of safe drinking water (a major source of stomach, liver, and intestinal cancers) continue to be huge problems. Nutrition-related diseases, parasitic diseases, tuberculosis, and hepatitis B are common.

China's health care system is currently undergoing a major privatization, but today it has many serious problems. Photo by Gregory Weiss.

China has rapidly increased its number of physicians in recent years, but a serious shortage remains in both urban and rural areas. With the onset of health insurance coverage there has been a significantly increased demand for services. This has, of course, dramatically increased health care costs. Some progress in assimilating advanced medical technology has been made, but expansion has come slowly, and few high-tech services are offered outside large urban areas. Overall, China spends about 5.5 percent of its gross domestic product on health care—a percentage that is high for developing nations but considerably less than what is spent in industrialized countries.

Recent Developments in Health Care

The commitment to a private-market health care system created profound problems for health and health care in China. In recent years, however, China's commitment to improving its health care system and to providing universal access to effective, safe, and low-cost health care has already had noticeable effects. Just since 2009, more than US$125 billion has been spent on building new clinics and hospitals throughout the country. State-subsidized health insurance for urban and rural residents has enabled more than 95 percent of Chinese people to be covered by some form of health insurance. Efforts to increase private market opportunities for international companies to build private hospitals, to engage in research and development activities, and to sell pharmaceuticals and medical devices in China have been very successful. In 2011, a public–private health care partnership between China and the United States was created to boost health care knowledge, technology, and development in China and to open a new lucrative market for U.S. medical goods. Several large pharmaceutical companies—including Eli Lilly, Merck, and AstraZeneca—have created manufacturing and research and development

facilities in China. These changes are very recent, and much has yet to be determined, but China has made significant progress in addressing issues in its health care system.

CANADA

The Historical, Political, and Philosophical Foundation

The nation of Canada is a federal system—its 35 million people are spread across a loose confederation of ten provinces, from Newfoundland off the east coast to British Columbia in the west, and two territories, the Yukon and the North West territories. Much of the political structure of Canada was created under the British North America (BNA) Act, which was passed by the British Parliament in 1867. It guarantees considerably greater autonomy to the Canadian provinces than that held by individual American states. The BNA Act allocated to the federal government all matters of national concern, plus others thought likely to be most costly. It allocated to the provinces more local and (presumably) less costly activities, such as education, roads, and health care.

Throughout the early decades of the twentieth century, limited programs for health insurance were offered by local governments, industries, and voluntary agencies. These programs covered only selected services and left much of the population uninsured. Not until the mid-1940s did Canada begin to earnestly consider universal health insurance. This consideration was stimulated by three factors—the extreme prevalence of poverty brought on by the Depression, the inability of local governments to offer substantial help due to their own state of near bankruptcy, and the despair of physicians who were frequently not paid. Significant disparities in wealth among the provinces led to additional inequalities in health services.

Although a universal plan was defeated at this time because of fears of federal infringement of provincial authority, the widespread health problems of Canadian people and the inadequacy of available health care facilities and programs were well documented. As a beginning but precedent-setting step, the federal government initiated financial assistance to the provinces for creating additional health care resources.

The transition to a universal health insurance plan occurred gradually. In 1946, the Saskatchewan government enacted legislation for a universal compulsory hospital care insurance plan for all its citizens. The success of this program led additional provinces to enact similar programs. These were quite successful and well received but very expensive—prompting the provinces to encourage the federal government to develop a national plan. However, as the concept was becoming more popular with the general citizenry and with political leaders, increasing reservations were expressed by physicians fearing a loss of professional autonomy, and by private insurance companies fearing their own elimination.

Finally, in 1968, Canada passed the Medical Care Act, which brought all the provinces together in a universal national health insurance program. The federal government agreed to pay for half of the health care costs in each province as long as their health care services complied with four conditions: (1) they provided *comprehensive* services with no benefits limitations; (2) benefits were *universal*—available to all—and provided uniformly; (3) benefits were *portable*, so that citizens were covered wherever they were in Canada; and (4) the plans had to be *publicly financed and administered by an agency accountable to the provincial government.*

Although the system worked well, the federal government soon realized that it not only lacked control over the amount of funds expended by the provinces (and the provinces had little incentive to control costs), but also received little political credit for its substantial contribution. In 1977, a key compromise, *Bill C-37*, was enacted. This legislation enabled the federal government to reduce its financial contribution (now at about 20 percent), with a corresponding reduction in federal and corporate taxes. The provinces, whose share increased (and is now at 80 percent), were able to increase their taxes so as to generate sufficient revenue to fund the program. In addition, the provinces were given greater latitude in managing the program, with the desired effect being that they would become more cost conscious.

The law pertaining to health insurance was modified again in 1984 in the Canada Health Act. Concerned that some physicians were "extra-billing" (i.e., directly charging patients fees above the reimbursement amount), this law mandated that physicians accept the reimbursement as their total payment. This legislation was not well received in the medical profession. For example, although only about 10 percent of physicians in Ontario were extra billing, a series of general strikes occurred to protest the government's increased regulation of physicians (Lewis, 2015).

Two key values underlie the Canadian national health insurance system. First, Canada has established a "right" to health care for all its citizens and eliminated financial barriers to care. In doing so, the Canadian people have made an important statement about the social unity of the country, the high value placed on social equity, and the worth of people independent of their ability to pay for a service. Many would say that these values are more reflective of Canadian than of American culture.

At the same time, Canada has maintained the private nature of the medical profession. Canadian physicians are not government employees and have considerably greater autonomy than their counterparts in Russia or even England. Canada's intention has been to offer publicly funded insurance for health care in a privately controlled system.

Organization of the Health Care System

Within the national government, the ultimate authority on health care is the health minister who directs national health care policy, works with the Parliament on relevant legislation, and serves as an important liaison with the health minister of each of the provinces. Because health is still primarily a provincial responsibility, much of the work related to medical education and medical licensure, hospitals, and public health occurs at the provincial level. Although policies, procedures, and standards among provinces tend to be comparable, this is not required and variations do occur.

About 75 to 80 percent of Canadian physicians are in office-based private practice, with most of the remainder based in hospitals. As in the United States, however, most office-based physicians (generalists and specialists) have hospital privileges, and admit and tend to patients there. Patients have free choice of physicians, and physicians have the option of accepting or rejecting any new patient.

The national health insurance plan is funded from federal and provincial tax revenues, and insurance premiums are paid by all tax-paying citizens. The government utilizes a variety of "supply-side" cost-containment measures. The most important of these mechanisms is prospective budgeting, whereby hospitals are financed on the basis of annually negotiated prospective budgets within each province. Once a budget is established, hospitals and other programs and providers are expected to live within it. Capital expenditures are handled separately and do not come out of the assigned allocation, but do require government approval.

Other key mechanisms that are used to regulate costs by controlling the supply of health care services include (1) determining the level of reimbursement for physicians (currently at 75 percent of established fees), (2) controlling the number of physicians by limiting enrollments in medical schools, and (3) minimizing the presence of private health insurance, which is available only to cover supplemental benefits (e.g., a semiprivate room in a hospital, dental and eye care, and prescription drugs).

A key issue within medicine in Canada is the degree of autonomy held by physicians. Policy discussions regarding national health insurance have typically been sensitive to preserving the "private" nature of the profession, and have avoided language which suggests that physicians are government employees.

In reality, however, the line is not so distinct. Physicians are reimbursed directly by the provincial government on a fee-for-service basis, but these fees are established in annual negotiations between the provincial medical association and the provincial government. Through these negotiations, prices are set for each medical service. The negotiated reimbursement schedules are binding, include little variation by medical specialty or complexity of care delivered to individual patients, and prohibit extra billing. Even physicians who have entirely "opted out" of national health insurance (an option taken by only a small percentage of Canadian physicians) are prevented from charging patients more than the specified reimbursement level.

All of this has led to continuing criticism that the medical professional has in reality been "de-privatized." Provincial governments reimburse physicians for only a percentage of the fee schedules set by the medical associations. This has been acceptable to most physicians, however, because they know that they spend considerably less time on billing and other administrative paperwork and pay significantly less for malpractice insurance than physicians in the United States.

Physicians enjoy high esteem in Canada, which is reflected in salaries in the top 1 percent of all professions. Although some physicians have complained that national health insurance has depressed their incomes, incomes have continued to increase at a reasonable level.

Accessibility of Health Care

All basic hospital and physician services and other services deemed to be necessary are covered for Canadian citizens. The only out-of-pocket health care expenses are for private insurance or direct payment for eye care, dental care, medication purchases for ambulatory patients, and, if a patient desires it, a semiprivate versus ward room in a hospital.

This system has enabled broad access to the health care system. Research has documented a greater use of physician and hospital services by Canadians than by Americans, especially among people with a lower income. One recent study found that residents of Ontario averaged 19 percent more visits than Americans to physicians (prior to the Affordable Care Act), and that this difference was even greater among those on a low income (who averaged 25–33 percent more visits) (Katz, Hofer, and Manning, 1996).

Critics of the Canadian system counter that accessibility of health care in Canada is limited by reduced availability of physicians, surgical procedures, and high-tech equipment. The relative lack of equipment and resources means that patients are not seen as promptly as they are in the United States, that queues (i.e., waiting lists) exist for many high-tech diagnostic and surgical procedures, and that fewer of these procedures are provided. One study of comparable hospitals in the United States and Canada found that U.S. medical patients received 22 percent more diagnostic tests than their Canadian counterparts, with almost all of the difference being accounted for by greater use of MRI and CT scanning (Katz, McMahon, and Manning, 1996). These delays in service provision lead some Canadians to cross the border to obtain services in the United States, although this practice is much less common than is often portrayed.

Performance of the Health Care System

Standard health indicators for Canada are very favorable. Canada is among the upper echelon of countries in the world with regard to life expectancy (longer than in the United States) and infant mortality (lower than in the United States). One recent study found that the health of wealthy Americans is about the same as the health of wealthy Canadians, but that the health of low-income Americans significantly lags behind that of low-income Canadians. In Canada, on most measures, the health of the rich and the poor is about the same, whereas in the United States there is a significant disparity, as people on a low income are much less healthy than those who are financially better off (McGrail et al., 2009).

The extent to which Canada has been able to maintain control over costs while providing high-quality comprehensive services to its people is an issue that has generated considerable controversy. Many advocates of the Canadian system emphasize that it has been able to guarantee services to all its people while spending a considerably smaller percentage of its gross domestic product (now about 11 percent) than does the United States (at about 18 percent). Canada's willingness to provide universal coverage for health care has given it the bargaining leverage to include mechanisms of cost control. Compared with the United States, Canada invests significantly less money per capita in administrative costs (the uniform billing system alone saves billions of dollars each year), profits, marketing, legal involvement in medicine, and other "medically irrelevant" areas. As noted in Chapter 14, while as much as 30 percent of the American health care dollar goes toward administrative costs, the corresponding figure in Canada is about 16 percent (Woolhandler, Campbell, and Himmelstein, 2004).

Critics of the Canadian system contend that these cost efficiencies come with a price. They argue that even after restricting the availability of services and sacrificing investment in sophisticated high-tech equipment, Canada has not had sufficient money to run the health care system.

The recent lack of growth in the Canadian economy along with a high rate of inflation and the aging of the Canadian population (producing greater medical needs and less tax revenue to fund the system) led to significant budget slashing in the mid-1990s. Provincial governments and their health authorities closed or merged some hospitals, removed selected non-essential medical services from the health care plans, made significant reductions in the number of health care jobs, became more assertive in negotiations for physician fee reimbursement (physicians in some provinces received pay cuts), and reduced budgets for outpatient diagnostic services. Both physicians and patients have lamented these developments.

Canadian citizens have long expressed great pride in their health care system, and this pride has consistently been expressed in public opinion polls. About 75 percent of Canadians consider their health care system to work well or very well. Prior to health care reform, only 25 percent of Americans rated their system as highly. Surveys show that 90 percent of Canadians prefer their health care system to that of the United States. Most people in the United States express a preference for the Canadian system.

Recent Developments in Health Care

The Canadian system will need to address two major pressure points in the coming years. First, a decision will have to be made about the level of funding for the system. After several years of budget slashing, cutbacks in available services, and increased dissatisfaction among providers and patients, the government did commit increased funding to health care in the early 2000s—a development that was received very favorably.

This issue relates to the other pressure point, namely the public–private mix in the health care system. Some medical professionals and ideological conservatives have long sought to reprivatize the system by shifting financial responsibility away from the government and back to patients (through private insurance), establishing less universal and less comprehensive health insurance plans, and emphasizing market forces in health care by deregulating the field. This position has not been supported by either a majority of the population or the government.

There is currently increased discussion of allowing a private health care system to develop alongside the public system. Proponents argue that movement in this direction is already occurring. Private health insurance has increased in Canada (about two-thirds of Canadians have private insurance to supplement the public system). Private insurance pays about 12 percent of all health care, mostly for services not covered in the public plan. By allowing patients who want to pay for private insurance to do so, some pressure on the public system is relieved (Allin and Rudoler, 2016). Opponents argue that this "two-tier" system would eventually lead to the destruction of the public system by eroding broad-based public support and increasing its costs. This issue will test the commitment of the Canadian people to their traditional health care system during the first decades of the twenty-first century (Steinbrook, 2006).

ENGLAND

The Historical, Political, and Philosophical Foundation

England has a total population of about 55 million people. England's strong commitment to public responsibility for the health and welfare of its citizens dates back to at least the mid-1800s. The foundation for today's National Health Service (NHS) was laid in 1867 when Parliament passed the Metropolitan Poor Act—a bill that obligated local governments to provide free hospital care for the poor. The measure appealed both to people's charitable interests and to a desire to protect the rest of society from contracting diseases from the untreated sick.

By the turn of the century, however, many were dissatisfied with the limited scope of the Poor Act, as England was confronted with the same pressures that existed throughout Europe to increase social welfare programs. The National Insurance Act (NHI) of 1911, one of several social reforms sponsored by the Liberal government, provided medical and disability benefits and income protection during sickness. The program was compulsory for all wage earners between the ages of 16 and 65 years earning less than a designated sum per year. However, the plan was less generous than similar programs in Germany and Japan in that it did not cover dependents of wage earners (except for a maternity plan), self-employed people (including farmers), or the unemployed. Although the NHI achieved its objectives as a limited plan, there was continued interest in a more comprehensive program.

In the early and mid-1940s, England suffered from the devastation of World War Two. Major parts of cities were destroyed, the economy was in chaos, a severe housing shortage existed, and the general health of the population was very poor. The prevailing system could not adequately handle these problems.

The *Beveridge Report* of 1942 analyzed these social problems and recommended major reform through increased government involvement in the economy, education, and health care. Strong sponsorship by the Labour Party and broad popular support for significant reform in health care existed, although not among physicians,

who fiercely resisted change. Eventually, the National Health Service Act of 1946 was passed by a wide margin and the National Health Service (NHS) was implemented in 1948. The NHS provided for the entire range of health care services to be available at no charge to the entire population in a system financed by general tax revenues. Despite several major adjustments, the basic health care system inaugurated in 1948 continues today.

England has a long history of extensive government involvement throughout society's institutions, and a commitment to providing for the basic needs of all citizens. Within this "welfare state," the NHS expresses the social value placed on a just distribution of essential resources (such as health care). Although the current health care system is not without its critics, the "National" is a source of great pride.

Organization of the Health Care System

The health care system has largely been government owned and government run. The government sets health care policy, raises funds and budgets for health care, owns health care facilities, employs physicians and other health care professionals, and purchases medical supplies and equipment. Ultimate authority rests with the Department of Health and the Secretary of State for Health.

The health care system underwent several significant changes in the 1990s and early 2000s. In the late 1980s, Prime Minister Margaret Thatcher commissioned a report, *Working for Patients* (Barr, Glennester, and Le Grand, 1989), which advocated making greater use of private-market forces to increase competition and efficiency in the system, while maintaining universal and free access.

At the heart of the reform were two basic changes. First, as of 2002, decision-making power was decentralized, with localized *primary care trusts (PCTs)* given responsibility for running the NHS and improving health in their areas; the PCTs receive 75 percent of the NHS budget. Regional *strategic health authorities* oversee the PCTs and engage in health planning. Second, increased competition among hospitals and other facilities was created, with the aim of reducing costs and increasing quality of services.

Medical settings are like those in the United States. Physicians work out of offices or clinics, or in hospitals. As is true in some managed-care networks in the United States, England mandates that an initial contact in the health care system be made with a general practitioner (GP).

The NHS is largely (more than 80 percent) financed by general tax revenues, with only about 4 percent of funds coming from out-of-pocket expenses. Patients do have co-payments for eyeglasses, dentures, and prescription drugs, although certain people (e.g., children and the elderly) are exempt from the fees. Health care is provided by physicians and hospitals to all citizens at no charge at the point of service.

Traditionally, there has been a small private health care sector. Recently, however, private health insurance has become more popular, with about 11 percent of the population now having a private policy. Physicians are not obligated to register with the NHS (although only a handful have not done so), and registered physicians may accept private patients, although rarely do private patients exceed 5 percent of the total patient load. Private insurance companies do exist and sell private health insurance for a premium. Hospitals reserve a small number of beds ("pay beds") for private patients. Why would anyone purchase private insurance? The main reason is to avoid long waits ("queues") that typically exist for elective surgery and that sometimes exist for more urgent surgery or even primary care.

Practicing physicians become either general practitioners or consultants. Patients have a free choice of GPs, but must get placed on one's roster in order to be seen. Once on a roster, that is the only GP that the patient can use. A patient can switch to another GP by registering with another physician, but this is rare. The GP offers comprehensive primary care and can prescribe medications, but must refer patients to a consultant for hospital care.

GPs contract with the NHS for reimbursement, which occurs in three ways. Each GP receives a base salary to cover the fixed costs of operating a practice, a certain amount of salary based on the number of patients accepted on the roster (called a **capitation system**), and additional income based on services such as vaccinations for which a fee is charged. The capitation system is the most controversial of the three sources of income. The NHS has established 3,500 patients as the maximum on a roster, although physicians average only about 1,900. Physicians are obligated to provide care for all patients on the roster, although neither the number of patients actually seen, the duration of the encounter, or the type of treatment dispensed affects salary. Physicians do receive a supplement for having certain categories of patient (e.g., the elderly, or people on low income) on their roster. Recently, the NHS has begun to experiment with "pay-for-performance" programs in which physicians receive some compensation when their patients hit designated health targets (McDonald, White, and Marmor, 2009).

Consultants, all of whom work in hospitals, are physicians trained in a medical or surgical specialty. They are salaried employees of the NHS. Salaries are the same for all specialties in all hospitals, and are determined in an annual negotiation with the NHS. Neither the number of patients seen nor the type of treatments provided affects salary earned.

Physicians are held in high esteem. Surveys report confidence in physician care, few patients seek a second opinion, and medical malpractice suits are rare. This high prestige is not reflected in salaries to the same extent that it is in the United States. Physicians earn considerably above the national average income, but not several times higher as they do in the United States.

However, the government maintains an important control by determining the amount of money allocated to the health care system. By limiting these funds (as a whole, England spends less money per capita on health care than any other country in Europe), the number of health care employees is restricted, and demand for services typically exceeds supply. When patients attempt to make an appointment, they may have to wait for several weeks. This situation is primarily responsible for the development of the private insurance sector, because the privately insured are seen promptly.

Performance of the Health Care System

Standard health indicators reflect positively on the general health of the people. Overall life expectancy is among the highest in the world (higher than in the United States), and infant mortality is very low (and lower than in the United States). Although no person is ever turned away due to an inability to pay, the NHS is considerably less expensive than the United States health care system. In recent years, England has spent a little more than 9 percent of its gross domestic product on health care—about half the U.S. level—and it has been criticized as being inappropriately low.

Accessibility of Health Care

Citizens can receive comprehensive health care without payment at the point of delivery. In this sense, services are maximally accessible. Moreover, the government offers incentives to physicians who establish practice in medically underserved areas—this has helped to ease the shortage of physicians in rural areas.

Recent Developments in Health Care

In England, the control of costs and cost increases is accomplished through use of a global budget for health. The amount of money to be spent on health in a year is determined in advance, and the system must then operate within the budgeted amount. A balanced budget is expected. The recent economic situation in England has resulted in only very minor increases in the budget in recent years (often less than a 1 percent annual increase)—an unprecedented occurrence. With an increased overall population and an increased elderly population, along with new medical technologies, demand for services has increasingly exceeded supply. Provider shortages, overworked workers, and longer waiting times have resulted. This has created frustration for patients, and has put pressure on the government to do better.

In response, several significant changes to the British health care system have been introduced in recent years, with the largest changes occurring in 2013 and 2014. The Health and Social Care Act 2012 created a new body, NHS England, with overall budgetary control and supervision of both *clinical commissioning groups* (which replaced the primary care trusts) and Monitor (an economic regulator of public and private providers). NHS England also now oversees primary care, national immunization and screening programs, health information technology, and some specialized low-volume services (Thorlby and Arora, 2016).

The primary objective of these recent changes is to increase efficiency, increase the power of physicians in allocating health care dollars, and increase private competition within the system. Efforts have been undertaken to reduce the provision of unnecessary services. Patients have been given increased choice of medical provider, and can choose between public and private facilities. Proponents hope that decentralization and added competition will create a more efficient health care system.

Critics of the changes express concern that the emphasis on competition and profit making will supersede the traditional closeness of the GP–patient relationship. For example, the increased importance of the capitation system gives physicians an incentive to take more patients onto the roster, thereby reducing the time available for each patient. Some suggest that the system may even increase rather than decrease costs if employers are forced to pay higher salaries in order to attract the best people. These are issues that will be followed closely in the coming years (Black, 2010).

RUSSIA

The Historical, Political, and Philosophical Foundation

Russia, with a population of about 144 million people (but changing little from year to year), is the largest of the countries that formed the Soviet Union. In many respects it falls between the level of modernization of the United States and Western Europe on the one hand, and that of developing countries on the other. Since the breakup of the Soviet Union in 1991, Russia has struggled to develop a sound economy and a workable health care system.

The roots of the socialized health care system of Russia can be traced back to the 1917 revolution. Overthrowing the tsar, Lenin and the Bolsheviks moved to establish a working-class society based on Communist principles. Given both the unstable political situation at home and throughout the world and the economic chaos within the country, the Bolsheviks moved quickly to consolidate their power in a totalitarian government. The power of the Communist party emerged from these events.

The health of the people was a primary concern of Lenin and the new government, and one of their priorities was to establish adequate preventive measures to counter the rampant disease epidemics of the time. In 1913, the mortality rate was 29 per 1,000 people, the infant mortality rate was 269 per 1,000, and an average life expectancy was no more than 32 years—all indicators of severe health problems (Leichter, 1979).

Lenin was also determined to sharply reduce the power of the medical profession. Under the tsar, physicians had substantial autonomy and had organized themselves into a medical corporation. This body was political as well as medical, and often spoke out against the tsar. Following the 1917 revolution, physicians attempted to alter the structure of medicine to make it more amenable to centralized planning (in accord with Lenin's wishes), but they also attempted to retain extensive professional control over clinical practice. This effort was denounced by the Communists, who were convinced that physicians would always serve the interests of the ruling class. In an effort to deprofessionalize physicians, the government created a medical union in which physicians had no greater say than other health care workers. By the mid-1920s, the medical profession had been transformed into a group of medical experts employed and largely controlled by the government.

The philosophical foundation for the health care system was developed in the first years after the revolution. The guiding principles were as follows: (1) the state has responsibility for public health and the provision of health care; (2) administration of the health care system is highly centralized and bureaucratized, but includes public participation; (3) health care is defined as a right of citizenship, and health care services are provided at no cost; (4) preventive medicine is to be emphasized; and (5) medical research must be oriented toward the solution of practical problems—for example, the reduction of industrial absenteeism (Barr and Field, 1996).

These principles guided the health care system in the succeeding decades. Although the government released little information to the outside world about health indicators, the general perception was that the health care system worked adequately, if not better.

However, when President Gorbachev began to open Russian society to the outside world in 1985, it became obvious that the health care system was in a badly deteriorated condition due to underfunding. While Soviet leaders had painted a glowing picture of their health care system, in reality they had concentrated their attention on rapid industrialization and militarization, and had failed to adequately support health care. Although the Soviet Union had more physicians and more hospital beds per capita than any other country, their quality was often very low. Unqualified students bribed their way into medical school, severe shortages of pharmaceuticals and other medical supplies existed, and many medical facilities were crumbling (Barr and Field, 1996).

During the summer of 1991, people throughout the Soviet Union demanded an end to centralized government control and insisted on autonomy for the republics. Their focus was largely on political and economic structures, but changes were initiated in every institutional sector. In medicine, an end was signaled to highly centralized decision making and planning, and efforts commenced to establish more free-market principles in the system. However, the transition to a workable and efficient health care system has been very difficult.

Organization of the Health Care System

Historically, the chief organizational characteristic of the health care system was its centralized administration. The ultimate authority in the system resided in the national Health Ministry led by a minister of health (typically a physician) and a Council of Health Ministers. This body had responsibility for the following: (1) all planning, coordination, and control of medical care and medical research; (2) medical education and standards of medical practice; (3) formulating the health care budget and allocating funds to republic, regional, district, and local medical resources. The government owned all health care facilities and employed all health care workers.

In urban areas, a network of polyclinics (large multiservice clinics) continues to represent the core of the health care system and serves most of the population. Until recently, each person was assigned to a particular polyclinic, but this requirement has now been eliminated. About 30 percent of the population, including the police, railroad employees, university employees, and high-level government officials, have their own clinics and hospitals.

The key ambulatory care providers in rural areas are the midwife and the feldsher—a mid-level practitioner approximately equivalent to a physician's assistant (but with even more responsibility), who provides immunizations, primary care, assistance with normal childbirth, and minor surgery.

The hospital sector contains both general and specialized hospitals (e.g., maternity and infectious diseases), most of which are fairly small. Few hospitals contain modern medical technology and adequate pharmaceuticals, or have high sanitary standards. Periodic reports of shortages of rubber gloves, surgical instruments, sterile needles, and other necessary supplies still occur. The emergency medical system, which was once the pride of the health care system, is in total disarray, with ambulances sometimes arriving half a day after being called.

Physicians enjoy some prestige in Russia, but they are not among the highest paid professionals. Salaries are approximately the same as those for starting teachers, but only 70 percent as much as those of industrial workers. This situation helps to explain the under-the-table payments from patients to physicians that have become common in order to secure more expedient care or additional services, or even to have an operation performed or medication prescribed. It should be noted that the government does provide many physicians with certain fringe benefits (e.g., preferred apartments, vacation benefits, and access to better schools for their children) that are not accorded to others (Lassey, Lassey, and Jinks, 1997).

About 70 percent of all physicians in Russia are female, and most of these women work out of the polyclinics. Male physicians are more likely to hold the more prestigious specialist positions in hospitals, academic positions, and most of the positions in the Ministry of Health. These patterns developed during the early 1930s, at a time when there was an overall shortage of workers that was especially acute among physicians. Medicine was determined to be an area where women could adequately replace men. The Soviet government perceived many of these new female physicians (who had been nurses or even hospital orderlies) as being satisfied with a small paycheck and an occupation with little professional status.

Accessibility of Health Care

According to the Russian constitution, free health care is guaranteed to all citizens (at the publicly funded polyclinics and hospitals), but only a small part of services are actually free. Services are provided on a first-come-first-served basis (often with long queues), and are limited by the chronic shortage of supplies and equipment. The primary problem with the public system is that it continues to be underfunded. Russia spends about 7 percent of its gross domestic product on health care, and this is not sufficient to elevate standards.

Laws passed in the early 1990s created a two-part government-run health insurance system. Workers were covered under one part (financed by a payroll tax), and non-workers (e.g., the unemployed, retirees, and children) were covered in the second part, which is financed through the national government's budget. All persons are required to have medical insurance. To date, however, the program has not worked as anticipated and has not generated the desired amount of funds.

In recent years, a private system has begun to emerge beside the public system. Physicians are permitted to treat private as well as public patients, and patients with adequate personal resources may prefer to pay a fee for service in order to get faster, more personalized, or more thorough care. A few pay-polyclinics have been started, and private health insurance is now available to help to subsidize these costs. Many patients avoid both the public and private systems by relying on informal access to physician friends or relatives. Not surprisingly, this resource is most readily available to people in the upper socioeconomic groups (Brown and Rusinova, 1997).

Performance of the Health Care System

Russia today has substantial problems with its health care system, and extremely concerning health indicators. Mortality rates are higher than in other industrialized countries. Life expectancy has actually decreased in some recent years, and infant mortality rates are two to three times higher than in Western countries. The death rate from heart disease is the highest in the developed world, and AIDS has increased rapidly (there are now about one million cases). Epidemics of diseases that were once thought to be under control in developed countries (e.g., tuberculosis, hepatitis, typhoid, cholera, and diphtheria) are all on the increase and occasionally at epidemic levels. Drug-related health problems have increased, while public sanitation, childhood immunizations, and health education programs are down. On average, life expectancy in Russia is about 13 years higher for women than for men.

These conditions relate to the deterioration of the health care system, but are traceable to a variety of other causes. Mark Field (1995) places the problem within the broad context of the collapse of the Soviet empire and the "systemic" breakdown of Russian society (a macro factor). He casts Russia as a country in a "post-war" mindset having experienced a humiliating national defeat. The deteriorating economic condition, with high rates of inflation, political instability, and feelings of social isolation and alienation, has contributed to a tearing of the social fabric.

The high rates of heart disease have been attributed to social stress and to harmful individual behaviors such as alcoholism, cigarette smoking, drug abuse, high-fat diets, and lack of adequate exercise. Russia also has high rates of homicide, suicide, traffic accidents, and alcohol poisoning (micro factors). The macro and micro factors have been mutually reinforcing. Poor economic conditions have had a negative impact on population health, and poor health has been one barrier to economic growth (Danton, 2013). King, Hamm, and Stuckler (2009) have shown that rapid implementation of large-scale private market programs reduced available health care resources *and* created considerable psychological stress, which has contributed to poorer health and lifestyles, increased rates of heart disease and suicide, and decreased life expectancy.

Recent Developments in Health Care

The leaders in Russia and in many of the countries that formed the Soviet Union intend to focus heavily on the application of free-market principles to the health care system. Many health care providers believe that the main problem with the system in the past—in addition to underfunding—has been its centrally controlled nature, and they now believe that the main priority is to complete the transition to a new health care-financing system. However, the focus to date in Russia has been on the economic system, and little attention has been directed to reforming the health care system and acquiring the basic medical supplies and equipment needed for quality clinical services.

In 2011, Prime Minister Putin announced that the government would contribute $10 billion to the health care system over the next few years, that the medical insurance tax paid by employers would increase in order to add funding to the health care system, and that increased privatization efforts would occur. In 2012, Putin promised to double the (very low) wages of health care workers by 2018. However, deepening economic problems have forced austerity measures throughout the country, and health care funding has been reduced. Privatization efforts thus far seem to be exacerbating the problem, as prices have increased and the quality of services has declined. An "optimization" plan which commenced in 2014 to try to eliminate waste has concentrated resources in large hospitals but led to the closing of many smaller facilities. Many hospital staff positions have been cut.

COMMON CHALLENGES TO HEALTH CARE SYSTEMS AROUND THE WORLD

Despite their profound differences, nations around the world are struggling with some of the same issues and questions with respect to their health care systems. Having briefly examined the health care systems of China, Canada, England, and Russia, the following emerge as common and very important issues that countries are dealing with at the time of writing:

1. What is the optimal level of involvement of the national government in the health care system, and in what ways should the government be involved?

2. Should there be both a public and private health care sector? What is the optimal

relationship between the government, employers, insurers, and providers?

3. What is the optimal number of physicians within the system, and what should be the distribution between primary care physicians and specialists?

4. Given considerations of cost and equitable distribution, what is the optimal commitment that should be made to the incorporation of health care technologies?

5. How can increases in health care costs most reasonably be controlled?

SUMMARY

Studying health care systems around the world offers insights into policy alternatives and an enhanced ability to understand the forces that shape health care. While every health care system is unique, all are shaped by some configuration of environmental, situational-historical, cultural, and structural factors.

The four systems examined in detail in this chapter represent alternative ways of structuring a health care system. China is an agriculture-based country with a huge and very poor rural population. Recently, the government has abandoned the cooperative system based on community health workers—a system that was effective in getting medical care to the people—in favor of a more privatized system. This change created a system in disarray, and one in which health care became unobtainable for much of the rural population. Recently, however, China has committed to a significantly enhanced health care system, and early results are promising.

Canada illustrates the national health insurance with private regulated services model. Canada's health care system has undergone a significant transformation that has shifted more financial and managerial control to the provincial governments, while maintaining a commitment to providing universal access to care. Health care personnel in Canada are not government employees, although the federal and provincial governments exercise significant influence on the conditions of medical practice. Health indicators are very positive, but difficult economic times in Canada have led to recent system cutbacks.

England illustrates the national health insurance with public regulated services model. It guarantees universal access to health care through a system that is substantially publicly owned and run. Health indicators for the British people are very favorable, and there is considerable pride in the "National." However, rapidly increasing costs have led to organizational changes and focused efforts on using competition and private-market forces to control cost increases.

Russia, when it was part of the Soviet Union, illustrated the national health insurance state-run system (socialized medicine) model. Russians took much pride in the emphasis on preventive care and on the provision of free care for all citizens. However, the health care system became greatly underfunded and has entered a crisis period. Efforts to address this by transitioning to a private-market economy have been fraught with difficulty. The health care system, like the general economy, is in a desperate condition, and several health indicators remain major concerns.

HEALTH ON THE INTERNET

Throughout this text we have discussed the World Health Organization and used data that it has collected. Learn more about the WHO by checking out its website at www.who.int.

When and by whom was the WHO created? How is the WHO structured and governed? Where is its main office located? What are the WHO's basic principles? What are the six programmatic areas in which the WHO works? What does the WHO have to say about reproductive health, child maltreatment, and environmental health?

DISCUSSION QUESTIONS

1. Determine which of the four major influences on health care systems (physical environment, historical and situational events, cultural norms and values, and the structure of society) had most impact on each of the four health care systems presented in detail in this chapter.
2. What are the common denominators in these four health care systems? How is each system unique?

3. Identify a major strength and a major concern for each of the four systems. Can you identify at least one feature in the health care system of each country that you would like to see incorporated in health care reform in the United States?

GLOSSARY

barefoot doctors
capitation system
global health

global health partnerships (GHPs)
socialized medicine

REFERENCES

Allin, Sara, and David Rudoler. 2016 "The Canadian Health Care System, 2015." *International Profiles of Health Care Systems*, Elias Mossialos, Martin Wenzl, Robin Osborn, and Dana Sarnak (eds.). New York: The Commonwealth Fund.

Anderson, Gerard, and Peter S. Hussey. 2001 "Comparing Health System Performance in OECD Countries." *Health Affairs*, 20: 219–232.

Barr, Donald A., and Mark G. Field. 1996 "The Current State of Health Care in the Former Soviet Union: Implications for Health Care Policy and Reform." *American Journal of Public Health*, 86:307–312.

Barr, Nicholas, Howard Glennester, and Julian Le Grand. 1989 "Working for Patients: The Right Approach?" *Social Policy and Administration*, 23:117–127.

Black, Nick. 2010 "'Liberating the NHS'— Another Attempt to Implement Market Forces in English Health Care." *New England Journal of Medicine*, 363:1103–1105.

Brown, Julie V., and Nina L. Rusinova. 1997 "Russian Medical Care in the 1990s: A User's Perspective." *Social Science and Medicine*, 45:1265–1276.

Campion, Edward W., and Stephen Morrissey. 2013 "A Different Model — Medical Care in Cuba." *New England Journal of Medicine*, 368:297–299.

Central Intelligence Agency. 2016a "Life Expectancy." *World Factbook*. www.cia.gov/library/publications/resources/the-world-factbook/rankorder/2102rank.html.

———. 2016b "Infant Mortality." *World Factbook*. www.cia.gov/library/publications/resources/the-world-factbook/rankorder/2091rank.html.

Crone, Robert K. 2008 "Flat Medicine? Exploring Trends in the Globalization of Health Care." *Academic Medicine*, 83:117–121.

Danton, Christine. 2013 "The Health Crisis in Russia." *Topical Research Digest: Human Rights in Russia and the Former Soviet Republics.* www.du.edu/korbel/hrhw/researchdigest/russia/health.pdf.

Edney, Anna. 2014 "U.S. Health Care System Among Least Efficient Before Obamacare." www.bloomberg.com/news/articles/2014-09-18/u-s-health-system-among-least-efficient-before-obamacare.

FamiliesUSA. 2010 "Why Global Health Matters—Here and Abroad." www.familiesusa.org/issues/global-health.

Fang, Hai. 2016 "The Chinese Health Care System, 2015." *International Profiles of Health Care Systems*, Elias Mossialos, Martin Wenzl, Robin Osborn, and Dana Sarnak (eds.). New York: The Commonwealth Fund.

Field, Mark G. 1995 "The Health Care Crisis in the Former Soviet Union: A Report from the 'Post-War' Zone." *Social Science and Medicine*, 41:1469–1478.

Himmelstein, David U., Miraya Jun, Reinhard Busse, Karine Chevreul, Alexander Geissler, Patrick Jeruissen, Sarah Thomson, Marie-Amelie Vinet, and Steffie Woolhandler. 2014 "A Comparison of Hospital Administrative Costs in Eight Nations: U.S. Costs Exceed All Others by Far." *Health Affairs*, 33:1586–1594.

Katz, Steven J., Timothy P. Hofer, and Willard G. Manning. 1996 "Physician Use in Ontario and the United States: The Impact of Socioeconomic Status and Health Status." *American Journal of Public Health*, 86:520–524.

Katz, Steven J., Laurence F. McMahon, and Willard G. Manning. 1996 "Comparing the Use of Diagnostic Tests in Canadian and U.S. Hospitals." *Medical Care*, 34:117–125.

King, Lawrence L., Patrick Hamm, and David Stuckler. 2009 "Rapid Large-Scale Privatization and Death Rates in Ex-Communist Countries: An Analysis of Stress-Related and Health System Mechanisms." *International Journal of Health Services*, 39:461–489.

Lassey, Marie L., William R. Lassey, and Martin J. Jinks. 1997 *Health Care Systems Around the World.* Upper Saddle River, NJ: Prentice Hall.

Leichter, Howard M. 1979 *A Comparative Approach to Policy Analysis: Health Care Policy in Four Nations.* Cambridge, UK: Cambridge University Press.

Lewis, Steven. 2015 "A System in Name Only—Access, Variation, and Reform in Canada's Provinces." *New England Journal of Medicine*, 372:497–500.

Light, Donald W. 1990 "Comparing Health Care Systems: Lessons from East and West Germany." Pp. 449–463 in *The Sociology of Health and Illness* (3rd ed.), Peter Conrad and Rochelle Kern (eds.). New York: St. Martin's Press.

McDonald, Ruth, Joseph White, and Theodore R. Marmor. 2009 "Paying for Performance in Primary Medical Care: Learning About and Learning From 'Success' and 'Failure' in England and California." *Journal of Health Politics, Policy, and Law*, 34:747–776.

McGrail, Kimberlyn M., Eddy van Doorslaer, Nancy A. Ross, and Claudia Sanmartin. 2009 "Income-Related Health Inequalities in Canada and the United States: A Decomposition Analysis." *American Journal of Public Health*, 99: 1856–1863.

Ngoasong, Michael Z. 2009 "The Emergence of Global Health Partnerships as Facilitators of Access to Medication in Africa: A Narrative Policy Analysis." *Social Science and Medicine*, 68:949–956.

Payer, Lynn. 1989 *Medicine and Culture.* New York: Holt, Rinehart and Winston.

Squires, David, and Chloe Anderson. 2015 "U.S. Health Care from a Global Perspective: Spending, Use of Services, Prices, and Health in 13 Countries." www.commonwealthfund.org/publications/issue-briefs/2015/oct/us-health-care-from-a-global-perspective.

Steinbrook, Robert. 2006 "Private Health Care in Canada." *New England Journal of Medicine*, 354:1661–1664.

Thorlby, Ruth, and Sandeepa Arora. 2016 "The English Health Care System, 2015." *International Profiles of Health Care Systems*, Elias Mossialos, Martin Wenzl, Robin Osborn, and Dana Sarnak (eds.). New York: The Commonwealth Fund.

Woolhandler, Steffie, Terry Campbell, and David U. Himmelstein. 2004 "Health Care Administration in the United States and Canada: Micromanagement, Macro Costs." *International Journal of Health Services*, 34:65–78.

World Bank. 2014a "World Development Indicators: Per Capital GDP." www.data.worldbank.org/indicator/SH.XPD.PCAP/countries.

————. 2014b "World Development Indicators: Per Capita Health Expenditures." www.data.worldbank.org/indicator/NY.GDP.PCAP.CD/countries.

World Health Organization. 2000 *World Health Report 2000—Health Systems: Improving Performance*. Geneva, Switzerland: World Health Organization.

————. 2010 *World Health Statistics*. Geneva, Switzerland: World Health Organization.

Yip, Winnie C., and William C. Hsiao. 2008 "The Chinese Health System at a Crossroads." *Health Affairs*, 27:460–468.

Name Index

Subject Index